CHINA AND THE CHRISTIAN COLLEGES
1850-1950

CHINA AND THE CHRISTIAN COLLEGES

1850-1950

Jessie Gregory Lutz

CORNELL UNIVERSITY PRESS
ITHACA AND LONDON

First published 1971 by Cornell University Press.
Published in the United Kingdom by Cornell University Press Ltd.,
2–4 Brook Street, London W1Y 1AA.

The map of nineteenth-century China is derived from the map on page 61 in *The Political History of China; 1840–1928* by Li-Chien-nung, translated and edited by Ssu-yü Teng and Jeremy Ingalls; copyright © 1956 by Litton Educational Publishing, Inc., published by Van Nostrand Reinhold Company. The maps of China in the 1920's, 1930, and 1939 are derived by permission of Charles Scribner's Sons from Map 31, THE AGELESS CHINESE, page 472, by Dun J. Li; copyright © 1965 Charles Scribner's Sons.

International Standard Book Number 0–8014–0626–9
Library of Congress Catalog Card Number 70–148022
PRINTED IN THE UNITED STATES OF AMERICA
BY VAIL-BALLOU PRESS, INC.

To my parents

To my parents

Preface

During the century from 1850 to 1950 the continuing revolution in China and the work of Protestant missionaries in higher education sometimes followed parallel but separate ways, sometimes merged, and sometimes met in violent confrontation. The nature and frequency of this interaction have influenced the emphasis of this study and the availability of sources. Missionaries were prolific writers and keepers of records; and those who engaged in education in China produced voluminous diaries, reports, letters, and surveys. Literate Chinese, on the other hand, until 1895 showed only occasional interest in the educational work of the Christian evangelists. Though the mission schools were a clear challenge to traditional Chinese education, the institutions remained largely isolated from the intellectual life of China and were seldom the subject of comment by Chinese writers. By the twentieth century the role of Christian education in revolutionizing China was beginning to receive recognition; the Christian educational institutions were serving as mediators of Western civilization, as examples of Western education, and as foci for anti-imperialist nationalism. They thus became the subject of numerous essays and critiques by Chinese, especially during the nationalistic movements of the 1920's and the early 1950's.

In defining my subject, I have concentrated on those schools, founded by Protestant missionaries, which eventually became institutions of higher education, omitting with regret the Roman Catholic colleges. I have, however, consulted a limited number of sources on the Catholic missions, and these materials were not out of line with my findings.[1]

Many of the Protestant schools evolved gradually into institutions of higher learning and changed their names, titles, and locales in the process. Because it would be impossible to state the time when each of the institutions attained college or university standards, I have adopted the designations used by the schools themselves. In the case of institutions which changed names several times, I have for the sake of simplicity used the one or two most common designations. A list of the various titles and locales of the institutions is provided for reference.

During the years that this study has been in progress, I have incurred numerous debts. I am grateful to all who have given aid even though it is not possible to thank each one separately. The study could not have been made without access to many library collections, and I appreciate the courteous assistance provided by the staffs of the following libraries in particular: the Missionary Research Library, the Wason Collection of Cornell University, the New Brunswick Theological Seminary Library, the Hoover Institution on War, Revolution, and Peace of Stanford University, and the Harvard-Yenching Institute of Harvard University. Financial aid given by the Rutgers Research Council, the Social Science Research Council, and the American Association of University Women made it possible to devote full time to research and writing, and I appreciate their generosity.

Knight Biggerstaff of Cornell University has been more than generous in providing encouragement and criticism; his assistance on numerous occasions has been invaluable. The late Charles Corbett of the United Board for Christian Higher Education in Asia made the use of the United Board archives a pleasanter and an easier task than it would have otherwise been. Others who were associated with China missions or the Christian colleges have graciously provided information in personal interviews and conversations, particularly

[1] Among the works consulted were Catholic University of Peking, *Bulletin*, 1926–1931, 1934; *Fu Jen Magazine*, 1932–1949; *Bulletin de l'Université l'Aurore*, 1927–1937, 1947–1949; *La Revue Nationale Chinoise*, 1929–1941; Catholic Church, China, *Collectanea Commissionis Synodalis*, 1927–1947; and *Relations de Chine*, Paris, 1914–1938.

M. Searle Bates of Union Theological Seminary, Harold Shadick of Cornell University, Anne Cochran of St. John's and Tunghai universities, K. S. Latourette of Yale University, and Wu Teh-yao of Tunghai University. Ray Lutz continued to believe that completion of this study was possible and worthwhile, and I am thankful.

JESSIE GREGORY LUTZ

Douglass College
Rutgers University
New Brunswick, N.J.

Contents

Maps

Tables

I | Confrontation in China

Despite the labors of thousands of Christian missionaries in China during the nineteenth and twentieth centuries, most Chinese showed little interest in either Christian doctrines or the Christian church. Many Chinese demonstrated open antagonism by making the missionary and his institutions the favorite targets of antiforeign attacks. Though the Christian community could boast a high rate of literacy and a number of prominent Chinese became Christians, the total number of converts never equaled 1 percent of the population; and after the communist assumption of power and the departure of Western missionaries, China was left with small and weak Christian communities. The Christian missionary, had, nevertheless, acted as a mediator of Western civilization in China and had participated in the Chinese definition of their nation. Through his personal life and through the schools, hospitals, printing presses, and other institutions he founded, the missionary became a propagator of ideals and customs from Western civilization. In opposition to the rights, privileges, and teachings of Westerners, educated Chinese began to seek a conscious definition of their own state and nation.

Such a secular role was not eagerly assumed by missionaries of the nineteenth century; nor has it been gladly acknowledged by Chinese scholars. It was out of dismay over the indifference of the Chinese to the Christian message that a few missionaries in the nineteenth century founded schools and other institutions. The schools were considered evangelistic agencies first and academic institutions second. Chinese families which could afford a traditional education for their sons paid little attention initially, but for some less fortunate families the schools' instruction in English and mathematics opened avenues to wealth and influence. Missionary educators cooperated with certain Chinese leaders in an attempt to provide special training in Western languages, science, and mathematics for a small number of Chinese gentry.[1]

A few of the mission institutions began to assume the title "college." Though the title was an expression of goals rather than of academic standards, the schools did increase in size and expand their course offerings. During the early twentieth century, several became important centers for training in science, mathematics, the English language, and Western civilization. Christian schools helped initiate college education for women and educational research in medicine and agriculture, and they remained leaders in these fields throughout their existence. Institutional pride and the natural desire of an institution to expand as proof of its usefulness and vitality were partially responsible for growth, but the schools also gained in popularity as Chinese attitudes toward Western civilization changed. With the disintegration of Chinese tradition, some Chinese turned to the mission schools as a source of Western learning. Others used the superior English language training of the institutions to prepare for study abroad, and the Christian colleges prepared a high percentage of those who went to the United States and England for advanced work. Mission boards in the twentieth century showed a greater willingness than their predecessors to allocate money and personnel to schools and other social services. The hope was that such service would demonstrate the spirit of Christianity and would help to Christianize many aspects of Chinese life; the institutions would be indirect agents of evangelism.

For a brief period during the early twentieth century both Chinese and Westerners considered the schools useful because they were alien to Chinese tradition in organization, methods, and ideals as well as in curriculum. The foreign character of the colleges and their isolation from Chinese life, however, became offensive to the rising nationalism of the 1920's. Consciousness of the Chinese nation

---

[1] In this work there is no attempt to use the term gentry in a precise fashion and limit it to either office holders or degree holders. It is used to designate the upper class, most of whom held land and were also literate. For a good brief discussion of the origins of the China Christian colleges, see Kwang-ching Liu, "Early Christian Colleges in China," *The Journal of Asian Studies*, XX (1960), 71–78 (cited as *JAS*).

and the politicizing of this consciousness developed in opposition to Western civilization and Western pressure. Nationalistic Chinese initiated a movement to "restore educational rights." With hesitancy, the colleges began to pass under Chinese administration and regulation. They were registered with the government, and Chinese assumed most of the faculty and administrative positions. Though significant financial support continued to come from the West, some colleges seemed to be gaining acceptance as legitimate Sino-Western syntheses within the Chinese environment. By the 1930's the sixteen Christian schools (thirteen Protestant, three Roman Catholic) which were generally acknowledged to be institutions of higher education enrolled 10 to 15 percent of the total number of students in colleges and universities in China. But the schools' chances for a permanent role in China were sharply reduced by the communist victory of 1949 and the focusing of nationalist resentment on the United States. By 1952 all of the Christian colleges on the Chinese mainland had disappeared, and most missionaries had been forced to leave. Mission boards were assessing the failure of the massive effort to convert China to Christianity. In line with the new orthodoxy, one explanation was that Christian missions had placed too much emphasis on social service activities and too little on Christian doctrines and the Christian church.

It is noteworthy, however, that the communist government did not simply disband the colleges but rather amalgamated them with other institutions. In some cases, the Christian college faculty, campus, and equipment became the core of a new national institution. One might say that the process of nationalization begun during the 1920's had been completed. Chinese communists had continued a habit of selective borrowing from the West; although they had rejected Christianity, they were still adapting much from Western civilization to Chinese needs. The mission boards likewise did not completely reject the past, for they founded new Chinese Christian colleges in Taiwan and Hong Kong during the 1950's.

The China Christian colleges may be studied then as mediators of Western civilization and participants in a continuing Chinese revolution. In their early years the colleges touched the Chinese scene at relatively few points; later the institutions and their leaders became more responsive to the Chinese environment and were integrated with the rapidly changing China of the twentieth century. Their history serves to document changing Chinese attitudes toward Western civilization and the development of a growing national consciousness. They played a role in both the destructive and constructive aspects of revolution in China, and the love-hate relationship which has often characterized Sino-American relations is articulated in their history. At the same time missionary approaches to their tasks are illustrative of changing Western attitudes toward the confrontation of Chinese and Western civilizations. The self-confident nineteenth-century evangelist was as expressive of the dynamism and assurance of the West at that time as the self-critical mission theorist was indicative of the loss of nerve in the West after two world wars, the rise of communism, and the disintegration of world empires.

Cultural Confrontation

Contact between China and the Western world has, of course, a long history, but until the late eighteenth century most contact had been limited and intermittent. Each civilization had evolved certain traditions about the other, and China had developed techniques for dealing with Westerners, but the knowledge which educated leaders in each culture had about the other was generally minimal. In so far as possible China had placed the Western peoples in the category of outer barbarians and had applied the techniques of the tributary system in her relations with the West. Though she acknowledged that there were nontributary trading states, the restrictions on ports of trade, length of trading season, and the right of individuals to engage in Sino-Western exchange were derived from the tributary system. For the West, China was exotic. Western images of China varied widely; there was the picture which the eighteenth-century philosophes painted on the basis of reports by Jesuit missionaries: the land of the sage king, of beautiful porcelains and fine silks. There was the picture held by merchant adventurers: a land of astute, inscrutable merchants who were hard bargainers but who kept their word, a land where profits were to be made. An assumption common to these Western views was the otherness of Chinese culture and peoples; in China Western norms did not apply.

During the late eighteenth and early nineteenth centuries, China and the West had more frequent and regular intercourse. Commerce

in opium, tea, and silk and cotton goods expanded so rapidly that
Westerners began to chafe over the restrictions on trade. At the
same time a new era for Christian missions began. The fact that
the nineteenth century was a period of growth in Christian missions
as well as political and economic expansion by the West was not
coincidence. There is a striking correlation between those nations
which were industrialized earliest and most completely and those
nations which were leaders in mission work. During the nineteenth
century, England and the United States sent out the most Protestant
missionaries, and Germany followed in third rank. France, in spite
of her anticlerical reputation, permitted no competitors in her role
as principal supporter and protector of Roman Catholic missions.
Improved communications contributed to an awareness of a world
beyond Europe and the Americas. Traders brought back interesting
tales along with the products of far-away lands. Many a Christian
who until then had hardly heard of China began to feel a responsibility for "the heathen masses of the Orient," and the new wealth
created by expanding agricultural and industrial production enabled
Western society to support approximately two thousand missionaries
(Roman Catholic and Protestant) in China by the 1890's.

The upswing in missionary activity was not, however, an inevitable
result of the growing interest in foreign lands and of the new wealth
and power generated by the industrial revolution. Without a religious revival, investment might have been confined to commercial
and colonial ventures. The church experienced a reawakening in
the eighteenth and nineteenth centuries. Among the Roman Catholics many mission societies were founded or revived. In 1814 the
Congregation for the Propagation of the Faith (generally known
as The Propaganda) was reconstituted. In 1816 the Lazarists were
reestablished in France, and the *Missions Étrangères* sent out their
first recruit since reorganization. Members of the Society for the
Propagation of the Faith, which was founded in 1822, pledged to
pray daily for foreign missions and to contribute two centimes a
week. Catholics, who had counted only 31 missionaries in China
in 1810, listed 639 in 1890.[2]

[2] Though published in 1929, Kenneth Scott Latourette, *A History of Christian
Missions in China* (New York, 1929), is still an indispensable source of information. I have relied on it for the brief summaries given here on the beginnings
of modern Catholic and Protestant missions; see especially pp. 180, 203–206,

The religious revival, known as the Great Awakening in North America and as the Evangelical Movement in Britain, began to affect Protestant communities in the eighteenth and early nineteenth centuries. John Wesley, George Whitefield, and other leaders emphasized the necessity for an individual emotional experience resulting from a sense of sin and a desire for forgiveness. The convert must determine to lead a new life and must seek the conversion of others. As the movement spread, practically every Protestant denomination founded its own mission organization. The English Baptists, organizing a mission society in 1792, were the first. Three years after came the London Missionary Society, originally undenominational, but later the agent of the English Congregational churches. A branch of the Anglicans formed the Church Missionary Society in 1799. In the United States the American Board of Commissioners for Foreign Missions was founded in 1810 and became the agent of the Congregationalists, while the Methodists and Presbyterians soon formed their own societies. With the growth of the Young Men's Christian Association later in the century and the founding of the Student Volunteer Movement for Foreign Missions in 1886, many college students were persuaded to enter mission work.

In 1724 the Yung-cheng Emperor had withdrawn imperial edicts granting tolerance to Christianity, and until the Sino-Western treaties of the mid-nineteenth century, the propagation of Christianity in interior China was forbidden. Thus, there were few Catholic missionaries and no Protestant ones in China in 1800. The first Protestant evangelist to reside in China was Robert Morrison, who arrived in Canton in September 1807. Received with hostility, he spent his early years studying the Chinese language; then, to make his position more secure, he accepted employment with the British East India Company. Widespread antagonism and Chinese restrictions on proselytism forced him to concentrate on translating Christian works into Chinese as his major evangelistic activity. Protestant colleagues joined Morrison in a few years, but only a score or so of Protestant missionaries were working in China in 1840. The number

---

329. Other works by Latourette which include the more recent history of China missions are *A History of the Expansion of Christianity*, 7 vols. (New York, 1937–1945), and *Christianity in a Revolutionary Age*, 5 vols. (New York, 1958–1962).

grew rapidly thereafter; in 1889 there were 1,296, and in 1905 there were 3,445 Protestant missionaries in China.[3]

In the mission field as in diplomatic and trading relations, Western desire for expansion rapidly outstripped Chinese willingness to make the necessary institutional and legal changes. The goal of Chinese officials during the early nineteenth century was to restrict and regulate contacts rather than encourage them. The tolerance once shown by a few court officials toward the religious teachings and secular knowledge of Jesuit missionaries in the sixteenth and seventeenth centuries had disappeared before a growing antagonism toward Christianity and its emissaries. Christian missionaries in the early nineteenth century were faced by imperial edicts against evangelism and also by an anti-Christian tradition which had already formulated the major Chinese objections to Christianity.[4] In the anti-Christian literature, the Christian heterodoxy was condemned because it was foreign; it contained many irrational teachings; it consciously opposed the traditional Chinese religions and placed itself above them; and it did not accord with the basic values of Confucian society and was, therefore, disruptive to social stability. Through the centuries these criticisms of Christianity were to show remarkable vitality and continuity.

Western traders, diplomats, and missionaries refused to be permanently deterred by the hostility and indifference of Chinese officials. They insisted on their right to bring China the blessings of Western civilization, both material and spiritual. They demanded that Westerners be permitted to enter China and not be restricted to trade at a single port on the fringe of the empire; they demanded that China enter the community of nations. Stubborn Chinese resistance was followed by military conflict. With the treaty settlements emerging from the Opium War (1839–1842) and the Anglo-French expedition (1856–1860), Western regulations, rather than Chinese, came to

[3] Records of the General Conference of the Protestant Missionaries held at Shanghai, May 7–20, 1890 (Shanghai 1890) p. 732 (cited as Records 1890); D. MacGillivray, ed., A Century of Protestant Missions in China (Shanghai, 1907), App. II, p. 1.

[4] For an excellent discussion of the literature and content of the anti-Christian tradition before the mid-nineteenth century, see Paul A. Cohen, China and Christianity The Missionary Movement and the Growth of Chinese Antiforeignism, 1860–1870 (Cambridge, Mass., 1963), ch. 1, pp. 3–60.

dominate contacts between the two civilizations. Missionaries, who helped negotiate the treaties, insisted on conditions which would permit the expansion of Christian evangelism. Four stipulations particularly affected the work of the missionaries. First, certain ports were opened to foreign trade and residence, and foreigners were permitted to build houses, hospitals, and places of worship in these ports. Next, foreigners with passports were permitted to travel in the empire outside the treaty ports. Third, foreigners were given permission to study the Chinese language. Finally, as a defendant, a foreigner would be tried under his own law and before an official of his own government.

Even more important was a treaty guarantee of toleration of Christianity and a promise of protection in the exercise of Christian faith, not only to missionaries, but by implication to Chinese converts as well. The Chinese text of the Sino-French agreement of 1860 gave Roman Catholic missionaries permission to buy property and to reside outside the treaty ports; by virtue of the most-favored-nation clause, Protestants quickly assumed the same right. Chinese officials were not unaware of the disruptive implications of these concessions, as is revealed in the comments of Grand Secretary Mu-chang-a and members of the Grand Council on the Sino-American treaty of 1844 (the Treaty of Wanghia). While accepting without protest practically all the commercial clauses of the treaty, they were deeply concerned over the concessions which allowed foreigners to study the Chinese language, purchase Chinese books, and establish their own churches and cemeteries in the treaty ports. They asked the Chinese administration to "take pains to cause the residents of the seacoast to understand that barbarian languages are not to be imitated and barbarian rites are not to be practiced."[5] Subsequent events would indicate that their consternation over these concessions and the much more serious ones of 1856–1860 were well founded.

After 1860, missionaries ceased to hover on the periphery of China. As they moved toward the interior and fanned out over the country-

---

[5] *Ch'ing-tai ch'ou-pan i-wu shih-mo* (The management of barbarian affairs of the Ch'ing dynasty from beginning to end) (Peiping, 1930), Tao-kuan series 72; 21a, 6–25a, 7 (cited as *IWSM*). Trans. of this memorial in Earl Swisher, *China's Management of the American Barbarians* (New Haven, Conn., 1953), pp. 166–170.

side, there were frequent conflicts with the populace. Missionaries could ordinarily count on the backing of their national governments in their insistence on their treaty rights and in their demands for redress, and missionary attempts to protect their converts often seemed to place Chinese Christians as well as missionaries under the aegis of foreign powers. Thus, the symbiotic relationship between Christian missions and the unequal treaties plus the activities in interior China of hundreds of propagandists from another culture aggravated the fear that Christian missionaries were a threat to the Chinese heritage. The anti-Christian tradition was revitalized and popularized.

Under these circumstances, there was no rapid expansion of accurate knowledge in China about Western civilization and of knowledge in the West about Chinese civilization, in spite of the expansion of trade and missions. The sense of cultural superiority held by both Chinese and Westerner encouraged in each a conspicuous lack of curiosity about the cultural heritage of the other, and the confrontation of the Middle Kingdom concept with the concept of the "white man's burden" seemed to generate friction rather than fruitful exchange. Though the British had insisted on a written commitment that they would no longer be referred to as "i" (barbarians) in official documents,[6] there were at first few indications that Chinese officials had ceased to think of Westerners as "i." The Westerners, on their part, often displayed arrogance and an impervious faith in the superiority of their own culture. Representatives of both civilizations had apparently adopted the maxim of Mencius: "I have heard of men using the doctrines of our great land to change barbarians, but I have never yet heard of any being changed by barbarians."[7]

But information and attitudes important to Sino-Western relations and the modernization of China accumulated during the nineteenth century. If few Chinese gentry had undertaken formal training in Western languages and history, in science and mathematics by 1900, many Chinese officials had been made aware of the exis-

[6] Article LI of the Treaty of Tientsin between China and Great Britain, June 26, 1858. See William F. Mayers, *Treaties between the Empire of China and Foreign Powers*, 3d ed. (Shanghai, 1901), p. 19.

[7] James Legge, trans., *Chinese Classics*, 5 vols. (Hong Kong, 1960), vol. II, *The Works of Mencius*, 3d ed., pp. 253–254.

tence of another powerful center of civilization. A considerable body of knowledge about the West had become available in China, and institutions and techniques for transmitting much more information had been created. Concepts and attitudes about the West which would continue to influence the revolutionizing of China during the twentieth century had already been formulated. For an explanation of the rapidity with which twentieth-century Chinese intellectuals abandoned their commitment to the Chinese heritage, one must look to the last decades of the nineteenth century. It might be said that the disasters of 1895 to 1905 forced educated Chinese to draw conclusions from many separate bits of information already attained. The pressures that brought the explosions of the twentieth century had been building throughout the preceding century.

Because much of the information that accumulated came incidentally through personal contacts, the missionary was a prime source. Because the Chinese gentry were reluctant to organize schools offering science, mathematics, and Western languages, the mission schools, hospitals, and printing presses were important both as purveyors of information and as examples of Western methodology and organization. Of all Westerners, it was, after all, the missionary who was most likely to travel and reside in the interior and thus serve as a primary source on Western customs and beliefs. The missionary was more likely than the trader to learn the Chinese language, and often both Chinese and Westerners used him as interpreter. Even those who feared Christian propaganda sometimes turned to the missionary for assistance as teacher or translator. That the missionary was Western civilization in concrete form for both gentry and peasant was demonstrated with alarming frequency by the many antiforeign attacks directed against the Christian evangelist.

Yet few of the early missionaries came to China with the intention of revolutionizing Chinese civilization. They at first showed little interest in Chinese culture, and even the founding of schools and hospitals was considered incidental to the task of evangelization. Many Protestant missionaries of the nineteenth century were under strong revivalist influences when they made the decision to go to China. For them, all the world was divided into the damned and the saved, and the millions of heathen standing on the brink of hell could be rescued only by a minister of the gospel with his message of grace. Fletcher Brockman, a missionary to China, quotes from some of the addresses which persuaded him to enter mission work. The following, taken from the records of the 1894 convention of the Student Volunteer Movement for Foreign Missions, is typical: "Why should I go to China? . . . One reason is because a million a month in that great land are dying without God. Can you picture what it is to die without God? Can you imagine it? . . . Another reason, because 300,000,000 in China are living without God. O brothers and sisters, can you picture what it is to live without God? Have you ever thought of it, to have no hope for the future and none for the present?" Brockman says that these words greatly influenced the attitude with which he approached his work in China; only after some years of residence in Asia did he develop a broader outlook. "From the standpoint of the religious need of the missionary fields, I looked upon all of the non-Christian countries as presenting the same problem. They were composed of heathen, and at the distance from which I viewed them all heathen were alike. I believed sincerely that all non-Christian religions should be destroyed root, stock, and branch. . . . The religious leaders of China were hostile to Christianity, I thought, and I must meet them with the same spirit. It was to be a fight to the finish between light and darkness. It is a fight for life. We must conquer them or they will conquer us." [8] Today it might be understood that the success of the missionaries would entail the destruction of much of the Chinese cultural heritage, but evangelists like Brockman did not consciously accept such a goal. They were interested in the conversion of individuals, and they frequently considered an individual's religious beliefs separable from other aspects of his culture. The great missionary Griffith John spoke for many when he told a China missionary conference in 1877: "We are here, not to develop the resources of the country, not for the advancement of commerce, not for mere promotion of civilization; but to do battle with the powers of darkness, to save men from sin, and conquer China for Christ." [9] Evangelists of this persuasion

---

[8] Fletcher Brockman, *I Discover the Orient* (New York, 1935), pp. 12, 16–17.

[9] *Records of the General Conference of the Protestant Missionaries of China held at Shanghai, May 10–24, 1877* (Shanghai, 1878), p. 32 (cited as *Records, 1877*).

approached their task with a deep sense of urgency; they worked fervently to achieve the slogan of the Student Volunteer Movement: "The evangelism of the world in this generation."

The indifference with which Chinese received the gospel of salvation must have been painful indeed for the evangelist. Robert Morrison baptized his first convert after being in China for seven years, and year after year missionary reports spoke of only one, two, or at most a dozen converts at a station; even these gains had to be set against losses through death or relapse, as the missionaries labeled it. Such meager returns amid frequent illness and appallingly high death rates, especially among the wives and children of missionaries, called for dedication to a cause beyond material considerations. It also demanded frequent reassessment of goals and methods and a constant search for new avenues of approach. It was out of frustration and the need for new mission techniques that some missionaries began to turn to educational work.

Turn to Education

Since theory generally lagged behind practice, theoretical justification for educational work as a legitimate phase of evangelism evolved slowly. The demands of the Chinese environment rather than studies in mission methodology first persuaded missionaries to found schools, translate Western works, and compile dictionaries. One consequence was that individuals who were already devoting much of their time and energy to educational work continued to consider that work decidedly secondary to evangelist activities. A more significant consequence was that gaps in communication developed between the educational missionaries and the evangelists and even wider ones between the missionaries in the field and the Western mission boards. The evangelists assumed the superiority of their work, so that educational missionaries were constantly on the defensive and felt obliged to give great emphasis to the evangelistic goals of their education. Such emphasis delayed the growth and theoretical justification of the schools as academic institutions. Calvin Mateer, for example, became known as one of the earliest advocates of higher education under Christian auspices; the institution which he founded in 1864 eventually became a component of Cheeloo University in Shantung province. Yet, in a speech to the 1877 conference of Protestant missionaries in China, Mateer felt it necessary to devote over half of his address to answering criticisms of educational work by missionaries, and before listing the many contributions of mission schools, he acknowledged the subsidiary nature of education. "While education as a mission agency, is highly important, it is not the *most* important. It cannot be made to take the place of preaching, which without controversy stands first in importance." Finally, Mateer, who was to devote much of his life in China to teaching, translating, and composing science and language textbooks, stated that he thought no missionary should give his whole time to teaching, to the neglect of preaching.[10] Even Mateer's cautious defense of education met with rebuttal by conference members.

The mission boards in the West were still more prone to give priority to evangelistic work. For them the outstanding characteristic of all mission fields was that they were heathen, and this one great similarity outweighed all cultural differences. Without the direct experience in China which had drawn missionaries into educational work, many mission boards expressed impatience with calls for teachers or school building funds. They cautioned against losing sight of the primacy of direct evangelism. The Reverend A. P. Happer's first proposal for the founding of a Christian college in Canton was not approved by the Presbyterian Board of Foreign Missions (U.S.A.) in 1885; permission was given only when he suggested that a separate board of trustees be made financially responsible for the institution.[11] Even the small classes sponsored by north China missionaries during the 1860's and 1870's brought warnings from the American Board of Commissioners for Foreign Missions (ABCFM) against losing sight of the supreme goal, "the salvation of souls from sin." In 1868 the governing body of the ABCFM recommended that its North China Mission accept no new pupils in its schools. Members of the China Mission not only protested; they even expanded their educational work and in 1883 supported an ambitious plan for an Anglo-Chinese college. Presum-

[10] *Records, 1877,* pp. 171–179.

[11] Happer's plans for a college were later published in a small pamphlet entitled *Prospectus of a Christian College in China* (no publisher, no date, but probably 1886; in Cornell University Wason Collection). Many of the records of the institution have been transferred from the New York office of the Board of Trustees of Lingnan University to Harvard University.

ably, they were disappointed but not surprised when the American Board refused to provide funds for the project.[12]

Despite the admonitions of the mission boards and fellow evangelists, some China missionaries continued to found schools and engage in other educational activities. Why? To a very considerable extent because of the indifference of the Chinese. It was all very well to talk of the importance of direct evangelism, but it was difficult to maintain enthusiasm for preaching tours which brought few tangible results.[13] What was to be accomplished by preaching in a street chapel to an audience of the missionary's helpers and servants? Or, if there were an audience, had not most of them come to gawk at the barbarian's strange blue eyes and long nose? Or perhaps to make sport of the foreigner's outlandish accent? Certainly few in the audience expressed interest in the foreigner's message, and most had lost interest by the next time the missionary came around on his itinerary. Aware of the great respect of Chinese for the written word, some missionaries sought to attract inquirers by distributing religious tracts. These were often gladly received; in fact, in some cases there was such a scramble for the books that missionaries resorted to tossing them in the air, to be caught by those who could reach them, "much as you would throw a handful of pennies among a crowd of beggars." [14] Unhappily, missionaries often discovered that their religious tracts were being sold for waste paper and used for wrapping parcels or making shoe soles. Experiences of these kinds persuaded some evangelists to turn to teaching.

Missionaries who were preaching to nonexistent congregations did not necessarily feel the need for well-reasoned theory justifying educational work. They found a permanent audience by drawing a few ragamuffins off the street, furnishing them with room and board, and instructing them in Bible and Chinese. If the Chinese were

[12] ABCFM, *Annual Report, 1889* (Boston, 1890), p. 82; also, Roberto Paterno, "Davello Z. Sheffield and the Founding of the North China College," in Harvard University, *Papers on China* (Cambridge, Mass., 1947–), XIV (1960), 110–130.

[13] See for example the statement of John Leighton Stuart, son of a China missionary and later president of Yenching University, in *Fifty Years in China: The Memoirs of John Leighton Stuart, Missionary and Ambassador* (New York, 1954), p. 28.

[14] Statement by the Reverend B. C. Henry in *The Cross and the Dragon or Light in the Broad East*, 2d ed. (New York, 1885), p. 249.

hostile or indifferent, then their desire for literacy could be used to establish contact. At least a regular class of students would provide an audience for the missionary's teachings, and he could hope in time to convey to his pupils some of the essentials of the Christian doctrine. Haphazardly then, numerous tiny schools were begun. Sometimes the missionary simply subsidized a tutor in Chinese, provided the tutor allow the missionary to speak on Christianity several times a week. Other missionaries opened classes in their own homes or rented a room in which they could offer Biblical instruction while a Chinese provided the traditional curriculum emphasizing the Confucian classics. Missionary wives gave instruction in needlework, Chinese characters, and the Christian religion to a few orphans or former slave girls. Since it was difficult to attract pupils without offering free room and board, many of the classes quickly evolved into boarding schools. Often, the missionaries were not satisfied until they had added courses in science and mathematics, world history and geography.

With the growth of the Chinese Christian community, missionaries desired schools in which to educate Christians and the children of Christians. They did not wish the children of their converts to attend non-Christian schools, where the Confucian classics were taught without Christian emendations and where all their Christian teachings might be undermined. And yet, if the missionaries did not provide the schools, it was the traditional education or none at all. In most cases, it would actually have been none at all, since the majority of the early converts were too poor to pay for any education. Another argument for mission schools, therefore, was that the Christians must provide free education for their converts if they were not to have an illiterate church. Since most Protestants believed that the Bible was the authoritative witness to the Christian faith, it followed that Chinese Christians should be taught to read it. Missionaries also hoped that by providing schools they could produce an intelligent church membership and thus raise the status of Christianity in the eyes of Chinese.[15]

[15] The arguments for establishing schools for Christians were frequently repeated; the following sources are two among many: Letter of Bishop William Bacon Stevens to Bishop H. Potter, March 5, 1877 (Wason Collection, pamphlet); N. G. Clark, "Higher Christian Education as a Missionary Agency," *Report of the Centenary Conference on the Protestant Missions of the World held in London, 1888* (London, 1888), II, 185–186.

The need to train Chinese assistants for evangelical work furnished another reason for establishing mission schools. Though most missionaries had at first given little thought to the creation of a Chinese pastorate, they soon discovered that they were heavily dependent on Chinese helpers. Chinese Christians could sometimes gain access to groups which would not accept the foreigners; they knew the language of the people and knew better than the missionaries, how to appeal to the people. In the drive to spread the message of salvation, many missionaries attempted to cover a wide territory; after they had made a few converts in one village, they sought Chinese helpers to look after the small congregation while they themselves went on to other villages to preach. Since Chinese frequently would not enter into contracts with Westerners, the missionaries used Chinese aides to rent or buy property for new mission centers. Some missionaries, therefore, organized schools in which they could educate future Christian workers in the Chinese classics, in Western history, science, and mathematics, and in Christian doctrines. The Chinese classics were necessary so that the minister could attain the status of an educated man; science and mathematics, the missionaries said, were essential to train the reasoning ability; and Western history and geography provided the necessary framework for Christian theology.

Many evangelists continued to find these arguments in favor of mission education unconvincing. They retained their belief that the first duty of the missionary was to convert Chinese to Christianity; they still hoped for the speedy adoption of Christianity by the Chinese nation and were impatient with the small number of conversions in the mission schools. Some evangelists believed, furthermore, that missionaries who spent their time teaching such secular subjects as science and mathematics were betraying a trust. Men who had received the commission to preach the Christian message and who were supported by funds given specifically for missionary work had no right to engage in such secular work as education. There was also opposition to the use of mission funds to teach the Chinese classics, for these heathen works were considered a deterrent to the acceptance of Christianity by Chinese. Still others argued that conversion depended on faith, not knowledge. Education in Western science and philosophy and in the Chinese classics was said to make a Chinese less receptive to Christian teaching. Finally, it was pointed out that many of those educated in mission schools did not enter Christian work, but sought lucrative positions in the treaty ports where they indulged in all manner of vice.[16]

At the Liverpool international missionary conference of 1860 and the Shanghai missionary conference of 1877 much time was spent in the defense of education as a facet of the evangelist's work.[17] When a missionary told the Liverpool conference that there was danger that money raised for preaching the gospel was being unduly spent on education, he was widely applauded. Cheers rose when he recommended that missions should "ever estimate their educational work according to its value and direct bearing upon the progress of the Redeemer's cause in the hearts of men." The opposition to education gradually declined, however. Though missionary educators remained on the defensive, their arguments carried the authority of experience. There were always some who objected in principle to educational work by missionaries, but by the 1890 Shanghai conference, the majority seems to have accepted education as a legitimate responsibility of China missions.

Goals of Mission Schools

Such acceptance did not end the controversy over mission education; rather, the arguments shifted ground. Instead of discussing whether mission schools should exist, missionaries turned to debates on the purpose and kind of education offered. Individual missionaries, after all, had founded schools without awaiting the outcome of the controversy over the legitimacy of mission education. By 1890 hundreds of tiny institutions were already in existence, and a few missionary educators had begun to nurture high ambitions for their

[16] *Ibid.*; T. W. Houston, "The Highest Efficiency of Educational Branch of Mission Work Dependent upon Cooperation of Evangelistic Branch," *The Chinese Recorder*, XXVIII (1897), 229. This magazine was first published in 1867 under the title *The Missionary Recorder*; it then became *The Chinese Recorder and Missionary Journal*; long before it officially shortened its title to *The Chinese Recorder* in 1911, it was familiarly known by its shorter name; cited as *CR*. See *Records, 1877*, pp. 198, 203; *Report of Centenary Conference, 1888*, II, 247; G. A. Stuart, "How Mission Money is Expended," *CR*, XXIII (1892), 262: A. J. Gordon, "Education and Missions," *CR*, XXV (1894), 68–69.

[17] See Thomas Gardiner, C. B. Leupolt, and Thomas Smith in *Conference on Missions Held in 1860 at Liverpool* (London, 1860), pp. 116–121, 145; *Records, 1877*, pp. 164, 179, 203.

creations. Thus, by the time mission schools had gained general assent, some educators had moved ahead to goals which stressed the academic standards of the education offered. Some were talking of raising the level of their schools to that of colleges or establishing a college to cap the middle schools already under their supervision. They were seeking to broaden the curriculum of the schools with the inclusion of more courses in science, mathematics, history, and philosophy. They wanted more teachers and better equipment. Their ambitions almost immediately gave rise to conflicts between the religious purpose and the academic goals of the institutions and to controversies over the relative weight to be given to each. This was to be a concern of the missionaries and mission boards throughout the history of the schools.

Since the missionary educators disagreed among themselves as to the purpose and kind of education to be offered, the reasons they gave for wishing to emphasize higher education were varied. One reason, not always mentioned, but generally present, was pride in the institutions already founded and pleasure in the academic work. Also contributing to academic ambitions was a sense of rivalry among Protestant denominations and various mission stations. A report that one group was planning to establish a college frequently acted as a stimulus for other denominations or mission centers; and in making their appeals for support, the China missionaries were aware that mission boards in the West were subject to this sense of competition. In 1888 it was proposed that the Methodist church (U.S. North) found a university in Peking. The following year the Congregationalists of the North China Mission reported the Methodist project and requested that T'ungchow High School be raised to the status of a college. The American Board gave its consent after having refused support for previous proposals.[18] In recommending the establishment of a Christian college at Canton, the Reverend B. C. Henry referred more than once to the institutions at Foochow and Shanghai.[19]

Most of the reasons given for higher education, however, emphasized the evangelistic goals of the missionaries, and the arguments

[18] I. T. Headland, "Sketch of the History of the North-China Mission of the Methodist Episcopal Church," *CR*, XXVI (1895), 420.
[19] Henry, *Cross and Dragon*, pp. 432, 454.

generally fell into three categories: conversion of the upper classes in the hope that their conversion would influence the masses; the need for college training for Christian converts and workers in Christian schools, hospitals, and churches; and the hope of Christianizing the whole Chinese nation. Though these purposes were not mutually exclusive, they did frequently lead to different conclusions concerning the clientele of the colleges and the kind of education to be offered. The famous missionary Timothy Richard was one of those who wanted colleges which would attract members of the upper classes. He felt that Protestant missionaries were mistaken in their concentration on the poorer classes. According to Richard, a widespread change in Chinese attitudes had occurred by the 1880's, and Christians should take advantage of the new interest in science, mathematics, and Western languages by offering such subjects under Christian auspices. The conversion of members of the gentry or even a favorable attitude on their part toward Christianity could strongly influence other classes to accept Christianity.[20] Richard's proposal for a Christian university in each provincial capital was rejected as impractical and extravagant, but more modest projects with similar goals did get a hearing at this time. The statements of purpose by Peking University (Methodist) and the Christian College at Canton indicated that they hoped to offer a broad educational program for both Christians and non-Christians. According to the catalogue of Peking University, it would operate under Christian, evangelical principles, but at the same time it hoped "to aid the youth of the Chinese Empire and other countries in obtaining a literary, scientific, and professional education."[21] The prospectus for the Canton school stated its intention "to raise up educated men to be Christian ministers, teachers and physicians, as well as for every other calling in life, by teaching Western science, medicine, and religion."[22]

D. Z. Sheffield represented those educators whose primary interest was in training Christians and church workers. Though he came to

[20] Timothy Richard, *Conversion by the Million in China, Being Biographies and Articles* (Shanghai, 1907), II, 66; William E. Soothill, *A Mission in China* (Edinburgh, 1907), pp. 149–150.

[21] *Calendar of Peking University, China, 1896–97* (Oswego, N.Y., n.d.), p. 11.

[22] *Prospectus of a Christian College in China*, p. 5.

China deeply committed to the techniques of direct evangelism, he was by 1889 prime mover behind the proposal to broaden the curriculum of his boy's school and raise it to the level of a college. Sheffield's arguments were based on the realization that the Chinese had an ancient and complex cultural heritage. Being heathen was not necessarily identical with being uncivilized, and furthermore, being Christian in a non-Christian civilization was quite different from being Christian in the Judeo-Christian society of the West. Though a sudden sense of conversion might seem sufficient for church membership in a Christian society, in China the convert's faith was likely to be quickly diluted by heathen influences, as Sheffield put it. "A strong, well-balanced Christian character is not a creation but a growth, not an act but a process," Sheffield wrote, and he concluded that certain missionaries should give themselves to intensive rather than extensive work since education of high quality was essential for faithful and intelligent Christians. Obviously Sheffield's experience in China not only had forced him to turn from direct evangelism to education, but had also broadened his definition of Christianity to include many aspects of Western civilization. Sheffield, nevertheless, remained in a middle-of-the-road position among missionary educators. His school was primarily for Christian converts, the sons of Christians, and future Christian workers. He could not accept the goals of the Peking and Canton colleges which hoped to attract non-Christians from gentry families. Nor did he have hope of Christianizing all Chinese society through education.[23]

A few missionary educators in the nineteenth century did talk of Christianizing Chinese society, and in their minds this was hardly distinguishable from Westernizing Chinese civilization. Religion, they had come to believe, was not something apart from all other aspects of culture. Since there was little hope of converting China to Christianity as long as Chinese lived in a heathen civilization, the

[23] The summary of Sheffield's views is based on the following sources: ABCFM, *Annual Report, 1889*, p. 82; Sheffield, "The Relation of Christian Education to the Present Condition and Needs of China," *Records, 1890*, pp. 470–474; Sheffield, "The Relation of Christian Education to other Branches of Mission Work," *CR*, XXI (1890), 253–254; Sheffield, "Christian Education: Its Place in Mission Work," *CR*, XXVIII (1897), 80; Paterno, "Sheffield and North China College," pp. 117, 119–120, 138–145.

whole Chinese culture must be Christianized. The following argument, for example, was given for establishing St. John's, one of the
early China Christian colleges: "Buddhism and Taonism [sic] and
Confucianism, the three religious sects of the Chinese, are interwoven throughout with false history, false science, false geography,
false chronology, false philosophy, yet all these falsities alleging
some divine basis; thus making a false theology uphold a defective
education, and a defective education uphold a false religion. . . .
Modern science and literature, by teaching a true history, chronology, geography, philosophy, etc., will necessarily displace the
false, and this removed, . . . their now boasted religions will of necessity topple and fall." [24] Such a thesis was based on several assumptions; one was the superiority of Western civilization to Chinese
civilization. This particular proposition was taken for granted by
most Westerners of the time and hardly seemed to require discussion, but there was the additional assumption that Western civilization was Christian and that Western political institutions, science,
and literature were dependent on, if not the products of, the Christian religion. Since Christianity and Western civilization thereby
became practically identical, the importation of Western knowledge
became a means of Christianizing China.

Calvin Mateer did not shrink from such propositions. In a speech
which in 1877 seemed far ahead of its time, Mateer argued that
Christian missionaries should teach the science and arts of the West
first because they were good in themselves and would bring untold
blessings to China and second because the commission to take the
gospel to all peoples meant "to make the *nations* Christian nations,
to destroy heathenism and to cause Christian faith and morals to
interpenetrate the whole structure of society." He gladly undertook
the task of revolutionizing Chinese society, and science could aid in
this task. It was not by accident that the great scientific discoveries
had all been made by Christian nations, he said; science belonged
to the church and should be used to open doors and prepare the way
for the acceptance of Christianity. Another argument not entirely
compatible with his previous ones was then added by Mateer: since
China would in any event import Western science and mathematics,

[24] Letter by Bishop Stevens to Potter, 1877.

missionaries should see that these subjects were studied under Christian rather than secular, materialist auspices.[25] Thus the controversy over the purpose and role of mission schools continued.

The manner in which Christian schools originated in China shaped their early history and contributed to their isolation from traditional Chinese education. Initiated reluctantly and almost incidentally by a few missionaries, Christian schools found theoretical justification only after they had acquired lives of their own as institutions. They arose out of the evangelistic needs of the missionaries rather than as a result of the demands of Chinese and they were only tangentially related to Chinese schools already in existence. Since there had been no overall planning and little concern with Chinese educational philosophy, they were disruptive intrusions. Their purpose was in direct opposition to that of Chinese academic institutions. As they grew, they tended to model their curricula, teaching methods, and organization after those of denominational institutions in the United States. Thus, they departed even further from traditional Chinese education.

Chinese education was normally oriented toward the civil service examinations. Through the examination system, the Chinese government encouraged private support of numerous small schools under one or two tutors while contributing little financial aid itself. Educating a bright lad could be a profitable investment for a family, since entrance to the bureaucracy opened doors to economic gain as well as political power. Through the examinations, the government also controlled the purpose and content of Chinese education. The creation of a cultivated gentleman of high moral character was, according to Confucian teachings, accomplished primarily by education, and such an individual could serve his government wherever needed, while clerks handled the more technical aspects of his job. Chinese education did actually attempt to fulfill this goal, but in a narrow and sometimes distorted fashion. Education consisted largely

[25] C. W. Mateer, "The Relation of Protestant Missions to Education," *Records, 1877*, pp. 171–179. Another statement of this viewpoint is F. L. H. Pott, "The Aim of a Christian School in China," *Records of the Third Triennial Meeting of the Educational Association of China* (Shanghai, 1899), p. 67 (cited as *Records, EAC, 1899*).

of the study and memorization of certain works designated as the Confucian classics and the reading of orthodox commentaries on these classics. In addition, a student was expected to attain a style of calligraphy that was handsome or at least accurate and to learn to compose poetry and essays in classical style. Since, however, success in the examinations opened the way to the most lucrative and prestigious of occupations, state service, most Chinese considered passing the civil service examinations the real goal of education. What was meant to be humanistic education was often transformed into professional training.

Those who passed the higher examinations were generally able, intelligent, and also conservative. By the time they had reached this pinnacle, they had been subjected to many years of indoctrination in the Confucian tradition and were inclined to believe that their prestige and position depended on the maintenance of the status quo. They were, under ordinary conditions, an important element in the safety and perpetuity of the dynasty and of China's cultural heritage; they were not generally receptive to proposals requiring rapid or fundamental change. Though education can normally be expected to uphold accepted social ideals, the bond between Chinese education and ethical indoctrination was unusually close. Everything about the educational system was calculated to encourage social orthodoxy; almost nothing was designed to create a consciousness of real alternatives.

Little wonder, then, that both Chinese and missionaries considered the mission schools quite outside the normal educational system. Though the early Christian schools, like those of the Chinese, were simple, one-room affairs in which the pupils shouted their lessons, and though Chinese tutors were hired to give instruction in the classics, the institutions were still not a part of Chinese educational tradition. Ethical indoctrination was the heart of both the Chinese and Christian schools, and in this fundamental area they were poles apart. The Christians taught doctrines which denied the basic values of Confucianism. Nineteenth-century Protestantism embodied individualism, an admiration for competition and the work ethic, and a belief in progress; these values stood in contrast to Confucian emphasis on stability, familism, and the status society and would, if put in practice, revolutionize China. Considering the Chinese heritage a deterrent to the conversion of China, missionaries had few compunctions about participating in its destruction, and they eagerly hailed signs of change. No matter how great the physical similarity of the Christian and Chinese schools, therefore, the mission schools were alien elements on the landscape.

II | Nineteenth-Century Origins

For the China Christian colleges, the nineteenth century was a time of beginnings, a time when administrative and academic patterns were laid down and when the institutions were still trying to justify their existence to the missionary and Chinese communities. Little work of actual college level was offered. Almost every important mission center included a primary school by the end of the century; many mission societies maintained secondary schools, and a few were supporting institutions called colleges or universities. It is sometimes difficult to determine the founding dates of these colleges. Though a few of them were founded as institutions of higher education, most grew out of primary schools that had become secondary schools and then junior colleges. In any case, the institutions often assumed the name college while they still had few or no students doing advanced work. The upper divisions were not separated from the lower; and with the majority of the students, faculty, and courses in the preparatory field, they had neither the atmosphere nor the academic standards of a college. The reports issued by the schools, however, naturally tended to give as early a founding date as possible. Because the schools claiming to be colleges were not clearly differentiated from other educational institutions and because the missionary educators often taught classes at different levels, the discussion of changing attitudes toward Christian education was not restricted to opinions concerning college level work. In the history of the founding of individual schools and of their academic work, it is possible, however, to limit the subject by concentrating on those institutions which eventually became recognized colleges or components of colleges.

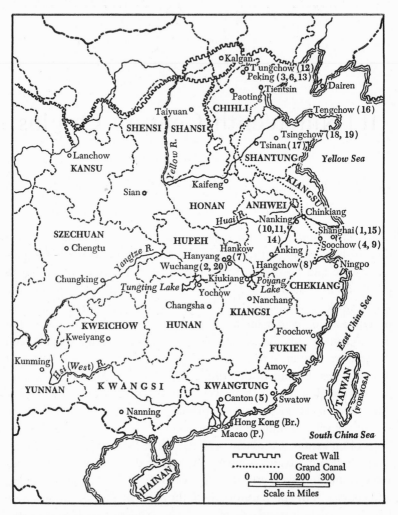

Nineteenth-Century China

Location of the Forerunners in 1900

1. Anglo-Chinese College of Shanghai, Shanghai
2. Boone School, Wuchang
3. Bridgman Academy, Peking
4. Buffington Institute of Soochow, Soochow
5. Christian College in Canton, Canton
6. Gordon Memorial Theological College, Peking
7. Griffith John College, Hankow
8. Hangchow Presbyterian College, Hangchow
9. Kung Hong School of Soochow, Soochow
10. Nanking Christian College, Nanking
11. Nanking University, Nanking
12. North China College, T'ungchow
13. Peking University, Peking
14. Presbyterian Academy, Nanking
15. St. John's University, Shanghai
16. Tengchow College, Tengchow
17. Tsinan Medical College, Tsinan
18. Tsingchow Boys' Boarding School, Tsingchow
19. Tsingchow Theological Institute, Tsingchow
20. Wesley College, Wuchang

The Forerunners

The earliest schools illustrate most clearly the view that education should be an adjunct of evangelism. Classes were begun by missionaries who were primarily concerned with gaining Christian converts, and it would often be a decade or more before the goal of college status was acknowledged by founder or institution. The schools which were the forerunners of Hangchow Christian University, Cheeloo University, and Yenching University fall into this category.

One year after the first American Presbyterian missionary arrived in Ningpo in 1844, the precursor of Hangchow Christian University (Chih-chiang ta-hsüeh) was founded. Ningpo Boys' Academy was designed primarily for training Christian ministers and assistants for the missionary work of that region. The school opened with thirty pupils and enrollment grew slowly, for the Chinese were reluctant to become associated with the foreigners, and many were convinced that the missionaries had evil motives for providing free schooling. Several epidemics in the school appeared to confirm their suspicions, so that by 1866–1867 the enrollment had declined to eighteen.[1] Only by providing food, housing, clothing, and medical care in addition to instruction could the missionaries persuade families to place their sons in the institution. Most of the pupils were from poor families and were not Christians, but a great deal of time was devoted to Christian instruction and worship, and a significant proportion of the students staying for any length of time became Christian converts. Among the minority who remained long enough to graduate, many entered church work or other activities associated with the mission. Of the first graduating class of eight in 1850, one pupil remained to teach in the school, one studied medicine under a medical missionary, four went to work for the Presbyterian Printing Press, and two returned to their homes.

[1] *Catalogue of Hangchow High School,* 1894 (Shanghai, 1894), pp. 1–2; D. N. Lyon and J. H. Judson, "Historical Sketch of the Hangchow High School," in *Jubilee Papers of the Central China Presbyterian Mission, 1844–94* (Shanghai, 1895), p. 93; also J. C. Garritt, "Historical Sketch of the Ningpo Station," in the same volume, pp. 5–13; Clarence B. Day, *Hangchow University: A Brief History* (New York, 1955), pp. 1–13. Though the river for which Hangchow University was named was generally known as Che-chiang, the school used an alternative name and transliteration, Chih-chiang.

When the Presbyterians (North) initiated work in Hangchow in 1867, the school was moved to that city and became known as Hangchow Presbyterian Boys' School. For many years there was no one identified with the institution who could act as its promoter and defender. Finally, in 1880 J. H. Judson was assigned to full-time educational work. While Mrs. Judson assumed responsibility for day schools which could be feeders for the academy, Mr. Judson worked to raise the academic level and broaden the curriculum. Increased Chinese interest in English, mathematics, and science contributed to a rise in enrollment and the lengthening of the school program. In 1888 the school was made the high school for the Central China Presbyterian Mission, and in 1897, under its newly adopted title Hangchow Presbyterian College, the institution offered a six-year course.[2] There were at the time approximately fifty students, most of them at the secondary school level.

Shantung Christian University, or Cheeloo University (Ch'i-lu ta-hsüeh) as it became known, was another institution with a long history. The foundation of its arts college was Tengchow School, opened by Calvin and Julia Mateer almost immediately upon their arrival in 1864 and dominated by Mateer for thirty years. In Mateer, the school had a dynamic leader who became an ardent and successful proponent of Christian higher education and who provided continuity of administration. The school began with eight pupils studying the Chinese classics and Christian ethics; it was enlarged to admit thirty students in 1869; and then, with the addition of courses in mathematics, geography, science, and music, it was divided into primary and secondary departments. The first class of three, which graduated in 1877, had attended the school almost from its inception and had received approximately the equivalent of a high school education. Two went to teach in mission schools and one became an evangelist's assistant, though all three later continued their education.[3]

[2] Day, Hangchow, pp. 14–19; "The Hangchow High School," CR, XXV (1894), 240: Lyon and Judson, "Historical Sketch," p. 93.
[3] Mrs. T. P. Crawford, "Protestant Missions in Tengchow," CR, VIII (1877), 389–391; Letter by Charles R. Mills, CR, XIII (1882), 151; William M. Decker, "The Foundations and Growth of Shantung Christian University, 1864–1917" (M.A. thesis, Columbia University, 1948), pp. 26–29.

Since Mateer believed that the sciences and mathematics would help the Chinese eradicate superstition and give them training in logical thought, he spent much of his time teaching in these fields. He also prepared Chinese-language texts in arithmetic, geometry, and algebra; and he constructed equipment so that he could give demonstration experiments in the sciences. The use of scientific experiments in the classroom was at that time a real innovation in Chinese education. Of all the Christian colleges in nineteenth-century China, Tengchow probably offered the widest range of mathematics courses, and its graduates were eagerly sought as teachers in Christian middle schools. The school adopted the name Tengchow College in 1882 and at the same time reorganized its curriculum to provide a six-year course. Its enrollment was one hundred in 1889.[4] With some justice, Cheeloo has claimed to be the first Christian institution in China to offer work of collegiate grade.

The English Baptists also founded schools which were eventually to become part of Cheeloo: a theological institute in Tsingchow in 1885 (later named the Gotch-Robinson Theological School) and a boys' boarding school in 1894.[5] By the end of the century, the coordination of the educational work of the English Baptists and American Presbyterians in Shantung was being discussed, though union as Shantung Christian University would be achieved only in the twentieth century after difficult negotiations.

Two of the four schools which were later to form Yenching University (Yen-ching ta-hsüeh) were North China College (Lu-ho shu-yüan) and Peking (Methodist) University,[6] both originating as

[4] Decker, "Foundations and Growth," p. 30; Charles H. Corbett, *Shantung Christian University (Cheeloo)* (New York, 1955), pp. 15–16, 20–21; *Catalogue of Tengchow College, 1891* (Shanghai, 1891), pp. 9–10; Daniel W. Fisher, *Calvin Wilson Mateer, Forty-five Years a Missionary in Shantung, China* (Philadelphia, 1911), pp. 207–209.

[5] By 1887 the theological school had added courses for training teachers for Christian elementary schools and a museum with scientific, medical, and religious exhibits. In 1893 a gift from Mr. and Mrs. Edward Robinson of Bristol, England, enabled the Baptist missionaries to erect a new plant for the school and museum and expand their work; the institute became known as Gotch-Robinson Theological College.

[6] In 1888 when the name Peking University was proposed, there was no government institution with this name. The imperial university founded in 1898 was first called Ching-shih ta-hsüeh-t'ang (literally, Capital University but

small primary schools in the nineteenth century. D. Z. Sheffield, who was to become so closely identified with North China College as to be considered its founder, arrived in T'ungchow in 1869 and discovered that classes for three or four boys had already been started. The school grew slowly. Because both the American Board and the Chinese were lukewarm toward mission education, it received little aid from the mission and nothing in tuition fees, and much of its support had to come from private sources, including the missionaries themselves. In 1875 it was reported that there were only thirteen students, but that the pupils were making fair progress in their classical and Christian studies and showed "marked spiritual growth".[7] Despite the small enrollment, a new school building was erected, and the curriculum was expanded to include Western subjects and courses in theology. A primary goal was to train evangelists' assistants who would be competent in both colloquial and classical styles of Chinese and could cooperate with the missionaries in producing Christian literature for China.

In 1889 the North China Mission voted to make the T'ungchow school a college serving the whole region. The American Board approved and offered modest support. Shortly thereafter, the financial position of the institution was improved by a gift of the proceeds from the sale of S. Wells Williams' Chinese dictionary.[8] When the first six college graduates received their diplomas in 1892, they had taken Bible classes, Christian evidences, mental philosophy, trigonometry, mathematics, international law, political economy, geology,

---

generally known in English as Imperial University); in 1912 this institution became Pei-ching ta-hsüeh (Peking University, familiarly called Pei-ta). The resulting confusion between the mission institution known as Peking University and the government school of the same name was one of the factors in the decision in 1925 to change the name of the Christian school to Yenching University. Where there is apt to be confusion, I shall use the names Peking (Methodist) University and National Peking University; otherwise, Peking University will refer to the Christian institution.

[7] ABCFM, *Annual Report, 1875*, p. 53. See also, Howard S. Galt, "Yenching University, Its Sources and Its History" (MS at the United Board for Christian Higher Education in Asia; New York, preface dated 1939), p. 30. Galt became president of North China Union College in 1910. T'ungchow was a city about fifteen miles east of Peking.

[8] ABCFM, *Annual Report, 1889*, p. 82; Paterno, "Sheffield and North China College," pp. 122–138; *The China Mission Hand-book* (Shanghai, 1896), pp. 158–159.

physical geography, universal history, and Chinese studies. They had not studied English, and all of their courses had been given in Chinese; in order to make the latter possible Sheffield was devoting much time to the composition and translation of textbooks into Chinese. A further reorganization in 1893 divided the institution into North China College (including a high school) and Gordon Memorial Theological Seminary. By 1898 North China College of T'ungchow reported thirty-six students in the college division and thirty-eight at the secondary level.[9] Though the American Board found satisfaction in the strong religious emphasis of the school, the preference of the home board for direct evangelism strained its relations with educational missionaries in the field on more than one occasion.

The primary school which was the forerunner of Peking (Methodist) University was established in 1870; the students were at first three boys who attended because the mission let it be known "that the school closed each day with a bowl of rice." [10] After several reorganizations under its part-time missionary teachers, the small school developed into a boarding school and then into a secondary school known as Wiley Institute. A medical course was added in 1886. Eighty students were enrolled in 1889, when a visiting Methodist bishop recommended that the institute become a university. With the organization of a board of trustees in New York and incorporation under New York state law in 1890, Peking University officially came into existence. In addition to a preparatory school and an industrial school, the three major divisions were the College of Liberal Arts, Wiley College of Theology, and the College of Medicine. The first class of five graduated in 1892.[11]

Though the goals of Peking University were stated in broad terms, the evangelistic purposes of the institution were not neglected; attendance at chapel services was required twice daily; there was required Bible study once a week, and revival meetings were held annually. To secure as many Christian teachers as possible, Peking

[9] Galt, "Yenching University," p. 32.

[10] Bishop I. W. Wiley, in Dwight W. Edwards, Yenching University (New York, 1959), p. 5.

[11] Calendar of Peking University, China, 1896–97, pp. 3, 11–12; Galt, "Yenching University," p. 8; Headland, "Sketch of North China Mission," CR, XXVI (1895), 418–420.

University, like several other Christian colleges, hired graduates of Mateer's Tengchow College as instructors in mathematics, science, and Chinese. H. H. Lowry assumed the presidency in 1894 and retained this position until the institution became a part of Yenching University in the twentieth century. During his leadership, Lowry emphasized raising the academic standing of the school and expanding its area of influence.

St. John's College (later St. John's University, Sheng-yüeh-han ta-hsüeh) was one of the first institutions to be founded as a college. Bishop Schereschewsky of the American Episcopal Church had opened a financial campaign for the college in 1877. One purpose of the institution, he said, was the education of Chinese ministers, but such education was not to be the usual Bible training supplemented by a few years of work on the primary school level. Schereschewsky contemplated a well-rounded, six-year course, and he hoped that his college would attract outstanding young Chinese to "our Christian religion and Christian civilization".[12] Though Schereschewsky was able to raise only US$26,000 of his $100,000 goal, the Board of Missions of the Episcopal Church promised an annual appropriation of $6,000 for three years. At Jessfield, just outside Shanghai, the cornerstone of the first college building was laid in April 1879, and the first students arrived the following September. About forty boys were transferred from two small Episcopal schools founded some years earlier.[13]

Though St. John's was founded as a college, its work for over a decade was at the secondary level. The majority of the first pupils were Christians, and they were provided with food, clothing, housing, books, and supplies. Living quarters were purposely simple, with no heat and only candles for light in the dormitories. The daily schedule was rigidly maintained: 6:45 A.M., prayers; 8:00–12:00 P.M., study and recitation; 12:00–2:00, recess; 2:00–5:00, study and recitation; 5:00, prayers, supper; 7:30–8:30, study; 9:00, lights out. A brief walk after supper was permitted, and a half-holiday was given on Saturday. In addition to three missionaries who taught part

[12] Samuel Schereschewsky, *An Appeal for Establishing a Missionary College in China* (Philadelphia, 1877), pp. 3–4 (Wason pamphlet).
[13] F. L. H. Pott, "History of St. John's University," in *St. John's University, 1879–1929* (Shanghai, 1929), pp. 1–2, 4.

time, the faculty included Yen Yung-chiung, who had been educated in the United States at Kenyon College and ordained to the
priesthood in 1870. Yen not only served as Proctor and Professor of
Mathematics and Natural Philosophy but also translated several
scientific works into Chinese. The English courses introduced in
1881–1882 proved of great importance in the history of the institution, for St. John's soon became a center for English language study.
Another important event was the arrival in 1886 of F. L. Hawks
Pott, who was to guide the school for fifty-two years and was to
become a leading advocate of Christian higher education in China.
Pott vigorously set to work to raise the standards of the institution;
he reorganized the course of study, established entrance examinations in Chinese and English, added a three-year collegiate course,
and secured funds for additional buildings and equipment. The first
college class graduated in 1895. St. John's included after 1896 the
preparatory school and three major departments: theology, medicine, and arts and sciences, which was by far the largest and which
attracted many non-Christians because of its excellent training in
the English language.[14]

Many other mission schools were established during the nineteenth century; some were called universities or colleges, and some
were later to develop into colleges, but none offered a full college
course before 1900. There was Nanking University, begun in the
home of its first president, John C. Ferguson. The founders apparently hoped to take advantage of the 1887 government decree that
mathematics might be included in the civil service examinations, for
the 1888 meeting of the Central China Mission of the Methodist
Episcopal Church stated that the school "was designed to teach
science for the higher degrees and thus to gain a standing with the
literary classes."[15] In 1871 in Wuchang a few boys were attracted

---

[14] Ibid., p. 4. See also, "An Historical Sketch of the China Mission of the
Protestant Episcopal Church, U.S.A.," in the same volume, p. 53, and Mary
Lamberton, St. John's University, Shanghai, 1879–1951 (New York, 1955),
pp. 11–45.

[15] B. C. Henry, "Editorial Notes and Missionary News," CR XIX (1888),
590. Actually the inclusion of mathematics in the civil service examinations
was hedged about with numerous restrictions, and exceedingly few candidates
ever offered the subject; see Knight Biggerstaff, The Earliest Modern Government Schools in China (Ithaca, N.Y.; 1961), pp. 28–30.

by the promise of free tuition and board plus a small subsidy to Boone school opened by the American Episcopal Mission. The school, founded to train Chinese clergymen and church leaders, added college-level courses in 1903 and adopted the name Boone University in 1909. Eventually Boone was to join several small schools in central China to form Huachung University (Hua-chung ta-hsüeh) in Wuchang.[16] Among the several Shanghai and Soochow schools associated with the Southern Methodists, Shanghai Anglo-Chinese College was founded in the 1880's by one of the most influential China missionaries, Young J. Allen. The Methodist Mission of East China recommended in 1889 that Anglo-Chinese College and its other institutions of higher education be merged to form Soochow University (Tung-wu ta-hsüeh), a union that, as it turned out, was actually accomplished in the twentieth century.

The story of the origins of the institution that became Lingnan University (Ling-nan ta-hsüeh) at Canton illustrated the continuing controversy over the purposes of mission education and the effect of the controversy on the school's growth. By the 1880's missionaries in Canton and Macao had already organized several small schools, a training institute for pastors, and informal medical instruction; and B. C. Henry and A. P. Happer of the American Presbyterian mission were beginning to envision a Christian college. Henry argued that since the Chinese wanted to learn the English language and Western science, the missionaries should see that they obtained the knowledge under Christian auspices. He advocated "not a theological school, not a school in which religious teaching is given undue prominence, but one after the model of our colleges at home, where the first thing would be the study of English and afterward a thorough training in the arts course." [17] Happer's plans were also broadly conceived; by teaching Western science, medicine, and religion, the college would contribute to the enlightenment and Christianization

---

[16] *Boone University Fiftieth Anniversary Report, 1871–1921*, pp. 1–4; MacGillivray, *Century of Protestant Missions*, p. 303; "Boone University, Wuchang," *The Educational Review*, X (1918), 25 (cited as *ER*). Though Hua Chung University would be the more correct form, I have followed the usage of the institution, Huachung University.

[17] Henry, "Shall We Assist the Chinese in Acquiring a Knowledge of the English Language," *CR*, XII (1881), 235–236; Henry, *Cross and Dragon*, see esp. pp. 427–450.

of China and would correct the many erroneous views resulting from exclusive study of the Confucian classics. Having secured the approval of the Presbyterian missionaries in Canton, Happer and Henry turned in 1885 to the United States for support.

In the meantime, a group of Cantonese who were interested in the school and feared that it might be located elsewhere, petitioned for its establishment in Canton.[18] The petition was signed by more than four hundred persons, most of them not Christians, and many from landed or merchant families. Since antagonism toward missionary activities was the norm, it is noteworthy that one-quarter of the signers were said to be government officials and ten were members of the Hanlin Academy. A reading of the petition, however, indicates that the Chinese wanted a specialized school that would provide scientific and technical training as well as instruction in the English language. Graduates would enter commerce, diplomacy, or other specific government positions. The school would be neither a competitor for regular instruction in the classics nor a model for future reorganization of Chinese education. Happer was understandably disillusioned by the amount of support offered by the Chinese petitioners as the goals of the two parties became clearer to each other.

A third view entered as the institution was organized. Happer was forced by illness to resign as president only two years after opening classes in 1888. The election of B. C. Henry as president and incorporation of the Presbyterian school, Pui Ying, gave Canton College a strong evangelistic emphasis. Though Henry had recommended a broad liberal arts program, he wanted to concentrate on evangelistic work and accepted the presidency on the condition that this be permitted. The student body of Pui Ying was largely drawn from Christian families in rural villages, and graduates looked forward to employment by the mission. Instead of the interdenominational board of directors anticipated by Happer, all were members of the Presbyterian mission and were unenthusiastic about fostering the English-language instruction sought by Chinese for commercial purposes. Happer was so deeply disturbed by what he considered a

[18] "A Petition to the Trustees of Canton Christian College by the Gentry of Kwangtung, Requesting the Establishment of a Scientific College in Canton" (typewritten copy of translation by son of one of the petitioners located at UB).

distortion of his original goals that he sought to withdraw his support and even considered founding another institution.[19] Though Canton Christian College eventually became a multipurpose institution under a nondenominational board, its growth was long delayed by conflict over the purpose of the institution, difficulty in building up loyal supporters, and lack of continuity in administration. Such problems were particularly acute at Canton, but many other Christian colleges faced similar difficulties during their early years.

The nineteenth century closed with more than a dozen Christian institutions of higher education in China. Other institutions founded during the nineteenth and twentieth centuries called themselves colleges, but did not regularly offer college courses, and many of them eventually disbanded or became high schools or junior colleges.[20]

A Tenuous Existence

Since there had been no overall plan for Christian higher education in China, and the schools had developed in a haphazard fashion, whether or not a school became a college often depended on the interest and ability of the head of the institution and the support which he could secure from his home society. A number of factors enabled a dynamic educator to have a decisive influence on the evolution of his school—the slow communications, the undeveloped state of mission theory, and the need to adjust methods to the Chinese environment. In addition, a minimum of administrative organization in the field during the nineteenth century gave ample scope to the individual; the stamp of the missionary leader on the character and development of the school was strong. At the same time the willingness of the home mission board to provide support was essen-

[19] *The Projection of the Christian College in China Located at Canton, Including a Review, Its Present Status and Prospects* (pamphlet located at UB; n.d. but probably 1897), pp. 8–12, 19; "The Christian College, Canton," *CR*, XXVII (1896), 136; Charles H. Corbett, *Lingnan University, A Short History* (New York, 1963), pp. 26–28.

[20] Among the others were William Nast College at Kiukiang in Kiangsi, Talmage College in Amoy, English Methodist College in Ningpo, and Lutheran College in Hunan. Oberlin-in-China, located at T'aiku, Shansi, also had its origins in the nineteenth century. Though it did not aspire to college status, it acquired considerable influence as a preparatory school during the twentieth century.

tial, since little income came from tuition or other contributions in China and most of the institutions had no endowment. The ability of the school president to persuade supporters in the West of the merit and urgency of his appeals was often crucial to the growth of the school. Despite some discussion of interdenominational cooperation, appeals to denominational loyalty and pride were more successful in gaining consistent support during the nineteenth century. The institutions might have begun to develop their individual images in China, but they had not yet established any such individual identities in the West, and aid was gained through identification with particular Protestant denominations.

Consequently, a relatively small number of mission societies sponsored the Christian colleges. Though the English Baptists maintained the Tsingchow schools in Shantung, most English missions of this period were little interested in fostering Christian higher education in China. Leaders in the founding of China Christian colleges during the nineteenth century were the American Methodists, Presbyterians, Congregationalists, and Episcopalians. These American societies were often larger and wealthier than the corresponding English organizations (with the exception, of course, of the Anglicans). Also, a large portion of the English funds and workers went into the China Inland Mission, a strongly evangelistic society which sponsored little educational work. Americans came from a country where many of the colleges were maintained by religious denominations, and many of the missionaries from the United States had graduated from these denominational colleges; they thus accepted higher education as a normal function of the church. Having seen the important role education played in the conversion of immigrants into Americans, these missionaries had great faith in the ability of education to change attitudes and ideals and to prepare the way for the acceptance of the Christian doctrine which they taught.

The Protestant colleges had been located in those sections of China which were earliest and most adequately penetrated by Protestant missionaries: north and east China. Most of the colleges were, in fact, located in a few cities near the coast: Peking, Tengchow, Shanghai, Soochow, Hangchow, and Canton. In these areas missionaries had established permanent residences; churches were being organized, and congregations were growing so that missionaries felt the need for educated Chinese ministers to carry on the work. The number of converts was thought to warrant institutions of higher education for Christians and children of Christians, and there were already in existence Christian primary and secondary schools which could act as feeders for the colleges. Finally, those few Chinese who were beginning to show some interest in Western languages and science were generally located in the eastern cities. In central and western China, missionary activities would not reach a comparable stage of development until after 1900.

Most of the schools were small; they drew students from families connected with the mission or poor families willing to risk identification with the missionaries in return for free support and education for their sons. The life of most schools was quite tenuous, in part because they depended on individual missionaries who might be transferred elsewhere, retire for health reasons, or be required to subordinate their educational activities to their evangelistic work. The antagonism of Chinese officials and gentry also made the survival of the institutions uncertain. Before the treaty settlement of 1858–1860, for example, the Reverend Justus Doolittle had opened a boy's school in Foochow; in 1853, when it was reported that a relative of the Chinese teacher had been imprisoned for cooperating with a Foochow missionary, both the teacher and the parents of the pupils became wary of being identified with missionary activities. The school had to close. Though Doolittle soon opened another school, it proved difficult to attract capable pupils even with free board and tuition, and in 1859 he abandoned the project.[21] During the 1860's the Reverend W. A. P. Martin secured an annual grant from Sir Robert Hart of the Chinese Maritime Customs for a school in Peking for students from the upper class. Somewhat ruefully, Martin had to admit that he was unable to spend all the funds at his disposal because of difficulty in attracting students.[22]

Hostility frequently led to opposition to missionary attempts to purchase property and buildings for their institutions. The Wesleyan Missionary Society, having decided to "provide a liberal Western education for the sons of officials and other Chinamen", sent a

[21] ABCFM, *Annual Report, 1853*, p. 132; *1854*, p. 145; *1856*, p. 170; *1859*, p. 116.

[22] W. A. P. Martin, *A Cycle of Cathay or China, South and North with Personal Reminiscences*, 2d ed. (New York, 1897), p. 235.

minister to central China in 1885 to establish Wesley College. A number of Chinese were indeed interested in learning mathematics, and some even came to inquire how many days it would take to master the subject. Their interest evidently was not great enough to overcome an aversion to an institution controlled by Western evangelists, for there was great difficulty in purchasing land. When a lot in Wuchang was finally secured in 1887, the seller was imprisoned, and the deeds remained without official seals for many years.[23] The students, furthermore, were few; and Wesley College had not yet attained full college status when Huachung University was opened in 1924 as the union Christian college for central China. Perhaps because of the resentment against Christianity left by the Taiping Rebellion, Hunan was well known as a center of anti-Christian sentiment, but missionaries found obstacles in their paths elsewhere also.

Though A. P. Happer and B. C. Henry had been encouraged by the request of some four hundred Chinese for a Canton college offering science, mathematics, and English, they too had difficulty in purchasing or renting property. Henry reported that some forms for deeds of sale or lease of property classed Christian schools and chapels with gambling houses, houses of prostitution, and houses for receiving stolen goods, and renting or selling for such evil purposes was forbidden.[24] One missionary stated that the governor-general had been disgusted by the petition asking foreigners to provide education for China, was attempting himself to foster training in science and mathematics, and was doing all that he could to obstruct the purchase of property for a Christian college.[25] Chinese who attended

[23] Arnold Foster, comp., *Christian Progress in China. Gleanings from the Writings and Speeches of Many Workers* (London, 1889), pp. 156–157; *The Educational Directory of China, 1916* (Shanghai, 1916), p. 118.

[24] Henry, *Cross and Dragon*, p. 358.

[25] Discussion by the Reverend Wilson Phraner, in *Report of Centenary Conference. 1888*, II, 205. Phraner does not give details, nor does he cite his source. Chang Chih-tung was governor-general of Liang-kuang from 1884 to 1889 and was at the time an aggressive advocate of a policy of resisting all infringements on Chinese sovereignty. He vigorously pushed the war with France and opposed the negotiations for settlement in 1885. At the same time he advocated the study of Western science and technology; and while governor-general of Liang-kuang took a special interest in the Hsi-hsüeh Kuan (School of Western Studies) at Canton, reorganizing it in 1884 and giving it the name of Po-hsüeh Kuan (School of Wide Learning), and then in 1887 converting it into a naval and military academy. See Biggerstaff, *Earliest Government Schools*, pp. 48–49, 54–57.

Christian schools or were otherwise associated with the missions were labeled "disciples of foreigners" or "followers of the red-haired devils," and it was often assumed that they were spies for the enemies of China. Since there was little recognition of the difference between Protestantism and Catholicism, Englishman and Frenchman, the misdeeds of one aroused antagonism toward all. During the conflict with France over Annam in 1884–1885, for example, Protestant converts in Canton were arrested as spies for France, and the attempt of the American Protestants to secure property for their college was made more difficult by the war.

These are only a few of the many concrete manifestations of hostility toward the missionary and his activities during the nineteenth century. As Paul A. Cohen has pointed out, the Chinese had developed an anti-Christian tradition well before the modern missions came to China, and the experience with Christian missionaries during the nineteenth century popularized and intensified this tradition.[26] Christianity suffered because it was foreign and taught doctrines that were considered superstitious and did not accord with the Confucian ethic; it was condemned, therefore, as subversive of social order and stability. Converts refused to support village festivals, which were usually closely associated with religious customs and beliefs as well as the agricultural cycle. In a culture where filial piety was basic to the whole ethical system, the demand for individual conversion and the demand that converts abandon the ancestor rites caused dissension within families. Missionaries ignored the requirements of *feng-shui* in the construction of chapels, churches, and school buildings; and they engaged in mysterious practices which led to wild rumors about missionaries' gouging out the eyes of children to make silver. Neither in their own lives nor in church activities did they observe the proper relationship between sexes as dictated by Chinese custom.

Moreover, missionaries seemed to have become rivals of the Chinese upper class for power and position.[27] In acting as teachers and

[26] Cohen, *China and Christianity*, esp. ch. x, "Chinese Xenophobia and the Foreign Missionary," pp. 262–273.

[27] See Lü Shih-ch'iang, *Chung-kuo kuan shen fan-chiao ti yüan-yin, 1860–1874* (The Origin and Cause of Anti-Christianism among Chinese Officials and Gentry) (Taipei, 1966). A translation of some of the anti-Christian tracts is available in *Death Blow to Corrupt Doctrines: A Plain Statement of Facts* (Shanghai, 1870).

ethical preceptors, they were usurping the functions of the gentry; some evangelists even assumed the dress of the Chinese scholar and demanded the scholar's privileges in matters of access to officials, mode of address, and travel. Missionaries traveled and resided in interior China, but were subject only to Western justice; they frequently came to the support of Christian converts who were thought to be persecuted and thus participated in the Chinese judicial process. Although Christians were subject to popular hostility, an official who sympathized with the hostility had to take care in calling for opposition. Violence against Christians would bring down upon his head the wrath of foreign consuls and even higher Chinese officials; the Chinese magistrate found himself caught between popular hostility toward the missionary and foreign pressure. B. C. Henry, while sympathizing with his converts and assuming their innocence, described the situation quite accurately in the 1880's: "If on the one hand, the officer fails to obtain redress and guarantee protection to Chinese Christians, as is sometimes the case, the people say, 'We have nothing to fear, we can treat them as we please; there is no one to call us to account.' If, on the other hand, the officers exert themselves and the offenders are punished, it is always treasured up as a grievance by the people, and made the occasion for secret assaults."[28] No matter what the magistrate's course of action, the result was likely to be loss of political authority and popular respect. That frequent incidents occurred despite the penalties they brought to the responsible Chinese official attests to the popularity of anti-Christian sentiment among both the masses and the gentry. The intervention of foreign consuls, in fact, aggravated existent ill will, and so incidents fed upon incidents.[29]

The missionary also received the blame for Western pressures on China and humiliating incidents in which he had no role. For many Chinese, missionary and businessman, Englishman and German, educator and evangelist were indistinguishable; they were all for-

[28] Henry, *Cross and Dragon*, p. 374.

[29] There are several studies of specific anti-Christian incidents during the nineteenth century: John K. Fairbank, "Patterns behind the Tientsin Massacre," *Harvard Journal of Asiatic Studies*, XX (1957), 480–511; James E. Kirby, Jr., "The Foochow Anti-Missionary Riot—August 30, 1878," *JAS*, XXV (1966), 665–680; Edmund S. Wehrle, *Britain, China and the Anti-Missionary Riots, 1891–1900* (Minneapolis, 1966); Ellsworth C. Carlson, "The Wu-shih-san Incident of 1878," *A Festschrift for Frederick B. Artz* (Durham, N.C., 1964).

eigners and all a threat to China. Since the missionary was the foreigner who most often came in contact with the populace, he was frequently looked upon as Western civilization personified and was resented both because of his own role as disrupter of Chinese society and because of the Western imperialism which he symbolized.

Educational Missions and Chinese Gentry

The Christian schools existed largely apart from the intellectual life of China during the 1870's and 1880's and in many cases had almost no contact with Chinese educational institutions or with Chinese officialdom. When, in a few instances during the 1890's, Chinese bureaucrats consented to attend graduation exercises or other ceremonies, the visits were hailed as indications of a significant change in official attitudes and in the standing of the mission schools. This paucity of official contact does not necessarily mean that the mission schools exercised no influence during the nineteenth century, but it does mean that the influence was not likely to be openly recognized and that the Chinese made contact with individual missionary educators rather than with the schools as institutions.

Anti-Christian sentiment was not the only reason Chinese gentry families showed no desire to enroll their sons in the Christian colleges. The mission schools seemed to serve none of the traditional goals of Chinese education, their training in the classics was inadequate to prepare students for the civil service examinations, and their graduates were accused of being unable to write in acceptable classical style. Instead of fostering orthodox values, the schools preached a religious doctrine which was at variance with much of the Chinese heritage. A major purpose of Chinese education was to make the pupil knowledgeable about the Chinese tradition and to inculcate in him respect for that tradition. The missionary, on the other hand, was constantly reminded that Chinese tradition was non-Christian, and so he could hardly afford to express any great admiration for China's past. Even those missionaries who became students of the Chinese classics and developed appreciation for Confucian teachings continued to be influenced by their original antagonism toward that which was heathen and stood in the way of Christian conversion. A certain ambivalence characterized their attitude; they had learned to respect the ethical teachings of the classics, but at the same time they believed that Confucianism was the major obstacle to acceptance of Christianity. Some tried to solve their dilemma by presenting Christianity as a more adequate fulfillment of Confucian teachings; others judged the Chinese heritage not by its ideals but by the customs they observed in nineteenth-century China; Chinese civilization in the nineteenth century was heathen, dead, tradition-bound—it must be Christianized and changed. Whereas one of the major purposes of Chinese education had been to teach respect for tradition, a major theme of mission education was the transformation of tradition. The inadequacy of the Chinese heritage and the need for change were the leitmotifs of the educational missionary.

During the second half of the nineteenth century, however, it began to be apparent even to Confucian scholars that the home of the Great Tradition was in trouble. The Taiping Rebellion, in which whole provinces were devastated and millions died, was only the most spectacular of numerous rebellions. Population growth, bureaucratic corruption, and natural disasters were making the position of the peasantry intolerable. Western nations had refused to accept the Middle Kingdom concept of foreign relations. Instead of becoming the tributary states of China, the Western nations had, in effect, made China their joint satellite. By the beginning of the T'ung Chih period (1862) a few Chinese leaders had recognized that China was faced with problems of unprecedented magnitude. At the same time they remained confident of the superiority and rightness of the Chinese tradition, and they had no thought of abandoning the Chinese heritage for Western civilization. No leader, in fact, advocated fundamental changes in the Great Tradition, and none demanded basic alterations in Chinese educational and civil service systems for the majority of the literati. Instead, they argued that revitalization of Confucian ideology and institutions was the first and most important task in the restoration of the dynasty.[30] They also favored

[30] For a perceptive study of the T'ung Chih period, see Mary C. Wright, *The Last Stand of Chinese Conservatism. The T'ung-Chih Restoration, 1862–1874* (Stanford, 1957). The brief summary given here is based on Wright's interpretation and also on Biggerstaff's excellent study of the special schools during the nineteenth century, *Earliest Government Schools*.

the importation of certain information from the West, information that would help China build up her defenses so that she would not have to accede to the demands of Westerners.

In January 1861 the throne received a famous memorial advocating the establishment of a foreign office, the Tsungli Yamen, and a language school for training interpreters and foreign relations officers. The Peking T'ung-wen Kuan opened the next year and was followed by similar schools at Canton and Shanghai. Soon thereafter, naval academies and schools for training engineers and technicians for ship yards and arsenals were approved by the throne. The advocates of self-strengthening quickly realized that training foreign language experts and military technicians was not enough; since science and mathematics were basic to the manufacture of armaments and machinery, China must educate men in these fields if she were to manufacture her own steamships and weapons instead of copying the foreigners. Science and mathematics, furthermore, were important elements of Western civilization and must be studied in order to understand the enemy. It was proposed therefore, that the Peking T'ung-wen Kuan add courses in these fields and that they be open only to Chinese with civil service degrees. Despite vociferous opposition, the new departments were sanctioned by the throne in 1867. Later in the century technical schools for training telegraph operators, army and naval officers, doctors for the army and navy, and mining engineers were founded.

Like the mission schools, these institutions were outside the normal educational program and did not prepare students for the civil service examinations. Graduation from these schools or passing examinations given by them did not ordinarily entitle one to the regular civil service degrees. Like many of the Christian colleges toward the end of the century, the government professional institutions stressed training in mathematics, science, English, and to a lesser extent French or German; and the Chinese gentry showed almost as great a reluctance to send their sons to the government schools as to the Christian institutions. One of the reasons was the same: mastery of this imported knowledge brought little prestige and rarely opened doors to influential political positions. The United States consul in Canton wrote in 1880 that fourteen students from the Canton T'ung-wen Kuan had been drafted a decade earlier for further study at the Peking T'ung-wen Kuan, but that since that time not one student from the Canton school had been called into government service.[31] Parents were generally willing to send only their least promising sons to the special schools.

Despite some similarity in curricula, the government institutes and the Christian colleges were expressions of different educational philosophies. The advocates of the government schools considered them specialized institutions for training experts; there was no intention of making their curriculum the norm. Missionary educators, on the other hand, thought of their college curriculum as furnishing the basic knowledge required of an educated man, and some had begun to talk of providing educational models for a changing China. Such assumptions, however, were far ahead of the thinking of most Chinese. It was not until the disasters of the 1890's that a few Chinese leaders began to advocate basic changes in the curriculum of traditional education.

On the other hand, the founding of the government institutions did offer individual missionary educators avenues of influence. The American Presbyterian W. A. P. Martin was president of Peking T'ung-wen Kuan from 1869 until 1895, and several missionaries closely connected with the early Christian colleges were employed in other government schools, A. P. Happer of Canton and Young J. Allen of Shanghai Anglo-Chinese College, for example. Some of the Christian educators worked for government institutes as translators of Western books on science, mathematics, international law, and economics. John Fryer was both general editor of the Christian School and Textbook Committee and a major translator for the government at the Kiangnan Arsenal from 1868 to 1896; between 1875 and 1891 he reached a fairly wide audience among literati in the eastern cities by publishing the *Ko-chih hui-pien* (The Chinese Scientific Magazine).[32] Both Fryer and Allen served as editors of *Hsi-kuo chin-shih hui-pien*, a foreign news periodical published by

[31] F. D. Chesire to George F. Seward, U.S. minister to China, March 29, 1880, in U.S. Dept. of Interior, Bureau of Education, *Progress of Western Education in China and Siam* (Washington, D.C., 1880), pp. 6–8 (Wason pamphlet).

[32] Though John Fryer came to China as a missionary educator in 1860 and remained closely associated with Christian educational work throughout his career in China, he was officially a government employee while at Kiangnan Arsenal. See Adrian A. Bennett, *John Fryer: The Introduction of Western Science and Technology in Nineteenth-Century China* (Cambridge, Mass., 1967).

the Kiangnan Arsenal for government officials, while Allen and Timothy Richard edited *Wan-kuo kung-pao* (Review of the Times), an influential monthly from which the Chinese press frequently reprinted. Despite its missionary origins, the *Wan-kuo kung-pao* was distributed for years at the civil service examinations and even received some financial assistance from Governor-General Chang Chih-tung and other officials desiring reform.[33]

Some of the textbooks used by the government schools were composed or translated by the Christian educators, and some translations reached an even wider audience. Several medical works by missionaries who were teachers as well as physicians were accepted as basic texts in medical training; and the scientific texts by Dr. A. P. Parker of Buffington Institute in Soochow and Calvin Mateer of Tengchow College were useful at a more elementary level. W. A. P. Martin's translation of *Elements of International Law* by Henry Wheaton was used as a guide in international disputes by high Chinese officials.[34] Finally, the editor of *The Chinese Recorder* reported in 1879 that Chinese officials and merchants had subscribed liberally to the work of the School and Textbook Series Committee, and John C. Ferguson, president of Nanking University, reported in 1892 "an immense sale of all kinds of mathematical and scientific books" by the Society for the Diffusion of Christian and General Knowledge, the Textbook Series Committee, and other mission groups.[35]

[33] Roswell S. Britton, *The Chinese Periodical Press, 1800–1912* (Shanghai, 1933), pp. 53–55; E. R. Hughes, *The Invasion of China by the Western World* (London, 1937), p. 110; Latourette, *Christian Missions in China*, p. 441. *Wan-kuo kung-pao* was published with occasional interruption from 1875 to 1907. Its original English title was "The Globe Magazine," but in 1889 it was changed to "A Review of the Times."

[34] Tsuen-hsuin Tsien, "Western Impact in China through Translation," *FEQ*, XIII (May, 1954), 305–327; Timothy Richard, *Forty-five Years in China* (London, 1916), pp. 218–223, 230.

[35] "Editor's Corner," *CR*, X (1879), 75; John C. Ferguson, "Higher Education in China," *CR*, XXIII (1892), 154. The Society for the Diffusion of Christian and General Knowledge among the Chinese was founded by Alexander Williamson in 1887 and in 1891 came under the leadership of Timothy Richard. Its purpose was to publish literature for Chinese officials and scholars and thus to explain the contribution of Christianity and other elements to the progress of Western civilization; in 1906 it became the Christian Literature Society for China.

Because many individuals and events were propelling Chinese leaders toward a reassessment of the Chinese heritage in the late nineteenth century, the influence of missionary educators and their publications in persuading Chinese officials of the necessity for reform cannot be isolated. It is worth noting, however, that the influential publicist Liang Ch'i-ch'ao spoke of 1890 as the year "the great world began to speak to him," and one of the important events in his life during this year was a visit to Shanghai and a chance to examine some of the European books translated into Chinese by John Fryer, Young J. Allen, and others from the Shanghai Kiangnan Arsenal.[36] K'ang Yu-wei is reported to have told the editor of the Hong Kong newspaper, *China Mail*, "I owe my conversion to reform chiefly to the writings of two missionaries, the Reverend Timothy Richard and the Reverend Dr. Young J. Allen." [37] One further evidence of the importance of translations was the statement in 1893 by a missionary at the Boone School: "We sometimes have men call upon us who are very well versed in science and mathematics, who have obtained their knowledge through the medium of books alone." [38]

The government institutions apparently drew at least a few of their students from the mission schools and became one avenue through which these students might gain minor positions in government agencies. The reluctance of gentry families to send their sons to the special schools and the attempt of the institutions to enroll students who already had some training in both Chinese and a foreign language frequently forced the schools to seek applicants among those who had little chance of entering government service through the normal examination route. In addition to the less promising sons of gentry or Manchu families, this group included sons of merchants in the treaty ports, sons of Christian families, and students in the mission schools. Though the latter groups had many handicaps in seeking admission to the special schools, they often

[36] Joseph R. Levenson, *Liang Ch'i-ch'ao and the Mind of Modern China* (Cambridge, Mass.; 1953), p. 17.

[37] Warren A. Candler, *Young J. Allen* (Nashville, 1931), pp. 174–175. For further information on contacts between missionary educators and the reform leaders of 1898, see Chapter IV.

[38] James Jackson, "Objects, Methods and Results of Higher Education in Our Mission Schools," *CR*, XXIV (1893), 7.

had the important asset of knowing some English. Schools kept few records on the backgrounds of individual students, and Chinese were reluctant to mention mission school training; these two facts make even an estimate of the number from Christian families or schools impossible. There is, however, the complaint of Hawks Pott in 1891 that many students were leaving St. John's to enter the newly founded naval academy in Nanking.[39] At least four individuals listed in *Who's Who in China, 1925,* attended St. John's or Shanghai Anglo-Chinese College before going on to one of the special government schools; three of these later entered government service and one went into business.

These contacts between the Christian educators and their institutions on the one hand and Chinese officials interested in Western learning and the special government schools on the other hand contributed to the flow of Western ideology and information into China. Until the last decade of the nineteenth century, however, the Christian institutions remained largely isolated. Though the founding of the special government schools and the growing interest in Western learning encouraged missionary educators to expand into higher education, the Christian colleges achieved no great popularity. Changes came slowly; only a small minority of the educated Chinese had gained any appreciation of Western learning by 1900, and this group had to work against a powerful and numerous opposition. The rapidity with which the Chinese heritage was abandoned in the twentieth century revealed the importance of the infiltration of disruptive ideas during the nineteenth century, but concrete evidences of basic change in the viewpoint of educated Chinese were few and far between in late nineteenth-century China. The nineteenth century was more important as a time of preparation for change than as a time of reforms deliberately undertaken.

The Chinese desire to import Western science and technology did not necessarily mean that they were ready to accept Christianity from the West. On the contrary, those who recommended changes did so because they were sensitive to infringements on Chinese sovereignty, and they often considered the missionary the personification of Western imperialist pressure. Both conservative and reformer, therefore, continued to hold anti-Christian attitudes. At the

[39] Lamberton, *St. John's,* p. 34.

same time, the evangelistic emphasis remained strong in all of the Christian colleges. Attendance was required at chapel services and Bible classes, and most missionaries agreed that religious goals should not be subordinated to secular or academic demands. When Chang Chih-tung offered to contribute handsomely to Boone if his grandson might attend the school but be excused from church services, he was turned down.[40] The grandson did not enroll. Mission educators supported the stand of the Boone authorities, just as most Chinese would have agreed with Chang Chih-tung. Submission to Christian propaganda was generally considered too high a price to pay for the privilege of instruction in Western languages and mathematics. In the eyes of some Chinese, the missionaries offered Western learning simply as a bait in order to obtain an audience for Christian teachings. Thus, Chinese antagonism and the tendency of the missionary to evaluate his work in evangelistic terms sometimes deterred recognition of the role of the Christian institutions or made their influence a negative one; it did not, however, eliminate their influence.

[40] Boone University, *Fiftieth Anniversary Report*, p. 4.

III | An Educational Alternative

The China Christian colleges of the nineteenth century experienced both the advantages and the disadvantages of being small pioneer institutions. They were poorly equipped. Many of their faculty members did not consider teaching their primary purpose and gave only part time to it. Their curricula were limited and their academic standards low. They were usually unable to attract superior students; a large proportion of their students failed to complete the course. The colleges did not fulfill the aims of traditional Chinese education, and in many ways their development and growth took place with little reference to the life and desires of the Chinese people. They were foreign institutions. On the other hand, many Chinese who would otherwise have been unable to obtain an education attended the colleges and thus raised their economic and social standing. In organization and purpose the colleges strove toward an ideal quite different from that of Chinese educational institutions: a residential academic community set apart from its neighboring environment and devoted to a liberal arts program of Western origin. The contact between student and teacher was close, and each student could receive individual attention. The schools were inexpensively run and were not yet heavy financial burdens on the supporting boards with whom they remained in close touch.

Administration and Finances

At first the institutions had little formal administration. They were run by one or more Western missionaries, who decided upon the courses to be offered and hired the Chinese teachers. The principal expense, the salary and residence of the missionaries themselves, was borne by the Western mission society; other expenses—for buildings, employment of Chinese tutors, and so forth—were also met by the mission board or by private donors. General supervision was exercised by the field board of the denomination to which the founder belonged or by the home mission board. When a school was raised to college status or when a "college" was founded, more formal organization was considered necessary.

This usually meant a board of managers in China and a board of trustees in the West. Members of both boards were ordinarily required to be Christians and, since the institutions were denominational, so were most boards.[1] The supporting mission society as a rule appointed the members of the China board of managers, though the board itself could co-opt members and occasionally the faculty of the college could elect representatives. In later years the alumni of the college were represented on the board. The China board usually consisted of the president and administrative officers of the college, representatives of the regional mission society, and interested members of the American or British diplomatic staff. During the nineteenth century there were few if any Chinese members. The duty of the China board could be loosely defined as the immediate supervision of the institution. It generally nominated the college administrators, drew up an annual budget for approval by the home board, appointed and removed the Chinese members of the faculty, sanctioned the courses of study, and superintended other matters requiring the attention of committees in the field. In the Episcopal schools, St. John's and Boone, the diocesan bishops assumed many of the supervisory duties.

Much of the administrative power lay in the hands of the boards of trustees in the West, and their approval was required in all major decisions on policy. With the aid of the mission societies, they

---

[1] There were some at least theoretical exceptions to this statement; according to the original bylaws of Peking University, the members of the China board of managers simply had to be members of a Protestant evangelical faith and residents of China; the bylaws were later modified to state that one-third of the board should be members of the Methodist Episcopal Church; in actual fact, Methodists retained control until the union to form Yenching University. Canton Christian College was organized under an interdenominational board of trustees in the West, but the majority of Western teachers and of the China board were Presbyterians.

formally appointed the president, the vice-president, and the non-Chinese members of the college faculties; in addition, they authorized the use of any Western funds for employing Chinese faculty members. Until the protests of Chinese nationalists during the 1920's and 1930's, college property was ordinarily held by the board of trustees rather than by the organization in China, and this body controlled the disposition of all property.[2] These boards accepted as a major function the raising of funds for the colleges.

In spite of the formal organization under boards of managers and boards of trustees, the foreign mission boards of the supporting denominations actually had ultimate control of the administration of the colleges. The mission societies held the purse strings. They provided a regular sum for the annual expenses of the school and paid the salaries of the missionary educators, who composed the majority of the Western college teachers. Though the missionary teachers were formally appointed by the boards of trustees, they were actually designated by the mission societies and were responsible to them. The letters and reports of college administrators to the mission boards and to the boards of trustees reveal the tight financial control exercised by the Western bodies; in fact, so much of the correspondence concerned minor financial transactions that a board secretary occasionally felt obliged to apologize for the disproportionate attention given to mercenary concerns and to assert that of course religious and educational matters were recognized as of primary importance. The Western boards really determined the budget of the colleges through their allocations, and they expected to pass on many individual expenditures. They handled the purchase of all supplies bought in the West, and they often sent salaries and funds for other regular expenses directly to the recipients rather than to the college. Slow communications, rather than policy, gave the college administrators in China some leeway in determining policy.

The split in the administration of the colleges, half in the West and half in China, partly under college boards and partly under mission boards, frequently hindered attempts to raise the academic standards of the schools; and the problems resulting from the divi-

[2] For additional detail, see Ralph Wellons, *The Organizations Set up for the Control of Mission Union Higher Educational Institutions* (New York, 1927), pp. 40–45, 92–106.

sion of authority were to reach serious proportions with the growth of the colleges in the twentieth century. Though the boards of trustees and the boards of the mission societies received annual reports from the schools, they sometimes found it difficult to understand the changing needs of China and the broadening views of the missionary educators there. The boards tended to consider the number of conversions a criterion of success, and the college presidents often found that their lack of control over the appointment and dismissal of faculty members thwarted efforts to emphasize educational goals.

During the nineteenth century, however, fairly close contacts were maintained between the home boards and China. The college presidents made frequent trips to the United States to report to supporters, and furloughs for missionaries came every seven to ten years. The colleges were not yet large enough or old enough to have strong traditions of their own. Since they had little or no endowment and had not yet attracted a sizable group of patrons who made regular contributions, they accepted the implications of their dependence on the annual appropriations of the mission societies and the gifts of a few benefactors. A fairly large percentage of the student body came from the Christian constituency, and the missionaries themselves sometimes supported individual pupils. Most of the Western faculty members accepted the primary emphasis on the religious purpose of the colleges. All these things helped to give the home boards an interest in the welfare of the colleges and a sense of satisfaction in their work. They enabled the administrative bodies on the two sides of the Pacific to maintain comparatively harmonious contact, and at the same time they created among the mission societies a strong feeling of proprietorship. The mission societies not only appreciated the dependence of the colleges upon them, but they believed that the societies had a stake in the future of Christian education in China. Though they often warned against undue emphasis on educational work, they generally felt that the schools were making a real contribution to the goal of missions in China.

After the creation of their governing boards, one more step was necessary before the colleges considered their organization complete. Each sought a charter from the West. Many of the schools were incorporated under the University of the State of New York; others secured charters in Canada, the District of Columbia, Tennessee, and elsewhere. Such charters of incorporation were advantageous for several reasons. The schools had no standing or recognition in China. With a charter, the institution could confer B.A. or B.S. degrees, designations of significance in the West and of growing importance in China; furthermore, incorporation facilitated the acceptance of mission school students by Western colleges and graduate schools, a fact of some importance as study abroad became the goal of many of the pupils. Many administrators believed that a Western charter put their institutions in a better position to solicit funds in the United States.

Financial support was not a problem of great magnitude during the early years. The missionary members of the faculties were paid on a maintenance basis, that is, their salaries were supposed to cover living expenses only. Since they were considered employees of the mission societies sponsoring the institutions, their wages were often not included in the formal budgets of the schools. Chinese faculty members during the nineteenth century were generally of two types: old-style Chinese tutors and graduates of the mission colleges; salaries in both cases were exceedingly modest. Though held in high esteem, the tutor in China was traditionally underpaid, and the mission schools followed tradition. For a number of reasons the institutions were able to hire their own graduates at low salaries; the person with a Western-type education found relatively few openings in China before 1900; the Christian college often engendered in its graduates a sense of obligation to the institution which had educated him, and mission school students frequently met with discrimination when seeking employment.

Most of the schools opened with meager accommodations, and it was a long time before they built up the extensive campus facilities which eventually became the hallmark of some Christian colleges. At Tengchow the Presbyterian mission had been able to rent a section of a Buddhist temple because the temple's income had declined, and it was here that the Mateers were living when they decided in 1864 to open a school; they simply set aside a portion of the temple for classrooms and dormitory.[3] The Peking school started with a single room; even after it adopted the designation Peking University, one building provided classrooms, the president's office, a library,

[3] Corbett, *Shantung*, pp. 16–17.

a room for social activities, and dormitory space. North China College considered the provision of central heating in its first college building a luxury.[4]

As the academic aspirations of the missionary educators grew, however, they gave greater attention to the building of campus facilities. Quite understandably, they pictured the isolated college community so typical in nineteenth-century America; then they started drawing their blueprints. They, therefore, sought property for a campus on the fringes of a city rather than within it, for they feared that the commercial and recreational opportunities of the city might divert the students from their goals. They wanted enough land for dormitories and faculty houses along with the classrooms, chapel, and administration buildings; and they expected that both students and faculty would reside on campus and would create a Christian academic community fostering all those extracurricular activities considered necessary for a self-sufficient unit. Such a scheme was quite different from the traditional Chinese concept of educational organization, and even the modern Chinese universities of the twentieth century are generally city institutions with a minimal campus.

Purchasing property within the city walls was difficult, and in a land so heavily populated by the living and the dead, a spacious college campus was not easily obtained under the best of circumstances. The Chinese literati often opposed the sale or lease of land to the foreign evangelists, and they were particularly adamant about the alienation of property where large permanent buildings were to be erected.[5] Missionaries and their helpers, therefore, spent much time scouting out property and negotiating its sale, and often even more time was required to arrange the removal of many scattered graves on the property.

By 1900 the process of purchasing a college site and erecting permanent buildings had just begun for many of the institutions. St.

[4] Edwards, *Yenching*, p. 21; D. Z. Sheffield, "The North China College and Theological Seminary," *CR*, XXVI (1895), 224–225.

[5] For an interesting discussion of opposition by Chinese literati to the residence of missionaries in Foochow, see Carlson, "The Wu-shih-shan Incident of 1878," pp. 72–97. A central issue in the controversy was the attempt of members of the Church Missionary Society of the Church of England to erect a large school building within the city walls of Foochow; they were finally forced to accept a site in a suburb of Foochow.

John's had been located on the edge of Shanghai in an area known as Jessfield; since it was situated along Soochow creek and thus accessible by water, there was general satisfaction over the fact that six miles separated the campus from the commercial district of Shanghai and yet it was not completely isolated. Soochow University and Boone had also found permanent locations on the edge of a city, but neither Canton nor Hangchow College purchased a permanent campus until the twentieth century.

Since little money was spent on libraries or scientific laboratories before 1900, buildings for classrooms and for student and faculty residences were the major items of capital expense once the campus had been purchased. Study of diagrams of the various colleges reveals that a surprisingly large number of the buildings were faculty residences, and such emphasis frequently elicited criticism by Chinese and by evaluation committees. Explanations were available, even if they were not always satisfactory to the questioner; faculty residences were essential for the community-type college desired; Western-style homes were an investment in the health and morale of the educators; and it was often easier to secure a donation for a faculty residence for a specific missionary family than for a classroom building or for current expenses. New buildings were usually financed by special contributions from the mission societies or by the fund-raising campaigns in the United States that seem to have been the particular responsibility of the presidents of the institutions. It was said of F. L. Hawks Pott that he never made a trip to the United States without returning with a building for St. John's in his pocket.

The students at first contributed nothing. In the special schools established by the Chinese government during the nineteenth century, the scholars received complete support, including even a spending allowance. Since Christian education was even less attractive to the Chinese, the first mission boarding schools were able to obtain students only by providing books, tuition, room, and board; at the beginning some had also to offer clothing, bedding, and travel expenses from home to school, though most schools dispensed with these after a few years.[6]

[6] ABCFM, *Annual Report, 1857*, p. 125; *1879*, p. 59; Robert E. Speer, *Report on the China Missions of the Presbyterian Board of Foreign Missions*, 2d ed. (New York, 1897); p. 48; Pott, "History," *St. John's*, p. 3.

Late in the nineteenth century, however, the addition of English-language courses by many of the Christian schools made possible changes in financial policies. St. John's, for example, introduced the study of English in 1881–1882. Though the course was open at first only to twelve special students paying Ch$8 a month for board and tuition, by 1884 English had become a regular part of the curriculum, and all students except those on mission scholarships were required to pay part of their expenses. The fees were Ch$2 a month for those agreeing to study eight years and Ch$4 for those staying four years.[7] Chinese living in the treaty ports had begun to realize that a knowledge of English had commercial value, for English-speaking Chinese could obtain well-paid positions with Western and Chinese firms. Accordingly, Chinese became willing to pay for training in the language.

Some missionaries hoped that income from tuition fees might soon cover all college expenses except their own salaries.[8] This view was especially popular among those evangelists who believed that education was absorbing too great a proportion of mission funds and men. Unfortunately for their hopes, there developed simultaneously a demand for more and better schools, so that the colleges were soon to cease to be relatively inexpensive institutions run for evangelistic purposes and requiring only a small part of the mission society budget. Educational work was to absorb an increasing proportion of the missions' men and money.

Faculty and Educational Methods

The perennial problem of obtaining trained and dedicated teachers assumed distinctive forms in the Christian colleges because of their duality of purpose. Nowhere was the conflict between academic and religious goals more clearly presented than in the selec-

[7] Pott, "History," p. 5. The numerous changes in the Chinese government during the period from 1850 to 1950 meant changes in the system of currency notation and fluctuations in the value of the currency. Since translation into Western equivalents would indicate little about buying power, I have simply used the notation Ch$ when referring to Chinese currency. During the nineteenth century the exchange value of Ch$1.00 generally fluctuated between US$0.50 and US$1.25; during the first decade of Kuomintang rule (1927–1937), its value ranged between US$0.25 and US$0.50; inflation thereafter led to a rapid decline.

[8] John C. Ferguson, "Higher Education in China," *CR*, XXIII (1892), 157; C. W. Mateer, "Self-Support," *Records, EAC, 1899*, p. 49.

tion of the college faculty. Practically none of the Westerners teaching in the China Christian colleges during the nineteenth century had chosen college teaching as a profession. Some had volunteered for mission work in general and some had specifically requested service in China; in nearly every instance, the missionaries expected to do evangelistic work. The mission boards made the final decision on placement. Those who became teachers either decided after they reached the field to organize Christian schools or were assigned by the mission board to educational work. Long after they had begun to devote most of their time to teaching and translating, both Sheffield and Mateer continued to think of their evangelistic activities as their primary task. Even one who was to become as closely identified with educational work as Hawks Pott, wrote: "You know, of course, of my being stationed here at St. John's and of being transferred to the college work. I will not say that I do not like the new work, for that would be untrue, but I will say that I *ought* to have been enabled to go on in the other department. As things stand there is no help for it." [9]

The college president and faculty rarely had a decisive voice in the selection of Western faculty members, and the complaint that unsuitable persons had been appointed to college teaching was occasionally heard. Most of the missionaries teaching in the colleges, however, were firmly convinced of the importance of education as a branch of missionary activity and expressed satisfaction in their work. The colleges may generally be said to have been fortunate in obtaining teachers who believed in their work and were willing to devote time and energy to their occupation. In the matter of their teachers' preparation, the colleges were in a less favorable position.

During the nineteenth century Protestant missionaries were ordinarily sent to China with no prior training in the language, institutions, and customs of the Chinese people. They generally came, says K. S. Latourette, from earnestly religious families and were of a rural or small-town background.[10] Though most of the American missionaries were graduates of denominational colleges or theological schools, British missionaries were usually not university graduates. Missionaries were expected to learn the spoken language

[9] Quoted in Lamberton, *St. John's*, p. 23.
[10] Latourette, *Christian Missions in China*, p. 408.

after arrival in China, and since they plunged immediately into religious work, language study with an individual tutor and evangelistic work through interpreters were carried on simultaneously. The Mateers, for example, opened their Tengchow school three months after arrival in China. Since they were not yet able to speak Chinese, their first pupils were taught by their language tutor, and the Mateers added courses as they gained language facility.

Toward the end of the nineteenth century many mission societies recommended that a new missionary devote his first year in China to learning the language. During this time the missionary was to assume no educational or evangelistic responsibilities. This policy, however, proved difficult to put into practice. A desire to convert China to Christianity as quickly as possible had led many missionaries to expand their activities more rapidly than the number of available evangelists warranted, and in their desire to help relieve the older workers, new missionaries often accepted evangelistic duties as soon as they reached China. After the colleges began to teach English and to teach Western subjects in English, mission boards found it especially difficult to allow a year of uninterrupted language study. There was always a shortage of teachers, and it seemed a simple and natural solution for the new missionary to teach a course or two. Hawks Pott in 1894 lamented the practice of appointing missionaries to teach at St. John's while they learned the language and then assigning them to other work as soon as they were competent in the tongue. Nevertheless, the practice was not wholly unwelcome, as one missionary pointed out: "St. John's was known at that time as 'the benevolent octopus,' from its habit of laying hold of every member of the Mission; so [B. L.] Ancell and I were soon hard at work teaching English classes—a blessed relief from the study of Chinese." [11]

Many, perhaps most, of the missionaries eventually became proficient in the spoken language, and some learned to read classical Chinese well, but only a handful became capable of writing good literary Chinese. Among the minority who developed a real appreciation of the culture and philosophy of China and made a contribution to Sinology were several missionaries closely connected with education: J. Percy Bruce, one of the founders of the Baptist theo-

[11] Quoted in Lamberton, St. John's, p. 49.

logical school in Shantung, later president of Shantung Christian University, and author of *Chu Hsi and His Masters;* Samuel Couling, who compiled the *Encyclopedia Sinica* and made one of the first collections of divination bones while teaching at Tsingchow High School and Shantung college; John C. Ferguson, founder of Nanking University and authority on Chinese art and folk religion; and Howard S. Galt, who served both North China Union College and Yenching University and who wrote one of the few works on early Chinese education. Though these individuals were exceptional, educational missionaries often became quite well informed about many aspects of Chinese culture; they had an advantage, of course, over the evangelists in that they generally worked in urban areas, had contact mostly with students, and needed to become acquainted with China's literary heritage because of the nature of their work.

Even so, administrative, instructional, and religious activities often left little time for scholarship. Mission societies frequently did not encourage the study of Chinese philosophical literature, assuming that heathen literature had no value, or fearing that evangelists might seek some compromise between Christianity and Confucianism.[12] Chinese students sometimes complained that missionaries came to China expecting to find poverty, sin, and dirt, and that this was what they found. Because of this outlook and because they associated only with the lower classes, it was said, the missionaries often overlooked the admirable elements of Chinese civilization.[13]

Both missionary and Chinese agreed that the Westerners were severely handicapped by inadequate preparation for work in China and that it was years before the missionary could make up for this handicap, if he ever did. The effectiveness of the Christian teacher during his early years in China was reduced by his difficulties with the language. Even those who taught in English needed to be able to explain complex points in Chinese, and a teacher could have greater influence if he could approach his students in their own language. To win the respect of their students, teachers needed to know something about the history and philosophy of China. They needed to know about Chinese social customs and economics as

[12] Brockman, *I Discover the Orient*, p. 13.
[13] "The Nationalism of a Chinese Christian," by a Chinese student in America, *CR*, XL (1909), 150–151.

well if they were to offer courses adapted to the needs of their students and China.

The early missionary educators labored under other disadvantages. Many held temporary or part-time appointments and few had advanced degrees; moreover, most missionaries appointed to college work lacked teaching experience and many were assigned to teach courses for which they were not prepared. In 1897 the missionaries at Canton Christian College stated that they had all had theological training and would like some trained educators to aid in the work,[14] while the Hangchow College teachers sent regular but unsuccessful pleas for someone with science training. At the 1889 meeting of the (Christian) Educational Association of China, the Bishop of Victoria gave a personal experience which was perhaps typical of many: "When I came to China in 1875, I was sent by the Church Missionary Society to establish and conduct a college for the training of native clergy, evangelists, and school masters. Being, of course, wholly without experience I went, as in duty bound, to my Bishop, the late Bishop Russell, and asked him what books and what methods I should employ." [15]

Both the faculties and the student bodies of the colleges were small. Hangchow had four faculty members in 1880, Junius Judson and three Chinese teachers; St. John's faculty in 1888 consisted of eight teachers. Though Tengchow listed one of the larger faculties in 1891 (seven foreign members and five Chinese), most of these were part-time workers or wives. In 1893 North China College's faculty of seven was attempting to offer courses in three major fields: Chinese classics, Western learning, and Bible.[16] Many a missionary with a B.D. degree was obliged to teach chemistry, physics, and mathematics, and it was generally accepted that anyone whose native tongue was English could teach English. Hawks Pott of St. John's wrote in 1902 that the time had not arrived when the school could use specialists; he needed all-around men who could teach anything, and his words were amply borne out by the facts; for example, Mr. M. P. Walker, an engineer by training, was assigned to teach mathe-

[14] Projection of Christian College at Canton, p. 7.
[15] "Training of Native Agents," in Records, EAC, 1899, p. 132.
[16] Day, Hangchow, p. 15; Catalogue of Tengchow College, 1891, first page; Galt, "Yenching University," p. 32; ABCFM, Annual Report, 1896, p. 83.

matics, economics, English literature, and history; in addition, he coached various sports. At this same time Mr. E. L. Mattox at Hangchow College was teaching: plan of salvation; organic, inorganic, and analytical chemistry; general history; arithmetic; and English. Another year he taught Leviticus, Numbers, Acts, Deuteronomy; chemistry, political economy, history, and English.[17]

The hiring of Chinese faculty members seems to have raised almost as many problems as the procuring of Western teachers. During the early years few Chinese Christians were capable of teaching advanced subjects, especially the Chinese classics, and so the missionaries had little choice but to employ old-style Chinese tutors. This was done in spite of the fact that many missionaries opposed allowing non-Christians to teach in the schools and feared that the tutor in Chinese classics would undo the work of the missionary in Bible classes. The Chinese scholars generally remained apart from the life of the school. Many did not enjoy teaching within a set schedule of classes and examinations such as the Westerners advocated and were frustrated by the limited amount of time devoted by the pupils to classical Chinese. They did not speak English and did not live on campus, and so communication with the Western faculty was maintained with difficulty. Since faculty meetings were ordinarily attended only by the foreign staff, Chinese tutors had no part in decisions on college policy.

In fields other than the classics, the colleges soon began to employ their own graduates. By the time Tengchow had graduated its third college class in 1881, it had provided a number of teachers for its own courses and was beginning to supply instructors in Chinese, mathematics, and science for other Christian institutions.[18] St. John's had begun to use its alumni by 1892, though Hawks Pott had discovered an additional source of Chinese teachers in the students who had been sent to the United States in 1872–1874 at the instigation of Yung Wing and then recalled in 1881.

Most tutors followed the traditional method of teaching literary Chinese; memorization of texts, practice in writing characters followed by explanation of the meaning of the characters, reading of

[17] Lamberton, "St. John's University" (preliminary ed.) p. 81; Day, *Hangchow*, p. 81.
[18] *Catalogue of Tengchow College*, 1891, p. 9.

commentaries on the classics, and composition of essays and poems. The missionaries of the nineteenth century were not yet in a position to alter this method of teaching Chinese to any significant extent; they lacked both the necessary assurance and the textbooks. They soon came to understand, furthermore, that an educated Chinese was expected to be able to quote large portions of the classics and that social position depended partly on the ability to ornament one's writings with classical allusions. Though Y. K. Yen of St. John's believed that the Chinese method involved waste of time and energy and that it placed too little emphasis on the exercise of reason, he advocated that the school "make haste slowly" in reforming the traditional methods. "A truly liberal curriculum and a scientific method of instruction cannot yet be carried out, without serious injury to the future of the student as regards his social position," said Yen in 1885.[19] Since Western schools employed memorization at this time, the China missionaries themselves had confidence in the "memoriter" method, as it was called. At Tengchow and Hangchow the students were required to memorize whole chapters and even complete books of the Bible in Chinese.[20] Missionaries did, however, recommend modification of the traditional method so that explanation would accompany, rather than follow, the memorization of the texts. Also, the missionaries divided the pupils into classes according to their knowledge and set up a required curriculum for each group, whereas the old-style tutor had taught each pupil in his class individually.

Even though the missionaries generally were willing to follow the traditional Chinese methods for teaching Chinese and the accepted Western techniques in teaching Western subjects, they were innovators within the context of nineteenth-century China. It was in their emphasis on mathematics and science and in their methods of teaching these subjects that the Westerners seemed most revolutionary. They brought from the West a belief in the importance of science and mathematics in cultivating logical thought, and they believed that the use of laboratory experiments in science was one

[19] "Echoes from Other Lands," CR, XVI (1885), 352.

[20] C. W. Mateer, "What is the Best Course of Study for a Mission School in China?" and George B. Smyth, "Discussion," in Records, EAC, 1896, pp. 47, 49; Catalogue of Tengchow College, 1891, pp. 1–2; Catalogue of Hangchow High School, 1894, pp. 7–8.

of the best ways of developing this. Ideally, the students themselves would conduct the experiments; if this were not possible, the teacher should perform demonstration experiments; and there should be as little emphasis as possible on memorization. Though inadequate equipment prevented the realization of these ideals during the early years, individual educators made strenuous efforts to overcome this handicap. Calvin Mateer spent part of his first furlough in the United States in 1879 at a locomotive factory studying the construction of steam locomotives; he also secured a ten-inch reflecting telescope for his school, and a dynamo to furnish electricity for the school buildings. Once back in China he used income from his book royalties to equip a workshop where he could construct scientific apparatus for the Tengchow laboratories.[21] St. John's erected a science building in 1898–1899, the first instance, Hawks Pott wrote, of a Christian college in China erecting a special building for the teaching of natural sciences.[22] He might have added that it was one of the few such facilities in all China. Though the equipment at Hangchow was still inadequate in 1899, J. H. Judson stated that his school was attempting with some success to introduce individual laboratory work in physics.[23] By the end of the century, therefore, some schools had enough equipment so that the instructors could perform most of the basic experiments in beginning chemistry and physics, and a few institutions were introducing laboratory work by the students themselves.

The lack of laboratory equipment was not the only obstacle the missionaries met. Students were strongly predisposed to memorize whatever material was presented to them and to accept it without question or personal interpretation, since this was the method of study with which they were acquainted. A favorite story of Dr. Harold Balme, a medical missionary teaching at Shantung Christian University, concerned the response of his fifth-year class in surgery to a question he asked on one of his examinations. "A man is brought to the hospital unconscious, as the result of a severe abdominal in-

[21] Fisher, *Mateer*, p. 211; Corbett, *Shantung*, p. 24.

[22] Pott, "History," *St. John's*, pp. 14–15.

[23] "Educational Department," *CR*, XXX (1899), pp. 39–40. For information on other schools, see *Calendar of Peking University, 1896–97*, pp. 15–16; J. W. Davis, "Protestant Missionary Work in China," *CR*, XXIII (1892), 508.

jury which he had received the same day. How would you proceed to investigate the case and determine the nature of his injuries?" In an earlier lecture Balme had given the proper procedure in investigating the case of a man brought in with a severe leg injury: ascertain how the injury was sustained, determine whether the patient can walk or stand, etc. "The mere fact of my having given a lecture on a rather similar topic some time previously, sent half the class racking their memories to think of the points which I had laid down as important on that occasion. The result was that quite a large number of those students commenced their answer to the question by the statement that it was first necessary to ascertain from him how he had met with this accident, and to find out whether he could stand or walk, etc., etc. They did not record what the unconscious man was likely to reply." [24] Though it would be difficult to estimate the influence of the missionary teaching techniques, they were clearly regarded by Chinese students and teachers as innovations, and not always welcome innovations at that.

The lack of textbooks encouraged missionaries to introduce other educational techniques from the West. Though Chinese traditionally made little use of graded textbooks, Christian educators desired works suited to the intellectual level of the students. China, furthermore, had neither the textbooks nor the terminology for chemistry, physics, world geography and other Western subjects, since these were not a part of the regular Chinese curriculum. During the second half of the nineteenth century a number of translations or original works on Western subjects did appear; the Translation Bureau of Kiangnan Arsenal, for example, issued approximately two hundred titles in Chinese, mostly on military and naval science, engineering, agriculture, medicine, and chemistry; many of these, however, were unsuitable or too expensive for use as textbooks for beginning students. During the early years missionaries often dictated to the students in Chinese from English texts, and this dictated material served in place of text, lecture notes, and outside reading.

Slowly, missionaries worked to supply the lack by translating English textbooks or by composing their own. D. Z. Sheffield of T'ungchow produced several widely used works on history and

---

[24] Harold Balme, "Some Problems of Higher Education in China, with particular Reference to Medical Training," ER, XI (1919), 10.

political economy and Mateer wrote or translated most of the text-books in mathematics used at Tengchow.[25] At the 1877 conference of Protestant missionaries, a School and Text Book Series Committee was formed to encourage the writing of textbooks, to prevent dupli-cate translations, and to aid in the publication of books.[26] The plan called for works which would not be mere translations, but adapta-tions using Chinese examples and illustrations. Though this was an ideal not always realized in the nineteenth century, mission teachers produced books on a wide range of subjects and thus contributed to the importation of Western knowledge to China.

When introducing courses or composing textbooks in fields like chemistry, physics, world geography, and history, educators had to devise Chinese terms for concepts, elements, and place-names lack-ing in Chinese; since Chinese was a nonalphabetic language, this was a task for which there were no simple and obvious guidelines. In the nineteenth century neither general principles nor specific lists of terms had been formulated and accepted by Chinese or Western-ers. The result was confusion, some translators approximating the sound of the Western term and others trying to convey its meaning. As one example of confusion, a missionary wrote to *The Chinese Recorder* that he had consulted four atlases published after 1885 and had discovered four different names for Arabia, Australia, and Calcutta and three for Siberia, Madras, and Turkey.[27] There were instances in which different texts used the same characters for dif-ferent chemical elements obviously presenting possibilities for inter-esting, if not disastrous, laboratory experiments. With the hope of devising uniform lists of scientific, medical, and geographic terms, missionary terminology committees were organized, and they made a start on what was to be a long and sometimes disputatious task. Eventually, many of the terms used by the missionary translators came into general use.[28] Acceptance and actual use of uniform terms, however, seemed to require the sanction of a national body;

[25] Decker, "Shantung," p. 30; *CR*, XXXIX (1908), 654.
[26] *Records*, 1877, p. 18; C. W. Mateer, "School Books for China," *CR*, VIII (1877), 427–431.
[27] Letter by Leonard Wigham to "Educational Department," *CR*, XXX (1899), 403.
[28] Tsien, "Western Impact on China through Translation," *FEQ*, XIII, 312.

and both missionary and government committees were still working at the task well into the twentieth century.

In spite of the efforts of the missionaries, textbooks remained expensive, scarce, and often unsatisfactory. Respectable Christian college libraries were largely nonexistent, and the book collections, in some cases, consisted primarily of the reference works owned by individual missionaries. Partly because of the inadequacy of textbooks and of laboratory and library facilities, students spent much of their time in the classroom. Most of their knowledge was acquired from lectures, and students often attended as many as thirty hours of classes a week. Taking notes on lectures and memorizing these notes occupied most of their waking hours. Another reason for the large amount of time spent attending lectures was the overcrowded curriculum. Though mastery of classical Chinese occupied the pupil's full time in traditional Chinese education, the missionary added to this Western subjects and religious courses. Chinese students made no complaint about the long hours in the classroom or the passive nature of their training, for this was what was expected. They were more likely to be disturbed by the discussion, recitation, laboratory work, and outside reading introduced by missionary educators.

Curriculum

Though the Christian colleges have rightly been called experiments in Sino-Western education and contributors to a Sino-Western civilization, they were not consciously conceived and planned experiments, at least not in the nineteenth century. And nothing reveals the haphazard, evolutionary nature of their origins so clearly as their curricula. In general organization and emphasis the curricula resembled those of small denominational colleges in the United States. This seeming anomaly, the target of much criticism in the twentieth century, had a simple explanation. The Western teachers, most of whom had graduated from church-related schools, looked to these institutions for guidance in organizing the course of study for the mission colleges. Most denominational colleges in the United States emphasized Latin and Greek, mathematics, philosophy, and religion, though courses in history, English literature, and the sciences began to receive somewhat greater attention toward the end of the century. In China the missionaries substituted Chinese and then English for Greek and Latin, but the emphasis on mathematics and religion was retained; and the goal was a humanistic, not a technical or professional education.

The Christian colleges generally offered a curriculum with few electives and advanced courses. There were too few courses to permit students to choose major and minor subjects in various fields. Except for Chinese, mathematics and religion were the only areas where there might be a variety of advanced courses. The 1891 catalogue of Tengchow College summarized the curriculum: "The course of study, as now taught, presents such a combination of Chinese classics, Western science, and Religious Instruction as has been found to best subserve the purpose for which the college was established." [29] The list of courses offered reveals that mathematics was included in the term Western science and was the most important feature thereof. The number of mathematics courses taught in the China Christian colleges seems quite remarkable today. At Tengchow College the students followed a six-year course including algebra, geometry and conic sections, trigonometry and mensuration, surveying and navigation, analytical geometry and mathematical physics, calculus, and astronomy. There were, in addition, two years of physics and one year of chemistry. Mathematics, Chinese, and religion were the only subjects studied by the pupils every year. Other Christian colleges were not far behind in their mathematics requirements. There was a widespread belief in the ability of such studies "to fix a wavering mind, to produce a habit of attention," and "to cultivate the faculties of reasoning and analysis in which the Chinese are so deficient." [30]

In their crowded curricula the Christian colleges gave scant attention to social sciences. Most students had a year of universal history, a year of Chinese history, and frequently a year of geography and/or political economy. These studies were said to rectify Chinese ig-

[29] *Catalogue of Tengchow College,* 1891, p. 23.

[30] George Loehr, "Foreign Studies in Higher Schools," in *Records, EAC, 1899,* p. 76; Mateer, "What is the Best Course of Study?" *Records, EAC, 1896,* p. 52.

norance of other nations and at the same time furnish opportunities for moral lessons.

In October 1881, St. John's first admitted students for the study of English. This move, along with the subsequent decision to teach Western subjects in the English language, was a major turning point in the history of the China Christian colleges. A year later, Young J. Allen of the American Southern Methodist Mission organized an Anglo-Chinese College in Shanghai, and other Anglo-Chinese schools began springing up elsewhere. As their name indicates, these institutions concentrated on two major fields: the English language and the Chinese classics. English soon became the chief subject in the Western curriculum of most Christian colleges. Some schools, notably Tengchow and North China College, which were somewhat isolated from the growing commercial centers of China, resisted for a time the pressures to include English. They summoned many arguments against its introduction: it meant the secularization of Christian education and a defeat for the missionary purpose of the school; the students studied English for commercial reasons and on leaving school went into commercial or diplomatic careers rather than into religious work; the students did not remain in school until graduation but left as soon as they had a smattering of English; the Chinese who studied English learned to express Western knowledge only in English, not in Chinese, and they became denationalized.[31]

The arguments had much truth in them, but the tide was in the opposite direction.[32] All of the China Christian colleges eventually yielded and introduced the study of English. Though the Central China Mission of the Presbyterian Church passed a resolution in

[31] The controversy over the teaching of English was long. Some of the numerous arguments against the introduction of English may be found in: H. C. DuBose, "Secularization in Kiangsu," and "Editorial Notes and Missionary News," CR, XVII (1886), 234, 321; C. W. Mateer, "How May Educational Work Be Made Most to Advance the Cause of Christianity in China?" Records, 1890, p. 461.

[32] President Bergen of Shantung reported to the board of directors in 1906, "Both teachers and students are studying the language privately. We could not prevent it if we would. We are begged to send for English textbooks. . . . We find English alphabets scribbled over blackboards" (Corbett, Shantung, pp. 74–75).

1884 discouraging the teaching of English in its schools, any reduction in English courses met with resistance from both faculty and students, and by the end of the century, the Hangchow school had increased the emphasis on English. Because of the commercial value of English, Chinese in the port cities were eager for the courses and were willing to pay for them. Since most of the early Christian institutions were in the coastal areas of east and north China, they were particularly subject to pressures exerted by this urban minority. At that time several institutions were acquiring campuses and erecting permanent buildings, and they were simultaneously struggling to raise their academic standards. Tuition fees to supplement the modest sums furnished by the mission boards seemed the answer to their financial problems. Some missionaries stated that by offering English they could draw students from the higher classes and thus secure an influential Christian laity or at least break down the prejudice against all things foreign. And finally, English was the course most desired by those students who attended a mission school instead of a traditional Chinese school.[33]

Even before English courses had become firmly established in the curriculum, the missionaries began to discuss using English as the medium of instruction in Western subjects. This too was to be a major controversy in the history of the Christian colleges and was in many ways a step of greater consequence than the introduction of English language courses. By 1894 the science courses at St. John's were being taught in English. Five years of English was a prerequisite for entrance to Peking University's English sequence; the Western subjects were taught in English, and students taking the English sequence were requested to complete their Chinese studies before entrance, if possible.[34] Though Tengchow and North China colleges were again holdouts, by the turn of the century many of the colleges were using English as the medium of instruction in all but their Chinese studies. There were several reasons for this. It was, of course, much easier for the missionaries to teach in

[33] Some of the numerous arguments in favor of English may be found in F. L. H. Pott, "The Teaching of English," Isaac T. Headland, "With Our Present Experience Does It Pay to Use Mission Funds for Teaching the English Language?" and the ensuing discussion by Y. K. Yen, John Fryer, and L. P. Peet in *Records, EAC, 1896*, pp. 59–85.

[34] *Calendar of Peking University, 1896–97*, p. 23.

their native tongue. Since there was a serious shortage of adequate Chinese textbooks, many schools were already using English texts. Some educators argued that the Chinese language was incapable of being adapted to scientific use and that a Western language would always be essential for advanced scientific research.

Such an emphasis on facility in English could not but affect the colleges in many ways. The colleges gradually ceased to draw most of their pupils from poor families closely related to a mission and began to attract students from an urban commercial background. They improved their financial status through tuition fees. To some extent the mission schools became a closed system, since Christian middle schools were almost the only institutions giving adequate preparation for classes taught in English. The popularity and reputation of some of the Christian colleges came to depend heavily on their excellent training in English. The study of literary Chinese was drastically curtailed and it was acknowledged by both missionary and Chinese that the average Christian college graduate was inferior to the Chinese degree holder in mastery of the literary language. Though the inferior education in Chinese was sometimes regretted, the missionary educators believed that in the Christian religion and in Western learning, they were offering something more valuable.

All students, Christian and non-Christian, received intensive exposure to Christian doctrines and rituals. Most schools required at least one course in religion every year, and the students were obliged to attend one or two daily chapel services as well as a mid-week prayer service in many cases. Sunday was almost entirely devoted to religious worship and education; the Sunday schedule at Tengchow, for example, was: a morning prayer meeting, followed by Bible reading classes, and then the eleven o'clock church service, Sunday school in the afternoon, and classes in the evening to examine the pupils on the morning sermon.[35] Not to be forgotten were extracurricular religious activities. There was pressure on Christians to take part in evangelistic work among their fellow students and outside

[35] *Catalogue of Tengchow College, 1891*, pp. 7–8. For information on other schools, see *Annual Report of the Christian College, Canton, China, 1894–95*, pp. 1–2; *Calendar of Peking University, 1896–97*, p. 12; D. Willard Lyon, "Biblical Instruction in the Colleges of China," *Records EAC*, 1902, pp. 81–85.

the college. The students conducted Sunday schools, preached in neighboring villages, distributed religious tracts and accompanied missionaries on summer evangelistic tours. Revival services were held once or twice a year in most colleges, and missionary educators devoted particular attention to their non-Christian pupils in the hope of obtaining their conversion.

The extent to which education was subordinated to religion is difficult to ascertain and doubtless varied from college to college and even from individual to individual. There were instances in which classes were suspended for several days or weeks during a successful revival.[36] Although the foreign teachers had come to China as missionaries and their qualifications, and frequently their goals, were those of evangelists, the degree to which instruction in the classroom was influenced by religious motive was an individual matter. D. Z. Sheffield of North China College requested an educational literature thoroughly permeated with the spirit of Christianity:

By this it is not meant that Christian themes should be introduced when they are out of place, but that they should not be avoided when they are in place. . . . General learning is the study of nature and providence. The exact sciences are a study of the divinely appointed laws of nature in their inter-related operations. Human history is a record of the activities of men under the providential limitations of the divine supervision. Thus, writers upon the various sciences and upon human history, if they are Christian men and write without restraint, speak of God and of His relationship to nature and human history as freely as would a writer discoursing upon the affairs of government speak of the ruler of a nation.[37]

W. T. A. Barber of Wesley College in Wuchang told the 1890 conference of Protestant missionaries that he was not a Christian first and a schoolmaster afterward, or vice versa, but he was a Christian schoolmaster and tried to preach Christ in all he did. He did not, he continued, talk religion while teaching algebra or natural science, but in the latter case he could not help "pointing to the one God

[36] B. A. Garside, *One Increasing Purpose, The Life of Henry Winters Luce* (New York, 1948), pp. 128–130; Corbett, *Shantung*, pp. 86–88; MacGillivray, *Century of Protestant Missions*, p. 434.

[37] Sheffield, "How Can the Ethical Element Be Best Introduced into the New Learning of China?" *Records, EAC, 1899*, p. 118.

who unifies all nature." [38] Hawks Pott felt that there was religious teaching and continuous exhortation unto nausea; students in the West, he said, would revolt against it.[39]

In their attempt to build a Christian academic community, the missionary educators gave attention to extracurricular activities; and here, too, they were guided by their own experiences in denominational liberal arts colleges in the United States. Physical exercise was required despite the Chinese ideal of the dignified scholar whose most strenuous activity was wielding his brush in painting and calligraphy. Archery, gymnastics, and military drill with the participation and supervision of Western teachers seemed the most satisfactory way of overcoming the reluctance of students to participate. The faculty fostered clubs and debating societies, choirs, the Y.M.C.A., student newspapers both in Chinese and English, and yearbooks. In addition, teachers were encouraged to arrange opportunities for meeting with the students on a social basis. The Christmas and Easter seasons became the focal points for a wide variety of social and religious activities, and each college community established traditions for these occasions. Most of the activities were those which missionaries had known in their homeland; for example, the decoration of Christmas trees and exchange of gifts, candlelight ceremonies, and special parties for the college servants were often a part of the Christmas festivities.

Since this concept of the academic community had no close counterpart in Chinese education, its importation with many details from Western Christendom contributed to the impression among Chinese literati that the missionary educators were building insulated foreign enclaves. At the same time Christian college alumni often indicated that such college traditions were the source of their fondest memories and their strongest ties to their alma mater.[40] The college as a residential community and the personal interest of teachers in individual students were among the distinctive characteristics of the Christian institutions.

[38] Discussion in *Records, 1890,* p. 499.

[39] F. L. H. Pott, "The Aim of the Christian School in China," *Records, EAC, 1899,* p. 67.

[40] *What My Education in Fukien Christian University Means to Me* (Foochow, 1938) (pamphlet in HI; it contains brief essays by a number of graduates of Fukien).

Students

Although information on the background of students attending the Christian institutions or the nature of their employment after leaving the schools is often fragmentary and imprecise, it is possible to make some general comments. The number of students who actually completed work at the collegiate level was only a fraction of those who enrolled in the institutions. Even after the schools began to call themselves colleges, they usually continued preparatory or middle school classes, and students in these classes formed the bulk of the enrollment. These students were not clearly separated from the college students in official attendance figures, in extracurricular activities, or in the physical organization of the school. Nor was there usually a separate college faculty. Records on the background of students refer to all enrolled students despite the fact that many never reached the collegiate level. Though one might wish statistics on the college students alone, the figures for the total enrollment are in some ways more meaningful, for the secondary level students often set the tone of the school. On the other hand, when giving information about the activities of their students after leaving school, the institutions usually provided statistics only for those who actually graduated.

During their early history the Christian colleges drew most of their students from families which could not afford a classical Chinese education for their sons; by the 1930's, however, a number of the Christian colleges had acquired a reputation as schools for rich men's sons, and all were relatively expensive. This transition was only beginning in the late nineteenth century and was perceptible primarily in those institutions like St. John's and Peking University where English language work received special emphasis. Since the first schools were established before there were many Protestant converts in China, most of the entering pupils were not Christians. Slowly, however, the number of Protestant converts in China increased; 13,035 communicants were reported by 1876; and by 1887 there were 32,260.[41] This meant, of course, that the schools could enroll a somewhat larger percentage of Christians; it also meant that

[41] *Records, 1877,* p. 486; "Statistics of Protestant Missions in China," *CR,* XIX (1888), 50.

fewer students were from families that were actually destitute. Most converts were farmers, shop keepers, artisans, and laborers, Chinese of the lower class and of the lower middle class. Though there were still converts from the poorest groups in the society, their proportion was apparently declining. Conversions among the literati were rare indeed.[42] Except for a somewhat larger representation from urban groups, Christian college pupils came from the same general background and economic status as the total Protestant community until the last decade of the century.

In all cases, the schools had difficulty retaining students once they were old enough to supplement the family income or to get married. The majority left before graduation. They were not particularly interested in the science or mathematics courses, which brought little prestige or influence in China, and once they had attained minimal literacy they saw little point in continuing their Chinese studies if they did not lead to success in the civil service examinations. In an effort to hold their students, many institutions adopted an indenture system whereby the parent agreed to keep his son in the school for a certain number of years or until graduation in return for the school's furnishing complete support. If the parent removed the pupil before the allotted time, he was to pay for his son's board during the period of attendance. The policy seems to have been partially successful, though broken contracts were fairly frequent, and the missionary had little recourse if the father refused to pay.

Christian pupils were somewhat more likely to complete the full academic course than were non-Christians. This, plus the fact that quite a number of students accepted Christianity while in school, meant that the advanced classes contained a high proportion of Christians, and a majority of graduates were Christians.[43] Once the giant step of accepting the foreign religion had been taken, fear of conversion was not a motive for withdrawal. In addition, Christians could generally expect mission employment after graduation; some Christian parents, as a matter of fact, seem to have considered attendance at mission schools an investment in a mission position

[42] R. H. Graves, *Forty Years in China, or China in Transition* (Baltimore, 1895), pp. 289–290; Soothill, *A Mission in China*, pp. 100–101, 116, 118.

[43] ABCFM, *Annual Report, 1878*, p. 81; *1881*, p. 70; *1892*, p. 68; Spear, *Report on China Missions, 1897*, p. 10.

for their son. Just as humanistic education in the Chinese classics had become professional training for entrance to the bureaucracy, so education in the liberal arts program of the Christian colleges often became vocational preparation for mission employment.

Such an attitude was a mixed blessing. Missionaries did everything possible to persuade the student to choose religious work, and they took pride in statistics showing that the majority of their graduates were teaching in Christian schools, working in mission hospitals, or directly engaged in evangelism.[44] On the other hand, the missionaries deplored the dependency of their pupils. Since the students were supported by the mission during their education and anticipated mission employment upon graduation, they tended to take support of the mission for granted, even to expect it as their due for having adopted Christianity. Many appeared content to accept the authority of the foreign missionary and to regard their duty as simply carrying out the orders of the evangelist.[45]

During the last decade of the nineteenth century, a growing number of educated Chinese began to show an interest in science, mathematics, and other Western subjects; a few Chinese turned to the Christian schools for information in these fields. The colleges began to enroll in advanced courses occasional students who had no intention of entering mission employ. This group, however, was too small to make a significant difference in the general make-up of the student body or the size of the college classes.

On the other hand, a considerable number of Chinese now wanted to learn English, and those Christian colleges which tried to meet this demand were dealing with new types of students and different problems. Most of the students who came to study English were ready to pay for their education, but they were not willing to be indentured. They expected to leave school as soon as they knew sufficient English and mathematics to obtain commercial positions in the treaty ports, minor government positions in the telegraph,

[44] Spear, *Report*, p. 11; *Catalogue of Tengchow College*, 1891, pp. 11–12; *Calendar of Peking University, 1896–97*, p. 37; "The Hangchow High School," *CR*, XXV (1894), 241; ABCFM, *Annual Report, 1899*, p. 127; Robert M. Mateer, *Character Building in China: The Life Story of Julia Brown Mateer* (New York, 1912), p. 63.

[45] "Editorial Notes," *CR*, XXIII (1892), 213–214; James Ware, "Annual Report of the Central China Christian Mission," *CR*, XXVI (1895), 298.

railway, or customs administration, or other jobs in which a knowledge of a foreign language was an asset. Usually they were from urban backgrounds, and though they were not generally from wealthy families, their circumstances were comfortable. Many were the sons of merchants or other businessmen in the treaty ports. Not only were they non-Christians, but they tended to feel little connection with or obligation to the missions. With a surplus of boys seeking admittance, the institutions could raise their entrance requirements and be more selective. The changes should not be exaggerated, however; the colleges still attracted few of the brightest students and few sons of scholars. A Western-type education was still for those who could not afford the classical Chinese training or who were not considered bright enough to pass the civil service examinations. In 1896 John C. Ferguson of Nanking University stated: "Fathers in placing their sons in [Christian] schools will often say that they cannot succeed in Chinese literature, but hope to be able to master the foreign language." [46]

Any assessment of the influence of the schools primarily on the basis of their graduates' accomplishments is misleading, since the majority of the students left before completing the course. Though most graduates accepted positions connected with the mission, most of those leaving school earlier seem to have entered other types of work. Many of the institutions offered a six-year course to follow the more elementary work; in some instances the whole six-year program was classified as college level work and in others only the last three years. It is not easy to determine either when the schools began to offer work of college grade or how many students took this work. Earl H. Cressy, long an official of the Christian Educational Association of China, has collected enrollment statistics that seem moderately accurate (*Table 1*). The figures are an attempt to indicate college students only and reveal the rather small amount of college work conducted by the Christian institutions during the nineteenth century.[47]

[46] Ferguson, "The Changed Aspect of China," *Records, EAC, 1896*, p. 37.

[47] Not listed by Cressy as having college students before 1900 were Peking University, Canton Christian College, Nanking University, and Boone. Cressy was undoubtedly correct in eliminating Nanking and Boone from the group. Canton, though, officially reported 105 students in 1894–1895; 41 in the primary department, 42 in the intermediate, and 22 in the highest (theological

Table 1. Enrollment of the China Christian colleges in the nineteenth century

Colleges	1873	1878	1882	1885	1887	1894	1896	1900
Tengchow Arts	10	15	23	24	26	55	48	56
Tengchow Theological	0	0	0	2	4	3	3	3
Tsingchow Theological	0	0	0	2	4	3	3	14
Tsingchow Normal	0	0	0	0	2	3	3	15
Medicine (Tsinan)	0	0	0	0	3	2	3	5
North China (T'ungchow)	0	0	7	13	9	17	14	23
St. John's	0	0	0	0	0	6	14	23
Hangchow	0	0	0	0	0	0	25	25
Totals	10	15	30	41	48	89	113	164

Source: Earl H. Cressy, *Christian Higher Education in China: A Study for the Year 1925–26,* CCEA Bull. no. 20 (Shanghai, 1928), pp. 26–27.

In actuality, only the foundation for Christian college education was laid during the nineteenth century. Mission work in China had been almost impossible before the wars of 1839–1842 and 1856–1858, and until the last quarter of the century, the missionaries were preoccupied with establishing their right to work and reside in various communities and with seeking effective techniques for approaching the Chinese. Even after the first schools were founded, the level of education they offered was limited by their rather narrow evangelistic purpose and by the hostility of most Chinese. Educational plants were, however, started; small faculties organized; student bodies collected, and traditions established. By 1900 Christian higher education had begun to attract increasing attention among the urban Chinese; even though literati and officials often remained hostile, many of them had been made aware of an educational program quite different from that of the traditional Chinese

and collegiate). Peking University would have disputed her exclusion from the list; her catalogue for 1896–1897 gave an enrollment of 194 students; of these, 17 were listed in the College of Liberal Arts and 9 in the College of Medicine. On the other hand, Cressy gave Tengchow and North China the benefit of the doubt in listing 1873 as the beginning date for college students at Tengchow and 1882 as the beginning date for college students at North China (T'ungchow), since Tengchow only assumed the name college in 1882 and North China in 1889.

schools. Through their work in education, publication, and translation, some of the missionary educators had become recognized as valuable sources of information about the West. Christian higher education had won the acceptance of many of the Protestant missionaries in China, and it had secured the support of several of the wealthier Protestant denominations in the United States. Even if most of the colleges had not yet offered much work on a college level, the goal had been proclaimed.

IV | Expansion and Consolidation in an Era of Change, 1895-1925

The period 1895–1925 is pivotal in Chinese history. It saw profound change in social custom and political structure, in cultural values, educational programs, and economic organization. As might be expected, Christian education in China was deeply affected. Missionaries had had a share in disrupting the Great Tradition and thus breaking the crust of custom, and they generally believed that a new era with rapidly expanding opportunities for Christian influence was opening. Indeed, Christian schools and their graduates did bask briefly in a new-found popularity; colleges were founded and existing institutions expanded their curricula and increased their enrollment. Mission educators and their publications were sought out as guides and as sources of information. Christian colleges became pioneers in medical education and in education for women in China; they exerted a far-reaching influence in such fields as agriculture and language instruction, and they were a valuable supplement to higher education supported by government funds.

Any hope of serving as models for a national system of higher education had, however, little basis in fact. Christian educators were in no position to control the accelerating process of change in China. Applying to the China Christian colleges Sidney Hook's distinction between the event-making man and the eventful man,[1] one might say that the mission institutions played the role of event-maker briefly and then became participants in a continuing revolution

[1] See ch. ix, "The Eventful Man and the Event-Making Man," *The Hero in History: A Study in Limitation and Possibility* (New York, 1943).

which they had helped to initiate. Christian educators lacked the political influence to do otherwise; their contacts with the Chinese bureaucratic and intellectual communities were limited; [2] they did not form a unified group either in organization or outlook; there was no agreement concerning the role of Christian education in revolutionary China; and even if there had been a consensus, the administrative organization to effect such a program was lacking. Individual educators and institutions could influence individual Chinese, but any program requiring national planning, organization, and resources was beyond the scope of the Christian colleges. By 1925 the problems of adjusting to the kaleidoscopic changes in Chinese politics and education overshadowed thoughts of acting as event-makers in China's revolution.

In education as in many other areas, Chinese leaders frequently agreed upon that which they did not want from the West before they agreed upon those elements which they did wish to adopt. The repercussions of this negative approach affected the Christian colleges. They were criticized for failing to meet the national needs of China, but the task of defining their role was made difficult by the absence of an effective and stable educational system in China. In moving from the traditional training in the classics to an educational system closely akin to that of the West, China was undertaking a transformation with far-reaching consequences; and consensus on goals and methods was not easily reached. Blueprints for national educational programs were drawn up in rapid succession and then discarded almost as quickly.[3] There is, however, one thread of continuity: the assumption that education should be subordinate to and should serve the national interest. The need of the state rather than the individual should determine the organization and content of education. The period 1895–1925 saw many changes in the definition

[2] The *Tung-fang tsa-chih* (The Eastern Miscellany) during its early years of publication had regular sections on religion and education, and I discovered no mention of Christian schools in either section for the first five years of publication, 1904–1909. The magazine is typical of many in that the section on religion is primarily devoted to *chiao-an* (lawsuits connected with the missions) during this period.

[3] Kuo Ping-wen, *The Chinese System of Public Education* (New York, 1915), pp. 78–135, gives details for several of the national educational programs drawn up between 1900 and 1915.

of the national interest, changes which played an essential part in the history of Chinese education.

Christian Educators and the Reform Programs of the 1890's

As related earlier, Chinese leaders had founded schools to teach Western languages, geography, science, and mathematics as part of the self-strengthening movement of the T'ung Chih Restoration, 1862–1874. Several contingents of students had been sent to the United States and Europe for military and technical training. In all cases, such education had been considered outside of and separate from the traditional education. The latter, in unaltered form, remained the norm. Study of "barbarian learning" by a limited number of scholars was a kind of insurance; these individuals would become foreign experts with the technical and diplomatic know-how to protect the tradition.

Such a program had quickly run into difficulties, and by the end of the century political reformers had moved on to other positions. Even where the reform slogans of the 1890's sounded similar to those of the T'ung Chih leaders, their internal content had been altered. Chang Chih-tung's *Chung-hsüeh wei t'i, hsi-hsüeh wei yung* (Chinese learning for the fundamental principles, Western learning for practical application) was the slogan for a program which differed significantly from that of Li Hung-chang and Tseng Kuo-fan; the province of those matters defined as fundamentals had receded, and a new political consciousness of China as a sovereign state rather than as a culture was emerging. Stunning blows toward the end of the century had revived the sense of emergency and forced reconsideration of reform programs. Most severe blow of all had been the defeat of the Sino-Japanese War of 1894–1895, followed by demands for concessions from all the major European powers. To many, the break-up of China seemed imminent. As the famous reformer K'ang Yu-wei put it: "The Russians are spying on us in the north and the English are peeping at us on the west; the French are staring at us in the south and the Japanese are watching us in the east. Living in the midst of these four strong neighbors, and being the Middle Kingdom, China is in imminent peril." [4] How different was K'ang Yu-wei's image of the Middle Kingdom from the traditional one!

[4] Trans. in Ssu-yü Teng and John F. Fairbank, *China's Response to the West: A Documentary Survey, 1839–1923* (Cambridge, Mass.; 1954), p. 152.

Calls for institutional change had begun to gain a hearing in certain limited but influential circles. Though the leading advocates of reform had all received a classical education, their world of ideas had not been formed solely on the basis of traditional learning; while still young, they had become aware of an alternative way, Western civilization. They had begun to seek information about the West, and they had not neglected mission sources. They had read translations of Western works issued by the Kiangnan Arsenal, missionary educators, and others. Some had established contact with Timothy Richard, John Ferguson, and Young J. Allen; Liang Ch'i-ch'ao, for example, served as Timothy Richard's Chinese secretary for some time before the Sino-Japanese War; and between 1895 and 1898 Timothy Richard met such prominent leaders as Li Hung-chang, K'ang Yu-wei, Chang Chih-tung, and Sun Chia-nai, tutor to the emperor. When K'ang Yu-wei organized the *Ch'iang-hsüeh hui* (Society for the Study of Self-strengthening, often called the Reform Club) in 1895, Timothy Richard and Gilbert Reid were asked by K'ang, Liang, T'an Ssu-t'ung, Yuan Shih-k'ai, and other members to discuss reform proposals with them.[5] The paper published by the reform society at first adopted the same title as the popular *Wan-kuo kung-pao* edited by Young J. Allen, and many of its articles were reprints from the mission journal.[6] Allen's periodical had itself greatly expanded its circulation among officials.

The reformers of the 1890's were not satisfied with information about ships and guns, or even mathematics and science; they wanted to know about the political and educational institutions of the West, and they wanted to convey their knowledge to other members of the gentry and even to the court. In order to convince the Chinese bureaucracy and the court of the urgent need for reform, they fostered educational and propaganda programs. Booksellers who

[5] Richard, *Forty-five Years in China*, pp. 234–238, 244–245, 253–256. Gilbert Reid of the American Presbyterian Board had become interested in working with educated groups in China and like Richard made a special effort to establish contact with officials and reform leaders. In 1894 he established the Mission among the Higher Classes of China and later with the approval of the Chinese government founded the International Institute to make available information about Western civilization.

[6] *Ibid.*, pp. 254–255; Levenson, *Liang Ch'i-ch'ao*, pp. 20–21. The journal was shortly replaced with *Chung-wai chi-wen* (The Chinese and Foreign Record). Richard implies that use of the title from the mission periodical was an attempt to protect the reform periodical from conservative opposition.

had formerly disdained works published by the Society for the Diffusion of Christian and General Knowledge (S.D.K.) now eagerly sought such books as John Fryer (Fu Lan-ya), *Tso-chih ch'u-yen* (Some Advice on How to Rule), Young J. Allen (Lin Le-chih), *Chung-tung chan-chi pen-mo* (Complete Account of the War), and Timothy Richard (Li T'i-mo-t'ai), *Hsi-to* (The Warning Bell from the West). Two of Richard's works were widely pirated: *Shih-shih hsin-lun* (Tracts for the Times), a reissue of essays he had written when he was editor of the Chinese daily *Shih pao*; and a translation of Robert Mackenzie's *Nineteenth Century—A History*. The latter work exudes optimism and faith in human progress as it contrasts the former barbarism and ignorance of Europe with the reign of science, enlightenment, and democracy in the nineteenth century; according to Richard, this book along with other S.D.K. publications were read by Sun Chia-nai and the emperor himself.[7]

In founding schools which would offer courses in current affairs and Western subjects, Chinese occasionally called on missionary educators for guidance. In 1896, for example, local authorities founded a new school in Hangchow and requested E. L. Mattox of the Hangchow Boys' School to help set up the curriculum and the laboratory equipment. John C. Ferguson of Nanking University served as foreign administrator for Nan-yang kung-hsüeh (Southern Public School); this Shanghai institution, founded by Sheng Hsüan-huai and supported by funds from the China Merchants Steam Navigation Company and the Imperial Telegraph Administration, was the forerunner of the famous technical school, Nanyang University. On request, Young J. Allen drew up a detailed outline for a national educational system for China. When in 1898 a group of Chinese in Shanghai founded a pioneer school for women, they sought the aid of Mrs. Timothy Richard and other wives of missionary and diplomatic personnel.[8] The school was modeled after the Methodist girls' school in Shanghai, McTyeire School; and maps, charts, and texts published by the S.D.K. and by the China Christian

[7] Richard, *Forty-five Years in China*, pp. 256–257. For a twentieth-century assessment of Mackenzie's history, see R. G. Collingwood, *The Idea of History* (Oxford, 1946), pp. 145–146. Collingwood calls it a third-rate work which illustrates the extremes to which the doctrine of progress was pushed.

[8] Mrs. T. Richard, "History and Working of the First Girls' School Opened by the Chinese," *Records, EAC, 1899*, pp. 155–158.

Educational Association (CCEA) were used. Among the teachers were two missionaries (one the daughter of Young J. Allen) and graduates of McTyeire School, Bridgman School, and St. Mary's Hall (sister school of St. John's). The Chinese administrators decided to follow the example of many of the mission schools and forbid foot-binding.

Though one can give specific examples of contacts between missionaries and reformers, it is not easy to assess the role of mission education in China's abandonment of the classical tradition and acceptance of change. There were, besides the missionaries, other sources of information about the West and other generators of reform sentiment. The humiliations suffered by China during the 1890's were doubtless more effective persuaders than either propaganda or education. The decade of the 1890's was the first time since the Jesuit missions of the seventeenth century that any but the most formal contacts between officials and missionaries had seemed acceptable, and there was still reluctance to admit that the relationship could be fruitful. Those who appeared most ready to establish contacts were the educational missionaries on the one hand and Chinese who were already convinced of the need to alter Chinese tradition, on the other hand. Neither Timothy Richard and Young J. Allen nor K'ang Yu-wei and Liang Ch'i-ch'ao were typical representatives of their communities, and those in the majority, conservative officials and evangelistic missionaries, continued to look upon each other as antagonists.

The exchange of ideas and information was not confined to a few prominent reformers and educational missionaries, however, and in many of the urban centers a variety of contacts was being established. At Foochow, for example, several officials and members of the literati attended the graduation ceremonies of the Anglo-Chinese College in 1898, and other officials sent tablets expressing appreciation of the devotion to teaching shown by the Christian educators.[9] Officials and other prominent Chinese in Soochow and Hangchow sent gifts to support the educational work of the missionaries in these cities. Several of the S.D.K. publications attained a circulation in the tens of thousands during the 1890's; and in connection with the reforms of 1898, the S.D.K. reported:

[9] "Educational Department," CR, XXIX (1898), 132. The "other officials" are listed as the salt intendant, the provincial judge, and the literary chancellor.

Missionaries were besieged in every province with Chinese students asking their help to teach them English, French, or German or some of the Western Sciences with the happiest results—friendship between the missionaries and the educated classes everywhere in place of the traditional hatred and opposition. . . . Ever since the Reform movement began in 1895 there were signs in the provinces of a similar tendency there also. As these Reformers gained sympathy and support among the provincial mandarins, news of Western schools and colleges appeared very frequently in the letters of correspondents in the interior. . . . Merchants and missionaries were constantly sought after for advice. Letters were sent to our Society from various places asking us to recommend foreign teachers to them.[10]

When there was an immediate need for detailed information about Western education, the missionaries, their institutions, and their publications were available sources.

The climax of the reform movement came with that brief period in 1898 known as the "Hundred Days," a summer of furious activity when one imperial edict followed hard upon the heels of another. It is only necessary to note here the prominent role given to educational reforms and the rationale of the promoters of educational changes. Under the guidance of K'ang, Liang, T'an Ssu-t'ung, Sun Chia-nai, and others, the Kuang-hsü Emperor called for a complete revamping of Chinese education. There was to be a national educational system with a curriculum which included classical learning plus science, mathematics, Western languages, history, and geography. The regular schools would be supplemented by special institutions for training in agriculture, mining, and railway construction; and they would be capped by an imperial university in Peking. To provide texts for the new school system, officials were encouraged to found translation bureaus; officials were also to urge and assist young Manchus to go abroad for a Western education. In the civil service examinations there would no longer be emphasis on calligraphy or the traditional style of exposition known as the "eight-legged essay"; instead, there would be essays on the history and government of China, "modern practical subjects" such as scientific problems and the governments of foreign countries, and the Confucian classics.

[10] *Eleventh Annual Report, 1898,* p. 11.

The reform movement was dominated by scholars who had already become deeply involved in educational and propaganda activities. They thought of these activities both as a means of persuading others of the need for reform and also as significant reforms in themselves; during the Hundred Days, therefore, they continued to hope that they could use education and propaganda to build support for their program. They accepted the traditional assumption that the major purpose of education was to inculcate in students those ideals and that information which would best serve China. Since good men were the means to good government and education was the means of creating good men, reforms in the educational and examination system were fundamental to the whole program.

If the reformers had their way, however, education would no longer be confined to the Confucian canon. Chang Chih-tung, generally considered one of the more conservative reformers, recommended that training in the classics be given first and that Confucian learning be considered fundamental, but he made no attempt to argue that it was all-sufficient. He argued, in fact, that it was incomplete and that training in Western subjects should be required of all students, not just a few specialists. He would require study of Western social, political, and economic institutions as well as Western technology, for the former were no longer considered separable from Western power and prosperity. Only men who could pass examinations in these subjects in addition to the classics would be considered educated men capable of guiding China. Chang's program was set forth in a book published in 1898 and reprinted at the emperor's request; *Ch'üan-hsüeh p'ien* (Exhortation to Study) [11] was distributed to officials and scholars throughout the empire and was used by reformers to seek support.

Even more radical were the reforms urged by K'ang Yu-wei and his pupil, Liang Ch'i-ch'ao. They were more acutely aware than Chang Chih-tung of the importance of China's survival as a political entity.[12] Though they hoped to protect the fundamentals of the

[11] Trans. by Samuel I. Woodbridge under the title, *China's Only Hope: An Appeal* (New York, 1900). See pp. 63–71, 97–109, for the educational program of Chang.

[12] See the thoughtful studies by Joseph Levenson, *Liang Ch'i-ch'ao and Confucian China and Its Modern Fate*, vol. I, *The Problem of Intellectual Continuity* (Berkeley, 1958); also Benjamin Schwartz, *In Search of Wealth*

Confucian way through preservation of the state, the latter was their primary concern, and they were willing to sacrifice elements of the Great Tradition for the sake of the state. Such an approach is quite different from that of the T'ung Chih reformers, who assumed that restoration of the Confucian way would insure the continuance of the state and therefore made restoration their first concern. For them the Confucian way was whole, was civilization; it was not a tradition from which truths or goods might be selected. As a broad generalization, one might say that the T'ung Chih leaders gave their loyalty to a culture, but that the reformers of the 1890's gave their loyalty to China as a political entity.

At least the beginnings of modern nationalism are here, and this definition of the Chinese nation-state was being worked out in opposition to Japan and the Western powers. Consciousness of the national self was emerging from a series of humiliating encounters with other selves. Antiforeignism became, therefore, both a preliminary to and an important facet of this incipient nationalism. The reformers might call for more and more importations from Western civilization, but Westerners and Western nations remained their antagonists. Fear and distrust of the West was parent of both reformism and nationalism. The kinship of antiforeignism, nationalism, and reformism was illustrated in the alternation between antiforeign outbursts and demands for reform between 1895 and 1905. It helps explain the ambivalence and frustration of many Chinese leaders during this period. Though many of the reformers sympathized with the widespread xenophobia, they believed it necessary to condemn violence against the foreigners because of the disastrous consequences of such incidents for the Chinese state.

Nor was a more favorable attitude toward Christianity generally a consequence of the reform movement. Chinese were, after all, primarily interested in importing sources of power and prosperity, and this purpose guided their selection and colored their view of Western civilization.[13] Even as they called for the organization of education along Western lines, with graded classes and prescribed

---

and Power: Yen Fu and the West (Cambridge, Mass.; 1964). The brief summary given here is largely based on these works.

[13] This thesis is developed in detail in André Chih, L'Occident "Chrétien" vu par les Chinois vers la fin du XIXe siècle, 1870–1900 (Paris, 1962).

curricula, even as they recommend the study of Western history, languages, and sciences, most reformers continued to think of these as techniques. Beyond their contributions to wealth and power, these Western elements lacked merit in themselves. That science, for example, embraced a whole approach to knowledge and also philosophical assumptions about the nature of the universe was rarely understood. Chang Chih-tung stated that any scholar could learn enough about foreign subjects in three months to teach in high school; he had only to read some of the many books being published in Shanghai.[14] Small wonder, then, that most Chinese scholars continued to show little interest in the Christian religion.

The assumption that they could ignore Christianity in their selection of imports seemed to be substantiated by their increasing knowledge about the West. Translators of Western materials and other "barbarian experts" became conscious of anti-Christian and anti-religious traditions in the West itself. While missionaries in China often identified progress and prosperity with the Christian heritage, Chinese in direct contact with Western society or literature were becoming aware of the secularization of Western civilization. They learned that there were Western scholars who looked upon religion in general and Christianity in particular as obstacles to progress and science. Their own pragmatic approach to religion and their utilitarian approach to Western civilization predisposed them to find Western criticisms of Christianity congenial. Little persuasion was needed to convince most that Christianity was not essential to national wealth and power. One of the early works translated by Yen Fu, for example, was *Missionaries in China* by Alexander Michie, an attack on mission methods in China. According to Benjamin Schwartz, Yen Fu was well aware of the usefulness of anti-missionary arguments by Westerners.[15] When Yen Fu translated Thomas Huxley's *Evolution and Ethic* and Herbert Spencer's *Study of Sociology,* he used both Chinese philosophy and Western positivism to attack Christianity.

Even when there was some realization of the importance of Chris-

---

[14] *China's Only Hope,* pp. 103–104.
[15] Schwartz, *In Search of Wealth and Power,* pp. 38, 255. See also, Chih, *L'Occident "Chrétien,"* for Chinese knowledge of anti-Christian and antireligious arguments in the West.

tianity to Western civilization, this rarely led to a recommendation that China adopt the Western religion. K'ang Yu-wei, for example, argued that religion was essential to national morality and that it was necessary in the definition and cohesion of a nation; Christianity had helped unify and therefore strengthen Western nations. The conclusion of K'ang, however, was not that China should import Christianity; though Christian teachings had merit, they were not suitable for China. A national religion must be one which had been widely practiced for many generations and was profoundly rooted in the people. After proving to his own satisfaction that Confucianism was a religion, K'ang called for the active propagation of Confucianism among the masses; he later advocated national ceremonies honoring Confucius and a weekly day of rest in which all Chinese would worship according to the Confucian religion. By means of Confucianism, China would retain her cultural identity while undergoing the many changes recommended by K'ang. When Liang Ch'i-ch'ao called K'ang "the Martin Luther of the Confucian religion," he was thinking of this connection between religion and nation.[16] In a petition to establish Confucianism as a state religion after the 1911 revolution, Liang, Yen Fu, and others used arguments quite similar to those of K'ang.[17] The Confucian way had ceased to be valued because it was universal; those who sought to resuscitate it, did so because it was Chinese rather than because it contained eternal truths suitable for all peoples.

The reform movement of the 1890's may be said to have sanctioned, at least indirectly, much of the educational program of the Christian colleges, but it did not change the critical attitude of Chinese toward the foreignness of the institutions nor toward their Christian emphasis. Those non-Christians who sought the guidance of missionary educators or studied at the Christian colleges often entered into such contacts with reluctance. They enrolled despite,

[16] For a discussion of K'ang's attitude toward religion, see Hsiao Kung-ch'üan, "K'ang Yu-wei and Confucianism," *Monumenta Serica*, XVIII (1959), 96–212; Chih, *L'Occident "Chrétien,"* pp. 71–76. Liang's comments may be found in "Nan-hai K'ang hsien-sheng chuan" (Biography of K'ang Yu-wei), *Yin-ping-shih ho-chi* (Collected Works and Essays of the Ice-Drinkers' Studio), Wen-chi (Collected Essays) (Shanghai, 1936), pp. 39, 64b.

[17] An English translation of the petition is available in *National Review*, Shanghai, XIV, 392–393.

not because of, the Christian and foreign character of the institutions; missionary and Chinese appraisals of the purpose and usefulness of the institutions were often far apart.

Within these limits, the Christian schools enjoyed a popularity they had not known before the Sino-Japanese War. Their graduates were sought as teachers of Western subjects in privately organized middle schools and in some of the new institutions of higher learning. Success in local fund-raising campaigns by St. John's and Foochow Anglo-Chinese College between 1895 and 1900 gave evidence of Chinese appreciation of the work of the institutions. When the China Mission of the American Methodists (Southern) decided in 1899–1900 to reorganize their educational work and establish a university in Soochow, they received gifts of land and money from Chinese officials and business leaders.[18] Many of the schools reported a significant increase in applications for admission, especially from well-to-do families. Nanking University had to rent another house in order to take care of its growing enrollment; Peking University announced in 1896 that 14 literati and relatives of several court officials had matriculated, and Boone listed a nephew of Chang Chih-tung among its students. St. John's reported in 1900–1901 that 155 took the entrance examinations but that a shortage of facilities prevented the admission of more than 50 new students.[19]

The attrition rate of the colleges continued high. Sons of businessmen and of Christians might complete the program of the mission institutions, but those preparing for official position frequently stayed only a short while. The year after Peking University announced the enrollment of more than a dozen students from official families, it reported that such students tended to drop out after a month or so. Most of these young men wanted a brief introduction to Western learning, not a four to six year program of study. This attitude was encouraged by the nature of the civil service examinations, which after the "Hundred Days" reform reverted to the time-honored pattern.

[18] Hampden C. DuBose, "Are Missionaries in Any Way Responsible for the Present Disturbances in China?" *CR*, XXXI (1900), 611.
[19] *Calendar of Peking University, 1896–97*, p. 13; Galt, "Yenching University," p. 16; Boone University, *50th Anniversary Report*, p. 4; St. John's College, *President's Report, 1900–1901*, pp. 28–29.

Others were unwilling to attend the required church services and religion courses or were reluctant to accept the status of student to a foreigner. The missionaries themselves recognized that the religious requirements deterred many from enrolling in the Christian institutions and that others simply tolerated these requirements as a kind of payment for the education they were receiving.[20] At Nanking two Chinese Muslims who objected to the religious requirements received considerable support among the student body; when they were told that attendance was a condition of enrollment, they left school; many other students threatened to quit but did not actually carry out their threat.[21]

In those institutions founded by Chinese but employing missionaries as teachers or administrators, the differing motives of the two groups often caused conflicts. A Hangchow institution initiated by R. F. Fitch (later president of Hangchow Christian College) at the request of several influential Chinese in 1898 was shortly withdrawn from missionary control. Somewhat later Watson Hayes, president of Tengchow College, was asked by Governor Yuan Shih-k'ai to help organize a provincial college at Tsinan, Shantung. Accepting the invitation, Hayes brought with him six Chinese Christian teachers and a number of Christian students. When a controversy developed over required Confucian ceremonies, the protests of Hayes received no official support, and so Hayes and the six Christian teachers resigned.[22] Even among those who appreciated the educational work of the missionaries, therefore, resentment over their religious purpose and foreign character was often just below the surface. Though the internal content of the anti-Christian and antiforeign traditions changed somewhat as China approached the twentieth century, the traditions themselves showed remarkable hardiness and continuity.

The Boxer Rebellion was one of several occasions when the negative side of the ambivalent Chinese attitude toward the Christian

[20] See discussion by L. P. Peet, *Records, EAC, 1899*, p. 109, and F. L. H. Pott, "Education," *China Centenary Missionary Conference Records, 1907* (Shanghai, 1907), p. 68 (cited as *CCMC Records*).

[21] Eddy L. Ford, *The History of the Educational Work of the Methodist Episcopal Church in China* (Foochow, 1938), p. 162.

[22] Isaac T. Headland, *China's New Day: A Study of Events that Have Led to Its Coming* (West Medford, Mass.; 1912), p. 108; Corbett, *Shantung*, pp. 71–72.

colleges gained ascendency. At all of the colleges the tide of animosity toward foreigners was felt. In those areas where Boxer groups ran rampant in 1900, there is little evidence of attempts by gentry to protect the Christian educational institutions or educational missionaries as distinct from other foreigners or Christian institutions. Those officials who disregarded the Empress Dowager's orders and kept the Boxers in check in their districts did so because they realized the futility of the Boxer rampage and feared the price which the foreigners would require of China. Protection was offered not because of appreciation for the work of the missionaries, but because anything less seemed to imperil the continued existence of China. Chang Chih-tung had made his attitude crystal clear in his earlier writings. When he cautioned against attacks on foreigners or Christians, he was careful to indicate that this was not because of approval of their doctrines or activities. He admitted that dissension and humiliation had come to China with the preaching of alien doctrines; but because of his concern for the survival of China as a political entity, he argued that China must strengthen Confucianism by reforming the government, not by combatting other religions.[23]

When in mid-June of 1900 there appeared in Shanghai placards saying that St. John's was to be burned, nervous fathers began calling their sons home. President Hawks Pott closed the school on July 3 without holding examinations, and the institution was not reopened until later than usual in the fall.[24] The Hangchow school was closed in the spring of 1900 and did not reopen until March 1901, not because of direct attack but because missionaries and Chinese Christians in Hangchow fled to Shanghai for protection. In the Yangtze Valley area, the viceroys Chang Chih-tung and Liu K'un-i had made it known that they would be responsible for the safety of foreign lives and property as long as the powers did not land troops there. Li Hung-chang and Yuan Shih-k'ai offered similar protection in the areas under their jurisdiction—Kwangtung, Kwangsi, and Shantung—and there was little violence in these sec-

---

[23] *China's Only Hope*, esp. chs. iii, "The Establishment of Schools," pp. 97–105; v, "The Extensive Translation of Books," pp. 110–115; and xi, "Religious Toleration," pp. 144–148.

[24] St. John's College, *President's Report, 1900–1901*, p. 4; also Lamberton, *St. John's*, p. 47.

tions. Since, however, foreigners and Chinese Christians had been attacked during the preceding year, most foreigners congregated in a few areas to facilitate protection. This meant, of course, the disruption of education and also considerable loss of property as a result of looting or burning during the absence of the missionaries. At Canton, the college moved to Macao and remained there until it could complete arrangements in 1904 for a permanent site on the island of Honam about two and a half miles from Canton.[25]

Those institutions around Peking suffered the greatest losses. Missionaries fled T'ungchow on June 8 after the local official warned that he could no longer guarantee their safety; they were accompanied by a number of Chinese Christians, including about a third of the student body of the college; other Chinese Christians scattered to the hinterlands. The college property was burned the next day, and approximately two-thirds of the business section was destroyed during the summer. Congregating initially at the Methodist mission in Peking, the T'ungchow refugees moved to the legation quarters after the murder of the German minister, Baron von Ketteler on June 20. There they remained until the siege was lifted August 14. Much foreign property, including that of Peking University and other mission schools, was destroyed during the summer.[26]

[25] Annual Report, Canton, 1900–1901, p. 1; 1904, p. 2.

[26] ABCFM, Annual Report, 1901, p. 104; D. Z. Sheffield, "Educational Reconstruction in Peking," CR, XXXII (1901), 619–620; Galt, "Yenching," pp. 17–18. The events of the summer provide interesting sidelights. One source of frequent comment was the organizational ability of the American Protestant missionaries; their activities helped to give some semblance of order and equity in the crowded legation quarters. Frank T. Gamewell of Peking University had had two years of engineering training before he turned to theology and so he assumed charge of building sandbag fortifications for the besieged area. E. G. Tewksbury of T'ungchow was chairman of the committee which had overall responsibility for the daily life of the community. And the Peking University students with their knowledge of both Chinese and English performed valuable service as messengers, interpreters, etc.; a number of these students secured lucrative positions as interpreters with the international forces after the siege was over.

The fact that the Chinese Christians numbered several hundred accounted in part for their separate treatment in the besieged legations; also, the diplomatic corps may have hesitated to assume responsibility for Chinese in a conflict with the Chinese government. It is, nevertheless, a commentary on prevalent attitudes that there was on June 20 reluctance to admit Chinese Christians along with foreign missionaries to the legation quarters. Though the Chinese provided

Works on the Boxer movement sometimes question whether the movement was primarily anti-foreign or anti-Christian.[27] Missionaries relating their experiences in 1900 have often emphasized the xenophobia of the Boxers, and scholars have agreed that Christians and Christian institutions were attacked because they were ever-present reminders of the Western threat to Chinese tradition. Missionaries personified the humiliation of China by the West. They were frequently the causes, or at least the excuses, for infringements on Chinese sovereignty; the German demand for a lease of Kiaochow Bay and other concessions after the murder of two missionaries on November 1, 1897, was only a flagrant example of similar incidents.

Most Chinese made no distinction between missionary and foreign businessman or diplomat. Thus, D. Z. Sheffield of T'ungchow College was requested by a wealthy Chinese to prevent a proposed Tientsin-Peking railway from cutting through his ancestral graveyard; when Sheffield protested that he had no influence in such matters, the Chinese remained unconvinced. Later, when the railway by-passed T'ungchow and the city ceased to be an important transfer center for tribute rice or examination candidates, Christian missionaries and T'ungchow College became the focus of resentment over economic decline caused by foreign communication techniques. Such was part of the background for the burning of the college buildings on June 9, 1900.[28] The confusion between foreign diplomat and Christian missionary and between Western techniques and Christianity was so great that the Kuang-hsü emperor was rumored to have been deposed in 1898 because he had become a Christian, and this rumor was said to have made Manchus afraid even to express an interest in the foreign religion.[29] Certainly the missionaries' edu-

---

valuable manual labor in constructing fortifications, they were housed and fed separately; toward the end of the siege, conditions in their quarters and their food rations left much to be desired.

Finally, the events of that long, hot summer contributed to the union of several Christian institutions.

[27] See, for example, Victor Purcell, *The Boxer Uprising: A Background Study* (Cambridge, 1963), pp. 121–138.

[28] Edwards, *Yenching*, p. 32.

[29] See letters of William H. Rees to C. D. Cousins (London Missionary Society), Sept. 15, 1899, and Oct. 13, 1899; also J. Stonehouse to C. D. Cousins, Oct. 17, 1899, quoted in Purcell, *Boxer Uprising*, pp. 288–289.

cational, medical, and journalistic activities and their share in the introduction of Western learning to China had contributed to the confusion.

At the same time, opposition to the missionaries and to Chinese Christians on specifically religious grounds should not be overlooked. Though Chinese officials might be concerned over dislocations in the cultural and political realms, peasants were often most directly affected by the religious teachings and activities of the Christians. Boxer placards frequently mentioned offenses against the local gods, destruction of Buddhist images by Christians, vilification of Chinese sages, and disregard for filial piety and the respect due the ancestors. According to the placards, all these activities had angered Heaven and had led to hardship and suffering on earth. To peasants and literati, Christianity seemed an offense because it was an exclusivist religion as well as a foreign heterodoxy.

Opportunities under the Ch'ing Reforms, 1900–1911

Those scholars who had predicted disastrous defeat for the Boxer rebels and their supporters proved only too accurate. International troops entered Peking on August 14, lifted the siege of the legations, and began an occupation which was almost as destructive to life and property as the fury of the Boxers. Fleeing the capital, the Empress Dowager and her court left old Li Hung-chang to negotiate the humiliating Boxer protocol of 1901. It was a sobered T'zu-hsi who returned from "her tour of inspection" to Peking on January 6, 1902. She was at last convinced of the necessity of reform, not only to save China from Western imperialism, but also to restore the prestige and power of the Ch'ing dynasty in China itself. One of the first reform decrees, issued even before the court had returned to the capital, stated: "Those who have recently been learning Western methods have limited themselves to the foreigners' written and spoken languages and to the manufacturing of machines. These are the skin and hair of Western technology, but not the fundamental source of Western government." [30]

As in 1898, changes in Chinese education were considered fundamental to political reform. Decrees ordered the cessation of the mili-

[30] Teng and Fairbank, *China's Response*, p. 196.

tary examination and the abolition of the "eight-legged essay" beginning in 1902. A memorial by the president of the Hanlin Academy recommended that the members study ancient and modern history, politics, mathematics, and the sciences rather than spend their time composing poetry; the memorial was approved by the throne. Students were encouraged to study abroad, and those who had already had training abroad were to be given special examinations leading to degrees and civil service positions. In 1903 a commission was appointed to draw up a detailed plan for a national school system. It was soon discovered, however, that as long as the civil service examination emphasizing classical learning was the main road to officialdom, the majority of the better students concentrated on the classics to the exclusion of modern studies. Few modern schools were being established; and according to Ferguson and Sheffield, most Chinese leaders still believed that Western learning was surface knowledge to be added to the profounder knowledge of nature and man handed down by the sages. Conservative reformers in Peking still hoped that it would be possible to control the introduction of Western subjects into the educational program so that the fundamentals of Confucian ethics would not be disrupted.[31]

On September 2, 1905, a decree ordered the cessation of old-style examinations. Instead, there was to be a national educational program modeled after the Japanese and Western public school systems. For over a thousand years the civil service examinations had played a determining role in Chinese education. Their abolition was a drastic reform. Students preparing for government service sought schools where they could obtain the new knowledge, and even conservative scholars had to attempt to add Western learning to the traditional Chinese studies. The historian Ku Chieh-kang, who was a young scholar at this time, speaks of the sense of cultural upheaval among students and of the constant discussion of current events and national salvation in "the most lofty and animated of moods."[32] Although for two years he had read every new work he could obtain,

[31] John Ferguson, "The Educational Outlook in China," and D. Z. Sheffield, "Christian Education in Relation to Educational Reform in China," *Records, EAC, 1902*, pp. 39, 51.

[32] Ku Chieh-kang, *Autobiography of a Chinese Historian*, ed. and trans. by Arthur Hummel (Leyden, 1931), pp. 16–21.

he joined thousands of others in seeking admission to one of the new schools.

Following a brief set-back between 1898 and 1900, then, educational reform was resumed, and the Christian colleges once more achieved a certain popularity. Of course, Chinese seeking educational models or desiring to study Western subjects had sources other than the mission institutions. After 1905 Chinese colleges were founded to teach these subjects along with the classical curriculum, and students often preferred these institutions, though they were at first deficient in equipment and faculty. Some students went to Europe or the United States. Many more crossed the East China Sea to Japan, a short cut to Western learning which became particularly popular after Japan's demonstration of technical and military skill in the Russo-Japanese War. Many, however, could not afford to go abroad, and others wished to obtain English-language training before studying in England or the United States. For some of these, the Christian colleges performed a valuable service.

After 1905, most Christian schools had more applicants than they could admit, and a larger proportion of students than before completed the course offered by the institutions. Responding with enthusiasm to the interest in modern schools, Christian leaders raised academic standards and enlarged existing institutions. They founded new schools. They broadened their goals and gave greater emphasis to educational purposes as distinct from evangelistic aims. As they acquired a greater knowledge of and respect for Chinese culture, they attempted to adapt Western learning and techniques to the Chinese scene. Though they were often criticized for failure to follow through in this realm, they did contribute to the definition of some of the problems and they did initiate some of the early attempts at a Sino-Western synthesis.

Expansion of Christian education in China was facilitated by changes in the home base as well as in China.[33] Christian missions achieved unprecedented popularity in the West, especially among Protestant denominations in the United States. Support for and

[33] For greater detail see Paul A. Varg, *Missionaries, Chinese and Diplomats: The American Protestant Missionary Movement in China, 1890–1952* (Princeton, 1958), pp. 52–67.

interest in Christian missions became so widespread that it truly deserved the appellation of a crusade. Thousands of congregations identified themselves in a very personal way with "their missionary" in China; this identification included more. than simply financial support; there were individual gifts sent to the missionary family at Christmas time, regular letters from the missionary relating the experiences of his family, and visits to the church congregations by the missionary on home furloughs. As wealthy businessmen were persuaded of their financial and administrative responsibility, mission boards included some of the most prominent financial leaders of the United States. From 1889 until the opening of World War I, the number of missionaries sent to China and the money invested in missions increased rapidly; in 1889, 1,296 Protestant missionaries were reported in China; by 1914, the number was 5,462.[34]

An increasing proportion of the missionaries were college graduates, and quite a number had taken a full liberal arts program before entering theological training. This came about partly through the work of the Student Volunteer Movement for Foreign Missions. Formally organized in July 1888, the Student Volunteer Movement directed its appeals to college students and encouraged the formation of such groups as the Yale Foreign Missionary Society and the Oberlin Band. The orientation of this younger generation of missionaries, changes in the intellectual climate at home, and the increase in numbers all contributed to a changing emphasis in mission theory and methods. Fewer of the great missionaries of the twentieth century were pioneer evangelists, and more of them achieved prominence as administrators and educators. Through emancipating men from superstition and introducing a higher concept of life, missions would promote the social regeneration of the world.[35] Assuming that Christianity had contributed to prosperity and growing humanitarianism in the West, missionaries hoped to convince Asians that Christianity was fundamental to Western civilization and should be adopted along with other sources of Western power and wealth.

[34] Latourette, *Christian Missions*, p. 606.
[35] An influential statement of this view was James S. Dennis, *Christian Missions and Social Progress: A Sociological Study of Foreign Missions*, 3 vols. (New York, 1897–1906).

Such theses were, of course, familiar to missionary educators and had already been voiced by some of them, but the popularity of such arguments was new.

Though missionaries welcomed the chance to expand Christian education, the actual expansion was accompanied by soul searching and by relatively little coordinated planning or unanimity of opinion. It was not easy to discover a satisfactory equilibrium between the evangelistic and educational purposes of the schools. Evangelization and the training of Christian workers remained important aims, but it was generally conceded that even the religious goals could be better served by broader educational aims. Realizing that the conversion of China might require many generations, missionaries acknowledged that the bulk of the work would have to be accomplished by Chinese, not foreign, evangelists. Greater attention would have to be given to building a Chinese church, and this church would need thoroughly trained Chinese leaders, not just Chinese helpers. These ministers should be able to keep abreast of church scholarship in the West and at the same time command respect in their communities through their Chinese learning. This meant that preministerial students should receive a higher level of education than had been the custom during the nineteenth century; missions began to recommend at least two years of college education prior to theological training.[36]

The schools also sought to train Christian teachers. The intention was at first simply to man the mission schools with Chinese Christians. As the Chinese government organized a school system, however, missionary educators believed they saw an opportunity for Christianizing China by furnishing Christian teachers for the national schools. This hope was more than once dampened by government regulations requiring attendance at Confucian ceremonies or by discrimination against mission school graduates, but it remained an important aim of the Christian colleges during the early years of the century.

[36] Arthur J. Brown, *Report on a Second Visit to China, Japan and Korea, 1909, with a Discussion of Some Problems of Mission Work* (New York, n.d.), pp. 184–185; Pott, "Education," *CCMC Records,* p. 66; Lord William Gascoyne-Cecil, *Changing China* (New York, 1912), pp. 255–257. Later surveys reveal that it was often difficult to make this recommendation effective.

The schools continued to make the education of the children of Christians a fundamental objective. Well-educated lay leaders were essential, it was said, if the Christian churches of China were to become independent of missionary control; thus, the colleges could contribute to the Christianization of China through training an intelligent church membership. As the enrollment of the Christian colleges grew, missionaries could no longer hope to provide mission employment for almost every graduate. Missionary educators believed it necessary to offer a well-rounded liberal arts education with a wide variety of majors, and some of the schools even added professional and vocational courses.

Whereas most evangelists still hoped to achieve the regeneration and Christianization of China through individual conversion, some of the educators were talking more about building Christian character and creating a climate of opinion favorable to Christianity than about conversion. Some spoke of educating Chinese, both Christians and non-Christians, to be citizens of new China. They believed that in the government schools students would learn only of the material progress of Western civilization and that it was the especial task of mission colleges to acquaint Chinese with Western philosophical and religious thought. After the 1911 revolution, particularly, Christian educators realized that contact with the West and with Christianity had seriously disrupted Chinese society, and they argued that Westerners had some responsibility for helping China evolve a new society. During these years, when the government educational system was in a state of disarray, some of the missionaries saw their task as limited only by the availability of teachers and funds; and these, they sought constantly to increase.[37]

Such broad conceptions of the purpose of the Christian colleges antagonized those missionaries who continued to believe in the primacy of direct evangelism, and the gulf between the educators

[37] Discussions of goals by educational missionaries are available in W. T. A. Barber, "The Place of Education in Foreign Missions," *Report of Ecumenical Missionary Conference*, 2 vols. (New York, c. 1900), II, 116–117; *World Missionary Conference, 1910*, vol. III, *Report of Commission III: Education in Relation to the Christianization of National Life* (Edinburgh, n.d.), p. 85; "Extracts from the Findings," *The Continuation Committee Conferences in Asia 1912–13* (New York, 1913), p. 225; Pott, "St. John's University," *ER*, IX (1917), 136.

and evangelists widened. Growing financial difficulties during the 1920's exacerbated the sense of competition between the two groups. In the prosperous years from 1890 to 1914, many continuing projects and expenses had been assumed; then, the disillusionment and cynicism which followed World War I and the isolationism of the United States led to a gradual decline in contributions to missions; people had answered so many appeals during and immediately after the war that they became somewhat immune to fund raising drives; many were no longer sure that the West should undertake to be moral teacher to the East. During much of the period after 1914 an unfavorable rate of exchange for United States currency in China and a rise in the price of silver further reduced the real income of missions.

As the rivalry between educator and evangelist for money and workers grew, criticism of the increasing costs of the China Christian colleges mounted. Some felt that the schools had departed from their original purposes. Only a small and declining percentage of the graduates were entering the ministry. A large number of the students were non-Christians; the conversions were too few; and many students who became Christians while in school deserted the church upon graduation.[38] It was pointed out that almost every one of the Christian colleges hoped eventually to become a university and that it was unrealistic to suppose that the churches could support over a dozen universities in China. Demands for a re-evaluation of the goals and accomplishments of the Christian colleges multiplied.

Well might both advocate and opponent of the mission schools request reappraisal. By 1914 less than half of the Protestant missionaries in China were engaged in direct evangelistic work. From a few schools with a total of 199 college students in 1900, the Christian educational work had grown to 16 colleges with almost 1700 college students in 1920.[39] Most of the new colleges were union institutions,

[38] Joseph Clemens, "Are We in Danger of Secularizing Our Missions?" *CR*, XLIV (1913), 660–661; Robert E. Speer, "The Relationship of Missionary Education to Evangelism," *Report of a Conference on the Preparation of Educational Missionaries, 1916* (New York, n.d.), pp. 193–195; Luella Miner, "What the Church Expects of the College," and M. T. Stauffer, "The Strength and Influence of the Church," *The Chinese Church as Revealed in the National Christian Conference, Shanghai, May, 1922* (Shanghai, 1922), pp. 221, 398.

[39] Cressy, *Christian Higher Education*, pp. 26–27.

but their formation, like that of the nineteenth-century colleges, had been based on individual agreements among missions rather than on a comprehensive plan for Christian education in China. Even the missionary educators themselves had reached no consensus concerning the role of Christian education in China.

As early as 1877 Calvin Mateer had recommended consolidation and division of labor in Christian education. He pled for cooperation in founding different grades of schools rather than duplication of types of schools in one area.[40] Two years later *The Chinese Recorder* printed a letter signed "Unitas" which called for a union of the various schools in and around Peking to form a college; such cooperation would mean a smaller financial burden for the supporting missions and a higher standard of education.[41] These two reasons were to form the core of all subsequent arguments in favor of union in missionary education.

Gaining support for the theory of union and actually effecting union proved to be two quite different things, however. Even Calvin Mateer later had difficulty in reconciling himself to a union which involved transferring the site of his own college and broadening its purpose. Strong personalities, differing emphases in the schools, and denominationalism, all deterred cooperation, and administrative bodies to facilitate collaboration were scarce.[42] Even the various China missions of a single denomination frequently had no central organization in China which could coordinate their efforts. The only unifying force was the home board. The denominations themselves were not united; the Canadian Methodists, the English Methodists, the American Methodists (South) and the American Methodists (North) had their separate mission societies and sent out their own missionaries; the same was true of other Protestant denominations such as the Baptists and Presbyterians.

Until 1890 Christian teachers in China had no educational organization except the School and Text Book Series Committee. At the 1890 conference of Protestant missionaries in China, however, the

[40] "The Relation of Protestant Missions to Education," *Records, 1877*, p. 180.

[41] "Correspondence," *CR*, X (1879), 465–467.

[42] E. C. Lobenstine complained in 1918 that to secure action on any given subject by the Protestant missionary societies in China, it was necessary to address over 125 separate missions. See "The Work of the China Continuation Committee," *CMYB, 1918*, p. 271.

(Christian) Educational Association of China was formed. The broad purpose of the association was "the promotion of educational interests in China and the fraternal cooperation of all those engaged in teaching." [43] More specifically, the organization should plan a course of study for all grades of mission schools, devise a uniform set of Chinese terms for science, geography, medicine, and other Western subjects, recommend methods of conducting schools and examinations, and promote union in education. The association held triennial meetings and maintained more or less continuous contact with teachers through an "Educational Department" in *The Chinese Recorder* and after 1907 through its own magazine, *The Educational Review*. It also fostered the publication of many evangelical and educational works.

As far as the aforementioned goals are concerned, however, the association had only limited success. Uniform examinations and courses of study were later used in various sections of China, but national law rather than mission programs proved to be the determining factor in setting up a uniform system. Until the second decade of the twentieth century, the association had no permanent organization or executive secretary with authority and time to survey educational needs and to carry out a coherent program for cooperation or union. The triennial meetings did help make the missionaries more conscious of the need for overall planning and for coordination.

One reason why the educational missionaries were often less conservative than the home boards in their attitude toward interdenominational cooperation was that the former felt the pressure of events in China more immediately than did their supporters in the West, and events in China seemed to emphasize the necessity of cooperation. The Boxer Rebellion, for example, served the cause of cooperation both in the theoretical and practical realms. According to one interpretation popular among missionaries, the anti-foreign attitudes of the Boxers were primarily the result of ignorance, and such xenophobia could be most effectively eradicated by Christian education. Christian educators in China should coordinate their activities so as to facilitate rapid and efficient expansion of mission

[43] "General Secretary's Report" and "Constitution of the Educational Association of China," *First Triennial Report, EAC, 1893*, pp. 6–7.

education. Flight from the Boxers, moreover, brought many educators together where they could discuss their mutual needs and problems; some of the earliest serious conversations regarding union in the north were initiated in Chefoo, Shantung, and in the Peking legation quarters during the summer of 1900.[44] Also significant was the fact that several of the institutions had their initial investment in buildings and equipment destroyed by Boxers or other looters. Union seemed more palatable than before 1900, since the continuity of the program had already been interrupted and a transfer in location would not involve abandoning expensive buildings and equipment.

Imperial edicts fostering modern education brought to the missionaries a new realization of the importance of cooperation. When detailed plans for a national school system were drawn up, the mission schools received no recognition; nor were Christian college degrees recognized when graduation from Western-type institutions was made a basis for the franchise and civil service appointments. Missionaries, on their part, could not support all the five stated aims of the new national education: loyalty to the emperor, reverence for Confucius, devotion to the public welfare, admiration for the martial spirit, and respect for industrial pursuits.[45] Except for the teaching of Confucian ethics, religious instruction was forbidden in schools accorded national recognition.

The missionary educators began to worry about "government competition" in education. Though it was generally recognized that the government would require some years to set up a nationwide school system, many feared that unless the missions pooled their resources, they would soon be outstripped by the national schools.[46] Without more adequate laboratories and libraries, more and better teachers, the mission colleges would lose the good students to the

[44] Decker, "Shantung," p. 54; E. W. Burt, *Fifty Years in China: The Story of the English Baptist Mission* (London, 1925), pp. 53–55; D. Z. Sheffield, "Coordination in Christian Education," *CR*, XXXIX (1908), 307; and Sheffield, "The Present Educational Status in North China," *Records, EAC, 1902*, pp. 182–183.

[45] Kuo, *Chinese Public Education*, pp. 74–78, 89.

[46] Pott, "Education," *CCMC Records, 1907*, p. 70; "Editorial," *The Monthly Bulletin of the Educational Association* (later *The Educational Review*), May 1908, p. 2.

government schools. Only as truly outstanding institutions of higher learning could the Christian colleges hope to serve as models for national universities and thus encourage a different emphasis in the national educational program. The majority of the missionaries and many Chinese Christians believed that Christians should not attend national schools if participation in the Confucian ceremonies were required. They were convinced of the necessity, therefore, of offering to Chinese Christians a Christian education which equaled that provided by the government. To provide education of such quality, the missionaries would have to maintain a few institutions supported by many denominations rather than many colleges supported by separate societies.

Expansion through Cooperation, 1900–1911

Though the Christian colleges never achieved the degree of unity considered desirable by many educators, a number of established institutions joined forces early in the twentieth century, and most new colleges were supported by several mission societies. The majority of the union institutions founded during this period were in the coastal section of China, also the main area of college work and intensive evangelism during the nineteenth century.

In the Peking district the buildings of North China College at T'ungchow and Peking University had been destroyed during the Boxer Rebellion. Since both schools expected to receive indemnity funds for reconstruction and were considering the purchase of a new campus site, it seemed natural to ask whether each should go its separate way and restore the pre-Boxer status quo. The answer of missionaries in the field was no, and so between 1900 and 1902 Protestant missions in the Peking vicinity held negotiations for the unification of their higher educational work. The home front, however, rejected the proposal for union. One obstacle was concern lest denominational differences and loyalties be lost in the federation. Other obstacles were the differing traditions of the two schools; Peking University offered instruction in the English language and admitted some non-Christians, whereas North China College had not yet introduced English courses and gave greater emphasis to religious goals. The union of the two institutions to form Yenching University was over a decade and many long conferences away.

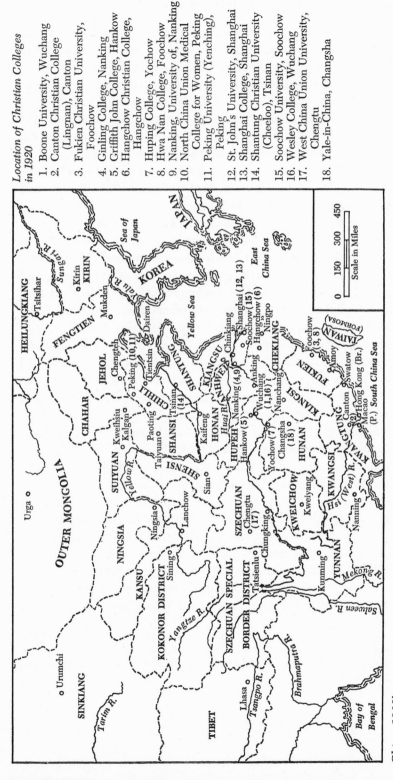

Location of Christian Colleges in 1920

1. Boone University, Wuchang
2. Canton Christian College (Lingnan), Canton
3. Fukien Christian University, Foochow
4. Ginling College, Nanking
5. Griffith John College, Hankow
6. Hangchow Christian College, Hangchow
7. Huping College, Yochow
8. Hwa Nan College, Foochow
9. Nanking, University of, Nanking
10. North China Union Medical College for Women, Peking
11. Peking University (Yenching), Peking
12. St. John's University, Shanghai
13. Shanghai College, Shanghai
14. Shantung Christian University (Cheeloo), Tsinan
15. Soochow University, Soochow
16. Wesley College, Wuchang
17. West China Union University, Chengtu
18. Yale-in-China, Changsha

China, 1920's

In the meantime, each school had begun rebuilding; North China College conducted its work briefly in Peking and then returned to T'ungchow in 1902; Peking University acquired additional property in Peking and began the construction of new college buildings. Hope for cooperation was not abandoned, and negotiations in 1903–1904 led to the cooperation of the American Congregationalists, the English Congregationalists, and the American Presbyterians in the North China Educational Union. These three missions agreed to coordinate their efforts in maintaining Gordon Memorial Theological College and Lockhart Medical College, both in Peking, and North China Union College in T'ungchow.[47] Within a year Peking University had agreed to cooperate in Lockhart Medical College. The scheme actually was not so much a union as a federation to prevent duplication of effort. Each mission furnished faculty members, a portion of the current expenses of each of the schools, and personnel for a joint board of managers, but the individual missions owned the separate educational plants. Since the three home mission boards had final say on all major decisions, the administration was cumbersome and important changes required lengthy and complex negotiations. Nevertheless, the North China Educational Union slowly acquired prestige and authority and, as an early example of educational cooperation among several denominations, it stimulated other attempts at cooperation.

In Shantung, also, several denominations began to coordinate their work in higher education. Even before the Boxer Rebellion some missionaries had proposed transferring Tengchow College to a more central location, and the destruction of the Tengchow campus during the Boxer rampage threw the balance in favor of those advocating a move to Weihsien. During the negotiations English Baptists expressed an interest in cooperating, and in 1902 the American Presbyterians and English Baptists reached an agreement whereby they would unite in three colleges: an arts college in Weihsien, a theological college at Tsingchow where the Baptists were already maintaining the Gotch-Robinson Theological School, and a medical col-

[47] Galt, "Yenching," pp. 36–37, 41–42; George A. Stuart, "Report of the Committee on Union Educational Establishments," *Records, EAC, 1909*, p. 37; Thomas Cochrane, *Survey of the Missionary Occupation of China* (Shanghai, 1913), p. 260.

lege, the location of which was to be determined later.[48] The plant at Weihsien was to be the property of the Presbyterians, and the plants of the theological and medical schools were to belong to the English Baptists. Current expenses of the colleges were to be shared equally. There was to be a joint board of directors, with the three colleges to be known as Shantung Protestant University (changed in 1909 to Shantung Christian University in English and Shan-tung chi-tu-chiao kung-ho ta-hsüeh in Chinese).

Despite opposition from Calvin Mateer and others, the federation took place, and the arts college moved to Weihsien in 1904. Five years later, the Society for the Propagation of the Gospel (Anglican) joined the union and transferred the upper class of the Anglican school at Taian to Weihsien. During the same period the medical college was set up at Tsinan, and the University Council recommended that all divisions of the university be consolidated in Tsinan; the move to the new campus actually took place in 1917.[49] As other denominations joined the union, Shantung Christian University (or Cheeloo as it was later known) came to have the support of more than a dozen mission societies and gained a reputation as the leading Christian college teaching in Mandarin.

A union agreement which led to the founding of the University of Nanking (Chin-ling ta-hsüeh) in 1910, made possible regular training on a college level for the first time. The upper classes of the Presbyterian Academy and Nanking Christian College (Disciples of Christ) joined to form Union Christian College in 1906, and then Union Christian College and Nanking University (Methodist) formed the University of Nanking in 1910. In establishing the new university, each mission agreed to turn over to it the equivalent of US$40,000 in land, buildings, equipment, or cash; to provide three teachers; and to make an annual grant of US$2,400. All university property was to be held by a joint board of trustees appointed by the home mission societies. The university received a charter from

[48] Decker, "Shantung," pp. 48–52; Garside, *Life of Luce*, pp. 100, 106–107; J. A. Silsby, "Proposed United Colleges in Shantung," *CR*, XXXIII (1902), 417–418.

[49] Cochrane, *Missionary Occupation of China*, pp. 273–274; Decker, "Shantung," pp. 88–90, 115; *Shantung Christian University* (pamphlet issued by the university in 1910, containing the "Basis of Union" and the annual report, located at UB), pp. 1, 9; H. W. Luce, "Shantung," *CMYB, 1917*, p. 228.

the State of New York in 1911.[50] As the university became known for its pioneer work in agriculture, it came to lead the Christian colleges in the amount of financial support received from Chinese sources, the proportion of Chinese teachers on its faculty, and the percentage of its students from government preparatory schools.

In several instances educational union took the form of cooperation by mission societies from one denomination rather than interdenominational collaboration. In 1909, for example, the American Southern Presbyterians joined the Northern Presbyterians in operating Hangchow Presbyterian College. Even with this broadened base of support, the college grew slowly and had difficulty in attaining and then maintaining full college status. The Presbyterian mission societies had joined in the responsibility for so many Christian colleges in China that the Hangchow administrators often found themselves competing for funds with other and seemingly more persuasive Christian college leaders. The institution, nevertheless, moved to a new site and new buildings in 1911, and changed its name to Hangchow Christian College in 1914. With the active support of the alumni, the college administrators resisted all arguments that it accept junior college status; and after enlarging the faculty and student body and expanding the curriculum, they were rewarded in 1920 by incorporation under the laws of the District of Columbia.[51] College leaders took especial pride in the large proportion of its alumni who entered the ministry.

Also the fruit of cooperation between sectors of the same denomination was the University of Shanghai (Hu-chiang ta-hsüeh). The original plans for the university were made while missionaries of the central and east China missions of the Baptist church were gathered in Shanghai because of the Boxer Rebellion. Representatives of the Northern Baptist and Southern Baptist churches, having agreed to cooperate in founding a seminary and a liberal arts college in Shanghai, secured the support of their home societies. In 1906 with the purchase of the first college property, Shanghai Baptist College and

[50] Report of the President of the University of Nanking, 1911; C. H. Hamilton, "The University of Nanking," ER, IX (1917), 226–228.

[51] Hangchow Presbyterian College, President's Report, 1912–13, p. 53; Day, Hangchow, pp. 18–37; Theodore E. Hsiao, The History of Modern Education in China (Peking, 1932), p. 120.

Seminary was officially founded. The first forty-nine students enrolled in 1909, and in 1917 the institution was incorporated under the laws of Virginia, though the name University of Shanghai was not officially adopted until 1931.[52]

The school became known for its work in sociology and social service. Daniel H. Kulp, head of the department of sociology, secured the support of several Shanghai business and educational leaders in organizing the Yangtzepoo Social Center as a laboratory for sociology students and as a social service center. Here, recreational, religious, and educational facilities were provided for factory workers and the children of working parents. College students helped conduct continuation and day schools for adults and children, Sunday schools and church services, a reading room, a playground, and other educational and recreational activities.[53] In addition to directing surveys of conditions in industrial sections of Shanghai, Kulp wrote one of the first China community studies based on modern scientific methodology, *Country Life in South China* (New York, 1925).

Soochow University evolved out of three separate schools, all maintained by the American Southern Methodists: a Soochow school which had been opened in 1871 by Rev. Tsao Tz-seh and transformed into Buffington Institute in 1884 by Dr. A. P. Parker; an Anglo-Chinese College in Shanghai founded by Young J. Allen in 1882; and the Kung Hong School established in Soochow in 1896 by D. L. Anderson. The curricula of Kung Hong and Anglo-Chinese College reflected the growth of Chinese interest in Western learning during the last two decades of the nineteenth century; the Anglo-Chinese College gave primary emphasis to English language instruction, and the Kung Hong School, begun fourteen years later, offered courses in European history, geography, science, and mathematics, as well as English. In 1899 Buffington Institute was discontinued, and many of the students and teachers transferred to Shanghai Anglo-Chinese College. That same year the China mission of the Southern Methodists voted to coordinate all their educational work into one system capped by a university in Soochow. When this plan

[52] University of Shanghai, *Catalogue, 1933*, pp. 15–16.
[53] D. H. Kulp, "Social Effort in Yangtzepoo, Shanghai," *CMYB, 1918*, pp. 346–348.

was presented to Chinese officials and literati by Young J. Allen and Timothy Richard, it was enthusiastically received, and Chinese subscribed approximately Ch$20,000 for the project. A letter from Viceroy Liu K'un-i promised to facilitate the purchase of land and welcomed the proposal with the statement, "In days to come your school's graduates will be the peaches and pears [i.e., the choice products] of Tung Wu." Apparently this reference to the classical name for the Soochow region, Tung Wu, suggested the Chinese title for the university.[54]

The next step of the missionaries was to present their plans to the 1901 general conference of the Methodist Episcopal Church (South), which donated US$50,150. D. L. Anderson was appointed president, and Soochow University opened in the buildings of the old Buffington Institute. All of the entering students were below college level, and the first college graduation with presentation of a B.A. degree took place in 1907; at that time there were eleven college students.[55] Foreshadowing the emphasis of the college on the natural sciences, N. Gist Gee began to build up the programs in biology and the physical sciences. Anglo-Chinese College in Shanghai continued until the death of Anderson in 1911 and the nomination of the president of the Anglo-Chinese College, John Cline, to be the new president of Soochow; at this time many of the students and teachers at the Shanghai school transferred to Soochow. After this, the number of students at the college level grew steadily, and the institution so strengthened its science program that several of its students, after study abroad, helped staff the science departments of other Christian colleges.

As the Chinese government assumed responsibility for a national educational system, mission schools generally tried to meet the requirements of the government curricula. Beyond this, however, there were few attempts to integrate the two educational programs. Official government documents ignored the existence of the mission

---

[54] W. B. Nance, *Soochow University* (New York, 1956), pp. 3–21; Soochow University, *Catalogue, 1909*, pp. 1–4; "Historical Sketch," *Soochow University Bulletin, 1934*, p. 13. Nance was closely associated with Soochow University and the antecedent colleges from the late nineteenth century until 1949.

[55] John Cline, "Soochow University," *ER*, XI (1919), 75–76; Soochow University, *Catalogue, 1909*, pp. 3–4; "Soochow University, Historical Statement," *Monthly Bulletin, EAC*, no. 5 (1907), pp. 11–12.

institutions, and mission groups evolved their own policies, with the result that significant differences between the two systems developed and students had difficulty transferring from one to the other. Contributing to the growth of closed systems were the care with which Christian colleges cultivated their feeder schools and the fact that many of the colleges included preparatory schools; most of the Christian college students came from these two sources. Soochow University, for example, had a group of schools known as Soochow University First Middle School, Second Middle School, etc., and Soochow University First Primary School, Second Primary School, etc.

A separate Christian educational system was perhaps most fully developed in southwest China. Here, mission schools were established later than in coastal China, and the missionaries profited from the absence of vested interests by founding an interdenominational educational union and limiting their work in higher education to one institution. As early as 1905 the missions which were engaged in educational work in Szechuan met to discuss cooperation. Reflecting the dual interest of the missions, the conference members organized both a committee for primary and secondary education and a temporary board of management for a union university.[56] Land just outside the south gate of Chengtu was purchased in 1908; a union middle school was established on the property the following year, and a constitution for the university was adopted. Missions representing denominations in Britain, the United States, and Canada took part in the project: the American Baptist Foreign Missionary Society (North), the Friends' Foreign Mission Association of Great Britain and Ireland, the General Board of Missions of the Methodist Church of Canada, and the Board of Foreign Missions of the Methodist Episcopal Church, U.S.A. The Church Missionary Society (English Anglican) later joined the union.

Since there was some conflict between the English concept of a university as a group of more or less independent colleges and the American idea of a glorified college, the duties of the central administration were only vaguely defined. The missions were to set up individual colleges for housing and religious instruction. Each mis-

[56] Joseph Taylor, *History of West China Union University, 1910–1935* (Chengtu, 1936), pp. 11–13; George A. Stuart, "Report of the Committee on Union Educational Establishments," *Records, EAC, 1909*, pp. 36–37.

sion would also aid in erecting classroom buildings, furnishing university faculty members, and appointing representatives to the local governing body, the University Senate. In fact, the centripetal tendencies were strong, and power steadily accrued to the president, the Reverend Joseph Beech, who was appointed after several years of negotiation.

West China Union University (Hua-hsi hsieh-ho ta-hsüeh) opened in 1910 with eleven students. It closed the following year because many foreign missionaries left the interior during the revolution but resumed college classes in 1913. Since Christian education was only in its initial stages in Szechuan and there were few feeder schools, the college grew slowly. The first permanent buildings were completed in 1915, and in the same year the first two students graduated. A year later the college reported an enrollment of forty-eight, seven in the senior college and forty-one in the junior college.[57] Though West China Union University had opened with only a faculty of arts and science, it added departments in medicine, religion, education, and dentistry during its first decade. For some years it was the only Protestant institution in China to offer a complete course in modern dentistry. The prominent role of British and Canadian mission personnel and the British organizational pattern with separate residential colleges distinguished West China from the other Protestant colleges, where United States influence was dominant.

Not all of the attempts at union during the early twentieth century were successful. Christian educators in north and central China would eventually unite in Yenching University and Huachung University, but for years they had to report failure. Another scheme which caused untold frustration was a proposal to form one union university in China to crown the Christian educational system. After an unsuccessful attempt to gain support for such an institution in 1906, proponents won approval at the 1909 meeting of the (Christian) Educational Association of China. The project was championed by Lord William Gascoyne-Cecil, later Bishop of Exeter. Having interested the universities of Oxford and Cambridge in the venture, he came to China in 1909 and helped draw a comprehensive plan

[57] CMYB, 1916, p. 253; West China Union University, Annual Report, 1910–11, p. 6; 1913–14, pp. 4–6; Taylor, West China, p. 30.

for a united university at Wuhan. A president was elected, and several men were even sent to begin instruction in existing institutions.

American support remained theoretical, however, and though Gascoyne-Cecil wrote a book pleading for the university,[58] British financial aid was meager. It was difficult to arouse enthusiasm for a project lacking an appeal to denominational loyalties. The proposal would have required the approval and support of numerous mission societies, and this depended on the project's being actively pushed by missionaries in the field. Many of the missionary educators were not willing to give up hope that their individual colleges might develop into universities offering graduate and professional courses. Some doubted that there were enough Chinese students ready for advanced work in Western subjects. The union university project, already languishing, died with the outbreak of World War I, and attempts to found one Christian university for all China ended. Cooperative projects were to proceed as before through the tedious process of negotiation among individual denominations and schools.

Growth and Consolidation, 1911–1925

The revolution of 1911 brought a new sense of urgency regarding the need to improve Christian education and to renew attempts at cooperation. The apparent ease with which the initial transfer of sovereignty occurred led many to believe that the republic would speedily achieve its goals, and among these goals was a literate populace on which to base a democratic government. Not only were new elementary and secondary school systems outlined, but there were plans for the reorganization of Peking University and the founding of new government universities at Wuchang, Nanking, and Canton. Concern over the competition of government schools again occupied the missionaries, and they insisted that the Christian colleges must improve the quality of their faculty and equipment or be outdistanced by the national universities.

The fears of the missionaries now had some basis in fact. Despite political disintegration and internal warfare, the government was making progress in the number and quality of its schools. Peking

[58] *Changing China.* The project was known first as the Oxford and Cambridge scheme and then as the United Universities plan.

University, or Peita as it was affectionately known, was about to enter upon its brief reign as the intellectual center of China. Students who had studied abroad and held advanced degrees in scientific and technical fields, were beginning to return to China in fairly large numbers. They could command high salaries, often more than the Christian colleges could offer, and many went to teach in government colleges. At the meetings of the missionary educators and in the pages of *The Educational Review* and *The Chinese Recorder*, there were frequent pleas that no additional Christian colleges be established and that the existing colleges raise their standards through union.[59]

In an attempt to achieve greater unity and uniformity, the (Christian) Educational Association of China was reorganized.[60] China was divided into eight regions, each with its own educational association which would elect delegates to a central advisory council. Plans were later made for four full-time secretaries, one each for religious education, primary and secondary education, higher education, and adult education. Whereas the association had been composed almost entirely of Westerners, it now sought Chinese members. An Association of Christian Colleges and Universities in China was organized in 1919 to help correlate the work of the colleges and to make a united appeal for funds in the West. In cooperation with the secretary for higher education, it sponsored a series of valuable surveys of the colleges in which information was collected on such matters as student-teacher ratio, faculty teaching load, academic training of instructors, annual budget, value of plant and equipment, and proportion of Christian students.[61] Individual colleges were thus able to make a comparative evaluation of their strengths and weaknesses and to plan more intelligently for future expansion. The

[59] See, for example, Cochrane, *Missionary Occupation of China*, pp. 359–360; "Union in Mission Education," *The Educational Directory of China, 1914*, p. 1; J. A. Silsby, "Cooperation in Educational Work," *ER*, VII (1915), 309–316.

[60] "Constitution of the China Educational Association," *ER*, VI (1913), 5–6. In 1915 the name was changed to China Christian Educational Association and thereafter the abbreviation CCEA was often used.

[61] Among the published surveys were Earl H. Cressy, *College and University Finance in China*, CCEA Bul. no. 1 (Shanghai, 1924); Cressy, *Christian Higher Education in China: A Survey for the Year, 1925–26*, CCEA Bul. no. 20 (Shanghai, 1928); Cressy, *Minimum Standards for Christian Colleges in China*, CCEA Bul. no. 21 (Shanghai, 1927).

two associations gave guidance to the colleges in working toward uniform entrance requirements and trying to prevent duplication in the special vocational and professional courses.

Negotiations among denominations enabled several of the colleges to broaden their support and strengthen their educational programs during the second decade of the twentieth century. In 1911 the American Baptists joined in supporting the University of Nanking's work in agriculture.[62] The Canadian Presbyterian Mission in 1916 furnished a professor for the College of Medicine of Shantung Christian University, and a few years later agreed to provide one teacher in the College of Theology and one in the College of Arts and Sciences.[63] Additional support encouraged Canton Christian College to offer a full college course for the first time.

Canton had been slow in attaining college status, and its history seemed to illustrate some of the difficulties of a nonsectarian institution at a time when union institutions were being advocated. Canton did not inherit a group of denominational primary and secondary schools that sent their graduates on to college. The only regular mission support of which it was assured was the maintenance of some of its faculty, and the lack of continuity in staff and small number of full-time staff members were undoubtedly related to its nondenominational status. Both the mission society supporting a faculty member and the missionary himself seemed more ready to accept transfer than in some of the other institutions. The college had no devoted and persuasive champion such as Hawks Pott of St. John's, Sheffield of North China College, or Calvin Mateer of Tengchow; rather, two of its early presidents accepted their positions reluctantly and on condition that they be allowed to devote much of their time to other activities.[64]

Interestingly enough, another factor which retarded the growth of Canton College was the long experience of the Cantonese with Westerners. The commercial value of English was so widely appreciated that the school seemed to have unusual difficulty in retaining

[62] University of Nanking, *Catalogue, 1917*, p. 13.

[63] Corbett, *Shantung*, pp. 102–104.

[64] B. C. Henry, president from 1893 to 1896, asked permission to continue many of his evangelistic activities; Charles K. Edmunds, president from 1908 to 1924, gave much of his time to research and tours of exploration on the earth's magnetism.

students after they had learned a smattering of English. Even the preparatory division reported that most students left before graduation; the school had offered one or two years of college-level work for a decade before the first three students completed a full college course in 1918. At the same time experience with foreigners had fostered the growth of xenophobia in Canton, and sentiment against Westerners and their institutions was easily aroused. Mission school students were not immune. During the 1905 boycott protesting United States exclusion acts and mistreatment of Orientals, students at Canton Christian College objected to the use of American textbooks and refused to wear as part of their school uniform shoes manufactured in the United States; a number of students refused to return to the school in the fall of 1905, and during the same period the college experienced what was one of the first student strikes in any of the Christian colleges.[65]

Despite handicaps, Canton Christian College began in 1915 a concerted campaign to raise its standards. The results were encouraging. At that time there were thirty students taking college level work; 115 college students were enrolled in 1920; and by 1925 there were 226.[66] Financial hardship had forced the institution to seek support from Chinese patrons, and this dependence on Chinese interest and aid became an asset. In 1908–1909 a local fund-raising campaign gained the support of a number of high officials and raised Ch$39,000 for a new dormitory. Shortly after the 1911 revolution Canton College students attracted favorable publicity for the institution by collecting Ch$55,000 for the new regime. Somewhat later Chung Wing-kwang (Chung Jung-kwang) of the department of Chinese, following the example of Sun Yat-sen, took advantage of the close ties between the Chinese of Kwangtung and of Southeast Asia to seek aid from wealthy Nanyang Chinese; at the same time the college established on its campus an Emigrant School (later called the Overseas School) to prepare the sons of overseas Chinese for education in the homeland. The college could also report additional aid from mission societies; the United Brethren in Christ, the

[65] Canton Christian College, *Catalogue, 1917–18*, p. 11; "Canton Christian College," *Educational Directory of China, 1918*, pp. 46–48; Corbett, *Lingnan*, pp. 37–42, 47, 67.

[66] Cressy, *Christian Higher Education in China*, pp. 26–27.

London Missionary Society (Congregational), and the Swatow Mission of the American Baptist Mission Union each offered to maintain a faculty member at the college.[67] It was on the basis of such assistance that the college curriculum was expanded to include agriculture and sericulture.

Though missionary educators were, during the second decade of the twentieth century, principally concerned with unification movements or with raising the academic standing of the existing colleges, several new colleges were founded to serve special purposes such as the education of women or medical training, or to serve areas without Christian institutions of college level. Fukien Christian University (Fu-chien hsieh-ho ta-hsüeh) was the major new institution in the latter category. It owed its inception to the 1910 World Missionary Conference at Edinburgh, which called for Protestant universities in strategic centers throughout the world; a sub-committee recommended that in China the cities be Peking, Nanking, Chengtu, and Foochow. Since Foochow was the only center which did not already have or at least plan a liberal arts college, a committee representing six interested Fukien missions was organized in 1911. Then began a period of negotiation which stretched into years as the home boards debated approval and support.

By 1915 four mission societies had promised aid, and in 1916 Fukien Christian College was formally opened with approximately eighty students. Its student body was composed of the upper classes of three preparatory schools in Foochow: St. Mark's Anglo-Chinese College supported by the Anglicans, Foochow College founded by the American Congregationalists, and Foochow Anglo-Chinese College of the Methodist Episcopal Mission. A few students were also to be drawn from Talmage College, maintained by the Reformed Church mission in Amoy. All of the preparatory schools continued as middle schools after their upper classes were transferred to Fukien Christian College, and they served as feeder schools for the new institution. Instruction was given in a rented tea hong by six foreign and two Chinese teachers; the library was borrowed from Foochow College, and science laboratories were made available by

[67] For details, see Canton Christian College, *Report of the President, 1911–1912*, pp. 28, 73; *Catalogue, 1923–24*, p. 15; Corbett, *Lingnan*, pp. 46–47, 68–70.

the Anglo-Chinese College in the mornings. The first president, Edwin C. Jones, and several of the teachers came from the preparatory schools. After acquiring a permanent site outside Foochow in 1917, the college received a provisional charter from the State University of New York in 1918 and was officially named Fukien Christian University.[68]

Unification efforts continued to occupy missionary educators in central China and in the two sections where Christian higher education had its beginnings, the Yangtze delta and northeast China. The east coast colleges achieved little more than agreement to consult about plans for expansion. Educators placed much of the blame on the home boards for refusing to delegate greater authority to the field and for putting denominational loyalties before cooperation. They pointed out that alterations in the administration of the colleges usually required the approval of each of the supporting missionary societies as well as the boards of trustees of the schools. Often a year lapsed before all the societies had met and had reached a decision on the proposed change. It took individuals truly dedicated to the cause of cooperation to push on to success. Even if the amalgamation were finally achieved, the administration of the union institution was cumbersome, for the board of trustees frequently sought the approval of each of the cooperating missions on matters of more than routine importance.

Many of the deterring factors were in the field, however. As faculty and alumni developed pride in their institution, they became unenthusiastic about absorption of the college into a union school. Some of the most vocal opponents of union were Chinese alumni. The schools differed in their religious emphases and in their policies for admission of non-Christians, and compromise was difficult on these matters. In east China there were St. John's University, the University of Shanghai, Soochow University, Hangchow Christian

[68] Fukien Christian University, *Report of the President, Oct. 10, 1919*, p. 5; Edwin C. Jones, "Fukien Christian University," *CMYB, 1918*, pp. 187–188; Roderick Scott, *Fukien Christian University* (New York, 1954), pp. 7–8, 15–18; John Gowdy, "Report of the Educational Association of Fukien Province," *ER*, X (1918), 205; Ford, *History of Educational Work*, pp. 256–257. During the first years various names were used for the school, Fukien Union University in 1914, Fukien Christian College in 1915, and Fukien Union College in 1916. The Chinese name means Fukien Union University.

University, the University of Nanking, and Ginling, a Christian college for women. Union of several or all of these schools would have formed a strong university with adequate financial backing, but even so the pressures for unity were less insistent than elsewhere. Though there were more Christian colleges in east China than in any other section, there were also more Christian middle schools to act as feeders and more Chinese interested in a Western-type education. Even if the east colleges were not yet large enough to be efficient units, they were generally larger than most of the other Christian colleges, and they were expanding, so each hoped that it could develop into an institution of acceptable size and standing. The prospects for union faded, therefore; and in 1922 an Advisory Council of the East China Christian Colleges and Universities was organized. Its purposes were modest: to devise uniform entrance examinations, to recommend similar curricula for the first two years of college and differing emphases for the upperclasses, and to organize cooperative work in professional and graduate studies.[69] Optimists still hoped that such a loose organization might grow towards union and pointed to the University of London as a model.

The negotiations for union in north China did not lead to the merging of all institutions into one, but the schools were reorganized into two interdenominational universities. There were in north China in 1911: (1) the confederation of schools known as Shantung Christian University and including the arts college at Weihsien, the theological and normal schools at Tsingchow, and the medical school at Tsinan; (2) the North China Educational Union schools which included the T'ungchow arts college and four institutions in Peking: Gordon Memorial Theological College, Lockhart Medical College, a women's college, and a women's medical school; and (3) Peking (Methodist) University, which cooperated in the theological and medical schools of the North China Union. Though the multiplicity of institutions made the situation appear similar to that in east China, north China had certain advantages in any unification movement. Most of the east China colleges were denominational, whereas most of the north China institutions had become interdenominational;

[69] Earl H. Cressy, *The University of London and Christian Higher Education in East China,* East China Studies in Education no. 1 (Shanghai, 1925), pp. 1–34.

denominational loyalties would not be so important a deterrent in north China. Alumni opposition, furthermore, had been undercut, since several of the north China schools had already changed names and sites. Perhaps, too, the Peking schools were especially fortunate in having leaders who believed in union and were willing to work many years to achieve it: D. Z. Sheffield and Howard S. Galt of T'ungchow, President H. H. Lowry of Peking University, and Frank Gamewell, superintendent of educational work of the Methodist Episcopal Church in China and secretary of the CCEA. Moreover, since several leading Chinese universities were in north China, the challenge to the mission institutions was immediate and visible.

The negotiations for union of Peking University and the North China Union schools, in abeyance since 1903, were resumed after the 1911 revolution, and two viewpoints emerged. Dr. Lowry desired essentially a continuation of Peking University on a nondenominational basis. The other missions preferred a federated university in which the cooperating colleges could maintain some of their individual traditions. A compromise was gradually worked out. In 1915 the Peking University charter was revised to fit the needs of the new union university, and in 1918 the students of Peking University and of the North China Union arts and theological schools were brought together on the Peking campus.[70]

Numerous problems remained unsolved, however: the selection of a university president, agreement on a name and permanent site, and a decision on whether to include North China Union College for Women. In 1919 J. Leighton Stuart of Union Theological Seminary in Nanking accepted the presidency. In the following year North China Union College for Women formally joined, though coeducational classes were not held for several years. After considerable controversy over the name, it was acknowledged that having two Peking Universities, one government and one Christian, was confusing and that the national institution had first claim on the name. The title Yenching University, using the literary name for

[70] Peking University, *Report of the Board of Managers, 1917*, p. 30; *Report of the President, 1919–1920*, p. 2; Edward L. Smith, *Fifty-two Days in China* (n.p., 1918), p. 3. Smith came to China as a representative of the board of trustees of Peking U.

Peking, was officially adopted in both English and Chinese.[71] In 1926 the university moved to its new site outside Peking; here, the university adopted an architecture which combined Western construction techniques with decorative elements from Chinese public buildings and built one of the handsomest college campuses in China. Yenching soon became the leader among the Christian colleges in China—the strongest, the largest, and the best endowed.

Meanwhile Shantung Christian University secured support from additional mission societies and consolidated all of its work in Tsinan, the home of the medical school. In 1915 it began to use a new Chinese name, Ch'i-lu ta-hsüeh (usually transliterated as Cheeloo); the name combined the titles of two dukedoms which had dominated the Shantung region in the time of Confucius, and it gradually came to be employed in English as well as Chinese.[72] Expansion strained both institutional and denominational loyalties. A number of Presbyterians in the seminary were unhappy with the work in theology and with the policies of President J. P. Bruce; in 1919 the acting dean and the Presbyterian seminarians withdrew from the university and established North China Theological Seminary, dedicated to conservative theology. On the other hand, Vice-President Henry W. Luce, who had pictured a great university to train leaders for a new China as he had raised funds for the new campus, was disappointed by what seemed to him a narrow definition of purpose. He resigned from the university in 1918 and soon thereafter turned his talents to securing funds for Yenching University.[73] Disagreements over theology, over the relationship of the university to the supporting denominations, and over a satisfactory balance between religious and educational goals seemed particularly sharp at Shantung, and apparently personality conflicts aggravated the discord.

[71] Though the official English name of the institution was Peking University until 1928, I have used Yenching University for the institution after 1918 in order to avoid confusion with the earlier Peking (Methodist) University.

[72] One reason for the change was that Shan-tung chi-tu-chiao kung-ho ta-hsüeh (Shantung Christian Union University) was cumbersome for daily use. Though generally used, the name Ch'i-lu ta-hsüeh was not officially adopted until registration with the Chinese government in 1931.

[73] Corbett, Shantung, pp. 133-134; Garside, Life of Luce, pp. 153-163.

Perhaps no attempt at union faced greater difficulties than the one which finally brought together five small institutions in central China; unfortunately, the institution which was created, Huachung University or Central China University, came into being so late that war and revolution disrupted much of its short life. With good reason, surveys of mission education in China invariably recommended the consolidation of Christian higher education in Hunan, Hupeh, and western Kiangsi. Though a few cities along the major communication routes had felt the impact of Western learning and technology and a few cities had become important mission centers, the countryside had remained heavily insulated from Western influences. Mission education at the secondary level was still very limited in central China. Since Christian institutions drew most of their students from mission schools, this meant that few students were being prepared for the Christian colleges, and even these students often preferred to go to the metropolitan centers in the east. As late as 1920, therefore, all the Christian "colleges" in central China were small and most of their work was at the secondary level.

Despite the strong arguments for cooperation, union was achieved only after years of effort by a few determined individuals. For one thing, the schools were supported by five different societies and had staff members from three foreign countries.[74] The two strongest schools, Yale in China at Changsha and Boone University at Wuchang, were two hundred miles apart, and each was reluctant to abandon its location. Institutional traditions, though young, were strong; some of the most vociferous opposition to union came from the Chinese alumni. Some schools enrolled few non-Christians and trained students almost exclusively for mission work; others admitted a student body which was 50 percent or more non-Christian and offered a liberal arts education. Some preferred English as the medium of instruction and others argued for Chinese.

[74] Before negotiations for the union university were concluded, the Church of Sweden Mission had proposed a sixth institution, Lutheran College at Yiyang, Hunan, and in 1923 had begun to offer some college courses. This presented the possibility of cooperation with yet another mission society representing an additional country. Because of differences in educational philosophy and the preference of the Swedish mission for Chinese as the language of instruction, union was never achieved. Lutheran College carried on separately for several years before abandoning college work in 1931.

The oldest Christian college in central China was Boone University, founded by the American Church Mission (Episcopal) as a boarding school with five pupils in 1871. It organized a three-year college department in 1903; and after incorporation as a university under the laws of the District of Columbia, awarded its first B.A. degrees to nine men in 1911.[75] Though the college grew slowly, it was fortunate in the continuity of its administration, two of its presidents serving a total of thirty years; it was able to build a fairly strong program in the humanities and to organize a library school which was to train some of the first modern librarians of China.

Three of the institutions did not offer a full college program on a regular basis, though they occasionally provided some college work for a few students. The institutions were: Wesley College established at Wuchang in 1885 by the Wesleyan Missionary Society; Griffith John College founded at Hankow in 1899 by the London Missionary Society; and Huping College (or Lakeside College) established at Yochow on the shores of Tungting Lake early in the twentieth century and supported by the Reformed Church in America.

The fifth institution, Yale-in-China, was distinctive both in its origins and support. It was a product of the upsurge of interest in missions among college students during the 1890's and 1900's. In 1901 several Yale students and alumni who had become interested in the Student Volunteer Movement for Foreign Missions decided to devise a plan for working as a group in a mission field. They chose China, partly because the first Chinese graduate of a United States college was Yung Wing, a Yale alumnus of 1854, and partly because of the recent death of a Yale man during the Boxer Rebellion. With the blessing of the Yale administration (though with the stipulation that there be no official connection with Yale University), the Yale Foreign Missionary Society came into being in 1902. That same year J. Lawrence Thurston went to China to survey the field and make recommendations concerning the locale and nature of the Yale mission.[76]

---

[75] Boone University, *Fiftieth Anniversary Report*, pp. 1–10; "Boone University, Wuchang," *ER*, X (1918), 25.

[76] Brownell Gage, "Yale in China," *Educational Directory of China, 1921*, p. 44; Reuben Holden, *Yale in China, The Mainland 1901–1951* (New Haven, 1964), pp. 3–24.

Since it had recently become possible to establish permanent mission stations in Hunan, numerous societies had begun to stake claims in the area, and missionaries held a conference in 1903 to discuss division of the Hunan field. The conference passed a resolution inviting the Yale mission to establish an educational center in Changsha, and the invitation was accepted.[77] The work was to be non-denominational and to depend for support primarily on the gifts of Yale students and alumni. The Yale mission stressed humanitarian rather than evangelistic goals in its statement of purpose; expression of the Christian spirit through service rather than doctrinal instruction was the goal. To make this emphasis quite clear, the Yale society soon changed the name from Yale Mission in China to simply Yale-in-China, and often the name was further shortened to Yali. In 1906 a middle school and a medical dispensary were opened; in 1914 the College of Arts and Science was added, and in 1916 the first class was admitted to the medical school. Yali held its first graduation in 1921; twenty B.A. degrees and ten M.D. degrees were awarded, the number including retroactive degrees to all students who had completed the college course since the founding of the institution.[78]

With the emphasis on the premedical course in the college and with substantial grants from the Rockefeller Foundation for science equipment and teachers, Yale-in-China gained a reputation in the sciences. The institution also became known for its close ties with Chinese educators and leaders in Hunan, a fact which may be best illustrated when discussing the medical school. At the same time Yali experienced considerable difficulty with student strikes and indiscipline and with the recruitment and retention of teachers. These problems were faced by all of the Christian colleges, and whether or not Yali was peculiarly plagued would be hard to say; nevertheless, Yali teachers faced a student strike only a few weeks after school was opened in 1906, and several other instances of student rebellion occurred during the first decades of existence. Tragic losses deprived the institution of two promising workers almost as soon as they had become oriented to the Chinese scene; Thurston died of

[77] "Missionary News, The Hunan Missionary Conference," CR, XXXIV (1903), 473.

[78] The Yale Mission, Annual Report, 1910, pp. 5–6; E. H. Hume, "First Graduation Exercises at Yale-in-China," ER, XIII (1921), 372; Gage, "Yale in China," Educational Directory of China, 1921, pp. 44–45.

tuberculosis in 1904 and Warren Seabury, one of the first teachers, was drowned in Hunan in 1907.[79]

When negotiations for union of Christian higher education in central China were undertaken in the early 1920's, the college division of Yale-in-China was still small (seventy-six students in 1920–1921). The Yale community, nevertheless, resisted abandonment or absorption of a project which they believed was on the threshold of attaining its goals. They took pride in the nonsectarian and broadly humanitarian definition of their work, and they were not eager to join forces with other educational projects which they considered more narrowly evangelistic or denominational.

Representatives of the five missions conducting Christian higher education in central China met in Hankow in 1922, and recommended union to form Huachung University at Wuchang.[80] Hoping that approval from the home boards would soon be forthcoming, the educators decided to open Huachung University for a three-year trial period on the Boone campus in September 1924. As it turned out, the Yale society voted against participation, and the Reformed Church still had not given approval by the fall of 1924, so that the university opened with only the support of the Wesleyan Missionary Society, the London Missionary Society, and the American Episcopal Mission.[81] Since the Wesleyan Mission was able to send only one faculty member and two students, and the rest of the students, faculty, and administration came from schools of the American Episcopal Mission, the institution seemed more like a continuation of Boone than the beginnings of a new university. It was expected, however, that Wesley College and Griffith John College would henceforth concentrate their work at the secondary level and would send their graduates to Huachung University.

[79] Laudatory but useful biographies of both these men have been written: Henry B. Wright, *A Life with a Purpose: A Memorial of John Lawrence Thurston, First Missionary of the Yale Mission* (New York, 1908); J. B. Seabury, *The Vision of a Short Life: A Memorial of Warren Bartlett Seabury* (Cambridge, Mass.; 1909).

[80] The Church of Sweden Mission, which was not prepared to join the union movement, sent an observer without voting rights. A detailed discussion of the negotiations is given in John L. Coe, *Huachung University* (New York, 1962), pp. 17–43.

[81] It may be noted that R. Holden considers 1929 as the year in which Huachung University was formed; see *Yale in China*, p. 185.

The three-year trial period proved to be a trial in unexpected ways. Only a few weeks after the beginning of classes, a nationwide anti-Christian and antiforeign movement among students interrupted academic work. The storm passed, but the more intense activities of the May 30th, 1925, movement followed so that Huachung had to close its first year without holding examinations. Huachung managed to complete the second year, though with its enrollment reduced from eighty-nine to seventy-five. The third year, 1926–1927, saw the eclipse of both Yale-in-China and Huachung during the Northern Expedition and the breakup of the Kuomintang-Chinese Communist Party accord. Many Huachung students enrolled elsewhere in the fall of 1927, and the union university plan seemed dead. Bishop Alfred A. Gilman, acting president of Huachung, continued to work on the assumption that the university would reopen, however; and he was rewarded when in September 1929 Huachung made a second start, this time with the cooperation of both Yale-in-China and the Reformed Church Mission.

There were no more major reorganizations of the China Christian colleges until World War II, and even the cooperative ventures undertaken during the war emergency were abandoned after the Japanese surrender. No new institutions were founded, and the existent institutions gave their attention to consolidating their work. As was true of China missions in general, the great upsurge of optimistic pioneering had given way to concern with the delimitation of goals and the adaptation of methods to the Chinese environment. The China colleges had, during the first quarter of the twentieth century, placed themselves in a much better position to fulfill their promise as institutions of higher learning. Though few institutions had actually disappeared, many small schools which had called themselves colleges had curbed their ambitions and reorganized as middle schools. Their more advanced pupils and some of their staff had been transferred to union institutions such as Yenching, Cheeloo, the University of Nanking, and West China Union University, and these expected to profit from their broadened base of support and larger student bodies and staff.

The extent to which the union institution could build on these assets depended partly upon its success in overcoming the disadvantages of a cumbersome administration and a decline in interest derived from denominational loyalty. Some institutions, notably Yenching and the University of Nanking, were able to create their own public image and clientele of Western supporters, so that the loss of sectarian identity and appeal was more than offset by support from other quarters. In some cases, strong leadership encouraged the flow of power to the university president and other university administrative bodies so that they, rather than the mission societies, generally determined policy; the president and the Senate had a decisive voice in the life of West China Union University, for example. Other schools, Cheeloo and Huachung for instance, moved more slowly toward recognition as entities deserving support in their own right. They remained dependent on separate missions and societies for support and policy decisions, and their growth was hampered by factionalism and an unwieldy administrative structure. Even these institutions, however, offered educational programs with higher standards than those of the schools from which they originated.

V | Special Emphases

Two areas in which the missionaries made significant contributions were higher education for women and training in modern medicine and nursing. The mission institutions not only initiated work in these fields, but continued to allocate to them a greater portion of their resources than did the national schools. Even after government universities and other private schools assumed some responsibility for medical training and for college education for women, several of the Christian schools remained among the leaders in these two fields.

In China little formal schooling had customarily been offered in medicine and nursing, and relatively few women had managed to obtain advanced training. The best hope of a girl who aspired to literacy was to benefit from the instruction of tutors hired to educate her brothers or to obtain instruction from her father and brothers. A girl became a member of her husband's family when she married, and her main duties were as housekeeper and mother; to the girl's family, therefore, it seemed a poor investment to spend money educating a daughter. Since the major goal of education was to pass the civil service examinations and enter the government bureaucracy and since this avenue was closed to women, advanced training for girls seemed pointless. The apprenticeship system was the accepted method of training physicians, but in the absence of provisions for government licensing, anyone who so desired could set up as a doctor. His acceptance depended upon his success. New remedies did not become the property of all physicians but were passed down from doctor to apprentice or from father to son. Since the sick were cared for by their servants or relatives, nursing as a profession was unknown.

Missionaries who founded medical schools and boarding schools for girls in Ch'ing China were undertaking pioneer work. Their defiance of tradition, however, went beyond the offering of formal academic training which had been lacking; the schools were direct challenges to the existing social structure, to widely accepted ideas about the role and status of doctors and women. These two areas of Christian education in China were prime examples of the confrontation of differing cultural traditions. Initial Chinese reactions covered a wide range of negative attitudes: indifference, resentment, contempt, alarm. The missionaries, on their part, tended to import the techniques, standards, and curricula of the West; and because Chinese education provided few precedents in these particular fields, Christian educators were subject to fewer pressures to adjust their program to the Chinese academic heritage than in other areas of education. At the same time the absence of vested educational interests contributed to the Christian institutions' leadership and influence.

Though Protestant missionaries began to establish boarding schools for girls in the middle of the nineteenth century, Chinese educators showed little inclination to follow suit; with few exceptions, the formal training available to girls was provided by missionaries. During the early twentieth century some Chinese began to talk of the importance of educating women, or rather of the importance of educating future mothers,[1] but action was slow. Though some provincial schools for girls were founded, it was 1907 before the Ministry of Education added primary and normal schools for girls to the national educational program. After the 1911 revolution, educated groups changed their attitudes more rapidly, and some even included females when talking of democracy and individual equality. The republican government recommended for the first time that the lower primary schools be made coeducational and that middle schools for girls be included in the national educational system.[2] Even so, girls formed only a fraction of the total number

---

[1] See, for example, "Lun nü-hsüeh suo-i hsing kuo" (Discussion of how female education contributes to the prosperity of the state), *Tung-fang tsa-chih*, II, pt. 3, no. 11 (1905–1906), pp. 254–257; also the publicity given to one of the early schools, "Pei-ching yü-chiao nü hsüeh-t'ang chang-ch'eng" (Regulations of the Peking Women's Preparatory School), *ibid.*, no. 12 (1906), pp. 336–342.

[2] Kuo, *Chinese Education*, pp. 101, 111, 121, 129.

of pupils at all levels of education, and the perennial shortage of educational funds meant that allocations for institutions with low priority, girl's middle schools for example, were invariably reduced. The government made no attempt to provide college education for women until after the May 4, 1919 movement.

Missionary education for women was well ahead of these developments. In the nineteenth century mission schools for girls, like those for boys, were considered effective instruments for establishing contact with Chinese and insuring a regular audience for Christian teachings. Wives of missionaries and single female missionaries often organized small schools for girls soon after arrival in China. A lack of knowledge about Chinese tradition and a conviction of the superiority of Western mores and ideals meant that most missionaries had few scruples about founding what were actually revolutionary institutions. They hardly realized the extent to which their work constituted a break with the Chinese heritage. They began with little thought of paving the way for college education for women, and it was not until the twentieth century that the possibility of Christian colleges for girls received serious consideration.

Christian Higher Education for Women

Though numerous primary and secondary schools for girls were founded during the nineteenth century, only those which were the predecessors of Christian colleges will receive consideration here. In 1864 Eliza Bridgman of the American Board opened a school for a few beggar girls in Peking, and for thirty years the school gave primary training in the Chinese classics, Christianity, domestic science, and mathematics.[3] Its enrollment during this period averaged about eighteen pupils, a figure kept low by regulations against footbinding and by a requirement that pupils furnish their own clothing. Even to Chinese Christians, the education of their daughters hardly seemed desirable enough to warrant a contribution, especially if the girl's chances of a good marriage were reduced because of big feet. In 1895 the institution became Bridgman Academy and began to offer work at the secondary level. The Boxer Rebellion brought a serious setback; the buildings were destroyed, one-third of the pupils

[3] ABCFM, *Annual Report*, 1866, p. 133; Margaret E. Burton, *The Education of Women in China* (New York, 1911), pp. 50–51, 55–57.

were killed, and several years elapsed before the school could be re-established in permanent quarters. The inclusion of the academy in the North China Educational Union in 1904 gave the school a new lease on life; under the guidance of its new principal, Miss Luella Miner, it steadily raised its academic standards and gained support among mission societies in the West, particularly women's missionary associations. Assuming the title North China Union College for Women, the institution began to offer a limited number of college level courses, and in 1909 it graduated four students who had completed the full college course. The college department continued to be small, however; it had eight pupils in 1910 and twenty in 1912. Despite considerable doubt about the advisability of coeducation in China, union with the new Yenching University was accepted in 1919–1920.[4]

Hwa Nan College in Foochow, though not officially founded until 1908, also built on the work of earlier boarding schools for girls. In 1859, Foochow Girls' Boarding School opened its doors; and from 1899 to 1906 there also existed Foochow Conference Seminary, organized to attract well-to-do girls desiring to learn English. Both of these institutions were sponsored by the Women's Foreign Missionary Society of the Methodist Episcopal Church; in addition, in Foochow there were schools supported by the American Board and the Church Missionary Society. Whatever the names of these institutions, much of their work was at the primary level.

Encouraged by the Women's Foreign Missionary Society and the CCEA, Lydia Trimble began in 1904 to solicit funds for a woman's college in Foochow. The major function of the institution, as Miss Trimble saw it, would be to train religious leaders for women of the less privileged classes, especially women in the rural villages of south China. Though the American Board and Anglican institutions

---

[4] *Yenching College, Peking, China, 1905–1921* (promotional brochure, NBT); Luella Miner, "Women's Work in Education," *CMYB, 1910*, pp. 299–300; Miner, "The Higher Education of Women," *CMYB, 1917*, pp. 384–385; Mary R. Anderson, *Protestant Mission Schools for Girls in South China* (Mobile, Ala.; 1943), p. 210. The secondary school continued in existence as Bridgman Academy. As early as 1920 the North China Union College for Women had begun to use the shorter name Yenching College, or Yenching College for Women, in its publicity material, though Yenching University was not adopted as the English name of the union university until several years later.

hoped to send their graduates to the projected college, neither mission promised support, and so the new institution opened in 1908 under the auspices of the Methodist women's society. All work was initially at the secondary level, and the school was known as The Foochow College Preparatory of Foochow Woman's College (*sic*). Not until 1917 did the school introduce a full college course. Hwa Nan College received a provisional charter from the University of the State of New York in 1922.[5]

During much of its history Hwa Nan closely resembled the early Christian colleges for men, displaying both their strengths and weaknesses. College classes were small, eighty being the highest enrollment before 1925. Library and laboratory facilities were meager; the number of staff members and the course offerings were severely limited, and the institution seemed to face perennial financial crises. The college, with its strong Christian atmosphere, remained insulated from the national life of China. On the other hand, each student received individual attention, and most alumnae retained a lively sense of loyalty to the institution, a number of graduates returning to teach at considerable financial sacrifice. The supporting mission took pride in the fact that practically all of the students were Christians and the majority of the graduates worked in mission schools, hospitals, or other church agencies. Though Hwa Nan attracted a limited number of girls from well-to-do families, a significant percentage of its graduates undertook advanced study. By 1926, Hwa Nan had graduated thirty-eight students, of whom twenty-four were teaching in Christian schools and nine were pursuing graduate studies. Of the twelve students who graduated in 1928, two entered medical school and three later obtained Ph.D. degrees. Hwa Nan often boasted that its graduates, although few, exerted a far-reaching influence among the Christian communities of south China.[6]

The third Christian college for women, Ginling, was one of the

[5] ABCFM, *Annual Report, 1882*, pp. 56–57; "Hwa Nan College, A Statement of the Founder and First Principal, Miss Lydia A. Trimble," 1920 (typewritten MS; UB); L. Ethel Wallace, *Hwa Nan College* (New York, 1956), pp. 1–25. As in other instances, I have followed the usage of the institution itself in transliterating the name.

[6] Wallace, *Hwa Nan*, pp. 34–43; Hwa Nan College, *Brief Book of the Woman's College of South China*, 1920, pp. 7–13; Cressy, *Christian Higher Education*, pp. 26–27.

few mission institutions to begin work as a college. In 1907 the China Centenary Missionary Conference had urged mission boards to cooperate in establishing a few women's colleges and normal schools in strategic centers, and in line with this recommendation conferences were held in Shanghai, 1911–1912, to discuss the founding of a union college for women in central China. Several missions pledged support, and in 1913 the first board of control elected Matilda C. Thurston president of the proposed college. Because it was believed that Nanking would be the new capital of China, this city was chosen as the site for the new institution.

The college, Chin-ling nü-tzu ta-hsüeh, opened its doors in 1915 with eight students, six teachers, and five supporting missions: the Northern Baptists, the Disciples of Christ, the Methodists (North and South), and the Presbyterians (North).[7] The following year Smith College adopted Ginling as her sister college and made her first contribution to the school; for some years, the largest annual cash grant received by Ginling was that of Smith College. Among the others joining in support of the institution was the Chinese YWCA, which transferred its Shanghai Physical Training School for women to Ginling. In 1923 the college moved to a new and handsome campus, a factor which contributed to its growing reputation as a school for the wealthy. Ginling alumnae, like the graduates of the other Christian colleges for women, considered themselves an elite group pioneering in the field of women's education, and many continued their studies in graduate schools in China and the West. Almost half of the first forty-three Ginling graduates, for example, obtained degrees abroad. The school grew fairly rapidly, and in 1925 it enrolled 137 women, more than any other Christian college.[8]

[7] Ginling College, *Report of the President, 1915–16*, p. 3; Matilda Thurston and Ruth M. Chester, *Ginling College* (New York, 1955), pp. 1–11; *CCMC Records*, p. 587; Laura M. White, "A Union Woman's College," *CR*, XLII (1911), 644–648. The Chinese name of the University of Nanking was Chin-ling ta-hsüeh and so the characters for "woman" were added to the Chinese name for Ginling College. Mrs. Thurston was the widow of J. Lawrence Thurston, who had helped initiate Yale-in-China; and she had herself taught at Yali from 1906 to 1911.

[8] Mrs. Matilda Thurston, "Ginling College," *ER*, X (1918), 242–243; Ginling College, *A Six-Year Review, 1915–1921* (Nanking, 1921); A. J. Bowen, "Tenth Anniversary of the Founding, Ginling College," *Ginling College Magazine* (Dec. 1925), p. 7.

During the second decade of the twentieth century, demand for coeducation at the college level developed. The doctrine of equality, so popular among educated youth in this period, reached the women as well as the men, and customs discriminating against women were among those often condemned as deterring change. Soon after the government primary schools adopted a coeducational policy in 1911 and Tsing Hua scholarships were opened to women in 1915, women requested admission to government universities. Two students at North China Union Women's College, inspired by their study of prominent American women, applied to Peking National University and became the first women admitted to that institution in 1919. Within two years the government Higher Normal College in Nanking (later Southeastern University) and Nankai College in Tientsin had become coeducational.[9] The missionaries, who had done much to create an interest in women's education, were encouraged by public opinion to open their men's colleges to women.

Canton Christian College had for some years admitted a few girls but had not made a regular practice of coeducation. Most of the girls were daughters of faculty members and were enrolled in the middle school. By 1920, however, Canton was ready to appoint a dean of women, open a women's dormitory, and admit women to the regular college classes. The first woman to graduate from Canton received a B.A. degree in 1921. Shanghai Baptist College, Soochow University, and Yale-in-China all admitted women in 1920. Yenching became coeducational with the addition of North China Union College for Women, and Shantung Christian University first admitted women when North China Union Medical College for Women joined the Shantung University College of Medicine in 1923.[10] In west China agitation for higher education for women had begun as early as 1908. When funds for a separate girls' school were not forthcoming, coeducation at West China Union University was suggested. The university, however, would not consent unless women's mission-

[9] *Christian Education in China, The Report of the China Educational Commission of 1921–22* (New York, 1922), p. 261; Edwards, *Yenching*, p. 95.

[10] Canton Christian College, *Report of the President, 1911–12*, pp. 70–71; Corbett, *Lingnan*, pp. 71–72; Anderson, *Protestant Mission Schools*, pp. 212–213; Soochow University, *Catalogue*, 1929, p. 19; Shantung Christian University, *President's Report*, 1923, p. 3. The Yali women were in the premedical course.

Table 2. Enrollment of women in the China Christian colleges

Colleges	1920	1925
Canton Christian College	23	29
Ginling College	55	137
Hwa Nan College	14	80
Shanghai University	9	68
Shantung Christian University	0	53
Soochow University	0	6
University of Nanking		
(Agriculture and Forestry)	0	27
West China Union University	0	8
Yale-in-China	2	6
Yenching (women)	14	116
Total	117	530

Source: Handbook of Christian Colleges, 1926, pp. 28, 32.

ary societies assumed financial responsibility; some of the faculty members, furthermore, were unenthusiastic about coeducation. Only after long negotiation were the first eight women admitted in 1924.[11]

By thus opening their doors to women, the Christian schools maintained their leadership in the relative emphasis given to female education, although in the actual number of women attending college in China, the government universities were ahead. In 1922 the national universities reported 405 women out of a total of 10,535 college students, or 3.8 percent. The provincial and private colleges had only 132 women in a total of 20,325 students, 0.6 percent. The mission and foreign colleges enrolled fewer women than the national schools, 350 in a total of 4,020 students, but the percentage of women was 8.71.[12] By 1925–1926 the number of women in Christian colleges had risen to 530 out of 3,489 students, or 15.2 percent. The enrollment of women in the Christian colleges quadrupled between 1920 and 1925 (*Table 2*).

Most of the students did not look upon a college education as simply an opportunity for individual, intellectual growth. Women's

[11] "Report of the West China Union University Senate to the Board of Governors," 1924–25 (typewritten MS; UB), p. 7; Taylor, *West China,* pp. 38–42.
[12] *Statistical Report of Christian Colleges and Universities in China, 1924,* CCEA bul. no. 8 (Shanghai, 1925), Table XVII.

chances of obtaining a college education were still slim enough so that many of those enrolled had professional goals. They were serious, ambitious students, conscious that the eyes of China were upon them; they were thinking of career training and social service. Perhaps this is one reason why such a high percentage of the early graduates undertook advanced studies. The most popular careers were teaching and educational administration, though a significant number became doctors or entered social service. Many found positions with their alma mater or with institutions connected with the missions, but others worked for government schools or agencies. Perhaps their consciousness of being a leadership group also helps explain why the dire predictions of immorality and promiscuity by opponents of coeducation proved largely unfounded. At least for some years and for most students, the lack of experience in social relations with the opposite sex and the absence of courtship mores seem to have contributed to reticence rather than aggressiveness.

Origins of Modern Medical Training

The difficulties faced by missionaries who pioneered in modern medical training were even greater than those met by the initiators of higher education for women. Medical education under any circumstances is an expensive undertaking which requires many years of study, hospitals with costly facilities, a low student-teacher ratio, science laboratories, and the like. In China where textbooks were nonexistent, few hospitals had even minimal equipment, staffs were small, and facilities for scientific experiments were a luxury, medical education of high quality would require years of expensive preparation. Moreover, Chinese and Westerner had different concepts of the medical profession. This, plus the widespread suspicion of foreigners in China, deterred the acceptance of medicine as a profession requiring advanced training.

The physician had not been held in high repute in traditional China. Some Chinese doctors were scholars who had been unsuccessful in the civil service examinations; many were sons of doctors and were brought up in the occupation; quite a few were simply quacks who chose doctoring as a means of earning a living. Though there were works on medical techniques and *materia medica* with which the literate practitioner might be acquainted, many learned their trade as apprentices, and no licensing agency regulated admission to the profession. The relationship between physician and patient differed from that of the West. To some extent at least, the Chinese doctor was held responsible for the death or recovery of the patient; he might be amply rewarded if the patient regained his health; it was less than certain that he would receive any payment if the patient died.

Dr. Edward H. Hume, one of the founders of Hsiang-Ya Medical College in Changsha, had been warned by Chinese advisers not to accept critically ill patients and above all not to attempt surgery in such cases. To have a patient die while Hume was just establishing a practice would undermine confidence and might inspire retaliation against the foreigner. When after some months the inevitable happened and a youth died shortly after an operation, members of the mission anxiously awaited the reaction of the villagers. On the advice of a Chinese member, the mission furnished a coffin and burial twice as expensive as the family would normally have provided. As a precaution, however, the governor sent a few soldiers to protect the mission. When the father accepted the death as the will of Heaven and thanked Hume for his services, there was a sigh of relief and a sense that a milestone had been passed.[13]

The Chinese doctor, lacking professional status, often could not assume control in the treatment of a patient and frequently found his recommendations overruled by relatives of the patient. Although the Chinese had considerable knowledge of drugs and accurate descriptions of the symptoms and the course of many diseases, there had been little scientific study of diseases or of the relation between sanitation, antiseptic practices, and the control of disease. Without dissection the misconceptions in the field of anatomy were many, and the Chinese belief in the importance of completing life with one's body intact had deterred the development of surgery. Both the growth and the reputation of medicine in China were hindered by the large portion of superstition mixed with the valuable information about diseases and drugs.

The medical techniques of the missionary doctor at first only compounded suspicion of things foreign. Rumors that the Westerner

[13] Edward H. Hume, *Doctors East Doctors West: An American Physician's Life in China* (New York, 1946), pp. 85–89.

used Chinese eyes to manufacture silver or to make photographs circulated widely, and the foreigner's free use of the scalpel seemed scandalous to most Chinese. As tales of the "cut-knife" miracles of the missionary doctors spread, however, increasing numbers of brave or desperate souls were willing to place themselves under the foreigner's care. Missionaries, recognizing that cured patients were their best advertisements, reprinted testimonials and letters of thanks. Though fear and suspicion remained just below the surface, the foreigner acquired a reputation for success in healing, and his reputation became greatest in fields such as surgery and ophthalmology, where Chinese medicine offered the least aid. Most Chinese continued to place greater trust in traditional Chinese medicine, but in critical cases many of the poor and some of the rich were willing to turn to the foreign doctor. Before many months the missionary had usually acquired more patients than he could treat with ease. Even so, Chinese who had some respect for Western medicine hesitated to study three to five years to become a doctor; during the nineteenth century the returns in wealth and in social standing did not seem great enough.

The many obstacles to initiating Western-type medical education in China left the early missionary educators undaunted. They believed that they were guided by God's will and had few qualms about the rectitude and beneficiality of their work; they were not inclined to question the superiority of Western civilization and the applicability of Western medical and educational techniques in China. Furthermore, the Christian medical colleges, like the liberal arts colleges, evolved slowly in China. Mission societies neither intended nor desired to establish medical schools in China; for them medical missions had three principal purposes: to relieve suffering, to eradicate prejudice against the foreigner and Christianity, and to attract an audience for proselytizing. Like the liberal arts colleges, the medical schools generally began with a few classes taught by one or two missionaries. An overworked doctor who needed aid in his hospital duties in the course of his work gave clinical training to a few helpers; these Chinese were considered medical practitioners rather than doctors, and often they continued to work in mission hospitals under the supervision of the medical missionaries. Before the missionaries had given serious consideration to the difficulties of importing Western-type medical training to China, they were already deeply involved in medical education.

Only as the commitment to medical education grew did missions begin to ask basic questions. What level of medical training should be imported to China? Could China support a highly trained medical profession similar to that in the West, or should medical schools concentrate on preparing practitioners and public health workers? If Christian medical colleges should be modeled on those of the West, what were the prerequisites of a good medical school? From whence could financial support be expected? Some of these questions did not actually receive serious consideration until the second quarter of the twentieth century. Only a few of the training programs, furthermore, evolved into medical colleges.

In 1837 the first Protestant medical missionary to China, Peter Parker, opened a medical class for three Chinese assistants in Canton. Parker gave a little theoretical instruction in English, but at that time there were no Chinese textbooks on modern medicine, and the emphasis was on practical training in medical techniques. To a considerable extent, the students simply picked up what information they could obtain in the hospital wards, the operating theater, and the outpatient dispensary.[14] An important contribution to the training of a medical profession in China was made by Dr. Benjamin Hobson, who translated numerous textbooks in medicine and science while stationed in south China by the London Missionary Society. His first volume, published in 1851, was a treatise on anatomy and physiology; it attracted so much attention that the Governor-General of Kwangtung-Kwangsi ordered its republication. Other translations and compilations by Hobson became standard works in China and were even reproduced in Japan; they included books or pamphlets on physics, astronomy, surgery, midwifery and diseases of children, and the practice of medicine and *materia medica*.[15]

Dr. Hobson had a worthy successor in Dr. John G. Kerr, who arrived in Canton in 1853 and who translated or wrote some twenty

[14] K. Chimin Wong and Wu Lien-te, *History of Chinese Medicine* (2d ed.; Shanghai, 1936), pp. 317–318.

[15] Harold Balme, "The History of Western Medical Education in China," *The China Medical Journal*, XL (1926), 700–701; Tsuen-hsuin Tsien, "Western Impact on China through Translation," *FEQ*, XIII (1954), 312–313.

textbooks in science and medicine during his forty-eight years of practice in Kwangtung. In 1866 Dr. Kerr began more or less regular medical classes at Canton Missionary Hospital and thus started to build on Dr. Peter Parker's earlier educational work. The pupils studied anatomy, physiology, surgery, *materia medica,* chemistry, and Western and Chinese medicine. Among the teachers were Dr. Kwan Ato, who had been one of Parker's pupils, and Dr. Wong Fun, who had earned an M.D. degree at the University of Edinburgh and had thereby become the first Chinese known to have graduated in medicine abroad. There were about a dozen pupils during the first years of the school; though Dr. Kerr was never able to admit many students at a time, he trained almost two hundred students during his years at Canton.[16] Sun Yat-sen's interest in medicine was stimulated through his work in Canton Hospital in 1884, and when the hospital and two other Christian institutions later united to form a medical college, the name of the new institution, Dr. Sun Yat-sen Medical College, commemorated this fact.[17] Also worth noting is the fact that many of Dr. Kerr's classes included women and that such coeducation appears to have caused no special comment.

Other small classes were trained at various mission hospitals in China. Beginning in 1880, Dr. H. W. Boone taught medical students at St. Luke's Hospital in Shanghai and tried to set up a systematic course of study, but he lacked texts, adequate laboratory equipment, and cadavers for dissection. In 1896 the school was transferred to St. John's where it persevered for years with insufficient staff and funds. With the aid of the London Missionary Society, the Hongkong College of Medicine was established in 1887, and it educated students under mission auspices until it was incorporated into Hongkong University.[18] Sun Yat-sen in 1892 became one of the first graduates of the Hongkong medical college, and the friendship he established there with Dr. James Cantlie later served him well.

By the 1880's the reputation of Western medicine enabled mission-

---

[16] Wong and Wu, *Chinese Medicine,* pp. 391–393.

[17] Letter by Dr. William W. Cadbury, Lingnan University, April 1, 1937 (Reproduced under the title, Lingnan University, "A Letter from William Penn Lodge," MRL); Corbett, *Lingnan,* p. 124.

[18] Omar L. Kilborn, *Heal the Sick, An Appeal for Medical Missions in China* (Toronto, c. 1910), p. 214; Harold Balme, *China and Modern Medicine. A Study in Medical Missionary Development* (London, 1921), p. 113.

ary doctors to extend their influence beyond the small communities they served, and some Chinese desired Western medical education, as the medical classes cited above illustrate. Another example of Chinese appreciation of modern medicine was Li Hung-chang's support of a medical school in Tientsin. Dr. John K. Mackenzie of the London Missionary Society had won the gratitude of the powerful viceroy by successfully treating Li's wife after Chinese practitioners had failed. Li thereupon aided Mackenzie in establishing a small hospital in Tientsin. When in 1881 Mackenzie proposed to provide medical instruction for some of the students recalled from the Educational Mission to the United States, the I-yao Kuan, or Viceroy's Hospital Medical School, was opened. Li was to pay all expenses from provincial defense funds and the graduates were to serve as medical officers in the armed forces. After Mackenzie's death in 1888, the school passed under Chinese control and became the nucleus for Pei-yang I-hsüeh T'ang (Peiyang Medical College).[19]

Having become inextricably involved in medical education, the missionaries soon became dissatisfied with what they considered the inadequate training of their students. This desire to raise the standards of mission medical education in China was one of the motives for the formation of the China Medical Missionary Association in 1886. The association, though founded to serve medical missionaries, came to perform a variety of the functions ordinarily undertaken by a national medical association or by government agencies. It established standards in equipment and staff for medical schools, and to some extent it served as a registration agency for those wishing to practice medicine in China. Its magazine *The China Medical Journal* discussed common problems faced by medical missionaries and also published scholarly articles based on research in China. The associaton fostered the translation and publication of medical texts, and in the twentieth century, it helped sponsor at Shantung Christian University a translation bureau which became a center for the publication of medical literature in Chinese.

At its first general meeting in 1890 the association established a

[19] This brief history of the Viceroy's Hospital Medical School is based on Wong and Wu, *Chinese Medicine,* pp. 440–442, 479; Biggerstaff, *Earliest Modern Schools,* pp. 68–69; Balme, *China and Modern Medicine,* pp. 112–113; and Mary F. Bryson, *John Kenneth Mackenzie: Medical Missionary to China* (London, 1891).

committee to draw up uniform lists of medical nomenclature in Chinese. For over twenty-five years its committees worked at creating and gaining acceptance for uniform terms in anatomy, surgery, histology, pharmacology, physiology, etc. After the formation of a National Medical Association in 1914, the two medical associations joined other parties in organizing a General Committee on Medical Terminology, and the work continued under this auspices. The government and the National Medical Association gradually assumed many of the functions formerly undertaken by the missionary organization, and in 1932 the two associations united in the Chinese Medical Association.[20]

The China Medical Missionary Association hoped to persuade the Chinese that medicine should be an honored profession deserving lengthy preparation. Though effecting such a change in attitude would take years, a heightened appreciation of Western medical education was created by the same events which had convinced Chinese reformers that Western scientific and mathematical knowledge were essential to national salvation. During the Sino-Japanese war, a member of the American Presbyterian Mission in Peking helped care for the wounded near Tientsin and created such a favorable impression that several generals requested that foreign-trained doctors be stationed at their camps.

Outbreaks of plague also increased the prestige of Western medicine. An epidemic of bubonic plague in which the death toll was estimated at 100,000 struck Canton in 1894. The Chinese became so disillusioned with Chinese methods in treating patients that a special plague hospital, emphasizing ventilation and sanitation, was opened. When the pneumonic plague invaded Manchuria and north China in 1910–1911, local officials entrusted the checking of the epidemic to modern-trained physicians and allowed such drastic measures as compulsory house-to-house visitation, segregation of exposed persons in camps or wagons, and cremation of thousands of corpses which

[20] Additional details may be found in J. L. Maxwell, "The Chinese Medical Association," *CCYB*, 1932–33, pp. 475–477; Wong and Wu, *Chinese Medicine*, pp. 468, 554–555, 641–645, 702; and H. Owen Chapman, "Christian Medical Cooperation in China," *International Review of Missions*, XXXVII (1948), 163–164. *The China Medical Journal*, 1909–1931, was entitled *The China Medical Missionary Journal*, 1887–1909; it was succeeded by *The Chinese Medical Journal*, 1932–.

had accumulated. Subsequently, an international medical conference was called at Mukden to study the little-known pneumonic plague, and the government established the Manchurian Plague Prevention Service to carry out the recommendations of the conference. Such official display of confidence in the methods of modern medicine increased the interest and desire of many Chinese for the medical knowledge of the West. In 1913 a presidential mandate legalized the performance of autopsies and of dissections. Two years later another presidential mandate, which announced the standards demanded for candidates in medicine, pharmacy, and veterinary science, in effect gave official recognition to Western medicine: the requirements were those of Western medical schools; no reference was made to old-style methods of medical practice.[21]

Both the Boxer Rebellion and the 1911 revolution made clear the need for medical schools with high standards. When the missionaries fled the interior on these two occasions, they were frequently able to find Chinese Christian ministers and teachers to carry on the work of the churches and schools, but the number of Chinese doctors with modern training was insufficient to keep the hospitals open. The missionaries returned to their positions with a new appreciation of the necessity for good medical schools to train well-qualified Chinese doctors rather than assistants.

The missions became increasingly aware that good schools would have to be union institutions and that the continuation of many small schools would mean that all would remain under-staffed and poorly equipped. In 1913 the China Medical Missionary Association recommended that no new medical colleges be established until the existing ones were made efficient. Listed were eight medical colleges for men and three for women. The staffing and equipment of all these were below the standard set by the Medical Missionary Association: "Only Peking College approximates to this standard and even there they have constant difficulty in keeping their teaching staff up to the point desired in numbers and efficiency." [22] The eight men's schools were located at Peking, Mukden, Tsinan, Chengtu,

[21] E. J. Stuckey, "First Graduation Ceremony of the Union Medical College, Peking," CR, XLII (1911), 368; Wong and Wu, Chinese Medicine, pp. 520, 592, 598, 600, 604–605, 618.
[22] J. B. Neal, "Medical Schools in China," CR, XLIV (1913), 595–596.

Hankow, Nanking-Hangchow, Foochow, and Canton. St. John's University and Soochow University also maintained medical departments, and the Yale mission was shortly to open a medical school. A number were already union institutions deriving their support from several denominations.

The Christian Medical Colleges, 1900–1930

Perhaps the best place to begin the story of some of the individual institutions is Peking College. Though the school was taken over by the China Medical Board of the Rockefeller Foundation in 1915 and officially ceased to be a mission institution, ties with Christian education remained. Shortly after the Boxer Rebellion, the North China Educational Union had recommended the founding of a union medical school in Peking. In 1904, therefore, the London Missionary Society, the American Board, and the American Presbyterian Board agreed to establish North China Union Medical College (also known as Lockhart Memorial) on London Mission premises in Peking. Peking University requested in 1905 to join the institution, which thenceforth became known as Peking Union Medical College; two other societies later joined the union: the Society for the Propagation of the Gospel and the Medical Missionary Association of London. The project had the additional support of the Empress Dowager, Chinese officials and scholars, and foreign residents, all of whom contributed substantial sums. Furthermore, the college had the unique privilege among missionary schools of recognition by the Chinese government: the Chinese board of education conferred a diploma upon the graduates. Teaching was in Mandarin, and the course lasted five years. At the first graduation ceremony on April 7, 1911, sixteen students received diplomas.[23]

By this time, the opportunity for aiding education in Asia had attracted the attention of John D. Rockefeller. A commission which had been sent in 1909 to study the educational situation in China, Japan, and India had recommended the establishment at Peking of

[23] Peking Union Medical College, *Addresses and Papers, Dedication Ceremonies and Medical Conference, September 15–22, 1921* (Peking, 1922), p. 12 (cited as *Peking Union Medical College Dedication*); Wong and Wu, *Chinese Medicine*, p. 547; Stuckey, "First Graduation Ceremony of the Union Medical College, Peking," *CR*, XLII (1911), 368.

an institution for the teaching of the natural sciences. After further consideration the project was narrowed to the teaching of medicine, and the China Medical Board was formed as a branch of the Rockefeller Foundation. On July 1, 1915, the China Medical Board assumed full support of Peking Union Medical College.[24] Missionary influence did not immediately end, however, for many of the missionary teachers were retained, and the new Board of Trustees included one person appointed by each of the six missionary organizations heretofore maintaining the institution and seven appointed by the China Medical Board.

Under the ambitious and expensive program formulated, the hospital and school in Peking were to be the equal of any in the West in equipment and standards. The school was to be a research and instruction institution; its main purpose was not to be treating patients.[25] The staff would be large enough to enable the professors to do research as well as teaching, especially research on diseases unique to or prevalent in China. English would replace Mandarin as the language of instruction because of the scarcity of doctors who could teach in Chinese and the paucity of modern medical literature in Chinese. The two upper classes could finish their work at Peking, but no new students were to be admitted to the medical school itself; rather, a three-year premedical school for middle school graduates with a good knowledge of English was initiated.

The medical school proper with its five-year course opened in 1919, and by the following year thirteen students had enrolled. The growth of the staff was much more rapid; by 1921 faculty and administration totaled 123 foreigners and 23 Chinese, all of whom had been trained abroad. In 1928 the Rockefeller Foundation made the China Medical Board an independent body with an endowment of US$12,000,000 and with title to the land, buildings, and equipment of the college.[26] Dr. Y. T. Tsur was elected chairman of the China Medical Board; the Board of Trustees was made self-perpetuating,

[24] China Medical Board of the Rockefeller Foundation, *First Annual Report, December 11, 1914–December 31, 1915* (New York, 1916), pp. 11–13.

[25] John D. Rockefeller, Jr., "Response for the Rockefeller Foundation," *Peking Union Medical College Dedication,* p. 61.

[26] China Medical Board, *Second Annual Report, January 1, 1916–December 31, 1916* (New York, 1917), pp. 10–11; *Peking Union Medical College Dedication,* p. 5; Wong and Wu, *Chinese Medicine,* pp. 635–636, 686.

and the administration of the school came to be increasingly in the hands of the Chinese.

During the first two decades of its existence the reorganized Peking Union Medical College fulfilled well the function that the Rockefeller Foundation had assigned it—a research and teaching institution in modern medicine. A League of Nations *Report on Medical Schools in China* characterized it as an excellent medical school with a hospital "extraordinarily well equipped with all the necessary facilities for pre-clinical and clinical teaching and research." [27] Only one other medical school in China really approached it in its standards, the Japanese Manchurian Medical College, which was attended almost exclusively by Japanese students. The college acted as a graduate school for teachers for other medical schools in China, and it also offered refresher courses for doctors who had been out of touch with Western medicine and wished to catch up on recent developments; between 1921 and 1933 more than 900 physicians, nurses, and other technical personnel registered for graduate or special work at Peking.

Nationalistic Chinese and even Westerners sometimes criticized the school's philosophy and the consequences thereof. The contribution of the institution was limited by the small size of its regular classes; only 64 students graduated between 1924 and 1930, and only 166 had received M.D. degrees by June 1936. These graduates were accused of having grown accustomed to working with modern and ample equipment and being unwilling to leave the port cities to work in the poorly equipped hospitals of the interior. They were subject to the standard criticism of Chinese educated in the English language—that of being unable to adapt their knowledge to the needs and conditions of China. Some stated that Peking Union Medical College had isolated itself by setting an educational standard far above that which government schools could attain, and they favored the training of a larger number of doctors on a lower level. In the 1930's the Rockefeller Foundation would reassess its philosophy and attempt to orient its work more toward the needs of rural China. [28]

[27] Knud Faber, *Report on Medical Schools in China*, League of Nations Publications Series, III, Health (Geneva, 1931), p. 14.

[28] Wong and Wu, *Chinese Medicine*, pp. 682–683; James C. Thomson, Jr., *While China Faced West: American Reformers in Nationalist China, 1928–1937* (Cambridge, Mass., 1969), pp. 130–139.

When the Rockefeller Foundation had first begun to plan for medical education in China, it had anticipated the organization of several medical colleges. Mission societies hoped that the China Medical Board would assume much of the financial burden for their medical schools, and for several years plans for expansion or unification of medical schools in the Yangtze Valley were held in abeyance. Much to the disappointment of the mission societies, the China Medical Board found the reconstruction of Peking Union Medical College such an expensive project that it decided against additional ventures.

Medical education and scientific instruction were, nevertheless, deeply affected by the Peking medical college and by the generous grants of the China Medical Board. Partly to improve the quality of its own entering students, the China Medical Board helped a number of the Christian colleges increase their scientific equipment and hire additional science teachers. The grants often required the colleges to secure matching funds, and thus several of the schools were able for the first time to erect adequately equipped science buildings. At Yenching, science students joined in the courses and laboratory experiments of the medical college's premedical program; and when the program was discontinued in 1925, its facilities were turned over to Yenching. Yenching, furthermore, received a five-year grant in aid, a promise of funds for a science building if the university matched the funds, and eventually an endowment of US$325,000 for Yenching's work in the natural sciences. By providing fellowships for study abroad to teachers of science and medicine, the China Medical Board enabled the Christian colleges to build up a more highly trained faculty. Finally, the medical board gave direct assistance to other medical schools and hospitals. During the first decade of its existence, for example, the Hsiang-Ya Medical College depended largely on the medical board for the salaries of its Western-trained faculty. The China Medical Missionary Association and the National Medical Association of China received assistance in their administrative expenses and in their work on medical terminology and translation. These grants to hospitals, colleges, medical schools, and organizations, individual doctors and teachers were largely confined to the period between 1913 and 1933; they totaled US$4 million, and they often meant the difference between maintaining the status quo and expanding.[29] Once higher standards had been attained, there was impetus to maintain these standards.

Competition with Peking Union Medical College helped raise the level of medical instruction in the Christian colleges. Far more potent than admonitions by the China Medical Missionary Association were the high standards set at Peking. The mission schools realized that they had the choice of raising their academic level, of seeing their degrees decline in value and prestige, or of recognizing two levels of medical education in China and ceasing to confer the M.D. degree. As far as they were able, they chose the first alternative. Several of the mission boards increased their appropriations to medical schools. The union movement, which had been lagging, received a new lease on life.

Perhaps the school most deeply affected was Shantung medical college, as the missions sought to make it the leader for instruction in Mandarin just as Peking had become the model for work in English. A medical school had been included in the 1902 plans for Shantung University, but the location and organization of the medical division had been left vague. Eventually the English Baptists secured a grant to purchase a site and erect medical buildings in Tsinan; both the English Baptists and the American Presbyterians agreed to support members of a medical faculty, and the medical school began work in 1910. When the formal opening took place in 1911, the interest of Chinese literati in modern medical education was demonstrated: the governor of the province, Sun Pao-ch'i, delivered an address and donated funds and for several years the government made an annual grant to the school.[30] A new hospital to accommodate 115 patients was built in 1914–1915, and a nurses'

[29] Further information concerning the assistance given by the China Medical Board to scientific and medical education may be found in the annual reports of the board; Peking Union Medical College Dedication, pp. 8–10; R. S. Greene, "The Work of the China Medical Board, 1917–18," CMYB, 1918, pp. 202–204; Greene, "The China Medical Board of the Rockefeller Foundation," CMYB, 1916, pp. 321–322; and the president's reports issued annually by the various Christian colleges. Among the recipients were two national universities and one (Nankai) private Chinese university in addition to ten Christian colleges. See Thomson, While China Faced West, pp. 39, 268 (n. 32).

[30] D. MacGillivray, "Mission Schools and Colleges and Universities for Men and Boys," CMYB, 1910, p. 79; "Missionary News," CR, XLII (1911), 430, 431; Decker, "Shantung," pp. 72–73.

school offering a four-year course opened in 1915. In 1917, all the divisions of Shantung Christian University united at Tsinan, the home of the medical college.

When the China Medical Board took over Peking Union Medical College in 1915, it transferred the three lower classes to Tsinan. With the sixty-five students came US$150,000 to house and educate them and to enable Shantung Medical College to increase its equipment and faculty. The student body and faculty, equipment and support thus multiplied with almost startling rapidity. Largely as a result of the high standard set by Peking, several of the weaker medical schools, including the University of Nanking medical department and the Hankow Union Medical College, decided to discontinue their institutions and transfer their work to Tsinan. The China Medical Missionary Association encouraged this concentration in the hope that the Christian missionaries could demonstrate the possibility of providing high quality medical education using the Chinese language.

For some years the North China Educational Union had maintained a women's medical school in Peking.[31] Instruction was in Mandarin, and the premedical work was given by North China Union College for Women. When the latter institution joined Yenching University and began to use the English language as a medium of instruction, the medical college had difficulty offering a full medical course. The institution therefore welcomed an invitation by Shantung Christian University to join the medical school at Tsinan, and in 1924 two classes of women and five faculty members transferred from Peking to Tsinan. The North China Union Medical College for Women brought with it an endowment of US$350,000.

Though the size of its faculty and the adequacy of its equipment could not equal those of Peking Union Medical College, Shantung maintained an academic standard as close as possible to that of the Peking school. The school, however, conferred an M.B. rather than an M.D. degree, and pending improvement of its facilities, it was granted only provisional registration by the China Medical Association in 1925. The League of Nations survey team in 1931 considered

[31] The institution opened in 1908 with two students; in 1920–1921 there were thirty-eight. See *North China Union Medical College for Women, Peking, China* (Boston, 1921) (promotional brochure, NBT).

it the best of the mission medical schools.[32] Entering students had to be middle school graduates and to pass a qualifying examination. The course consisted of two years of premedical education and five of medical study. Though instruction was in Mandarin, students were required to learn English so that they could use English text books and other medical literature. In 1920 there were ninety-nine students in the school of medicine and forty-five in the premedical department. Of the hundred students who had already graduated, between sixty and seventy were working in mission hospitals, and the rest were holding government medical posts or were doing private work.[33] By 1925 there were twenty-five full-time teachers on the faculty—eighteen foreigners and seven Chinese; these staff members had already initiated a number of social service and research projects: a leper hospital, a baby clinic, research on kala-azar and other diseases caused by parasites.

Though the China Medical Board was not able to establish its proposed school in Shanghai, medical education at St. John's was strengthened. Medical training had been established at St. John's in 1896 by Dr. H. W. Boone, who offered a four-year course to graduates of St. John's preparatory department. In 1906 the medical school raised its entrance requirement to two years of college level work and lengthened its course to five years. An additional year as an intern was strongly recommended.[34] The medical school remained starved for funds, its existence precarious; because of the smallness of the teaching staff, classes were admitted only in alternate years. Then in 1914, the University of Pennsylvania, which had been aiding medical education at Canton Christian College, transferred its work to St. John's, and in 1920 the Rockefeller Foundation announced that it had abandoned its plans for Shanghai and offered US$80,000 to strengthen St. John's work in science. The medical school was thus able to improve its facilities, though both staff and student body

[32] R. T. Shields, "The Origin and Development of the School of Medicine of Shantung Christian University," *The China Medical Journal*, XL (1926), 759, 761; Faber, *Report on Medical Schools*, p. 16.

[33] Harold Balme, "Facts Concerning the School of Medicine, Shantung," *ER*, XII (1920), 224–225.

[34] J. C. McCracken, "Pennsylvania Medical College, being the Medical Department of St. John's University, Shanghai," *The China Medical Journal*, XL (1926), 753–755; Pott, "History," *St. John's*, pp. 6, 13.

remained small; between 1901 and 1920 fifteen students received medical diplomas, and twenty-five received certificates. Among the alumni of St. John's were some of the most prominent men in the Chinese medical profession at that time, with many of them having pursued graduate work in the United States or England and enjoying the prestige accorded "returned students." [35]

In Szechuan, West China Union University pioneered in the organization of a medical department in 1914. This school like others, however, suffered for years from inadequate equipment and staff. A member of the medical faculty wrote: "For the first 4 or 5 years of our existence we did not have an average budget annual [sic] outside the teachers salaries of $200 gold a year! Of needs and necessities—, our first classes in physiology, had test tubes, a few beakers and bottles, spirit lamps and matches! As for reference books and library, the first volume purchased and the only one for several years was a Gray's anatomy." [36] The one medical school building was erected, he said, only because the university officials were afraid to allow dissection in the regular college buildings. Seven students were enrolled in the medical and premedical courses at the end of the first year, twenty-one in 1920, and fifty-eight in 1924.[37] Because of illnesses, furloughs, and transfers by the mission society, the number of faculty members varied from one or two to twenty or more during the first decade. With the awarding of the first five M.B. degrees in 1919, however, the school began to grow slowly but steadily; it is indicative of increasing interest in modern medicine even in interior China that by the 1930's approximately half the students were enrolled in medical or premedical curricula. One important contribution of West China was the organization in 1920 of a faculty of dentistry in conjunction with the medical school.

[35] St. John's alumni included such influential physicians as Yen Fu-ch'ing, Dean of Hsiang-Ya Medical College; S. M. Woo, secretary to the Joint Council on Public Health Education; T. M. Li, G. Y. Char, and E. T. H. Tsen, all on the staff of Peking Union Medical College; P. C. Chiang of the medical school at Tsinan; and E. S. Tyau, U. K. Koo, W. S. New, and L. S. Woo, all at St. Luke's Hospital or the Pennsylvania Medical School of St. John's. See Wong and Wu, Chinese Medicine, pp. 622–623.

[36] W. R. Morse, The Three Crosses in the Purple Mists (Shanghai, 1928), pp. 175–176.

[37] Ibid., pp. 188, 211; W. R. Morse, "The Medical School of Union University Chengtu, West China," The China Medical Journal, XL (1926), 766.

The university offered the first college-level course in modern dentistry in China and hoped that graduates of its seven-year program would help establish standards for this new profession in China.

The Hsiang-Ya Medical College at Changsha had a unique history in that it originated as a joint venture of the Yale mission and local Chinese leaders. Ever since arriving in China in 1905, Dr. Edward H. Hume had looked forward to the establishment of a medical school as part of the Yale program in Changsha; this hope seemed a possibility in 1912 when a Yale alumnus offered to donate funds for a modern hospital. The conditions of the gift were that the hospital be supported by local Chinese and that it be an educational center. The Yale Mission seemed in a position to fulfill these requirements. It had already broken precedent and hired a Chinese, Yen Fu-ch'ing (Dr. F. C. Yen), as an equal member of the mission on the same salary scale as Westerners; Dr. Yen had attended St. John's medical school, obtained an M.D. degree from Yale University in 1909, and done graduate work in tropical medicine at the University of Liverpool; he was, furthermore, a devout Christian; despite the misgivings of some missionaries that such an appointment was premature, he seemed eminently suited for membership in the Yale Mission and had quickly become an influential colleague of Dr. Hume.[38] In 1912 Dr. Yen had helped the Hunan government organize an inspection system to prevent the spread of the pneumonic plague in Wuhan, and other contacts with provincial and municipal officials had soon followed. The Yali physicians gave physical examinations to students taking the government examinations for study abroad; they began research on remedies for opium addiction and acted as advisers to the Changsha Municipal Bureau of Hygiene. On the basis of such contacts Dr. Yen undertook negotiations to secure local Chinese participation and support.

The negotiations, however, became involved in a long-standing controversy over the division of authority between central and provincial governments in China. Peking repudiated the original agreement with the Hunan provincial government on the grounds that the provincial officials had not consulted the central administration

[38] Hume, *Doctors East*, p. 144; William Reeves, Jr., "Sino-American Cooperation in Medicine: The Origins of Hsing-Ya (1902–1914)," in Harvard University, *Papers on China*, XIV (1960), 174–176.

prior to signing the contract and had exceeded their authority in negotiating directly with a private foreign institution. Other objections concerned academic standards and provisions for appointment of teachers and for religious instruction. The trustees of the Yale Mission also expressed reservations and requested assurances on such matters as ownership of the hospital and freedom in the selection of faculty members. A face-saving compromise was worked out whereby local gentry formed a private association, Hu-nan yü-ch'ün hsüeh-hui (Hunan Ru-chun Educational Association); with this organization acting as an intermediary for the provincial government, the agreement was re-negotiated and signed in 1914.[39] The Yale Mission was to provide the hospital and equipment plus support for the Western-educated staff; the Hunan society was to provide the site, a medical college building, and an annual sum for running expenses; there was to be a board of managers, with each party appointing ten members, and the agreement could be revised after ten years.

In 1914 a two-year premedical course was initiated, and the first class of medical students began a five-year course in English in 1916. Within four years the new hospital had opened and a new science building, the gift of the China Medical Board, had been erected. One of the governors of Hunan took a personal interest in the school and helped secure a new power plant at Changsha so that the hospital could have adequate electricity for illumination and x-ray work. Various social service projects were initiated, including rat extermination campaigns, inoculation against smallpox and diphtheria, and the maintenance of a cholera hospital during summer months. When the agreement between the Yale Mission and the Hunan Ruchun Educational Association came up for renewal in 1925, a majority of the faculty members were Chinese and there was agitation for Chinese control. Somewhat reluctantly, the Yale mission withdrew from direct administrative control and turned the jurisdiction over to a Chinese board. The medical college had fifty-one students and the premedical course thirty-four in 1925. Between the first commencement in 1921 and the sixth in 1926, forty-three

[39] Reeves, "Sino-American Cooperation in Medicine," pp. 187–195, 203–207; Hume, *Doctors East*, pp. 177–178; E. H. Hume, "Developments at the Hunan-Yale College of Medicine, Changsha," *CMYB, 1916*, pp. 324–325.

students graduated. Two were in public health work, and the rest were working in hospitals; of the latter, over half were either at Hsiang-Ya or Peking Union Medical College.[40]

Since Chinese women were reluctant to permit medical examination by male doctors, there was a need for female physicians, and this was one of the first professions to be opened to women in China. The percentage of women with higher education entering the medical profession was much higher in China than in the West, and female physicians, along with hospitals for women, were quickly accepted once modern medicine had won recognition. Medical training for women, nevertheless, long remained the province of mission education, for it was initiated by Christian missionaries and it continued into the twentieth century to be largely under mission auspices. The medical colleges were even more undernourished than the men's schools, and financial difficulties eventually persuaded most of the women's schools to join other institutions.

The founding of North China Union Medical College for Women and its amalgamation with the medical school of Shantung Christian University have been related. In Soochow various missionaries had given medical instruction for both men and women during the nineteenth century, and in 1894 the Soochow Hospital and the Mary Black Hospital for Women and Children organized a program for both sexes. Men and women attended lectures in the same hall, though a screen divided the sexes so that they coud not see each other. In the twentieth century the men's division was organized as the medical department of Soochow University, but insufficient funds led to its closing in 1909. The women's section, which had operated alone since 1901, continued in Soochow for another decade and then transferred to Shanghai to unite with Margaret Williamson Hospital. The school, now known as Women's Christian Medical College (Shang-hai nü-tzu i-hsüeh-yüan) was officially opened in 1924. Entering students were required to have completed two years of college work and were expected to take a four-year course taught in English. Supported by the Women's Union Missionary Society of America and the Women's Foreign Missionary Society of the Meth-

[40] F. C. Yen, "The Hsiang-Ya Medical College," *The China Medical Journal,* XL (1926), 776–779; E. H. Hume, "First Graduation Exercises at Yale in China," *ER,* XIII (1921), 372.

odist Episcopal Church (South), the institution remained small, but tried to maintain high standards. There were two classes in 1926: the class of 1929 had five students and the class of 1930 had four; in 1933–1934 the enrollment was twenty.[41]

Farther south in Canton was Hackett Medical College for Women (Hsia-ko i-hsüeh-yüan). Dr. John Kerr in Canton had admitted women to his medical classes as early as 1879. When Dr. Kerr retired from Canton Hospital in 1899, however, and devoted his time to a refuge for the insane, he took the young men in his medical class with him, and the provisions for continuing medical education for women were most inadequate. The first building used was the ground floor of the First Presbyterian Church, where the students shared living quarters with the out-patient clinic. When in 1903 and 1905 E. A. Hackett of Indiana provided funds for the first college buildings, the school adopted the name Hackett Medical College for Women in his honor. The academic standards of the school were gradually raised; by 1907 the curriculum had been extended to four years; and with the premedical work and a year of internship, it eventually became a six-year course for middle school graduates; an M.B. degree was awarded. Though instruction was given in the Cantonese dialect, students were required to take courses in English so that they could use medical literature in English. Fifty-eight student were enrolled in 1926, and 155 had already graduated; of the graduates, approximately one hundred were in private practice and thirty in the employ of missions. In the 1930's Hackett Medical College joined with Lingnan University and Canton Hospital to form Sun Yat-sen Medical College.[42]

As many of the medical colleges, including Peking Union Medical College, West China Union University, Cheeloo, and Hsiang-Ya, became coeducational, the need for separate women's medical

[41] Francis W. King, "Women's Christian Medical College, Shanghai," *The China Medical Journal*, XL (1926), 756–758; Wong and Wu, *Chinese Medicine*, p. 545; Chuang Wen-ya (W. Y. Chyne), ed., *Handbook of Cultural Institutions in China* (Shanghai, 1936), pp. 273–274.

[42] J. Allen Hofmann, "A Short Historical Sketch of Hackett Medical College and Affiliated Institutions," *The China Medical Journal*, XL (1926), 776–779; J. A. Hofmann, "The Work in Hackett Medical College," *ER*, XXV (1933), 64; "Prospectus of Medical Colleges and Schools," *The Chinese Medical Journal*, XLIX (1935), 1006–1007.

schools seemed less urgent, and the Women's Christian Medical College in Shanghai was left almost alone as a mission medical school for women. The women's schools, like the medical colleges for men, had, however, brought modern medical training to China and had trained some of the most prominent physicians of China in the first decades of the twentieth century. Though Peita and the national medical college in Shanghai were beginning to surpass many of the Christian medical schools in equipment and support, the mission institutions had pioneered in the field, and they continued to educate a significant proportion of the physicians of China.

Nursing as a Profession

Almost inevitably, the nursing profession was brought to China along with modern medicine and Western-type hospitals. The profession was unknown to China, since patients were normally cared for by relatives or servants in the home. Even when medical missionaries began to found hospitals, patients were at first responsible for their own food, bedding, and nursing care. Doctors soon realized that it was impossible to insure proper diet or sanitation under these conditions and therefore began to hire individuals to help care for patients, of necessity offering these nursing assistants or orderlies rudimentary instruction. At first most of the workers were male and had the status of servants. They could provide only minimal assistance to the doctor in the operating room or in any other situation requiring literacy or medical knowledge. They were in an inferior position vis-à-vis the patients, and controversies over diet or ventilation easily led to the nursing assistant's being overruled by the patient or relatives unless the doctor intervened. In emergencies, the doctor had to turn to the few Western-trained nurses who had come out as missionaries or as the wives of missionaries.

To initiate nurse's training in China was no simple task. Nursing was only slowly gaining acceptance in the West as a profession, and in China there was even greater reluctance to accord professional status to individuals who performed the menial duties required of nurses. Chinese who had some education were at first unwilling to consider such an occupation, and neither hospitals nor patients could support a salary scale which might make the position attractive. The need, however, was great. As formal medical schools began to be organized, it seemed impossible to attain satisfactory medical standards in the teaching hospital without nurse's training programs. In the twentieth century, therefore, many of the Christian medical colleges added schools of nursing and attempted to present nursing as a respectable occupation worthy of professional training. A Chinese term for nurse (hu shih) was invented, and student nurses came to resent being addressed in terms implying servile status. Leaflets explaining the function and status of the nurse in the West were sent out by nursing schools. There was also present the example of educated Western women who performed the duties expected of nurses in the mission hospitals. Missions appealed to the ideals of social service and of service to China and hired servants for the more menial tasks. Within the Chinese Christian communities, at least, these appeals had some effect, since practically all of the first students came from mission schools.

Appreciation of the profession, however, grew slowly, and the nursing schools often had to accept graduates of junior middle schools or even higher primary schools. Students complained of the hard work and especially of night duty; they were easily irritated by condescension on the part of patients. Gradually, a few schools were able to offer more advanced programs. As was true in medical training, Peking Union Medical College served as a graduate school to train teachers of nursing and hospital administrators. In collaboration with Yenching, the Medical College provided a five-year program whereby middle school graduates took a two-year pre-nursing course at Yenching and then a three-year nursing course at the Medical College. Graduates received both a diploma in nursing and a B.S. degree. After some years of experimenting Hsiang-Ya offered a three-year course to middle school graduates, and Cheeloo organized a four-year course. Other schools continued to accept junior middle school graduates.

As part of the attempt to introduce the nursing profession, missionaries helped organize the Nurses Association of China. This private association, under the guidance of Nina Gage of Hsiang-Ya, worked to establish national standards for nurse's training. In 1915 it set up a national examination system for nurses seeking admission to the organization, and it thereby served as a nurse's registry until the National Health Administration assumed this responsibility in 1935.[43] Social service activities such as public health clinics, health education programs, and vaccination campaigns were encouraged. The great majority of trained nurses, both male and female, worked in hospitals rather than as private nurses.

[43] Holden, *Yale-in-China*, p. 141; Evelyn S. Lin, "Schools of Nursing in China," *CCYB*, *1936–37*, pp. 363–364; Gertrude E. Hodgman, "Comments on the Tentative Regulations for the Higher Vocational Nursing Schools," *The Chinese Medical Journal*, XLIX (1935), 903.

VI | Educational Response
in an Era of Change

Factors Affecting Growth Rate of the Colleges

In 1900 the Christian colleges of China were small institutions enrolling a total of 164 college students. Though most mission colleges maintained middle schools with sizable student bodies, not a single institution had as many as 60 college-level students. After 1900, however, the number of students increased fairly rapidly; this growth is related to changes in the emphases of the colleges, Chinese attitudes toward Western-type education and mission schools, and sources of the student body. In 1910 there were 898 students in the Christian colleges. Though several new colleges were added during the first decade of the twentieth century, these were small institutions with mostly middle school students. The older schools were the ones contributing to the increase in college-level students. During the next decade the size of the colleges fluctuated from year to year, but in general growth was steady, and the 1919 enrollment was almost double that of 1910. Another period of rapid growth occurred between 1920 and 1924, when the number of college students again doubled; by 1925 approximately 3,500 college students were enrolled in the Protestant colleges.[1]

Many of the same factors which persuaded missionaries to found new colleges during the early twentieth century enabled the Chris-

[1] *Handbook of Christian Colleges and Universities, 1926,* CCEA Bul. no. 14 (Shanghai, 1926), pp. 35–37. This number does not include the students enrolled in the separate professional colleges such as Hackett Women's Medical College and Women's Christian Medical College, nor does it include the much larger number of middle school students who were enrolled in schools sharing the faculty and facilities of the colleges.

tian schools to increase their enrollments. Chinese interest in Western civilization continued to expand, and American educational theories and methods received particular attention. This interest redounded to the benefit of the Christian colleges, which were considered examples of American education in China. In 1908 the United States remitted a portion of its Boxer indemnity funds for scholarships to study in the United States, and between 1910 and 1925 over 1,000 Chinese made use of the scholarships. A number of these students studied educational theory at Columbia University Teachers College and returned to China with the hope of implementing their new pedagogical ideas. As the republic floundered, some Chinese intellectuals turned to education as a panacea.[2] The ethical basis of Chinese government had been lost with the abolition of the examinations based on the classics, the overthrow of the monarchy, and the decline of the gentry class, and Chinese scholars were looking for a new ethic that would accord with republican government. No longer did the education and indoctrination of the elite seem sufficient; a literate and patriotic citizenry was considered essential to the salvation of China. Popular education as exemplified in the United States seemed one way of strengthening China. All these factors increased interest in Western-type education in China, but internal warfare slowed the attempts of the government to provide adequate schools and teachers. Students who could not gain admission to the national schools and others who desired English-language instruction as preparation for study abroad turned to the mission institutions.

Though all the Christian colleges expanded between 1915 and 1925, the rate of growth of the institutions varied.[3] Several grew

[2] See, for example, Wen Tsung-yao, "On Education," *Hsin ch'ing-nien* (La Jeunesse), II, no. 1 (Sept. 1916).

[3] Yenching University (including North China Union College for Women) had 508 students in 1925; University of Nanking, 461; Shanghai Baptist College, 400; Shantung Christian University (Cheeloo), 392; Soochow University, 265; West China Union University, 258; Canton Christian College, 226; St. John's University, 218; Fukien Christian University, 175; Hangchow Christian College, 148; Ginling College, 137; Yale-in-China, 91; Hwa Nan College, 80; Huachung University, 74; Lutheran College, 32; and Huping Christian College, 24. The total enrollment was 3,489. (*Handbook of Christian Colleges, 1926*, Table I, p. 28). It seems impossible to obtain an accurate list of college enrollments. Some of the colleges which had six-year programs included the two

fairly rapidly, among them Nanking, Yenching, Shanghai, Soochow, and St. John's. Other schools experienced a moderate, though steady increase in their student enrollments: Shantung, Ginling, Hangchow, Fukien, Yale-in-China, Canton, and West China. Five of the institutions had a very slow rate of growth: Huping, Huachung, Lutheran, Hwa Nan, and North China Union College for Women. It may be noted that all of the colleges with a rapid rate of growth were in large cities and all but Yenching were in east China.[4] In this area Chinese contact with foreigners was most frequent, the interest in Western education was greatest, and the commercial value of such education was most apparent. Possibly a larger proportion of the Chinese in this area could afford to send their sons to college; at any rate, the average fees paid by students in these four eastern colleges were unusually high for mission schools. With such financial support the colleges could serve a larger number of students and they could more easily expand their faculties and facilities to accommodate a growing enrollment. This same section of China was the one with the most students in Christian middle schools, an important consideration, since the Christian middle schools were the major feeder institutions for the colleges.

The particular colleges in east China that had stressed the development of general rather than religious education were Soochow, Shanghai, St. John's, and Nanking. Once the Christian colleges had helped staff the missions of east and north China, the annual need for Chinese Christian graduates in mission work was not great. The Protestant community did not grow rapidly enough to require many new workers every year, and since a large proportion of the Christian alumni could no longer expect to enter mission employ, they desired a broad education which would prepare them for other

---

subfreshmen classes in their college enrollments. The figures given here differ somewhat from those of Cressy, *Christian Higher Education*, pp. 26–27, where Soochow is credited with 392 students. It should be pointed out that in 1925 both St. John's and Yali had unusually small enrollments because of dissension and withdrawal of part of the student body. St. John's had 398 students in 1923, 447 in 1924, 218 in 1925, and 313 in 1926. Yali had 184 in 1923, 182 in 1924, 91 in 1925, and 102 in 1926.

[4] For purposes of discussion, I have followed the 1922 China Christian Educational Commission in dividing China into six areas: north, south, east, west, and central China plus Fukien. Comparisons are made in terms of these regions.

occupations. Many college students who came from Christian middle schools were not Christians, and these too were attracted to the schools offering general education as distinct from sectarian education. The same was true of students from government middle schools. In 1925 Soochow, Shanghai, St. John's, and Nanking enrolled the lowest proportion of Christian students of any of the colleges; Christians constituted half or less than half of their enrollment.[5] The other two institutions of some size, Yenching University and Cheeloo, had a larger proportion of Christians. These two schools, however, had the advantage of being in north China, which had a relatively large number of Protestant communicants and of students in Christian middle schools. Yenching offered a broad liberal arts program, and it had adequate financial support for expansion as the need arose. Cheeloo's curriculum was strongly influenced by religious objectives. This helps explain why much of Cheeloo's growth had been in the medical school rather than the college of arts and sciences and why much of this growth had come through the addition of such institutions as North China Union Medical College for Women and Hankow Union Medical College. The Cheeloo liberal arts program had grown slowly and was to continue to do so; in 1925 over one-third of Cheeloo's students were enrolled in medical and premedical curricula.[6]

Most of the six larger institutions—Soochow, Shanghai, Nanking, St. John's, Yenching, and Shantung—had enjoyed continuity of leadership during the years of growth; several had had strong, even outstanding, men as presidents. F. L. Hawks Pott had been head of St. John's since 1888. Peking University had been under H. H. Lowry most of its life, and North China Union College had been under two well-known missionaries, D. Z. Sheffield and Howard S. Galt; when the two colleges united as Yenching University, they were able to secure as president J. Leighton Stuart, who served from 1919 until 1946 when he became U.S. Ambassador to China. D. L. Anderson, one of the more foresighted missionaries of his time, was president of Soochow from its founding until his death in 1911; his successor John Cline directed the college for over a decade.

Two of the colleges which had grown slowly, Hwa Nan and North

---

[5] *Handbook of Christian Colleges, 1926,* p. 28.
[6] *Ibid.,* p. 30.

China Union College for Women, were women's schools, and their smallness can be largely explained by the status of women's education in China during the first quarter of the twentieth century. The other small schools with a slow growth rate, Lutheran, Huping, and Huachung, were located in central China, which had relatively few Protestant communicants or Christian middle schools. Both government and mission school students preferred to go east to Shanghai or north to Peking for higher education, if it was at all possible. Huping and Lutheran were denominational institutions with a strong religious atmosphere and purpose, and they attracted few non-Christians. Huachung had only recently been formed from three denominational schools which had remained small (Boone, Wesley, and Griffith John), and it had not yet created an image of its own as a nonsectarian institution.

Of the colleges experiencing a steady but moderate growth, Hangchow and Fukien had quite recently begun to emphasize a broad curriculum of arts and sciences. They continued to prefer Protestant applicants; and at both schools in 1925 over three quarters of the student body was Christian. A major handicap of Canton Christian College and West China seems to have been the scarcity of Christian middle schools. West China had both few Protestants and few students in Christian middle schools. South China had the second largest number of Protestants of any region, but the development of mission secondary education had been particularly slow in this area. The growth of Canton, as has already been indicated, was also delayed by frequent changes in location and personnel during its early years and by difficulty in securing financial support for the nondenominational institution.

Though the enrollment of the Christian colleges doubled several times between 1900 and 1925, none of the schools was large. The average enrollment in 1925 was only 218, and even the largest, Yenching, had only 508 students. The discrepancy between the graduation requirements of the national middle schools and the entrance requirements of the Christian colleges furnishes one explanation for their small size. The Christian colleges did much of their teaching in English, whereas the government institutions used English primarily for their science courses. In addition, many of the graduates of government middle schools had not had as much mathematics and science as the Christian colleges required for entrance. Concerning the difference in the mid-1920's, Cressy stated: "The emphasis put by the Christian colleges upon English as the medium of instruction . . . makes it impossible to admit graduates from government and private middle schools direct to the first regular college year, save in the most exceptional circumstances. . . . Students from non-Christian schools generally lose about two years, being admitted to the attached middle school or to the sub-freshman years, from which there is, however, a very heavy elimination."[7] Graduates of government middle schools resented this delay in their education and often considered it discrimination against government school students. They generally preferred to attend a national or provincial university where they were not at such a disadvantage. The emphasis on English and science accentuated the dependence of the Christian colleges on the Christian middle schools, whose curricula corresponded with their entrance requirements. In 1925 over four-fifths of the college students came from Christian middle schools.[8]

The emphasis of the colleges on religion and the required Bible classes and church attendance alienated many non-Christians and reduced the number of qualified applicants. Nym Wales (Helen F. Snow) gives one example of such alienation in her interview with Wu Liang-p'ing, an official of the People's Republic and one-time member of the Politburo of the Chinese Communist Party. Wu said that he had once applied to Shanghai Baptist College, but then decided not to go there because of the emphasis on Christianity. "I could not face hearing prayers and blessings said all the time."[9]

One other reason why the colleges remained small was the unusually high loss of students between their freshman and senior years. In 1922 Warren H. Stuart, president of Hangchow Christian College, estimated that the students who did not graduate from the Christian colleges were five to ten times as numerous as the graduates. Shanghai Baptist College felt that real progress had been made when 40 percent of its freshman class reached the senior year.[10]

[7] Cressy, *Christian Higher Education*, p. 181.
[8] *Handbook of Christian Colleges, 1926*, p. 34.
[9] *Red Dust, Autobiographies of Chinese Communists* (Stanford, 1952), p. 51. Wu was director of propaganda, CCP Central Committee in 1940, vice-minister of the chemical industry, 1958–1963.
[10] Stuart, "What the Colleges Have Done for the Church," *NCC, 1922*, p. 393; Shanghai Baptist College, *Annual Report, 1925*, p. 6.

By 1925 the colleges were more successful in retaining students than during the early years of the century; even so, only three or four colleges were listed as having a hundred students or more in the two upper classes, and half of the colleges were credited with less than fifty.[11]

Student Origins

Though the Protestant colleges drew the majority of their students from Christian middle schools, additional information about the background of these students is minimal. There appears to have been some differentiation between the students of the larger eastern schools and those of the smaller, sectarian colleges. As early as 1901 about half of the college students at St. John's were the sons of merchants. Next came those who listed their fathers as scholars or members of the professions; only a few were the sons of farmers and clergymen. Soochow University and Shanghai Baptist College likewise drew a large portion of their pupils from merchant and scholar families.[12]

Since each of these schools had the limited financial backing of one denomination, it had to charge high tuition or else sharply curtail its enrollment. All three chose the former course. Among the Christian colleges, St. John's was the second highest in the average educational fees paid per student, and it soon began to acquire a reputation as the "rich boys' school." By 1922 there was concern lest some of the mission colleges price themselves out of the reach of the average Chinese Christian.[13] St. John's, Soochow, Nanking, and Shanghai tried a compromise; they charged high tuition, but in order to maintain a certain proportion of Christian students, they

[11] Handbook of Christian Colleges, 1926, Table II, p. 29. The Handbook lists Yenching, Shantung, and Shanghai as having over a hundred students in the upper division; Cressy lists Yenching, Shanghai, and Nanking, p. 38. In 1925 the Christian colleges had a total of 435 subfreshmen, 1,146 freshmen, 687 sophomores, 540 juniors, and 412 seniors.

[12] St. John's University, Report of the President, 1900–01, pp. 9–10; J. W. Davis, "Schools for Teaching Western Learning in Soochow," CR, XXXIV (1903), 32; "Soochow University," Monthly Bulletin, EAC, Sept. 1907, p. 14; Handbook of Christian Colleges, p. 38.

[13] NCC, 1922; Commission II, The Future Task of the Church, p. 291; Ralph A. Ward, "Making Christian Schools More Christian," ER, XVIII (1926), 480–481; Report of Conference on the Church in China Today (Shanghai, 1926), p. 127.

offered loans and scholarships to preministerial students and to sons of Christian ministers and other religious workers. Approximately 20 to 25 percent of their students came from Christian homes; the remainder came from families which could afford to pay high tuition. Such a policy was in contrast to that of earlier times, when the mission schools had to provide free room and board as well as free tuition in order to attract students. It was also in contrast with the practice of the national universities, most of which were tuition free. All four of these Kiangsu colleges attracted almost half of their pupils from other provinces, principally from southern and central China. The Nanking constituency was particularly widespread; in 1925, for example, it had ten or more students from nine different provinces.

The colleges in north China drew a large portion of their students from the Protestant communities. These Protestant groups were strongest in villages; even Peking University, located in the capital of China, was said to receive the majority of its students from farming families.[14] The occupational listing for students' parents by North China Union College in 1915 would seem to have been fairly typical for Peking and Shantung universities as well. Out of eighty-two parents, thirty-eight were farmers, seventeen merchants, nine teachers, seven evangelists, six laborers, and five were not actively engaged in any vocation.[15] In 1915 Shantung Christian University admitted a special preparatory class composed mostly of non-Christians. Concerning these, it was stated: "On the other hand, these boys coming, as they do, chiefly from well-to-do families of the upper middle class, introduce an element into the school which has salutary influences. As a rule these young men are better versed in the common civilities of life than are our own boys and they usually have a better grounding in the Chinese language and literature and exert no small influence to stimulate our own students to more worthy achievements in that direction."[16] After North China Union College and Peking University joined to form Yenching, the sources

[14] D. MacGillivray, "Mission Schools, Colleges, and Universities for Men and Boys," *CMYB, 1910*, p. 75.

[15] North China Union College, *Annual Report, 1915*, p. 11.

[16] William P. Chalfant, "The Arts College of Shantung Christian University," *ER*, VII (1915), 20.

of the student body shifted somewhat. In 1925–1926 Yenching drew over 42 percent of its students from outside north China. Howard Galt, former president of North China College, said that among Yenching's students the literati and the business and Christian communities were the groups most largely represented.[17] As Shantung's national reputation grew, this college also broadened the area from which it drew students; by 1925 about one-half of its students came from outside Shantung province. Shantung, however, seems to have remained a center for educating the sons of rural Christian families. Practically all of its instruction was in Mandarin and so it did not attract many businessmen's sons seeking a knowledge of English. Its tuition was low and its proportion of Christian students was high.

Ginling College, like Cheeloo, drew over half its pupils from outside the local province, and it too had a high percentage of students from Christian homes and Christian middle schools. Ginling, though, was one of the more expensive mission schools, and many of the Christian students could attend only on scholarships. The expense and the fact that education for women first appealed to the wealthier classes and to Christians meant that the student body was largely drawn from two sources: well-to-do non-Christian families and Christian families of modest means. In 1921 the Ginling enrollment was said to include girls from professional and wealthy merchant families, several orphans reared in mission schools, daughters of Christian ministers, the niece of a former premier, and the granddaughter of a viceroy.[18] Yale-in-China seems to have been rather successful in winning the support of the Chinese and in drawing students from non-Christian families, especially from the official and scholar classes.[19]

The remaining mission colleges, Fukien, Hangchow, West China, Hwa Nan, Huachung, Lutheran, Huping, and Canton, may be treated as a group. Each served primarily the Christian families of the province in which it was located. As a rule, their admissions policies favored Christian rather than non-Christian pupils, and their primary purpose was to train future ministers, social workers, doctors, and teachers for mission schools.

[17] Galt, "Yenching," pp. 316–317.
[18] Ginling College, A Six Year Review, 1915–21, p. 36.
[19] The Yale Mission, Annual Report, 1910, p. 3.

Hsüeh-ch'ao—Student Storms

Whatever the social and cultural background of the students, they did not always prove to be a docile group with whom to work. Well before the famous movement of May 4, 1919, Chinese college students had used various techniques for bringing pressure on college authorities and for giving expression to their dissatisfaction. Though the students did not ordinarily take their cause outside the academic community as they did in 1919, they recognized the power of petitions, strikes, demonstrations, and threats of mass withdrawal and used these techniques with considerable frequency during the first two decades of the twentieth century. Difficulties of communication between Chinese and Westerner do not provide a sufficient explanation for the outbursts, for national universities also experienced "student storms" (hsüeh-ch'ao), as they came to be called. Nor can the outbursts be explained solely as the normal complaints of college students against college authorities. Many a fracas did ostensibly originate in dissatisfaction with food, an unpopular teacher, or some administrative decision, but the question is why the dissatisfaction often ballooned into a major incident. Why could a student who was being disciplined by the administration easily secure widespread support from his colleagues? Why were dozens of students willing to go on strike, or even withdraw from the institution?

The prominent educator and college administrator Chiang Monlin has argued that incidents as early as 1902–1903 were part of a general revolt of youth against authority.[20] Dismayed by internal disorder and foreign humiliation, students blamed those in power and struck out against the older generation. The Great Tradition was no longer sufficient for China, and neither it nor its upholders could command respect simply on the basis of past accomplishments. A challenge to school authorities was an expression of disillusionment and also evidence that traditional norms governing relations between generations were no longer accepted without question. Westerners in positions of power were especially vulnerable, since they represented both foreign imperialism and the older generation.

Though the annual reports of Christian college administrators

[20] *Tides from the West: A Chinese Autobiography* (New Haven, 1947), pp. 47–49.

were generally reticent about such unpleasant outbursts, they mention a number of challenges to authority over substantive as well as seemingly insignificant issues. There were strikes at St. John's in 1903 or 1904, at Canton Christian College in 1905, at Shanghai Baptist College in 1911–1912, and at the University of Nanking in 1915. In several cases students withdrew or were expelled, but the subjects of dispute are not made clear. The acting president of Shanghai, for example, simply reported that a strike during the mid-term examinations in 1911–1912 had been amicably settled, and the president of the University of Nanking stated in 1915–1916 that a strike of the previous year had enabled the school to get rid of disruptive elements.[21] Annual reports give somewhat greater detail on a controversy at Shantung in 1906 and a succession of incidents at Yali between 1906 and 1912 and thus provide insights concerning the grievances of the students and the difficulties of communication between the two generations.

At Shantung students had long agitated for the introduction of English language courses; when in 1906 the Board of Directors postponed action despite a favorable report by the president, the students decided to force the hand of the administration. They, in fact, used the occasion to bring forward an accumulation of grievances. Presenting nine demands, they stated that they would attend no more classes until their requests were granted. In addition to English language courses, students wanted an instructor appointed in athletics and military drill, freedom to go to Weihsien on Saturday afternoons without securing permission, modifications in the administration of examinations, and elimination of certain courses which they considered nonessential. Finally, they asked for changes in the teaching of Chinese: less emphasis on the classics and repudiation of the requirement by one of the traditional style tutors that students kneel when reciting. The latter, though often required in previous generations, the students now considered an indignity. The faculty rejected the demands as improper, and the strike lasted a week. After nine students had been expelled and nine suspended until they made public apology, the rest returned to classes, and it looked as if the college administration had won. The unpopular Chinese tutor

---

[21] University of Nanking, *Report of the President, 1915–16;* pp. 2–3; John B. Hipps, *A History of the University of Shanghai* (Richmond, 1964), p. 26.

was soon dismissed, however, the requirements in Chinese were modified, and English courses were introduced within a year or two.[22]

The conflicts at Yali included a potpourri of ingredients, though the difficulties were compounded by problems of communication and of "face" between Westerner and Chinese and between the student generation and their elders. Shortly after the school opened in 1906, the students complained that the syllabus of one science teacher was not written in elegant *wen-yen* or classical style. Though the faculty attributed the protest to provincialism and resentment of the science teacher (who was not from Hunan), they later decided that it was the work of a local educational leader who hoped to destroy the foreign mission institution. Discussions between faculty and students appeared to resolve the difficulties, but resentment soon found expression in the chapel service when a number of students deliberately hesitated to rise for the opening hymn. The dean, Warren Seabury, struck the table and impatiently motioned the pupils to stand. The whole student body was outraged at what was interpreted as a deliberate insult, and all left school. After a few days, however, most of the students returned, often, it seems, as a result of parental pressure.

Another *hsüeh-ch'ao* occurred in March 1910, after several pupils had been given demerits by Dean William J. Hail. When Hail directed the students to apologize to their proctor Mr. Wang, the students replied that Wang was only the equivalent of a comprador, i.e., a Chinese servant who acted as an agent for Westerners; they as students could hardly be expected to apologize to someone of comprador status. Hail answered by giving Wang a title with greater prestige, and the students then demonstrated their contempt for him by refusing to sing the next time he led chapel services. Classes were suspended, and both parties took a position of no compromise. After a four-day contest of wills, however, the students agreed to apologize through middlemen. The third incident, which occurred in 1912, became so involved that only the main issues can be sketched here. The controversy arose over the amount of released time stu-

[22] *Annual Report of the President of Shantung Union College, 1907,* pp. 29–30, 40, 47; *Minutes of the Board of Directors, Feb. 1907,* pp. 13–14; *Dec. 1907,* p. 8; Corbett, *Shantung,* pp. 74–79.

dents should have for national celebrations, and the incident grew to major proportions because of failure to work out a face-saving compromise. In the course of the *hsüeh-ch'ao* the foreign administrators were accused of trying to undermine Chinese patriotism, the dean abolished the student self-government association, rebel students withdrew from Yali to form a school of their own, and a large number of students were expelled or suspended from Yali.[23]

A number of aspects of these and other student storms may be noted. In the first place, a new group had appeared on the Chinese scene: the new-style student or the New Youth. With the decline of the gentry class, the students often thought of themselves as its successors, but there were obvious differences. The academies of old China had been for relatively mature scholars whose goal had been to pass the civil service examinations and move into the bureaucracy. The new-style students were often younger, and they were concentrated in a few urban centers where they formed a separate community. Though quite a few had hopes of state service, other occupations for the educated were opening up at the same time that the normal routes to political power were closing. The young students were less knowledgeable about the Chinese heritage and less closely tied to it, and their residence in that sector of China where tradition was disintegrating most rapidly seemed to substantiate their view of tradition as an impediment to their ambitions.

They did, however, consider themselves a privileged elite and were cognizant of the importance of protecting the interests of their group. Though they had not yet developed nation-wide student unions, they were beginning to become nationally conscious. They were beginning to found their own organizations such as the self-government association at Yali, and their concentration in a few dormitories made it fairly easy for them to bring concerted pressure on those in authority. They were becoming adept at using appeals which could not be easily denied, and by 1912 they had learned that demands in the name of patriotism undercut the resistance of student opponents and the self-assurance of the older generation. Impatient with tradition and resentful of authority based on age or office, they deliberately flouted the respect ordinarily accorded their

[23] The summaries of the Yali incidents are based on Yale Mission, *Annual Report, 1908* and *1911*; Holden, *Yale-in-China*, pp. 50–52, 68–71.

elders. They showed remarkable confidence in youth and considerable sensitivity to any seeming slight to the New Youth. Such group consciousness encouraged the majority to come to the defense of a member, and thus a minor dispute easily burgeoned into a conflict of generations.

They were, however, like their fathers in the sophistication with which they could make known their lack of respect for an individual, especially a foreigner. Perhaps it is significant that the students in the Christian colleges often chose to express their contempt or resentment at chapel services. These were not only public gatherings where group action was easy and effective; they were foreign ceremonies required of Chinese. In many cases the Western administrators had to turn to Chinese members of the faculty for middlemen to help negotiate a settlement. The *hsüeh-ch'ao* of the first fifteen years of the twentieth century thus provide an introduction to the new-style students who were to demand the attention of the nation in 1919. They also provide a background for the student-led anti-Christian movements of the 1920's.

College Curricula: Emphases, Expansion, Problems

Students attending the Christian colleges during the first decade of the twentieth century did not find the curriculum essentially different from that of the late nineteenth century. Many of the courses were taught on a more advanced level than before, and the colleges generally offered a wider variety of courses. Quite a few of the colleges had increased their scientific equipment, and textbooks were more easily available. Essentially, however, the curriculum was still a combination of literary Chinese, English, mathematics and the sciences, religion, and a little history and philosophy. Though the schools offered professional and vocational courses in medicine, theology, and nursing, they offered little in law, agriculture, business administration, education, or engineering prior to 1910. The century was well into its second decade before many basic changes were made in the curriculum.

In their attempt to become senior colleges and to evolve a curriculum appropriate to their Chinese students, the institutions faced many problems. There was the dilemma presented by the tension between religious and educational goals, which has already been discussed; and there was the persistant controversy over the relative importance of English and Chinese in the curriculum. By 1910 the controversy had been temporarily decided in favor of English, and the emphasis on English was having consequences both for the individual graduates of the Christian colleges and for the history of mission education in general. During the decade 1910–1920, thousands of Chinese went to Europe and the United States to study. Since a knowledge of English was an important part of the scholarship examinations, the student from the Christian colleges had a real advantage, and mission school students constituted a high percentage of the successful candidates. A knowledge of English was also an asset in seeking positions in the diplomatic corps, the telegraphic, railway, and customs administrations; and a number of Christian college graduates went into this work. Quite a number of non-Christian students chose Christian colleges because of the record of their students in the scholarship examinations and in obtaining jobs requiring a knowledge of English.

Those who went abroad to study or who secured government positions were a small minority, however; most graduates entered teaching. The latter had difficulty translating their knowledge into Chinese and sometimes they resorted to teaching in English, especially if they were science instructors. The insistence of the Christian colleges that applicants for entrance be able to read, write, and speak English put pressure on the middle schools to stress the teaching of English. In many of the mission schools the study of English was begun in the primary grades and received increasing emphasis as the student progressed. In spite of this great emphasis, many missionaries maintained that few students achieved real facility in the use of the language. In history, science, literature, and other courses, the students had to give as much time and energy to translation as to mastering the content. It was said to be difficult for courses taught in English to attain a high intellectual level.[24]

The Christian colleges employing English as a medium of instruction regarded it as a temporary expedient, but having achieved a *modus operandi* with English, they did little to encourage its replace-

[24] Galt, "The North China Union College," *ER*, VIII (1916), 303; J. Taylor, "Our Aim in Teaching English: Are We Realizing It?" *ER*, X (1918), 101; *Christian Education in China*, 1922, p. 345.

ment by Chinese. Though most schools allocated many hours to courses in Chinese language and literature, they did not change the educational organization, and the Chinese department remained a division apart from the college. The manner in which the college budget was organized gave the college only a small fund for hiring Chinese teachers, and so the schools frequently could not afford good instructors in Chinese. Even if the students had five, ten, or even fifteen hours a week for Chinese studies, this was but a fraction of the time traditionally given to the subject. In some cases all courses on China—its history, geography, literature, and language— were placed in the Chinese department, and the Chinese tutors were responsible for whatever work was done in these fields. The attitude of the students themselves fostered the neglect of Chinese. When chided for lack of interest in Chinese studies, they were likely to answer that they had come to the Christian college to learn English and Western subjects; they could learn their Chinese better elsewhere and would do so when the need arose.[25] Foreign knowledge had acquired prestige and monetary value in China, and the students concentrated their energies on gaining this knowledge.

Some of the schools made a special effort to secure good instructors in Chinese even when they had to pay salaries as high as those paid Chinese teachers in the sciences and other fields.[26] Yenching University attempted to raise the level of Chinese studies and secured Chou Tso-jen, essayist, translator, and a leader in the New Culture Movement, to offer literature and composition courses. To meet the criticisms of Chinese training was no simple matter, however. In the first place, the Christian colleges were unlikely to attract students who wanted to major in Chinese language and literature; even at Yenching where a fairly strong department of Chinese was built up, the number of majors in Chinese was consistently less than 5 percent of the total student body. In many of the other institutions

[25] Conversation with Charles H. Corbett, member of the physics staff of North China Union College and Yenching, 1908–1921, and author of *Shantung Christian College* and *Lingnan University* (Jan. 5, 1954); Shanghai Baptist College, *Annual Report, 1914*, p. 5.

[26] University of Nanking, *Report of the President, 1915–16*, p. 5, and *1918–19*, p. 27; Peking University, *Report of the President, 1921–22*, p. 5; "Resolutions in the East China Christian Educational Association," *ER, XIII* (1921), 179; *Chinese Christian Education, A Report of a Conference Held in New York City, April, 1925* (New York, 1925), pp. 19, 20, 40.

it proved impossible to attract eminent Chinese scholars to the faculty because of inadequate salaries, the Christian and foreign atmosphere, and the paucity of majors. Chinese courses, therefore, continued to be taught by old-style tutors or by Christian college graduates. Administrators ruefully admitted that their work in Chinese continued to be inadequate.

More satisfactory were attempts to raise educational standards in other fields. After 1915 most schools replaced their prescribed curricula with a system of majors, minors, and electives; several began to offer a B.S. degree as well as a B.A. Though few schools were yet able to offer majors in specific subjects such as chemistry, history, or physics, most colleges provided a major in the sciences, the social sciences, Western languages and literature, or religion.

At first, the number of advanced courses was limited, and library facilities and scientific equipment for senior college work were inadequate. The colleges had been particularly lax about building up their libraries. In 1925–1926 five of the colleges had fewer than 10,000 volumes of Chinese and English books, and only six had 25,000 or more.[27] Over half the colleges allocated less than 4 percent of their educational budgets to libraries. The science training in many middle schools was so poor that the college courses generally had to assume that almost no science work had been done,[28] and a person who majored in the sciences often did the bulk of his work in introductory courses in biology, chemistry, physics, geology, etc. With the aid of funds from the China Medical Board, however, several of the Christian colleges made real progress after 1916 in improving their scientific equipment. A 1925 survey of scientific equipment based on the standards employed for accreditation of small colleges in the United States listed eight Christian colleges as having sufficient biology equipment; nine had adequate chemistry laboratories, and five came up to standards in physics.[29] Nanking,

---

[27] Cressy, *Christian Higher Education*, pp. 226–227. Even these figures are deceptively favorable since gifts had helped build many of the libraries, and the number of books unsuited for college use was large.

[28] Leonard G. Morgan, *The Teaching of Science to the Chinese* (Hong Kong, 1933), p. 1927.

[29] Cressy, *Christian Higher Education*, pp. 229–331. Statistics for Yenching and West China universities are not included. West China's equipment at the time was limited; before the transfer to the new campus in 1926, Yenching's laboratories were modest but were supplemented by those of Peking Union

Shanghai, Shantung, St. John's, Soochow, and Canton had the best equipped laboratories. Yali, Hangchow, and Ginling were each up to standard in only one field; Huping, Huachung, and Hwa Nan were below standard in all fields. By 1925 the well-equipped colleges were offering the basic courses necessary for a science major and were requiring laboratory experiments of the students.

Curricula: Professional and Vocational

The colleges also expanded their professional and vocational education. Though courses in medicine and theology had been offered, the missions had not generally supported professional and vocational education in other fields. Among most missionaries, vocational education was considered secular work which contributed little to the growth of Protestantism in China, and so Christian schools were not justified in spending mission money to train engineers, agriculturalists, lawyers, and the like.[30] Some educators maintained that few Chinese were interested in college-level work in these fields. Traditional education in China was humanistic, and its purpose was preparation for government service. Scholars looked upon manual labor as degrading. Attitudes slowly changed, however. Missions felt responsible for providing Christians with the means to earn a living, and when the missions could no longer offer employment to all their graduates, the latter often discovered that they were poorly equipped for other positions. Christian educators pointed out that, since a large portion of their converts were farmers, both the sons of farmers and Chinese ministers who were to work in rural areas would benefit from agricultural training. Government competition was compelling the Christian primary and middle schools to raise their standards by employing teachers trained in education, and so the missionaries became interested in organizing normal schools and instituting educational courses. As professional and technical education became popular in the West, institutional pride encouraged the educators to add courses and raise their colleges to the status of universities.

Medical College. According to the standards, the minimum value of scientific equipment should be US$10,000 for biology, $10,000 for chemistry, and $12,000 for physics.

[30] George A. Stuart, "The Relation of Christian Schools to Racial and National Movements in China," *Records, EAC, 1909*, p. 12; H. B. Graybill, "The Next Step in Christian Education in Kwangtung," *ER*, VIII (1916), 269.

Rivalry with government institutions was an important factor in changing attitudes. Though most Chinese students still preferred a liberal arts education, a number of influential Chinese educators had become advocates of "education for life." At the invitation of the Ministry of Education, John Dewey came to China in 1919 to deliver a series of lectures on education. These addresses advocating freedom of thought, experimental methodology, and the relation of education to civic life and social experience were widely publicized; with Hu Shih as interpreter, Dewey managed to reach hundreds of students, newspaper correspondents, teachers, and other educated groups. The lectures were first reprinted in magazines and newspapers and then published as a book which went through fourteen printings of 10,000 copies each in two years. During Dewey's one-year visit to China many of his other works were translated into Chinese and were widely read.[31] American educational theory thus influenced the formulation of a new set of aims for the national educational system in 1922: to adapt itself to a new and changing society; to promote the spirit of democracy; to develop individuality; to take into special consideration the economic status of the average citizen; to adjust education to the needs of life; to facilitate the spread of universal education; and to make itself flexible enough to allow for local variation. Neither the humanistic education of traditional China nor the humanistic emphasis of the Western-type liberal arts college was considered sufficient; specialized vocational and professional training should be added to the curriculum.

Other Chinese educators were influenced by materialist and utilitarian theories, and these groups added their voices to the demand for practical education, for education to strengthen China economically and politically. Ch'en Tu-hsiu, one of the most influential educators of this period, was an advocate of utilitarianism years before he accepted Marxian materialism. In a "Call to Youth" issued in 1915, Ch'en attributed Europe's material progress to the fact that Westerners had made usefulness a major criterion in education, government, literature, and the crafts; they had applied scientific methodology to all fields of endeavor. Ts'ai Yüan-p'ei, minister of educa-

[31] Chow Tse-tsung, *The May Fourth Movement Intellectual Revolution in Modern China* (Cambridge, Mass.; 1960), p. 192; Hughes, *The Invasion of China*, pp. 184–185. The reactions of Dewey and his wife to their experiences in China are contained in Evelyn Dewey, ed., *Letters from China and Japan* (London, 1920).

tion (1912–1913) and then chancellor of Peking National University (1917–1927), listed five kinds of education as necessary for China: military, utilitarian, moral, asthetic, and education for a world view.[32] Of these, he said, utilitarian education should receive the greatest emphasis, for it was necessary to develop the mineral wealth and industrial potential of China and to raise the general economic level of the people.

Practical vocational education thus became a popular theme among Chinese educators. A Chinese Association for Vocational Education (Chung-hua chih-yeh chiao-yü she) was founded in 1917, and the National Association of Vocational Schools (Ch'üan-kuo chih-yeh hsüeh-hsiao lien-ho-hui) was organized in 1922. The Chinese Society for the Survey of Practical Education (Hsi-chih chiao-yü tiao-ch'a she) invited Paul Monroe of Columbia Teachers College to China in 1921, and it was with Monroe's aid that the aims of Chinese education were restated in 1922.[33] Vocational and technical training were not to be confined to middle schools or special institutes, but were also to be offered at the university level. Peking National University anticipated adding schools of agriculture, commerce, medicine, and applied science. The Christian colleges, which had generally hesitated to offer technical courses, were coming under fire for providing only theoretical work. Even the Christian college alumni were recommending more practical courses; specifically, they asked for courses which would enable graduates to raise their standard of living and increase the wealth of China.[34]

The University of Nanking was a pioneer in vocational education. Its program in agriculture and forestry grew out of famine relief work led by Joseph Bailie, a professor, and it actually began without much theorizing about China's need for practical education. During

[32] Trans. of statements by Ch'en and Ts'ai are in Teng and Fairbank, *China's Response*, pp. 235–238, 240–245. See also, Wen Tsung-yao, "On Education," *Hsin ch'ing-nien*, II, no. 1 (Sept. 1916).

[33] Two works by Monroe reveal something of his experiences in China: *Essays in Comparative Education* (New York, 1927) and *China: A Nation in Evolution* (New York, 1928).

[34] Djang Siao-mei, "Ginling College from Five Angles" and M. S. Hwang Cha "The Daughters Speak to their Alma Mater," *Ginling College Magazine*, II (1925), 38, 43; T. Z. Koo in *Chinese Christian Education, 1925*, pp. 49, 53; Pott, "Present Educational Tendencies in China," *ER*, XII (1920), 111; Hsiao, *History of Modern Education*, pp. 130–131.

the drought of 1911, the college was able to obtain low rental lands, where it settled refugees, who were given seed and implements and were instructed in improved agricultural methods. Attention, praise, and money quickly came to the project. When the government granted the college Purple Mountain as an experimental station, the college established a colony there and guided the colonists in constructing fire breaks, manufacturing bricks, building roads and houses, and undertaking afforestation. Upon the urging of Bailie, a school of agriculture and forestry was opened in 1914–1915. The school gained widespread Chinese support. The Chinese government gave its sanction to the mission school, closed its own forestry school in Peking, and transferred eighteen students to the University of Nanking. A financial grant accompanied the pupils. The governors of Anhwei, Shantung, Shansi, Yunnan, Kweichow, and Kiangsu sent scholarship students; and the cotton mill owners' association of China made grants for experiments to improve cotton seed and methods of cotton cultivation.

The school had its troubles, however. In such a new field the language problem was acute; there were practically no suitable Chinese books on agricultural methods, and the government students were not competent in English. To obtain teachers was difficult; to obtain teachers who were fluent in Chinese was almost impossible. The students, who considered themselves members of the educated elite, were most unenthusiastic about the required field work. Nevertheless, the school grew quite rapidly in size and support. Entrance requirements were the same as for the regular arts course, and a five-year program was offered. The school received an unexpected boost in 1923 with the grant of $675,000 from the unexpended balance of the China Famine Fund, and by 1924–1925 there were 126 students and 78 staff members. The school was also aided by an arrangement with the International Education Board and the Plant Breeding Department of the New York State College of Agriculture at Cornell University. Cornell agreed to send out a member of its Plant Breeding Department for approximately six months each year to help with plant improvement work.

Since many staff members concentrated on research, the Nanking school was able to undertake a wide variety of projects: plant disease control; animal disease studies, especially the control of rinderpest and of silkworm diseases; economic and social studies of tenancy, marketing, production, and indebtedness; crop improvement, particularly of the most common Chinese grains; forestry work such as reforestation and erosion control; and the development of a Chinese agricultural literature. The school helped develop and distribute improved cotton, wheat, and corn seed; it produced certified silkworm eggs; and it conducted short term courses in sericulture and summer school courses for rural teachers. By 1926 the school had graduated 109 students; almost half were teaching, and a third were engaged in agricultural work.[35]

Canton Christian College began work in agriculture when a trained horticulturist joined the staff in 1907. The work, which was for middle-school and primary students, gradually expanded to include school gardens, a model dairy with native buffaloes, goats, and Holstein cows, experiments with citrus fruits, and a herbarium. By 1918 several college students were taking agricultural courses, and the school was eager to develop a separate agricultural faculty. The request of French and American silk exporters for the college's cooperation in improving and standardizing the quality of Chinese raw silk inspired the college to propose a broad program of research and teaching in sericulture. The Association of Christian Colleges and Universities in China, however, considered the cost of agricultural schools so high and the commitments for liberal arts already so great that it recommended that the missions maintain only one college of agriculture, that of the University of Nanking. Canton should attempt only junior college work in agriculture.[36]

C. K. Edmunds, president of Canton, protested that the agricultural problems of south China were quite different from those of central China and that a second Christian agricultural college was justified. He secured the support of the Kwangtung provincial gov-

[35] The history of the origins of the College of Agriculture and Forestry of the University of Nanking was based on the following: University of Nanking, *Report of the President, 1912, 1915, 1924–25; CMYB, 1915,* pp. 402–404: *Educational Directory, 1915,* pp. 48–50; C. J. Hamilton, "The University of Nanking," *ER,* IX (1917), 232; J. H. Reisner, "Recent Developments in Agricultural Education under Mission Auspices," *CMYB,* 1919, pp. 158, 169–172; Cressy, *Christian Higher Education,* pp. 137–140.

[36] H. C. Brownell, "The Canton Christian College," *ER,* IX (1917), 301; E. C. Lobenstine, "The Association of Christian Colleges and Universities in China," *CMYB, 1919,* pp. 154–156.

ernment, of Kwangtung Christian Educational Association, and of several prominent Chinese businessmen; and in 1921 the Lingnan Agricultural College was organized under a separate Chinese board of managers. Financial aid also came from the United States Department of Agriculture and The Pennsylvania State College of Agriculture. By 1925 the agricultural college had a student body of thirty-three and a staff of sixteen. As was true of the agricultural school at Nanking, faculty members taught a relatively small number of students and could devote much of their time to research. One of the most important projects of the college was the production and sale of large quantities of improved, disease-free silkworm eggs. In horticulture it conducted experiments with the lichee, the papaya, and citrus fruits and imported a number of new strains of fruit trees from Hawaii and Southeast Asia. Stock breeding and attempts to improve rice seed and methods of rice cultivation were also undertaken.[37]

Between 1915 and 1925 the Christian colleges broadened their curricula in other fields. The Comparative Law School of Soochow University had an interesting history and claimed among its graduates several prominent jurists and educators. When the students of Shanghai Anglo-Chinese College and Tungwu College were combined in 1912 to form the Arts and Science College of Soochow University, the Anglo-Chinese institution was permitted to continue and become affiliated with Soochow University as its Second Middle School. In 1914 Charles W. Rankin, a political science teacher at Soochow, was appointed head of the middle school. It was understood that he could expand the work of the institution if he did not commit Soochow University to any extra expenditure. Rankin, a lawyer by training, was impressed with the complexity of the Shanghai legal system, which included Chinese, Anglo-American, European, and mixed courts. Certainly there seemed a need for training in comparative law and for the preparation of jurists who could modernize the Chinese legal system; during the next decade or so China would require experts who could develop a system of civil

[37] S. H. Taam, "A Letter from a Chinese Agricola," *ER*, X (1918), 36–37; C. K. Edmunds, "Agricultural Education in China," *ER*, XII (1920), 154; "Colleges of Agriculture in China," *Lingnam Agricultural Review*, I (1922–23), 101–102; C. K. Edmunds, *Modern Education in China*, U.S. Bureau of Education Bulletin no. 44 (Washington, D.C., 1919), p. 60.

law, codify laws, and organize a hierarchy of courts and judges. The consular courts, the British Supreme Court in China, and the American Court for China, all located in Shanghai, formed a reservoir of talent which might be tapped for legal instruction. There were also, Rankin believed, ambitious young Chinese in Shanghai who would welcome the opportunity to study law on a part time basis as a means to a more profitable and interesting career. All these factors persuaded Rankin to open the Comparative Law School of China in 1915.[38]

Classes were held in the late afternoon and evening; and except for Rankin, all instructors were practicing jurists—English, American, and Chinese. Beginning with fewer than a dozen students, the institution expanded gradually from 1915 to 1925 and then experienced such rapid growth that by 1930 it had become the largest of all the special schools under the auspices of the China Christian colleges. Soochow University had, in truth, begun to fear that the tail might wag the dog. Whereas the law school enrolled 594 students in 1930, Soochow had only 450, and 186 of the latter were prelaw students who would leave for the law school after two years.[39] The Shanghai school, furthermore, was adding commercial studies. Soochow, however, could hardly complain of unauthorized expenditure, for the school was quite an inexpensive operation. The majority of the instructors continued to be practicing lawyers who taught part-time and did not demand a high salary scale. Most of the students were also part-time, and they worked and resided in the city; thus the institution had to furnish only a minimum of dormitory, dining, and extra-curricular facilities.

For entrance the student was required to present two years of college work plus an ability to use English. He then undertook a three-year study of Chinese, Roman, and Anglo-American law. The school adopted the case study method generally used in the United

[38] Soochow University, *Catalogue, 1915–16*, pp. 2, 25; Nance, *Soochow*, pp. 70–72; *CMYB*, 1916, p. 273.

[39] Cressy, *Christian Higher Education*, p. 141; *Statistical Report—China Colleges and Professional Schools of China, 1930–31*, CCEA Bulletin no. 28 (Shanghai, 1931); for further detail, see Soochow University, *Catalogue, 1919–20*, pp. 31–32 and W. W. Blume, "The Comparative Law School" in Nance, *Soochow*, pp. 73–80. Blume was dean of the law school from 1920 to 1927.

States, and students participated regularly in practice courts which employed in rotation Chinese, Anglo-American, and mixed court procedure. At the end of the three-year course, the student received an LL.B. degree.

Boone University gave the only Christian college program in library methods and one of the first such courses in China. A three-year sequence for students of sophomore standing was offered by Mary E. Wood, and by Samuel T. Y. Tseng and Thomas C. S. Hu, Boone graduates who had studied library science in the United States. Since China had not developed scientific methods for cataloguing books and organizing a library, students trained at the Boone Library School easily secured positions, and the course became one of the more popular ones offered there during the 1920's.[40] Yenching University in 1923 opened the first home economics department among the Christian colleges; its goal was to train social workers and teachers and to prepare college girls to be better homemakers. Such subjects as child care, nutrition, sanitation, and household management were emphasized, and an effort was made to adjust the program to the needs of China; the practice house, erected on the new campus, was built in Chinese style and included Chinese-style furniture and equipment.[41]

Most Christian colleges were financially unable to offer complete programs in fields which required extensive equipment, engineering and specialized work in the sciences, for example. Soochow and Shanghai did offer a few courses in industrial chemistry, and St. John's gave some work in engineering. The money for St. John's engineering department, however, came largely from Chinese sources. Hangchow in 1920 opened a construction department in which students served as apprentices; as part of their training the pupils helped design new mission buildings in the area and then supervised their construction. Commercial courses were introduced by Shang-

[40] T. C. Tai, *The Library Movement in China,* Bulletins on Chinese Education, 1923, II, no. 3 (Shanghai, 1923), p. 17; Coe, *Huachung,* pp. 18, 78–79.
[41] Ava B. Milam, "Home Economics—The Fourth R," *ER,* XV (1923), 229; Camilla Mills (Mrs. Knight Biggerstaff), "Home Economics in China," *Journal of Home Economics,* XVI (1924), 394, "Home Economics at Yenching College, Peking University," XVII (1925), 160, and "Yenching Progresses," XIX (1927), 456.

hai, Canton, Huachung, and St. John's and were more popular with the Chinese students than most of the other vocational or professional courses.

A field which gained support with the missionary educators was teacher training, for the missions had developed a system of education extending from kindergarten through college. Though their schools had at first been manned by missionaries, old-style Chinese tutors, and mission school graduates, competition of government education made it necessary to improve the training of their teachers and the missions wanted as many of their teachers as possible educated in a Christian environment. Surveys of Christian education during the 1920's showed that over one-third of the Christian college graduates did actually become teachers, often in mission schools, but the Christian colleges were providing little specific training for this profession.[42] All but one of the Christian colleges, therefore, introduced courses in education. Despite the fact that many of the graduates became teachers, the courses were not popular with the Chinese students. Two explanations may be offered: many of the alumni became teachers by default rather than by choice, and the traditional Chinese preference for a humanistic education rather than specialized training was still influential among college students. Neither the pay nor the prestige of primary school work was great enough to interest college graduates, and the same was largely true of middle school teaching. Many college students hoped to secure academic positions or government jobs where prestige and income were high; in college, therefore, they elected a humanities course and did not take teacher training or other vocational courses. When the majority of them were not able to obtain the coveted government jobs, they had little choice but to teach in the middle schools; even this was often seen as only a stepping stone to a better position.

One innovation which the Christian colleges brought to the Chinese curriculum was physical education. The stereotype of the stoop-shouldered Chinese scholar with long gown and long fingernails had considerable basis in fact. Westerners brought their love of sports

[42] Handbook of Christian Colleges, Table XI, p. 38; Christian Education in China: A Study Made by an Educational Commission Representing the Mission Boards and Societies Conducting Work in China (New York, c 1922), pp. 138–142.

and of action with them to China, and St. John's introduced track only a few years after its founding. Believing in the usefulness of sports in building both character and bodies, other missionary educators followed suit, and sports and athletic contests slowly won favor among students despite their initial reluctance to take part in such undignified activities. In 1904 the first intercollegiate athletic meet in north China was held between Peking University and North China Union College. While military drill and calisthenics were emphasized in some colleges, tennis, baseball, and soccer were more popular and were even introduced in the government schools.[43] Both Ginling and Soochow added physical education courses to train leaders in physical education and public health work for schools, colleges, the YMCA, the YWCA, and other mission organizations.

Curricula: A Critique

The Christian college curricula as a whole call forth several criticisms. The missionaries had transferred to China the curricula of the small denominational colleges in the West with which they were familiar, and many of the shortcomings arose from the laxity of the Christian educators in adapting the curricula to the needs of Chinese students. The missionaries had even been somewhat slow about keeping up with educational changes in the West. Overcrowding of the curriculum had plagued the colleges from the first. Whereas the standard number of semester hours required for graduation in most United States colleges was 120, the number ranged from 128 to 163 among the Christian colleges in 1926, and over half of the schools required more than 150 semester hours for graduation.[44] Not only did the students try to absorb the Western curriculum in addition to the Chinese classics and courses on Christianity, but they were also required to spend an unusually large number of class hours on a foreign language, English.

When Christian colleges had been established in China, Western education was emphasizing the languages, mathematics, and the sciences; the mission schools followed this tradition. In a summary of instruction offered by the liberal arts colleges in 1925–1926, the

[43] Hugh A. Moon, "Physical Training in China," *CMYB, 1912*, p. 356; Pott, "History," *St. John's*, p. 9; Galt, "Yenching," p. 25.

[44] Cressy, *Christian Higher Education*, p. 51.

four subjects in which the largest number of semester hours were offered were English, chemistry, Chinese, and biology.[45] Several of the colleges placed unusual emphasis on science and mathematics. Shantung, Fukien, Nanking, Soochow, and Canton all gave over 40 percent of their instruction in these fields, and the average for the colleges as a whole was one-third. The demand of Chinese students for science was actually not this great during the 1920's. Though science as the source of the West's power had been emphasized, interest had generally centered on technology and applied science or on scientism as a weapon against tradition. Except for teaching, China had relatively few positions to offer the scientist, and the prestige traditionally accorded the humanistic studies remained strong. Timothy T'ingfang Lew, dean of Yenching School of Religion, wrote in 1926: "The fact still remains that the students who specialize in science have not increased in considerable numbers under the present strenuous effort to advocate science. . . . With the exception of certain technical institutions, students in colleges of arts and sciences have not chosen subjects in the sciences as they have literature, law, politics, history, sociology, economics, and the like. There is still lurking in their minds the notion that physical sciences are somewhat philistine compared with literary work." [46] Over half of the total instruction in mathematics, chemistry, and biology was given to classes with less than ten students.

Though few Chinese students majored in the natural sciences, they were interested in the social sciences, especially political theory. China's internal and international difficulties fostered this interest among a group who considered themselves the country's future leaders. After the revolution of 1911, many Chinese wanted to study the problems involved in establishing a democratic government for China. It became only too apparent that writing a constitution and organizing a legislature did not create a working democratic government and that much more information and many more social and political changes were essential. World War I and the organization

[45] Ibid., pp. 44–46.
[46] The Christian College in New China: Report of the Second Biennial Conference of Christian Colleges and Universities in China, 1926, CCEA Bulletin no. 16 (Shanghai, 1926), p. 17. For detail on the Chinese attitude toward science, see D. W. Y. Kwok, Scientism in Chinese Thought, 1900–1950 (New Haven, 1965).

of the League of Nations at first gave China hope of entering the family of nations on equal terms with the Western states; after the war Chinese were negotiating for the return of the Shantung concessions seized by the Japanese and for the termination of the unequal treaties. Concern with these matters encouraged the study of international law and international relations. A sense of competition with the industrialized nations and the industrial growth which occurred in China during World War I fostered interest in the field of economics. Economic determinism became popular.

The Christian colleges were slow in responding to this interest; in 1925–1926 only 14 percent of their total instruction was given in the social sciences. In the leading non-Christian colleges in China three times as much work in politics and economics was offered as in the Christian schools; the small American college provided twice as much work in politics and three times as much in economics.[47] Courses in the social sciences were relatively popular; and in the Christian colleges only a small proportion of the instruction in economics, politics, history, and sociology was given to classes of five or fewer. Even those social science courses seem to have been designed for Western rather than Chinese students. Although practically all of the schools offered courses in modern European history, English history, and American history, not all of them gave courses in modern Chinese history. Introductory courses in sociology, economics, and other social sciences frequently were transferred with little alteration from the Western colleges to the China Christian colleges, and little information on conditions in China was included. One widely used textbook, *The Science of Government* by D. Z. Sheffield of North China Union College, included three chapters on Greek government, five on Roman law and government and their influence, seven on modern Western governments, and one chapter on Chinese government and its historical development.[48]

[47] Cressy, *Christian Higher Education,* pp. 58–59. In compiling these statistics Cressy obtained catalogues (1926–1927) for thirty government and private colleges in China; only fifteen of the stronger institutions included science departments and only the curricula of these fifteen schools were used in making comparisons. In making comparisons with American colleges, Cressy used the catalogues of thirty-one accredited institutions with student enrollments between 200 and 600. A list of the schools is on page 61 of Cressy.

[48] "Our Book Table," review by A. P. Parker, *CR*, XLII (1911), 299–300.

By the time of the New Culture Movement, however, both Christian and Chinese educators were becoming aware of the inadequacy of such courses and texts once they were divorced from their Western frame of reference. Teachers stated that the information and principles seemed abstract and theoretical to their students, without practical application in the Chinese context. During the second decade of the twentieth century a few Christian educators initiated the research essential to the reorientation of the social science courses. Daniel H. Kulp of Shanghai Baptist College, for example, organized the research for his book, *Country Life in China,* and J. Lossing Buck was soon to undertake his surveys of the agricultural economy of the Yangtze delta. Field research of this type would be necessary before social science courses and texts could be adapted to the Chinese scene.

Staffing and Financing

Another concern of Christian college administrators during this period was the securing of a more highly trained faculty. Though improvement in the teaching staffs had been made since 1900, many administrative and financial obstacles to obtaining qualified instructors had not yet been eliminated. In the appointment of a Western faculty member, the first step was usually a request by the college president and the board of managers in China for a man competent in a certain field of study; the mission society, complying with this request in so far as possible, often designated one of its evangelists in the field or a missionary newly assigned to China. The teacher was then formally appointed by the Western board of trustees, though he continued to be supported by the mission society. If the man were not competent to teach the needed subjects, teaching loads were reallocated to accord as closely as possible with the competence of the various teachers and still enable the full gamut of courses to be offered. For the home societies the overriding purpose of the Christian colleges remained religious rather than educational, and they responded slowly to requests for teachers with specialized training and experience. They also pointed out the difficulties of complying with such requests. Missionaries were not selected from among the best suited ministers of the church; they volunteered for evangelistic work, and quite frequently they volunteered at the end, not at the beginning of their ministerial studies. To require special training for those entering educational work would increase the financial burden of the supporting board and delay the productive work of the missionary.

The desire for better trained men grew stronger among the missionary educators, however. In 1909 Hawks Pott of St. John's protested against carrying on educational work by a policy of make-shifts.[49] The schools could not progress without continuity of personnel, he said. Sometimes the head of the school was needed for other work in the mission and so he was transferred. Even when the president remained, there was constant change in the teaching staff. New missionaries were still assigned to a school to teach in English while they learned the Chinese language and then were sent to other work. Canton Christian College estimated its faculty turn-over at 50 percent in four years.[50] *The Chinese Recorder* remarked in 1910 that there was little excuse for missionaries who had been in the field for several years and still lacked a knowledge of Chinese history and culture.[51] Upon investigation it was discovered that a relatively small percentage of the missionaries were really proficient in Chinese, possibly a smaller percentage than in the preceding century. The early missionaries had found few Chinese who would listen to them and so had devoted considerable time to studying the language and translating. Those who came later found themselves quickly absorbed into the mission organization; instead of being isolated in a Chinese village, they frequently lived in a mission compound with other English-speaking people. Though they were supposed to give their first year to the study of the language, they found it difficult to avoid acquiring other obligations. They might in time learn to speak Chinese fluently, but mastery of written Chinese could be obtained only with years of regular application.

The 1911 revolution enabled the missionaries to make a start toward rectifying the language problem. Missionaries who had fled the interior joined with new missionaries in holding a four-weeks language school in Shanghai. Convinced of the benefits of such a

[49] Pott, "The Present Status of Missionary Schools," *Report, EAC, 1909,* pp. 27–28.
[50] Canton Christian College, *Report of the President, 1919–24,* p. 11.
[51] "Editorial," *CR,* XLI (1910), iii.

program, they planned a permanent department of missionary training at the University of Nanking and in 1912 organized a one-year course.[52] A language school in Peking, founded in 1910 by the London Missionary Society, was enlarged in 1913 to a union enterprise; and other schools were begun in Chengtu and Canton. Though one could hardly acquire competence in Chinese in a year, the schools had two merits in particular: the teaching methods were generally more efficient than those of a private tutor with no knowledge of pedagogy; while in school the new missionary was likely to devote his whole time to language study.

Having somewhat improved the language situation, the missionaries returned to the problem of adequate training for their teachers. College administrators requested greater authority in the selection of teachers. They reiterated that a degree in theology did not prepare a man to teach the sciences. They requested that missionaries be trained for specific countries so that a teacher would not come to China ignorant of its history, geography, and culture. They asked for more teachers so that one man would not have to teach in several departments.

Though the method of selecting teachers remained unchanged, several less basic changes were made. One was the employment of short-term teachers—men who wished to come to China for the experience or wished to try missionary work before definitely volunteering. Short-term instructors enlarged the inadequate faculties, and sometimes the colleges were able to bring in specialists who were a real benefit to the schools. Yenching invited the dean of the department of home economics at Oregon State College to come out for a year to help organize a home economics curriculum, and the University of Nanking had an exchange program with the School of Agriculture of Cornell University whereby they secured specialists who helped initiate research projects. If the short-term teachers had had no special training, they usually taught English. As long as the colleges hired only a small proportion of these workers, the policy seems to have been beneficial. A few of the institutions had more short-term workers than seemed advisable for the continuity of the

[52] "Missionary News," CR, XLIII (1912), 183–184; A. P. Parker, "The Nanking Language School," CR, XLIV (1913), 471–473.

college community, however; in 1925–1927 almost half of Yenching's Western faculty members were short-term teachers.

After 1915 increasing numbers of missionary educators used their furlough periods for advanced study rather than evangelistic work and fund raising. The mission boards began to acknowledge the need for graduate work and to provide support for advanced study; the China Medical Board granted fellowships to a number of the Christian educators for graduate study. An editorial in the *Educational Review* for 1918 remarked upon the distinct advance in the professional qualifications of those engaged in educational work.[53] Subsequent complaints, however, reminded the missionaries that the situation left something to be desired. Shanghai Baptist College reported in 1919 that the head of the mathematics department taught thirteen hours of English and only three of mathematics. The rest of the work in mathematics was given by an assistant history instructor. The acting head of the department of Biblical literature and ethics taught one course in elementary economics and one in the history of industry and commerce.[54]

Unfortunately, qualified Chinese teachers seemed as scarce as qualified missionary teachers. Again, much of the trouble was apparently the result of the religious emphasis, the dual administration, and the poverty of the individual colleges. The Chinese teachers were selected by the board of managers in China and the president of the college, and they were supported by tuition fees or by special allotments made by the home boards. Though most colleges had no restriction against using non-Christians if necessary, all preferred Christians. Chinese teachers were at first set apart from the Western faculty members. In some early college catalogues the missionary teachers with their ranks were listed individually, and then there followed the simple statement that there were also a certain number of Chinese instructors and assistants. The Chinese usually did not take part in faculty meetings during the early twentieth century. Soochow University, for example, had a governing faculty and a nongoverning one; the members of the Chinese department and of the middle school (except the Bible teachers) composed the non-

[53] "Editorial Notes," *ER*, X (1918), 277.
[54] Shanghai Baptist College, *Annual Report, 1919*, pp. 16–17.

governing faculty.[55] Relatively few Chinese attained a rank above instructor or assistant. The Chinese teachers frequently lived in towns apart from the college community; when homes were provided, they were smaller and simpler than the missionary houses. Their salaries were low, even for China. The attitude of the missionaries in 1905 toward the Chinese teachers may perhaps be best illustrated by quotations from a speech by Paul D. Bergen, president of Shantung Christian University, to the Christian Educational Association. The speech, said Bergen, was a plea for the Chinese teachers, who were often criticised, but who did a large part of the classroom work: "The teacher stands in a position of subordination to the foreign missionary. This situation is one of peculiar hardship and that mostly though nobody's fault. . . . As long as school and teacher are supported by mission funds, so long and perhaps longer, will authority rest with the missionary. . . . [The missionary] engages and dismisses Chinese teachers, has the final word in the regulations of the school, etc." This situation was somewhat justified, Bergen said, because: "The missionary knows what he wants to do and has the initiative, devotion and courage to go about it. The average Chinese teacher's range is narrow. . . . Nearly all are deficient in strength of character as well as in body. . . . Of a theory of teaching they have little notion." In comparing the status of the missionary with that of the Chinese teacher, Bergen stated:

We foreign missionaries are rich, though we may not feel so. We live in big houses and enjoy many bodily comforts. But the majority of our teachers have little at best. We can pinch him. . . . We often have him in a corner where he must bow to our will. But it is best to be liberal. Let his room be neat, sanitary, and decently furnished in Chinese style. . . . Grant him small privileges, which after all are little to you and much to him. . . . What is it that breaks down our precious nerves? It is the rack and strain of trying to fix the status of teachers . . . and to keep it fixed. . . . The fact that we hold the purse strings and are dealing with men in our employ and who belong to a decadent civilization, inevitably makes us autocratic to the verge of tyranny unless we faithfully examine ourselves.[56]

[55] Soochow University, *Catalogue, 1915–16*, pp. 4–5.
[56] Bergen, "Status of Chinese Teachers in Mission Schools," *Report, EAC, 1905*, pp. 152–155, 158.

As the twentieth century wore on, Christian college administrators became increasingly aware that the salaries, status, and working conditions of the Chinese teachers would have to be improved if the schools were to attract and retain good teachers. Though the old-style Chinese tutor was still employed in many institutions, neither tutor nor missionary administrator was, as a rule, happy with the arrangement. The colleges preferred mission school graduates if they were competent in Chinese or government school graduates if they were favorably inclined toward Christianity. After 1905, however, the customs administration, commercial firms, national schools, and government bureaucracy were making greater use of Chinese with a modern education, and they were able to outbid the colleges. Though a sense of obligation to the mission held some of the Christian college graduates, missionary educators complained that they were losing their best teachers to higher paying positions. In 1910 Shanghai College reported that not a single Chinese member of the teaching staff had been rehired; some were leaving; others were being fired. In 1918 the North China Union College for Women reported that they had secured five men for the chair of Chinese literature during the preceding three years and none had been satisfactory. The president of Fukien Christian University stated in 1919 that one of his most difficult problems was securing Chinese teachers with suitable training and character; even Fukien graduates were leaving for lucrative positions in Shanghai or Peking.[57]

The colleges were handicapped because funds from tuition fees were insufficient to hire many Chinese at good salaries and the mission societies were reluctant to donate funds for Chinese salaries. As a rule, the societies were more willing to designate one of their evangelists for educational work than to support a Chinese Christian teacher, who was actually less expensive to the mission. Chinese nationalists, however, were insisting that the Christian colleges use a larger percentage of Chinese teachers and accord them higher status. Amid much talk about raising the status and salary of Chinese teachers, several colleges took steps in this direction. Cheeloo, which had already added Chinese members to the university council, made

[57] Shanghai Baptist College, *Trustee's Report, 1909–10*, p. 5; North China Union Women's College, *Annual Report, 1916–18*, p. 4; Fukien Christian University, *Report of the President, 1919*, p. 2.

Table 3. Faculty of Canton Christian College in 1920–1921

Rank	Westerners	Chinese	Total
Administrators	7	2	9
Professors	10	1	11
Associate professors	3	1	4
Instructors	7	3	10
	27	7	34
Counted twice	3	0	3
Total	24	7	31

Source: Canton Christian College, *Catalogue, 1920–1921*, pp. 5–11.

Li T'ien-lu dean of the College of Arts and Science in 1923. Dr. Li had graduated from Peking (Methodist) University in 1908 and had a doctor's degree from Vanderbilt University; he had served as secretary to the Chinese delegation at the Washington Conference on Disarmament in 1921–1922 and was in 1923 principal of a Methodist middle school. In 1922–1923 Soochow University made Chao Tzu-ch'en, one of its former students who had done graduate study at Vanderbilt University, dean of the college and chairman of the faculty. Yenching agreed that there should be no differentiation between Chinese and Westerners in housing. Most of the Christian colleges, furthermore, increased the ratio of Chinese teachers, though it was not until the anti-foreign outbursts accompanying the Northern Expedition of 1926–1928 that the balance of power in the college administrations began to shift in favor of the Chinese.

In 1925–1926 the Christian colleges listed a total faculty of 465, of whom 181 were Chinese.[58] Over half the faculty members at Soochow, Cheeloo, and St. John's were Chinese. Less than a third of the teachers at West China, Fukien, Yali, and Lutheran colleges were Chinese; and the other colleges had 33 percent to 45 percent Chinese teachers. Of the 181 Chinese faculty members, 79 had studied abroad, and from this latter group Chinese leadership in faculty and administration generally came. The majority of the returned students were at four institutions: Shanghai, Canton, Yenching, and St. John's. Unfortunately, few statistics on the proportion of Chinese holding administrative and professorial positions are available. A report on Christian education in China in 1921–1922 spoke of the "strikingly

[58] Cressy, *Christian Higher Education,* p. 99.

Table 4. Faculty of Shanghai Baptist College in 1921–1922

Rank	Westerners	Chinese	Total
Professors	15	2	17
Assistant professors	2	1	3
Instructors	3	3	6
Associates (wives)	6	1	7
Assistants	0	8	8
Total	26	15	41

Source: Shanghai Baptist College, *Catalogue, 1921–1922*, pp. 5–8.

small proportion of Chinese in executive or responsible teaching positions," [59] and a study of the catalogues of several Christian colleges during the 1920's confirms this impression. The faculties of Canton Christian College and of Shanghai Baptist College in 1920–1922, for example, show a preponderance of Westerners in the higher ranks (*Tables 3* and *4*). The two Chinese holding professional rank at Canton, one full professor and one associate, were both in the Chinese department and held official degrees awarded under the traditional civil service examinations. Two of the Chinese instructors and one of the Chinese administrators had studied abroad. At Shanghai, the dominance of the Westerners was even more striking. Most of the assistants there had been educated in the China Christian colleges or government universities and did not have advanced degrees. In 1925 all of the college presidents were Westerners. The majority of the members of the boards of managers were appointed by the mission societies and were generally Western missionaries. In every college except Nanking, at least half the Chinese faculty members were Christians, an indication that the Christian colleges still depended heavily on their graduates for teachers.

A study of the Christian college faculties as a whole in 1925–1926 leads to the division of the schools into three groups according to size.[60] Yenching stood alone with eighty-four faculty members.

[59] *Christian Education in China, 1922*, p. 114.

[60] See Cressy, *Christian Higher Education*, pp. 99–113. In most cases the figures do not include the faculties of the professional colleges attached to the universities; nor do they seem to include the missionaries' wives, who frequently assisted with class instruction. The statistics on degrees include the traditional Chinese degrees, the three major degrees being equated to B.A., M.A., and Ph.D.

Cheeloo, West China, Canton, and the stronger eastern schools (St. John's, Shanghai, Soochow, and Nanking) each had twenty-seven to thirty-six teachers. The colleges of central China, plus Hangchow and Fukien, had faculties ranging from fourteen to twenty-one members. According to the minimum standard set by the Association of Christian Colleges and the Universities in China, 80 percent of the faculty should have had at least one year of graduate study; only two colleges met this requirement. Of the 465 teachers, 198 had a B.A. degree or no degree. Only seventy teachers held Ph.D. degrees.

The Christian colleges were frequently criticized for being overly ambitious and attempting more than they could do well. Most of them, it was said, were too small to carry on their work economically, and statistics were cited to substantiate these criticisms. The institutions had established more departments than the number of instructors, teaching hours, or students warranted. The number of departments in the arts colleges ranged from twenty-seven at Yenching to twelve at Ginling, and over half the college departments had no full-time instructor and offered less than twenty-four semester hours in courses. Though the teachers complained with some justice about the variety of courses which they had to teach, the median student-faculty ratio ranged between five and six pupils per instructor, and in many subjects the cost per student hour (i.e., one hour of instruction given to one student) was higher in the China Christian colleges than in comparable colleges in the United States.[61] The smallest Christian colleges almost invariably showed the highest cost to the mission per student.

Though the Christian colleges had originated as institutions inexpensive to both mission societies and Chinese students, they had ceased to be so. The total expenses of the colleges, of course, were not great in comparison with those of large institutions in the West. But in terms of the number of students educated and the ability of the students to pay as well as the number of mission societies supporting the colleges and the funds available for Christian higher education in China, the colleges were expensive. In 1925–1926 the total annual budget of the arts colleges, exclusive of capital expenditures, was slightly under US$2,000,000.[62] The total arts college en-

[61] Ibid., p. 248.
[62] Ibid., pp. 234–236.

rollment at the time was approximately 3,500. About half the total budget was included in the accounts of Yenching, St. John's, Shanghai, and Canton, each having accounts between $200,000 and $300,000. Most of the other schools had budgets of less than $100,000 a year. In 1925, only 2 percent of the educational income of the colleges came from endowment funds.

Canton received significant contributions from Chinese sources, as did Hsiang-Ya Medical School; and Yenching, Nanking, and Soochow managed to secure a small portion of their income from Chinese benefactors. St. John's alumni were quite generous in helping the school acquire new buildings; Chinese paid approximately one-third of the cost of two new dormitories, made a contribution toward a new science hall, largely financed a new library, and endowed the department of engineering.[63] In general, however, the colleges were unsuccessful in winning financial support from Chinese benefactors, and the Chinese Protestant churches were too small and too poor to give support. A partial explanation for the lack of Chinese support was that many of the alumni worked for mission institutions and were financially unable to make large contributions to the colleges. The larger eastern colleges charged high tuition fees and had a low proportion of Christian students on reduced or free tuition, and so they secured approximately one-third to one-half of their educational income from student fees. The other colleges received thirty percent or less from tuition fees.

The burden of support lay with the mission societies, which contributed 63 percent of the educational expenses. Some societies were faced with the responsibility for several colleges, each trying to raise its standards to that of a fully accredited institution of higher learning. Eleven mission boards gave support to three or more institutions. If one includes the theological seminaries and the medical colleges as well as the arts colleges, the following statistics are obtained: the American Presbyterians (North) supported nine institutions in China; the Methodists (North, U.S.A.), seven; the London Mission (Great Britain, Congregational), six; the Church Missionary Society (Anglican), six; and Congregational (U.S.A.), five. Colleges found themselves competing for the inadequate funds of the boards. Mission societies found themselves committed to devoting a larger portion

[63] Pott, "St. John's University," *ER*, IX (1917), 128–130.

of their income to educational purposes than they felt justified. Little wonder that the Christian colleges had difficulty securing the funds necessary to raise their academic standards. Little wonder that pleas for union recurred with predictable regularity.

Academic Standards

To determine the level of education offered by the Christian colleges in China is not easy. Enough has been said concerning the training of the teachers, the library holdings and laboratory facilities, and the proportion of students in the upper classes to indicate that most of the schools did not equal the small denominational colleges in the United States. On the other hand, the Christian educators were genuinely concerned with raising academic standards and much was accomplished during the first quarter of the twentieth century. In 1900 most of the colleges had been overshadowed by their attached middle schools, and the atmosphere and quality of work given in the colleges resembled those of a middle school. In 1925 several of the colleges had no attached middle schools; in many of the others the work was now carried on separately. Though missionary educators still cautioned against subordinating education to evangelism, the need for the Christian colleges to raise their academic standards was increasingly recognized by mission societies both in China and the West. Throughout this period the colleges were raising their entrance requirements and lengthening the course of study. St. John's changed its college course from three to four years in 1904, and in 1914–1915 raised the entrance requirements of the preparatory department and of the college one year; in 1919 the University of Nanking for the first time required formal, written examinations for entrance; and Yali, when it failed to attract well prepared students, organized a preparatory department rather than lower the level of the first-year work in college.[64]

The wide variation in education offered by the middle schools was a serious obstacle to the maintenance of educational standards. Some Christian middle schools were well run and efficient, whereas

[64] St. John's College, *Annual Report, 1905–1906*, p. 7; Pott, "History," *St. John's*, p. 19; Lamberton, *St. John's*, pp. 82–83; University of Nanking, *Report of the President, 1918–19*, p. 11; Bernard Upward, "University Missions in China," *CMYB*, 1911, p. 157.

others were poorly equipped, with inadequately trained teachers and administrators. Though the CCEA attempted to set up a uniform curriculum for the middle schools and uniform college entrance requirements, effective coordination was thwarted by denominational and national differences and by the variation between the schools stressing English and those emphasizing Chinese. The standard of education in the government middle schools was still more uneven. To lessen the difference in the qualifications of their entrants, some Christian colleges offered preparatory courses emphasizing English and the sciences; others drew up lists of accredited middle schools from which graduates might gain admission to college without examination.

The China Association for Christian Higher Education began in 1924 to establish minimum standards and to issue ratings to the Christian colleges.[65] On the basis of requirements close to but slightly below those of accrediting agencies in the United States, the Christian educators worked out the following ratings: Class A (fully up to minimum standards), 4 colleges; Class B (slightly below minimum standards), 5 colleges; Class C (considerably below minimum standards), 2 colleges; and no rating (too low to permit rating), 5 colleges. The ratings of the individual colleges were not made public, but were for the benefit of the institutions themselves, to stimulate greater effort to raise standards.

Another rating of the Christian colleges during the 1920's is available. In 1928 Yoshi S. Kuno of the University of California issued a work discussing educational institutions in East Asia and their standing with relation to the acceptance of their graduates by universities in the United States.[66] Although his study was based partially on the curricula and equipment of the colleges, he gave especial emphasis to the number of years required for graduation and to the records of graduates who studied in American schools. Analysis of the basis for his assessments indicates that he may have underestimated the

[65] A list of the requirements is given in Earl H. Cressy, *Minimum Standards for Christian Colleges in China*, CCEA Bulletin no. 21 (Shanghai, 1927), pp. 1–8.

[66] Yoshi S. Kuno, *Educational Institutions in the Orient with Special Reference to Colleges and Universities in the U.S.*, Part II, "Chinese Educational Institutions: A Preliminary Statement" (Berkeley, 1928). The ratings are on pages 56–66.

importance of adequate training in the English language and that he may sometimes have taken the announcements of the government universities for accomplishments. Disruption of some of the government institutions by political and military activities frequently led to a significant gap between catalogue prospectus and academic achievement; this was less likely to be true in the Christian colleges before 1927. Nevertheless, Kuno's ratings seem to have considerable validity.

Of the Christian colleges Kuno gave only the University of Nanking and Yenching University after 1925 a Class A or B rating, that is, their graduates might be permitted to enter graduate schools in the United States without deficiencies. Seven government institutions received this rating. A Class C rating was given to Huachung University, Ginling College, Canton Christian College, Shanghai University, St. John's University, Yale-in-China after 1926, Yenching before 1925, and Shantung Christian University. Graduates of these schools might be admitted to graduate schools in the United States with deficiencies of thirty undergraduate units. According to Kuno, college administrators in the United States would generally accord St. John's and Ginling a higher standing than that he had given.[67] Graduates of other Christian colleges in China, thought Kuno, should only be admitted as undergraduates, some to the junior or senior classes, others as sophomores. Kuno thus considered the majority of the Christian colleges below the standard of their counterparts in the West; on the other hand, it is indicative of the gains made by many of the Christian colleges between 1915 and 1925 that Kuno would have the ratings apply only to graduates in 1925 or after. Earlier graduates of practically all the institutions, said Kuno, should be accorded undergraduate status in United States colleges.

The Christian colleges might not have attained the standards desired, but during the first quarter of the twentieth century they had expanded their faculties and facilities. They were more numerous in 1925 and they enrolled almost 3,500 college students instead

[67] *Ibid.*, pp. 69–70. A significant percentage of the Chinese students who studied in the U.S. between 1900 and 1925 were from St. John's and their record in comparison with the records of students from other Chinese institutions would also seem to indicate a higher rating for St. John's than Kuno has given. See Chapter XIII. St. John's did suffer from some disruption during the 1920's.

of less than two hundred as in 1900. Most of the schools had charged little or no tuition at the beginning of the century and had concentrated on serving the Christian community; though there were still a few institutions of this type in 1925, most of the colleges required substantial fees and drew their students from a constituency extending beyond the Christian community. In one respect, however, the institutions had not changed greatly. They were, as in 1900, under the dominance of Westerners; both financial support and policy decisions were the responsibility of mission societies in the West. Missionary educators generally looked to Western institutions rather than Chinese ones for their guides, and standards of achievement were determined in comparison with Western schools. Changes in curriculum, faculty, and administration, there had been, but changes which required altering the role of the Westerners or the practices of the mission societies had been few. The schools had been looked upon by Chinese as foreign Christian institutions in 1900; they evoked a similar image in 1925. China, however, had changed, and what had been accepted or tolerated in 1900 would be challenged by Chinese nationalists during the 1920's.

VII | The Challenge of Chinese Nationalism, 1919-1930

The decade of the 1920's was crucial for the China Christian colleges, as it was for China as a civilization and as a political entity. In 1920 the Christian colleges were, in many ways, foreign institutions operating outside the national educational system; by 1930 most of the missionary educators had acknowledged the right of the government to supervise all educational institutions in China, both public and private; Christian educators were, furthermore, reorganizing their programs to meet standards set by the Chinese Ministry of Education. In 1920 Westerners generally determined the policy of the colleges and administered the educational program; by 1930 most of the schools were under a dual administration, Chinese and Western. Until 1920 the history of the colleges could be told largely on the basis of Western sources, and their history might be considered one aspect of the history of Christian missions in China. After 1920 the life of the institutions became intertwined with the decisive events of modern Chinese history: the search for a viable Sino-Western synthesis, the Japanese invasion, and the conflict between the Kuomintang and the Chinese Communist Party.

The Anti-Christian Movement and the Restore Educational Rights campaign during the 1920's, for example, deeply affected the organization and role of the Christian colleges in China; and they also aided educated Chinese in their definition of the Chinese nation. The movements illustrate the growing popularity of leftist ideologies among young Chinese intellectuals and the effective use of nationalist appeals by Chinese communist groups. Study of the two movements clarifies the essentially negative emphasis of Chinese nationalism during the 1920's. The tradition of confrontation politics, exemplified by students in the May 4th Movement, is substantiated.

The Separate Educational Communities

Certainly the life of the Christian colleges had been linked with political and cultural changes in China before the 1920's, but generally the mission schools had maintained only limited contact with the Chinese educational community. Christian educators, however, had good reason to seek government recognition of their work, and some had sought such recognition without success. After the abolition of the traditional examinations in 1905, graduation from a modern school was made an avenue to government position. The Christian schools were not, however, recognized by the government, and graduates of mission schools were not accorded the privileges of graduates from government institutions. Until 1911, graduates of national colleges received literary degrees from the government and were enfranchised for the election of provincial assemblies, but not Christian college alumni. When students returned to China from study abroad, they were permitted to take examinations leading to government appointment, but graduates of Christian colleges were said to have been barred from government examinations on occasion.[1] The prohibitions do not seem to have been strictly enforced, since there was no religious qualification for the examinations held for returned students in 1906, and many of the students who went abroad on government scholarships were from Christian middle schools and colleges.

Missionaries were unhappy, nevertheless, that their protégés were not accorded the same status as graduates of public schools. They did not wish Chinese Christians to attend government schools, where there were bi-monthly ceremonies honoring Confucius, and Confucianism was taught. They preferred that Chinese Christians attend mission schools, where they could receive Christian instruction. After 1905, therefore, some of the missionary educators decided that the Christian colleges should seek government recognition, and they proposed to register their schools with the imperial administration.

Several missionaries approached W. W. Rockhill, the United

[1] Kuo, *Chinese Education*, p. 138; Gilbert Reid, "The Chinese Government and Education," *ER*, II (1909), 5–6.

States minister at Peking, for advice on procedure in applying for government recognition of Christian schools. Though Rockhill recommended that the Christian educational association confer directly with the government board of education, the missionaries preferred diplomatic channels. Accordingly, in a petition delivered by the British and American ministers to the Chinese government, the missionaries expressed willingness to conform to the regulations of the board and to submit to government inspection.[2] In return, they asked that graduates from missionary schools and colleges be entitled to all rights and privileges accorded graduates of government institutions. Recognition was not granted. The reply to a similar petition by missionaries in Fukien stated: "The Board of Education in Peking has issued definite instructions to the effect that no mission or other schools controlled or established by foreigners will be allowed to be registered at the Board, nor recognition be vouchsafed to the graduates, on the ground that China does not wish to encourage foreign interference in her education, as it may have the effect of hindering the attainment of extraterritorial abolition."[3] The Chinese government obviously regarded the mission schools as foreign institutions with extraterritorial rights and refused to classify the Christian colleges along with the private Chinese schools. Since it did not feel powerful enough to control the mission institutions, it attempted to ignore them. The fact that the Christian educational association had sent its petition through the American and British ministers did little to dispel the belief that the schools were alien institutions under Western protection.

Some missionaries had opposed the attempt to secure government recognition on the grounds that it would restrict the freedom of the schools and contribute to their secularization; when the Chinese government turned a cold shoulder, the Westerners were not inclined to pursue the matter. Chinese Christians, in contrast, were not content to leave the status of mission schools and their graduates unaltered. At the 1909 meeting of the CCEA, Fong F. Sec of the Commercial Press urged missionary educators to cooperate with the Chinese government. He argued that missionaries must register

[2] A. S. Mann, "Foreign Schools and the Chinese Government," *CR*, XXXVII (1906), 147; F. L. H. Pott, "Education," *CCMC, Records,* 1907, p. 74.

[3] "Educational Department," *CR*, XXXVIII (1907), 104.

their schools if the schools were to continue work in China. A similar recommendation was presented to the same meeting by a group of Chinese educators.[4] They considered it a real hardship that a Christian preparing for government service should have to enter a government school where Confucian ceremonies were held, and they were distressed that mission school graduates had not been included among the recently enfranchised groups. The association referred the subject to its executive committee, and there the matter rested for several years. During the decade 1911–1921, the republican government issued several sets of regulations providing for official registration and recognition of private schools, but did not enforce them. Though the Chinese Christians were interested in clarifying the status of mission schools, neither the Westerners nor the Chinese government seemed to consider action urgent.

Toward Confrontation Politics

After 1917, however, events in China moved rapidly to make the separate and special position of the Christian schools untenable. Chinese who had pinned their hopes for China's salvation on political revolution were becoming disillusioned. Not increasing strength and unity, but continued disintegration characterized China. Young intellectuals and students, seeking to displace an eroding gentry class, thought of themselves as spokesmen for China, and began to call for revolution. They entered a time of searching and of destruction, a time when, it might be said, real ideological revolution occurred. In the intellectual ferment no doctrine was too sacred to be questioned; no philosophy seemed too outlandish to receive serious consideration. The intellectual atmosphere included so many extremes as to make it difficult to characterize; iconoclasm and nationalism, however, left their mark on almost every program or demonstration.

At the core of Chinese nationalism were anti-imperialism and anticapitalism. Chinese intellectuals were first defining China in terms of what she was not, and they generally agreed that she was not to be the China of tradition. But just as surely, she was not to

[4] Sec, "The Cooperation of Chinese and Foreign Educationalists in the Work of the Association" and "Appeal of Chinese Educationalists to the Educational Association," *Records, EAC, 1909*, pp. 60, 69–70.

be simply a replica of the West. Though many aspects of Western civilization were considered essential to the new China, China as a nation was being defined in contradistinction to Western civilization, nation-states, and ideologies. For a number of Chinese intellectuals, the rejection of Christianity was part of the process of defining China, as well as part of the search for a guide for China; two movements, one directed against Christianity and one directed against the mission schools, expressed the negative nationalism of the 1920's. Government regulation of Christian schools was a primary goal of the second movement. Though the nationalism of the 1920's seems inchoate and lacking in positive content, a comparison of the anti-Christian movements of this decade with the Boxer Rebellion points up the dramatic and drastic changes which had occurred in China since 1900. The Boxer Rebellion, led by traditionalists in the name of orthodoxy, had the support of many peasants and the opposition of many progressive officials and intellectuals. It was a protest against disruption of Chinese tradition by foreigners. By the 1920's the national consciousness of educated and articulate Chinese had grown perceptibly, and the anti-Christian movements were launched in the name of antitraditionalism. Initiated by radicals committed to change, the movements found support among urban, academic groups.

Both the *pai hua* movement to give literary status to vernacular Chinese and the May 4th Movement against the Versailles settlement were influential in the origins of the anti-Christian campaigns. Chinese intellectuals in general assumed that education should be an instrument of China's salvation. It should be the principal means of creating a nationally conscious citizenry, of helping the masses achieve a sense of identity and of self-respect as Chinese. It should lay the foundation for the social and ideological revolution which must precede successful political revolution. Education should be made available to all. Textbooks and literature should have relevance to every day life and should be written in a language which the people were capable of mastering in a few years. Chinese scholars thus began to seek to adapt the Chinese language to the needs of modern China.

During the nineteenth century when the missionaries had worked primarily with the poor and illiterate, they had faced similar problems in their attempt to achieve a literate church membership, and they had tried several solutions. They had, for example, translated books of the Bible and Christian tracts into romanized dialects and into the vernacular. A few Christian educators had even predicted that the vernacular would eventually replace classical Chinese as the literary language and had required their students to learn to write essays in the vernacular.[5] Chinese scholars, however, had generally considered all Christian works, both those in the vernacular and those in classical style, crude and foreignized, and the works had received scant attention among educated groups.

In a series of articles between 1916 and 1918, the scholars Hu Shih and Ch'en Tu-hsiu advocated using the vernacular as the literary language of China.[6] Among the arguments in favor of *pai hua,* several reveal the national consciousness of the proponents and the national purpose of the campaign. Hu Shih, for example, emphasized the need for one spoken language to help unify China; this could be achieved only if *pai hua* were accepted as the national literary language, he thought. Only through the adoption of *pai hua* could China hope to emancipate Chinese scholarship from the Confucian heritage. The movement gained adherents with amazing rapidity, and vernacular editions of the Bible suddenly became popular as models for intellectuals attempting to write in *pai hua.*[7] In 1922 the Ministry of Education ordered that all elementary and secondary school texts be written in the vernacular.

The adoption of *pai hua* did apparently make it easier to substitute Chinese for English as the language for textbooks and lectures on Western subjects. Government universities which had previously used English in many science courses began to use the Chinese vernacular, but the switch to Chinese as a medium of instruction

[5] C. W. Mateer, "What is the best course of study for a mission school in China?" *Records, EAC, 1896,* p. 51; J. C. Ferguson, "Chinese Studies," *Records, EAC, 1899,* p. 74.

[6] Hu Shih (Suh Hu), "The Problem of the Chinese Language," *The Chinese Students' Monthly,* XI (1915–1916), 567–572; Hu Shih, "Wen-hsüeh kai-liang ch'u-i" (Some Tentative Suggestions for the Reform of Chinese Literature), *Hsin ch'ing-nien,* II, no. 5, pp. 1–11; also, Ch'en Tu-hsiu, "Wen-hsüeh ko-ming lun" (On Literary Revolution), no. 6, pp. 1–4; Hu Shih, "Chien-she ti wen-hsüeh ko-ming lun" (On Constructive Revolution in Chinese Literature), IV, no. 4, pp. 290–306.

[7] Hu Shih, *The Chinese Renaissance* (Chicago, 1934), p. 54.

was slower and more difficult in the Christian colleges. As long as Westerners or Christian college alumni whose training had been largely in English taught most science courses, they found it easier to continue to use English. Students who had enrolled in mission schools with the express purpose of mastering the English language resisted any diminution of emphasis on English, and the colleges had difficulty attracting outstanding teachers and scholars in Chinese language and literature. Increasingly, the teaching of Chinese in the Christian colleges was criticized as outdated and inadequate; and the inadequacies of Christian college students and faculty in Chinese became cause for reproach. Since such criticisms carried nationalist undertones, they contained a sting which other curricular criticisms lacked, and their emotional dimension gave them a potential for widespread appeal. In the minds of some Chinese, the *pai hua* movement sharpened the contrast between the government universities as centers of Chinese nationalism and the Christian colleges as foreign institutions.

The May 4th Movement of 1919 likewise heightened nationalism among educated Chinese and placed the Christian colleges in an unfavorable light.[8] It demonstrated the power of nationalist appeals in urban China and raised by several decibels the anti-imperialist and anti-Western content of Chinese nationalism. Even before Versailles, the image of the West had been tarnished by the awesome tragedy of total war. That such a war should occur at all was catastrophic; that the peace settlement should bring injury, not benefit to China deepened the disillusionment. The decision to allow Japan to retain the German concessions in Shantung set up shock waves among New Youth. Some intellectual leaders accepted the Marxist interpretation of the war as a struggle of imperialists;[9] even if they

[8] The standard monograph is Chow Tse-tsung, *The May Fourth Movement, Intellectual Revolution in China;* earlier works are Chiang Wen-han (Kiang Wen-han), *The Ideological Background of the Chinese Student Movement* (New York, 1948) and Tsi C. Wang, *The Youth Movement in China* (New York, 1927).

[9] Li Ta-chao, "Bolshevism ti sheng-li" (The Victory of Bolshevism), *Hsin ch'ing-nien*, V, no. 5, pp. 442–448, trans. in Teng and Fairbank, *China's Response*, pp. 246–249. One indication of the influence of Marxist theory after the Russian revolution is the fact that a magazine such as the *Tung-fang tsa-chih* ran articles on Lenin, Kautsky, socialism, etc., through the 1920's and that articles on many subjects refer to socialist writers and incorporate socialist

continued to advocate modernization, they wanted a highly selective borrowing from the West. Heartened by the example of the Bolshevik Revolution, they showed a readiness to accept heterodox or left-wing ideologies from the West and to criticize the more orthodox democratic and liberal programs. Though few committed themselves wholly to communism, translations of Lenin's writings on imperialism were issued, and the vocabulary of Marxism was on the tip of many tongues. All used the umbrella of nationalism to shelter their ideas. The May 4th Movement had made the students acutely aware of the popularity of the nationalist issue and of the political influence they could exercise by making use of this appeal. With the corruption of the Peking regime and the closing of traditional avenues to state service, educated Chinese had felt frustrated in their attempts to make their voices heard. The government's acceptance of the demonstrators' demands, however, encouraged students to believe that they had discovered in demonstrations, strikes, and boycotts substitute techniques by which they could act as formulators of public opinion in China, and the traditional Chinese concept of the superiority of men to law helped justify their use of such techniques. Confrontation politics was to become a significant factor in student-government relations.

At the same time, government arrests had enhanced the sense of cohesion among students and young intellectuals, and the founding of numerous organizations had increased the means for concerted action. Student unions had been established in the major cities of China and had united in a parent Student Union of the Republic of China (Chung-hua min-kuo hsüeh-sheng lien-ho-hui). The youths thus had the mechanism for starting protest movements which could quickly and easily be taken up by students throughout China. They also had means of broadcasting their demands, for they established magazines and newspapers on the slightest pretext.[10] Though Chinese teachers and students were split many ways by their competing

---

theories. See, for example, Sun Sho-chang, "Nung-yeh yü chung-kuo" (Agriculture and China), XX, no. 17, pp. 17–30, where there is frequent reference to Kautsky; also the series of articles on Lenin and socialism at the time of Lenin's death, XXI, nos. 3 and 6.

[10] Chow Tse-tsung, *Research Guide to the May Fourth Movement* (Cambridge, Mass.; 1963) lists 587 new magazines founded in China between 1915 and 1923.

programs for China's salvation, most of them were concentrated in a few urban centers and remained in frequent contact. A campaign in the name of nationalism could readily gain the support of numerous groups with their ready-made instruments of influence and propaganda. Even a protest confined to one institution could often be effective as the students learned to use the power of the student union and the issues of nationalism and group loyalty. Student strikes and direct action became frequent occurrences. Though many strikes concerned political matters, they at times degenerated into strikes over internal school affairs.

At first, the May 4 demonstration had been welcomed by certain students and administrators in the Christian colleges as an opportunity to show their support of Chinese nationalism and their common cause with the academic community. As the movement expanded and student activities continued to disrupt academic routine, however, Christian college administrators lost their enthusiasm and exerted pressure to keep the students in the classrooms. The net effect of the movement for the Christian colleges was to call attention to their special position among Chinese educational institutions. Students at many of the Christian colleges participated in the initial demonstrations in May and June of 1919, and classes and examinations were temporarily suspended. At Foochow, government and mission school students formed a league whose president and secretary were both from Fukien Christian University.[11] One of two delegates sent from Peking to Shanghai to help organize a national student council was a student in the School of Theology of Peking (Methodist) University.[12] The president of the University of Nanking praised the participation of his students in the hope that it had "demonstrated to the public . . . the patriotic loyalty, the effective leadership, and the unselfish devotion of mission students."[13]

At St. John's students received permission to go on strike, and for approximately ten days in early June 1919 they held campus meetings twice a day, published a daily newspaper, and conducted educational campaigns in neighboring villages. In time, St. John's

[11] Fukien Christian University, *Report of the President, 1919*, p. 2.
[12] Peking University, *Annual Report, 1918–19*, p. 5.
[13] University of Nanking, *Report of the President, 1918–19*, p. 3.

administrators began to feel that the student activities were placing the school in an embarrassing position: here was an institution on Chinese soil with extraterritorial rights, and its students were using the campus for a campaign against government officials and policies. When the students requested suspension of academic work for the rest of the term so that they could give full time to political activities, the administration ended the academic year and closed the school without examinations or graduation ceremonies. Six months later, Shanghai students called a four-day strike to protest injury to a group of Foochow students by a crowd of Japanese and Koreans. The faculty of St. John's refused on this occasion to sanction the movement by formally suspending classes. Though the teachers went to their classrooms, the students did not; rather, they demonstrated in Shanghai. No disciplinary action was taken against the students, and classes were resumed at the end of the four-day period. Another strike was called by the national student union in April 1920 to express opposition to the opening of negotiations with Japan on the Shantung question. In this third *hsüeh-ch'ao*, the St. John's administration not only refused to authorize the strike, but they forbade demonstrations on campus and required participating students to leave campus and reside elsewhere for the duration of the strike. Since only eight students remained in residence, academic work was disrupted for three weeks.[14]

Other Christian college administrators had similar experiences. Students at Hangchow Christian College participated in the strikes of May and June, 1919, and in demonstrations during the fall, but later, when the student union ordered a strike on what the missionaries considered "obscure issues," the faculty forbade the strike. Seventy or more students left school and only about half of these eventually returned. The president called the affair a severe blow to the institution.[15] When Cheeloo had an administrative shake-up in 1919 and the president and deans were asked to resign, the theology students from the Presbyterian missions demanded reinstatement of the dean of the College of Theology and withdrew from school when this was refused. Only with much persuasion were

[14] Pott, "History," *St. John's*, pp. 29–30; Lamberton, *St. John's*, pp. 77–81.
[15] Hangchow Christian College, *Report of the President, 1919–20*, p. 10.

the Presbyterian students in the arts college prevented from following suit.[16] Even the girls at Ginling caught the independent spirit and, when founding a student government association, demanded extensive privileges and few restrictions. Taking authority into their own hands, they treated the dormitory matron like a servant and requested her dismissal. The president of the college, Mrs. Thurston, was finally forced to replace the matron with a housekeeper of less education and of lower social class.[17]

Each new student storm seems to have diminished the readiness of school authorities to give sympathetic support. They resented the influence which the national student union could exercise over the students, and they were concerned over the irresponsible use of demonstrations and strikes. Since the Christian college administrators were not subject to the same political pressures as their counterparts in the government institutions, they generally had greater success in maintaining discipline among their students. The level of academic work in the Christian colleges was, therefore, frequently above that of the government schools during the 1920's. At the same time, their insistence that study, rather than politics, was the first duty of the student and their attempt to maintain a neutral position on political questions caused misunderstandings and alienation. Some Chinese Christians argued that it was a mistake for the mission colleges to attempt to carry on their work as if the situation were normal; these Chinese believed that under the circumstances the students were serving a more useful function in arousing and educating the populace than in pursuing their studies.[18] When the missionary educators for academic reasons refused to sanction participation in some of the patriotic demonstrations, numerous Chinese interpreted it as an attempt by foreigners to quell nationalism. Lei Ying-lam, secretary of the Canton YMCA and later president of Lingnan University, stated in an address before the 1925 missionary conference of Kwangtung: "In the last two years there were many open demonstrations against outside countries or for home affairs.

[16] Corbett, *Shantung*, pp. 139–143.

[17] Thurston, *Ginling College*, pp. 30–32.

[18] Timothy Tingfang Lew, "Some of the Factors, Dangers, and Problems in the Christian Missionary Enterprise in China Today through Chinese Eyes," *The Foreign Missions Conference of North America, 1927* (New York, 1927), p. 257.

The students of the Christian schools were found absent practically on every occasion. This has increased the bad feeling of the government school students." [19]

The Anti-Christian Movement of 1922

Interestingly enough, one of the earliest antireligious movements led by young intellectuals during the twentieth century was directed against Confucianism and not Christianity. There is, however, kinship between the anti-Confucian campaign of 1916–1919 and the Anti-Christian Movement of 1922. Both were led by Chinese who had rejected much of the Chinese heritage, not by traditionalists, and both were part of China's national identity crisis. Many of the arguments which were formulated in the attack on Confucianism were later used in the anti-Christian movements. It was the writing of a constitution for the new republic in 1913 that stirred up controversy over the status of Confucianism. Though supporters of Confucianism argued for its establishment as a state religion, they were only able to secure a statement that Confucian principles should be the basis for character training in national education. Then, in 1916 such conservative reformers as Yen Fu, Liang Ch'i-ch'ao, Ch'en Huan-chang, and Hsia Tseng-yu sent to parliament a "Petition to Establish Confucianism as a State Religion." [20] According to the petition, Confucianism had been the basis for Chinese morality since the time of the sage emperors and in the present era of ethical chaos it was imperative that China return to her national foundations. In Confucianism could be found that national essence which distin-

[19] Y. L. Lee (Lee Ying-lam), "The Anti-Christian Movement in China," *CR*, LVI (1925), 221.

[20] An English translation of the petition is available in the *National Review*, Shanghai, XIV, 392–393. For the arguments of K'ang Yu-wei, see *Ni chung-hua min-kuo hsien-fa ts'ao-an* (A Proposed Draft Constitution for the Republic of China), 2d printing (Shanghai, 1916), esp. pp. 1–5, 134–140, and "K'ang Nan-hai chih Tsung-t'ung Tsung-li shu" (Letter from K'ang Yu-wei to the President and Premier), *K'ung-chiao wen-t'i* (Problems of Confucianism), no. 17, supplement (Taiyuan, 1916). I have drawn on the following sources in my discussion: Chow Tse-tsung, "The Anti-Confucian Movement in Early Republican China," *The Confucian Persuasion*, ed. Arthur F. Wright (Stanford, 1960); and Joseph R. Levenson, *Confucian China and its Modern Fate*, vol. II, *The Problem of Monarchical Decay* (Berkeley, 1964), esp. pp. 10–21, 119–130.

guished China from other nations. With the argument that most of the great Western powers had a national religion came the clear implication that a unifying ideology was an essential source of strength for nation states.

Though they clothed their ideas in nationalist garb, the Confucianists met strenuous opposition. Critics included leaders of the New Culture Movement, in addition to Protestant, Catholic, and other religious groups. While Christians denounced the Confucianists in the name of religious freedom, the young intellectuals launched their attacks as part of their crusade against the Chinese heritage. The influential magazine *Hsin ch'ing-nien* directed attention to the issue in articles by Wu Yü, Ch'en Tu-hsiu, and Yi Pai-sha between 1916 and 1919.[21] Confucianism, it was argued, was the product of a feudal society; the ethical principles it taught were, therefore, inappropriate to modern society. Since Confucianism emphasized inequalities and insisted on obedience by subordinate groups such as youth and women, it could never serve as the ideology of revolution. Sharp attacks on filial piety lashed out at the power and conservatism of the older generation. In 1918 Lu Hsün (Chou Shu-jen) published in *Hsin ch'ing-nien* his first short story, "K'uang-jen jih-chi" (The Diary of a Madman); the satire was a vicious condemnation of Chinese tradition, which consumed its members; hope for China lay with its children, who had not yet learned cannibalism.

The attack on Confucianism broadened into an attack on religion in general and then into one on the Christian schools in what were perhaps logical steps. Critics of tradition had already begun to condemn faith in the existence of spirits and in the immortality of the soul. In 1918 one of the editors of *Hsin ch'ing-nien* planted a letter inquiring why the magazine concentrated its assault on Confucianism and ignored Western religions; another editor, Liu Fu, replied that the poison spread by Confucianism was so much greater than that spread by Western religions that discussion of the latter could

[21] See Yi Pai-sha, "K'ung-tzu p'ing-i" (A Discussion of Confucius), *Hsin ch'ing-nien*, I, no. 6; II, no. 1; Ch'en Tu-hsiu, "K'ung-tzu chih tao yü hsien-tai sheng-huo" (Confucius' Principles and Modern Life), II, no. 4, and "Tsai lun K'ung-chiao wen-t'i" (Another Discussion of the Problem of Confucianism), II, no. 5; Wu Yü, "Chia-tsu chih-tu wei chuan-chih-chu-i chih ken-chü lun" (The Old Family and Clan System is the Basis of Despotism), II, no. 6.

be postponed.[22] The Young China Association (Shao-nien chung-kuo hsüeh-hui), a loose association of anti-imperialist nationalists, initiated a campaign for criticism of all religions and helped prepare for a movement specifically against Christianity. Founded in 1918, the association had as its stated purpose the creation of a new China through emphasis on social service under the guidance of the scientific spirit, and it began in 1919 to publish its own organ, *Shao-nien chung-kuo* (Young China). A significant number of its leaders received part of their education abroad, particularly in France and Japan; among its influential members were Li Huang, Li Ta-chao, Tseng Ch'i, and Chou T'ai-hsüan.

In 1920 Li Huang and other members of the Young China Association studying in Paris sent to the Peking executive committee a recommendation that persons with religious faith be excluded from membership in the organization.[23] Following a number of protests, the association in 1921 canceled the resolution and began an investigation into the religious question. The results of the research were hardly calculated to bolster the position of religion; instead, the young intellectuals became acutely aware that religion was under attack in the West. Early in 1921 several members of the association in France sent a circular letter to University of Paris professors asking about the compatibility of religion and modern society and about China's need for religion. They received replies from Marcel Granet, professor of Chinese history at the Sorbonne; Henri Barbusse, novelist; and Célestin Bouglé, professor of sociology and social philosophy at the Sorbonne; and all three answers were negative. Religion, the French scholars said, might have been necessary for primitive man, but it was no longer needed by modern man; religion had been discredited by science.[24] Bertrand Russell was at this time (1920–

---

[22] Wang Ching-hsüan, "Wen-hsüeh ko-ming chih fan-hsiang" (A Reaction to the Literary Revolution), *Hsin ch'ing-nien*, IV, no. 3, pp. 265–268. The answer of Liu Fu follows on pp. 268–285. Chow Tse-tsung, *May Fourth Movement*, p. 321, is authority for the statement that the letter was by Ch'ien Hsüan-t'ung though it was signed Wang Ching-hsüan.

[23] Chang Ch'in-shih, *Kuo-nei chin-shih-nien-lai chih tsung-chiao ssu-ch'ao* (The Tide of Religious Thought in China during the last Decade) (Peking, 1927), pp. 184 (cited as Chang, *TCSC*). This collection includes many of the important documents of the anti-Christian movements.

[24] *Ibid.*, pp. 147–154.

1921) lecturing in China and building up a wide following through his addresses and translations of his works. He argued that modern society had no use for religion, which encouraged strife, reinforced the status quo, handicapped individual development, and substituted the emotions for objective evidence. The Young China Association published Russell's statements on religion along with its other findings in a series of three issues devoted to the religious question.[25] Other magazines, especially *Hsin ch'ing-nien*, took up the matter.

Between 1919 and 1922 articles specifically attacking Christianity had also been published. Christianity was condemned as an outdated superstition, the agent of imperialism, and the enemy of the Chinese nation in a special edition of the *Canton Times*, called the "Jesus Number," published on Christmas Eve, 1919; similar criticisms were made in an issue on Jesus in *Min hua chou pao* (The Mind of the People) published in Shanghai in 1920.[26] In the same year, Ch'en Tu-hsiu, searching for an ideology for new China, had briefly considered Christianity in an article entitled "Chi-tu-chiao yü chung-kuo-jen" (Christianity and the Chinese People). Though critical of the church, its doctrines, and missionary activities, Ch'en had found the teachings and personality of Jesus attractive. Perhaps, he thought, one of the major sources of Western power and greatness lay in the ethical teachings of Christ. Rebuttal came from Shen Ting-i, who was soon to join Ch'en in founding the Chinese Communist Party. According to Shen, the new China would have no use for any religion, certainly not a foreign one.[27]

An article which was to be widely reprinted during the anti-

[25] *Shao-nien chung-kuo*, II, no. 8 (Feb. 1921); II, no. 11 (May 1921); and III, no. 1 (Aug. 1921). See also, Russell's report on his visit to China, *The Problem of China* (New York, 1922). Some of the other leading magazines publishing articles on religion during 1920–1921 were: *Hsin chiao-yü* (New Education), *Philosophia*, and *Chüeh-wu* (The Awakening).

[26] Wang, *The Youth Movement*, pp. 192–193.

[27] For Ch'en's article, see *Hsin ch'ing-nien*, VII, no. 3. Translated selections from this article and a discussion of Ch'en's attitude toward Christianity are in Jessie G. Lutz, ed., *Christian Missions in China, Evangelists of What?* (Boston, 1965). Ch'en was not so much seeking a personal faith as a national ideology to guide a new China. Shen Hsüan-lu (Shen Ting-i), "Tui-yü 'Chi-tu-chiao yü chung-kuo-jen' ti huai-i" (My Doubts about "Christianity and the Chinese People"), *Hsing-ch'i p'ing-lun* (Weekly Review, Shanghai), no. 36 (Feb. 8, 1920).

Christian movements was "What is Jesus?" by Chu Chih-hsin, member of the Kuomintang and manager of *Chien-she* (The Construction).[28] Chu reveals a more than passing acquaintance with Christian literature and with Western criticisms of Christianity. On the authority of the German biologist, Ernst Haeckel, he states that Jesus was the illegitimate son of Mary by a Roman centurion. He argues that trustworthy information about the historical Jesus is scant and that reliable sources reveal Jesus as "a hypocritical, selfish, narrow-minded, easily-provoked man, with a strong desire for revenge." Chu is equally critical of the Christian church. He cites Luther's turning against the German peasants as proof that the freedom and equality advocated by Christians is false, and then indicates that a comparable example of hypocrisy in the twentieth century is the attitude of Western imperialists and missionaries toward the non-Christian peoples of Asia.

The intellectual ferment and the politicization of youth during the May 4th Movement had obviously fed the anti-Christian tradition of China rather than depleted it; the young intellectuals had, in fact, added Western criticisms to Chinese anti-Christian attitudes and had already formulated many of the accusations to be heard during the campaigns of the 1920's. The movements of the 1920's were led by antitraditionalists, and they condemned Christianity in the name of nationalism and science; their motivation was more exclusively political than in the case of the Boxers, whose objections were also religious; nevertheless, many of their basic criticisms show continuity with the earlier anti-Christian tradition of China.

The response of Christians to the criticisms actually provided the spark to light the anti-Christian explosion of 1922. The World's Student Christian Federation had decided to hold its 1922 meeting at Tsing Hua University near Peking, and it devoted the January issue of its magazine, *The Student World,* to articles on the Chinese church, modern education in China, Christian education in China, and the outlook of Chinese students. Many of these articles, though written by Chinese Christians and different in tone from anti-Christian denunciations, were critical of the Chinese church and

[28] Chang, *TCSC*, pp. 23–37, The article was reprinted in *Fan-tui chi-tu-chiao yün-tung* (The Anti-Christian Movement), a pamphlet published in Shanghai in 1924 and reprinted in 1925.

of Christian education and could easily be quoted by anti-Christians. Ch'eng Ching-i, for example, complained that the Christian church in China was a foreign institution dominated by foreigners, and he called for the Sinification of the church in organization and personnel.[29] The Chinese YMCA in February 1922 also published a special edition of its magazine, *Ch'ing-nien chin-pu* (Association Progress), in preparation for the conference; this issue contained articles both on the World's Student Christian Federation and its activities in China, and on the work of the YMCA and other Christian groups among students in China.[30] It was this publication which came to the attention of a small group of Shanghai students who in response formed the *Fei chi-tu-chiao hsüeh-sheng t'ung-meng* (Anti-Christian Student Federation) and issued a manifesto on March 9, 1922. The language of the proclamation indicated that the students were under the influence of Marxist-Leninist writings on imperialism:

We are opposed to the World's Student Christian Federation. We oppose it because we are resolved to protect the welfare and happiness of humanity. . . .

We know that in the past Christianity and the Christian church have been the cause of many evils and have committed many crimes against humanity. . . .

We know that in the world today, it is Capitalism that rules. Society is organized so that there are the class of property-holders who eat without working and the class of proletarians who work without obtaining the means to eat. In other words, on one side robbers and oppressors, on the other side the robbed and oppressed. Christianity and the Christian church are the evil demons who aid the capitalists in robbing the proletarians, who encourage those who possess, to oppress those who have nothing.

[29] "The Chinese Church," *The Student World*, XV (Jan. 1922), 27–31. Ch'eng later became a leader of the Church of Christ in China, a union of several Protestant denominations in China.

[30] This issue, no. 50 (Feb. 1922), and others are available at the Day Missions Library, Yale University. *Association Progress* was the English title generally used, though a literal translation would be Progress of Youth; it was founded in March 1917 and advocated patriotism and social reform. The YMCA at this time was one of the few Christian organizations in China in which Chinese leaders played a decisive role.

We are convinced that capitalist society today, tyrannical and cruel, unreasonable and inhumane, ought to be destroyed without mercy. Consequently we declare that Christianity and the Christian church today, evil demons which aid the merchants in doing wrong, are our enemies. We must battle against them in a war to the death. . . .

The capitalists of every country . . . invade China in order to cut her to pieces and exploit her economically. And the Christian church is the head of their assault column. . . .

The World's Student Christian Federation is the offspring of the Christianity of our day. It proposes to hold a Christian conference on April 4 at Tsing Hua University in Peking. The purpose of this conference is to search for the best means to uphold world capitalism and to secure its access to China. It will thus be a congress of robbers who profane our youth, who deceive our people, and steal our money. This being so and being offended to the quick, we have formed an Anti-Christian Federation and we declare war against the Student Christian Federation.

Students! Youth! Workers! Who of you can ignore the misdeeds of capitalism? Who of you can ignore that capitalists are cruel and heartless beings? How can we fail to rise against them when we see with our own eyes their spies holding a conference for our loss? Arise! Arise! Arise! [31]

The Shanghai students sent telegrams to other schools and student organizations advocating the separation of religion and education and calling for support in their opposition to the W.S.C.F. conference. They issued a booklet entitled, "Why We Oppose the World's Student Christian Federation."

The campaign was taken up by Peking scholars who believed that the movement should be broadened to combat all religions and so adopted the name Fei tsung-chiao ta-t'ung-meng (Great Federation of Antireligionists). In their proclamations they condemned religion for teaching men obedience, which is the moral code of slaves, and for propagating superstitions, which hinder the search for truth.[32] On March 21 they sent to student groups throughout China a telegram protesting the holding of the W.S.C.F. conference at Tsing Hua. Heading the list of seventy-nine teachers and students who signed the telegram was the name of Li Shih-tseng, well-known

[31] Chang, TCSC, pp. 187–188.
[32] Quoted in Milton T. Stauffer, ed., Youth and Renaissance Movements (New York, 1923), p. 34.

anarchist, a member of the Kuomintang, and former leader of the Society for Frugal Study in France. Other anarchists, communists, and members of the Kuomintang left wing also sponsored the telegram: Ch'en Tu-hsiu, Ts'ai Yüan-p'ei, Chu Chih-hsin, Wu Chih-hui (Wu Ching-heng), Wang Ching-wei, Li Ta-chao, Hsiao Tzu-sheng, and Tai Chi-t'ao. Chinese who sympathized with the views of the antireligious federation were urged to contact Chin Chia-feng, a former anarchist who had turned to communism.

The appeal of the Peking federation fell on fertile soil. Through the existing student organizations in the major cities of China, branches of the association were founded in many middle schools and colleges. *Pei-ching ch'en-pao* (Peking Morning Post) published declarations by approximately thirty organizations that had taken up the discussion, and students at numerous government schools issued anti-Christian manifestoes. Support was also given by prominent educators, by members of the Kuomintang and the Chinese Communist Party, and by labor unions and workers' groups. Even Liang Ch'i-ch'ao welcomed the movement as a sign that the Chinese nation was awake, and he criticized Christianity for its exclusiveness and its use of education for religious purposes.[33] The Chinese government, by attempting to suppress student mass meetings, made the movement more popular.

In the midst of the storm the W.S.C.F. held its conference at Tsing Hua University from April 4 to 9. On the opening day, the Peking anti-Christian federation sent the Tsing Hua students a letter protesting the use of the facilities of a government university to aid religion. It was a shameful humiliation, they said, that the Chinese government had allowed a group of Christian students to install themselves in the capital; and it was also an offense against the principle of separation of church and state. Repeating an argument in the original manifesto of the Shanghai anti-Christian association, they stated that Christianity had so declined in the West that missionaries had to try to make up the loss by "implanting in foreign areas the remnants of their superstitions in order to prolong their parasitic existence. Their governments and big business favor these enterprises because they open the way to colonization. . . . Gold and

[33] Quoted in Léon Wieger, *Chine Moderne*, vol. III, *Remous et Écume* (Hsien-hsien, 1922), pp. 86–87.

iron make our bodies slaves of the foreigner; the Gospel enslaves our souls." [34] This condemnation was to be echoed many times during the next few months.

Chinese Christian students at the W.S.C.F. conference themselves presented a memoir to the delegates. After pointing out the gap between Christian ideals and the actions of so-called Christian nations, the students repeated popular criticisms of mission schools: the schools were isolated from Chinese life, ignored the recommendations of the Ministry of Education, and failed to keep their students abreast of current events. Their students were taught obedience to autocratic missionaries and, whether Christian or not, were forced to participate in religious ceremonies. The education which the students received was more religious than national. Though admitting that the criticisms were exaggerated, the Chinese students concluded that many accusations had some truth in them. They asked that Christian missions and schools alter their policies in order to meet the criticisms. On the last day of the congress, the antireligious federation held a mass meeting at Peking University. More than a thousand students came to hear Hsiao Tzu-sheng and Li Shih-tseng condemn religion in the name of science. A speech by Ts'ai Yüan-p'ei criticized all religions as corrupt, advocated the separation of education and religion, and defended the freedom of atheists to work against religion. [35]

The Young China Association fed the movement by publishing many of the antireligious speeches, proclamations, and telegrams; it also published a number of antireligious articles by Japanese scholars and by Chinese abroad. [36] A student in the United States, Yün Chen, wrote that the missionaries who had founded Chinese schools and

[34] *Ibid.*, pp. 42–43.

[35] Chang, *TCSC*, pp. 199–207. Sources disagree as to whether Ts'ai Yüan-p'ei was actually present or whether his speech was read by someone else. Hsiao Tzu-sheng, listed by Wieger (III, 74–75) as president of the antireligious federation, was a follower of Li Shih-tseng. He had helped found the *Hsin-min hsüeh-tseng* in France, but when it split into left and right wings in July 1920, he led the anarchist, anticommunist wing; he later became an official in the Kuomintang government, Chow, *May Fourth Movement*, pp. 249–251.

[36] Yün Chen, "Lü-mei kung-hsüeh tsa-t'an" (Comments by an engineering student abroad in America), *Shao-nien chung-kuo*, III, no. 11; Yü Chia-chü, "Chi-tu-chiao yü kan-ch'ing sheng-huo" (Christianity and the Emotional Life), *ibid.*

had created the impression that the church was an educational leader in America had painted a false picture. Most American educational institutions had no connection with the church, and most students in the United States were indifferent to religion, Yün said. Yü Chia-chü, who was to help initiate the educational rights movement against mission schools, sent an article to *Shao-nien chung-kuo* from Paris; he tried to demonstrate that religion was simply a creation of man out of his own needs and God was a projection of oneself. Other magazines and organizations focused their attention on the anti-Christian issue during the late spring and early summer.

Christians themselves probably helped keep the campaign alive by the publication in 1922 of a volume surveying the progress of Protestantism in China; its very title, *The Christian Occupation of China*, nettled many nationalists. The wording of the survey was sometimes equally tactless: "About three-fourths of China Proper is now claimed by Protestant forces, and seven provinces report no unclaimed area whatever. . . . All of the cities with populations of 50,000 or more are occupied except eighteen." [37] The volume emphasized the rapid growth of Christianity in China since 1900; it pointed out, for example, that the number of residential mission centers opened since 1900 equaled the total opened in the previous ninety-three years. One of its maps showing the location and extent of the work of the mission societies in China was reprinted by the Peking antireligious federation under the caption, "The Spreading Infection of Religious Poison." [38] The volume's optimistic tone seemed to anti-Christian Chinese to leave little room for indifference; the aggressiveness of Christian missions made active opposition necessary. Eventually, the antireligious federation collected many of the anti-Christian essays and published them in a single volume so that they could reach a wider audience. Though some government officials tried to restrain the students, especially when demonstrations seemed likely to provoke disorders, few Chinese expressed opposition to the arguments against religion or Christianity. Five Peking university professors did protest the anti-Christian activities in the name of

[37] Milton T. Stauffer, ed., *The Christian Occupation of China* (Shanghai, 1922), pp. 33–34. There was a Chinese edition as well as an English edition.
[38] C. S. Chang (Chang Ch'in-shih), "The Anti-Religious Movement," *CR*, LIV (1923), 467.

religious freedom and did raise some questions about the origins of the movement, but they were quickly answered by a telegram from the Great Federation of Antireligionists. The federation explained that it was neither antiforeign nor Bolshevik; its goal was to free the people from the fetters of religion and to foster the truth of science.[39]

Though the anti-Christian and antireligious campaign had widespread appeal among college and middle school students, the Great Federation of Antireligionists was not able to maintain a high pitch of excitement for long. After mid-1922, demonstrations and strikes declined, though anti-Christian articles continued to appear in youth magazines during the two-year interim between the anti-Christian movement in 1922 and the rise of the educational rights movement in 1924. The students divided their energies among numerous associations which were often loosely organized; when they dispersed for the summer vacation, most organizations suspended activities, and some were not revived in the fall. Though Chinese students had many associations and publications for propagating their ideas, they lacked at this time effective means for a long-term campaign or continuing political influence. Their main weapons were strikes, boycotts, and the backing of public opinion; but frequent strikes so disrupted school work that they alienated supporters among the liberal professors. Boycotts became less effective as merchants became increasingly reluctant to incur financial losses, and public opinion could be galvanized only on major and dramatic issues. Chinese youth, though critics of their own and Western civilization, were seeking a guide for the salvation of China, and the 1922 campaign was primarily negative in emphasis; it had no positive program and no immediate goals.

The campaign was of great importance in the history of the colleges, however, for it laid the foundations of the educational rights movement, a movement with specific aims and one which profoundly affected the status and function of the colleges. Literature, organizations, and attitudes fostered in the anti-Christian movement of 1922 were revived in the educational rights campaign; the two campaigns show continuity both of personnel and of *Weltanschauung*, and, making their appeals in the name of nationalism and modernization, they derived their support from the same urban, educated groups.

[39] Chang, *TCSC*, p. 198.

The 1922 Campaign: Leadership, Support, Responses

Unfortunately, little information about the leadership and support of the 1922 eruption is available, and only tentative conclusions may be presented. Much of the work of the anti-Christian association and the antireligious federation was conducted informally or in secret. Students took much of the initiative, and even when their names are available, it is not always possible to identify them; either they failed to become well known or for other reasons disappeared from the stage; often they indulged the Chinese penchant for changing names.

The March 9, 1922 manifesto of the Anti-Christian Student Federation is clearly within the context of Marxist-Leninist ideology, but the names of the founders of the association are not available, and the vocabulary of Marxism was widely popular among students at that time. Youth seeking to revolutionize China felt a sense of identity with the Russian revolutionists, and after 1917, they could easily obtain inexpensive translations of Lenin's works, especially his theses on imperialism. In Canton, for example, a "Communist Library" (a brief selection of basic communist writings) and the collected works of Marx and Lenin were published in 1921. To conclude solely from the language of the March 9 manifesto that the anti-Christian association was founded by communist groups or individuals would not seem warranted; however, additional evidence indicates that much of the initiative and early support did come from individuals and societies committed at the time to ideologies of the radical left. Left-wing groups, it may be assumed, welcomed an opportunity to attack doctrines and individuals associated with the Western capitalist powers and used the 1922 campaign to establish avenues of contact and to identify possible supporters and leaders. Ch'en Tu-hsiu and Li Ta-chao both aided in the early phases of the anti-Christian movement; and according to one source, Ch'en Tu-hsiu's article "Why do we oppose the World's Student Christian Federation?" was printed in the first publication of the Anti-Christian Student Federation.[40]

[40] Tatsuro and Sumiko Yamamoto, "The Anti-Christian Movement in China, 1922–1927," *FEQ*, XII (1953), 144. Articles about communism and by communists were popular throughout the period from 1917 to 1927. See, for example, Ch'ü Ch'iu-pai, "Li-ning yü she-hui chu-i" (Lenin and Socialism), *Tung-fang tsa-chih*, XXI, no. 6, pp. 7–32.

A colleague of Ch'en in the founding of the Chinese Communist Party, Shen Ting-i (Shen Hsüan-lu), published one of the initial attacks on Christianity and religion in the *Hsing-ch'i p'ing-lun*. The Socialist Youth Corps, an organ of the Communist Party, gave its support to both the anti-Christian and the antireligious associations; and its first national conference, held in Canton in May 1922, passed a resolution supporting the campaign.

Much of the literature and activity in Shanghai and Canton were specifically against Christianity rather than religion in general at a time when these two cities were centers of intense activity by Ch'en, Li, Gregori Voitinsky, and other communist organizers. Young China Association, which played a vital role in initiating and nourishing the campaign, had been founded as a nationalist organization, but it was by 1922 deeply influenced by individuals of the left wing and would soon split over attempts to convert it into a socialist or communist association; Li Ta-chao was one of the editors of its journal. Two early supporters of the campaign were Chin Chia-feng, secretary of the Great Federation of Antireligionists, and Tai Chi-t'ao (Tai Ch'uan-hsien), who had translated Karl Kautsky's work on Marxian economic theory into Chinese in 1919. Both these individuals followed a rather well trod path from anarchism to communism, and though communism might not be the end of their intellectual journeying, they both were in the early 1920's closely associated with Ch'en and communist organizations. Ts'ai Ho-sen, whose article on modern Christianity was widely reprinted, had been one of the founders of the Young China Communist Party (Shao-nien Chung-kuo kung-ch'an-tang) and a member of the Socialist Youth Corps in France in 1921.

In the writings of these individuals, the Marxist argument that Christianity was an instrument of the ruling capitalist class to oppress the people was frequently repeated. Ts'ai Ho-sen saw a relationship between United States leadership in supporting Christian missions and its leadership as a capitalist state; only science and socialism could overthrow the twin enemies of progress—capitalism and Christianity. "In recent years many students have come back from America to spread this ill-smelling murderous superstition among our young people. And they have dared to hold in Peking at Tsing Hua University a conference of the World's Student Christian

Federation. All you misled young people had better wake up and oppose this Federation which is only the toy dog of capitalism." [41] A manifesto issued on April 4, 1922, by socialist groups in Peking also pictured an alliance of Christianity and capitalism under United States leadership. It called on proletarians to end their submission to the slavery of militarism, capitalism, and religion, and it summoned all comrades to launch a general reform movement. "The [W.S.C.F.] Congress wishes a restoration; it shall have it. It desires it under the cross of Christ; we shall make it under the red flag. It desires a new era; it shall have it, that of communism. Arise proletarians of the entire world." [42]

Obviously, individuals and organs closely associated with communism played a prominent role in the anti-Christian campaign of 1922. Whether or not Chinese Communist Party leaders deliberately initiated the campaign in order to extend the influence of the fledgling party is an unresolved question. A number of authors who condemned Christianity within the context of Marxism-Leninism can be identified as members of the left wing, but the affiliation of many is unknown. Despite the tendency of the Chinese Communist Party today to claim the initiative for practically all the student movements of the 1920's and 1930's and despite the general use of Marxist vocabulary, the facts thus far established would seem to be that communist influence was especially important during the early part of the campaign and that much of the specifically anti-Christian literature was by left-wing authors.

Once the campaign had been launched, it quickly gained widespread support among educated urban Chinese. Praise came from individuals who were far apart in their politics as well as intellectual orientation: Liang Ch'i-ch'ao, who might be called a conservative reformer in the 1920's; Hu Shih and Ts'ai Yüan-p'ei, influential liberals of that time; Li Huang, Yü Chia-chü, and Ch'en Ch'i-t'ien, leaders of the anticommunist wing of the Young China Association; the writer Mao Tun; and such well known members of the Kuomin-

[41] For a translation of Ts'ai's article see *The Anti Christian Movement*, pp. 18–24. *Fan-tui chi-tu-chiao yün-tung* was compiled by the Fei chi-tu-chiao t'ung-meng and the Chung-kuo ch'ing-nien she and published in 1924. The translation, somewhat toned down, is by the China YMCA and YWCA and is located in MRL.

[42] Quoted in Wieger, *Chine Moderne*, III, 43–44.

tang as Wang Ching-wei and Wu Chih-hui. The veteran anarchist Li Shih-tseng was leader of the Great Federation of Antireligionists. Significant shifts in the emphasis of the movement came with the broadening of its support, however. One difference is indicated in the change in name from anti-Christian federation to antireligious federation. Another is the prominence given to the criticism of religion as antiscientific and antidemocratic. Such criticism was not new in China, but it had not been part of the Shanghai manifesto of March 9, nor was it emphasized in the left-wing articles.

The argument in the name of democracy and science was primarily a nationalist one; it had been used in the attempt to disintegrate Chinese tradition and was now being turned against elements of the Western tradition which seemed unessential to China's modernization. According to the proclamation of the Great Federation of Antireligionists, science explained the origins of mankind through evolution, but religion repeated the story of creation; China needed to concentrate on economic growth, but religion emphasized the next world and the problem of sin; man was meant to be free and equal, but religion demanded the worship of idols and subservience to one master. The federation had only one goal: the destruction of all religion in order to foster the scientific spirit.[43] Over and over again, nationalistic Chinese condemned Christianity for fostering outdated superstitions discredited by science and inhibiting the growth of freedom and equality through its exclusiveness and racial prejudice. Even when the anti-imperialist arguments of the left wing were used, the emphasis was more nationalist than anticapitalist. Undoubtedly, Chinese who had rejected much of their own heritage could derive satisfaction from condemning Christian tradition along with Confucian tradition. Putting Christianity and Confucianism in the same category, i.e., the rejected, made it possible to maintain one's self respect while advocating importations from the West.[44]

The response of Christians to the movement is instructive. Certain missionaries, especially those in close contact with students, expressed dissatisfaction at being in China under the protection of the unequal treaties. Such protection, they said, seemed to substantiate

[43] Chang, *TCSC*, pp. 193–194.
[44] This hypothesis is developed in some detail in Levenson, *Confucian China and Its Modern Fate*, I, esp. ch. ix.

the charge that missionaries were the agents of Western imperialism, and it had become an obstacle to their work. They advocated the revision of the treaties, or they stated that they as individuals no longer desired treaty protection or extraterritorial rights. Reaction along these lines was, however, rare until after the outburst of May 30, 1925. Many missionaries were hardly aware of the anti-Christian campaign of 1922; and even when anti-Christian literature and activities came to their attention, they often did not appreciate the depth and breadth of the sentiment. Either they saw nothing new in the movement and interpreted it as simply part of the long Chinese anti-Christian tradition, or they attributed the movement to a few Chinese under Bolshevik influence. At a national Christian conference held in Shanghai in July 1922, the commission on the current state of Christianity in China found that "opportunities for religious teaching in our Christian schools are practically unlimited, for nowhere is there any serious prejudice against it." [45] Upon receiving an inquiry from the British embassy about an increase in antiforeign sentiment, the United States minister to China in May 1922 requested information from United States representatives in various Chinese cities. The responses provided no evidence of heightened antiforeignism, though the American minister did add an emendation to his report: "There is no indication in Peking of anti-foreign sentiment except for an anti-Christian agitation which is regarded less as an anti-foreign outbreak than as a reassertion of Chinese civilization as opposed to occidental civilization." [46]

Ignorance or lack of concern about the Anti-Christian Movement is the more surprising since 1922 was a year in which Protestants were completing surveys of both the general missionary movement in China and the whole Christian educational program. Perhaps the missionaries were misled by the rapidity with which the anti-Christian campaign subsided; more significant as the source of inattention were the lack of contact between Western missionaries and Chinese intellectuals and the gulf between nationalistic, urban China and the inarticulate countryside, where many of the missionaries worked. Such insensitivity did not bode well for the perti-

[45] NCC, 1922, p. 117.

[46] J. V. MacMurray, U.S. Minister to China, to R. Leslie Craigie, British Minister to China, May 20, 1922, Dept. of State Archives, Files on China.

nence of the surveys nor for the adequacy of missionary response to subsequent anti-Christian campaigns.

Some urban Chinese also refused to take the movement seriously, and newspapers scolded the students in a number of editorials. Embarrassment seems to have been a principal reason for negative response, concern lest the activities of the students humiliate China while numerous foreign visitors were in the capital.[47] Many Chinese Christians, however, were deeply disturbed by the movement; and their response reveals the gap between their outlook and that of the Western missionaries. Even though critical of the movement, they recommended that the church study the anti-Christian literature in order to understand the principal objections of educated Chinese to Christianity and Christian missions. Chinese Christians were, after all, Chinese as well as Christian, and they sometimes felt caught between the demands of Chinese nationalism and Christian faith. All too often, the two seemed to work at cross purposes, and in some anti-Christian activities a willingness to condemn Christianity became almost a test of Chinese patriotism.

In general, Chinese Christians distinguished between attacks on Christian teachings and attacks on mission methods and church practices. The former they attempted to refute, but the latter they often considered well founded. They argued that many missionaries had been slow to adjust their thinking to the findings of science and that many Chinese pastors were too poorly educated to deal with questions on the conflict between religion and science.[48] They denied that Christian doctrine was selfish and antinationalist because it emphasized individual salvation, but they asked that the Christian church give greater attention to social service work and other activities to strengthen the Chinese nation. Few Chinese Christians would deny the interdependence of Christian missions and Western imperialism; nor were they happy with individual relations between Westerners and Chinese. Too many of the Chinese Christians had personally experienced discrimination. They felt frustrated in their

[47] See, for example, the clipping from the *Peking Leader*, March 26, 1922, entitled "Student Daily Thinks Non-Christian Chinese Attack Very Discourteous," included in A. B. Ruddock, Secretary, U.S. Embassy in Peking, to Dept. of State, April 10, 1922, *ibid.*

[48] Chao Tzu-ch'en, "The Strength and Weakness of the Church in China," *NCC, 1922*, pp. 208–209.

attempts to make themselves heard in the church councils of China. Agreeing that the church was a foreign institution dominated by authoritarian Westerners, they renewed their pleas for Sinification of Christianity and Christian education. Wu Yao-tsung, a Congregational minister who was to become a prominent YMCA leader, called for the training of more Chinese leaders, for, he said, half the mistakes of the missions came from the lack of Chinese leadership.[49]

Origins of the Restore Educational Rights Movement

In 1924 a new anti-Christian campaign was launched. While building on the 1922 movement and reissuing earlier literature, the leaders focused on Christian schools and adopted as their slogan *Shou-hui chiao-yü ch'üan* (Restore Educational Rights). Movements by students and young intellectuals quite naturally turned to educational concerns, and, as a matter of fact, in a number of articles and speeches during 1922, Christian education had been condemned as an encroachment on national sovereignty and religious freedom. Behind the condemnation lay two fundamental factors. One was the assumption that a major function of education was to serve the state. The theme of an essay in the second volume of *Hsin ch'ing-nien*, for example, was that compulsory education largely accounted for Western strength, whereas illiteracy and ignorance led to the poverty and political servitude of Asia; a country which did not provide for the education of her people could not progress politically, industrially, or morally.[50] With such a concept of the function of education, Chinese would inevitably resent their lack of control over Christian schools. The separateness and autonomy of the mission institutions thus was a second major factor contributing to the educational rights movement. Chinese wanted to insure that Christian schools served national purposes.

In 1921, Minister of Education Fan Yüan-lien had stated before the Chihli-Shansi Christian Educational Association that compulsory chapel and Bible study were contrary to the Chinese constitution, which guaranteed freedom of worship.[51] Furthermore, he said, stu-

[49] Wu, "How the Church Can Meet the Challenge of the Movement," *Chinese Social and Political Science Review*, VII (1923), 111.

[50] Wen Tsung-yao, "On Education," *Hsin ch'ing-nien*, II (1916).

[51] Fan Yüan-lien, "Speech Given before the Chihli-Shansi Christian Educational Association," *ER*, XIII (1921), 131–133.

dents educated in Christian schools were generally lacking in knowledge of their own country; they were not equipped for a role as leaders in China's national life. Ts'ai Yüan-p'ei's speech before the antireligious federation on April 9, 1922, had stressed separation of religion and education, and in an article entitled "Chiao-yü tu-li i" (Independence of Education) he had urged that Chinese education be controlled by educators free from both religious and political influence.[52] Although the first part of his article calling for education independent of politics was frequently ignored, his cry for schools free from control by religious sects found many echoes. In July 1922 the Anti-Christian Federation sent a lengthy telegram denouncing mission schools to the conference of the National Association for the Advancement of Education (Chung-hua chiao-yü kai-chin she). Several of its statements exuded hatred of the Christian institutions: "The number of students whose intelligence and native talents are stunted and fettered by the shackles of Christian education is simply astounding. . . . The Christian preachers induce them to accept the Christian faith and worship God without questionings . . . and they will be unable to see the light of day for the remainder of their lives. This sort of education differs in no way from burying a man alive." [53] Hu Shih and several other members of the National Association for the Advancement of Education recommended to the conference the separation of religion and education and the forbidding of religious education in all primary schools.[54] In the same year a campaign for return of the remainder of the United States Boxer funds fostered resentment of the Christian schools, for it seemed likely that some of the income would go to mission institutions, and Chinese educators wanted allocations only to national schools.

As was true in the 1922 anti-Christian campaign, a publication by the Christians themselves fed the fears and resentments; in this case it was a volume entitled *Christian Education in China.* Statements in the work encouraged Chinese to believe that the missionaries were about to move toward a coordinated educational system, which was viewed as a much greater threat to Chinese sovereignty than

[52] *Hsin chiao-yü,* IV (1922), 317–319.
[53] Tseu Yih Zan, "Government Notes," *ER,* XIV (1922), 404.
[54] Ch'en I-lin, *Tsui-chin san-shih-nien chung-kuo chiao-yü shih* (History of Chinese Education during the Last Thirty Years) (Shanghai, 1930), p. 368.

the current haphazard groups of schools run by missionaries. Actually, Christian educators had for almost a decade regularly requested a survey of all educational work by mission societies in China, and the publication of the survey in the midst of a rising tide of anti-Christian sentiment was coincidental. A survey commission of Western educators and theologians, Chinese Christians, and missionaries had begun work in 1921 under the chairmanship of Ernest D. Burton, professor of theology at the University of Chicago. The surveyors revealed an awareness of the growing nationalist feeling in China and redefined the role of Christian education vis-à-vis national education. The time had come, they said, when Christian educators should realize that the missions could not furnish education for more than a small portion of the Chinese students. With the goal of building a strong Christian community, the Christian schools should henceforth concentrate on that Chinese minority which desired education under Christian auspices. Though the curricula and standards of the national school system should be adopted and Chinese patriotism fostered, the Christian schools would furnish a healthy variant from the norm and thus find a permanent place in China.[55] Unlike the government schools, they would provide education in a religious atmosphere; they would not be hampered by political pressure and could experiment in educational technique and curricula. A closer relationship with the government educational system, such as registration, was not yet considered urgent by the surveyors.

If Christian education were to become permanent in China, however, several reforms would have to be made to meet the demands of the Chinese, the home mission boards, and the financial situation. The reforms were summarized under the slogan "Missionary education must be more efficient, more Christian, and more Chinese." Chinese, it was said, were no longer satisfied with a foreign curriculum taught by foreigners. The number of Chinese teachers, administrators, and board members must be increased. In order to adapt the college curricula to the needs of China, there should be less emphasis on the liberal arts and more on vocational and professional

[55] *Christian Education in China*, pp. 37–38, 45. A summary of the recommendations is given on pp. 361–375.

education. Sociology, education, commerce, and business administration were among the fields suggested.

The best way of improving the quality of education, according to the commission, would be to insure greater efficiency through coordination and unification of colleges. Uniform entrance and graduation requirements and standard curricula should be established; schools in the same locale which were duplicating each other's work should be united. Among the suggestions for improving the quality of the teachers were several which the Christian college administrators themselves had requested. One was that missionaries be trained for a particular type of position and a particular country. The commission commended the practice of allowing missionaries to spend their first two years in the field learning the language and their furlough periods doing graduate study related to their particular work. It encouraged the missions to make as few exceptions as possible to this policy. Finally, the commission recommended that the missions grant fiscal autonomy to the universities; thus the university administrators rather than the mission societies would select the teachers and determine the salaries.

The recommendation that mission education be made more Christian expressed the concern of mission societies and evangelists that a large proportion of mission funds was being allocated to educational work without commensurate returns in Christianizing China. In many schools, according to the survey, the required chapel services and the religion courses had become dull routine. Henceforth, only the best teachers should be assigned courses in religion, and they should be given teaching loads light enough so that they could plan interesting and well-organized classes. Greater effort to adapt the courses to the needs of China should be made, and the courses should be graded and taught in a definite sequence. The Burton commission, while it approved of a few required courses in religion, suggested that most such classes be made elective and that the whole question of compulsory religious courses receive serious study. Above all, the spirit of Christianity should pervade every aspect of Christian college work.

The suggestions of the survey were in many ways sound; some proved controversial. Though to say that reactions followed ethnic lines would be an oversimplification, many Chinese Christians thought that the suggestions for making the colleges more Chinese did not go far enough, whereas many missionaries believed that they went too far. Even had the surveyors shown greater awareness of Chinese criticisms of religion, Christianity, and Christian education, however, they could hardly have met the demands of anti-Christian groups. Although criticisms by the latter were often directed against specific practices of mission schools, such as compulsory attendance at chapel, in actuality the object of attack was the whole concept of education under the auspices of a foreign religious society. This is demonstrated in the use made of quotations from *Christian Education in China* by initiators of the Restore Educational Rights Movement.

As in the 1922 anti-Christian campaign, opening salvoes came from the Young China Association. In October 1923 the association held a conference in which it sought agreement on a guide for political action. After sharp controversies between communist members and more moderate nationalists, the conference reached a fragile and temporary compromise and adopted a nine-point program which included advocacy of nationalistic education and opposition to the establishment of schools by religious groups. In the same month the association issued a booklet entitled *Kuo-chia chu-i ti chiao-yü* (Nationalistic Education), and one leading member, Yü Chia-chü published an article, "Chiao-hui chiao-yü wen-t'i" (The Question of Religious Education) in *Chung-hua chiao-yü chieh* (Chung Hwa Educational Review); the slogan "Restore Educational Rights" seems to have been coined in Yü's article.[56]

Both works condemned compulsory courses in religion as infringements on religious freedom, but they went much further and found Christian education a threat to the very existence of the Chinese nation. Quotations from *Christian Education in China* were cited as proof: "Now is the hour of opportunity so to strengthen the Christian schools of China that from them shall come the men and

[56] Ch'en, *Chung-kuo chiao-yü shih*, p. 369; Chiang, *Chinese Student Movement*, pp. 88–89; Chow, *May Fourth Movement*, p. 252. The first sentence of Yü's article reads: "Among the very great perils to the future of China, one ought to put religious Christian education first." See *Chung-hua chiao-yü chieh*, Oct. 1923.

women who will make China a Christian nation" (p. 15). "It is not yet settled whether Christian education is to be the determining force or a relatively insignificant and diminishing factor in Chinese life. On the answer to this question will largely hang the decision whether China will become a Christian nation, perhaps the stronghold of Christianity in future centuries" (p. 61). The writers revealed resentment and a sense of shame that Westerners should be able to organize an educational program independent of government control, and the Burton commission's emphasis on coordination of Christian education had aggravated their fears. Yü Chia-chü protested that China was not "an uncivilized place," not a "nation without men of learning" that foreigners should come to propagate their religion and to foster education. At the core of the protests, however, was the concept that the creation of nationally conscious citizens was a primary purpose of education, and Christian education could not fulfill this purpose. Many seemed to agree with an earlier writer who had found Christianity and Chinese nationalism incompatible and had said: "Rather China without Christianity than Christianity without China." [57] Nationalistic Chinese were disturbed, of course, when the Burton Commission recommended making Christian education more Christian by improving the religion courses and chapel programs; but what really alarmed Chinese educators was the recommendation that the spirit of Christianity pervade the whole educational program.

The Two-Pronged Attack

Such were the origins of the Restore Educational Rights Movement, a two-pronged attack on Christian education in China. One group of critics was dominated by the student generation, and its demands were far reaching: government take-over of the Christian schools and the ousting of foreigners. Its techniques included the strike, demonstrations, and ultimatums to school administrators. The second, somewhat older group of critics tried to influence government policy through its numerous educational associations. These men were primarily interested in government regulation and supervision of all Chinese education, and in many cases their demands had already been promulgated by the government; they were asking

[57] "The Nationalism of a Chinese Christian," *CR*, XL (1909), 152.

for enforcement. The demands were: no required religious instruction or activities in higher education and no religious instruction at all in primary education; acknowledgment of the primacy of educational rather than religious goals by the school; government registration and supervision of all schools; and a Chinese majority in the administration of the institutions. The extent to which the two groups coordinated their activities is difficult to discover. There was some overlapping of personnel, with more radical members of the older generation giving guidance and support to the students; student groups sent petitions to the educational associations and reprinted essays by well-known scholars and nationalist spokesmen. In general, however, the concerted campaign attacking specific schools and calling for direct action was the work of the student generation, whereas the older group exerted pressure on the government and on the Christian institutions through the recommendations and resolutions of their associations and through magazine articles. The campaign of the younger group contributed to the attainment of the goals of the educators, for it helped persuade both missionary educators and Kuomintang leaders of the urgency and necessity of government supervision. In most cases the campaign did not lead to Chinese take-over of Christian institutions, as many youth had desired.

Some of the first incidents in the student campaign began with protests by mission school students themselves against alleged insults by foreign administrators and against restrictions on participation in patriotic demonstrations. Several of the protests occurring in urban centers where left-wing influence was strong and receiving support from communist and left-Kuomintang organs blossomed into criticisms of the whole concept of Christian education. These incidents took place in the spring of 1924, after Kuomintang and Communist Party leaders had agreed to collaborate and the reorganization of the Kuomintang under Comintern guidance had begun. At its first national congress in January 1924, the Kuomintang had set as a goal the end of unequal treaties and the restoration of China's sovereign rights.[58] Nationalistic Chinese, therefore, had reason to

[58] A translation of the "Declaration by the First National Congress of the Kuomintang, 1924," is available in Li Chien-nung, *The Political History of China, 1840–1928,* trans. and ed. by Ssu-yü Teng and Jeremy Ingalls (Princeton, 1956), pp. 450–458.

believe that they would receive support in their demand for government control of all educational institutions, and communists could work more openly than before in their efforts to build up support among Chinese youth.

On April 22, 1924, Chinese journals in Canton published a manifesto by students of Holy Trinity College (Kuang-chou sheng-san-i) demanding the restoration of China's educational rights.[59] According to the manifesto the students had decided to introduce a system of student self-government and had organized a committee to work out the details. When the principal of the school was informed, he reprimanded them for establishing a committee without his consent and argued that since Holy Trinity was an English school under the protection of the English consul at Canton, he could not accede to their request for student government. The school was closed and a number of pupils were expelled. The students asked: "Is China no longer China? Is Canton an English colony?" Foreign schools were established to enslave young Chinese, not for altruistic motives, said the students, and they would no longer submit to the foreigner's tyranny. They were humiliated that the Chinese government could not protect the educational rights of the nation, and they called on all comrades to rise against the oppressors in order to return to China a monopoly over education. Though the students were obviously inspired by anti-imperialist nationalism as well as personal grievances, they were somewhat vague as to their specific and immediate goals; this is revealed in a rather contradictory petition presented to Sun Yat-sen on April 26. Although they demanded suppression of all foreign education of a "servile form," they also asked Sun Yat-sen to require the principal to reopen Trinity, readmit all students and apologize to those whom he had insulted.

The Holy Trinity students received encouragement and publicity from the Canton Student Union, from *Chung-kuo ch'ing-nien* (Chinese Youth), Communist Party organ published in Canton, and from the Kuomintang organ, *Min-kuo jih-pao* (Republic Daily) with its weekly supplement, *Chüeh-wu* (Awakening). During this same pe-

[59] Yang Hsiao-ch'un, "Chi-tu-chiao chih hsüan-ch'uan yü shou-hui chiao-yü-ch'üan yün-tung" (Protestant Propaganda and the Restore Educational Rights Movement), *CHCYC*, vol. XIV, no. 8 (Feb. 1925); manifesto quoted in Wieger, *Chine Moderne*, vol. V, *Nationalisme, Xenophobie, Anti-Christianisme,* pp. 134–135.

riod Chinese journals gave wide publicity to a May 5 communiqué from Moscow telling of the closing of foreign schools by Turkey; the lead line in the articles revealed what the action meant to Chinese: "The Turkish Government closes foreign schools. The United States, Italy, and France protest, but world opinion is with the Turks." [60] Emboldened by the protests of the Holy Trinity students and the support they received, pupils at Sacred Heart School in Canton and at Christian middle schools in Nanking, Foochow, and Soochow also stirred up student storms. Similar themes ran through the manifestoes and articles: the mission schools served the cause of the imperialist powers, making denationalized servants of the pupils and acting as a vanguard for the capitalists and militarists; the Christian administrators were autocratic and respected neither Chinese students nor Chinese nationalism. The depth of animosity expressed by some former pupils must have been shocking to the missionaries; one student wrote anonymously that he despised the vermin of the church, that he had breathed to satiety the slavish atmosphere of mission schools, and that the Chinese should close the foreign schools just as the Turks had done.[61]

By the summer of 1924 the drive against mission schools had begun to gain cohesion, and specific goals and techniques of the educational rights movement were being spelled out. As in previous campaigns, the organizational know-how of the students and the communication links among students were impressive. In July, for example, students in Canton announced the launching of a movement to restore educational rights and issued a proclamation demanding government registration and inspection of all schools operated by foreigners, the elimination of required religion courses and required attendance at church services, and freedom of organization, press, and assembly for students. The Young China Association, though politically divided, united in support of the educational rights movement and published both new anti-Christian articles and reprints of articles issued during the 1922 campaign. In August, a group meeting in Shanghai revived the anti-Christian federation,

---

[60] Wieger, *Chine Moderne*, V, 129–131, 138–150. Some articles also mention the Japanese use of schools in Manchuria for imperialist purposes.

[61] *Ibid.*, pp. 137–139, 142; see also Yang Hsiao-ch'un, "Chi-tu-chiao yü chiao-yü ch'üan," *CHCYC*, XIV, no. 8.

which soon began to put out its own anti-Christian periodical. The Sixth Congress of the Student Union of China, meeting in August, condemned schools like Holy Trinity for making their students the "running dogs" of the foreigners; it called for the closing of foreign schools and a national monopoly over education. A move by the older generation also came during the summer when several leaders of the 1922 anti-Christian campaign brought the issue of educational rights before the third annual meeting of the National Association for the Advancement of Chinese Education. After a sharp debate between radicals and moderates, the demand of Yu Chia-chü, Ch'en Ch'i-t'ien, and others for deletion of all courses in religion was tabled, and the association simply urged strict enforcement of registration requirements; these requirements included, of course, the elimination of required religion courses and required attendance at religious ceremonies.[62]

The recurrent theme was that education should serve the Chinese nation, and since Christianity was a foreign religion and an outdated one, schools founded for evangelistic purposes were more of a danger to China than an aid. The manifestoes also revealed that student organizations generally wanted to go further than government supervision of the schools; they wanted Chinese control. How did they propose to attain their goal? Partly by publicity; as the opinion makers of new China, they would make known the evils of mission education through demonstrations, handbills, periodicals, resolutions, and public telegrams. Increasingly, however, the students turned to direct action, encouraging strikes in the mission schools and attempting to force the hand of Chinese in taking control of the institutions. Two nationalist outbursts—the movement of May 30, 1925, and the Northern Expedition of 1926–1928—enhanced the opportunities of the students; during these events the activities of the older generation and of New Youth coincided briefly, though the gap between the two groups soon opened again. A few highlights of the educational rights campaign will illustrate its course.

[62] Material on the activities of the summer of 1924 may be found in Yang, CHCYC, XIV, no. 8; in Chang TCSC (see pp. 376–380 for the proclamation and constitution of the Anti-Christian Federation); in Wieger, Chine Moderne, V, 155, 233–238 and VI, 79–80; in Ch'en Ch'i-t'ien, "Wo-men chu-chang chou-hui chiao-yü-ch'üan," CHCYC, XIV, no. 8; and in Sanford C. C. Chen, "The Anti-Christian Education Movement," ER, XVII (April 1925), 141–143.

Student associations had chosen the Christmas season of 1924 for the first major battle of the campaign. In preparation the Anti-Christian Federation and the China Youth Society (Chung-kuo ch'ing-nien she) had compiled and distributed a pamphlet of anti-Christian articles.[63] There was also an outburst of anti-Christian articles in the magazines, *Chüeh-wu* and *Chung-kuo ch'ing nien*. On December 24–25, protest meetings were held and manifestoes issued in many cities throughout China, especially the centers of left-wing influence, Canton, Changsha, and Shanghai. Canton students gathered on December 25, 1924, at Kwangtung University (later Sun Yat-sen University) to hear Chou Lu, president of the university, and Liao Chung-k'ai, chief of the Bureau of Labor of the Sun Yat-sen regime, condemn all religions in general and Christianity in particular; they argued that all religions had become anachronistic, and Christianity was particularly harmful because of its link with the imperialistic powers; there was no room in China for schools founded to preach Christianity. Members of the anti-Christian federation visited Christian schools and other mission institutions to distribute handbills, harangue students, and disrupt church services if possible. A few cases of disorder and jostling occurred where students tried to force their way onto school premises or to drown out church services, but no violence developed. Among the student leaders was Liao Ch'eng-chih, son of Liao Chung-k'ai and a student at Lingnan, and among the participants were groups of Whampoa cadets.[64]

[63] See note 41, preceding. The China Youth Society was an organ of the Communist Party and published *Chung-kuo ch'ing-nien*; it is to be distinguished from the Chung-kuo ch'ing-nien tang (Chinese Youth Party).

[64] Douglas Jenkins, U.S. Consul General, sent a report concerning the anti-Christian activities in Canton on Dec. 24–26, 1924, to the Dept. of State. The report also includes a translation of the regulations of the Kwangtung Anti-Christian Association and a declaration by the I Chung Young Men's Education Association distributed on Dec. 25, 1924. Mr. Jenkins protested informally about the anti-Christian activities to Fu Ping-ch'ang, Commissioner of Foreign Affairs in Canton. (See Dept. of State Archives, File on China, Jan. 7, 1925; also Wieger, *Chine Moderne*, VI, 143–148.) Liao Chung-k'ai, who was assassinated in 1925 was a close associate of Sun Yat-sen and had been influential in Comintern negotiations with Sun; he strongly supported collaboration between the Kuomintang and the Communist Party. His son, Liao Ch'eng-chih, was later to become a high official in the Communist Party. Liao Ch'eng-chih told Nym Wales in 1937, however, that he was sympathetic with communism in 1924–1925 and a

More serious was a strike at Yali which led to the departure of approximately one-third of the student body. The storm began in the late fall with a minor fracas during a football game between Yali and Boone; a faculty member, while trying to end the melee, cuffed one of the Yali students. Public apology by the teacher, who was an American of Chinese descent, was demanded and given. Other grievances, however, became cause for conflict between student leaders and the administration; Yali students held a protest meeting without permission, and the Yali administrators in response expelled one student leader and placed two others on probation. The local anti-Christian association, the Hunan branch of the Society for the Maintenance of Educational Rights (Chiao-yü chu-ch'üan wei-ch'ih hui), and the Hunan Student Union took up the Yali student cause. Just at the Christmas season, therefore, Yali students called a strike, public demonstrations were organized, and about two hundred middle school students left the institution. Manifestoes issued by Yali students and other groups interpreted the specific grievances of the mission school pupils as insults to the Chinese nation and race, urged parents to withdraw their sons from Christian institutions, asked public schools to make special dispensations in order to admit the students who had withdrawn, and encouraged the minister of education to reclaim a monopoly over Chinese education by ousting foreigners from the schools. The situation had by this time gotten out of control. Radicals, many of them not from Yali, acted as spokesmen for the students and sought confrontations rather than negotiations. Finally, several local citizens helped arrange conferences between Yali administrators and the parents of Yali students where a compromise settlement was reached. Penalties for certain students were reduced, and the parents expressed support of Yali and urged students to return to classes. A number of teachers were so deeply disturbed by the concessions of President Hume that they resigned and Hume felt impelled to call for a vote of confidence from his faculty. Though a semblance of normalcy was restored and

member of the left Kuomintang, but that he did not join the Communist Party until some years later. See Snow, *Red Dust*, pp. 25–34; also Clarence M. Wilbur, ed., *Documents on Communism, Nationalism, and Soviet Advisers in China, 1918–1927* (New York, 1956), p. 503.

244 | CHINA AND THE CHRISTIAN COLLEGES, 1850–1950

Yali reopened after the holidays, only about two-thirds of the student body returned and Yali was to experience two more *hsüeh-ch'ao* before the academic year ended.[65]

The Christmas agitation provides useful insights concerning the orientation of students and the status of Christian colleges in 1924. The doctrines of the left wing were already influential among student activists and their organizations had already established communication with student associations and had come to dominate them in some cases.[66] The fact that the Christmas protests were particularly disruptive in Canton and Changsha probably had less to do with the ineptness of the Christian college administrators than with the effectiveness and strength of left-wing leadership in these cities. This did not mean that all or most of the leftist students were communists, for the line between the Chinese Communist Party, the left Kuomintang, and other more ephemeral organizations was vague. In 1924 New Youth was not primarily interested in the discipline and organization of the Communist Party, nor its doctrine of dialectical materialism. The most effective appeal of communism, as of the left Kuomintang, was to student nationalism, and the emphasis of the two parties in their nationalist propaganda was similar. As they defined Chinese nationalism in anti-imperialist, anti-capitalist, and anti-Western terms, they gave it powerful emotional overtones. They helped to justify attacks on the foreigners who had been the source of both individual and national humiliation. Many of the manifestoes and articles of the educational rights movement of late 1924 and early 1925 indicated that activist students were well acquainted with the Leninist doctrine of imperialism and its

[65] "The Recent Student 'Strike,'" *The Yali Quarterly*, vol. VIII, no. 3 (March 1925), p. 6; "Annual Report, 1924–25" *The Yali Quarterly*, IX, no. 1 (Sept. 1925), pp. 4–5; Wieger, *Chine Moderne*, VI, 135–136, 148–149; Holden, *Yale-in-China*, pp. 147–153; Correspondence of E. H. Hume to Palmer Bevis, Dec. 14, 17, 19, 23, 1924; Jan. 13, 1925 (Yali Archives, Box 28).

[66] According to Jerome Ch'en, *Mao and the Chinese Revolution* (London, 1965), Mao Tse-tung in 1919 edited three issues of the *Hsin Hunan* (New Hunan), weekly of the Yali student union, and approximately a year later he rented three rooms from the Medical College of Yali for his "Culture Bookshop" to distribute socialist literature (see pp. 64, 72). Li Chien-nung, *Political History of China*, says that propaganda and recruiting activities of the Kuomintang and Communist Party were largely carried out by the student unions (see pp. 438–439 of English translation). For a list of some of the articles showing the influence of left-wing theory, see following footnote.

relation to nationalism and with Marxist theories on the relation between Christian religion and bourgeois capitalism. Some of the protests seem little more than a paraphrase of Marxist-Leninist writings, with specific illustrations drawn from experiences with Christian missions in China.[67] Thus, although the anti-Christian and educational rights movements were basically expressions of Chinese nationalism, the definition of nationalism was generally within the context of Marxist-Leninist theory. Left-wing groups were using the appeal of nationalism to gain influence in student associations and to acquaint them with the orientation and value system of Marxism.

There was a deeply rooted antiforeignism on which negative nationalism could build; this antagonism toward the Westerner was prevalent among students in Christian institutions as well as among students in public schools. At Yali, for example, the initial protest was over alleged mistreatment of a student by a teacher, but by the time of the strike students were treating the incident as symbolic of the imperialists' humiliation of China and typical of the capitalists' use of Christianity as an opiate to keep China weak. Unless a Yali student were willing to be identified as unpatriotic by leaders of

[67] The argument that Christianity had been used by feudal lords to oppress the common people and that Christianity was currently used by bourgeois capitalists as an opiate to keep the downtrodden masses quiet was repeated frequently. See, for example, the "Declaration of the I Chung Men's Educational Association," in Jenkins to Dept. of State, Jan. 7, 1925; the "Manifesto of the Anti-Christian Federation, Aug. 19, 1924," in Chang, TCSC, pp. 376–380; Ts'ai Ho-shen on "Modern Christianity" in Fan-tui chi-tu-chiao yün-tung. The theory that imperialism arose from the economic needs of capitalism was generally accepted by Chinese nationalists of all persuasion; there were, though, several interesting variants of this theme as it was applied in Chinese anti-Christian literature. In one, Christianity as well as capitalism was in serious difficulty in the West; missionaries were sent, then, as the vanguard of imperialism to help revive capitalism and also as the emissaries of a dying Christian church trying to find new life in less advanced civilizations. Another argument seemed to identify the colonial and semicolonial nations with the proletarian class. Just as Christianity was used by capitalists to oppress the working class so it was used by the imperialists to keep colonial peoples quiet and prevent the growth of a strong China. See Ts'ai Ho-shen, "Modern Christianity," Fan-tui chi-tu-chiao yün-tung, and Li Ch'un-fan, "Evangelism and Imperialism," in ibid.; article on the Anti-Christian Federation published in Chung-kuo ch'ing-nien, fall, 1924, and translated in Wieger, Chine Moderne, VI, 143–144, also, the manifesto of the Shantung branch of the Anti-Christian Federation, Dec. 25, 1924, VI, 148; and Yang Hsiao-ch'un, "Chi-tu-chiao yü chiao yü-ch'üan," CHCYC, XIV, no. 8.

the Hunan student union, the educational rights association, and many of his colleagues, he gave support to the protest movement. Though Christian college students were benefiting from the educational work of Christian missions, their public declarations revealed that they often harbored deep resentment over the dominance of foreigners in the schools, the religious requirements, and the isolation of the institutions from Chinese cultural and national life. Their very experiences in the Christian schools made them responsive to an antiforeign, anti-imperialist nationalism, and so they were often ready to support the educational rights movement; they themselves wanted changes in the status of the Christian colleges. When they supported demands for the integration of the mission institutions with the national educational system, their own integration with the New Youth of China was begun.

May 30, 1925

Both the May 30th Movement of 1925 and the Northern Expedition of 1926–1928 speeded up the educational rights movement as they inflamed national sentiment. To students, the facts of the May incident seemed simple; unarmed students demonstrating in the International Settlement of Shanghai to protest the killing of a Chinese worker had been fired on by foreign troops. The students had deliberately defied regulations against demonstrations in the International Settlement in the hope of securing greater publicity and they had been warned before they surged toward the police, but these details faded into insignificance before the death of twelve Chinese. The insults of Western imperialism to China seemed epitomized in the affair of May 30; even when aliens slaughtered innocent youth on Chinese soil, the Chinese government lacked jurisdiction over the murderers, students said. A cry for an end to extraterritoriality, an end to all special privileges for foreigners and the whole treaty system echoed through urban China. Students hastily organized demonstrations, strikes, boycotts of Japanese and British goods, and protest campaigns in the major cities of China. Subsequent conflicts at Hankow and Canton further roused passions, and widespread support came from workers, merchants, educators, and Kuomintang and Communist Party leaders.

In effect, Chinese said to Westerners: right is on our side; stand up and be counted. At Soochow University a student interrupted class to ask the instructor to state his position on the incident, and a group of young Chinese teachers requested American members of the faculty for a public statement of their views. A number of Chinese Christians in Chefoo issued an open letter asking for public support of the Chinese position from missionaries; when we deny that Christian missions are the vanguard of imperialism, they said, other Chinese are not convinced; you Western missionaries can now help undermine the anti-Christian movement by condemning the action of the British troops.[68] Students in the Christian schools were asked to join in the demonstrations as proof that they were patriotic Chinese, not the lackeys of Westerners.

To many associated with the Christian missions, however, the issue was not so simple, and there was great variety in their reactions. Certain missionaries followed a line of argument often used by the Western business community: the students were deliberately flouting the law on May 30; when they got out of hand, force was regrettable but necessary; otherwise, there would be no security for life and property in China. More frequently, missionaries expressed sympathy with the Chinese over the loss of life; they refused, however, to make a judgment in the case, sometimes on the grounds that they should not interfere in politics and sometimes on the grounds that they were awaiting an impartial investigation. Yenching faculty members went further, and while calling for an impartial inquiry, protested the readiness of troops to resort to force; they also urged efforts to improve relations between Chinese and Westerners by treaty revision. A number of. missionaries publicly condemned the action of the British officer and wrote to the United States Department of State urging the renegotiation of treaties on

[68] Wieger, *Chine Moderne*, VI, 224–225; Nance, *Soochow*, p. 100. Executives of the National Christian Council, formed in 1922 as a coordinating body for Protestantism in China, sent a letter to the Shanghai Municipal Council asking an impartial investigation and also Chinese representation on the Municipal Council and any court of inquiry. The executives were sharply criticized by some missionaries for having exceeded their authority and for interfering in politics. See *The National Christian Council: A Five Year's Review, 1922–27* (Shanghai, n.d.), p. 22.

an equal basis; they no longer wished to be protected by United States gunboats, extraterritoriality, or other special privileges, they said.[69]

To most students the missionary response seemed far from satisfactory. They saw no need for investigation of what appeared to them a clear-cut case; they considered the repudiation of treaty rights by individuals as an expedient to win a friendly audience for evangelism. In the Christian colleges many students were restless, for even sympathetic administrators tried to minimize the disruption of academic work. The administrators had varying success. A few of the institutions—Ginling, Fukien, and Soochow—were able to complete the school year after permitting brief expressions of support for the movement. Many of the institutions—the University of Shanghai, Hwa Nan, and Huachung among others—closed early because regular school work proved impossible; by dispersing the students, the faculty hoped to avoid further incidents. At Changsha a mass meeting of students demanded that all foreigners in the city be brought to the execution ground and shot within twenty-four hours. Though a declaration of martial law by the Hunan governor helped avert violence, Yali closed precipitately, and anyone associated with the mission or other Western installations was fair game for public revilement. At St. John's and Lingnan open conflict between Western administrators and Chinese students occurred, and both schools suffered as a result of unfavorable publicity and loss of students.

The initial incidents at St. John's and Lingnan were minor and might have been settled peaceably in other years, but they were exacerbated by the current identification of the conflicts between Western officials and Chinese subordinates with the conflict between Western imperialism and the Chinese nation. There was a series of clashes between President Hawks Pott and the St. John's students over their role in the movement of May 30. Controversies over participation in the strike called by Shanghai students, over attendance at a concert instead of a memorial service for the Chinese worker killed, and over the flying of the Chinese flag at half mast developed

[69] Edwards, *Yenching*, pp. 146-48. For further detail on missionary response to Chinese nationalism, see Varg, *Missionaries, Chinese, and Diplomats*, pp. 180-211, and frequent articles in *CR* and *ER* for 1925-1926.

into a contest of wills and a test of authority. Communication between the two broke down, and on June 3 the president declared the school closed and ordered the students to leave immediately. The students issued a manifesto accusing President Pott of insulting the flag, and more than half of the student body vowed never to return to St. John's. They secured the support of many of the Chinese faculty who were offended because they had not been consulted in the decision to close the school and declared that national pride compelled them to resign. As students and faculty joined in founding a new institution, Kwang Hua University, praise for their actions came from student and educational associations in many sections of China.[70]

Canton in June of 1925 was a tinder box, with endemic warfare among local troops, shifting political authority, and hardship and ill will because of the boycott of British goods and unemployment. With the backing of the Kuomintang, a great protest parade had been scheduled for June 23, and the firing that broke out between the demonstrators and British and French ships lit the tinder. A Lingnan teacher and a freshman from the college were among those killed. Confusion, disorder, and the wildest of rumors reigned; students and all workers and servants employed by Westerners were called out on strike. Lingnan students and some of the Chinese faculty and alumni now found it reprehensible that Alexander Baxter, vice-president of Lingnan, had originally opposed participation of Lingnan students in the protest parade, that he withheld judgment concerning the student version of the incident, and that he was a Britisher. Leaflets demanding that Chinese take over Lingnan, expel all imperialists, and eliminate Christianity from the school appeared on campus. Baxter was forced to leave Lingnan, and relations between Lingnan and the Canton community remained strained for months to come.[71]

In 1925, it seems, most Christian college students were responsive to patriotic appeals, but not yet ready to assume initiative in nation-

[70] Shu Hsin-ch'eng, ed., *Chin-tai chung-kuo chiao-yü shih-liao* (Historical Materials on Modern Chinese Education), 4 vols. (Shanghai, 1923 ff.), III, 180–183; this contains the manifesto of the Chinese faculty along with other materials; Lambert, *St. John's*, pp. 100–102.

[71] Corbett, *Lingnan*, pp. 89–94.

alist movements. Some extra ingredient was required for the students to move from the role of sympathetic supporters to that of organizers of concerted action; this ingredient might be personal conflict with a Western administrator or special pressure exerted by outside organizations. Lacking these, most students participated briefly in demonstrations and then returned to their academic responsibilities, or they accepted the closing of the school and dispersal of the students. Some, however, were so dissatisfied with the actions of their colleagues that they transferred to public institutions, and enrollment dropped in many Christian colleges in the fall of 1925. As a result, complained nationalist critics, Christian college students were usually missing from the protest demonstrations.[72]

This absence fed the animosity of youth toward the mission schools; to them it seemed new proof of the denationalizing influence of the institutions. Thus, the demands of the educational rights campaign were renewed with an added vehemence. The seventh congress of the Student Union of China, meeting in Shanghai in June and July, called for new attacks on Christianity and the mission schools, especially during the Christmas season. Tactics recommended were: instigating mission school students to rebel against college officials; planting spies and *agents provocateurs* in mission institutions; making repeated appeals to the Ministry of Education to suppress or confiscate the schools; encouraging apostasy and publicizing instances of apostasy; aiding students who could be persuaded to withdraw from Christian schools; and disrupting Christian meetings and conferences by public questioning. In August the Anti-Christian Federation reanimated its campaign against Christianity and mission schools. The Peking branch of the federation called for the closing or appropriation of all schools run by foreigners and condemned mission school administrators for having repressed

---

[72] See the discussion of the May 30th Movement under "Chiao-yü she hsiao-hsi," *Chiao-yü tsa-chih* (Aug. 1925), XVII, no. 8; also "Wai-kuo chiao-yü ti ya-p'o" (Oppression of Foreign Education) and Fan Yüan-lien, "Hu-an yü chiao-yü" (The Shanghai [case] and Education), in *CHCYC* (Aug. 1925), XV, no. 2. According to the annual reports of the president of Yenching (p. 6) and of the president of Nanking (p. 3) for 1924–1925, these schools discontinued classes but allowed their students to remain in residence while participating in the demonstrations. For enrollment figures of the Christian colleges, see Cressy, *Christian Higher Education*, p. 27.

students wishing to participate in the May 30th Movement. To some extent, it seems, the heightened nationalism was transferred from that movement to the educational rights movement; by late summer student demonstrations against the British had begun to seem aimless, and the cries of June that the students would not quit their protests until England and Japan had been humiliated and imperialism defeated appeared unrealistic. More concrete objects of attack and other techniques for giving expression to nationalism were needed.[73] The campaign against the Christian schools helped fill the need.

Simultaneously the intensified nationalism of May 30 seemed to widen the gap between Western and Chinese faculty members in the colleges. The division was primarily over the manner and timing of the response to registration requirements. While the younger generation had concentrated attacks on the mission schools, the older generation had increased its pressure on the government to bring the schools under national supervision. In October 1924, the National Federation of Provincial Educational Associations had passed resolutions demanding immediate registration of all schools in China, discrimination against students in unregistered schools after a certain date, and the elimination of religious teaching and worship from all schools. These demands were renewed by the federation at its annual meeting the following year and also by the National Association for the Advancement of Education. The influential *Chung hua chiao-yü chieh* devoted its February 1925 issue to the educational rights movement. The arguments supporting the resolutions did not usually emphasize the imperialist goals of the mission schools so much as their inability to fulfill the national purpose of Chinese education: education, they said, was an important aspect of national sovereignty and should not be under foreign control; a primary aim of education was the instilling of national ideals and the cultivation of unique Chinese characteristics, and foreigners from a different culture could not do this; education should not be

---

[73] See the call of the Student Union for a review of tactics in the continuing struggle against imperialism, "Chiao-yü she hsiao-hsi," *Chiao-yü tsa-chih*, Aug. 1925. The resolutions of the Student Union Congress are in Chang, *TCSC*, pp. 395–400. The Student Union was reorganized under the influence of its left wing at this Congress. The resolutions of the Peking branch of the Anti-Christian Federation are in Wieger, *Chine Moderne*, VI, 237–238.

subordinated to religious goals.[74] Responding to the pressures of
the educators, the Peking and Canton regimes and several provincial
governments issued registration requirements. Minimal prerequisites
for registration were similar: Chinese participation in the administration of the schools, elimination of requirements concerning religious worship and study, equality in the treatment of Chinese and
Western faculty members, and an acknowledgment that the purpose
of the school was educational rather than evangelistic. Many Chinese
Christians were convinced that immediate and rapid steps toward
meeting registration requirements were essential if Christian education were to continue in China.

Chinese Christians pointed out that in 1925 not one Christian
college had a Chinese president. Much of the real power of administration, furthermore, lay with the college board of governors which
met in a foreign country and rarely included a Chinese member.
Such an organization could hardly be expected to understand the
needs and problems of the Christian colleges in China; administrative control should be transferred to China. Chinese criticized the
tendency in hiring faculty to give preference to Christian college
graduates even if they had only a B.A. degree. Such Chinese, said
the critics, were not trained to hold responsible positions; their sense
of obligation to the mission and their lack of contact with Chinese
intellectual life prevented them from questioning the dictates of the
foreign president. There should be one salary scale and equality in
residence facilities and other fringe benefits. The talk about Chinese
control had gone on long enough; the time had come for action.[75]

Western administrators tended to emphasize the merits of gradu-
alism. They feared that Chinese placed in control during a period
of intense nationalism might allow patriotism rather than Christianity to become the guiding principle of Christian higher education,
and this would betray the trust of the home supporters. Chinese administrators, it was said, would be more subject than Western ones

[74] Harold Balme to J. H. Oldham, Jan. 21, 1925, Dept. of State Archives; Yü
Chia-chü, "Shou-hui-chiao-yü-ch'üan wen-ti ta-pien," CHCYC, Feb. 1925, gives
the typical arguments.
[75] Y. S. Tsao, "Chinese Cooperation in Mission Schools," ER, XVII (1925),
338–339; P. C. Hsu, "What Is on the Student's Mind," ER, XVIII (1926), 94;
"Tentative Findings of the Conference of Chinese Administrators in Christian
Colleges and Universities," Chinese Christian Education, 1925, p. 19.

to political pressures and the influence of student demands, and they would have difficulty maintaining academic discipline and academic standards. The missionaries pointed out the difficulty of securing competent Chinese. They bespoke the patience of Chinese while they tried to obtain reforms in methods of hiring and more adequate appropriations for salaries. They reminded the Chinese that opinion among home mission societies was behind opinion in the field and the transfer to Chinese control must await the education of the churches in the West. Important duties of the college president were to lead fund-raising campaigns in the United States and to maintain relations with the board of governors, who helped secure much of the financial support. Since it would be difficult for a Chinese president to carry out these functions, Chinese administrative control should perhaps await the development of further financial resources in China.[76]

Even more divisive was the issue of response to the registration requirements concerning religion. The first reaction of most missionaries was that the Christian institutions simply could not meet such conditions and that they would have to seek modification of the requirements. The schools, they said, were trying to provide education of high quality, but as long as most of the financial support came from Christian churches in the West, the religious purpose of the schools could not be relegated to the background. The missionaries disagreed with the argument that compulsory religious courses in private schools violated the constitutional guarantee of religious freedom. Students, they said, were free not to attend the Christian institutions; those who entered the schools did so with the knowledge that they were entering Christian institutions where courses on Christianity and attendance at chapel would be expected. It would be a denial of the religious freedom of Christian parents if they were not able to send their children to schools where religious instruction was given.

Most Chinese, both Christian and non-Christian, could not accept

[76] J. L. Stuart, "Some Administrative Problems," *ER*, XV (1923), 336; Pott, "Some Principles Contained in the Report of the China Educational Commission," *ibid.*, p. 218; Mrs. Lawrence Thurston, "Ginling College," *ibid.*, XVI (1924), 30; F. J. White, "Making the Christian Colleges More Chinese," *The Christian College in New China*, pp. 34–35.

the arguments of the missionaries. Actually, they said, the inadequate educational facilities meant that Chinese students were often not free to go to other institutions if they objected to the religious requirements. Moreover, compulsion was foreign to the spirit of Christianity and of democracy. Forcing non-Christians to participate in worship services was especially unwise. Quite frequently it resulted in revulsion toward Christianity, as was evidenced by the fact that several leaders of the anti-Christian movement were mission school students who harbored resentment over such compulsion. Chinese Christians generally believed that the spirit of the times demanded that the Christian schools register as soon as possible. Delays by Christian educators as they sought concessions on the religious question could only result in further misunderstanding and loss of sympathy. Chinese Christians also pointed out the discrimination which mission school graduates met because the institutions were not registered. Missionaries were doing their schools no favor, they said, by placing such difficulties upon their graduates.[77]

A number of missionary educators came to agree with Chinese Christians that the colleges would lose more than they would gain by refusing to register without modification of the religious requirements. This group was still a minority in 1925, however. The CCEA acknowledged the advisability of registration with the government and recommended that the mission schools prepare for it by increasing the number of Chinese teachers and administrators and adapting their curricula to government standards. The CCEA still hoped for concessions on the religious clauses, though, and urged that no school seek registration until a suitable agreement had been reached. The atmosphere in China was changing so rapidly that in 1926 the CCEA urged individual schools to do as they thought best, and quite a few of the colleges had already made attendance at chapel services voluntary. By 1927 several of the institutions had also made the courses on Christianity and the Bible elective: Cheeloo, Yenching, the University of Nanking, Soochow, Shanghai, Yali, Huachung, and West China. Some of the colleges had also opened negotiations for registration with Peking or with the Nationalist government.

[77] "Editorial Notes," ER, XVII (1925), 101–102; "Tentative Findings of Chinese Administrators," ibid., p. 174; Some Friendly Critics, "Christian Education from the Standpoint of Government Educators," ibid., p. 217; Sanford C. C. Chen, "Toward a Better Understanding," ibid., XVIII (1926), 404.

The Northern Expedition and Registration

At this time political developments in China rather than the desires of missionary educators were determining the fate of the Christian colleges. The Northern Expedition of the Kuomintang, begun in the summer of 1926, seemed to be exceeding the expectations of even the most ambitious Whampoa commanders, and a mood of exhilaration swept nationalist groups. Once again, hope for unity, peace, and progress was kindled. Many of the educated looked upon the Kuomintang armies as liberators who would free China from imperialism as well as warlordism; the humiliation of China would be ended and China would be sovereign once more. Students wanted to share in the great national campaign, and both the Kuomintang and the Chinese Communist Party were more than willing to accept their aid. In fact, the Kuomintang had encouraged students to join the party, with the result that many local student unions served as branches of the Kuomintang. The Chinese Communist Party had also continued to gain influence in student associations. The major function of students in the Northern Expedition was to prepare the way for Kuomintang troops by broadcasting nationalist propaganda. They were to whip up patriotic sentiment among workers and peasants, infiltrate the ranks of warlord troops to encourage defection, and organize demonstrations against imperialism and warlordism.

To leaders of the educational rights campaign, the ideal opportunity for obtaining their goals seemed to have arrived. Students charged with organizing demonstrations turned to institutions and associations with which they already had contact and attacked Western missionaries and their installations as the omnipresent symbols of imperialism. Thus, the timing and locale of the *hsüeh-ch'ao* in the Christian colleges correlated with the movement of the southern troops; there was also correlation with left-wing influence. Lingnan in Canton, Yali in Changsha, and Huachung in Wuchang were disrupted by strikes and protests through much of the fall of 1926 and spring of 1927; in Hankow a group of Chinese Christians formed an Association of Christian Revolutionaries and petitioned the leftist government to take control of all mission schools. Somewhat less serious attempts to take control of Hangchow, Fukien, and St. John's occurred during the spring of 1927. At Ginling the girls presented their faculty with a set of demands, and at Shanghai the school workmen went out on strike and briefly seized control of the campus as Nationalist troops approached. Yenching and Cheeloo in north China, on the other hand, experienced greater difficulty from the evacuation of foreigners than from *hsüeh-ch'ao*.

In these actions the students believed that they had the support of the southern regime, for the second congress of the Kuomintang in January 1926 had come out forcefully in favor of a national monopoly over education. The Central Committee of the Chinese Communist Party had directed members to spread propaganda against the Christian church as the vanguard of imperialism and to incite the populace against the church when the opportunity arose. Some members of the Kuomintang army had received from their political departments leaflets blaming missionaries for all China's losses during the nineteenth and twentieth centuries and condemning mission schools for making slaves of their students; soldiers were encouraged to help establish centers for anti-Christian activities.[78] Though the leaders of the Northern Expedition encouraged and profited from the nationalist storms which preceded or accompanied the troops, they were not always in control of the outbursts. Students and young intellectuals arrogated to themselves an authority far beyond what their actual experience or power enabled them to exercise, and at several colleges they sought to oust all foreigners and assume control themselves rather than simply bring the institutions under government supervision. Their demands and techniques closely resembled those recommended by the Student Union. Where possible, they used as instigators Christian college students and young Chinese teachers who were already in contact with the Kuo-

[78] Wilbur, *Documents on Communism,* pp. 299–300; Wieger, *Chine Moderne,* vol. VII, *Boum!* pp. 98, 115. On p. 115 Wieger gives a translation of a leaflet issued by the political department of the Fourth Army Corps (Cantonese) of the National Revolutionary Army, August 25, 1926. The Student Union of Shanghai set forth demands that students share authority in the affairs of the schools; that where the head of the school had quit, the student association should run the school until the government had appointed a new head; that fees be reduced and the accounts of the school be made public; that examinations be abolished and students be graded on the basis of their notes; that there be coeducation from the primary school to the university; that students help choose the professors; that students be free to organize, publish, hold meetings, strike, etc. See Wieger, *Chine Moderne,* VII, pp. 235–236.

mintang, the Chinese Communist Party, or nationalistic student organizations; sometimes they seem to have planted agents in the schools. These activists helped organize the students and occasionally the workers of the institution, played upon their specific grievances, and encouraged them to make impossible demands on the college authorities. Refusal to meet the demands then became reason to strike and force the closing of the school or the transfer of control.

At Yali the local youth branch of the Kuomintang established contact with leaders of the student union and with a young middle school teacher who was a Kuomintang member. Through these individuals student meetings were called in the fall of 1926 to persuade the students of the need to reform Yali and bring it into the national revolutionary system. At first, according to a Kuomintang report, the students did not realize that they had been made the slaves of foreigners, but after several meetings the truth dawned and they were ready to demand the reorganization of Yali. Actually, a variety of techniques seem to have been necessary to move the students to action: there were emotional appeals to patriotism which carried the implication that it was a privilege for Christian college students to be included in the nationalist revolution and thereby give proof that they were not foreignized; students who refused support found their names published in local newspapers, an unusually effective technique of persuasion in Chinese society. The use of committee rule in the student union, furthermore, enabled a small group of dedicated, active student leaders to make decisions in the name of the student body and then brand opposition in public meetings as unpatriotic. These techniques, as evolved during the student movements of the 1920's, were to be refined and used over and over again in the student campaigns of the 1930's and 1940's.

At Yali students demanded the abolition of the Y.M.C.A., the right to force the resignation of any faculty member by a two-thirds vote and to compel teachers to participate in demonstrations, a reduction of tuition fees, a subsidy for the student union, student representation on the board of governors, a student voice in the determination of curriculum, and expulsion or demotion of a student only with the consent of his colleagues. Whether these demands were presented in good faith or in the hope of an impasse leading to a strike is hard to say, but many demands were similar to those made at other

schools in the area.[79] At any rate, neither Chinese nor Western
faculty members believed it possible to run the school under the
conditions proposed. A strike followed rejection, and the school was
closed on December 13, 1926. The resignation of President Edward
Hume, tendered earlier, was accepted by the board of trustees in the
midst of the controversy; and F. C. Yen, head of the medical school,
was forced to depart because of his close association with Westerners and with W. W. Yen of the Peking government. The situation in
Hunan had grown so tense by January 1927 that all Americans were
ordered by their consul to leave. This proved to be the end of the
college division of Yali at Changsha; though it was possible to reopen
the middle school in 1928 and to reopen the nursing and medical
schools in 1929, college work was transferred to Wuchang and
henceforth supported as a part of Huachung University.[80]

Lingnan's experience was somewhat similar, though strikes by the
workers' and clerks' unions were more influential in the closing of
the school than the student strikes. Here, too, much of the initiative
and organization appear to have come from a small group of students with outside contacts. In a strike called by workmen on March
9, 1926, the college was able to get the local labor bureau to arbi-
trate, but a month later some Lingnan students who had publicly
condemned their school and aroused the ire of their colleagues
secured the support of the workers' union and Canton education
authorities. Though the students had been expelled on the recommendation of the student body, a face-saving compromise for the
offenders had to be devised. Another strike by workmen in November 1926 temporarily cut the food and water supplies of the school,
and finally a strike by both workmen and clerks in the spring of

[79] Actually, there were several sets of demands, one presented by the middle
school on October 28 and settled by compromise within a few days, and another
more extreme set presented on November 12 by the middle school and supported in part by the nursing school and the college; the strike began on
December 1, 1926. See "Standing By-Statement by the Trustees," *The Yali
Quarterly*, X (Dec. 1926), 2–4; "The Resignation of President Hume," *ibid.*,
X (March 1927), 2; William J. Hail, "Yali and the Chinese Revolution," *ibid.*,
X (June 1927), 4–14; letters of E. D. Harvey to Palmer Bevis, Nov. 30, 1926
and to F. W. Williams, Dec. 13, 1926 (Yali Archives, Box 13).

[80] In addition to the articles in the *Yali Quarterly*, listed above, see Holden,
Yale-in-China, pp. 156–162; letters of D. H. Leavens to Palmer Bevis, Feb. 2,
March 5, 14, April 4, 30, 1927 (Yali Archives, Box 30).

1927 made it impossible to continue academic work. Not only did the clerks want higher pay and better working conditions, but they also demanded a tenure and sabbatical system plus a union closed shop. With a small group of students as advisers, the clerks and workers took possession of the college gates to prevent the passage of food, baggage, and other goods, closed the library and some of the school offices, sealed administrative files, shut off the supply of fuel, and took control of one of the college buildings as their headquarters. Lingnan was officially closed on April 14, 1927, and most of the students left campus, but not until after Chiang Kai-shek's break with the communists was it possible to oust the strike leaders from school property; at that time three of the leaders were arrested as communists. Many students who had not desired disruption of their schooling managed to continue their work through informal arrangements with instructors, although the school was not officially reopened until the fall semester of 1927. By that time Lingnan had acquired a Chinese president and vice-president, and a board of directors that was predominantly Chinese.[81]

At Hangchow and Foochow in March 1927 small groups of students attempted to take control of the Christian colleges and make them into government institutions. Students from Kwang Hua University, the institution formed by St. John's dissidents after the May 30th Movement, threatened to take over St. John's. Except at Hua-chung University in Wuchang, however, none of the protest movements received as much support from official sources as those in Canton and Changsha, and they were, as a rule, less successful.

For many of the Christian institutions the action of southern troops proved more disruptive than the agitation of youth because it was the former that led to the departure of Westerners and the closing of schools. During the Northern Expedition, confiscation of school and church properties was widespread; some foreigners were injured or publicly humiliated, and a few were killed. Perhaps even more terrifying were the rumors about murder, rape, and looting by

[81] A brief report issued by Lingnan University in 1927, entitled "Carrying On," gives details on the strikes; located at MRL. See also, Corbett, *Lingnan University*, pp. 100–112; Lingnan University, *Catalogue, 1928–29*, p. 13. An English translation of the "Demands of the Staff Union of Canton Christian College" is included in the correspondence of D. H. Leavens, April 23, 1927 (Yali Archives, Box 30).

troops and local populace and the uncertainty about what would happen when the fighting reached one's own city. Though some Chinese offered what protection they could by hiding missionary friends or persuading troops not to enter foreign compounds, such action was unpopular and even dangerous before the wave of anti-foreign nationalism. Other Chinese joined in the attacks on the foreigners either because of personal animosity, because the missionary seemed the ever-present reminder of China's humiliation, or because it was the popular and profitable thing to do under the circumstances. In addition, mission installations along with Buddhist compounds were frequently the most attractive facilities available for housing troops or setting up officers' quarters; their hospitals were the best equipped in the countryside; troop commanders found it natural and justifiable to press these into service of the nationalist cause.

The most widely publicized incident occurred at Nanking on March 24, 1927, when southern troops occupied the city and inaugurated a reign of terror against foreigners, a reign which was quickly ended by a barrage from United States and British gunboats. Five residences at the University of Nanking were burned, and many more buildings were looted; John E. Williams, vice-president of the university, was shot to death when he hesitated to hand over a gold watch demanded by a soldier, and all foreigners feared for their lives until they could escape to the foreign ships. The Nanking incident persuaded most missionaries who had remained in the interior despite advice from their governments, to leave. Only about 500 of the approximately 8,000 Protestant missionaries who had been in China were still in the interior in July 1927.[82] The campuses of the Christian colleges in the coastal cities were used as refuges for missionaries from the interior. With the depletion of teaching

[82] Latourette, *History of Christian Missions*, p. 820. There are available a number of reports on the Nanking incident by foreigners in China at the time; see Pearl Buck, *My Several Worlds* (New York, 1954), pp. 206–210; M. Searle Bates, "The Ordeal of Nanking," *The Missionary Review of the World*, Aug. 1927, p. 587; and the file, "Conditions in China, 1927," MRL. H. Owen Chapman, *The Chinese Revolution, 1926–27* (London, 1928) gives an eye witness account of Hankow while it was under left-wing control. For a study of these events as they relate to United States foreign policy, see Dorothy Borg, *American Policy and the Chinese Revolution, 1925–1928* (New York, 1947).

and administrative staffs, most of the colleges closed. In many cases the departing college presidents hurriedly appointed Chinese as acting deans, department heads, and presidents and delegated to them authority to make decisions appropriate to the emergency situation. The Chinese members of the boards of managers were empowered to assume the duties of the full board and to coopt additional members if they desired. Some Chinese resented their being asked to take control at such a difficult time; they pointed out that shortly before, missionaries had argued that there were not enough experienced Chinese to administer the colleges. Non-Christian Chinese were little inclined to give credit to the Westerners for acceding under duress to demands which had earlier been resisted.

In spite of misunderstandings the Chinese and the few remaining missionaries made every effort to keep their institutions alive, and in the fall of 1927 most of the colleges reopened. Several small institutions which had been struggling to attain college standards now gave up hope of becoming colleges; they decided to concentrate on work at the middle school level; Lutheran College at Iyang, Huping College at Yochow, and Talmage College at Amoy were in this category; as mentioned, Yali transferred college level work to Huachung University when the latter reopened in 1929.

Class work at some schools was still upon occasion disrupted by student unrest. At Hangchow in the fall of 1927 eight outstanding students in the college were accused of being communists, and when the accusing document was discovered to be forgery, thirty students were dismissed. Cheeloo was kept in a state of uproar by strikes and demonstrations during most of the fall of 1929. Though the movement began in October with a request for a Chinese dean for the College of Arts and Science in order to speed registration, a few radical students in contact with outside organizations appear to have gained control. In fact, the techniques and demands would have seemed quite familiar to any one who had experienced the student storms in Changsha or Canton in 1926–1927. A parade on October 22 was followed on October 28 by a mass meeting at which the students voted to strike until a suitable dean had been appointed and to leave school en masse if any student were expelled for his actions in support of the movement. The new dean, according to some of the more radical students, should be a well-educated man with a Ph.D.

from a Chinese institution, a man of long experience and of outstanding reputation in educational circles, not a member of the present University staff, not a medical man and not an adherent of any religion." [83] Then, while students and administrators were seeking a compromise settlement, came a demand for the resignation of President Li T'ien-lu and threats to burn college buildings if the resignation were not immediately forthcoming. President Li resigned despite the protests of the Westerners, and peace returned briefly.

On November 18, however, the students went on strike again to renew the pressure for progress toward registration, and on December 31 the workmen walked off their jobs in a dispute over wages and working conditions. Power lines were cut, pickets posted to enforce the strike, and attempts made to cut the supplies of food and water to the hospital and college. Students were urged to launch special anti-Christian activities during the Christmas season, and some of the literature attacking Cheeloo equaled in violence the most extreme statements of the educational rights campaign: "We all want to recover the educational rights vested in Cheeloo, and we wish to destroy all the nests of cultural penetration. Cheeloo was established by the English and the Americans, and it serves as an organ of cultural aggression and destruction of the Chinese race. . . . Cheeloo, a cooperative undertaking of thirteen missions, is the headquarters of the imperialists of North China. The influence of this institution in destroying Chinese intellectual life is more dangerous than big Krupp guns pointed at our breasts. Now that we are awake we solemnly vow to eliminate this obstacle to China's progress." [84] The university was officially closed on January 7, though some of the strikers refused to leave campus. Only after Nanking sent orders demanding an immediate settlement did the workers' strike end in February 1930; the College of Medicine and the hospital reopened immediately; the liberal arts divisions opened the following fall.

[83] Quoted in Corbett, *Shantung*, p. 173.

[84] *Ibid.*, p. 174. According to Corbett, the Propaganda Department of the Provincial Committee of the Kuomintang in Tsinan aided and advised a small group of Cheeloo students, and negotiations had to be conducted with party representatives as well as student leaders; pickets at the school displayed the Nationalist colors as they tried to cut supplies of food and water. On page 175 Corbett quotes from a party directive urging students to step up their attacks during the Christmas season.

St. John's was also the object of attack by groups demanding restoration of educational rights. When St. John's, which had been officially closed during most of 1927, proposed to reopen without changing to meet the registration requirements, activists founded associations to oppose the resumption of operations. A Union of Ex-St. John's Students and a Federation of Schools Opposed to the Opening of St. John's University joined with Kwang Hua University students in petitioning the government to take control of St. John's. The youth received little support from Nanking, however, and the university reopened without public announcement in the fall of 1928; only a small and very carefully selected student body was admitted.

Despite occasional storms such as those at Cheeloo and Hangchow, the educational rights campaign declined rapidly after the Kuomintang had completed the Northern Expedition. Christian colleges were still under pressure to accept government supervision, and misunderstandings between Westerner and Chinese could easily grow into open confrontation; nevertheless, the concerted campaign to end the separate identity of the Christian institutions had ebbed, and most of the schools found that if they made perceptible progress toward meeting the demands of the older generation for registration, they could avoid the student storms of the younger generation. The educational rights campaign and the Northern Expedition had convinced most missionary educators of the urgency of meeting nationalist demands, and the flight of the missionaries in 1927 had placed Chinese in most of the top administrative positions in the colleges. Under Chinese leadership and with the support of the returning missionaries, therefore, most of the Christian colleges moved toward fulfilling the registration requirements. The process was often difficult and lengthy, for changes in the Nanking educational administration and in registration requirements were frequent and some home mission boards were still reluctant to accept the regulations.[85]

[85] Ch'iang Shu-ko, *Chung-kuo chin-tai chiao-yü chih-tu* (The Modern Education System of China) (Shanghai, 1934), devotes chapter vii to "The Regulation of Private Schools and the Restoration of Educational Rights"; see esp. pp. 158–167 for a discussion of various registration requirements. During the late 1920's various groups, factions of the Kuomintang and of the educational community, were competing for control of educational administration; there

By 1929 most colleges had made religious worship and instruction voluntary, and most of them had a Chinese president or chancellor and a Chinese majority on the board of managers. Since the schools could not list the propagation of religion as one of their purposes, a number of them stated that they offered education in a spirit of "love, sacrifice, and service." This phrase, coined by Lin Ching-jun of Fukien Christian College, satisfied the Ministry of Education and at the same time expressed the Christian purpose of the schools for the missionaries.

New government rules, however, listed minimum requirements in budget, library, and laboratory facilities, number and type of departments, and faculty training before an institution could be registered as a college or a university. Some of the smaller colleges needed several years in which to achieve the standards set. Even Shantung Christian University was judged substandard. The provincial inspection committee which visited Tsinan in 1929 said that the library of 24,000 volumes was inadequate, the training of a number of the teachers was below par, the college should offer more than one foreign language, the College of Theology should be separated from the rest of the university, the university must have at least three faculties whereas it now had only two (the College of Theology was not counted), and two-thirds, not just a majority of the board of directors must be Chinese. Shantung took two years to satisfy the requirements of the government and obtain registration. Hangchow, which had been closed in 1928 because of reluctance by the American board of trustees to meet the religious requirements, reopened in 1929 with a Chinese as acting president and with voluntary religious instruction. Since Hangchow's former students had already transferred to other schools and did not return, the institution was at first able to maintain only a middle school and a junior college. This meant that the college was now below government academic standards and still unable to register. The University of Nanking and Shanghai College (the University of Shanghai as of 1931) were among the first to be registered; they completed the process in 1929. By 1931 Yenching, Ginling, Soochow, Fukien, and Canton had also

were, therefore, frequent changes in educational policy, see Allen B. Linden, "Politics and Education in Nationalist China: The Case of the University Council, 1927–28," *JAS*, XXVII (Aug. 1968), 763–776.

registered. With the exception of St. John's, which chose to function as an unregistered institution, the remaining Christian colleges were negotiating with the government, but had not yet satisfied the authorities on all requirements.[86]

The fact that most of the Christian colleges were making a real effort to register with the government certainly contributed to the decline of the educational rights campaign; the schools were beginning to meet many of the demands of the older generation. The goals of the younger generation went far beyond the registration requirements, however, and additional explanations must be provided for the abatement of student strikes and demonstrations. For one thing the youth never ceased to think of themselves as students working for academic degrees, those essential passports to civil service and educational positions. Though they felt a responsibility in an emergency to act as the conscience of China, few students were willing to become full-time revolutionaries. Few were even willing to become full-time political activists for more than a short period. Emotional fatigue and concern about academic careers became factors of increasing importance as activist students called for new demonstrations which would disrupt school work and perhaps lead to the closing of the institution. Establishment of the Nanking government and a decline in the revolutionary atmosphere meant that it was more difficult to persuade students of the necessity and legitimacy of extra-legal activity. In more than one case, therefore, techniques which had formerly been successful in securing support for a student storm failed after the summer of 1927.

Also significant was the reduction of assistance to students by outside groups. In Canton, Changsha, and other centers, the Kuomintang and the Chinese Communist Party had furnished aid, advice, and even leadership to the students. With the break between the Chinese Communist Party and the Kuomintang, communists had to go underground; many of the young leaders had to abandon their followers and seek safety in the countryside or the international concessions. Even so, many communists and suspected communists were jailed or executed in the purge; among those who lost their lives was T'ang Chien, the leader of the national student union and a communist. The student union itself split into procommunist and

[86] C. S. Miao, "Status of Registration," *CCYB, 1931*, p. 250.

anticommunist factions in the spring of 1927 and could no longer provide unified guidance to its branches. The Chinese communist leadership, in its disorientation, not only lost contact with many youth groups but seemed uncertain about the reliability of intellectuals and the desirability of incorporating them in the party; there was a drastic decline in membership in the Communist Youth Corps during 1927. The party could no longer give the kind of direction and assistance to youth that it had before the split with the Kuomintang.

In the spring of 1927 Kuomintang leaders were having second thoughts about the political activism of students, and various factions were debating the proper relationship between students and the party and between students and politics.[87] Though the Kuomintang had encouraged and benefited from student-initiated demonstrations during the Northern Expedition, party leaders had discovered that they could not always control student demands, which often exceeded the goals of the party, at least the goals of that faction seeking dominance after the Kuomintang-Chinese Communist Party split. Most Kuomintang leaders, for example, were happy to see the Christian schools made subject to government supervision and to have Chinese placed in the top administrative positions, but the party government was not prepared to assume administrative responsibility for the institutions; nor did it want to reduce the already inadequate educational facilities of China by destroying the Christian schools. Local left-wing leaders whose actions threatened the existence of the Christian colleges did not always gain the support of the central party administration. At Fukien Christian College in 1927, the Kuomintang leader who sparked the attempt to take control of the institution was transferred to another party post, and at Cheeloo in 1929–1930 the Nanking government forced a reduction in demands so that a settlement could be reached and the school reopened.

As the Kuomintang became the party of the responsible government, it became less enthusiastic about the extra-legal activities and political activism of students. The party was deeply disturbed, more-

---

[87] For an analysis of student-Kuomintang relations during the first years of Nationalist rule, see Israel, *Student Nationalism*, ch. ii, "Time for Decision; 1927–1931."

over, by the influence exercised by the Communist Party and other left-wing groups upon student associations, and it began a campaign to bring the student union and other student organizations under tight Kuomintang surveillance and control. In April and May, 1927, Chiang Kai-shek blamed the communists for the excesses of the Northern Expedition and called for a purge of communists from the student union; in 1928 the Kuomintang prescribed the reorganization of the student unions as student self-government associations having no political functions. Henceforth, college youth could join the Kuomintang only as individuals. In his speeches to student groups and educational associations Chiang argued that student campaigns were legitimate when they were in support of a revolutionary party, i.e., the Kuomintang, seeking to overturn a reactionary government; now that the revolutionary party represented the government, student campaigns against authority were reactionary and illegal. Students should, therefore, end mass movements, demonstrations, and strikes and should concentrate on constructive endeavors, that is, academic work. Discipline and obedience became the virtues emphasized by Chiang Kai-shek.[88] Student campaigning did move into a period of relative quietude which lasted until the flare-up in 1931 over the Japanese invasion of Manchuria. With the decline in the revolutionary atmosphere, both student activism and the exhilaration of 1926–1927 ebbed. The coincidence between the decline of student activism and the change in Kuomintang and Chinese Communist Party policies is indicative of the importance of party aid in the anti-Christian and educational rights campaigns.

The anti-Christian and educational rights campaigns of the 1920's forcefully illustrate the power of nationalism among Chinese intellectuals and the strong strain of anti-Westernism in Chinese nationalism. None dared oppose arguments presented in the name of nationalism, and when nationalistic arguments were used against Christianity and its works, few came to the defense. The unforgivable sins of Christianity in the eyes of most Chinese were that it was

[88] "To Provincial and Municipal Educational Authorities, University Districts and Presidents of Government Universities," *ER*, XX (1928), 394–395; "Order of the National Government Regarding Discipline of Students," *ibid.*, XXI (1929), 197–198. For translations of several of Chiang Kai-shek's speeches on this subject, see Wieger, *Chine Moderne*, VIII, 126–129, 163.

foreign and that it was an obstacle to the building of a powerful and unified China. Conservatives might criticize Christianity because it destroyed Chinese tradition; liberals might emphasize the conflict between religion and modern science, and radicals might stress the ties between Christian missions and the Western imperialist nations, but they all agreed that Christianity and Chinese nationalism were incompatible. Almost no one questioned the theses that the major goal of education was to serve the nation and that China had no room for institutions with the dual purpose of evangelism and education. Though Chinese were offended by the Christian college requirements concerning courses in religion and attendance at worship, they were even more disturbed by the idea of a foreign religion pervading the whole educational program of the schools.[89] Common to all the emphases in Chinese nationalism was a deep resentment of superior Western power.

During the early 1920's missionaries generally underestimated the depth and popularity of anti-Christian sentiment. They offered specific explanations for incidents: a particular Western administrator had shown himself insensitive to rising Chinese nationalism; Chinese were ignorant of the true goals of Christian missions and the real teachings of Christianity; Christians must show that there was no real conflict between Christianity and science or between Christianity and Chinese nationalism. Or, there was the familiar thesis that the anti-Christian campaigns were simply the creations of the Bolsheviks. In all of these explanations there was an element of truth. Baxter of Lingnan and Hawks Pott of St. John's did find negotiating with students difficult, if not humiliating, and they did try to insist on fulfillment of academic obligations in what was a revolutionary situation; in one instance, a faculty member at Yali did use physical force against a student. But certainly the inadequacies of a few administrators do not provide a sufficient explanation for the *hsüeh-ch'ao* which struck practically all the Christian colleges. At least some of the schools were under the leadership of individuals who made an extraordinary effort to understand and meet the demands

[89] Typical are the criticisms in Li Ju-mien, "Chiao-hui ta-hsüeh wen-t'i" (The Problem of the Christian Colleges) and in Ch'ang Tao-chih, "Tui-yü chiao-hui ta-hsüeh wen-t'i chih kuan-chien" (Opinion Concerning the Problem of the Christian Colleges), *CHCYC*, XIV, no. 8.

of the students, and their schools were also the objects of attack. Baxter and Hawks Pott were not newcomers to China, and they were using techniques which had gotten them through difficult situations in previous years; the atmosphere among the students was new, however, and old techniques were no longer adequate. Though the aid of the Kuomintang and the Communist Party helps explain the organizational know-how and the power behind the student movements, it does not explain why Christianity and Christian institutions were singled out for attack.

As the demonstrations and strikes spread to most of the Christian colleges and as participants came from the Christian college communities themselves, missionaries had to admit that specific explanations claiming ignorance, outside initiative, or administrative mismanagement were no longer sufficient. They were forced to acknowledge the popularity of the thesis that Christianity and Christian schools were an offense to Chinese nationalism and the necessity of adjusting to nationalist demands. If the anti-Christian movements reveal anything, they illustrate the emotional base of Chinese nationalism, an emotional base heavily dependent on negativism. A recital of Chinese losses arising out of missionary incidents could feed resentment against Westerners just as an insult by a Westerner could trigger a student storm, but the resentment was essentially an outgrowth of the unequal relationship between China and the West, of the inequality built into the assumptions of Christian missionaries who came to bring their knowledge and doctrines to China. Resentment toward the Westerners, therefore, could not be dissipated by rational explanations of the benefits of Christian missions brought to China in the way of hospitals, schools, and social service activities. For most Chinese the benefits could not offset the implication of inferiority and humiliation underlying both the treaty system and the missionary venture.

The anti-Christian campaigns of the 1920's contributed to a tradition linking youth movements, political parties, and political decisions. Both the Kuomintang and the Chinese Communist Party understood something of the power of nationalism and the significance of anti-imperialism and anti-Westernism as the basis of nationalism. They encouraged and aided students in developing techniques of public demonstration, and they even made use of pressure tactics for their own political benefit. These experiences were significant in the evolution of a role for the New Youth and the development of their concept of themselves as a separate generation. The May 4th Movement became not just an incident but a tradition, a model to be followed by subsequent generations of students. The Kuomintang and the Chinese Communist Party were willing to use the May 4 tradition in specific instances, though neither had yet committed itself to a definite policy toward the New Youth and political activism by students.

In the history of the China Christian colleges the events of the 1920's closed an era. The schools ceased to be foreign institutions run by foreigners for the propagation of a foreign doctrine. The process of Sinification had been abruptly accelerated in 1926–1928 as Chinese acquired top administrative positions and became a majority in the teaching ranks. Educational goals were to be primary, and the evangelical goals would have to find a place within the context of an educational program supervised by the government. This reversal of emphasis was accepted only after much soul searching; for some, it was accepted out of necessity as the educational rights campaign revealed that the alternative was the end of Christian education in China; for others, it became an opportunity to demonstrate the value of Christianity to the Chinese nation. Certain features distinguishing the Christian colleges from other institutions of higher education in China did remain: the foreign financial support and with it a degree of influence in policy decisions, the Christian atmosphere which the Christian teachers sought to maintain, the international character of the faculty, the liberal arts orientation, and the emphasis on campus community life. As a rule, however, the Christian colleges entered increasingly into the educational life of the nation.

VIII | Sinification and Secularization, the 1930's

Despite disappointment over Kuomintang actions against left-wing groups and dismay at the Manchurian incident of 1931, many nationalistic Chinese during the early 1930's kept alive the hope that a revitalized China was moving toward national unity and power. They anticipated that the creation of a Sino-Western synthesis would give form and content to that amorphous Chinese nation which had already captured their loyalty. Research projects were undertaken to gather the empirical knowledge necessary for economic policies and theories relevant to the Chinese environment. Political unity seemed a possibility as the Kuomintang bent every effort to eliminate alternative foci of power. The party government fostered educational expansion as a means of instilling national loyalty; it promoted a national economy by improving railways and highways, creating a national fiscal system, encouraging industrialization, and gaining control of Chinese customs. In the international realm it sought recognition as an equal and sovereign state. Though Japan refused to accord China such recognition and even augmented her demands for special privileges, the Western powers were moving hesitantly toward ending the unequal treaties.

Admittedly, much of this activity was still at the talking stage, but even so intellectuals believed that China had awakened. Many Chinese found a new pride and self respect as they identified themselves with the new China and worked to define and form her. These educated Chinese were not always masters of the Chinese heritage; many had been abroad to study, and others had received a modern education in the national institutions or the Christian

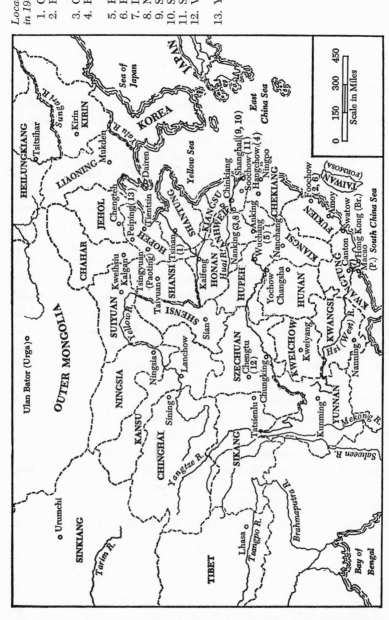

Location of Christian Colleges
in 1930

1. Cheeloo University, Tsinan
2. Fukien Christian University,
   Foochow
3. Ginling College, Nanking
4. Hangchow Christian College,
   Hangchow
5. Huachung University, Wuchang
6. Hwa Nan College, Foochow
7. Lingnan University, Canton
8. Nanking University of, Nanking
9. St. John's University, Shanghai
10. Shanghai College, Shanghai
11. Soochow University, Soochow
12. West China Union University,
    Chengtu
13. Yenching University, Peiping

China, 1930

colleges. They, better than the old gentry, understood the sources of Western power. At the same time they were intensely conscious that they were Chinese, for their very contact with non-Chinese people and customs had sharpened their awareness of the existence of a Chinese nation. It had also made them more desirous of altering China so that she could compete as an equal in the international ring. They were not so tightly tied to the Chinese heritage that they could not bear to change. They talked much about the worth of a Sino-Western synthesis, but when conflict developed between elements of the old and the new, they generally came down on the side of the new. Although they often spoke of the importance of "the people," the gap between them and the peasants was wide and deep. They had trouble remembering to include the peasants in their thinking and planning. Idealistic and nationalistic as many Chinese intellectuals were, their orientation was urban and Western. Western-type education in an urban environment had been the wellspring of their nationalism, and they often continued to use a Western framework as they tried to place their knowledge at the service of China; they wanted to continue to live in the bustling, modernizing cities of China rather than go to the slower-paced interior towns to work.

In a nation still overwhelmingly agrarian, this gap between peasant and intellectual was a serious weakness; educated Chinese have been criticized for failing China because of their physical and mental isolation from the bulk of the nation. There were, however, a few Chinese and Westerners who understood the importance of revolution in rural China and were willing to work for it. In addition to the activities of the Chinese communists, there were rural reconstruction projects fostered by a number of educated Chinese and their Western colleagues. These rural reconstruction projects were small and few, and what they managed to accomplish before they were swept away by the Sino-Japanese conflict and civil war was meager; nevertheless, they are among the more interesting aspects of Chinese history during the 1930's.

Many of the strengths and weaknesses and many of the emphases of the new China found expression in the Christian colleges. After the turbulence and humiliation of the 1920's came a brief period of hope, even optimism. Perhaps, after all, the Christian colleges would

274 | CHINA AND THE CHRISTIAN COLLEGES, 1850–1950

find a permanent place on the Chinese scene. Efforts were made to adapt the curricula to the needs of modern China and at the same time to give greater attention to the Chinese heritage. Most of the institutions grew in strength. Their student enrollment climbed, and the proportion of faculty members with graduate degrees increased. Where most of the schools had formerly had one or two-man departments and had offered majors in such general areas as the social sciences or the physical sciences, many now expanded their staffs and offered majors in specific subjects. Several of the institutions developed special areas of strength, for example, the School of Dentistry at West China Union University, the College of Agriculture at the University of Nanking, and the Department of Biology at Soochow University. Slowly, most colleges were completing the process of registering with the government; and a number of schools established cordial relations with the provincial and national administrations. They received financial support from the Chinese government and from individual Chinese patrons, and they were awarded contracts by the government or business concerns for research and training projects. A number of the colleges tried to channel the patriotic sentiment of their students into social service projects for peasants and workers.

This assimilation was generally conducted under the leadership of Chinese administrators. Government registration had required that either the college president or vice-president be Chinese, and transfer of title had frequently occurred during the chaos of 1926–1928. The schools continued during the 1930's to raise the percentage of Chinese faculty members and to increase the number of Chinese in responsible positions. Not that Westerners ceased to have influence in the Christian colleges; they still played an important role, partly because they included able individuals who identified themselves with the life of the college and provided continuity and partly because significant financial support came from the West. The presidents of two of the best known Christian colleges were Americans: J. Leighton Stuart of Yenching and F. L. Hawks Pott of St. John's. Religious education and activities were generally in the hands of Westerners.

Except for some of the instructors in classical Chinese, the Chinese teachers and administrators in the Christian colleges had secured a

Western-type education. They, like many Chinese intellectuals, were partially Western in orientation, but intensely Chinese in their national loyalty. A sizeable proportion of the college staff had, in fact, attended one of the Christian colleges and then had gone abroad for further training. They too were seeking a synthesis between East and West, and they hoped that their institutions might become educational models or at least experimental centers in the search for an educational system for new China. Their task was complicated by the fact that in the college communities Christianity was considered a necessary part of the Western heritage. As in earlier years, they sometimes found the needs of the schools as educational institutions in conflict with evangelistic goals. In most of the colleges, though, the educational demands received priority, and the aim of the institution came to be defined in such broad terms as the provision of a quality education in a Christian atmosphere. Concern over the secularization of the colleges was, however, widespread both in China and abroad.

Despite hope and even some real accomplishments, neither the Kuomintang government nor the Christian colleges moved as rapidly toward strength and a new Chinese synthesis as many educated Chinese demanded. The college administrators, like the government leaders, lived increasingly under the shadow of Japanese ambitions. They found themselves caught between the students' demands for active nationalist expression and their own concern with the tasks at hand and, like the government leaders, were irritated by criticisms from what they considered the irresponsible opposition. For the colleges, there loomed the discouraging possibility that external events rather than their own efforts would largely determine their future.

One characteristic of the Christian colleges during the 1930's, their growing individuality, makes generalization increasingly difficult. Differences among the early Christian colleges had often resulted from the influence of the college president. Calvin Mateer of Tengchow, Hawks Pott of St. John's, and Mrs. Lawrence Thurston of Ginling had dominated their institutions and thus had contributed to their differing emphases. All of the small, struggling schools, however, were at first concerned with the basic tasks of building a curriculum and a campus, collecting a faculty and a student clientele, and finding a satisfactory relationship between evangelism and education. The very similarity of their concerns dictated a certain similarity in the institutions and their policies. By the 1930's the separate schools had fashioned their individual reputations and were building their own special areas of strength. They had developed their own clientele and alumni who tended to accentuate the separate traditions. Several of the colleges were now growing quite rapidly in size and strength, whereas others remained small and poor. Some came to be dominated by secular interests, whereas a few remained deeply religious in orientation and closely tied to the mission boards in the West. Many of them had become so large and had acquired such vigorous traditions that they could no longer be shaped by a single individual. The institutions were as different as the prosperous and influential Yenching, proud of its growing integration in the intellectual life of Peiping, and Hwa Nan, a small girls' school, evangelistic in purpose and ever struggling to attain and retain college status. Cheeloo, with a medical school that almost overwhelmed the other divisions of the university, stood in contrast to St. John's, still attractive as an entrée to study abroad and positions of influence. Though generalizations can be induced from the histories of the institutions, the individuality of the schools should be kept in mind.

Redefinition of Goals: Service to the Chinese Nation

One concern of all the Christian colleges during the early 1930's was a redefinition of their role. The conclusions which the individual schools reached might differ, but the anti-Christian movement and the educational rights campaign had made obvious the need for rethinking goals. The campaigns had demonstrated that most Chinese students did not consider Christianity a universal religion. When many condemned Christian missions as the vanguard of Western imperialism, missionaries saw Christianity cast in the role of enemy to the Chinese nation. A conflict of loyalties between Christianity and nationalism confronted the student contemplating Christian conversion; and he, like many other individuals throughout the twentieth-century world, generally chose to bow down before nationalism. Clearly, a conscious effort to interpret Christianity within the context of Chinese nationalism was imperative.

Christianity would have to be presented as compatible with Chinese nationalism, even as a source of strength for the Chinese nation-state.

At the same time the means by which the Christian message was presented in the colleges had to be altered. The educators could no longer hope to reach each student by compulsory chapel attendance and required religious courses, since government registration regulations permitted only voluntary religious activities and insisted on primary emphasis on the educational goal of the institution. In view of these restrictions, a number of difficult questions had to be answered. What were the aims of the Christian colleges? Were these goals different from those of secular institutions? Could the colleges any longer be considered a part of the missionary effort and be given the support of the mission boards? How best to exercise Christian influence within the government regulations?

A few schools decided that the government regulations and their religious goals and educational independence were incompatible. St. John's University, for example, refused to seek registration until the late 1930's and did not complete the process until after the war, but even it moved toward voluntary religious activities. In the 1928–1929 and 1929–1930 college catalogues, requirements included attendance at daily morning chapel and at either a divine worship service or an ethical lecture on Sunday. A note stated that chapel attendance was voluntary for non-Christians, but clearly abstention would not be looked upon with favor and would set apart those who took advantage of the option; Christians had no choice. By 1932–1933 morning chapel had been replaced by morning roll call, and the requirement concerning Sunday services had been dropped. These regulations remained unchanged from 1933 to 1937, and then with the application for registration in 1937, the whole section on extracurricular requirements was omitted.[1] Lutheran College in central China had closed in 1926 because of the nationalist and anti-Christian campaign and because of opposition to registration requirements. Though the mission talked of reopening Lutheran as a small private college with strong evangelistic emphasis, it never

[1] See St. John's Catalogues, 1928–1929, p. 68; 1929–30, pp. 62–63; 1930–1931, p. 76; 1932–1933, pp. 76–77; 1933–1934, p. 80; 1934–1935, p. 83; 1935–1936; p. 86, 1936–1937, p. 88.

did so. Certain would-be colleges such as Ningpo Methodist and Talmage (Reformed Church in America) near Amoy altered their goals; some became middle schools subject to government supervision and some remained private middle schools serving a limited constitutency.

The other Christian colleges resumed their activities and worked toward finding a role within the national educational program. Christianity, they said, would be best served if it were demonstrated that Christianity served the needs of China. Education in the Christian colleges must contribute to the strength and greatness of China, and for Christian educators such education necessarily included Christian moral standards and values. Cheeloo, which had been known for its close ties with the church, stated that its original purpose had been to serve the Christian constituency and the Christian movement, but now its purpose must become the service of the Chinese people as a whole.[2] But how were such goals to be translated into practical policy?

One popular theme of the 1930's was character building. China needed trained leaders in all fields of work, and if the Christian colleges could train leaders who were both expert in technical and professional fields and Christian in character and personality, they would be serving the Christian cause by serving China. An article by N. Z. Zia of Lingnan is illustrative of many attempts to redefine the function of Christian higher education and of the broad, even nebulous goals set forth. Zia argued that schools which made education a tool for religion were examples of cultural exploitation and should be abolished. Christian education, he maintained, should be a matter of spirit, not form; like many Chinese Christians, he differentiated between Christianity as the teachings of Christ and Christianity as an institutionalized religion. The former, with a minimum of cultural baggage from the West, he could accept and attempt to translate into a meaningful guide for China; the church as a middle-class Western institution had little appeal. Zia's article ended with

[2] "Statements Concerning Christian Higher Education in China, July, 1928" (mimeo., MRL pamphlet), p. 24. These are quite frank evaluations by the colleges themselves in preparation for an attempt to work out a correlated program for the schools.

the hope that the infusion of the spirit of Christ among Kuomintang leaders would revitalize, purify, and unify the Kuomintang.[3] One finds much the same emphasis on character building in the writings of missionary educators, though Westerners were more likely to add the hope that influential Chinese Christians would contribute to a favorable attitude toward the church.

To most mission boards such definitions of the colleges' role seemed to be compatible with the missionary goals of the Western churches and to justify continued financial support. The question of how one built Christian character still had to be answered, however. Influenced by popular theories about the importance of environment in molding the individual, many answered: by creating a Christian environment for the students. And so, the CCEA expressed concern over the percentage of Christians among students and recommended that the colleges maintain a faculty that was three-quarters Christian.[4] Here the educators came into conflict with other goals: the desire to raise educational standards and to Sinify the institutions, and the attempt to increase the proportion of financial support from Chinese sources. Since less than 1 percent of the Chinese population was Christian, the number of qualified Christian students seeking admission to the colleges was limited. Most of these came from Christian middle schools and many came from relatively poor families. Could one justify admitting a Christian student who would require financial aid in preference to a non-Christian able to pay tuition and presenting a better transcript? If one chose to admit students almost exclusively from the Christian feeder schools, was not one fostering a separate educational system which could exert little influence on the educational system of China? Would not one be cultivating a group of hothouse Christians? The demand was for Chinese teachers and administrators, and yet it was not easy to find Chinese with both a Ph.D. degree and a baptismal certificate. Which was more important? College

[3] "Are Christian Education and Party Education Conflicting?" *ER*, XX (April 1928), 181–187.
[4] "News," *ER*, XX (July 1928), 303–304; "Christian Education," *ER*, XXI (Jan. 1929), 23–25; George H. Betts, "The Need of Better Defined Objectives in Religious Education," *ER*, XXIII (Jan. 1931), 14–17.

administrators found themselves caught again on the horns of the old dilemma. Which should be given primacy, the schools' needs as educational institutions or as instruments of Christian evangelism?

All colleges sought a compromise in their answers, but the policies of some were much more secular in emphasis than others. It seems clear that those institutions which chose to maintain a high percentage of Christian students were also making the choice, consciously or unconsciously, to remain small. In 1930–1931, the 13 Protestant colleges listed 3,239 students in their arts and science divisions; 6 of the 7 colleges with enrollments of less than 200 had student bodies which were more than 70 percent Christian. In contrast, the 6 colleges with more than 200 students each had a student body which was less than half Christian, and by 1935 some of the larger colleges reported a decline in this proportion to one-quarter. In many of the colleges less than one-third of the students attended the voluntary worship services or elected the courses in religion. Despite a recommendation that three-fourths of the faculty be Christian, 6 of the arts colleges in 1930 failed to attain this goal, and any increase in the proportion of Chinese teachers was likely to decrease the ratio.[5]

Such statistics were hardly calculated to bring joy to Christian evangelists and mission board members. Even committed Christian teachers had difficulty maintaining a Christian atmosphere when less than half of the students were Christian. The colleges, furthermore, were not experiencing any great success in converting their students to Christianity; most of those who were Christians had become so before entering college. Also disturbing was the realization that many of the students who were Christian did not maintain their ties with the church after graduation.

By the mid-1930's the colleges were talking of demonstrating the spirit of Christianity by supplementing the educational system of China, instilling an ideal of social service among Christian college

[5] CCEA, *Statistical Report, 1930–31*, Tables 2, 4, 5, 7, 8. The six largest schools were Nanking, Yenching, Soochow, St. John's, Shanghai, and Lingnan. The three colleges where more than 80 percent of the students were Christian were Cheeloo, with 129 students, Fukien with 126, and Hwa Nan with 97 (CCEA, *Report on the Religious Life in the Christian Colleges in China*, Bul. no. 37 [Shanghai, 1936], pp. 6–7).

students, and contributing to the rural reconstruction of China. Certainly, such a concept of purpose was a far cry from that of the founding fathers, and even in the 1930's it was sharply attacked by conservative Christian groups and by many evangelists. The Christian educators were accused of neglecting the conversion of China and of contributing little to the growth of the church. The gap between those missionaries emphasizing the social gospel and those primarily concerned with the salvation of souls was, in part, a reflection of division within the church in the West, but the gap between the two wings was broader and deeper in China than in most of Christendom.[6] This was because of a tendency toward segregation of conservatives and liberals in different types of activities and because the Chinese environment seemed to encourage the liberals in an unusually broad interpretation of their work. The liberal wing of the Christian church had traditionally dominated in the colleges, while conservatives generally preferred more direct means of evangelism. Missionary educators argued that religion could not be disembodied theory; it must be intimately related to the environment in which it existed,[7] and there was little chance of Christianizing China unless a new society were created and Christianity had a role in forming and buttressing that society. Thus, contributions by the Christian colleges to the modernization of Chinese agriculture and industry and to the acceptance of ideals of social service and responsible citizenship were contributions to the missionary goal.

The expanding role of Chinese in the colleges was also conducive to an emphasis on service to society and nation. A political and social interpretation of religion could be expected to find a congenial reception in China. Such an interpretation of the role of religion might be only one thread in the Christian tapestry but it

[6] For a discussion of the divisions within the Protestant churches of the United States as they found expression in China missions, see Varg, *Missionaries, Chinese, and Diplomats,* esp. ch. ix, "The Crusade Runs into Stumbling Blocks at Home Base, 1919–1931," and ch. xiii, "The Rise of the Christian Socialization Wing of Missionaries, 1920–1931."

[7] One of the more interesting and thoughtful discussions along these lines is Joseph Rutten, "Les Obstacles à l'évangélisation de la Chine," in Museum Lessianum, Section Missiologique, *Obstacles à l'apostolat* (Louvain, 1929), pp. 30–49 (trans. selections in Lutz, *Christian Missions in China,* pp. 26–33).

was the very warp of traditional Chinese philosophy. One of the more frequent criticisms of Christianity during the 1920's had been that it was an escapist religion. Consciously or unconsciously echoing Marx, Chinese had accused the Christian church of offering little guidance in this life and of concentrating on the next life so that present troubles and injustices would seem bearable.[8] Chinese Christians naturally welcomed the social humanism of liberal Christianity; this interpretation they could understand and appreciate. As they became administrators in the Christian colleges, they helped redefine the role of the institutions, and no more laudable goal seemed possible than the service of Christianity through service to Chinese society.

Finally, the influence of nationalism on the popularity of the social service theme should not be overlooked. Both the nationalist and religious loyalties of Chinese educators could find expression in the goal of creating a new Chinese society. Some college administrators also hoped that by emphasizing social service they could channel the energies of students away from less acceptable activities, such as public demonstrations and participation in left-wing associations. College youth were still looking for an effective program to make China strong and respected and for a clear delineation of their role in the creation of a new China.[9] Many were already becoming disillusioned with the Kuomintang government, and the Chinese Communist Party, despite its weakness and confusion during the early 1930's, continued to represent for many educated Chinese the major alternative to the Kuomintang. The social service emphasis of the Christian colleges was based partly on a sense of conscious competition with communist programs and a desire to provide students with an alternative.[10] Since the students sought concrete expression of their nationalism, the educators would en-

[8] Li Huang, "Lun li-chiao-yü yü tsung-chiao chiao-yü," *CHCYC*, XIV, no. 8; Li Ju-mien, "Chiao-hui ta-hsüeh wen-t'i," *ibid.*; Tsai Ho-sun, "Modern Christianity," trans. in *The Anti-Christian Movement*, pp. 18–24.

[9] A fairly typical expression of this search is Tso I-li, "Wo ti ta-hsüeh shenghuo" (My University Life), *Wen-hua* (Culture), I, no. 5 (June 1934).

[10] See, for example, Y. C. Yang, "Crisis in the Christian Movement," *CCYB*, 1932–33, pp. 65–75; "Report of the College Conference," *ER*, XXII (1930), 338; Yu-kwang Chu, "A Proposed Theory of Education for the Reconstruction of China," *ER*, XXV (1933), 21–34.

courage the students to participate in village reconstruction projects, literacy schools for workers, sanitation campaigns, and the like. By encouraging students to major in subjects which could be of direct benefit to the Chinese nation, college administrators hoped to link the social and ethical teachings of Christianity with Chinese aspirations and to enable students to fulfill their desire for national service under Christian rather than communist auspices.

The Rural Reconstruction Movement and the Colleges

Agreement on the goal of service to Chinese society and nation was easier to obtain than agreement on specific steps for implementation. For over a decade the Christian schools had admitted that their contribution in terms of numbers of graduates would be minor; the national and provincial colleges were growing more rapidly than the Christian colleges, and during the 1930's the Christian institutions usually accounted for approximately 15 percent of the total number of college students.[11] Christian schools, it was argued, should concentrate on special fields of knowledge and serve as models and experimental centers. One area of agreement was the need for research and experiment in rural reconstruction, and this field received the attention of the Christian colleges during the 1930's. Approximately three-fourths of China's population lived in villages and depended on agriculture for their livelihood. As was true in much of Asia, the lives of the peasants had been deeply disrupted by political conflict, by population growth, and by the increasing concentration of landholding and the shortage of credit. The lot of the Chinese farmer, never easy, had apparently deteriorated during the past century. Unrest among the peasantry was widespread, and though scholars may disagree about the level of conscious revolutionary sentiment in the countryside, there is little question about the revolutionary potential.

Without necessarily realizing the urgency of the situation, every Chinese political group acknowledged the need for aid to the peas-

[11] T. L. Tan, "Status of Christian Higher Education in China," *ER*, XXX (1938), 4. One exception to this generalization might be noted; the Christian colleges, which admitted a high percentage of women (more than 25 percent) in comparison with other Chinese schools, continued to make a significant contribution to the education of women.

ants. Minority parties and private organizations, in particular, tried to work out plans for village reconstruction, and their leaders took the initiative in fostering mass education movements such as the 1,000 character program of James Y. C. Yen (Yen Yang-ch'u). During the 1930's, the communists used a land reform program to displace traditional village authorities and build a peasant base for the party. Even the Kuomintang included in its program an elaborate plan for aid to the peasants. In 1930 the Nanking government passed a land law setting the maximum rent at 37½ percent of the value of the main crop; it helped finance agricultural research on farming techniques and plant strains; and it gave assistance to several rural reconstruction projects. Workers in the field, however, soon discovered that fundamental institutional change had to accompany new agricultural techniques if the peasants were to benefit; proposals for changes in the power structure or in social mores met with opposition from local interests. The Kuomintang, not willing to risk social revolution or the loss of support among those who seemed to bring stability to the countryside, lost its enthusiasm for village reconstruction projects. It argued that full implementation of its agrarian program should be delayed until after the communists and the warload rivals had been defeated and unity achieved. Since the Japanese holocaust descended before the latter was accomplished, there never was a time when the Kuomintang concentrated its attention on agrarian China and its problems.

The reconstruction of rural China was a task of such magnitude that strong government support was probably essential for significant progress. Though the Christian colleges could not accomplish a revolution in the countryside, could hardly even make a major contribution toward reconstruction of agrarian China, they were aware of the significance of the task and tried to generate interest among other segments of Chinese society. Moreover, their pilot projects and rural surveys contributed much information necessary for the evolution of an intelligent program of rural reconstruction.[12]

[12] The work of the Joint Commission on Rural Reconstruction on Taiwan during the 1950's benefited from the findings of the projects of the 1930's. There was some carry over of both personnel and techniques from the University of Nanking and National Central University, with which Nanking cooperated.

Research by their schools of agriculture on better farming techniques and improved strains of silkworms and grains contributed to increased productivity.

The Christian colleges concentrated on two approaches to rural reconstruction: agricultural research and education, and village aid programs. In agriculture the work of the University of Nanking was outstanding, though Lingnan, Fukien, West China, and others conducted less ambitious programs. The organization of the University of Nanking's agricultural studies and the special areas of interest had been outlined during the 1920's, but during the following decade its activities expanded and the results of its research began to benefit neighboring farmers. Especially interesting was the close coordination between the university agricultural staff and the government department of agriculture. For some years the University of Nanking served as the center for registration of new hybrids of small grains and operated the National Bureau of Agricultural Research for the government. It undertook for the central administration research studies such as the survey of flood damage along the Yangtze after the disaster of 1931, and it organized summer institutes for agricultural agents. A large proportion of the agricultural specialists in the Ministry of Agriculture and in the departments of agriculture of the national and provincial universities were graduates of the University of Nanking College of Agriculture and Forestry.[13] In return, the college derived a substantial portion of its budget from government agencies.

The University of Nanking initiated a broad range of activities, including the organization of a wool weaving center, with improved handicraft machines for workers unemployed because of the decline in the silk industry; the collection of traditional Chinese literature on agriculture and the publication of an index to agricultural literature in China; the distribution of disease-free silkworm eggs; and aid in the organization of rural credit societies. There were forestry

[13] One source stated that at one time Nanking graduates headed five of the seven technical departments and three of the five national research institutes in the Ministry of Agriculture; Nanking graduates also administered seven agricultural colleges of government universities and comprised almost one half of those agriculturists going abroad for advanced study. See UB paper entitled, "Instruction, Research and Extension in Agriculture in the China Colleges" (typewritten, n.d.), 15 pp.

surveys and the distribution of nursery trees for reforestation, and there were attempts to encourage farmers to grow their own fruits and vegetables by the sale of improved seeds and seedlings at minimal prices. Using a thousand character vocabulary, the college published pamphlets on improved techniques for growing rice, the use of copper carbonate for treating smut, and other subjects which would interest the farmer who had just learned to read.[14] The principal areas of concentration, however, were plant breeding and studies of land utilization, population, and food in China.

An agreement with Cornell University and the International Education Board of the Rockefeller Foundation in 1924 had brought to Nanking Clyde H. Myers of the Cornell department of plant breeding. He and the dean of the Nanking College of Agriculture, John H. Reisner, organized a comprehensive crop improvement program involving the major food crops of central and north China. Since the poverty of the peasants and the small industrial base of China made the widespread manufacture and use of chemical fertilizers and pesticides impracticable, they concentrated on the hybridization of seeds to increase yields and produce disease resistant varieties of plants. Within a decade they had obtained superior strains of wheat, soybeans, kaoliang, millet, and rice.

The agricultural scientists quickly discovered that producing new hybrid grains was only the beginning. They had to try to close the gap between the intellectual, who had knowledge of scientific principles in agricultural research but little experience in farming, and the farmer, who had experience and a willingness to get his hands dirty but no conception of scientific methodology. In other words, the agricultural students had to be persuaded to work in the fields, and the workers in the university fields had to be given some understanding of scientific techniques. After the development of an experimental strain which needed to be tested under varying conditions, the farmers had to be persuaded to try the new seed and keep records of yields. The understanding of the complexity of introducing improved seed strains and the evolution of techniques

[14] K. S. Sie, "Rural Reconstruction," *CCYB, 1932–33,* pp. 369–379; Y. G. Chen, "A Brief Survey of the Contribution the University of Nanking Is Making to the Life of the Community," *ER,* XXV (1933), 62: "News," *ER,* XXVII (1935), 184–185.

to accomplish the task were valuable preliminary steps toward an overall program for rural reconstruction.

Since most peasants felt that they could not risk trying unknown varieties, the agriculturists had to demonstrate the superiority of the new seed and at the same time make it financially worthwhile for the farmer to try the seed. Thus, seed was at first provided free; through cooperation with the College of Agriculture of National Central University, agricultural experiment stations with demonstration fields were distributed through central China; and short term institutes for farmers and agricultural agents were organized. In some cases the Nanking agriculturists began by working through country churches where Christians could be prevailed upon to experiment with the new seeds. Shortly after the superiority of the new strains had been demonstrated, however, the specialists' problems changed to those accompanying popularity. How were they to keep the seed strains pure? Who should have the right to distribute the seed? Should the college take the responsibility for nomenclature and regulation in the absence of other agencies? How deeply involved should the university become in the commercial enterprise of producing and selling seed? At first the university did assume wide-ranging responsibility. It set up a registration bureau for new strains of seed, and it prohibited distribution of its strains without registration at the university. The school itself grew and distributed large quantities of seeds; it tried to keep its strains pure by distributing seed on a community basis so that all farmers in one village would grow one strain of wheat, rice, or cotton; and it trained personnel in record keeping and crop reporting. At the same time the university helped found a National Bureau of Agricultural Research which could eventually take over some of the work.[15]

The university collected information on conditions in the villages, a subject on which there were broad generalizations but little specific detail. Many surveys were conducted in collaboration with the Chinese government; for example, there was government aid for a complete agricultural census of the Chu Yung district of Kiangsu.

[15] C. H. Myers, *Final Report of the Plant Improvement Project Conducted by the University of Nanking, Cornell University, and the International Education Board* (Nanking, 1934), 56 pp. See also, K. S. Sie, "Rural Reconstruction," *CCYB, 1932–33,* 369–379.

Studies of price changes in major food crops and of the marketing and transportation of these crops convinced Nanking teachers that rural credit and cooperative marketing were fundamental to improving the standard of living of the peasants, and so they used famine relief funds to organize cooperative societies. Probably the best known of the surveys were those supervised by J. Lossing Buck; these were summarized in two works: *Land Utilization in China,* a descriptive study of China's agricultural economy based on a survey of 16,786 farms in twenty-two provinces from 1929 to 1933, and *Chinese Farm Economy,* a study of farm management and other socioeconomic aspects of farm life in selected areas of north, central, and southeastern China. These works remain the most comprehensive studies in English on Chinese agriculture before reorganization under the communists.

The University of Nanking also cooperated with other institutions engaged in agricultural work. It aided in the organization and management of the crop improvement program of Cheeloo Rural Institute. At the urging of Myers, Yenching University gradually turned over to Nanking its agricultural experiment work and concentrated on urban studies and the broader village reconstruction work. The University of Nanking and Nanking Theological Seminary cooperated in providing literacy classes and courses on agriculture, rural sociology, and the organization of cooperatives for rural pastors.[16] Several vocational and middle schools became regional centers for testing seed varieties under local conditions. They received guidance in agricultural techniques from the Nanking staff, and their graduates were encouraged to enroll in the agricultural courses at the University.

Though the Nanking College of Agriculture and Forestry devoted approximately half its budget to research and a fifth to extension work, it also trained agriculturists for China and offered a wide

[16] The Seminary and the University cooperated in the Shunhuachen experiment, an attempt to make the market town of Shunhuachen a model for a church-centered rural reconstruction program and a training area for theological students preparing for rural work. See Frank W. Price, "History of Nanking Theological Seminary, 1911 to 1961: A Tentative Draft" (New York, 1961); also William A. Brown, "The Protestant Rural Movement in China (1920–1937)," in *American Missionaries in China: Papers from Harvard Seminars,* ed. by Kwang-ching Liu (Cambridge, Mass.; 1966), pp. 217–248.

variety of courses in such fields as plant breeding, sericulture, horticulture, and agricultural economics. To give students experience with farming techniques and problems, the college required all students to spend one summer in field practice. During the 1930's the university offered a B.S. and a M.S. degree in agriculture, a teacher training program organized in cooperation with the Ministry of Education, a two-year extension program to prepare cooperative supervisors and agricultural agents, and frequent short term courses. The College of Agriculture and Forestry, the College of Arts, and the College of Science each had an undergraduate enrollment of about 250 in the mid-1930's.

What the University of Nanking tried to do for central and northern China, Lingnan and West China Union University attempted on a smaller scale for southern and southwestern China. Much of the research at Lingnan was devoted to sericulture; the silk industry and the provincial government gave support for the university's research and for its production and distribution of disease-free silk worm eggs. West China Union University did some research in animal husbandry and plant breeding, but made contributions particularly in the fields of fruit growing and transportation. In both schools the number of students enrolled in the agricultural curriculum remained small. None of the other Christian colleges undertook such expensive and specialized agricultural work as the University of Nanking; they turned rather to social service and village reconstruction projects.

Contributing to this emphasis was the discouraging experience of trying to aid the populace in one phase of their lives and having that effort defeated by the incongruity of the change with other aspects of village life. That formal training and research in agriculture could perform an important, but limited service was undeniable. The Nanking College of Agriculture and Forestry could develop Nanking 2905, a wheat strain that was 20 percent more productive than the varieties traditionally planted by the farmers; but this did not automatically mean that its yield would be higher on peasant plots or that the farmer would receive the benefit if there were increased productivity. The graduates of Nanking College of Agriculture, furthermore, had no intention of becoming dirt farmers; they had become members of the educated elite and wanted government or teaching positions; they would work with their heads, not their hands. Once they had gotten this far they were on their way to a larger world, usually an urban one, and they had no intention of returning to their rural villages.[17] Agricultural schools, then, could serve as research centers and train professional specialists in agriculture, but there still remained the problem of enabling the farmer to use and benefit from the findings. Many hoped that broad village reconstruction projects were the solution, and so the University of Nanking along with other Christian colleges began to plan such programs. They talked of sending the teachers to the peasants rather than bringing the peasants to the college farms, and they thought in terms of studying and altering many aspects of village life.

Educators in the Christian colleges were not, of course, the only ones learning the prerequisites and techniques of change in rural China. James Y. C. Yen had attained prominence during the 1920's as leader of a mass literacy movement based on his "thousand character" vocabulary; by the 1930's he had expanded his goals to a fourfold attack on ignorance, poverty, disease, and civic disintegration in rural China, and his Tinghsien center was becoming a model for others interested in rural reconstruction. Liang Shu-ming (Liang Sou-ming) had left the faculty of Peita in the 1920's to work for the revival of traditional Chinese values in rural China, but he too had moved to a multifaceted program; he and Liang Chung-hua had helped found the Shantung Rural Reconstruction Institute, which made the village of Tsouping (Chou-p'ing) near Tsinan its experimental center for rural reconstruction. The Rockefeller Foundation, which had devoted most of its China funds to Peking Union Medical College and to the improvement of scientific and medical education in the China colleges, reassessed its priorities during the 1930's and decided to transfer much of its aid to rural reconstruction projects. The Kuomintang began in 1934 to foster a rural reconstruction program in sections of Kiangsi recently freed of communist control. Thus, numerous groups in China appeared to be following a similar path, and there was both exchange of information and personnel. Eventually, several of these groups

[17] This was a frequent lament of educators; see, for example, Chang Fu-liang, "Agricultural Education and Country Life," *ER*, XXII (1930), 188–193; Corbett, *Lingnan*, p. 123; P. Buck, *My Several Worlds*, p. 188.

organized rural reconstruction unions to coordinate their activities and to husband their limited funds and personnel. Many Christian leaders welcomed such cooperation as indicating acceptance of their institutions as partners in building a new China, though some feared the implications of joint participation with government agencies and others questioned the church's devoting funds and personnel to projects with so little emphasis on evangelism. For all those working for rural reconstruction, the problems were awesome.[18]

A discussion of the program of Cheeloo University will reveal some of the difficulties and opportunities in rural reconstruction work and also point up certain fundamental problems of the Christian colleges during the 1930's. The decade 1925 to 1935 was not a happy or prosperous one for Cheeloo. Various factors contributed to its frustration and even to a decline in its prestige and influence. There had been confusion and discontinuity in the administration partly because of rapid turnover in leadership and a cumbersome administrative structure. There was, in addition, a decline in funds from the West because of the depression and the disillusionment with educational missions following the anti-Christian movements. Relations between Cheeloo and the churches had been particularly close, and the great majority of her graduates had gone into Christian work. To prepare students for this work, Cheeloo had given especial attention to Chinese language training and had taught many courses in Chinese. It maintained a high percentage of Christion students by drawing most of its pupils from Christian middle schools. Few of its alumni, therefore, were equipped or encouraged to study abroad or to enter commerce in the treaty ports. At a time when a Western Ph.D. or a substantial bank account were passports to influence, Cheeloo found itself with few influential alumni. Since its own graduates seldom went abroad for graduate study, it had difficulty finding Chinese Christians with higher degrees for its faculty, and in 1930 over three-quarters of its arts faculty held no graduate degrees.[19] As a crowning blow, a decline in Christian primary and middle schools, the slow growth of the Chinese church,

[18] Detailed information on the rural reconstruction movement is available in Thomson, *While China Faced West*.

[19] CCEA, *Statistical Report, Christian Colleges and Professional Schools of China, 1930–31*, Bul. no. 28, Tables 15, 16.

and the reluctance or inability of parishes to employ college educated pastors meant that openings for Cheeloo alumni in Christian work lagged behind the number of graduates. All of this was translated for Cheeloo into decreasing enrollments and falling academic standards.[20]

Cheeloo had to evolve a new role for itself, one which did not place it in competition with the more prosperous Yenching. Recommendations were not lacking. The CCEA had in 1928 issued the first version of a correlated program for all the colleges. Cheeloo was advised to concentrate on serving rural China, on preparing "men and women to meet the needs of the rural and town populations through the training of teachers, preachers, doctors, nurses, and other social and religious workers."[21] Cheeloo, however, was not to develop her own department of agriculture but was to depend on the University of Nanking for work in this field. These recommendations were received with dismay by students, faculty, and alumni, who accused the educational association of wanting to make Cheeloo a "cow college" or rural institute. The Cheeloo governing boards, who understood somewhat more clearly the intent of the proposal and the overall problems of the college, accepted the recommendations with reluctance, hoping to modify them. Despite the faculty members' noncooperation and even opposition, a rural program was gradually organized and slowly won support.

In 1927 the Cheeloo College of Theology had started rural work at Lungshan, a town east of Tsinan, and it seemed natural for the university to take over and expand the work there. Lungshan, with 460 households, was a market center for numerous hamlets within a five-mile radius. Accepting the necessity of simultaneous change in many facets of life, the Rural Institute organized departments of agriculture and economics, education, health, and homemaking. Members of the institute worked with the farmers in their own hamlets and on their own farm plots, on the theory that model farms created artificial conditions. They introduced improved seed strains (wheat from the University of Nanking and cotton from the

---

[20] "Statements Concerning Christian Higher Educational Institutions in China," see p. 21 for a self-analysis by Cheeloo.

[21] Corbett, *Shantung*, pp. 214–217; CCEA, *The Correlated Program, 1930, as Adopted by the Council of Higher Education* (Shanghai, n.d.).

United States), and encouraged the expansion of poultry production and the use of waste lands for orchards. To reduce underemployment among farming families, the institute aided the local wool weaving industry. The organization of cooperative credit societies received especial attention, since many economists maintained that expensive credit was a major reason for the farmer's slowness in altering agricultural techniques. The hope was that the farmers would make loans at moderate interest rates for productive purposes such as the purchase of better seed or of draft animals rather than for economically nonproductive expenses such as wedding and funeral ceremonies. Profits of the credit unions were to be used for schools, roads, and other welfare activities. The credit societies, which charged interest of 1.5 percent a month, did force the customary interest rate in the local area down from 4 percent to 2 percent a month.[22]

The studies of Gerald F. Winfield of the Cheeloo biology department and Stanley Wilson of the Yenching chemistry department on human parasites demonstrate the attempt to orient research toward service to rural China. Winfield and Wilson traced the life cycles of several common human parasites and discovered the principal source of infection for the farmers. Night soil proved the culprit in certain cases, and yet there seemed no possibility of discontinuing its use while both chemical fertilizer and manure remained expensive and scarce. Winfield and Wilson therefore sought a cheap and effective technique of composting waste so as to kill disease organisms and parasite eggs. They were ready to organize a pilot project in one of the hamlets when the Japanese invasion halted the work.[23]

The Cheeloo College of Medicine cooperated in other health and welfare projects: the operation of a dispensary, a midwife service, and a baby clinic; health work in the schools; the circulation of information on nutrition and sanitation. The head of the depart-

[22] For further information, see P. C. Hsu, "Christian Rural Reconstruction in China," *CCYB*, 1926–27, pp. 319–329; E. H. Cressy, "Council of Higher Education," *ER*, XXVI (1934), 205; "The Cheeloo Rural Institute," *ER*, XXV (1933), 201–204; Corbett, *Shantung*, pp. 209–229; and numerous issues of the *Cheeloo Monthly Bulletin* during the 1930's, especially nos. 24–25, 29, 35.

[23] Winfield gives information on his work in *China, The Land and the People* (New York, 1948); see report in *Cheeloo Monthly Bulletin*, May 31, 1936, pp. 6–8.

ment of home economics tried to devise a diet for young children which was both nutritious and economically feasible; in the absence of a dairy industry, for example, she encouraged the use of soybean milk. Finally, the publication *T'ien-chia* (The Christian Farmer) should be mentioned; though it was not an official organ of the Cheeloo Rural Institute, one of its editors was T. H. Sun, a Cheeloo graduate and former teacher, and its offices were adjacent to the Cheeloo campus; thus close contact between the magazine and the Rural Institute was maintained. The magazine had a dual purpose: to convey agricultural information and to help farmers who had recently learned to read in night courses or winter schools to retain their literacy. The magazine, using a limited vocabulary of common words, quickly became popular, and its subscription list of 5,000 or more extended far beyond Shantung province. Religion was not a major department of the institute for a variety of reasons: the Nationalist government, which provided some financial support, was opposed to aiding religious work; some evangelists resented the intrusion of educational personnel in what they considered their province, and the social service workers anticipated a more favorable reception by villagers if, initially, there were no overt evangelistic activities. As friendships developed, however, individual members of the Rural Institute staff were able to undertake informal work in this field.

The activities initiated by the Cheeloo Rural Institute might be considered typical of the more ambitious village reconstruction projects in which several of the Christian colleges participated. Typical also was cooperation with local and national government agencies or private groups. Fukien Christian University, which had begun a program at a village near campus, agreed in 1935 to take over the provincial rural experiment station at Wulitien, a project that included ten nearby villages. When in 1934 the Kuomintang began reconstruction projects in Kiangsi centers recently under communist control, the Kiangsi Christian Rural Service Union assumed responsibility for one center in the Lichuan area of southeastern Kiangsi. The National Economic Council provided some financial support, but the project's organization and personnel were the responsibility of the members of the union: several church and mission groups, the YMCA and the National Christian Council, the

Mass Education Movement of James Yen, plus Yenching University and Nanking Theological Seminary. Yenching had also undertaken work at the nearby town of Ch'ing Ho in 1930 and was developing a program for training rural administrators.

When the Rockefeller Foundation decided in 1934 to make rural reconstruction its major focus in China, many looked forward to substantial financial aid and the coordination of the fragmented efforts at rural reconstruction in north China.[24] Selskar Gunn of the foundation drew up a detailed plan both for research and training in rural reconstruction and for reform programs in village centers. Since the intent was to support and build on efforts already under way, the North China Council for Rural Reconstruction was formed in 1936. The cooperating institutions included many of the leaders in the field: James Yen's Mass Education Movement with its center at Tinghsien, the Department of Preventive Medicine of Peking Union Medical College, Nankai University's Institute of Economics, the College of Agriculture of the University of Nanking, Yenching University, Tsing Hua University, and the North China Industrial Service Union, which worked with Yenching, Nankai, and Cheeloo in the development of village industries. The two major village centers were to be Tinghsien in Hopei and Tsining in Shantung. In the division of labor, the University of Nanking was responsible for agricultural extension and was to make available its experimental farms in the north, while Yenching was to aid in organizing cooperatives, in providing vocational courses, and in training civil administrators. The appointment of North China Council workers in Tinghsien and Tsining to official administrative posts seemed to ensure government participation and support. Despite initial optimism, problems remained. Personnel conflicts and differences of approach and emphasis between newcomers and some of the project founders delayed implementation of programs. Local authorities were often less than enthusiastic about the "do-gooders" from outside. Most important of all, the Sino-Japanese conflict broke out before even the planning stage could be completed. It was typical that plans for inclusion of rural health programs under Cheeloo's

[24] Details on the Rockefeller effort are in Thomson, *While China Faced West*, ch. vi, "From Models to Training Programs: The Rockefeller Effort."

direction were interrupted by news of the Marco Polo Bridge incident.[25]

Some Christian colleges did not participate in such ambitious programs, but rather encouraged their students and faculty to undertake small social service projects. At almost every college, extra-curricular activities included adult literacy classes, kindergartens, community recreation programs, the distribution of information on sanitation, nutrition, and child care, and leadership in health and clean-up campaigns.

What did the reconstruction programs of the Christian colleges accomplish? While acknowledging the good will and sacrifice of the students, one can probably conclude that the isolated social service projects were as much for the benefit of the students as the peasants. Most Chinese students were still elitist; they went to the villages to work for the peasants, not with them, and the difference in the status of the educated leaders and the illiterate peasants was a tangible thing not to be overlooked by either party.[26] A college education often proved to be poor preparation for rural reconstruction work. Some students were quickly disillusioned by the slowness and meagerness of the changes and by the discomfort of being in a situation where their knowledge seemed inadequate or irrelevant; others earnestly continued their efforts. In the latter cases individual peasants were assisted, though the pressures to return to old ways after the departure of the outsider were often overwhelming. The student was richer for having given concrete expression to his sense of responsibility for the welfare of the poor and for having experienced directly something of peasant life and problems.

[25] Further information concerning cooperative ventures is available in *ibid.*; National Christian Council of China, *Annual and Biennial Reports, 1933–35* (Shanghai, 1935), pp. 113–121; E. H. Ballou, *Dangerous Opportunity* (New York, 1940), pp. 111–114; Lyman P. Van Slyke, "Liang Sou-ming and the Rural Reconstruction Movement," *JAS,* XVIII (1959), 457–474; Timothy Ting-fang Lew, "The Christian Movement in China under Protestant Auspices," *The Chinese Year Book, 1936–37* (Shanghai, 1936), pp. 1493–1494; James Y. C. Yen, *The Ting Hsien Experiment* (Peiping, 1934); *Princeton-Peking Gazette,* V, nos. 2, 3.

[26] Concerning the agricultural students at the University of Nanking, Pearl Buck wrote in *My Several Worlds:* "They not only knew nothing about their own country people, they did not even know how to talk with them or address them. My blood used to boil when a callow young intellectual would address a dignified old peasant with the equivalent of 'Hey, you—' " (p. 188).

The more extensive programs would seem to have much to recommend them; they made use of recent scholarship in sociology and cultural anthropology, and their techniques foreshadowed many of those now in use in rural assistance programs in Asia and Latin America. By the mid-1930's their work had amply demonstrated the complexity of change at the village level and the necessity of attacking many facets of the poverty cycle simultaneously if there were to be long term results; they had learned of the importance of peasant participation in the planning and initiation of reform projects. Their surveys have been valuable sources of information for students of China and for those interested in rural reconstruction in general. Specific contributions that they made would be valuable under almost any circumstances; for example, discovery of improved strains of small grains, inexpensive chemical compounds for control of barley smut, and effective techniques for composting fertilizer. And yet the student of the modernization of China can hardly avoid a sense of disappointment over their accomplishments. This disappointment was also felt by the students seeking national salvation. After a few years of popularity, the village reform projects ceased to arouse great enthusiasm. Though the reconstruction programs continued and some of them in 1936–1937 seemed to be evolving promising techniques and effective personnel policies, students were searching for other programs for national revival. Leftist doctrines, especially the holistic philosophy of communism, were attractive to some of the most idealistic and nationalistic students.

Why did the enthusiasm and support decline? First, the issue of resistence to Japan increasingly occupied the students after December 1935. Then, there was admittedly sometimes more talk than action in the reconstruction work. Although the college staff quite naturally was concerned primarily with educating students, when reporting to the outside world, especially to mission boards and the Chinese public, the colleges stressed their service to China. Since the thesis that the colleges could best serve Christianity through serving Chinese society had been widely accepted, the college administrators were likely to devote a considerable portion of their reports and fund appeals to the social welfare work of the colleges. Despite this emphasis, such activities never became a major function of the colleges (few would maintain that they should have done so); thus many projects received insufficient funds and inadequate planning; and work on them often came out of the spare time of both teachers and students. Though reformers were learning much about the essentials of a successful reconstruction program, lack of funds or personnel forestalled application of their knowledge. The Lichuan project undertaken by the Kiangsi Christian Rural Service Union, for example, languished after its enthusiastic leader George Shepherd left to become an adviser to the New Life Movement. The Rural Life Department of the National Christian Council nearly ceased to function when its leader, Chang Fu-liang, accepted a position with the National Economic Council. Too much depended on a few individuals willing to work long hours with inadequate staff and funds.[27] By 1937, when the Japanese invasion disrupted practically all reconstruction work, some programs were just reaching the stage where productive results might be expected. A partial explanation for the failure of the programs to meet expectations is similar to that given for so many disappointed hopes in China during this period—not enough time.

Certainly rural reconstruction could not attain widespread success without a stable political environment. This, China did not enjoy during the 1930's. Probably a really effective program would have required the support and guidance of a centralized administration; the magnitude of the task necessitated concerted planning, liberal financial resources, and the ability to bring political power to bear at local levels. The Nationalist government was, however, either unwilling or unable to give unqualified support to a far-reaching rural program. The research of the University of Nanking College of Agriculture secured regular financial backing from the government, and close cooperation characterized the work of university and government agriculturists. Pilot projects such as those of Cheeloo and of the North China Council for Rural Reconstruction received the blessing of the government initially but met opposition as they expanded and sought basic changes in social and economic relationships between peasants and the gentry-landlord class. In many cases opposition came first from local groups who saw their economic and social dominance of the countryside threat-

[27] William Brown, "The Protestant Rural Movement," *American Missionaries in China*, pp. 226, 234–244; Thomson, *While China Faced West*, pp. 107–108, 116–121.

ened. Some reconstruction leaders therefore delayed tackling one of the fundamental problems of rural China: the concentration and conditions of land tenure. Those who sought land reform needed the backing of Nanking, and this was not forthcoming, either because the Kuomintang did not wish to alienate local leaders, or because it feared that a land reform program would gain such momentum that it could not be controlled. The government law restricting rent to 37½ percent of the value of the principal crop was rarely enforced. In some cases, the Kuomintang used the reconstruction program for its own political purposes, thereby distorting the program and alienating its leaders. In the Cheeloo project, the Rural Institute leaders who wanted to organize separate, specialized associations for different community functions came into conflict with the government's desire to have one multi-faceted organization whose work and philosophy would accord with that of the New Life Movement. During the 1930's the likelihood of an effective national program of rural reconstruction was slim; the individual programs helped individual villagers and gathered information and experience in the techniques of such work, but they had little chance of tackling what was a national problem needing nationwide support and planning. A political party which had the will and the power to carry out a rural reform program would receive a sympathetic hearing among Christian reformers who felt frustrated in their attempts to express Christianity through service to China.[28]

Factors Affecting Curricular Emphases

Another national aim, industrialization, also necessitated a reappraisal of educational goals and techniques. The Kuomintang, which derived much of its support before the Sino-Japanese War from the urban communities, worked to create conditions it con-

[28] See the writings of Wu Yao-tsung, who became leader of the "Three Self Reform Movement" to build a Chinese Protestant church independent of the West after 1949, quoted in Lutz, Christian Missions in China, pp. 67-70, and Francis P. Jones, ed., Documents of the Three-Self Movement (New York, 1963), pp. 1-5, 12-14. See also the statement issued by the National Christian Council in China, Dec. 19, 1949, quoted in Jones, Documents, pp. 9-11. The Council stated that "the Church has been unable to undertake responsibility for service on any vast scale" and it should therefore welcome the lead of the People's Government in assuming responsibility for service to the people.

sidered conducive to industrial growth. Political unity, a national currency and banking system, a coherent body of civil law, and improved communications and transportation received particular attention. Concern about the scarcity of Chinese scientists and technicians led the government to encourage more students to major in professional and vocational fields. Of government aid to private colleges in 1934, four-fifths was for scientific and technical fields and less than one-fifth for the humanities; the Ministry of Education also decreed that colleges should admit no more students in arts courses than in science courses. Government scholarships for study abroad were increasingly restricted to graduate study in scientific and technical fields, and Chinese educational and news magazines, which frequently deplored China's dependence on foreigners for technical know-how, called on Chinese youth to contribute to China's strength and independence by preparing for specific vocations.[29]

The reaction of both the Christian colleges and Chinese students to such pleas was mixed. Chinese youth were sensitive to arguments couched in nationalist terms and agreed on the importance of industrialization in the strengthening of China. On the other hand, many Chinese students still considered political leadership their natural role, and state service was still a prestige position ranking far above factory management, medicine, or bridge building. Though Chinese academic youth were similar to other intelligentsias in their alienation from surrounding society, they were not, like the Russian intelligentsia before the 1917 revolution, generally alienated from the state.[30] They expected and hoped to enter government service; even if they studied agriculture or engineering, they were more likely to secure a position with a government ministry or a university than one on a farm or in a factory. Despite the iconoclasm of Chinese intellectuals, the tradition of the scholar-bureaucrat still had influence in twentieth-century China. Students, furthermore, had been

[29] P. C. Kuo, "College Men in Depression," *China Critic*, VII (1934), 775–777; You-kuang Chu, *Some Problems of a National System of Education in China* (Shanghai, 1933), pp. 206–207; Yu Shan-han, "Research Movements and Institutions," *CCYB*, 1936–37, p. 62; Herman C. E. Liu, "Higher Education in China," *School and Society*, XLII (1935), 676–677.

[30] Benjamin Schwartz develops this thesis in "The Intelligentsia in Communist China," *Daedalus* (Summer 1960), pp. 604–621.

convinced by the disastrous warlord years that political unity and stability were prerequisites to progress in all fields. They usually had no deep prejudice against state capitalism or socialism and expected that industrialization would be accomplished under government guidance. Many thought of themselves, therefore, as future political leaders who needed broad knowledge for directing national programs and guiding personnel.[31] Lesser individuals from somewhere would provide the necessary technical service.

Another factor must also have entered the thinking of Chinese students. Personal contacts had always played a role in an individual's rise through the government bureaucracy; with the decline of the examination system the role of personal influence had been enhanced, and one's admission to state service depended heavily on recommendation. Students were well aware that personal influence was often more important than technical knowledge in securing a position; they knew of instances in which scientists were serving in positions unrelated to their training because an uncle or a friend had recommended employment. They knew too that despite the government's call for more specialists, the number of young graduates without jobs was disturbingly large; the expansion of attractive positions in industry and commerce did not always keep pace with the increase in technically trained personnel.[32] They were likely to conclude that a broad program of study which would enable them to serve wherever they happened to find employment through personal influence was preferable to a more specialized program.

Not all students, of course, expected to enter the government;

[31] Various expressions of the nationalism and elitism of students during the 1930's are available; see Tso I-li, "Wo ti ta-hsüeh sheng-huo," *Wen-hua* (June 1934), pp. 95–97; Ts'ao I, "'Shih-erh-chiu' kei-wo ti chiao-hsün" (The Lesson of "December 9th" for Me), *Shih-erh-chiu chou-nien chi-nien t'e-k'an* (Special Issue on the Anniversary of Dec. 9th), issued by Yenching Student Government Association (Peiping, 1936), pp. 31–33 (cited as *SECCN*); E. E. Liu, "Complaints of a College Graduate," *China Critic*, VIII (1935), 129–131; Zia Yi-chen (Hsieh I-chen), "Thoughts of an Undergraduate," *ibid.*, pp. 131–132.

[32] In 1934, 1935, 1936, articles deploring the high rate of unemployment among college graduates appeared frequently; see P. C. Kuo, "College Men in Depression," and "Chief Events," in *China Critic*, VII (1934), 690, 775–777, in which it is reported that college graduates were forming an employment association; for the government response, see "Jobs for College Graduates," *ibid.*, XIV (1936), 77.

numerous college graduates entered the teaching profession. Though education did not have the prestige of state service, it was an acceptable occupation for an intellectual and could be a way station until a more desirable position became available. Those for whom teaching was a second choice or a temporary expedient did not generally take a professional course in education. Youth from the urban families of the treaty ports often planned to carry on their fathers' business enterprise. These students were interested in English language facility, in the social sciences and some legal training; they were not generally enthusiastic about such specialized fields as engineering, agriculture, or business administration; nor did they often major in a science. They wanted to belong to the managerial class and work with their brains, not with their hands.

A combination of nationalist and personal goals, then, guided students in their selection of majors. The humanities, social sciences, and law were popular; science attracted a fair number of students, many of whom expected to teach; professional and technical courses attracted only a few. In 1930–1931 only 25 percent of the students were majoring in scientific or technical subjects. With government pressure the proportion in engineering, medicine, agriculture, and science had risen to 38 percent in 1937, but well over half the students continued to enroll in the humanities, law, commerce, and education. The general picture in the Christian colleges was similar to the overall picture, though there were some interesting variations in detail (Table 5). The Christian colleges drew a larger proportion of students into the liberal arts, but this is partially offset by the very low percentage in the educational curriculum. Since education was considered an important tool of nationalism, the government sought to monopolize the training of teachers and severely restricted the founding or expansion of departments of education by private institutions. Almost one-third of the Christian school graduates entered teaching, however, and the combined percentages for liberal arts and education in the Christian colleges and in all the colleges are not significantly different. Many Christian educators had difficulty justifying work in such areas as commerce, engineering, and law by church related schools, and so practically all work by Christian institutions in these fields was by three or four schools in east China. The Christian colleges, which had pioneered

Table 5. Majors of university students in China, 1937 (in percent)

Major subjects	Christian colleges	All (incl. the Christian colleges)
Liberal arts	32.7	19.0
Law	10.3	26.4
Education	0.2	9.7
Commerce	5.8	7.3
Total	51.3	62.4
Engineering	0.2	14.16
Medicine and pharmacy	6.5	6.31
Agriculture	6.8	4.39
Science	33.8	12.75
Total	48.7	37.61

Source: T. L. Tan, "Status of Christian Higher Education in China," *ER* XXX (1938), 17–19.[33]

in modern medical education, had not expanded their medical schools significantly and now trained only about the same proportion in medicine as the national average. Though most of the Christian colleges, like most of the other Chinese universities, did not offer work in agriculture, the departments of Nanking and Lingnan were large enough to bring the enrollment of the Christian schools above the national ratio.

The most significant divergence was in science, where the proportion of majors in the Christian colleges was almost three times that of all the universities. A number of factors may account for the contrast; many of the Christian institutions had emphasized the sciences ever since their founding, and several schools had built their reputations on their work in scientific fields. The sciences, more than many fields, required a knowledge of Western languages and necessitated study abroad at the graduate level; since the Christian colleges were known both for their English language

[33] Tan does not make clear whether the term Christian colleges includes both Protestant and Roman Catholic institutions or only the Protestant colleges. It is probable that the figures are only for the Protestant schools since the CCEA was generally the organization which gathered such statistics and it was concerned only with Protestant schools. The totals for the Christian colleges are obviously incorrect, but I have not altered Tan's figures.

training and their preparation for study abroad, they would attract students planning to major in science. The Christian schools, moreover, had greater success in attracting outside funds for the support of science teaching and equipment than for any other purpose. Finally, in a few institutions like Cheeloo, West China, and Yenching, many of the science students were actually preparing for admission to medical school.

As the enrollment figures indicate, most of the Christian colleges during the 1930's continued their traditional emphasis on the humanities and to a lesser extent on the sciences. At the same time, the institutions were not unresponsive to government pressure for expansion of work in professional and technical fields. When Christian educators were defining their goals in terms of service to Chinese society and the nation, they could hardly ignore Nanking's recommendations concerning the orientation of higher education. Institutional ambition and fiscal need also encouraged certain schools to initiate professional and technical training. College administrators were not unaware of the expensiveness of such work, and they were certainly conscious of their own college's fiscal difficulties. Despite, and sometimes even because of these factors, they were occasionally persuaded by promises of support to undertake professional and technical training. They were reluctant to turn down such windfalls as an alumni gift to help found an engineering school or a Boxer indemnity grant to expand work in library science. A few comments on the financial status of the colleges is, therefore, a necessary preface to detail on new curricula.

Though the Christian colleges had never been free of financial worries, the severity of their problems during the 1930's decisively affected curriculum planning. Most of the colleges had exceedingly small endowments and lived almost wholly from current income. In 1929 over 75 percent of this income came from the West.[34] As a consequence, the depression in the West worked a real hardship on the China Christian colleges. It not only cut the total income of the churches so that they had to slash mission budgets, but it made special fund-raising campaigns liable to failure. Years of preparatory work for a cooperative campaign to raise $8,000,000 for the colleges

[34] *The China Colleges* (publ. by the Associated Boards for Christian Colleges in China), I (Oct. 1934), 1.

went by the board when the stock market came tumbling down in the fall of 1929. Since funds were short, some church leaders asked that available resources be concentrated on direct evangelistic work rather than educational institutions. The fact that the Educational Rights Movement had been directed against Christian schools did not help the colleges combat such requests.

The Sinification of the colleges did not make the task of fund raising in the West any easier. Mission boards often assumed that self-control and self-support should proceed at the same rate. Proof of readiness for independence was an ability to pay one's own way. Since most of the colleges now had Chinese presidents, deans, and department chairmen, the churches expected a growth in Chinese support, and a decline in interest accompanied the decline in the sense of proprietorship. Mission boards which might have been persuaded to support another missionary on the college staff were not so ready to grant additional funds for a Western instructor in commercial law or a Chinese sociologist.

Some of the colleges offset the loosening of ties with the missions by attracting secular supporters. The Rockefeller Foundation continued to be an important source of assistance, especially for science, medicine, agriculture, and rural reconstruction activities. Though the Harvard-Yenching Institute used the bulk of its income for Chinese studies at Harvard and Yenching, it aided several Christian institutions in their work in Chinese. Also fruitful were other relationships established between the China colleges and American institutions. Often these contacts took the form of support for technical and professional studies. The affiliation of Cornell University and the University of Nanking College of Agriculture was one of the best known, but other ties were noteworthy: the Princeton-Yenching College of Public Affairs, The Pennsylvania State College and the Lingnan College of Agriculture, the Yale School of Science of Huachung University, and the Schools of Journalism of Yenching and of the University of Missouri. In some cases the United States partner furnished one or more instructors on a regular basis; sometimes there was exchange of instructors or an opportunity for the Christian college teacher to pursue graduate studies abroad; and in most instances the China institution could expect a fairly regular financial contribution.

Most Christian colleges realized, however, that they would have to look to increasing Chinese support if they were to expand their curricula. The tuition and room rates of the Christian colleges were already above those of the national universities and of many of the better private colleges, and so they did not desire significant increases in tuition. Nor did it seem possible to turn to the Chinese Christian churches for support, since they were having fiscal problems of their own. Most congregations had formerly relied on the mission boards to furnish missionaries as pastors, but Westerners had become less acceptable with the trend toward Chinese control. Since the mission boards frequently asked churches desiring to select their own leaders to pay the salaries of these men, many congregations were already in serious financial difficulty.

Some of the schools focused on building loyalty and support among alumni. St. John's could boast a number of prominent Johanneans, as they were dubbed, and was fairly successful in this endeavor. Work in engineering had been expanded in the mid-1920's through the donation of Alfred Sao-ke Sze (Shih Chao-chi), Minister to Great Britain and then to the United States. In connection with the college's fiftieth anniversary celebration in 1929 and Pott's seventieth birthday in 1934, alumni made contributions toward an endowment fund and the erecting and equipping of needed buildings. Yenching made use of influential connections to have H. H. Kung, minister of finance, Yenching alumnus, and chairman of the Yenching board of managers, and Wang Ching-wei (Wang Chao-ming), president of the Executive Yuan and minister for foreign affairs, launch her endowment campaign in 1935. Lingnan University was also quite successful in building up a sense of loyalty among the Chinese and in gaining financial support locally. Those colleges which had been most successful in persuading their graduates to enter Christian work, on the other hand, had relatively few wealthy alumni to whom they could appeal.

One of the most promising sources of support was the Chinese government itself, an indication of the growing domestication and acceptance of the Christian colleges in China. As the controversy over registration died down, as the left-wing elements were eliminated from the government, and as several of the Christian colleges became known in special fields, Nanking began to include the

Christian institutions in its grants to private schools. J. L. Stuart stated that approximately half of the Ch$720,000 allocated by the Ministry of Education to private universities in 1934–1935 went to Christian institutions, most of it for the support of professional and scientific programs.[35] Gradually these allocations came to be annual contributions, and the colleges began to count on them in their yearly budgets. National and provincial governments also provided scholarships for students in forestry, sericulture, dentistry, and microbiology.

The Boxer funds returned by the Western governments became important sources of income. United States Boxer funds were administered by the China Foundation for the Promotion of Education and Culture, which before the 1930's had usually ignored the Christian schools. With the registration of the colleges, however, the China Foundation began to make regular grants. The Boone Library School of Huachung University relied on the China Foundation for the greater portion of its support, generally $13,000 to $15,000 a year. The Lingnan and Nanking schools of agriculture and sericulture began to receive regular subsidies in 1930, and Yenching's department of chemistry received annual support for research in ceramics. By 1935 the medical schools of Cheeloo and West China and the science departments of many of the institutions could expect yearly contributions for equipment and research. Arrangements for the remission of British Boxer funds were made in 1930, and several universities, including Huachung and Cheeloo, received assistance for equipment or personnel in medicine and natural science.[36] Finally, special programs such as the Soochow School of Commerce and the Lingnan sericulture institute were founded with the aid of Chinese business associations and continued to receive their support.

The Christian colleges were thus fairly successful in increasing

[35] Stuart, "Foundations of Christian Higher Education," *CCYB, 1934–35,* pp. 273–275; *The China Colleges,* I (1934), 1.

[36] China Foundation for the Promotion of Education and Culture, *Annual Reports, 1930–1939.* Because of fiancial difficulties, all grants were suspended in 1932 but were subsequently renewed. *Cheeloo Monthly Bulletin,* no. 31 (1936), p. 4; Chu Chia-hua, "British Boxer Indemnity Fund Activities," *China Quarterly,* V (1941), 437–441. Chu was administrator of the British Boxer Funds during the 1930's.

their support among Chinese, and between 1929 and 1936–1937 the proportion of Chinese contributions to the total income of the colleges rose from 24 percent to 53 percent.[37] Most of the new contributors, both Chinese and Western, were secular in orientation. Nationalistic Chinese gave their aid in the expectation that the colleges would serve the needs of China; they supported scientific and professional work rather than the humanities, and they might be uninterested or even antagonistic toward the evangelistic work of the colleges. Administrators could not help but be cognizant of the intent of the donors. Since the grants were not as a rule given for the normal operating expenses of the colleges but for the expansion of certain fields of study or the addition of new ones, they helped overcome reluctance to undertake expensive operations or professional work. They sometimes helped institutions raise their standards in scientific and medical work already begun, but they certainly did not solve the financial problems of the colleges. Rather, as frequently happens with aid programs, the expenses of the new commitments threatened to expand more rapidly than the support.

If institutional ambition and financial aid persuaded the administrators in China to expand, these factors had less influence with the Christian organizations in the West. Many of the mission boards were less than enthusiastic about programs in commerce, law, journalism, or engineering, for to the boards such work seemed more suitable for secular institutions than for Christian ones. Even they, however, were responsive to appeals to institutional pride and could become caught up in plans for expansion in certain fields such as medicine or education.

The Associated Boards for Christian Colleges in China, organized as a loose federation to coordinate promotional and administrative work in the United States, tried to foster a correlated educational program for the colleges as a prerequisite for joint fund-raising campaigns.[38] It firmly maintained that not all colleges could hope

[37] Associated Boards, An Impressive Service: The Story of the Christian Colleges in China (brochure with no pub. data, c. 1939), pp. 14–15.

[38] "Review of the First Year of the Associated Boards for Christian Colleges in China, June, 1933" (mimeo.; 3 pp. by B. A. Garside, Secretary; NBT pamphlet collection on missions, Box 1); E. H. Cressy, "The Present Status of the Correlated Program," ER, XXV (1933), 35–40. Some of the difficulties facing attempts at coordination are revealed in the following letters: F. J. White to

to become full-fledged universities and used its influence to persuade the various colleges to accept limitations. With the Council
of Higher Education of the CCEA, it called for a division of labor
in professional and graduate work and coordination or amalgamation of work by colleges in close proximity. Most of the college administrators agreed with the theoretical merits of such a plan, but
found implementation difficult. The union of colleges in central
China into Huachung University, begun in the 1920's but interrupted
by the 1926–1928 campaigns, had been revived and enlarged, with
Yale-in-China now participating. The coordination of work among
the eastern colleges in Shanghai and Soochow, however, made little
progress until the Sino-Japanese war forced cohabitation. Both the
pairs of colleges in Nanking (Ginling and the University of
Nanking) and in Foochow (Hwa Nan and Fukien Christian University) maintained that differences in clientele and emphasis made
integration undesirable. Cheeloo accepted an emphasis on serving
the rural community, but retained its liberal arts and medical programs. While recommendations about the division of professional
and graduate work acted as an inhibiting influence, each of the
colleges was, in the final analysis, guided by loyalty to itself and its
future. Where special donations, area needs, public pressure, or the
interest of a dynamic professor encouraged expansion, the college
often accepted the opportunity.

New Secular Programs and Interests

Yenching undertook a number of projects in vocational and professional fields, and a comparison of the histories of those that
flourished and those that languished may be useful. A description
of several special departments will also reveal their often unpre-
meditated origins. As early as 1919 a wealthy Chinese businessman
had offered a 1,200-acre farm for work in animal husbandry. Yenching therefore employed Walter E. Chamberlain, who argued that
separation of animal husbandry and agricultural studies would be
artificial and Yenching should undertake work in horticulture, poul-

Eric M. North, 9/10/1926; B. A. Garside to Herman C. E. Liu, 6/28/1931;
E. H. Cressy to Liu, 6/29/1931; Liu to Garside, 12/27/1932 (UB Correspondence on U. of Shanghai); Hawks Pott to Garside, 5/25/1935; Garside to Pott,
6/14/1935 (UB Correspondence on St. John's).

try raising, agriculture, and animal husbandry. Troubles began to rain upon the work almost immediately. Speculation and famine conditions brought bankruptcy to the Chinese benefactor and left Yenching with a farm mortgaged at a high rate of interest. Yenching, however, received a grant from the China International Famine Relief Commission, organized in 1921, and so was able to continue with plans for a department of agriculture. After many vicissitudes fifteen head of cattle, six hogs, two sheep, three goats, and twenty chickens were imported from the United States. It soon became apparent that effective work would require a greatly expanded staff, as well as additional equipment and land, and Yenching was at this time deeply involved in constructing its new campus and in building its basic curriculum. Neither funds nor ambitious leadership in the field of agriculture was forthcoming, and so Yenching acceded to the recommendation of the CCEA that it concentrate on studies suitable to its urban environment and turn over its agricultural work to the University of Nanking.

A brief attempt in the 1920's to set up a separate department for training and research in leather tanning perished for want of support, though some training in leather tanning continued to be given by the department of chemistry. A course in business training which emphasized typing, bookkeeping, and stenography was abandoned after a few years on the grounds that it was not a legitimate part of university curriculum. Finally, among the abortive projects might be mentioned a course in pre-engineering which never led to an engineering curriculum and was eventually dropped.[39]

More prosperous and long lived were the School of Journalism, the Harvard-Yenching Institute, and the College of Public Affairs, all developed in cooperation with universities in the United States. A realization of the need for training in journalism grew out of the literary activity of the New Culture Movement. The substitution of pai hua for wen yen and the ardent nationalism of young intellec-

[39] Information on these programs and some of their difficulties may be found in Peking University, President's Report, 1921–22, p. 3; letter of Howard S. Galt to J. L. Stuart, 3/17/1931 (UB Correspondence on Yenching); Myers, Report on Plant Improvement Project, pp. 8–17; Edwards, Yenching, ch. xx, "Vocational Training."

tuals had encouraged an amazing expansion in publication during the May 4th Movement, and students and faculty alike founded organs for expression of opinion or advocacy of a particular theory. Many publications were one- or two-sheet affairs, hurriedly put together by a few individuals for a local audience and expiring after a few issues. Others such as *Hsin ch'ing-nien* and *Shao-nien chung-kuo* caught the mood of the time and exercised great influence among young intellectuals. Some set exemplary standards of journalism; other were highly irresponsible in their interpretations, accusations, and even misrepresentations. Two Yenching teachers decided in 1924 that China needed professional courses in journalism and, despite opposition among the liberal arts faculty, were able to secure from the Willard Straight family and from the Lions Club of Kansas City funds to offer a few courses. Departure of interested teachers and depletion of support forced suspension of the work after three years.

One of the teachers, Vernon Nash, retained his interest in the field, however, and campaigned in the United States for funds. With $70,000 and an agreement with the University of Missouri School of Journalism for exchange of professors and students, Nash returned to Yenching in 1929 to revive the work in journalism. The school continued to operate on somewhat shaky foundations; by 1934 when the $70,000 had been expended, the depression had made significant aid from the United States or the general university budget unlikely. Members of the department, therefore, sought teaching assistance and monetary contributions from the newspaper world in the Chinese treaty ports. Under the chairmanship of Hubert Liang, they secured the services of such journalists as Sun Ju-ch'i of Reuters, Chang Chi-luan, editor-in-chief of *Pei-ping ch'en-pao*, H. J. Timperley of the *Manchester Guardian,* and Edgar Snow of the *New York Sun.* Only one exchange of professors between Yenching and the University of Missouri took place, but a number of student exchanges maintained the ties between the two schools. Though the department did not graduate many majors, it could claim among its alumni several influential editors and correspondents; with their facility in the English language, Yenching graduates often secured positions as heads of the Chinese news services in foreign cities or as China-based correspondents for Western news services.[40]

The history of the College of Public Affairs of Yenching University is also one of plans partially fulfilled but of pride in prominent graduates. It too demonstrates the determinative influence exercised initially by a few individuals and the rather surprising degree of interest in Chinese higher education among the American academic community. In 1906 Princeton students had established Princeton-in-Peking, a center cooperating with the Peking YMCA in social work. John S. Burgess, a Princeton graduate and a staff member of Princeton-in-Peking, tried to coordinate all the social service activities of Protestant groups in the city and soon realized the need for more accurate information about urban social conditions. In 1918 Burgess was joined by a fellow Princetonian, Sidney D. Gamble; the two initiated a course on Peking social conditions at Yenching and the North China Union Language School. Students in this course conducted a comprehensive survey of Peking as their field work, and the results were published in the pioneering study Peking, A Social Survey (New York, 1921). In 1923 when Princeton-in-Peking decided to transfer the bulk of its work to Yenching, it offered to support two instructors in sociology as an initial step toward a Yenching school of social sciences. A grant of $145,000 from the Laura Spelman Rockefeller Memorial Fund seemed to presage a bright future for the school.[41]

At this point the reorganization of the university to meet registration requirements influenced the course of events. The government had ruled that an institution must have at least three colleges for university status and it took at least three departments to make a college. In 1929, therefore, Yenching organized its curriculum into

[40] Information on the work in journalism at Yenching may be found in Edwards, Yenching, pp. 293–299; "On the Field," CR, LIX (1928), 397; "They Get Some of Your News," Yenching News, XIV (1935), 2; Edgar Snow, Journey to the Beginning (New York, 1958), pp. 139–145; Helen F. Snow, Notes on the Chinese Student Movement, 1935–36 (Stanford, 1959), p. 85.

[41] Princeton-Peking Gazette, I (1925–1926); Edwards, Yenching, pp. 167–169, 230. For examples of research publications, see in addition to Peking: A Social Survey, Sidney D. Gamble, How Chinese Families Live in Peiping (New York, 1933), and Yenching University, Ching Ho: A Sociological Analysis (Peiping, 1930).

a College of Arts and Letters, a College of Natural Sciences, and a College of Applied Social Sciences which included departments of economics, sociology and social work, and political science. A Ministry of Education ruling that sociology belonged in the College of Arts and Letters brought consternation since this would leave the College of Applied Social Sciences without three departments and Yenching without three colleges. A temporary solution was found by creating a department of jurisprudence and renaming the third college the College of Public Affairs (Fa-hsüeh yüan).[42]

Princeton was at this same time establishing a School of Public and International Affairs and also organizing a Princeton-Yenching Foundation. Plans called for exchange of fellows between Princeton and Yenching in the hope that study in Peking would "serve as a kind of laboratory" for Princeton graduate students and that the fellows would help China assume her proper place in the world by adding the ideals of "the Christian West to the spiritual heritage of China."[43] To further this goal Princeton would assist Yenching in its College of Public Affairs and in graduate programs in economics, political science, and sociology. Events both at Princeton and in China thus conspired to broaden the initial program and to orient it more toward political science than sociology.

A number of Princeton fellows were sent to Yenching to study in 1931, but the depression forced suspension of this aspect of the program. Yenching did build up its faculty in the social sciences, and approximately a third of the student body of Yenching majored in the College of Public Affairs. When the rural reconstruction ideal caught fire during the mid-1930's, the Princeton-Yenching Foundation secured a grant from the Rockefeller Foundation for expansion into this field, particularly the training of rural administrators. Most of the students chose economics as a major in preparation for a business career or political science in preparation for state service.

[42] While Yenching was making a vain effort to get a new ruling from the Ministry of Education, sociology remained in the College of Public Affairs; upon failure it was transferred to the College of Arts and Letters; and finally in 1936 was put back in the College of Public Affairs with government permission. At that time the unwanted child, department of jurisprudence, was abandoned.
[43] See brochure issued by Princeton-in-Peking, *Men and Events in Peking* (1929), p. 3; also, *Princeton-Peking Gazette*, IV (1929), 1–2.

The college began publication of the *Yenching Journal of Social Studies* in 1938; and though it had to suspend activities as a result of the war, some valuable articles on Chinese economic and social history, on rural reconstruction projects and techniques, and on the findings of current social surveys were issued during its short life (1938–1941, 1948–1949). During the 1930's, therefore, the College of Public Affairs became one of the strong divisons of the university, and members of the department fostered the use of scientific techniques for gathering basic factual information about Chinese society.[44]

The Harvard-Yenching Institute was one of the best known instances of cooperation between a Chinese and an American university and was one of the few examples of major expansion in the humanities. Contributing to its prominence were the funds of the Charles M. Hall estate and the strength of the participating institutions. On the basis of the bequest by the aluminum magnate for the support of education in foreign lands, plans were made in 1925 for a Harvard-Yenching Institute to foster research, instruction, and publication in the field of Chinese culture.[45] The first grants by the Hall estate, however, were made under a liberal interpretation of the donor's intent, with most of the China Christian colleges receiving funds for immediate expenses or endowment. Yenching, for example, received $345,000 in 1926–1927 for the construction of faculty residences, for the completion of a new power plant and heating system, for the historical museum, and for the general purposes of the university. Two years later six colleges received $2,400,000 to strengthen their work in Chinese studies. Cheeloo used

[44] A number of individuals who might be called members of the first generation of modern sociologists and anthropologists in China were associated with Yenching, for example, Wu Wen-tsao, Li An-che, and Leonard Shihlien Hsü. Fei Hsiao-t'ung received his undergraduate training in social studies at Yenching. For further information on the college, see the *Princeton-Yenching Gazette*, especially VI (May 1936), and VII (June 1937). The title was changed from *Princeton-Peking Gazette* to *Princeton-Yenching Gazette* in 1930.

[45] The title was Harvard-Peking Institute for Chinese Studies until the name Yenching University became the university's official designation. For further information, see *Yen-ching hsüeh-pao* publ. by the institute, 1927–1941, 1946–1950; also Stuart, *Fifty Years*, pp. 63–64; "Harvard-Yenching Institute," *School and Society*, XXVII (1928), 197, and "The Harvard-Yenching Institute for Chinese Studies," XL (1934), 485–486.

her share to expand her library holdings in Chinese and to add four new staff members who would teach in the Chinese department part time and conduct research in the area of Chinese humanities and social sciences. About $4,500,000 of the Hall bequest was set aside to support the general work of the Harvard-Yenching Institute, especially the activities at Harvard, while $1,900,000 became an endowment for six of the China Christian colleges and Allahabad Agricultural Institute in India.[46]

The group of scholars gathered by Yenching undertook a number of valuable projects. Among the activities of professors Hung Wei-lien (William Hung), Jung Keng, Ku Chieh-kang, and Wu Wen-tsao were archaeological research in Honan, Shensi, and Shantung, the study of Chinese bronzes and bronze inscriptions, the indexing of Chinese classics and belles-lettres, and the compilation of a dictionary of frequently abbreviated characters. Much of their work was published in the Harvard-Yenching Sinological Index Series, the Monograph Series, and the *Yen-ching hsüeh-pao* (in English first called the *Yenching Journal* and then the *Yenching Journal of Chinese Studies*). The latter, founded in 1927, soon established a reputation as an outstanding periodical on premodern China.

Yenching had difficulty attracting students to its program of Chinese studies. A small number of Western students of China came from Harvard to continue their work, and several of these subsequently pioneered in building programs for study of Chinese civilization at their academic institutions. For a number of reasons, however, few Chinese students enrolled as majors. The Yenching research and teaching was oriented toward ancient China, and Chinese youth during the 1930's were often more interested in destroying old China than studying it. Those students who did desire to study the classical tradition were likely to go to a national university with an established reputation in the field. Somewhat ironically, government policy probably also discouraged graduate students in Chinese studies at Yenching. When the national government issued regulations for graduate work in 1934, Yenching was authorized to conduct graduate work only in history, biology, chemistry, and po-

[46] Yenching was to receive approximately one fourth of the income from the endowment funds; the other five Christian colleges that were to share the remainder were Lingnan, Fukien, Nanking, West China, and Cheeloo.

litical science. Though Yenching continued to offer master's programs in Chinese and other areas, only degrees in the four authorized fields received official recognition in government appointments, scholarships, and so forth. In view of the government ruling and the increasing international tension, it is not surprising that the total number of Yenching's graduate students declined from 94 in 1930–1931 to 48 in 1936–1937.[47] Nor is it surprising that the greatest decline came in those areas not receiving government recognition. The number of undergraduate majors in the department of Chinese, furthermore, was consistently below 25. The department's contribution lay in the research of its faculty members and in the training of a few influential scholars, not in the number of students graduating in the field.

Perhaps one other special curriculum initiated by a Christian college should be mentioned because it offers a number of contrasts with most programs already discussed. This was the Comparative Law School of Soochow University, which quickly attracted a large enrollment, which was supported almost entirely by tuition fees and received little or no aid from foundations or even from Soochow University funds, and which catered specifically to the professional goals of urban Chinese. The origins of the law school as a modest evening program in Shanghai have already been discussed.[48] By 1930 the school was the largest of the special schools attached to the Christian colleges; its enrollment of 594 was a fourth larger than the total undergraduate enrollment of Soochow University. Despite the popularity and prosperity of the law school, Soochow University administrators found some aspects of the law division in Shanghai worrisome. One was its secularism. Religious instruction and chapel attendance had been compulsory for law students during the 1920's, but after the general abandonment of these requirements, the school had become almost completely secular in atmosphere. Few of its instructors were committed to evangelism, and only a fraction of its students were Christian; there was no campus community which could give the school a Christian orientation. Another disturbing factor was the school's independence of Soochow University. Since

[47] Cressy, *Information for Admissions Officers*, pp. 27–28; *Peking-Yenching Gazette*, V (Feb. 1931), 1; Edwards, *Yenching*, p. 262.
[48] See Chapter VI.

the school was located in a different city from the university, employed a faculty which was almost entirely separate, and was largely self-supporting, the institution developed a life of its own. It leaned only lightly on Soochow for guidance, and it had the wherewithal to make its own policy decisions.

The academic standing of the school was also a problem. Many in the university would have liked the school to concentrate on graduate training leading to the LL.D. degree; such a goal, however, faced many obstacles. When the school first opened, its requirements were ostensibly the same as those of most American law schools: two years of college plus three years of legal training. Actually, the levels of training were quite different. Most of the Chinese students were part-time evening scholars, and though they took fifteen course hours a week, they could hardly be expected to do much individual study in addition. The inadequacies of the library, the use of English as a medium of instruction in most courses, and the reliance on part-time instructors who were practicing jurists also affected the quality of instruction. The contrast between the levels of training at the Comparative Law School and at law schools in the United States sharpened as it became common in the United States to require four years of college and three years of law school. To offer work at this level, the Comparative Law School would have had to undertake a more expensive program with full-time graduate faculty, expanded library facilities, and daytime operations. The supporters of Soochow University, though they were unhappy about the level of instruction at the law school, were not prepared to furnish funds for such a costly operation. Furthermore, most of the law school clientele apparently preferred the short course; when the institution began offering a master of laws degree, few students enrolled. For the majority, the LL.B. was sufficient in that it served their business needs or it enabled them to practice law in the treaty ports. Those few who desired more advanced training found that a doctor's degree from a Western university carried greater prestige and opened more doors to employment than a similar one from a Chinese institution, and so they preferred to go abroad for graduate work.

A number of the graduates of the Comparative Law School did, in fact, study abroad; most of these gained influential positions as college teachers or government employees; seven alumni were members of the Codification Commission of the Legislative Yuan during the 1930's, and seven of the nine advocates of the Municipal Court of the International Settlement were graduates of the Comparative Law School.[49] John Ching-hsiung Wu, an alumnus of Soochow and principal of the law school during the 1930's, helped write the 1936 draft constitution which was promulgated in January 1947; he also was co-author of a standard work on the background of the 1936 draft constitution, *Chung-kuo chih hsien shih* (A History of Constitution-Making in China) (Shanghai, 1937). The law review published by the school contained most of the codes worked out during the modernization attempts of the 1920's and 1930's, as well as commentaries by both Chinese and Western jurists. It has thus become a valuable source for one of the creative periods in Chinese legal history. Despite the ambivalence of the Soochow University administration toward the school, therefore, the popularity of the institution and the contribution of its graduates and its faculty would indicate that it was performing a service desired by many Chinese.

For the Christian colleges as for the Kuomintang and the Chinese Communist Party, the decade 1927 to 1937 was one of transition, of questioning, and tentative steps in numerous directions. Sinification and service to China were acknowledged as essential goals if the disasters of the 1920's were not to be repeated. And yet, to know how best to achieve these aims was no easy task for the Westernized, urban leaders of the Christian institutions. They were hampered by lack of information about actual conditions in China and about the process of modernization, by the continuous disruption of Chinese political life, and by financial stringency. During the brief time available for exploration before the Japanese invasion, the colleges undertook a variety of research and service programs in agricultural and rural reconstruction, jurisprudence and library science, Chinese history and literature, and sociology. The major contribution of most of these projects was information. Some of the lacunae in knowledge about China and the modernization process were filled, and a number of individuals who had gained a new understanding of the complexity of rural reform had become deeply committed to recon-

[49] W. W. Blume, "The Comparative Law School," in Nance, *Soochow*, pp. 79–80.

struction work. Such modest accomplishments might be considered the necessary initial steps in the adaptation of Western techniques and knowledge to Chinese uses, and in the Sinification of the colleges.

The new or exploratory ventures of the colleges do not, however, compose the whole story of Christian higher education during the 1930's. The schools continued to educate students in increasing numbers. The enrollment of the Christian colleges, which had totaled approximately 3,500 in 1926–1927, had doubled by 1936–1937. Perhaps more significant was the fact that the increase had been due to the growth of existent institutions rather than the founding of new ones; the rate of growth had been highest in the upper classes of the colleges, and college administrators found satisfaction in the improving record of retaining students until graduation. In contrast with 1920, when none of the Christian colleges had as many as 300 students, and with 1925, when only two enrolled 500, eight colleges enrolled over 500 students in 1936.[50] Library collections, scientific equipment, and classroom facilities had increased steadily, if slowly, at most colleges. The two largest schools, Yenching and Nanking, could compare quite favorably with the better government institutions in their standards of teaching and research, though some of the smaller schools were still struggling to achieve college standards.[51]

Working out the basis for a new relationship between the colleges and their Western supporters and between the colleges and the Nanking government occupied the time and energy of the Christian college administrators during the 1930's. The result was that by 1937 a distinct shift of emphasis in matters of support and policy making

[50] CCEA, *Handbook, 1926*, Table I, p. 28; Table X, p. 37; Chester S. Miao, "Christian Education in China," *CCYB, 1938–39*, p. 207.

[51] In some of the smaller schools illness or a furlough could still mean that basic courses in a department had to be dropped temporarily or taught by substitutes from another department. Dean Theodore Chen wrote: "Many a time a whole department had temporarily disappeared from the curriculum on account of the furlough year or the sudden departure of a professor" (*Annual Report of Fukien Christian University, 1930*, p. 19). See also the lament of Hwa Nan's president over the lack of a teacher for physical education and for religious education in 1933–1934 and the emergency measures taken to provide basic courses in English and history in 1932–1933; *President's Report, 1932–1933*, p. 4; *1933–1934*, pp. 5, 6.

had occurred. Mission boards continued to exercise influence through providing funds for the colleges and members for the governing board, but the direct role of the mission societies was steadily declining. For one thing, the proportion of support contributed by the mission societies decreased as the colleges secured aid from other organizations and individuals in China and the West. The new sources of support found representation on the administrative boards, and by 1936–1937, when a third to a half of the colleges' income was coming from China, many policy decisions were being made by the board of directors on the scene. At the same time the paternalistic interest of the mission societies diminished somewhat as Chinese assumed most administrative positions and as faculty membership became 80 percent Chinese. Two new groups partially displaced the mission societies in interest and control: the Associated Boards for Christian Colleges in China took increasing responsibility for fund-raising campaigns and coordination of fiscal and administrative policy in the West, and the Nanking government assumed increasing control over curriculum, educational standards, textbooks, budget allocations, and many other aspects of the educational process.

The Sinification and secularization of the colleges did not occur without some apprehension and misunderstanding on both sides. College presidents and treasurers complained that they could hardly use Western funds to purchase a box of chalk without authorization from the Western office, and in a few embarrassing instances public decisions by college authorities in China were repudiated by Western boards.[52] On the other hand, Western supporters were concerned lest the colleges lose their distinctive Christian character. In comparison with the resistance and acrimony of the 1920's, however, the transfer occurred with considerable equanimity and good will. One indication that the change in the orientation of the colleges

[52] E. H. Cressy, "Council of Higher Education, Annual Meeting," *ER*, XXVIII (1936), 117–118; Edward H. Hume, "An Impression of the Meeting of the Council of Higher Education," *ibid.*, 121. See also, the correspondence of Stephen O. I. Ts'ai with the Associated Boards when Ts'ai was assistant treasurer and then controller at Yenching, Ts'ai to B. A. Garside, 2/24/1931; Ts'ai to J. L. Stuart, 3/3/1931; also Howard S. Galt to Garside, 12/30/1930; and Garside to Galt, 1/23/1931 and 2/9/1931 (UB, Yenching Correspondence File).

was of significant proportions is the fact that by the mid-1930's many of the Christian colleges had become accepted as Chinese, not foreign institutions. Their students were gaining acceptance as legitimate spokesmen for the Chinese nation. Instead of having their schools attacked in anti-Christian movements, the Christian college students were in some cases becoming important participants in student nationalist campaigns.

IX | The Colleges and the Student Movements of the 1930's

Despite Nanking's concentration on political and military unification, Japanese demands continually forced problems in foreign affairs upon its attention. During the 1930's Japan was making steady inroads on Chinese territory and sovereignty, and the Kuomintang's policy of compromise contributed to the students' loss of confidence in the government. Relations between the government and much of the academic world deteriorated perceptibly between 1927 and 1937. The students, who had earlier played an influential role as articulators of nationalist sentiment, continued to think of themselves as formulators of public opinion even after the establishment of the Nationalist regime. They were openly critical of Kuomintang foreign policy and assumed responsibility for trying to alter that policy. As in the movements of May 4 and May 30, their tactics included demonstrations, petitions, boycotts, and strikes.

There was, however, a major difference between the situation in the 1920's and that in the 1930's. During the 1930's the students had a rival spokesman for Chinese nationalism, the Kuomintang, and the government of this party was widely accepted at home and abroad as the legitimate defender of Chinese sovereignty; during the 1920's the Peking government had had less effective control over China and had generated little enthusiasm among nationalistic Chinese. Student protests during the 1930's did not ordinarily receive the popular support which they had in the 1920's, and the students were in a contest with a party which had a substantial power base. One important discovery of students during the movements of the 1930's was their dependence on Nanking for opposition to Japan. They might condemn the Kuomintang and its policies, but at the same time the Kuomintang was essential to national resistance to Japan. When Nanking censured student tactics and policies, student resentment and frustration were only aggravated by their dependence on the Kuomintang as a power base. The Chinese Communist Party, though not an effective national instrument for military resistance, had the advantage of not being the responsible authority. It could win favor among nationalists by verbal support for resistance. Along with the students, it accepted the necessity of a united front including the Kuomintang some time before the Kuomintang did. By 1936 the sense of alienation between students and the Kuomintang was being accentuated by a sense of rapport between the Communist Party and many student activists.

Christian college students had been criticized for failure to participate in many of the nationalist demonstrations of the 1920's. During the 1930's the story was different. Students at certain Christion colleges participated actively in the demonstrations during the Manchurian crisis, and Yenching student government leaders helped initiate the demonstration of December 9, 1935 against Japanese aggression and Kuomintang compromise. Such participation is an indication of the integration of certain Christian colleges into the Chinese educational community and the acceptance of their students as Chinese. At the same time, the foreign ties of the Christian schools were also relevant in the students' participation. With the greater immunity to Kuomintang and Japanese pressures brought by the foreign connections, Christian college students were freer than other groups to vent their nationalist sentiments and organize for protest movements. Perhaps also, the fact that they were students at Christian schools led some to try to prove their patriotism by being even more nationalistic than their colleagues at government institutions.

The Waning of Political Activism, 1927–1931

Between 1927 and the student campaign of 1931, Kuomintang-student relations were characterized by uneasiness and ambivalence. Many of the student unions and other student associations had until 1927 been under the influence of left-wing groups. They were critical of the more conservative elements that gained dominance in the Kuomintang and of the harsh measures taken against leftists after the split between the Kuomintang and the Communist Party. They had expected, or at least hoped, that Kuomintang rule marked a new era. Unity would bring peace, prosperity, and international respect. Education and the intellectuals would once more receive their due; perhaps influenced by their heritage more than they would admit, some seem to have hoped that China would be guided once more by the scholar elite. Their high expectations were, of course, doomed to disappointment. The displacement of the Peking government by the Nanking government did not automatically solve all problems. Instead of unity, factionalism and personal competition for control of the Kuomintang continued to dominate political relations. Military campaigns against dissident groups continued to deplete budgets so that funds allocated to education and social welfare were transferred to other uses.

During these years when there were few clear-cut nationalist issues, students frequently expressed their frustration in campaigns over local irritants. At Yenching in 1928 the students, especially the males, protested bitterly and long over the university's decision to discontinue the girls' middle school. They were unimpressed by the university's argument that it needed the facilities for the expanding college population and that it preferred to concentrate its limited resources on college level work. In 1928 and again in the spring of 1929 the rejection of a request by a Yenching student committee that required courses be abolished or reduced produced heated exchanges. The Representative Council of the Men's Self-Government Association blamed the college dean for the rejection and demanded his immediate resignation. When the faculty called for a retraction of the demand, the student association organized a publicity campaign attacking the dean and the university administration. The student leaders were finally persuaded to make a mild apology for "failure to follow the regular procedure, such as not having communicated the action in due form to the proper authorities before making it public," but the dean resigned shortly thereafter.[1] The following year, the dean of the women's college,

---

[1] Edwards, *Yenching*, pp. 341–343.

Mrs. Murray Frame, received the brunt of the attack. She was accused of high-handed and unfair treatment of a student, and there were threats of coercion if she did not resign within three days. She stayed beyond the time limit of three days and then left campus for a short vacation while the matter blew over. The student leader was expelled from the university.

At other schools protest movements also remained local in extent, but some had nationalist overtones in that a major goal was to increase Chinese control over the institution. Education was disrupted at Cheeloo during much of 1929 and 1930 by protests over the slowness with which the school was meeting registration requirements. Students at Fukien and Hangchow demanded greater power for the student association and less emphasis on the Christian purposes of the institution.

The students had unquestionably fostered a conscious nationalism which had contributed greatly to Kuomintang unification efforts, but just as surely, the frequent demonstrations had seriously disrupted education. Thus, government leaders and educators were divided over policy toward student associations and student political activity after mid-1927.[2] Ts'ai Yüan-p'ei, influential educator and head of the national educational administration from mid-1927 to mid-1928, advocated that students return to their classrooms. Ts'ai seems to have been motivated by a desire both to restore order to the school system and to prevent the students from being used as the tool of any political party. Certain Kuomintang leaders such as Ch'en Kuo-fan and Ch'en Li-fu wished to encourage continued political action by students but wanted tight Kuomintang control over student associations; the Kuomintang faction led by Chiang Kai-shek generally favored a policy of restricting student political activity while fostering its own version of Chinese nationalism.

The government soon moved to undermine the students' facilities for organizing strikes and demonstrations. It attempted to destroy the nationwide organization of the student union and to transform

[2] For greater detail, see Israel, *Student Nationalism* and Linden, "Politics and Education," *JAS*, XXVII, 763–776. Also Wieger, *Chine Moderne*, VIII, 126–129, 163; H. C. Tsao, "The Nationalist Government and Education," *ER*, XX (1928), 188–200.

the local student unions into student self-government associations. The latter were to deal only with such matters as dormitory and dining facilities, social activities, and literacy classes. They were not to conduct demonstrations off campus nor to try to influence national policy; they were not to establish connections with student associations in other universities. Student organizations were to register with the government as well as university authorities, and school administrations were warned that they should enforce discipline, for they would henceforth be held responsible for student disorders. A concerted effort was made to eliminate the influence of left-wing groups in the student associations. The Kuomintang leaders continued, however, to accept the thesis that a major purpose of education was to instill nationalism. Thus, the Nanking government found itself encouraging anti-Japanese attitudes in required San Min Chu I (Three Principles of the People) courses while officially forbidding student protests against conciliation of Japan. The result was that the Kuomintang was not always consistent in condemning student demonstrations after 1927. Specific Japanese demands could bolster the influence of those advocating use of student protests for political purposes, and the Kuomintang might try to strengthen its position in negotiations with Japan by fostering public protest.

Kuomintang factionalism and ambivalence concerning the role of students on the national scene was paralleled by confusion in both the student associations and the Chinese Communist Party. Between 1928 and 1931 student political activities did decline; there were no nationwide campaigns by student associations, partly because of effective Kuomintang control and partly because the students were themselves badly split over policy and deeply depressed over the failure of their dreams to be realized with the Kuomintang victory. Many students, furthermore, had been dismayed by the extreme demands made during the student campaigns of 1926–1927 and welcomed an opportunity to concentrate on their own academic careers. Student leaders did not find it easy to provide guidance or find followers.[3] Though Marxist and communist works remained

[3] Numerous articles written between 1928 and 1931 comment on the depression and confusion among students; see for example, *Chung-yang jih-pao*, July 20, Aug. 30, 1928, on divisions within the National Student Union; also Neander

popular, few students seemed willing to accept the risks and discipline incumbent upon Communist Party membership. The divided and disoriented Communist Party could offer neither protection nor direction.

The Manchurian Crisis

The Japanese attack in Manchuria on September 18, 1931, reawakened the political instincts of the students. Or, to put it more accurately, the issue of resistance to Japanese aggression overcame depression and galvanized students for a national political movement once again. Temporarily at least, divisions were glossed over as the New Youth recovered their identity as public spokesmen for China. On September 20, newspapers in the major cities of China announced the Japanese attack in headlines calculated to stir public indignation; within a few hours of the news students were calling protest meetings, dispatching telegrams to Nanking to demand defense of Chinese sovereignty, and planning a boycott of Japanese goods. Resist Japan National Salvation Associations were hastily organized to provide an administrative framework for coordinating programs and activities, and before a week was out Shanghai students had evolved the publicity technique that was to typify the 1931 movement: the trip to Nanking to petition in person for immediate military resistance to Japan. The Kuomintang, during the period of initial indignation over Japanese aggression, generally encouraged public expressions of anti-Japanese sentiment; party officials gave support to student attempts to organize a boycott of Japanese goods, and student petitioners to Nanking were assured that the government would never sacrifice the sovereignty of China. The Kuomintang turned to the League of Nations for support.

As it became apparent that Japan was not going to retreat and that League action would probably be limited to expressions of moral indignation, China had to face the question of what she could do alone. The Nanking government rejected the possibility of military defense of Manchuria without Western aid. This placed

Chang, "What of the Students?" *CR*, LIX (1928), 440–441; Chester Miao and Frank W. Price, "Religion and Character in Christian Middle Schools," *ER*, XXI (1929), 424; Daniel Fu, "The 1930 Special Study of the YMCA of China" (Shanghai, 1930), located in YMCA Historical Library, III, 21–33.

students in a quandary as to the future direction and tactics of their movement. The boycott, though effective, had not forced Japan to retreat and was meeting opposition from merchants whose businesses had been hurt.[4] Though the petition campaign and student strikes continued, Nanking showed no sign of accepting student recommendations for military resistance. In December, a group of left-wing students from Peita advocated a trip to Nanking to demonstrate against the government. They would not recognize Kuomintang officials as representatives of a legitimate government by petitioning for alteration of foreign policy, but they would demonstrate in order to censure the government itself and bring about its downfall.[5] Immediately upon arrival in Nanking, they came into conflict with government officials over lodging; and on December 5 a demonstration calling for overthrow of the government and armed rebellion by the masses ended in the arrest of most of their members.

Even students who had not agreed with the Peita corps' demands and tactics believed it necessary to come to the defense of the May 4 tradition; they had to defend the right of New Youth to immunity while acting as spokesmen for China. For a brief moment, the student generation closed ranks. Demonstrations condemning government arrests and maltreatment were launched in Nanking and Shanghai, and violence erupted in both cities. Government reaction was decisive; renewed attempts at demonstration were dispersed with armed forces, and both petitioners and demonstrators were rounded up, placed on railway cars, and dispatched home. In its action the Kuomintang had widespread support. Even nationalistic students had been dismayed by the new violence, and renewed exhortations for the support of injured youth fell on deaf ears. Not until the Japanese attack on Shanghai, January 28, 1932, did the movement show signs of reviving, and even with the new threat the revival proved temporary and ill-coordinated.

The whole Manchurian crisis emphasized the limitations of

[4] Actually the boycott was continued until the summer of 1933; see Japanese protests in Japanese Chamber of Commerce, Shanghai, *Aspects of Anti-Japanese Movements in China* (Shanghai, 1932), NW Collection pamphlet. For comments on student violence, see editorials and articles in *North China Daily News*, Dec. 11 and 17, 1931.

[5] I have followed the interpretation of Israel here; see *Student Nationalism*, pp. 65–69.

Kuomintang control over China, but the important revelation of the 1931 student movement was the tenuous nature of the loyalty of young intellectuals to the Kuomintang. Students were reluctant to accept the Kuomintang as champion of Chinese nationalism when the policies of the two groups diverged; yet the power of the Kuomintang forced students to turn to it as executor of policy. The Kuomintang as formulator and executor of national policy could not sanction the extralegal role sought by New Youth; yet it fostered and tried to use student nationalism. As these conflicts were brought out during the 1931 movement, the alienation between intellectuals and the Kuomintang grew; the failure of the Kuomintang to resist in Manchuria undercut the creditability of its primary appeal—nationalism. Though the student movement failed in its goals and students retired in disarray, the effects of the movement on relations between the Kuomintang and New Youth were long lasting.

The transitional status of the Christian colleges from foreign mission institutions to Chinese institutions is indicated in their divergent reactions. Students in certain Christian schools were active participants in the movement, but nationalistic activities in other colleges were minimal. Some of the schools were still isolated from the intellectual community of China, whereas others were still recovering from the Educational Rights Movement and were preoccupied with the task of government registration. At Ginling the girls organized a branch of the Resist Japan National Salvation Association but did not hold demonstrations.[6] The students of Fukien Christian University participated in mass demonstrations in Foochow and, according to the dean, even assumed leadership in certain activities, but their protests did not disrupt academic work for any extended period of time.[7] At Hwa Nan, which was just beginning to accept the necessity of registration and which was still insulated from Chinese political life, no participation in the 1931 student movement was reported.

The lukewarm concern in some institutions is also a reminder of the potency of regional interests and the relative weakness of nationalist appeals even in 1931. To many in interior China, Japanese

[6] Thurston, *Ginling*, p. 73.
[7] Fukien Christian University, *Annual Report, 1932*, p. 13.

aggression in Manchuria seemed the concern of Manchuria, not of the nation. They had more immediate and pressing problems. Warlord leaders in some cases forbade demonstrations and were powerful enough to enforce the prohibition. In Shantung, Governor Han Fu-chü ordered all schools closed temporarily as soon as news of the Mukden incident reached him. This action, together with the influence of the Japanese in the Tsinan area and the administrative difficulties of Cheeloo, helps explain why little was heard from Cheeloo students during most of the movement. Many in the Yangtze Valley were struggling to save life and property in the midst of the disastrous 1931 flood. In Wuchang the main city dikes had broken on August 18, and the last flood refugees were just leaving the Huachung campus at the time of the Japanese attack. When classes did begin on September 24, only sixty-seven college students were enrolled.[8] The institution, furthermore, was just re-establishing itself after the turmoil of 1926–1928, and both students and administrators gave priority to securing government registration. Instead of students traveling to Nanking to protest government policy, the school was trying to persuade Ministry of Education representatives to travel to Wuchang to sanction the Huachung program. The Mukden affair did not have high priority in the concerns of Huachung students during the fall of 1931.

The active centers of the movement for the Christian colleges, as for the national institutions, were the cities of east China, especially Peiping and Shanghai; and the reasons were similar. The greatest concentrations of students were in these centers; students in these cities were particularly conscious of the May 4 tradition; and these were the areas where the Japanese threat seemed real and the students' sense of involvement in politics was most acute. Also influencing the role of Christian college students in these areas was the Sinification of the institutions. A few schools had already begun to gain acceptance as Chinese institutions, and their students participated freely in the nationalistic movement as members of the New Youth. For students in all of the Christian colleges, participation was made easier by the fact that the enemy was neither Western nor Christian.

[8] Coe, *Huachung*, pp. 97–99.

In general, Christian college students taking part in demonstrations and petition tours belonged to the moderate wing, and disruption of academic work was briefer than in many of the national universities. Though several national universities could conduct no effective academic work during the fall of 1931, none of the Christian colleges was disrupted for more than a week or two. This may be attributed at least partially to the Christian college tradition of cultivating a campus community and maintaining rather tight administrative control over the extracurricular activities of the students.[9] Since the administrative personnel were not government appointees their tenure of office was more secure; and they were likely to make fewer concessions to student demands and to exert more pressure on students to give priority to academic obligations. The 1931 movement lacked a nationwide organization which could coordinate action and coerce students into continued participation, and so administrative appeals for academic responsibility could more easily offset appeals to nationalism. Christian college students often joined demonstrations in a spontaneous burst of outrage but returned to class when confusion over tactics dulled their enthusiasm and sense of purpose.

Students at the University of Shanghai (Hu-chiang), for example, helped initiate the first coordinated response by Shanghai students to the Mukden incident; on September 20 at a meeting held on Hu-chiang campus, approximately a hundred students from thirty colleges and universities in the area founded the Shanghai Resist Japan National Salvation Association. Protest meetings were planned, telegrams dispatched to Nanking, and students sent out to arouse the countryside and organize local Salvation Associations. When Shanghai student leaders called for petition tours to Nanking and an indefinite strike, however, most Hu-chiang students questioned the efficacy and propriety of such activities. They voted instead to concentrate on a week of civic forums, drills, special dis-

[9] A report on the activities of the Yenching students stated: "It is remarkable that our students controlled themselves so splendidly and did not make any more trouble for the University than they did. The Patriotic Week conducted by the University with the assistance of student representatives from November 30 to December 5 is a very conspicuous demonstration of the possibility of faculty-student cooperation even under the most difficult situations." Yenching University, *Annual Report of the Director of Studies, 1931–32*, p. 2.

cussions under the auspices of the International Relations Club, and lectures in surrounding villages. A few individuals joined the trips to Nanking, but no large delegations were sent by the Hu-chiang student body. Two months later, Japanese aggression in Heilungkiang prompted a revival of strikes and petition tours, and Hu-chiang students were eager to protest but divided over tactics. While the middle school students of Hu-chiang went on strike, the college students voted against a strike; and in fact, many students sought safety by returning to their homes.[10]

In Hangchow, on the other hand, appeals to patriotism and to loyalty to New Youth were more successful in overcoming factionalism and confusion; in a few instances coordinated leadership used organizational tactics similar to those of the 1920's to back up appeals. In November 1931, when Hangchow Christian College students decided to join other Hangchow youth in a petition tour to Nanking, they insured mass participation by levying a fine of Ch$10 on all refusing to go. Some 1,400 Hangchow students boarded trains for Nanking on November 22. Since this was one of the earliest groups to arrive in Nanking during the second wave of petitions, the youth were able to present Chiang Kai-shek personally with a request for immediate declaration of war against Japan and arming of student volunteer units. Chiang assured the students that the government was formulating a plan of action against Japan and then expressed his belief that the students could make a greater contribution by completing their education than by going to the front lines at that time.

Though the students were impressed by the government's expressions of anti-Japanese sentiment and the sympathy with which officials apparently listened to their protests, they were also dismayed by their inability to move the government to action. Discipline was difficult to maintain; the next step, difficult to determine. By the time the Hangchow group was ready to return home, students were pouring into Nanking, violent incidents had occurred, and the government was trying to halt the movement. The home-

[10] University of Shanghai, *Annual Report, 1932*; "Minutes of the Executive Committee of the Board of Directors, Shanghai," Oct. 31, 1931, p. 37, and Dec. 23, pp. 42–43; University of Shanghai, *Newsletter of the President*, no. 9, Dec. 4, 1931.

ward-bound Hangchow students met four trainloads of students who had been prevented from proceeding to the capital. One Hangchow Christian College youth expressed chagrin over the riotous behavior of some of the petitioners; even some of the Hangchow students had refused to ride in third-class coaches. Such sensitivity to privilege and status, he protested, hardly seemed congruent with their view of themselves as martyrs in the nationalist cause. Embarrassment over student behavior, however, was not great enough to kill the desire for continued pressure on the government. At the same time, the Hangchow students were not so deeply alienated from the government that they were ready to call for its overthrow as some of the Peita students were doing. They voted a strike. The reasoning of Hangchow Christian College students in joining the strike was made clear in an article in the student newspaper, *Campus Life*.

It is not without cause that we Chinese should be very much disappointed at the inability our Government has shown in its attitude toward the Manchurian crisis since September. Students from different parts of the country over and over again petitioned the Government to act its part as a faithful servant of the people, but none of these petitions has brought any better effects. Under these circumstances we were impelled, though unwillingly, to stop our study as a warning to the Government, the last and only step we can take.

Our College has joined this strike because, under the organization of the Hangchow Students' Anti-Japanese National Saving [Salvation] Organization, we had to take the same step with our fellow students to show that we in Hangchow are of one mind and heart with all students of the country, to oppose the invaders and save our country.[11]

Among the active participants in the movement were the Yenching students. Believing themselves the leaders among the Christian college students, they were eager to demonstrate the nationalism of Christian college pupils and their loyalty to the New Youth. They were close enough to the scene of warfare to feel directly threatened, and the flow of Tungpei refugee students to Peiping heightened their concern. Their actions also illustrate the factionalism and confusion of students as they sought to exercise influence despite the inflexibility of the Kuomintang and the absence of an effective national student union. One of the first moves by Yenching students

[11] Day, *Hangchow*, pp. 78–79.

was to publish a daily newspaper, *P'ing hsi pao*, in order to provide information about the Manchurian crisis at a time when rumors flew thick and fast but facts about the activities of the Japanese and the Kuomintang were difficult to obtain. For some months the Yenching newspaper was an important source of news for many in Peiping who had no connection with the Yenching community. The youths worked to enforce the boycott of Japanese goods and they went to the surrounding villages to lecture to the populace. They tried to organize military drill under the auspices of the Resist Japan National Salvation Association, and in mid-October they fostered a series of lectures by prominent historians and youth leaders, most of whom counseled patience. All this seemed less than satisfactory.

As disillusionment deepened with the fall of Tsitsihar, the Yenching students voted to join the new wave of petition tours to Nanking. They immediately met opposition from Yenching faculty and administration, who recommended instead local protests which would be less disruptive to academic work. The Peiping Student Union, though encouraging students to go to Nanking, could not agree on whether the purpose of the trip was to demonstrate against the government or petition the government to alter its policy. It left the various university associations to translate their protests into action as they saw fit. Obviously, the government's attempts to cut the nationwide ties of the student organizations had had their effect; spontaneous action by school associations was possible, but fractured communication lines and confusion in the face of Kuomintang power made unified action unobtainable. Yenching students, their certainty already undermined, agreed to reconsider their decision to go to Nanking when Chancellor Wu Lei-ch'uan resigned. Chancellor Wu, who had led the initial attempt to dissuade the students from the tour, had resigned on the grounds that he had not fulfilled his duty; now his resignation made possible resumption of negotiations between Yenching students and faculty.

As part of a compromise settlement, a week of no classes was set aside for a campus protest program and Chancellor Wu was persuaded to withdraw his resignation. Those students who still wished to go to Nanking were permitted to do so, and 130 boarded a train for the capital. Their experience during the expedition was typical in its frustrating inconclusiveness. By this time Chiang Kai-shek was attempting to stem the tide of students flowing to Nanking, and he refused to give the students an audience; they returned to Peiping with little sense of accomplishment, bewildered as to the next move. Most of the Yenching students had been persuaded to remain in Peiping where they organized a series of mass meetings and went out to the countryside to arouse the peasants to the Japanese threat. A parade of about seven hundred students led by Chancellor Wu and President Stuart marched through the neighborhood as a sign of patriotic protest, and the university agreed to admit thirty Tungpei refugee students. Embittered at being driven from their homes, the refugees kept alive resentment over Japanese aggression.[12]

After the 1931 experience, the government renewed its effort to tighten control over students and schools while expanding its support of education. The Ministry of Education drew up specific course requirements for various majors, and in most cases the hours of class work and the number of specialized courses necessary for a degree were so high that students would have little time for extracurricular activities. Highly competitive examinations for admission to college and for scholarships to study abroad, a National Institute for Compilation and Translation to authorize and issue acceptable textbooks, and the required courses in San Min Chu I were other means of exercising control. With greater consistency than before 1931, the government enforced its ban on nationwide student associations and renewed its attempt to eliminate left-wing students from positions of influence. Raids, arrests, and dormitory searches made life uneasy for student leaders. Student associations were not chartered without the sanction of the local Kuomintang headquarters, and they were expected to look to the party and government for guidance and supervision. In the New Life Movement the Kuomintang tried to provide an ideology and program that would fill the vacuum left by the disintegration of the Confucian tradition and offset the appeal of Marxism. By 1933 a degree of order seemed to have come to the academic community, and many college administrators could look forward to a brief period of growth.

[12] Account based on Edwards, *Yenching*, pp. 338–339; Israel, *Student Nationalism*, pp. 54–56, 64–65; Yenching University, *Annual Report of the Director of Studies, 1931–32*.

Student reactions to the 1931 movement and government educational policies were varied; they were not happy with Kuomintang compromises in foreign affairs or ambivalence toward domestic reform, but they knew no way to alter either.[13] Many retreated into a kind of privatism; they would stay out of trouble by concentrating on their personal interests and careers; political activism was dangerous for the individual and could accomplish nothing for the nation. A few turned to rural reconstruction and social service programs as a means of serving China. For some, the opposition of the New Life Movement to total Westernization and its attempt to evolve an ideology that was uniquely Chinese seemed briefly to offer hope and guidance. Marxism continued to hold appeal, and despite censorship students managed to obtain communist literature.[14]

Since conscious nationalism was to a very great extent the product of educational experience, however, students remained responsive to patriotic pleas, and Japan's repeated demands for concessions made it difficult for students to ignore the claims of nationalism. The government, they said, preached the Three Principles of the People but had not remained true to the first of these principles. Kuomintang-student relations were in that dangerous stage where real communication was difficult because neither trusted the good will of the other. Students were, furthermore, resentful of Nanking's growing influence over their lives and education. Their very dependence on the Kuomintang for both national and personal security often seemed to enhance their antagonism. Restricted as to legitimate

[13] Kiang Wen-han, "The Challenge of Communism in China," *Chinese Students and Religion* (Pamphlet issued by China YMCA in 1936), pp. 27–35; Hubert Freyn, *Prelude to War: The Chinese Student Rebellion of 1935–36* (Shanghai, 1936), pp. 3–10; Y. C. Yang, "The Missionary and Current Trends in Schools and Colleges," *The Tung Wu Magazine of Soochow University*, III (1935), 118–119. The titles of numerous articles in *The China Critic* for 1934–1935 reveal the mood of students: "College Men in Depression," "Complaints of a College Graduate," etc.

[14] Kiang Wen-han wrote that the book market was flooded with works on Marxism and that communist literature could circulate if elementary techniques of subterfuge were observed; a volume with the cover title, "Paul, the Friend of Youth," might actually contain the monthly of the Comintern, for example. See "The Challenge of Communism," *Chinese Students and Religion*, pp. 27–28.

avenues for patriotic expression and yet not trusting the Kuomintang
to defend China, students sometimes used minor, even petty incidents to give vent to their nationalism. In May of 1934, for example,
Mayor Yüan Liang of Peiping invited sixty Yenching girls to act as
hostesses at a party on May 9. The girls replied that May 9 was
National Humiliation Day, and on a day commemorating the acceptance of the Twenty-One Demands, they would hardly be in a
mood for merriment, and they would certainly not want to participate in festivities where Japanese officials would be present. With
patriotic zeal, the Yenching students also published an open letter
demanding a formal apology from the mayor. One periodical pointed
out that the mayor's previous condemnation of coeducation and
advocacy of traditional mores in relations between the sexes undoubtedly contributed to the self-righteous indignation of the
Yenching girls. Nevertheless, the students knew that the patriotic
argument was a powerful one, and this was the one they turned
against the mayor.[15] Not until December 9, 1935, however, was
there such a serious challenge to Chinese sovereignty that students
rose out of their lethargy and attempted once more to influence
foreign policy by nation-wide public demonstrations. The issue was
the Japanese attempt to organize north China into an autonomous
regime under Japanese influence; the hope of the students was that
public pressure would persuade the Kuomintang to resist Japan's
demands.

Launching of the December 9th Movement

Though there are many similarities between the student movements of 1931 and of December 9, 1935, the significant differences
between the two movements document the changing relations between the Kuomintang and the New Youth. The December 9th
Movement was distinctive because of the prominent roles played by
Christian college students [16] and by the Chinese Communist Party;
it was different also because it operated within the shadow of the

[15] Editorial: Mayor Yüan and the Yenching Girls," *The China Critic*, VII
(May 17, 1934), 1463; also, *The Peiping Chronicle*, May 6, 1934.
[16] For a more detailed discussion, see Jessie G. Lutz, "December 9, 1935:
Student Nationalism and the China Christian Colleges," *JAS*, XXVI (Aug.
1967), 627–648.

1931 movement and the increasing alienation between Nanking and the students. The period from 1931 to 1935 had been a time of growth and Sinification for most of the Christian colleges. In 1931, students at several of the Christian institutions had taken an active part in the student movement, and Christian administrators had shown a certain pride in the nationalism of their protégés even while expressing concern over academic disruption. With the continued integration of the Christian institutions, one could expect participation by a larger number of Christian colleges; education in a Christian school, like education in the government institutions, was increasingly the generator of national consciousness. A frequent theme in essays by Christian college students was a sense of awakening as the writers committed themselves to nationalism after a happy but parochial childhood. One Yenching student wrote that contact with "right-thinking" youth, with their magazines and newspapers, and with the urban environment had brought the dawn of light.[17] A young girl who had been at Yenching until the Mukden incident and then had transferred to the University of Shanghai was typical of many.[18] Writing in 1934, she said that she had lived for herself until she had become aware of the deformities of Chinese society and of the suffering of the nation under imperialism. She then decided to dedicate herself to serving the nation and she resisted romantic love because, in a time of emergency, patriotism should come first. Once having concluded that she must sacrifice for China, though, she found no specific course of action except to return to her studies, no outlet for her emotionally charged nationalism until the December 9th Movement. When students massed in the streets of Peiping on December 9, 1935, Christian college students were more than participants following the lead of youth from the national universities. Yenching students played a leading role in launching the movement; they helped inspire and plan the December 9 demonstration; and they, along with students at other Christian colleges, were to continue to play an active part in the protests throughout December and into January.

In the Japanese proposal to inaugurate an autonomous north China regime, the students had an issue with explosive potential.

[17] Ts'ao I, " 'Shih-erh-chiu' kei wo ti chiao-hsün," SECCN, pp. 31–33.
[18] Tso I-li, "Wo ti ta-hsüeh sheng-huo," Wen-hua (June 1934), pp. 95–97.

Here was a threat to the intellectual and cultural capital of China, not simply to the three northeastern provinces. Here was a threat, furthermore, to the safety and livelihood of the students themselves. What was to be gained by currying favor with the Kuomintang government if Nanking ceased to control political appointments, scholarships, and education in the north China area? Here was an issue which could overcome fear of government reprisal. The theme that the time for talk was over and the time for action had arrived was heard more and more frequently.[19] At this moment in the fall of 1935, Yenching students helped transform verbal protest into public demonstration, individual criticism into concerted action. On November 1, 1935, eleven student self-government associations in Peiping and Tientsin sent a petition to the Sixth Plenum of the Kuomintang Central Executive Committee protesting against arbitrary arrests and infringements on freedom.[20] The petition had been drawn up by members of the Yenching student government association, passed at a Yenching mass meeting, and supported by representatives from Tsing Hua, National Peiping Normal University, and eight other schools. About a week later the Yenching student association newspaper, Yen-ta chou-k'an, devoted its entire issue to the Japanese problem and protests against Japanese aggression and Chinese compromise. Students at Tsing Hua, Yenching, and other schools were also working to revive an interschool organization which could coordinate student protests. As they made progress in this illegal venture and student leaders from other universities joined, the possibility of a public demonstration was broached.

Helen F. Snow (Nym Wales) says that the first serious discussions of a public demonstration occurred about this time in her home with Ch'en Han-po, editor of the Yenching newspaper; Chang Chao-lin, president of the Yenching student body; Wang Ju-mei, vice-president of the Yenching student body; and her husband, Edgar

[19] Huang Hua (Wang Ju-mei), "Chung-kuo fa-hsi-szu yün-tung hsien-chuang" (The present status of the Chinese Fascist movement), Yen-ta chou-k'an (Dec. 6, 1935), pp. 12–14: "Yen-ching ta-hsüeh ching-kao t'ung-pao" (An open letter from Yenching students to all countrymen) NW Collection: broadside; n.d., probably Dec. 1935).
[20] X.A.N. (Pseudonym), "Shih-erh-chiu hui-i-lu" (Reminiscences of December 9th), SECCN, pp. 1–3; a translation of the petition is quoted in H. Snow, Notes, pp. 13–15.

Snow.[21] A definite decision to hold the mass protest rally in early December seems to have been made after the inauguration of the East Hopei Autonomous Council by Major General Doihara Kenji on November 25. The tempo of meetings, petitions, and public telegrams picked up momentum as educators, other student groups, and newspaper editors protested. A student meeting at Tsing Hua to plan strategy in detail and a meeting at Yenching on December 8 to complete arrangements for the demonstration created a mood of high excitement.[22]

What was there about Yenching and the Peiping environment which contributed to the prominent role of the Christian school in December? Though the attitudes of Yenching students were generally typical of those of the New Youth, Yenching University and its students were also distinctive in certain ways. Yenching was physically separated from Peiping, and this location on the fringes of China's cultural center was symbolic of the position of most of the Christian colleges in Chinese intellectual and educational life. The missionary origin, the foreign support, the large number of Western teachers, and the heavy dependence on English all set Yenching apart. The attempt by administrators to build a cohesive campus

[21] H. Snow, *Notes*, pp. 1–3; E. Snow, *Journey to the Beginning*, p. 139. E. Snow was at the time teaching courses in the Yenching department of journalism; H. Snow was taking courses at Yenching. Though sources available in the United States may encourage some overemphasis of the role of Yenching students in the early stages of the movement, writers in both the Soviet Union and China have specifically acknowledged their contribution. See Chiang Nan-hsing and others, *The Roar of a Nation: Reminiscences of the December 9th Student Movement* (Peking, 1963), especially Wan Lin, "In Memory of Comrade Huang Ching," p. 132; V. P. Ilyushchechkin, "Studentcheskoe dvizhenie 9 dekabria 1935 g.v. Kitae" (The Student Movement of December 9, 1935 in China), Institut Vostokovedenia (Institute of Eastern Studies), *Kratkie soobshcheniia* (Brief Commentaries), VII (1952), 3–19. The official communist interpretation, of course, emphasizes the role of the Chinese Communist Party in the movement; see "30th Anniversary of December 9th Movement," *Peking Review*, no. 51 (Dec. 17, 1965), pp. 7–9; Li Ch'ang, "Recollections of the National Liberation Vanguard of China," in *SCMM*, nos. 296, 297 (1961).

[22] "Ho Ying-ch'in pei shang jen-wu" (Ho Ying-ch'in's Mission in Peiping), editorial in *Yen-ta chou-k'an* (Dec. 6, 1935), pp. 1–2; X.A.N., "Shih-erh-chiu hui-i-lu," *SECCN*, pp. 5–13. X.A.N. says that during the planning stages he and several other students were so afraid of detection and arrest that they avoided sleeping in their own dormitory rooms; once they slept in a dining room and another time they tried the infirmary.

community in the tradition of church-related colleges in the United States contributed to the sense of separateness. At the same time, the writings of Yenching students in 1935–1936 reveal that efforts to acclimate the university to its Chinese environment had had some success. Integration had gone far enough so that they were no longer likely to be condemned as denationalized "running dogs" of the foreigners. Even so, they felt the separateness of Yenching enough so that they desired to be first and loudest in expressions of Chinese nationalism. They had reason to want to prove their patriotism. An essay written for the first anniversary of the movement conveys both the pride and insecurity of a Yenching student. Twice the writer mentions similarities in the role of Yenching in the December 9th Movement and the role of National Peking University in the May 4th Movement, and his pride in the similarities is obvious.[23]

In assuming their role in the December 9th Movement, Yenching students had certain advantages, and ironically these advantages were related to two characteristics for which Yenching was often criticized: its semi-extraterritorial status and the affluence of its students. Under ordinary circumstances, affluence might have made for a conservative student body; but in the Chinese environment of 1935 membership in the well-to-do classes could also encourage intense nationalism and defiance of political authority. For one thing, a large proportion of the Yenching students came from a commercial background, and urban China felt the threat of Japan keenly; the business community, in particular, was being hurt by the flow of Japanese goods into north China via Manchuria. Students preparing for state service, for teaching, and even for a business career—that is, the majority—saw their future livelihood threatened by Japanese domination of a north China regime.

For another thing, students who demonstrated in defiance of Nanking would need the protection of powerful interests. The young intellectuals, in fact, were the only group in China who had the prestige and influential connections to demonstrate against the policies of the older generation with any impunity. Laborers or peasants who called for direct action against a government program

[23] *SECCN*, pp. 3, 6–7.

would pay a dear price. Educators, journalists, and civil servants of
the older generation would jeopardize their jobs, and some of them
apparently knew this and were happy to have the students say what
they did not dare. Chancellor Lu Chih-wei of Yenching wrote, for
instance: "I cannot handle the students in a detached way. I am
quite in sympathy with their actions. When a pig is slaughtered, it
is natural that there be some squeaking, though perfectly useless.
The students are the only people that can do the squeaking." [24]
Students were well aware that the government would hesitate to
turn unbridled force against them once they had massed for demonstration; in a state where moral force was still important to political
power, the loss to the government would be too great. The students,
furthermore, often turned to their fathers to extricate them when
they ran into trouble. This, despite the fact that it was often against
their own fathers that they were rebelling. In more than one instance, intervention by an influential relative secured the release of
an arrested student.[25]

The Christian college students had a functioning student government to channel nationalist fervor. Not all of the public institutions
could say the same at the time of the December 9th Movement.
Since 1931 a tight watch on student associations in public universities had been maintained, and there had been frequent government
raids to arrest dissident students. Even National Peking University,
the traditional leader of student movements, no longer had an effective student government association in 1935. But Yenching's foreign
affiliation had served as a buffer against government interference.
The Kuomintang might exercise control over the curricula of the
Christian colleges, but it had limited influence over the administration or the extracurricular activities in these institutions.

The Yenching student association, furthermore, had reason to
believe that the college administration sympathized with student
attitudes. The student government was fostered by the faculty as a
part of campus community life and as training in democracy.

[24] C. W. Luh to J. Leighton Stuart, letter dated Jan. 16, 1936 (Yenching
Correspondence, UB File). See also the letter of Luh to Stuart, Dec. 9, 1935,
written while Luh was awaiting the return of the students to campus after the
demonstration.
[25] Heng (pseudonym?), "Shih-erh-chiu hou shang-hai" (Shanghai after December 9th), SECCN, pp. 28–29; H. Snow, Notes, p. 55.

President Stuart had publicly stated his belief that only forceful resistance would stop Japanese aggression and had, in fact, called on England and the United States to join Nanking in opposition to Japan.[26] On more than one occasion he had commended Yenching students for patriotic actions in defense of China. As an expression of patriotic protest, the Yenching administration had admitted a number of Tungpei refugee students, and this action was not without significance for the December 9th Movement, since several Tungpei students were Yenching leaders in 1935.[27] These youth, driven from their homeland by the conquest of Manchuria, were bitterly anti-Japanese and highly critical of Nanking's foreign policy. At a time when most presidents of public institutions felt obliged to accede to Nanking's demands, Yenching administrators could support the students without fearing loss of position. The differing responses to a conference of students, educators, and government officials called by Chiang Kai-shek for January 1936 can serve as an illustration of Yenching's independence. The Peiping student associations refused to elect delegates to the conference. In one editorial, a Yenching student asked: "Why should we go to be cheated? Haven't we already been cheated enough?"[28] Actions, not words, would be accepted as proof of Nanking's intention to protect Chinese sovereignty. Most university presidents thereupon met Nanking's request by appointing student delegates to the conference and themselves going to the meeting with Chiang Kai-shek. Chancellor Lu of Yenching alone acceded to the will of his students and appointed no representatives.

[26] Letters of J. Leighton Stuart to Yenching Advisory Council, Jan. 26, 1933 and March 1, 1935 (Yenching Correspondence, UB file).

[27] H. Snow, Notes, pp. 1–2. Among the Tungpei leaders were Chang Chao-lin, president of the Yenching student body; Wang Ju-mei (Huang Hua), vice-president and also chairman of the executive committee of the student council; and Ch'en Han-p'o, editor of the Yenching student newspaper.

[28] Pien, "Wo-men ying-tang chin tai-piao chin ching ma!?" (Should We Send Representatives to the Capital!?), Shih-erh-chiu t'e-k'an (The December 9th Special) (Jan. 9, 1936), pp. 1–2. Other reactions to the conference are given in "A Word to the Students," The China Critic, XII (Jan. 2, 1936), 6; "The Students' Conference," ibid. (Jan. 23, 1936), pp. 78–79; "On the Student Front in Peiping," China Weekly Review, LXXVI (March 7, 1936). Among the older generation, some viewed Chiang's invitation as a conciliatory move, evidence of Chiang's desire to establish a dialogue between Nanking and the New Youth.

Yenching students thus already had in existence a strong association which could act as their spokesman and could provide organization and discipline for concerted action. The emphasis on campus life gave Yenching students a sense of cohesiveness which was difficult to maintain in schools lacking either an isolated campus or an effective student union. And a number of Yenching student leaders were openly critical of Kuomintang policies but had enjoyed immunity because of the unique position of the Christian school and because of faculty sympathy and support.[29]

One interesting facet of Yenching's participation in the December 9th Movement is the important role of the university's department of journalism; and related to this is the fact that the first petitions of November and December gave almost as much attention to demands for freedom of speech, press, and association as they did to Japanese aggression and Nanking's policy of compromise. What was the relation between these demands and the decision to launch a protest movement? Public demonstrations were deemed necessary because in 1935 the news in Chinese language newspapers was severely restricted. Editors who published material offensive to Nanking or to Japanese military officers in China quickly found themselves in difficulty; the students hoped, therefore, to make known the facts of Sino-Japanese relations through publicized demonstration. Mass support would be forthcoming and would force the adoption of new policies.[30] At the same time the students realized that with the current press control, the effectiveness of their demonstrations would be limited unless they found other avenues of publicity. Chinese

[29] In Huang Hua, "Chung-kuo fa-hsi-szu yün-tung hsien-chuang," and Wang Hsiao-feng, "Chung-kuo fa-hsi-szu yü jih-pen" (Chinese Fascism and Japan), *Yen-ta chou-k'an* (Dec. 6, 1935), pp. 12–14, 23–25, there are thinly veiled attacks on Chiang Kai-shek and other Kuomintang leaders; XXX and XX are substituted for the actual names.

[30] Mo Ning, " 'Shih-erh-chiu' ti chiao-hsün," and I Ch'ien, "Kao ch'üan-kuo t'ung-hsüeh" (To All Fellow Students of the Whole Country), *Shih-erh-chiu t'e-k'an* (Dec. 17, 1935), pp. 1–2, 4–5; "To the American Students' League," issued by Peiping SU, Dec. 15, 1935 (NW Collection); Yen-ching tzu-chih-hui, "Kao p'ing ching t'ung hsüeh-shu" (Letter to Peiping and Tientsin Students), Dec. 14, 1935 (broadside in NW Collection, which also contains English translations of some of the Dec. 9th broadsides); W. C. J., "Peiping Students Stage Demonstration Against Autonomy Move," *China Weekly Review* (Dec. 21, 1935), p. 100.

language newspapers and even education journals were generally unable to report student protest activities. Students understood that publicity through English language newspapers and foreign correspondents would be essential.

Under Hubert S. Liang, Yenching had an active department of journalism dedicated to the principle of a free press and deeply concerned about the welfare of China. On several occasions the department had published newspapers with a circulation beyond the university, and the Yenching student newspaper, *Yen-ta chou-k'an,* put out special editions on national and social issues: fascism, the Japanese threat, and rural reconstruction.[31] Through its journalism department, Yenching had contact with some of the major newspapers of China and with several correspondents for Western wire services. A significant number of the Chinese newspapermen working for English language newspapers in China and for foreign news services were graduates of Yenching for the simple reason that such graduates had an unusual combination of talents—training in journalism and facility in both Chinese and English. Several editors and correspondents for Peiping newspapers served as part-time faculty members or advisers for the Yenching department of journalism. The writers and journalists, Edgar and Helen Snow, were associated with Yenching at this time. They were deeply sympathetic with the students and encouraged the December 9 demonstration by promising publicity. Edgar Snow says that he and his wife spent the night of December 8 translating student broadsides into English so that the protests could be published in the foreign press.[32] In addition,

---

[31] H. Snow, *Notes,* p. 85; Edwards, *Yenching,* p. 296; X.A.N., "Shih-erh-chiu hui-i-lu," *SECCN,* says that many people came to read news items which were regularly posted in late November and early December by Yenching students. Examples of special editions of *Yen-ta chou-k'an* are the issues of Dec. 6, 1935, on Fascism; Feb. 9, 1936, on emergency education; and May 30, 1936, on rural reconstruction. *P'ing hsi pao,* issued for a few months in the fall of 1931, served as a valuable source of information on the Manchurian Crisis until it was suspended to avoid political complications. In 1932, when the chief English language newspaper, *The Peiping Leader,* had to cease publication, the department of journalism again published a daily which served many Peiping residents briefly.

[32] E. Snow, *Journey to the Beginning,* p. 143. Hubert Liang was a staunch and vocal advocate of freedom of the press; and on Jan. 1, 1936, he helped organize the Chinese Journalists Association to fight for this goal.

they sent numerous articles to the *China Weekly Review, Asia Magazine,* the London *Daily Herald,* and the New York *Sun;* they also served as liaison among student leaders. On December 9, the Snows along with such correspondents as James White of the Associated Press, Mac Fisher of United Press, and C. M. MacDonald of the London *Times* joined the paraders. They expected to gather news stories, but they also believed that the presence of foreign journalists, especially ones with cameras, would have a restraining influence on police and gendarmes. In Hubert Liang, the Snows, and other journalists associated with Yenching, the students knew that they would have support for their demands for a free press and resistance to Japan; they would also have means of publicity and a degree of protection.

Several of the initiators of the December 9 demonstration, it may be noted, were simultaneously Tungpei refugees, journalism majors, leaders in Yenching's student government, and staff members of the student newspaper. These Yenching activists were nationalistic and bitterly critical of Kuomintang compromises with Japan; they believed in the possibility of forcing a policy change through publicity and pressure; and they had the protection of a Christian college in the planning stages of the demonstration. They epitomize much that is distinctive about Yenching and the origins of the December 9 campaign.

The movement opened December 9 with approximately eight hundred Peiping students marching in the streets to protest the north China autonomous regime and Nanking's appeasement of Japan. It continued the next day with a strike of most university and middle school students in Peiping and Tientsin, and it reached a climax in a massive demonstration of some 5,000 students on December 16.[33] Throughout the rest of December and into January, students spent their time lecturing, writing manifestoes and petitions, contacting students in other cities, and founding protest

[33] For descriptions by participants see "Hsüeh-sheng lien-ho ch'ing-yüan hou ti yi-ke ts'an-chia-che ti pao-k'ao" (Report by a Participant in the Joint Student Petition), *Shih-erh-chiu t'e-k'an* (Dec. 17, 1935), pp. 5–8; "Chinese Students under Fire," *The Student Advocate* (March 1936), pp. 11–13. On Dec. 9 there were, in addition to the 800 students who demonstrated in Peiping, some 800 or more Yenching and Tsing Hua students who demonstrated outside the city walls when they could not enter. The estimates for the Dec. 16 demonstration range all the way from 2,500 to 8,000 students.

associations. The organization and discipline of the students during this period left little to be desired.

Response of New Youth to December 9

Once launched, the movement quickly became national in scope, gaining support from youth throughout urban China. According to one count, there were sixty-five demonstrations in thirty-two cities between December 9 and December 31, 1935.[34] Study of these early protests in other cities reveals that the youth generally thought of themselves as playing a supporting role for the main actors, the Peiping students. Their demands were certainly in the name of nationalism, and they condemned infringements on Chinese sovereignty and compromise with Japan. A theme given equal prominence, however, was indignation over mistreatment and arrest of students.[35] Loyalty to the New Youth was a major reason for the demonstrations after December 9. Like their Peiping colleagues, these students were a self-conscious elite, and they believed that in fulfilling their duty as spokesmen for China, students were not to be treated simply as individuals. While articulating the will of the masses, they became a corporate national group that could demand resignation of an official or public apology for insult or injury. They thus believed that in supporting their Peiping colleagues they were defending the unique position of the New Youth in Chinese society. They could not afford to allow the Kuomintang to destroy the May 4 tradition of students' using the streets as a public forum. The fact that many of the youth felt alienated from the generation of their fathers and from the Nanking regime only enhanced their loyalty to the student generation.[36]

Such student attitudes help explain the variety of responses to the December 9 movement among the Christian college students. In all of the Christian institutions there was verbal support for the Peiping students and their goals, but for the students to pass over to direct action seems to have required both a highly conscious nationalism

[34] A list of demonstrations with the place and approximate number of schools and students participating in each demonstration is included in the NW Collection; see also Freyn, Prelude to War, pp. 29–31.

[35] Freyn, Prelude, pp. 29–31; Heng, "Shih-erh-chiu hou shang-hai," SECCN, pp. 23–24.

[36] Yen-ching tzu-chih-hui, "K'ao p'ing ching t'ung hsüeh-shu."

and a sense of loyalty to the New Youth. Christian colleges which had made considerable progress toward integration with the Chinese environment and schools in areas that had felt Japanese pressure directly were likely to participate in demonstrations. Their students were responsive to calls for proof of their patriotism and their loyalty to the New Youth. Where the Christian institutions were still isolated physically or culturally, protests generally remained verbal, and academic schedules were not seriously disrupted. In these institutions the students' sense of identity with the New Youth was not strong enough to overcome the administration's demand for order and fulfillment of academic obligations. Or, it was not strong enough to offset the fact that Japanese aggression in north China seemed remote. These differences in response were to be expected in a country where national consciousness was, to a large extent, the product of education in urban centers. In China there were still areas and institutions where national loyalty remained a vague ideal rather than a concrete reality for students. The traditional loyalties based on provincialism and familism continued to have force, and even the educated elite in certain instances could consider the Japanese threat more the concern of north Chinese than of the whole Chinese nation. Such attitudes could be found among students in regions or institutions cut off from the main stream of Chinese national affairs. In the Yangtze Valley, where Kuomintang control was strongest, some students were hesitant to resort to direct action because the risk of government reprisal was high and because the Kuomintang seemed clearly the legitimate authority contributing to stability in central China. There were variants, then, in the persuasiveness of appeals to patriotism and group loyalty and in the threshold of resistance to direct action.[37]

A student at West China Union University in Chengtu described

[37] When a paper on Yenching and the December 9th movement was presented at the April 1966 meeting of the Association for Asian Studies, M. Searle Bates of Union Theological Seminary emphasized that there were important regional differences in China in 1935 and that these differences might well influence student reactions to Japanese pressure in north China; James T. C. Liu of Princeton University commented that in concentrating on the alienated, activist students, one should not ignore the fact that many students in 1935 remained loyal to the Kuomintang and supported its policies. I have found these comments useful and should like to express my appreciation.

the pride and excitement of his colleagues as they learned of the December 9 demonstration in Peiping.[38] Other Szechwan students urged a strike as expression of support. A mass meeting was called at the university, but then at the meeting the Dean of Students urged restraint in patriotic actions, and some students said that the movement was simply being used by "a certain political party" to gain control of Peiping. Caught between contradictory interpretations, the West China students awaited further information. None was forthcoming; even the newspapers reported nothing. Excitement subsided and academic routine took over. In Canton, news of the movement coincided with special meetings sponsored by the China Y.M.C.A. in a Youth and Religion campaign. While the students of Chung Shan (National Sun Yat-sen University) went out on strike and organized propaganda tours, the students at the Christian school, Lingnan University, expressed sympathy and support but met their classes. The Y.M.C.A. report on its campaign expressed regret over the gulf between Christian and government schools and complained that in some cities there was little or no contact between the two.[39] At Huachung University in Wuchang, students postponed a performance of Handel's *Messiah* from December 21 to December 28, but the academic schedule was disrupted only briefly, and annual reports spoke of a year of quiet growth after the turbulence of previous years.[40]

Students in several Christian colleges did, however, give active support to the movement. Cheeloo students in Shantung were close to the scene of Japanese aggression; on the other hand, they were under heavy pressure to continue school work, for the provincial government had ordered all schools not holding normal classes to close immediately. After sending a telegram of support to Peiping,

[38] Yün, "Cheng-tu ti 'Shih-erh-chiu' " ("December 9th" at Chengtu), *SECCN*, pp. 30–31.

[39] E. H. Munson, "Youth and Religion Movement, Report of Campaign at Foo-chow, November 26–December 2; Hangchow, Canton and Toyshan, December 13–26, 1935" (in YMCA Historical Library, NYC, World Service Folders, Correspondence for 1935–1936).

[40] "Patriotic Wuhan Students Clash with Government Officials," *China Weekly Review* (Dec. 28, 1935), p. 142. According to the report: "Hua Chung Students returned to classes and did not continue the more wild and extravagant propaganda of students of government schools."

Cheeloo students agreed to shorten Christmas and New Year's vacation in order to complete the semester's examinations early. Those who desired to do so could devote the winter recess to propaganda work. The Peiping students, however, sent representatives to Cheeloo to call for an immediate strike as evidence of patriotism and student solidarity. Though most students were studying for examinations, a minority attended a special meeting and voted a strike. The Cheeloo administration thereupon declared winter recess, effective immediately.

Shanghai too had been the object of Japanese attentions, and nationalism had acquired a personal meaning for many in this urban center. Herman C. E. Liu, president of Hu Chiang (University of Shanghai) was typical of many Chinese Christians who had moved from pacifism to a belief in resistance as the only deterrent to the Japanese. In December 1935 he led a group of Christian leaders in issuing a manifesto supporting the student movement and calling for a united front against Japan.[41] Students organized numerous demonstrations in Shanghai, but there were risks, and students looked to Peiping for encouragement. A Shanghai youth described one protest rally where he had great difficulty gaining admission because he lacked a ticket.[42] The Shanghai student leaders trusted only bonafide students or individuals vouched for by students, and they posted guards outside meetings to admit only those with passes. In December 1935, the author Agnes Smedley was in Shanghai, and she wrote to Helen Snow requesting materials about the Peiping student activities. She commented: "Every student demonstration in Peiping acts like a long-distance Big Bertha down here. . . . It is Peiping that is the leader, and what Peiping does the students in the rest of the country will do, though lagging behind and hampered at every step by the Blue Shirts. . . . Every time they [the Peiping students] do anything or send down a magazine or a leaflet, I get these to those I can. A St. Johns boy grabs them and disappears from his house in a trail of smoke, going from house to house with these, showing

[41] Carbon copy of English version of the manifesto with list of signatures is located at YMCA Historical Library, World Service Folders, Correspondence for 1935–1936.

[42] Heng, "Shih-erh-chiu hou shang-hai," SECCN, p. 21.

friends, trying to organize, trying to shame them for their backwardness."[43]

After the wave of demonstrations in response to the December 9 and December 16 protests, the focus of the movement quickly returned to Peiping. In the public institutions as well as the Christian colleges, activist students had little success in keeping the movement alive outside Peiping after mid-January. President Liu in his report on the year at Hu Chiang spoke of a very successful academic year with all going well; similar reports came from Cheeloo, Huachung, and other Christian colleges.[44] A number of factors explain the dissipation of student protests: the pressure of academic obligations, the effectiveness of Kuomintang control in central China, and the blurring of the nationalist issue after the Hopei-Chahar Political Council had been organized and there were no longer specific Japanese demands to oppose. Perhaps most important, however, was confusion over a redefinition of goals and tactics for the movement. This confusion extended to Peiping itself, where the student union was rent by factionalism and could no longer provide clear guidance to the New Youth of China.[45]

Toward a United Front Policy

In truth, the students faced a dilemma. They had demanded an end to the civil war between the Kuomintang and the communists and a declaration of war against Japan; they had demanded freedom of press, speech, and association; they had protested against the organization of a north China autonomous regime; and they had called for a mass uprising against the Japanese. The students had heroically presented themselves as opinion makers in the faith that once the masses knew the true facts of Japanese aggression, they

[43] Helen Snow, *Notes*, pp. 195–196.
[44] Herman C. E. Liu, letters to B. A. Garside, June 3, 1936, and June 29, 1936 (Correspondence File, University of Shanghai, UB); Y. G. Chen, letter to B. A. Garside, May 1, 1936 (Correspondence File, University of Nanking, UB); *Yali Quarterly*, March 1936 and June 1936.
[45] Mu Han, "Fei-ch'ang shih-ch'i chiao-yü yü hsüeh-sheng yün-tung" (Emergency Education and the Student Movement), *Yen-ta chou-k'an* (Feb. 9, 1936), pp. 3–4; Fan Ping, "Hsüeh-sheng yün-tung nei ti fen-hua" (Internal Divisions within the Student Movement), *ibid.*, pp. 5–6.

would join in exerting pressure on the Nanking government. Student protests had undoubtedly strengthened the hand of General Sung Che-yüan so that his Hopei-Chahar Political Council was not the puppet regime anticipated by the Japanese. Some support had come from the intellectual world where numerous National Salvation Associations had been founded to urge resistance to Japanese aggression. But there had been no mass protest, and the Kuomintang showed no disposition to meet student demands. What next? Clearly, the protest movement of 1935 was taking place in a milieu different from that of the 1920's; there was in the mid-1930's a power structure that was more effective and more nearly nationwide than in the previous decade, and it too claimed to speak for China. The logic of the situation in the 1930's pointed toward a united front against Japan. Only gradually, however, did the Peiping student leaders accept the idea of a united front as their primary goal and concentrate on building organizations and a propaganda program for its attainment. As the goals of the Chinese Communist Party and of the students began to converge, a sense of rapport between the two groups developed, and it was not difficult for members of the left wing to gain ascendancy in student councils.

The student movement during the first half of 1936 was characterized by a search for new techniques to induce resistance to Japan, a search that led eventually to increased emphasis on the united front. A propaganda tour to the countryside in January 1936 is illustrative. Four corps of students left Peiping-Tientsin early in January to arouse the rural masses to the Japanese threat through lectures, songs, skits, and stories; the youth met with indifference or idle curiosity; the Japanese demands, even the concept of the Chinese nation, meant little to most villagers. The urban-oriented youth, however, learned much; they gained a new awareness of the harshness of the peasants' lot; and they learned that there was a way to gain the attention of the peasants. A hotly debated argument over strategy ended in a decision on January 9 to reorient the appeals made to the villagers; the Japanese would be associated with the tax collector and the landlord, and protests against all three would be urged.[46] The response of the peasants was immediate and

[46] Freyn, *Prelude to War*, pp. 34–50; see letters of Yenching student Li Min to H. Snow, quoted in *Notes*, pp. 150–151; also, a letter (probably by Wang

even overwhelming; they asked only that the students remain in the countryside to help them organize protest movements.

In 1936, though, most students were not yet willing to abandon academic careers in order to organize mass resistance. Even had they been willing, the power of the Kuomintang in north China was still strong enough to prevent such revolutionary activity, and, as a matter of fact, all of the propaganda corps were forcibly returned to Peiping after less than two weeks in the countryside. The tour was, nevertheless, important in the growth of organizations and programs to foster a united front and in the expanding influence of the left wing. On their return from the countryside, members of the propaganda corps formed the Chinese Youth Salvation Vanguard Corps and the National Liberation Vanguard, and these organizations joined on February 1 to become the National Liberation Vanguard of China, a major communist front organization. These associations were organized along communist lines; and according to one Yenching student, "advanced members" were to be invited to enter the Chinese Communist Party or Youth Corps.[47]

Some students proposed a boycott of Japanese goods, but discovered that they would receive little or no support from the hardpressed merchants of north China. Others turned to a demand for emergency education, a complete reorganization of the college

Ju-mei, according to H. Snow), in NW Collection; Wang Nien-chi, "Tao nungts'un ch'ü" (Off to the Countryside) in Li Ch'ang, ed., *I-erh-chiu hui-i lu* (Memoirs of December 9th) (Peking, 1961), pp. 141–147 (trans. in Chiang Nan-hsiang, *Roar of a Nation*, pp. 109–129); Li Ch'ang, "Recollections of National Liberation Vanguard," *SCMM*, nos. 296, 297.

[47] See the letter of Li Min to H. Snow, Jan. 18, 1936, in *Notes*, p. 151; also Li Ch'ang, "Recollections of the National Liberation Vanguard," *SCMM*, nos. 296, 297. It is not easy to pinpoint communist influence on the discussion of tactics, etc., during the propaganda tour. Wang Ju-mei (Huang Hua), Li Ch'ang, Yang Hsüeh-cheng, and others who went on tour do not seem to have been Communist Party members at the time, though all three joined the party shortly thereafter. They were in touch with Chiang Nan-hsiang and Huang Ching (Yü Ch'i-wei), who were Communist Party members working with students in the Peiping area in 1935–1936, but I do not know that Chiang and Huang actually went on the tour. Wang Nien-chi, who was a member of an advance group for the second propaganda brigade, was apparently a party member at the time. The appeals and slogans adopted were identical with those used by the communists in establishing anti-Japanese regimes in the countryside during the Sino-Japanese War.

curriculum to emphasize skills and information useful in organizing resistance to Japan.[48] A number of the more deeply alienated Yenching student leaders left college in the spring of 1936 to find other avenues of nationalist expression, and some later appeared in Sian as propagandists for a united front among Chang Hsüeh-liang's troops.[49] New moves by Japanese or Chinese authorities occasionally persuaded students to fall back once more on the familiar tactic of the strike or mass demonstration. It seemed increasingly difficult, though, to obtain majority support, and the dispersal of students for summer holidays may be considered the end of the December 9th Movement per se.

Much of the factionalism after December was derived from confusion over goals after the very limited success of the demonstrations and reluctance to accept a united front as the first prerequisite to resistance. Those of the older generation who had sympathized with the initial student protests argued that the students had fulfilled their function of making public opinion known; they should now return to their studies and leave policy-making to Nanking. Many of the less committed students agreed, and they could be persuaded to participate in new protests only by student pressure and Kuomintang reprisals. Among the activists there was a search for new tactics, but disagreement over whether the tactics were designed to exert additional pressure on Nanking to change its policy or designed to inspire opposition to the Japanese without Kuomintang participation. Weeks and months passed before student leaders were forced to the conclusion that a united front including the Kuomintang was essential and that their main job was to induce the Kuomintang to accept this thesis. One theme dominated a memorial volume, *Shih-*

[48] Hsüeh-lien t'ung-kuo ti fei-ch'ang shih-ch'i chiao-yü fang-an yüan-tse" (The Principles of the Emergency Education Platform Passed by the Student Union), editorial in *Yen-ta chou-k'an* (Feb. 9, 1936), pp. 1–2: Mu Han, "Fei-ch'ang shih-ch'i chiao-yü yü hsüeh-sheng yün-tung," *ibid.*, pp. 3–4.

[49] Among these was Chang Chao-lin, former president of the Yenching student body; in December 1936 Chang was in Sian editing a daily newspaper and doing radio broadcasting to foster an anti-Japanese united front. James Bertram, *First Act in China, The Story of the Sian Mutiny* (New York, 1938), p. 167. Bertram also mentions another Peiping student engaged in propaganda work in Sian but gives his name as simply Liu (p. 169); it is possible that this was Liu Yü-hsing of Tsing Hua University.

erh-chiu chou-nien chi-nien t'e-k'an (Special Issue on the Anniversary of December 9th), published by the Yenching Student Self-Government Association in 1936; the theme was the importance of concerted effort to unite all parties against Japan. The December 9th Movement, the authors insisted, had illustrated the futility of individual heroism and of actions by a single group such as the students; power would come only as a nationwide organization worked to save China.[50] Thus, increasing numbers of students were joining the national salvation associations and the liberation vanguard to work for a united front. The former president of the Yenching student body, Chang Chao-lin, had by this time reached a simple definition of friend and enemy: those who were for or against a united front. Such a definition, of course, placed the Kuomintang in the category of enemy as long as it opposed a united front. As a matter of fact, acceptance of a united front policy by the students did not generally seem to mitigate their antagonism toward Nanking; if anything, their very dependence on the Kuomintang for resistance to Japan and their frustration over Nanking's concentration on the war against the communists increased student resentment. The staunchest advocates of a united front often were the harshest critics of the Kuomintang.

The Chinese Communist Party was during mid-1935 to mid-1936 also coming to recognize the necessity of the Kuomintang to any national opposition to Japan. Though a declaration issued by the Central Committee of the Chinese Communist Party on August 1, 1935, was entitled "Appeal to the Whole People to Resist Japan and Save the Country," the party had not at this time evolved a clear definition of the united front or of the conditions of cooperation with the Kuomintang. Only during the first half of 1936 did the Communist Party leadership accept the united front as a major goal and acknowledge the necessity of including Chiang Kai-shek in such a

[50] Chang Chao-lin, "Shih-erh-chiu yün-tung yi chou-chi nien-tz'u" (A Statement on the First Anniversary of the December 9th Movement), *SECCN*, pp. 1–3; Ts'ao I, " 'Shih-erh-chiu' kei-wo ti chiao-hsün (The Lesson of "December 9th" for Me), *ibid.*, pp. 31–33; Yüan I, "Shih-erh-chiu i-lai chih yen-yüan (Yen Yüan after December 9th), *ibid.*, pp. 16–20; Mien Chih, "Chung-hua min-tsu chiai-fang yün-tung tsui-yen-chung ti i-yeh" (A Comment on the Great Importance of the Chinese National Liberation Movement), *ibid.*, pp. 13–16.

coalition.[51] Some of the student leaders of the Peiping-Tientsin Student Union were in contact with the Communist Party or front organizations, and they undoubtedly used their influence to guide students toward a united front policy.[52] A few leftist leaders could hardly have transformed a policy with little or no appeal into a popular and accepted policy however. What is important is not to try to prove a causal relationship between Chinese communist policy and the movement of youth leaders toward a united front program. The events of the winter and spring of 1936 amply demonstrated the logic of such a policy, if not indeed, the inevitability of such a policy. What is important is that the Chinese Communist Party and many of the New Youth were on converging paths during the December 9th Movement, and the sense of common goal made students more ready to give the benefit of the doubt to the Communist Party rather than the Kuomintang. The Kuomintang seemed to be losing the nationalist issue to the communists despite the fact that the importance of the Kuomintang to a coalition against Japan was gaining recognition.

The communists were, however, gaining more than a reservoir of good will. Student activists were concentrating on permanent organizations as well as sporadic demonstrations as a means of exercising influence; and nationalistic, anti-Japanese associations like the National Liberation Vanguard and the National Salvation Association were expanding in membership and prestige. Because the immediate goals of the Communist Party and of young nationalists coincided, members of the left wing and even party members could obtain

[51] "Appeal to the Whole People to Resist Japan and Save the Country (August 1, 1935)," *International Press Correspondence* (Inprecor), XV, no. 64 (Nov. 30, 1935), pp. 1595–1597; Wan Min (Wang Ming), "The New Policy of the Communist Party of China," *ibid.*, no. 70 (Dec. 21, 1935), pp. 1728–1729. In this discussion of the evolution of the united front policy by the Chinese Communist Party, I have followed the argument of Charles B. McLane, *Soviet Policy and the Chinese Communists, 1931–1946* (New York, 1958), pp. 66–76.

[52] Huang Ching (Yü Ch'i-wei), who participated in the Decmber 9th Movement, was secretary of the Chinese Communist Party Municipal Committee from 1935 to 1937 and was also director of the propaganda department for this committee from 1936 to 1937; Chiang Nan-hsiang was an important member of the Communist Party branch at Tsing Hua in 1935–1936. See *Who's Who in Communist China* (Hong Kong, 1966). Wang Nien-chi, who helped organize the January propaganda tour, was apparently a party member at the time.

leadership positions in these associations. The New Youth wanted guidance as they muddled toward a united front policy; they were willing to accept it from activists who seemed to be speaking the same language as they. A number of the students who had helped launch the demonstrations of December 9 and 16 had left the academic community of Peiping because of Kuomintang pressure or because of a desire to do more to foster cooperation against Japan; some had moved to other cities and were devoting full time to propaganda and organizational work; Chang Chao-lin and others had moved to Sian to propagandize among Chang Hsüeh-liang's soldiers; members of both groups, it seems, were in contact with the Communist Party.[53] The party was evolving a tactic it was to use during World War II and the subsequent civil war: it was using members of the New Youth to build a communist infrastructure in areas where the power of the nominal authority was limited and superficial; whether the areas were units of soldiers, university communities, or rural villages, anti-imperialist nationalism was one important basis of appeal.[54] The party was learning about the techniques of mass urban demonstrations as a means of exerting pressure and discrediting the responsible authority.[55]

The outbreak of war between China and Japan in July 1937 made Chiang Kai-shek the man of the hour, and educated youth hailed the Kuomintang as defender of the Chinese nation; the united front seemed finally a reality. The 1931 student movement and the December 9 movement had left their legacy, however. Just as the Chinese Communist Party had laid the groundwork for policies to

[53] See note 49, preceding. Huang Ching (Yü Ch'i-wei) seems to have gone to Tientsin in May 1936 to organize protests; other leaders, possibly including Huang Ching, went to Shanghai to set up national offices for the student unions and the salvation associations (Helen Snow, *Notes*, pp. 37–41, 60–61, 197–198).

[54] A detailed study is available in Chalmers A. Johnson, *Peasant Nationalism and Communist Power* (Stanford, 1962). See also, the review of this work, Donald G. Gillin, " 'Peasant Nationalism' in the History of Chinese Communism," *JAS*, XXIII (Feb. 1964), 269–289.

[55] This thesis is developed in John Israel, *Student Nationalism*. Numerous student protest demonstrations between 1945 and 1949 helped to create the impression that the Kuomintang had lost the Mandate of Heaven; there is evidence of communist influence and guidance in a number of the movements. See Chapter XI and also Jessie G. Lutz, "Student Activism: China, 1946–1948," Working Paper no. 2, Rutgers Seminar on Asian Studies, 1969.

be followed regarding educated youth during and immediately after the war, so Kuomintang-student relations were built on the experiences of the 1930's. The policies of both parties toward the New Youth were to become one factor in their power struggle after the breakdown of the united front. During most of the war the Kuomintang was to give the same advice to students that it had given for a decade: stay in school, concentrate on your studies, and thus prepare to serve China; this is your patriotic duty as the educated elite. A heritage of mistrust was one of the bases of this policy, and it eventually contributed to an almost total breakdown in communication between the Kuomintang and the New Youth. There was to be continuity also in the relation of the Christian colleges to the educational community and the relation of the Christian college students to the New Youth. Though the Christian institutions used their foreign connections to secure some protection from the Japanese during the early years of conflict, the war was actually to accelerate the integration of the Christian colleges with the Chinese environment. For almost all Christian college students, nationalism and loyalty to the New Youth became effective appeals to action just as they had been for the students of Yenching and a few other Christian schools during the movement of December 9.

X | The Impact of the War, 1937-1945

Seeking the loyalty of the Chinese college student in mid-1937 were the Kuomintang, the Chinese Communist Party, the Chinese nation-state, and the institution of higher learning he was attending. In a manner typical of institutions, each had acquired a life of its own; each had its own needs and sources of support and its own will to survive. The emergency of Japanese invasion in July 1937, however, seemed to unite their destinies. Only if the Chinese nation-state survived could the other organizations hope to continue in existence. All loyalties, even loyalty to one's individual destiny, became identified with patriotism, and the united front of Kuomintang and Communist Party finally seemed to have been achieved. The desires of students, the Communist Party, and the Kuomintang for resistance to Japan had converged with the outbreak of war, and the Nanking government under Chiang Kai-shek was hailed as leader of this resistance. Morale was high, conflicts in goals appeared minimal, and both students and colleges eagerly sought ways to serve China in her hour of need.

The hour of need, unfortunately, stretched into years. As the war dragged on, the atmosphere of emergency dissipated, and the separate interests of the various groupings reasserted themselves. The Kuomintang and the Chinese Communist Party began to concentrate on insuring postwar survival while the colleges struggled to keep intact their faculties, their traditions, and their individual identities. Perhaps more importantly, individual students could find few avenues for expression of their patriotism; and as the elementary tasks of securing food and shelter grew more difficult in interior

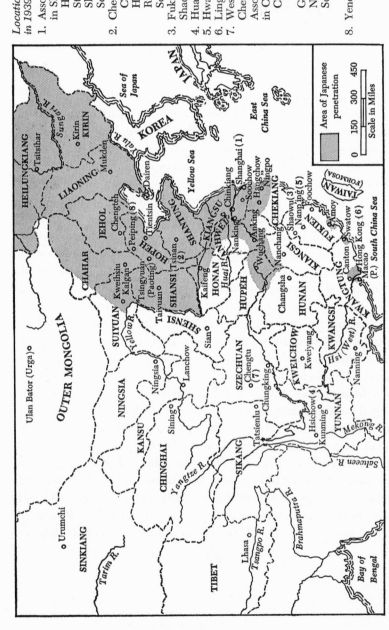

Location of Christian Colleges in 1939

1. Associated Christian Colleges in Shanghai, Shanghai
   Hangchow Christian College
   St. John's University
   Shanghai, University of Soochow University
2. Cheeloo University, Tsinan
   College of Theology
   Hospital
   Rural Institute
   School of Nursing
3. Fukien Christian University, Shaowu
4. Huachung University, Hsichow
5. Hwa Nan College, Nanp'ing
6. Lingnan University, Hong Kong
7. West China Union University, Chengtu
   Associated with West China in Chengtu:
   Cheeloo Colleges of Arts, Science, and Medicine
   Ginling College
   Nanking, University of
   Soochow University Department of Biology
8. Yenching University, Peiping

China, 1939

China, many resorted to a kind of privatism. Day-to-day survival became the preoccupation of many. Most of the Christian colleges were after 1941 located in sectors of China under Kuomintang governance, and their sharp descent from exhilaration to anomie is an indication of their integration with Chinese life. Like other Chinese, many in the Christian schools tried to survive current hardships by feeding their hopes for a better life when peace returned.

The Migrations of the Colleges

The Marco Polo Bridge (Lukouch'iao) incident of July 7, 1937, has generally been accepted as the beginning of the Sino-Japanese War. There was, however, no formal declaration of war; and by 1937 there were so many Japanese troops in north China that incidents were frequent. As on previous occasions, negotiations for a settlement were undertaken. Many Chinese, therefore, did not at first recognize July 7 as the beginning of the long expected conflict. Even those who had called for opposition to the Japanese and now hailed the moment of conflict did not seem sure that it had arrived. Accurate information about troop movements and diplomatic negotiations was impossible to obtain, and for a period of three weeks occasional clashes alternated with periods of relative quiet.[1] College administrators awaited the turn of events before altering plans for the academic year.

By mid-August, however, large scale operations in north China and the Japanese invasion of Shanghai left little doubt that a major conflict had begun, and most of the national universities in the war zones were unable to open. Many of the Christian colleges, on the other hand, did attempt to open for the regular academic year; they flew the United States flag as protection against raids or confiscation by the Japanese; and in one or two instances Westerners were asked to reassume top administrative positions. Several institutions transferred their classes to areas under Western control. The students were apparently less sure than the college administrators about their proper role and their safety, for many of the schools reported a sharp

[1] See the day by day reactions to events in the Peiping area during July and August, 1937, by Grace Boynton of Yenching University. Her letter describing her experiences was issued as a pamphlet entitled, *At Yenching University, August 1937* (no pub. data; HI).

drop in enrollment. Only about a third of the University of Nanking and the Yenching students registered and slightly over half of the Shanghai and Cheeloo students. A number of absences in the eastern colleges were due to transportation difficulties or the desire of parents to keep the family together in the emergency, and schools in the interior such as Huachung actually gained students as youth decided to enroll near their homes or refugees from battle areas sought admission. In sections of east China where the war situation became somewhat stabilized, students soon began to drift back to their institutions. Lingnan held a special session to enable students registering late to catch up with their course work, and Yenching's enrollment for the second semester rose from 300 to 588.

The central government gave every encouragement to students to continue their education. According to the Kuomintang, China suffered from no manpower shortage, for there were plenty of peasant sons who could serve as soldiers. China did have a paucity of trained talent. The need for professional and technical skills in the postwar reconstruction would be acute, and students could best serve their country by completing their education and preparing for the job of national reconstruction. Students were, therefore, exempt from conscription and were urged to find outlets for patriotism in the required military drill and in propaganda and relief work. During the early years of the war, government officials made sporadic attempts to organize the war activities of students. The provincial government of Fukien, for example, ordered colleges and senior middle schools to reorganize academic work so that the schools could close during the first three months of 1938 while students participated in a massive propaganda effort. After three weeks of training, students were to go in groups to nearby villages to lecture on the meaning of the war and on first aid and sanitation. They were to teach the populace patriotic songs and to perform plays encouraging army volunteers and explaining the duties of citizenship.[2] In August 1937 the Third Route Army enrolled more than a thousand students in the Shantung area for training in propaganda work.[3] When Tsinan fell and the army evacuated in

[2] Fukien Christian University, *Report of the President, 1939*, p. 1; Scott, *Fukien Christian University*, p. 80; Wallace, *Hwa Nan*, pp. 78–81.
[3] Y. Y. Tsu, "The Youth Movement," *CCYB, 1938–39*, p. 61.

December, however, the students were left without guidance or support. Neither constancy nor efficiency characterized government policy toward student war activities; nor was a revolutionary response, either in terms of educational program or the role of the New Youth, sought.

By the end of 1937 the Japanese had occupied the Peiping-Tientsin area and had moved up the Yangtze valley as far as Nanking. Since most of China's colleges were in eastern China, students and faculty found themselves preoccupied with the challenges of a rapidly changing political and military environment. Administrators of national universities had three options: to close for the duration of the war, to remain in east China with the probability of frequent Japanese interference, or to flee to the unconquered interior. Most of the government institutions chose the latter alternative, and the migration of the schools to Free China was undertaken with high morale. It was accepted as a patriotic sacrifice to help keep the Chinese nation alive; it became a symbol of defiance of the Japanese who had deliberately destroyed the campus of Nankai University and had billeted soldiers at Tsing Hua, Peita, and other schools. In truth, the trek to west China by tens of thousands of Chinese made a heroic story.

The decision as to how to respond to Japanese conquest was, however, more complex for the Christian colleges. They could hope to use their foreign connections to gain immunity from Japanese pressure, and thus the option of remaining in east China seemed more real to them than to the government institutions. Though a number of the Christian schools followed the preference of the Kuomintang for migration to the interior, several Christian colleges near enclaves of Western power moved to these protected areas; others hoisted the United States flag and tried to make themselves into islands of extraterritoriality. Since the Japanese did not wish to offend the Western powers during the early years of the war, neither the Nanking puppet government nor the Japanese ignored completely the privileged position of Westerners in the treaty ports, and several Christian colleges were able to carry on their work in east China until 1941. Then, the Pearl Harbor attack made the Western nations combatants in the Pacific War, and the colleges were no longer considered neutral ground. A second wave of migrations to the interior began. During their operation in east China, the Christian colleges were in the paradoxical position of serving Chinese youth by stressing their foreign connections and extraterritorial rights. Their role was not an easy one; the possibility of misunderstanding was always present, uncertainty about Japanese actions an unremitting worry, and the suspicion of collaboration never completely absent from the minds of those in Free China. Many Chinese, nevertheless, appreciated the opportunity to continue education in east China. After the fluctuation of 1937–1938, enrollments in the Christian colleges in the Shanghai, Peiping, and Hong Kong areas rose rapidly.

The Associated Christian Colleges in the Shanghai International Settlement and Lingnan University in Hong Kong were the two major examples of Christian colleges operating in the Western concessions. Both St. John's and the University of Shanghai had begun the school year 1937–1938 with classes in the International Settlement rather than in their buildings on the city outskirts, whereas Soochow had opened in its Hu-chou middle school buildings and Hangchow was on its own campus. After a few weeks, Japanese victories forced Soochow and Hangchow personnel to flee; and by November each school had given up the attempt to maintain a separate campus. Most of the faculty and students moved to the International Settlement, where they joined St. John's and the University of Shanghai in forming the Associated Christian Colleges in Shanghai.

The title, Associated Christian Colleges in Shanghai, indicated the institutions' relationship.[4] The schools were cooperating in an emergency situation to provide the best education they could to as many students as possible; but retention of legal and historical continuity by the separate schools seemed important for their future roles in postwar China; they were not forming a union university. Each institution admitted its own students, maintained its own graduation requirements, and retained its separate faculty and ad-

---

[4] For details, see University of Shanghai, *Annual Report, 1937*, pp. 1–8; *1939*, p. 2; mimeo. letter signed by representatives of the four schools to B. A. Garside of the Associated Boards, Nov. 22, 1938 (UB); Carleton Lacy, "Union Movements," *CCYB, 1938–1939*, pp. 123–124; V. L. Wong, "A Year of College Library Activities in War-Torn East China," *CR*, LXX (1939), 315.

ministration. Though students could elect courses offered by other units of the Associated Colleges, each school tried to offer the full gamut of courses at least on the freshman and sophomore levels. In addition to facilities secured by the individual institutions, the colleges shared the Emporium Building for classes, and they were able to provide skeletal library and laboratory facilities by pooling their resources. Conditions were crowded and inadequate. All the Christian colleges felt a patriotic obligation to admit as many qualified students as they could handle, and the pressure was especially great in occupied China, which had been practically denuded of government universities. The enrollment in the Associated Colleges expanded so rapidly that Shanghai became the largest center of Christian education in China; there were over 3,000 students in 1940.[5]

With enrollments rising while dormitory space was practically nonexistent, great stress was placed on the small area allocated for reading and studying. Servants having no place to go slept on tables at night and tucked their bedding in an odd corner during the day; refugee families who had been permitted to make their home in the Emporium Building added to the noise level. Maintenance of peace and quiet or even reservation of the reading room for those primarily interested in studying proved almost impossible, and little individual work could be done outside the classrooms. Though extracurricular activities were minimal, each institution observed as many of its traditional ceremonies as possible, and joint commencement exercises were sometimes followed by separate ceremonies by the separate schools. Retaining an individual identity while cooperating during the emergency was not an easy feat, and frictions seemed unavoidable. Retaining personal and institutional independence without offending either the Japanese or the Kuomintang was not easy either. On April 7, 1938, President Herman C. E. Liu of the University of Shanghai was assassinated, presumably by Japanese agents for his patriotic activities and his aid to refugees.[6]

Lingnan University had been able to complete the academic year

[5] "Educational News," *CR*, LXXI (1940), 579.

[6] See letter by John Y. Lee, chairman of the University of Shanghai board of directors, April 25, 1938, and a statement entitled, "Herman C. E. Liu—In Memorium," April 7, 1939 (Correspondence File, U. of Shanghai, UB).

1937–1938 on its own campus. When the Japanese launched a campaign in the Canton area during the fall of 1938, however, Lingnan decided to transfer to Hong Kong. President Lei Ying-lam (Y. L. Lee) made arrangements with the University of Hong Kong for the use of classroom and library facilities in the afternoons and evenings; space for science laboratories was rented in an apartment house and was gradually equipped. Thus, many Lingnan teachers and students were able to continue their work under an arrangement that protected the continuity of Lingnan as an institution. The flight of national schools from the Canton area greatly increased the pressure for admission to both Lingnan and the University of Hong Kong, and despite inadequate facilities for extracurricular activities, housing, and even studying, Lingnan's enrollment had reached 800 by the time of Pearl Harbor.[7]

Yenching University also sought the protection of extraterritoriality; without migrating to an area of Western control, it did what it could between 1937 and 1941 to identify its campus as a foreign enclave. It flew the United States flag at its front gate and pointed out to the Japanese that it was registered as an institution of higher learning in the United States. It maintained that it could have no official relations with the provisional government organized by the Japanese because the government was not recognized by the United States. Replacing Chancellor H. H. Kung and Acting Chancellor Lu, J. L. Stuart became both president and chancellor. Protests against Japanese demands or unwanted visits were sometimes channeled through the American embassy.

Though such a policy might have seemed contrary to Chinese nationalism under other circumstances, it inspired few protests from Chinese in Peiping and in fact was presented as a contribution to China's national welfare. Stuart argued that by continuing operation in Peiping, Yenching expressed its faith that Chinese control would eventually return to the area. Also, he said, the government colleges had all been closed or taken over by the Japanese, and thus Yenching and Fu Jen were almost the only institutions in northeast China offering university training free of Japanese control. The policy was

---

[7] *Lingnan*, X (1938), 1; *Lingnan University, Canton and Kukong, 1942–43* (pamphlet, n.d.), pp. 11–13; Corbett, *Lingnan*, pp. 131–137; Associated Boards, *Annual Reports, 1939–1942.*

not unreservedly welcome in Chungking, where the official line was that the Japanese occupation should be made as untenable as possible and that patriotic Chinese should migrate to Free China. In any literal sense, however, the Kuomintang policy was not feasible for all of occupied China, and Yenching's enrollment figures indicate that many in north China were grateful for its continued operation in the area. Her student body increased as rapidly as facilities could be expanded, from a normal enrollment of 800 to 1156 in the fall of 1941.[8] Now, however, the students came from the local area rather than from all sectors of China. Except for a number who accepted government work or other positions, the Yenching faculty remained intact. Individuals who left campus for Peiping faced inspection and sometimes detention for questioning, but as long as they remained on campus they could lead a relatively quiet academic life within the college community. One member of the faculty wrote, "We came dangerously near to an epicurean philosophy," as available pleasures, teaching, and research were savored in the knowledge that these opportunities might disappear at any time.[9]

Since the colleges could not afford to antagonize the Japanese, all of those remaining in east China had to screen the extracurricular activities of their students. War and propaganda work was restricted or forbidden. Soochow University, for example, instituted the following rules concerning extracurricular activities: no notices could be posted and no lectures or meetings held without prior approval; all extracurricular organizations must register and must limit their activities to those of an educational, religious, or social nature; students must not use the college name to form organizations or to publish outside the college.[10] Students did contribute time and money to war relief projects; in Shanghai under the leadership of President Herman C. E. Liu, student relief committees assisted student refugees with travel funds, hostel accommodations, and temporary classes. Yenching's welfare program and field research at Ch'ing Ho were transferred to a village nearer campus and were

[8] "Why Yenching Has Not Moved," Yenching News, XVIII (1939), 1; Edwards, Yenching, pp. 348–358.
[9] Claire and William Band, Two Years with the Chinese Communists (New Haven, 1948), pp. 2–3.
[10] "Educational News," CR, LXXI (1940), 381.

continued on a restricted basis, but Yenching's regulations concerning extracurricular activities were even more stringent than those of Soochow. The student union was discontinued except for committees on food, dormitories, and social life; all other student organizations had to register and to obtain authorization for meetings. Students could not subscribe to or hold literature unsatisfactory to the authorities; they could not post notices; they had to have manuscripts approved before publication; and they were to register before leaving campus.[11] Yenching authorities thus sought to prevent the campus from becoming a center of subversion of Japanese rule, and the result was that the campus became an island largely isolated from national and international events. Under the circumstances, reiteration of the patriotic goals of Yenching and other schools in east China never completely allayed the suspicions and criticisms of those in Free China.

The experience of Cheeloo University illustrates even more vividly than that of Yenching the gap in viewpoint between those in occupied China and those in Kuomintang China. Disagreement arose over the proper course of action as Japanese troops invaded Shantung and moved toward Tsinan in October 1937. Rejecting university migration as too expensive, the Cheeloo administration agreed to transfer the three upper classes of the medical school with fourteen staff members to West China Union University and to encourage the rest of the students to enroll as guest students in other institutions. Except for the hospital, the university had closed down by mid-November. It soon became evident that there would be no quick conclusion to the war and that a long range policy was needed. Alumni and faculty desired tangible evidence of the continuation of Cheeloo, and by the fall of 1938, a few staff members at Tsinan thought that the situation had calmed down enough to warrant reopening. They argued that many in occupied China had to make the best of a difficult situation until liberation, and that these individuals did not consider themselves collaborators; they could not accept the thesis that migration or open defiance of the Japanese were the only acceptable courses of action for patriotic Chinese.

[11] "Word from the Colleges," *ER*, XXIX (1937), 247; "What the Students Think about It All," *Yenching News*, XVII (1938), 4; Edwards, *Yenching*, p. 351.

Since opposition to reopening at Tsinan was still strong, President Liu Shu-ming decided to go to Chungking to consult with H. H. Kung, chairman of the board of directors. In Chungking President Liu found quite a difference in attitude, a difference which was to grow and poison relations between the Kuomintang and the formerly occupied sectors after 1945. Liu was given to understand that reopening in Tsinan might well be interpreted as collaboration and the institution might lose government recognition and support. On the other hand, Cheeloo alumni maintained that the institution could not be satisfied with having its students as guest students of other universities and must open a unit of Cheeloo in west China if the school were to continue in existence. Aided by a donation of Ch$20,000 from H. H. Kung, President Liu proposed to erect dormitories for Cheeloo students in Chengtu and to gather a faculty so that Cheeloo would become a separate entity cooperating with West China Union University.

Faculty members and administrators at Tsinan protested that President Liu had acted without proper authorization and continued to urge the reopening of classes at Tsinan as an alternative to Japanese dominated education. Finally, the two Cheeloo factions agreed that work could be done at Tsinan if it did not duplicate work in Chengtu and if it did not include departments registered with the government; the College of Theology, the Rural Institute, and the Nursing School reopened in the fall of 1939. The medical faculty at Tsinan remained dissatisfied, however, and despite the agreement accepted classes in medicine and pharmacy in 1941. The dual existence of Cheeloo ended temporarily only with the suspension of work at Tsinan upon the outbreak of the Pacific war and the departure of Westerners. Cheeloo factionalism was not dead, though, for the university had three different presidents between 1942 and 1945 and again operated on two campuses between 1945 and 1947.[12] The difficulties of Cheeloo were fed by long-standing internal conflicts, especially between the medical school and other divisions of the university, but the conflicts over policy for the con-

[12] Account based on Corbett, *Shantung*, pp. 230–252; Chester S. Miao, "Christian Education in China," *CCYB, 1938–39*, pp. 200, 206–207; Associated Boards, *Annual Report, 1939;* "Some Special Courses Offered by Cheeloo University, Tsinan," *CR*, LXXI (1940), 472–473; "News from Cheeloo," *The China Colleges*, XII (1944), 3.

tinuing emergency and the opposing viewpoints of those in Free China and those in occupied China plagued the other colleges as well; in most cases, open disagreement was delayed until after the migration had ceased to absorb all thought and energy.

The saga of the trek by the universities to West China was often told, and its retelling served for many months to maintain the morale of academic communities amidst the hardships of the interior.[13] The story was also told in the Western world, where it fostered sympathy for the Chinese cause and antagonism toward the Japanese. It inspired generous contributions to the China Relief Fund and more especially to the Far Eastern Student Service Fund and the National Emergency Committee for Christian Colleges. Perhaps for these reasons the tale was repeated long after the universities had turned their attention to problems of a different nature. A few comments about the exodus are in order, therefore. Under the best circumstances China's inadequate transportation facilities meant that the transfer of thousands of students and teachers, of books, records, and laboratory equipment to interior China was a herculean task. War-time conditions compounded the difficulties. Even the decision to move was not a simple one. The students and teachers of China considered themselves the public voice of the nation and they took seriously their responsibility for sustaining national morale. While there was a chance that the area might remain under Chinese control, the academic community felt that it should demonstrate its confidence in the Chinese defense by continuing operations. Actual preparations for evacuation could be made only after the situation had become hopeless, and by this time transportation facilities had become clogged or unavailable. Railway cars and river boats had in many cases been requisitioned by military and government officials; even if one gained passage, Japanese bombing made daytime travel hazardous. There was thus little time for packing books, records, and equipment, and there were almost no facilities for transporting

[13] Among the accounts of the migration are Hubert Freyn, *Chinese Education in the War* (Shanghai, 1940); Y. K. Chu, "Effects of the Present Sino-Japanese War on Higher Education in China," *School and Society*, XLVII (1938), 443–446; Kiang Wen-han, "The Educational Trek," *CCYB*, 1938–39, pp. 179–198; Carleton Lacy, "Immigrant Colleges and Middle Schools," *CR*, LXXI (1940), 557–566.

them. Under favorable conditions only the most essential materials could be taken.

Family commitments, ill health, and financial distress prevented many students and teachers from accompanying their schools, but it has been estimated that approximately a third of the total enrollment of the migrating universities made the journey. More than one group was attacked by bandits and malaria. Despite the hardships, the leading national universities and many of the Christian colleges made the trek. Several of the institutions made two or even three separate moves.

In the first wave of 1937, students and teachers from Ginling, Cheeloo Medical College, Soochow Department of Biology and the University of Nanking congregated around West China Union University in Chengtu. Then in the spring of 1938 Japanese campaigns forced Hwa Nan and Fukien Christian University to move inland, though neither made the long trek to West China. Hwa Nan decided after the fall of Amoy in May 1938 to move 120 miles up the Min River to Nanp'ing (formerly called Yenp'ing). On the way soldiers attempted to commandeer their boat and even arrested the boatman; only the personal intervention of President Lucy Wang at the local military headquarters secured the release of the boatman and enabled the college community to complete the trip.[14] Hwa Nan was more fortunate than many other colleges in that it was able to remain at its first refuge throughout the war. Fukien Christian University also moved to the interior of Fukien province to the town of Shaowu, where it was also able to carry on until 1945. Though Huachung personnel were not forced to leave the home campus until the fall of 1938, they had to make two separate moves and one of the longest total journeys. They settled first in Kweilin, Kwangsi, and then moved to Hsichow, west of K'unming, in the spring of 1939. For a couple of years thereafter the stalemate on the China front enabled most institutions to remain stationary.

Then came the Pearl Harbor attack, the involvement of the West in the Pacific war, and subsequent Japanese advances. As Westerners lost their extraterritorial privileges, the Christian colleges were forced into the same status as the national institutions. Schools in

[14] See the description by Frances Fulton, department of chemistry, quoted in Wallace, *Hwa Nan*, pp. 81–83.

areas taken over by the Japanese were not permitted to operate if they were registered with the Kuomintang government in Chungking. The Christian colleges that had remained in east China dispersed, and it is not easy to follow their peregrinations as they fled Japanese control. Teachers and students from Yenching joined the Associated Colleges in Chengtu. Hangchow, Soochow, and Lingnan moved beyond Japanese lines and continued class work until the Japanese offensive of 1944 forced them to abandon the attempt to carry on as separate institutions; students were encouraged to enroll as guest students in other colleges. In 1942 faculty members from Soochow Law School had organized an evening law school in Chungking, and this division of the university continued until the end of the war. Except for classes in biology at Chengtu, the University of Shanghai suspended formal operations in February 1942. Alumni and faculty were unhappy over the official termination of the University of Shanghai, however, and after vain attempts to reopen in Chengtu, university representatives secured permission from the government to offer commercial courses at Chungking in cooperation with the law classes of Soochow.

In Shanghai various devices were used to continue instruction without acknowledging the legitimacy of rule by the Japanese or by the Nanking government of Wang Ching-wei. A number of Chinese teachers from the University of Shanghai and other colleges organized underground classes and eventually formed a temporary school known as Hu-kiang shu-yuan (Shanghai Institute); a coalition of Hangchow and Soochow faculty operated an institution known as Hua-tung ta-hsüeh or East China University. Individuals from the Soochow Law School advertised the opening of Chung-kuo pi-chiao fa hsüeh-hsiao, a literal translation of the English title, Comparative Law School of China, but a name that had never been used in Chinese. Those connected with the institution understood its origins; others considered it a new school having no affiliation with the Kuomintang government, and it was thus able to continue operations throughout the war. The understanding in some cases was that students would receive retroactive credit for their work from the mother institution after the war.

Such unauthorized schools faced serious difficulties, however. Enrollment in some equaled that of the mother college before 1937.

Since the successor institutions had no formal standing with either the Chungking government or the boards of trustees in the United States, they did not generally receive financial aid, and the faculty had to depend for their salaries on student fees and supplementary employment. Lacking library and laboratory facilities and an effective administration to regulate entrance examinations, grading, and course requirements, they could not maintain academic standards. Faculty and administration were under constant suspicion of collaboration; President T. K. Van of the University of Shanghai, for instance, met severe criticism because of his decision to remain in Shanghai rather than go to Free China to organize a branch there. Perhaps the schism between the two China's was widest in the case of St. John's. St. John's was the one Christian college that had never registered with the Chinese government, and so it continued formal operations in Shanghai despite criticism by many in Free China. Though accurate information about the link between St. John's and the occupation government was difficult to obtain, some believed that St. John's administrators went too far in acceding to demands of the Wang Ching-wei government and the Japanese. President William Z. L. Sung, however, denied the charges of collaboration and argued that he was serving China by providing educational opportunity regardless of the political situation.[15] The gulf between those in Free China and occupied China and the substandard training of the Shanghai schools pointed to a difficult transition during the postwar period.

The migrations were made in a spirit of patriotic sacrifice. Despite hardship and real physical danger, complaints were few and morale was high. Formerly unruly students willingly submitted to the military-type organization and discipline imposed by some leaders during the migration. The Kuomintang government tried to ease the hardships and to encourage migration by financial assistance to destitute students who were willing to accompany their colleges.

[15] Some alumni were so disturbed by the reports from Shanghai that they made an unsuccessful attempt to open a division of St. John's in Chengtu. It was reported that supervisory officials from the Nanking government visited St. John's campus and that President Sung went to Nanking and reached an agreement concerning operating conditions in Shanghai. After the war Sung was tried as a collaborator by the Kuomintang and exonerated. For details, see Lamberton, *St. John's*, pp. 212–213, 247–248.

Some of the school units even held classes during rest periods on the journey, and both students and faculty showed ingenuity in using available materials to substitute for standard school supplies. In the absence of gas, the Huachung chemistry department distilled local wine to obtain alcohol as a fuel; packing boxes became tables and cupboards. Instructors in agriculture, sociology, and linguistics engaged in field work as they moved into an environment quite different from the university's urban home in east China. As they passed through villages, students lectured to the peasants about the national emergency and the duty to save China from Japanese imperialism. Even relief missions to aid soldiers and other refugees occasionally interrupted the trek to the interior. In most cases the response of the populace was favorable. Though both students and villagers remained cognizant of the social and educational gap between the two groups, the populace often aided the academic groups; temples and schools were opened to the migrants for shelter and classrooms, and assistance was given in the transportation of equipment. Segments of the peasantry seemed to be becoming aware of the need for national resistance. In interior China the refugees brought much that was new. West China, so long insulated from modernizing influences, was to feel the impact of the New Culture Movement and nationalism as a result of the migrations.

In the New Environment

Once in their western homes, the colleges had to seek a balance between their regular academic programs and programs related to the national emergency. Many of the institutions altered their curricula so as to contribute more directly to China's needs. This usually meant giving greater emphasis to the scientific and technical fields. The Ministry of Education officially recommended such a policy and gave substance to its recommendations by establishing enrollment quotas in various fields and contributing financial aid to specific studies; unless one were a student in a scientific or technical area, it was almost impossible to secure a visa to study abroad. Illustrative of this emphasis among the Christian colleges was West China Union University, which expanded its colleges of medicine and dentistry from 33 faculty members and 194 students in 1935 to

94 faculty members and over 500 students in 1943.[16] With aid from many sources, a new hospital, a new outpatient building, and a new chemistry building were constructed and a medical library was organized. West China's program in pharmacy also grew. In all three fields students and teachers attempted to correlate their studies with the war effort. Laboratory work included the manufacture of drugs in short supply, and several research projects on the analysis and clinical testing of traditional remedies were undertaken. Much of Hangchow's expansion during the early years of the war was in the field of engineering, and by 1941 it had organized a separate College of Engineering with four departments: architecture, civil engineering, mechanical engineering, and chemical engineering.

Schools tried to give a practical orientation to regular courses or they added courses directly related to the war effort. Since west China was almost devoid of railways, truck transportation was vital for both military and civilian movement, and China had no mechanical-minded youth who had tinkered with cars for recreation. Mechanics and drivers who knew something about the proper use and maintenance of machines were urgently needed. With government aid, the University of Nanking began in 1938 to offer a four-month course in mechanics and a two-month course in driving and maintenance of vehicles. Before graduation, Hwa Nan chemistry majors were required to carry out a month of practical laboratory work in a factory, a hospital, or other institution; for their laboratory work in their chemistry courses Hwa Nan students made shoe polish, paste, soap, and also pure alcohol for three nearby hospitals.[17] West China Union University offered a special leather tanning course because of the shortage of leather in west China; and in cooperation with national and provincial officials they trained craftsmen in leather manufacture and helped design simplified leather tanning machinery for use by Chinese Industrial Cooperatives. The agricultural departments of Fukien Christian University, Lingnan, and

[16] W. R. Morse, "Medical Education in a Mission School," *Chinese Medical Journal*, XLIX (Sept. 1935), 877–878; *The China Colleges*, XI (March 1944), 2. The figures in both cases include undergraduates registered for the premedical curriculum. The 1943 figures include guest students from Cheeloo and National Central University.

[17] Hwa Nan, *Report of the President, 1942–43*, p. 1.

the University of Nanking tackled such problems as improving the storage and transportation of oranges, helping to organize farmers' credit cooperatives, eradicating the citrus fruit fly, and developing an improved type of rice nursery.[18]

Students and faculty were urged and sometimes even required to participate in social service and war relief activities, especially during the early years of the war. Lingnan, for example, set aside the first two weeks of the semester for propaganda and social service work among neighboring villages and refugee groups; students were encouraged to continue their activities on Saturdays during the school year, and those who fulfilled certain requirements concerning reports, work under faculty supervision, and investment of time could receive three hours of course credit.[19] Students at West China Union University took courses on first aid and then organized public health teams to visit slums and villages and provide instruction in infant care, hygiene, and protection of life during air raids. To keep refugee students occupied during the summer and also encourage social service activities, the Ministry of Education sponsored educational work among the tribal peoples of Szechuan.[20] The University of Nanking visual education department set up a two-year program on motion pictures and radio technology for men in the provincial bureaus of education, and it also produced educational and propaganda films. One report in 1942 estimated that the University of Nanking alone was engaged in more than one hundred service projects.[21]

Intellectuals undertaking social service programs in interior China faced difficulties similar to those met in the rural reconstruction projects, now terminated by Japanese occupation of east China. Creating a national consciousness among the peasants and persuad-

[18] William Band, "Science in the Christian Universities at Chengtu, China" (pamphlet issued by Associated Boards, n.d.), pp. 4–6; "Work and Workers: Agricultural Research and Experimentation in Chengtu," *CR*, LXXI (1940), 537; "The Present Situation: University in Exile: Fukien Christian University," *CR*, LXXI, 789–790.

[19] Y. K. Chu, "Effects of the Present Sino-Japanese War on Higher Education in China," *School and Society*, XLVII (1938), 445–446.

[20] Liu En-lan, *Calls from Szechwan's Wilderness* (New York, 1942); Freyn, *Chinese Education in the War*, pp. 13–14.

[21] Oliver J. Caldwell, "Chinese Universities and the War," *School and Society*, LX (1942), 233; Band, "Science in Christian Universities," pp. 4, 16–17.

ing them to alter long-established custom was not easy; the cultural and social gap between students and peasants was wide; initial distrust could almost be expected, and more often than not the impact of student activity was quickly dissipated as villagers reverted to traditional customs and attitudes. When Hwa Nan girls first visited nearby communities, the peasant women were said to have fled for fear they would be forced to bob their hair and take military training; by the end of the propaganda tour, however, suspicions had been allayed so that the villagers expressed their gratitude in traditional fashion: lighting firecrackers and presenting silk banners.[22] A visitor to Hsichow some years after Huachung had returned to its home in Wuchang reported that the buildings erected by the university in Hsichow were unused and in disrepair, the town no longer had a post office, and the inhabitants seemed to have erased all memory of Huachung's seven-year stay.[23] As in the rural reconstruction program, the most valuable product of the social service work was perhaps the direct experience of faculty and students with the life and outlook of the villagers. Some of the educated youth were offended and dismayed by the apathy, superstition, and squalor they found in the villages, but others were persuaded to devote their lives to trying to alter conditions in rural China.[24]

Closely associated with relief and social service was a new emphasis on part-time work by students. As the students required increasing amounts of financial aid, many of the Christian colleges asked that the students contribute labor service in payment. Sometimes the work was typing or other clerical duties, but often it was manual labor of the kind usually performed by servants: dishwashing, bed-making, or gardening. Administrators in setting such a requirement hoped, first, to prevent the financial assistance from becoming a dole and, second, to undermine the traditional aversion of educated Chinese to manual labor. The extent to which labor service accomplished these goals is hard to say, but some of the Christian college administrators did continue and extend the practice

[22] Wallace, *Hwa Nan*, pp. 79–80.

[23] Coe, *Huachung*, pp. 168–169.

[24] Helen Snow points out that many of the founders and leaders of the Chinese Industrial Cooperatives were graduates of the Christian colleges or were associated with either the Christian colleges or the YMCA. See *China Builds for Democracy: A Story of Cooperative Industry* (New York, 1941).

after the war in the hope that required manual labor would counter-act the elitism of the students.

The war experience meant changes in personnel and in the make-up of the student body as well as different emphases in the curriculum. Like the Northern Expedition of 1927, World War II contributed to an increase in the number and influence of Chinese personnel at the expense of Westerners. Some Westerners joined the migrations of 1937–1938, and until 1941 Westerners played im-portant roles in the administration of those colleges in the foreign concessions, but in many cases Americans remained on the old campuses to protect the property from the Japanese and other plunderers. Since Ginling, Lingnan, Hangchow, and other Christian college campuses served as refugee centers during the early war years, former teachers became responsible for collecting and dis-tributing relief and administering the refugee programs. After Pearl Harbor the internment or repatriation of many Americans and Ca-nadians left practically all administrative and teaching positions in Chinese hands. Americans who retired or left the Christian colleges could not generally be replaced during the war so that courses in certain fields, for example, English, medicine, and dentistry, became increasingly difficult to staff. By 1944 Fukien Christian University had no Westerners on its staff and Hwa Nan had only one.[25]

Emergencies and difficulties in communication forced the Chinese leaders to act without prior consultation with their boards of direc-tors in China or the boards of trustees in the United States. At the same time an increasing proportion of the college budgets came from emergency relief funds rather than from mission societies, and as a rule the college administrations had greater latitude in allocat-ing emergency funds than they had had in dispensing mission funds. In consequence the ties between the colleges and the Western churches were further loosened and the identity of the colleges as Chinese institutions under de facto Chinese control was strength-ened.

Two interesting trends in the composition of the student body of the Christian colleges developed during the war. The first was a growing percentage of women students. Although the Christian

[25] Associated Boards, *Annual Report, 1945*, p. 2.

colleges had traditionally shown leadership in this area, only a small proportion of their students had been women. By 1941, however, almost one-third of Yenching's students were women; and St. John's, which had admitted seven girls in 1936, enrolled four hundred girls in a total of 1,200 students in 1941.[26] Similar increases were reported at Chengtu. Such growth in women's education, predictable during the war, was nevertheless significant because it was not likely to be reversible after the war.

The colleges, in the second place, increasingly drew their students from the local population. Migrant institutions began to admit most of their students from interior China, and with the paucity of Christian middle schools in western China, they had to draw heavily on the public schools and other secular institutions. The typical student soon ceased to be the product of a Christian middle school in the urban east. Sections of China that had received little Western influence through education, trade, or residence became centers of modern education. Families for whom higher education had been a utopian dream could now consider a Western-type college education for their sons. The socially disruptive effects of inflation meant, furthermore, that the families which could afford to educate their sons were not always from the old gentry class; though the powerful were generally the ones best able to ride the crest of inflation, merchants and even farmers became wealthy enough to finance an education for their sons. The composition of the student body of the coordinate colleges in Chengtu in 1945 was quite different from that in 1937.

Attrition

Two matters of growing concern to all the colleges were the declining morale of students and faculty and the lowering of academic standards. By 1945 most colleges had to admit that they were fighting a losing battle on both fronts. Though many difficulties were inherent in the war situation, some were the direct consequence of college and government policies.

The change in the locale of most Christian colleges meant the loss of all or part of their library and laboratory materials. As has been

[26] *Yenching News*, XX (Dec. 1941), p. 2; "Historical Sketch of St. John's University, Shanghai" (mimeo., n.d.; UB).

pointed out above, there were severe shortages even among those institutions that moved only a few miles to the Shanghai International Settlement. At a time when enrollment in the Shanghai Associated Colleges was 3,000, the library reading room could accommodate fewer than a hundred students, and laboratory experience was generally limited to science majors. Classes often ran to more than a hundred. The universities that had to flee long distances suffered even greater losses; despite the generosity of West China Union University in sharing its facilities with guest institutions, the equipment was far from adequate. Even relief funds from abroad were of limited assistance because of transportation difficulties; cargo space could not ordinarily be used for laboratory supplies or current books and periodicals from abroad. West China Union University in collaboration with the University of Nanking and Soochow and with government support initiated a project to manufacture minimal apparatus and supplies for introductory scientific work in west China, but materials for more advanced courses were often unobtainable. Inability to keep the library holdings up to date contributed to a sense of intellectual isolation among scholars in west China. Expanding enrollment in the Chengtu area compounded the difficulties; between 1937 and 1942 the number of students in the Christian colleges at Chengtu increased from 500 to 2,800.[27] In most of the educational centers, space was at such a premium that institutions had to take turns, one school using the facilities in the morning, another in the afternoon, and sometimes still another in the evening if the electric lighting were adequate. Of necessity, students had to depend heavily on textbooks and class lectures for information, and yet textbooks were in short supply and by 1945 were worn and outdated. Teachers had to rely almost exclusively on their accumulated knowledge in preparing lectures, and even the amount of time for classwork was restricted by the shortage of classrooms.

The war brought other problems, not the least of which was irregularity of attendance. Disruption of college calendars did not cease after the migrations; students were frequently unable to attend classes for other reasons: family responsibilities, financial difficulties,

[27] Edwards, *Yenching*, p. 378; *The China Colleges* gave frequent reports on college enrollment, see IX (Oct. 1942), p. 2 and XI (Jan. 1944), p. 4.

bombings by the Japanese, and toward the end of the war, illness and malnutrition. Students were called from the classroom for a short military course or instruction in first aid; they organized propaganda and relief expeditions and were absent for a few days or weeks, and penalizing them for such absences was considered unpatriotic. As partial remedy colleges held inter-calendar sessions or extended the school year. West China reported in 1939, for example, that all upperclassmen in the College of Arts had been absent at the beginning of the academic year for two months of military training; the school had tried to make up the work by extending the first term and foregoing most of the New Year holiday, but even so academic life had been disrupted by propaganda tours, by the obligation to help relatives coming from the war zone, and by numerous other responsibilities.[28]

The Christian colleges usually were not able to maintain their prewar admissions standards.[29] Patriotism demanded the admission of guest students from other institutions with little question as to the adequacy of their training or the availability of academic facilities. Since a refugee student received a government subsidy only as long as he was enrolled in a college, dismissing a homeless student and thereby cutting him off from all support seemed almost criminal. Schools that migrated, furthermore, brought only a portion of their students and so had to admit many new students in their new locale; this meant an imbalance between freshmen and upper classmen. More serious, perhaps, was the fact that the colleges were cut off from their traditional clientele, the Christian middle schools of east China. Since other middle schools generally provided less training in English and science and were also experiencing a decline in educational standards, the difficulties of the Christian colleges were compounded. Christian colleges were no longer able to maintain a quota of Christian students or serve specific Christian constituencies. At other times these facts would have led Christian educators to serious questioning about the purpose of the institutions, but the

[28] "The West China Union University" (pamphlet, no pub. data; MRL), p. 13.

[29] Associated Boards, *Annual Report, 1945*, p. 5. Soochow reported in 1939 that over 50 percent of its arts and sciences students attained only a fourth- or fifth-grade level in one or more of their subjects. "Educational News," *CR*, LXXI (1940), 381–382.

desire to contribute to the war effort muffled the rumblings. Some schools tried to mitigate the great inequality in the preparation of entering students by instituting sub-freshmen classes or remedial courses.

Students and faculty initially felt that they were participating in a patriotic crusade and redoubled their efforts so as to compensate for shortages. A number of factors, however, began to undercut morale so that there no longer appeared to be identity of student goals, university and government policies, and the good of the Chinese nation. Both students and teachers seemed less capable of making the extra effort to maintain academic standards. One burden was simply psychological fatigue; as the war dragged on it was difficult to retain the atmosphere of emergency. Sacrifice for the future of China was fairly easy on a short-term basis but much harder over the long haul. Closely connected was the brevity of academic generations and of youthful memories. To an eighteen-year-old in 1945 the war probably seemed more like the norm than a temporary emergency; he could hardly be expected to respond to patriotic appeals in the same fashion as the eighteen-year-old of 1937. Students in west China during the last years of the war were isolated from the major offensive against Japan. As the United States assumed primary responsibility for the defeat of Japan, students and faculty could find little relation between their personal sacrifices and the war against the enemy. In addition, physical debilitation undoubtedly contributed to lowered morale. Malnutrition, overcrowded housing, and inadequate medical care all were conducive to a high incidence of illness, especially tuberculosis, among academic communities during the 1940's.

Some policies of the colleges and of the Kuomintang government also contributed to the decline in morale and in academic standards. Both institutions tended to live in the future and be guided by the desire to provide for the life of the institution in postwar China. Such an orientation strengthened the decision not to surrender to the Japanese and to continue work at all costs, but it could also conflict with the war effort and with a rational adjustment to the emergency. There was, for example, the question of how to invest emergency funds sent the colleges from abroad. The desire of each school to retain its identity and the temporary nature of the cooperation at Shanghai and Chengtu deeply influenced decisions on allocations. Though a permanent science building and a hospital were built at Chengtu, the guest colleges generally gave preference to temporary buildings and to dormitories rather than classrooms. Building dormitories made it possible to house students of one institution together and create a sense of group identity. In most cases the schools tried to provide their own freshman courses but encouraged cross registration in the upper level courses. Even so, courses with small enrollments were duplicated. Institutions tried to retain their stockpiles of faculty talent, and therefore the associated colleges as a group could not work toward a balanced and complementary faculty.

Many specific instances of the primacy of institutional interests might be cited. In 1941 Hangchow Christian University fled to Shaowu where it rented classroom and library space from Fukien Christian University, but built its own temporary dormitories. The dormitories were approximately ten to fifteen minutes from the Fukien University campus, a location that President Lee said gave "the advantage of a separate existence to promote college spirit." [30] Fukien University decided to increase its own enrollment, however, and this meant that it would no longer be able to share space with Hangchow. Hangchow would have to construct its own classrooms or suspend operations. The rapid rise in construction costs forced acceptance of the second alternative in 1944. At Chengtu the colleges experimented with joint entrance examinations but gave up the attempt because of the differing emphases of the cooperating institutions. It proved possible to coordinate the academic calendar but not the degree requirements of the Chengtu institutions. Although a joint administrative committee worked toward common solutions for common problems, each college generally maintained its separate administration and faculty and its own salary scale.

The students themselves were not immune to institutional competition. Despite joint commencement exercises by the Associated Christian Colleges in Shanghai, the seniors at St. John's requested and obtained their own graduation program in 1940. Other member colleges also tried to maintain their separate and traditional ceremonies at Christmas time, commencement, or founder's day. Because

[30] Day, *Hangchow*, p. 111.

factionalism had split the Cheeloo faculty and the school had been slow in organizing a separate administration at Chengtu, Cheeloo did not have some of its most prominent professors in west China. Both alumni and students felt that Cheeloo was not making as good a showing as the other institutions at Chengtu, and this dissatisfaction found expression in various ways. President Liu was criticized because his Chengtu faculty included few full professors and relatively few Chinese who had graduate degrees from the West; eventually the administrative committee refused to cooperate with Liu and forced him from office in 1943. Later, the discontent contributed to student strikes which were partially responsible for the departure in 1945 of Liu's successor, President Edgar Chi-ho T'ang.[31]

After Yenching's move to Chengtu, the sense of institutional competition quickened. Yenching made a strenuous effort to maintain academic standards and with her reputation was able to draw to her faculty a number of prominent scholars from dislocated institutions such as Tsing Hua and to attract a significant proportion of the most promising student applicants to the associated colleges in Chengtu. Feeding the envy of the other schools was Yenching's ability to obtain funds from a wide variety of sources. Yenching administrators, on the other hand, had their troubles with their trustees and the Associated Boards in New York. The administrators were unhappy that as a newcomer to Chengtu, Yenching was held to an enrollment of four hundred despite the preference of many of the best qualified applicants for Yenching. They felt that their trustees were mistaken in reserving one-third of the regular budget for interned staff and for teachers temporarily separated from the institution, and they repeatedly requested that a larger portion of the funds be allocated for Yenching's work in Chengtu. It was obviously difficult to live in the present and the future at the same time, and yet most colleges believed that they could not sacrifice the future existence of the institution to the exigencies of the present. Thus, institutional interests sometimes thrust aside immediate academic considerations.

Alienation between the student generation and the Kuomintang government had found conspicuous expression in the December 9th Movement. Then the formation of the united front and the Kuo-

[31] Corbett, *Shantung*, pp. 246–248.

mintang resistence had once more inspired the hope and loyalty of students. The government had signified its confidence in teachers and students by financial assistance to refugees and, despite heavy military expenses, had even increased the amounts budgeted for education. By 1945, however, distrust between the academic community and the Kuomintang had again become widespread. Many students and teachers were questioning whether the Kuomintang spoke for the Chinese nation; others had adopted a cynical, apolitical attitude that justified concentration on the immediate problems of existence. Though the work in the Christian colleges was only occasionally interrupted by strikes, students were, during the last years of the war, asking whether their sacrifices were contributing either to the good of China or to their own personal welfare. Normal avenues for advancement seemed to be closing and the students tended to blame the Kuomintang government for their frustrations. A variety of explanations can be given as to why the Nationalist administration once more had come to be the focal point of student dissatisfaction.

To some extent the Kuomintang leaders were paying for their own claim to complete authority and to some extent Chinese students were simply acting within Chinese tradition when they made the government all responsible for disasters. But the Kuomintang was not all powerful and the party had continued to be riven by factionalism. The flight to the West had increased its dependence on conservative groupings, especially the warlords and their military units and the landlords who controlled most of the taxable income. A loyal and efficient civil service had not been achieved, and rational procedures for promotion and recruitment had not been followed. Students who had at first accepted the Kuomintang's definition of their contribution to the war effort became discouraged over the limited military effort exerted against Japan and their own isolation from activities that seemed vital to China's future. As respectable academic work became less and less possible and as graduates found little use for their training, then retreatism, *ressentiment,* and other expressions of anomie became widespread.

Some argued that government educational regulations contributed to the decline in morale and in academic standards. Under Ch'en Li-fu, the Ministry of Education continued to extend its control over the content and organization of education. The task of establishing standard requirements for specific majors, begun in the mid-1930's, was gradually being accomplished. On the thesis that the war emergency made graduate study too expensive, the Ministry required a high degree of specialization in the undergraduate curriculum. No minors were permitted and requirements in the major often ran as high as eighty credit hours. Other requirements included two hours a week of military training, physical and health education, a course in San Min Chu I, approximately sixty credit hours in basic courses, and, after 1940, a certain number of hours a week of labor service. Few opportunities for electives remained, and even the electives had to be chosen from courses approved by the government for the specific major. In 1940 schools were informed that they should require comprehensive final examinations and that the examinations should be kept for government inspection at any time.[32] Students and teachers complained that they were given little leeway in working out an academic program. Roderick Scott of Fukien Christian University said, for example, that few students were any longer able to elect a course in philosophy; the course had to be dropped and he could give his students training in philosophy only by including some in his English courses.[33] The Ministry of Education regulated the number and kinds of majors a college could offer. It decreed that only medical schools could provide premedical training, thereby placing Hwa Nan in a difficult position, since graduate study in medicine had often been the goal of Hwa Nan chemistry majors. In 1939 the government announced its intention of taking complete control of teacher training; no private institutions were to be permitted to add a major in the field.

Students were concerned about restrictions on their freedom of expression and association. As had been true during the mid-1930's, alienation between students and government led to ever more strenuous attempts to regulate the thought and actions of students, but the government lacked the wherewithal for effective control, and

[32] "Educational News," CR, LXXI (1940), 663. Early specialization had been common in the national universities and government regulations were simply accentuating an existent trend. The Christian collges, modeled on American liberal arts institutions, had to make significant alterations in their curricula to meet government requirements.

[33] Scott, Fukien, p. 90.

the sporadic enforcement by the government and the defiance of the students fed the antagonism of both groups. During the war, for example, the Ministry of Education called for a return to the tutorial method of instruction in colleges and senior middle schools; the goal was to restore the traditional emphasis on moral teaching by personal example. A tutor was to be held responsible for his student's thought and behavior, and a student's graduation certificate should include the tutor's estimate of his academic standing, thought, and behavior. Tutors would receive honor for their students who later won distinction and blame for those who went astray.[34] This program might be viewed as a combination of the sponsorship system of the old civil service with the loyalties of the traditional student-teacher relationship. It was wholly unacceptable to the New Youth of twentieth-century China, who saw it as an attempt to organize an educational spy system. Ironically, even though the regulation proved unenforceable in the chaotic conditions of west China, it heightened antagonism toward the Kuomintang government.

All college youth were under heavy pressure to become members of the San Min Chu I Youth Corps, established in 1938. According to official regulations, members should participate weekly in discussions based on Sun Yat-sen's Three Principles and other required reading, should receive military training and attend summer camp, and should contribute labor service to the war effort. The Kuomintang hoped to make the association an instrument for instilling Chinese nationalism as interpreted by the party, for training future party members, and for communicating information on service to wartime China. Critics likened the corps to a gestapo, the communist youth corps, or the Hitlerjugend. According to one scholar, however, the political indecision and laxness of the Kuomintang kept the corps from becoming like any of these associations and it was "at best a laggard bid to young men, and a belated competition with the Left.[35] Some youth in 1938 did try to channel their patriotism into work for the San Min Chu I Corps, but by 1944–1945

[34] "Educational News," CR, LXXI (1940), 251–252; Band, Two Years with Chinese Communists, p. 323.

[35] Paul M. A. Linebarger, The China of Chiang Kai-shek: A Political Study (Boston, 1941), pp. 132–133. See pp. 332–353 for the constitution of the San Min Chu I Youth Corps and General Ch'en Ch'eng's lecture of 1940 on the duties and activities of the corps.

the corps was more likely to be the object of cynicism than an effective instrument of terror or of patriotism. Other evidence of the growing distrust between the party government and the academic community might be cited. There were restrictions on the activity of student government associations, arbitrarily enforced censorship regulations, and occasional police raids. Public demonstrations were forbidden, but sporadic protests occurred nevertheless.

Discontent with the government's educational policy, however, was only a part of the general demoralization in West China by 1944–1945. Much of this demoralization had an economic base, and few groups had less protection against economic hardship than teachers and students. At first the Christian colleges were in a favorable financial position in comparison with other universities, for they received their regular support from the West plus substantial aid from special campaigns. The Associated Boards for Christian Colleges contributed emergency funds of US$250,000 or more annually between 1937 and 1940. The Rockefeller Foundation, the China Relief Fund, and various sister colleges of the Christian institutions were generous in their aid. Smith College, for example, made contributions totaling almost one-fourth of the Ginling budget.[36] The International Student Service Fund in Geneva and the Far Eastern Service Fund in the United States offered aid, and in some years Christian colleges reported that half or more of their students were receiving scholarships.

The debilitating hardship really came during the 1940's with the uncontrolled inflation. The Christian colleges were at a special disadvantage because the official exchange rate of Ch$20 for US$1 was far below the market rate. Though the government eventually permitted a higher rate for educational and philanthropic funds (40 to 1 and then 128 to 1), this was still well below the market rate of exchange. The steady inflation with the fixed exchange rate meant that the operations of the Christian colleges became ever more expensive in US dollars. By 1943 construction costs in US dollars had

[36] Chester S. Miao, "Christian Education in China," *CCYB, 1938–39,* pp. 214–215; "Educational Events," *School and Society,* LI (1940), 701; *The China Colleges,* VIII (June 1942), 4; Associated Boards, *Annual Report, 1939,* pp. 6–7; *1941,* pp. 6–7; *1942,* pp. 6–7.

become almost prohibitive, and fixed income in US dollars for operating expenses bought less and less. Salary scales could not be maintained, and the most essential equipment—textbooks, chalk, blackboards, paper, electricity, and the like—became unobtainable luxuries. Payments in rice, government subsidies, and other aids could not compensate for runaway inflation. When teachers took two or even three jobs in order to feed their families, the college administrators regretted the decline in teaching standards and the cessation of research; they could, however, say little. There undoubtedly were some teachers who engaged in black market activities despite stern warnings from college and government officials; no matter what the extenuating circumstances, their actions undermined the authority of the older generation and their attempts to inculcate a sense of social morality among youth.

Such harsh conditions, onerous even when they seemed to contribute to a worthy cause, appeared intolerable as the relation between personal sacrifice and national welfare seemed to evaporate. Graduates found it exceedingly difficult to obtain positions that made use of their training. Though many Chinese students assumed that they would make their contribution to China by entering state service or teaching, graduates in east China quickly discovered that this meant accepting employment with the puppet government or escaping to Southwest China in the hope of securing employment. In Free China, however, college graduates found government positions increasingly difficult to obtain for a variety of reasons: the mutual suspicion between the Kuomintang and the educated class, the fact that a large percentage of the refugees had been members of the white collar class and so there was no shortage of government personnel, and the importance of personal influence in securing a job. Even those who managed to gain government employment discovered that much of Chungking's attention was being diverted from the war effort; time, energy, and money went rather into trying to insure the dominance of the Kuomintang in postwar China.

In the unhealthy atmosphere, students reacted variously. Some of the Christian colleges at first reported a new interest in Christianity; this interest took the form of a search for a personal faith and found expression in small fellowship groups.[37] These groups, organized informally and directed by the students themselves, emphasized worship and discussion of personal problems and experiences. Some of them sponsored social service activities and tried to define the role of the Christian in wartime China, but they established no direct relation with the church. As the war continued, there were fewer reports about students' readiness to learn about Christianity and more complaints about the difficulty of fitting religion courses into heavy schedules or the lack of facilities and trained leaders for religious work.[38]

Many students grew cynical. They retreated from idealism and from responsibility and concentrated on obtaining the necessities of daily existence. The response to evangelistic efforts was: "Let's be practical; we need bread and clothes. Why talk about spiritual values?"[39] What was more unusual was the growing apathy toward nationalistic appeals. Some appeared to have lost all sense of involvement in the war effort; they felt that not only they but all of West China was isolated from the real fight against Japan. Without nationalism, they were without direction, and they were unwilling to sacrifice any longer.

As students observed the benefits that deviant behavior brought others, some became willing to follow suit. Graduates accepted positions and assignments that had nothing to do with the war effort, even undermined it, but they still talked of national sacrifice. Students condemned poor teaching and inadequate training while they engaged in strikes and demonstrations which made orderly academic work impossible. Toward the end of the war, for example, there was a mass demonstration in Chengtu. While Cheeloo students

[37] Stanton Lautenschlager, *Far West in China* (New York, 1941), pp. 37–48; W. Y. Chen, "The Christian Movement in National Life," *CCYB*, 1938–39, pp. 100–104; J. L. Stuart, "College Graduates and the Church," *CR*, LXXI (1940), 292–293; John S. Barr, "Christian Activities in War-Torn China," *CR*, LXXII (1941), 477.

[38] David F. Anderson, "What Makes a College Christian," *CR*, LXXII (1941), 120–121; "A Survey of the Year, 1943," *International Review of Missions*, XXXIII (1944), 21.

[39] Luther Shao (Shao Ching-san), "Jesus and the Cynical Attitude," *CR*, LXXII (1941), 491–492; see also, the comments on the growing cynicism by David M. Paton, "Christian Work in Chinese Government Universities," *International Review of Missions*, XXXIII (1944), 152.

obeyed the law and the command of their president not to participate in public demonstration, students in all the other Chengtu
colleges joined the protest. It was not, however, the students who
broke the law who were ridiculed, but rather the Cheeloo students.
Cheeloo students felt humiliated that they alone had lacked the
spirit to defy the authorities, and they blamed their college president
for his pressure on them to conform. Student enmity toward President T'ang eventually found expression in an accusation that he had
misappropriated the rice subsidy for students and teachers. Though
an investigating committee exonerated T'ang, he had lost much of
his influence; he was granted a leave of absence and then replaced.[40]
At Fukien Christian University in 1945 students called a week long
strike when a controversy developed over a proposal to alter the
sitting room in one of the women's dormitories.[41]

Even in the midst of *ressentiment* and retreatism, many students
would still respond to a nationalist appeal that included a positive
course of action. The Kuomintang in November 1943 reversed previous policy and launched a "student join the army movement."[42]
The response far exceeded the government's expectations and also
its capacity. Tens of thousands of middle school and college youth
volunteered for military service, but only a fraction of these could
be accepted. Though various explanations were offered for the many
rejections—the youth of many volunteers, their poor physical condition, the shortage of training facilities—disappointment was keen.
A year later, the Kuomintang launched another drive for student
volunteers. Many again responded; at Yenching approximately 13
percent of the male students volunteered during the winter of 1944-
1945. Some became members of China's expanding air force and
others entered officer's training. The increasing numbers of American soldiers used in military training programs and construction
projects had created a demand for English language interpreters,
and so quite a few Christian college students served in this capacity.
Three Fukien Christian University students, for example, served as

[40] Corbett, *Shantung*, pp. 246-248.
[41] Fukien Christian University, "President's Report on Conditions, 1945"
(mimeo., MRL).
[42] The Chungking government had earlier drafted graduates only in certain
special fields such as medicine and dentistry.

interpreters for General Joseph Stilwell in his preparations for the Burma campaign, and a number of Ginling and Yenching girls worked as typists, telephone operators, and accountants at an American air base near Chengtu.[43]

Many, however, found their attempt to contribute to the war effort a frustrating experience. Those who entered the army discovered that discipline, training, and basic services were inadequate or totally lacking. Still other volunteers awaited assignment but never received word that a program had been organized. The one-hundred Ginling girls, who volunteered for a nurse's aid course that met at 7 A.M. throughout December and January, found that, after completing the program, they were given few opportunities to put their training to use.[44] Two Ginling students entered a government training program for nurses only to discover that the participants varied so widely in their educational background that no effective course was possible.

As dissatisfaction with Kuomintang rule in Southwest China grew, students contrasted their experience with what they heard about the Chinese Communist Party in North China. They actually had only sparse information about Yenan and the guerrilla resistance, for censorship and restrictions on travel and communication made concrete factual detail difficult to obtain. The scarcity of information in combination with the multiple sources of discontent in West China sometimes encouraged youth to romanticize life in Yenan and exaggerate the communist contribution to resistance. Even during the early years of the war, however, a number of students had found communist policy on the role of youth in the war effort more attractive than Kuomintang policy, and from the time of the December 9th Movement some of the activist youth had looked to the Communist Party as mentor.

During the war the Chinese communists concentrated on those activities that would disrupt Japanese rule and at the same time increase the party's influence and authority in North China. As the party of revolution, they could pursue policies which altered the socio-economic structure of rural China and they did not worry

[43] Letter of Acting-President Y. P. Mei, *Yenching News*, XXIII (June 1945); Scott, *Fukien*, p. 93: Edwards, *Yenching*, p. 391; Thurston, *Ginling*, p. 120.
[44] Thurston, *Ginling*, p. 121.

unduly about the maintenance of institutions which would be important to order and continuity in postwar China. Unlike the Kuomintang, the Communist Party did not attempt to support a regular educational system and stockpile professional talent for the reconstruction of postwar China. The schools which they entitled colleges and universities made no pretense of offering the curriculum or attaining the academic standards of an accredited institution of higher education; in short-term courses they trained cadres for the immediate tasks of instigating guerrilla warfare against the Japanese and organizing procommunist administrations in the villages behind the lines. For some of the youth who had demanded military resistance to the Japanese and who had seen first hand the ravages of the Japanese army, the policy of the Communist Party provided emotional satisfaction.[45]

In the chaos of the early fighting, some students deliberately sought the guidance of communist units in organizing resistance, whereas others came under communist aegis almost by default. In August 1937, for example, more than a thousand youths in Shantung volunteered to conduct propaganda work in collaboration with the government's Third Route Army. When Tsinan fell without a battle and the army retreated, the youth were left without guidance or leadership. Some drifted back to their schools; others made contact with guerrilla forces and gladly accepted the training and advice offered by the Communist Party.[46] William and Claire Band, who fled from Yenching after Pearl Harbor and spent two years with the communists in northwest China, recorded the story of a group of Peiping students who attempted to organize guerrilla activities under an officer of the Twenty-Ninth Route Army; the core group was soon overwhelmed by three hundred prisoners whom they helped release, and the unit became scarcely distinguishable from a band of outlaws living off the countryside. When guerrillas of the Eighth Route Army established contact, many of the former

[45] In a speech delivered at a youth rally on Dec. 9, 1944, Liu Shao-ch'i stated: "Many of those who had participated in the December 9th movement now [1937] became military commanders, political workers, and local administrators, directing the economic and cultural work" ("Unite with the Broad Masses of Workers, Peasants, and Soldiers," reprinted in SCMP, no. 36 [Dec. 22–24, 1950], pp. 26–27).

[46] Y. Y. Tsu, "The Youth Movement," CCYB, 1938–39, p. 61.

students willingly transferred to the communist unit.[47] Chang Yu-yü of Yenching's department of journalism was one of the Peiping activists who worked as a propagandist with guerrilla units behind Japanese lines in Hopei, Shantung, and Chahar and then moved to Chungking in 1941 to become editor of the communist organ, *Hsin-hua jih-pao* and secretary of the Szechuan Provincial Committee of the Communist Party.[48]

During each war year that Yenching remained in Peiping a number of graduates who did not wish to serve the puppet regime made their way to Yenan or joined resistance groups in the occupied area. They organized National Salvation Associations and acted as guides for communist military and party personnel; they helped in the collection of taxes and operation of literacy schools and land reform programs. An estimate of the numbers of youths who entered such work is almost impossible. During the first year of the war when morale and enthusiasm were high throughout China, it was stated that Sian was processing seven hundred volunteers a week on their way to Yenan; not all of these were students and the numbers declined after the initial burst of enthusiasm, but the training institutes run by the communists continued to have enrollments of several thousand.[49] When the blockade between Kuomintang and communist territory made travel to Yenan dangerous, institutes were organized in the border regions behind Japanese lines so that youth could continue to join the guerrilla work. For a minority of youth at least, the call to hardship, adventure, and danger was more attractive than the call to studies.

By 1945 relations between educated youth and the competing parties were not unlike those following the December 9th Movement. The idealization of Chiang Kai-shek as savior of China, so typical of youth in 1937, had largely disappeared. Student ill will toward the Kuomintang was based on specific grievances and gen-

[47] Band, *Two Years with the Chinese Communists*, pp. 91–92.
[48] Freyn, *Chinese Education in the War*, pp. 81–88.
[49] "Student Pilgrims in China," *School and Society*, XLVIII (1938), 310–311. Edgar Snow in *The Battle for Asia* (New York, 1941) states that the various "resist Japan institutes" graduated nearly 10,000 a year (see pp. 273–274). The communists claimed 20,000 enrolled in these institutes (see Lautenschlager, *Far West in China*, pp. 14–16). Some of the institutes and programs were highly informal, of course.

eral condemnation of the responsible authority for personal hardships; the Kuomintang increasingly turned to censorship and repression in response to criticism. The Chinese Communist Party, on the other hand, benefited from a generally favorable attitude even among many who had little interest in communist ideology and only sketchy knowledge of Communist Party policies in north China. The sense of rapport that developed between youth and the Communist Party seemed partly a function of the growing alienation between youth and the Kuomintang.

There were, however, differences between 1936 and 1945. During the war the Chinese Communist Party had become larger and more influential; many peasants in North China had accepted governments under Communist Party tutelage as "the authority." The contrast with the weakness of the Communist Party shortly after the Long March was dramatic. The Kuomintang, on the other hand, had lost many of its sources of support in east China, and by 1945 its effectiveness as a political instrument had deteriorated because of indiscipline, corruption, and demoralization. In 1945 cynicism seemed more prevalent among youth and idealism rarer than in 1936, a phenomenon that would play into the hands of the disciplined few. In 1936 the call of nationalistic youth was for war, and in 1945 it was for peace. The Kuomintang seemed more essential to the making of war in 1936 than to the making of peace in 1945.

XI | Civil Conflict and the Politicizing of College Youth, 1945-1948

Though the end of World War II had long been dreamed of, the Japanese surrender in August 1945 caught many Chinese by surprise. Neither students nor faculty in the Christian colleges had detailed plans for the immediate postwar period. Like many other Chinese, they at first anticipated a prompt return to normalcy. They were eager to forget the hardships of the war years and the social disintegration of almost half a century of revolution. They wanted peace and quiet; they hoped for prosperity and the opportunity to fulfill personal and institutional goals; national and international events had dominated individual lives long enough.

The reaction of Christian college students at Chengtu was typical; torchlight parades, patriotic songs, and victory rallies gave spontaneous expression to their joy. And through all ran the refrain: Now we can go home; now we can see our parents; now there will be peace at last. Many students were ready to pack their belongings and start eastward immediately. An idealized picture of China before 1937 captured the imagination of college personnel. Morale, educational standards, living conditions, all would be different as they returned to the handsome and spacious campuses in the east. A new era lay ahead for the China Christian colleges, an era of cooperation and understanding with other Chinese educationalists and government leaders, an era in which the colleges would be an accepted part of the Chinese scene. College leaders, like the students, could hardly wait to begin the migration and the restoration.

But the price of decades of war and revolution could not be so easily discounted. Even the simplest tasks presented time-consuming difficulties. Return to the home campus involved numerous delays and complex planning. Inflation made the rehabilitation of college buildings, libraries, and laboratories almost impossible. As political and economic disintegration gathered momentum, the daily problems of holding together an academic institution seemed to occupy every hour. At the same time, national politics became increasingly difficult to ignore. A political or military resolution of the dispute between the Kuomintang and the Chinese communists seemed a prerequisite to rehabilitation in all realms. Plans for expanding curricula, campaigns for increased local support, student demands for larger rice subsidies, all acquired a political orientation. Normalcy, it appeared, would remain an ever receding dream.

Among students in particular, there was a growing preoccupation with politics and the civil war. By 1947 student demonstrations and strikes in the Shanghai and Peiping areas were occurring with such frequency that college administrators could scarcely maintain a functioning academic program, and the destiny of the colleges was becoming a function of national events, not of the actions of Christian educators. The outcome of the struggle between the Chinese Communist Party and the Kuomintang became the only issue that mattered, and the students often seemed to understand this sooner than the educators. While Christian college administrators concentrated on their academic problems, student leaders in Shanghai and Peiping demanded priority for political activities. Students might overestimate their ability to influence the outcome of the Kuomintang-Communist conflict, but they were correct in their estimate of the overriding importance of the outcome.

The students' politicization was accompanied by their loss of faith in the ability of the Kuomintang to guide China's modernization. The first student protests in the immediate postwar years had emphasized specific demands to be met by the Kuomintang, but the character of the campaigns soon changed. The students began making such far-reaching demands and sweeping condemnations that their purpose seemed to be embarrassment of the regime rather than attainment of definite requests. Leftist organizations deliberately used the student protests, so that participation in them contributed to polarization. If the students were barometers of public opinion in urban China, then their mood in 1948 clearly indicated that the Mandate of Heaven was passing from the Kuomintang to the Chinese communists, for the alienation from the Kuomintang was attended by a readiness to acknowledge the legitimacy of communist rule. Student campaigns between 1946 and 1949 helped create the impression of general disaffection from Kuomintang rule, and then leftist students helped ease the transition to the People's Republic of China.

By 1949 the Christian college leaders found that their control over the future of the institutions had so diminished that they had only two choices: to close the schools or try to continue work under conditions prescribed by the Chinese Communist Party. The latter course was elected by all. Unfortunately for the future of the Christian colleges, one legacy of the civil war had been to make the United States the focus of nationalist and anti-foreign sentiment. The United States had been tainted by its association with the Kuomintang so that it had become identified with the demoralization of the regime, the runaway inflation, and the continuance of the civil war. The student movement of 1946–1948 with its virulent anti-Americanism did not bode well for the future of the Christian colleges or of Sino-American relations under the People's Republic of China.

Postwar Reorientation

While there had still been hope for a peaceful period of postwar rehabilitation, some long-range planning for the Christian colleges in China had been initiated. In 1943 planning committees had been organized by the Associated Boards for Christian Colleges in China, the British Committee, and the boards of managers in China; and after three years of consultation these groups agreed on a design for development for the China colleges.[1] Their program gave greater emphasis to evangelistic goals than corresponding statements during the 1930's. The expression of the Christian spirit through social

[1] "Design for Development," *The China Colleges*, XII (June 1946), 4–5; Tan Jen-mei, "The Situation in Christian Education," in Miao Chu-seng (Chester S. Miao), ed., *Christian Voices in China* (New York, 1948), pp. 57–62. It should be noted that Westerners had much to do with initiating the planning. Not all of the leading Chinese Christian educators would have agreed with the emphasis on evangelism and on strengthening the church as an institution.

service was not considered sufficient. In accord with the new ortho-doxy then popular in theological circles,[2] the planners stressed the need to re-emphasize the Christian purpose of the colleges in edu-cational policy and practice. Furthermore, definite goals for the proportion of Christian to non-Christian teachers and students were set forth. The planners also looked to the Christian colleges to help eliminate two major weaknesses of the Chinese Protestant churches: the frail, hothouse character of many rural parishes and the tendency of college students to drift away from the church upon graduation. One recommendation was for more appropriate training for minis-ters in rural areas so that the parishes could become more nearly self-sustaining. At the same time, raising the educational level of pastors seemed imperative if the latter were to present a theology attractive to college students. The trend toward separation of the theological schools and the Christian colleges should be reversed in order to give a more liberal atmosphere to the seminaries; theologi-cal training of at least college level should be the minimum require-ment for a minister.

Between 1945 and 1949 several steps were taken toward these goals. In the revival of village reconstruction work, Christian leaders sought to make the local church the center of community activities. The North China Christian Rural Service Union, which included representatives of Yenching, Cheeloo, the College of Agriculture of the University of Nanking, and Peking Theological Seminary se-lected three centers in Hopei. In this province, they helped organize cooperatives and village health committees; they ran a workshop for rural pastors from communist-controlled areas; they illustrated the use of fertilizers, insecticides, and other agricultural techniques through demonstration plots; they dug a well with funds from

[2] The views of Karl Barth were a frequent topic for discussion at foreign mis-sions conferences during the 1940's, and they obviously influenced the thinking of some churchmen primarily concerned with China missions. See, for example, Luman J. Shafer, "The Meaning of the World Revolution for the Christian Movement: I, In China and Japan," *Report of the 49th Annual Meeting of the Conference of Foreign Mission Boards in Canada and the U.S.* (New York, 1943), pp. 18–19; Willard Brewing, "The New Imperialism," *Report of the Jubilee Meeting of the Conference of Foreign Mission Boards in Canada and the U.S.* (New York, 1944), p. 25; R. O. Jolliffe, "Recent Religious Thinking and Its Significance for Christian Education," *CR*, LXX (1939), 27–29.

the Chinese National Relief and Rehabilitation Administration (CNRRA), and they resumed publication of the *Christian Farmer*. They hoped thereby to make the local churches self-supporting and at the same time to make them the means to a better life for the villagers. This, they stated, was the Christian answer to communism in north China.[3] Huachung University launched a five-year course combining training in theology and the liberal arts for ministers as well as teachers in Christian middle schools. Attempts to strengthen Nanking Theological Seminary as a center both for the preparation of rural pastors and for theological education at the college and graduate levels were undertaken.

In academic matters, the planning committees emphasized setting limits to the ambitions of the individual institutions and guiding them in coordinating their programs. To aid in this coordination and also to provide a more efficient instrument for fund raising, the Associated Boards for Christian Colleges in China was transformed into the United Board for Christian Colleges in China in 1947. Whereas the Associated Boards had consisted of members of the separate college corporations and had acted as a coordinating agency, the United Board would be incorporated as a single body and would, it was anticipated, have the authority to act with efficiency and expedition. Hardy perennials in the proposals of the planning committees were the union of the four east China colleges —St. John's, Soochow, Shanghai, and Hangchow—into one university, and greater collaboration between Hwa Nan and Fukien and between Ginling and the University of Nanking. The coordination of Yenching and Cheeloo, also a frequent proposal, was omitted in the 1946 plan, but Cheeloo was urged to transform its Arts and Science College into a College of Rural Reconstruction and let Yenching be the center for liberal arts training in north China. Other limitations recommended were that graduate work be offered only at Yenching, the University of Nanking, Lingnan, and the east China university (if organized); that colleges of agriculture be

[3] *China Bulletin*, no. 23 (Jan. 6, 1948) gives considerable detail on the project. There had, of course, been concern about the weakness of the rural church before the war; see the results of a survey undertaken by the Nanking Seminary in 1936–1937: Frank W. Price, *The Rural Church in China* (New York, 1948).

developed only at Nanking and Lingnan; that all medical training be concentrated in five centers; and that there be only one college each in other professional fields.

The traditional disciplines and structure of Western education were to remain the framework, and the Christian college administrators could argue that they were given little encouragement to experiment by the government or the students. The Kuomintang government controlled the degree-granting powers of every registered institution and set up detailed course requirements for each degree. Students wanted recognized degrees that would lead to government positions or to admission to graduate schools in the West. Chinese educators and students both felt the need to prove that they were capable of mastering the learning of the West. The proposal for a College of Rural Reconstruction at Cheeloo was the one clear recognition of the continuing revolution in China and of the need for educational experiments specifically tailored to China. The fate of this proposal was not encouraging. The idea met strenuous opposition from Cheeloo alumni and students who were afraid that their degrees might decline in value. Fearing that Cheeloo might be relegated to the status of a technical institute, the faculty jealously guarded the humanities program and gave little aid in the search for staff for the new college. Even if the teachers had not been recalcitrant, however, the execution of the plan would have been difficult. Warfare and lack of trained personnel undercut President Wu K'e-ming's efforts at reorganization, and the Nanking government refused to recognize such a program as worthy of a college degree. The College of Rural Reconstruction was far from a reality when in 1948 civil war disrupted academic work in Tsinan.

Even the more conservative proposals proved difficult of attainment. In east China a vast amount of time and energy was given to working out the coordination plans. Though the University of Shanghai soon opted to go alone, President Lee Ba-en (Li Pei-en) of Hangchow, W. B. Nance of Soochow, President Y. C. Tu of St. John's, and other members of a special planning board spent many hours devising a scheme which would assure the alumni of the survival of their alma maters and would also lay the basis for one strong university. By 1947 they had agreed on the name East China Union University (Hua Tung), the constitution, and the election of a board of managers representing the three institutions. It was also agreed that in the fall of 1947 only St. John's would admit freshmen in liberal arts, whereas Soochow would admit science students, and Hangchow potential majors in engineering.

At this point the union scheme floundered. Decision on a site proved impossible. Previous understandings were disregarded, as the Medical School of St. John's admitted freshmen in the pre-medical program and Hangchow enrolled freshmen in liberal arts. The first meeting of the Board of Managers of East China Union University, scheduled for May 14, 1948, failed to secure a quorum; and during the rest of the academic year, student demonstrations and strikes so disrupted academic life that planning for the future had to be indefinitely postponed.[4] These incidents indicated that influential groups continued to oppose a course of action which had been bandied about since the 1920's. Until the establishment of the communist regime there was no authoritative body which could and would force amalgamation. With the realization that East China Union University would not come into being, many regretted that preoccupation with this issue had slowed rehabilitation and had perhaps contributed to student restlessness and dissatisfaction.

The first task facing most of the Christian colleges in August 1945 was the return to the home campus. As attention turned from victory celebrations to the eastward migration, both teachers and students realized the magnitude of the task. Schools had added extensively to the equipment they had brought west. Long distance travel, never easy in China, was complicated by wartime destruction of transportation facilities, especially the railway system of east China, and by the competition of the Kuomintang and Communist Party for territorial control. Whereas the migration westward had often taken place in stages, all the displaced Chinese hoped to return immediately in the fall of 1945. Obviously, government and military personnel would have priority, and others would have to wait. The journey would be a hard one. Fukien resorted to buying logs and constructing rafts on which to float equipment down the

[4] Nance gives his version of the negotiations in *Soochow*, pp. 127–134. Other views are given in Day, *Hangchow*, pp. 123–126; Lamberton, *St. John's*, pp. 231–233; *The China Colleges*, XV (Sept. 1947), 1; and "Historical Sketch of St. John's University, Shanghai," (mimeo., 1948, UB).

Min River; the logs were the pay of the river men who sold some of them back to the college for reconstruction.[5] Ginling discovered that if she waited until she were allotted space on river boats by the Ministry of Education she would not be able to return until October 1946, and so made private arrangements in April of that year for a journey by chartered truck, railway, and bus from Chengtu to Paochi to Sian to Hsüchow and finally south to Nanking.

Not one of the schools found its campus in any condition to receive students and faculty. There had been looting by both Japanese and Chinese; practically all metal objects—radiators, water pipes, and door fixtures—had been contributed to the war effort; wooden doors, furniture, and window frames had been used for fuel. The Japanese had used many of the buildings for military barracks and hospitals and had made few repairs. The books and laboratory equipment left on campus had generally disappeared. In some cases fire or fighting in the vicinity had caused serious losses; Hwa Nan's principal building had gone up in flames in 1941. College officials felt fortunate to find the shells of most buildings still standing. Funds would have to be raised and reconstruction begun. Estimates placed the cost of immediate property repairs at almost US$5,000,000. Most colleges reluctantly decided to delay transfer to the home campus until the spring or fall of 1946.

The Struggle to Restore Academic Standards

Despite the delay in returning to the home campus, conditions were far from ideal when the move was finally made. Students who had heard of the beauty and luxury of Christian college facilities were disappointed by what they found, and there was restiveness over the continuing hardships. At both Hangchow and Ginling students had to sleep on the floor, and students enrolling in Shanghai in 1946 had to bring all their own necessities, including wash basin, desk, and desk lamp. Economic problems had steadily mounted and were complicating the task of rehabilitation. It would be difficult to exaggerate the importance of inflation in the deterioration of all aspects of academic life between 1945 and 1948. Any delay in securing pledged funds meant that the money had lost

[5] Scott, *Fukien*, pp. 94–95.

much of its buying power by the time it could be put to use. Since the Chinese dollar was pegged at an artificially high rate in relation to the US dollar, colleges had to resort to black market operations or see a large portion of their real income go into the coffers of bankers and money changers. The United Board calculated that between 1945 and 1948, more than US$3,240,000 was spent on rehabilitating the colleges, but in the fall of 1946 the US dollar had only about 20 percent of its prewar purchasing power; by the fall of 1947 this had been reduced to 15 percent.[6] Building materials and food products were especially scarce and dear. College administrators, faculty members, and students, forced by the inflation to spend a whole semester's budget in order to survive a few weeks, often found themselves in desperate straits. The president of Lingnan reported in late 1945 that the funds he had on hand would carry him only through January 1946.[7]

Tuition fees contributed relatively little toward the budgets of the colleges. Government institutions charged little or nothing, and in view of the economic difficulties of many students, the Christian colleges could ask only minimal fees if they were to attract good students. Furthermore, a tuition fee set in September might lose half its real value before the semester ended. Some of the colleges resorted to collecting fees in kind, and so students journeyed to school with their belongings in one wheelbarrow and bags of rice for tuition in another. Even so, more than one student demonstration was occasioned by attempts to raise fees or to levy additional charges in mid-semester. In the spring of 1946, for example, sudden and rapid inflation left Soochow University without funds to pay salaries until the end of the term. When students were asked to pay an additional tuition fee, they argued that they had already paid the fee in advance and could not be required to pay another. After long discussions, the students finally suggested that they raise an "Honoring the Teachers Fund." Though the administration was not happy over a proposal with connotations of charity, the students collected enough to meet the deficit, and the faculty had little choice but to

[6] *The China Colleges,* XV (Feb. 1948), 4.
[7] *Lingnan,* XII (Jan. 1946) (a news bulletin published by the trustees of Lingnan in NYC, MRL).

accept the contribution. The worth of the Chinese dollar is indicated by the Ch$140,000 bonus received by one administrator.[8]

Paradoxically, the low tuition fees and government rice subsidies enabled more students than ever before to go to college. Thousands of youths were encouraged to seek a college education by its inexpensiveness, by the promise of aid, and perhaps by a wish to retreat from the deteriorating political and economic environment to the academic community. Thus, in a time of revolution, enrollments steadily increased. The Christian colleges, which had about 6,000 students in 1936, had almost doubled in size by 1947.[9] Such growth often seemed to compound the difficulties. Economic problems increased because student fees did not approach the cost of educating the students. Heavy pressures for expansion undercut steps to restore academic standards. The additional students meant continued use of improvised laboratories and libraries or the omission of library and laboratory work for many. Colleges in the Shanghai area felt obliged to admit students who had attended the underground schools and to grant them credit for their work despite its poor and uneven quality. Since dismissal for academic deficiency meant loss of economic support as well as humiliation, teachers who set high grading standards were sometimes the object of public criticism or even boycott. At Hangchow in 1947, for instance, students struck to obtain a lowering of the passing grade to 60 and elimination of the system requiring a certain number of grade points in order to graduate; according to President Lee, the protest was initiated by students from the Shanghai wartime schools.[10]

In some cases malnutrition contributed to the lowering of academic standards. Yenching, one of the few colleges to open on its own campus in the fall of 1945, was one of the first schools to feel the effects of inflation and food shortages. In north China, the

[8] Nance, *Soochow*, pp. 125–126. The Soochow University students did not act alone. Student associations in the Shanghai area had been officially encouraged to launch such a campaign after teachers in some schools went on strike to protest inadequate salaries. See C. P. Choi, "Students Unite to Put over $2 Billion Drive as Initial Campaign Flops at $300,000,000," *China Weekly Review*, June 1, 1946, pp. 7–8.

[9] *The China Colleges*, XV (Nov. 1947), 2.

[10] Day, *Hangchow*, pp. 121–122.

stronghold of Chinese communist influence, the communists used their control of the countryside to disrupt communications and transportation of supplies to the cities. Thus, Yenching students and faculty along with many other urban dwellers experienced serious shortages of food and coal during the winter of 1945–1946. With the renewal of civil war the situation worsened, and by 1947 the board fees were sufficient to provide only steamed bread and a few vegetables. Relief supplies sometimes supplemented the menu, and those students who could afford it bought extra rations, but even so, according to reports in the fall of 1947, most Yenching students were so undernourished that they could not stand the fatigue of required gymnastics.[11] As a result of the sharp economic crisis in the spring of 1947, academic work in much of east China was impaired by the fatigue of ill-fed students and faculty and by student strikes demanding an increase in rice rations.

For those who had survived the hardships of the war in the hope of better days, it was disillusioning to find the causes of decline in academic standards multiplying rather than disappearing. Problems in staffing continued. It was not until late 1946 or early 1947 that missionaries in any numbers could obtain return passage to China. Meanwhile, Chinese instructors who had postponed graduate training or who had not had the chance to keep up with the scholarship in their fields, wanted to make up for lost time. The doors to the United States were open, and thousands of Chinese left for graduate studies abroad. College administrators, hoping that the eventual result would be a more highly qualified faculty, could only applaud the desire of instructors to undertake further study. The immediate result, however, was an intensification of staffing problems. In 1947, for instance, more than 10 percent of the Christian college teachers were in England or the United States taking graduate work.[12] The communist victory in 1949 meant that the Christian colleges never enjoyed the fruits of their investment, for many of the graduate students either never returned to the mainland or did not renew their association with the Christian colleges if they did return. Those teachers who remained with their institutions during the postwar years often could not devote full time to their academic responsibili-

[11] Edwards, Yenching, p. 411.
[12] The China Colleges, XV (Nov. 1947), 3.

ties. With the inflation, professors had to continue to hold several jobs at once. Though institutions supplemented salaries that sounded astronomical with payments in kind, college salaries had only a fraction of the prewar buying power. Such conditions were conducive to neither high morale nor excellence in teaching; even in the Christian colleges there were threats of strikes by the faculty.

For many of the Christian colleges the postwar years were a time of rapid turnover in the administration, and this too disrupted efforts to restore academic standards. The various reasons for lack of continuity in personnel were all somehow related to the rapidly changing environment in China. College executives, like their faculty, often desired a refresher year abroad after the strain of the war, or the Western board requested a visit to the United States to renew ties with supporters and to aid in fund raising campaigns. Hwa Nan and Huachung granted their presidents a year's leave of absence for these purposes. President Y. C. Yang of Soochow University spent most of the period between 1941 and 1948 in the United States. While holding the office of university president, Yang served first in the Chinese Information Service and then in the United Nations Secretariat. He worked also to secure support for Soochow in the United States, and he made brief trips to China to handle college administrative matters. Some, however, felt that Yang's prolonged absences during the crucial postwar years were a handicap to the college, and faculty criticism became vocal and public on several occasions.

At the University of Shanghai and St. John's the fissure between occupied and Free China during the war continued to complicate the lives of the institutions. In 1945 the University of Shanghai was in the embarrassing position of having two boards of directors, each recognizing a different president. After Pearl Harbor a board had been organized in west China to consider founding a branch there and to guide the School of Commerce at Chungking; this board in 1944 elected the director of the School of Commerce, Henry H. Lin, acting president of the university and charged him with restoration of the university in east China. Neither the original board of directors nor President T. K. Van (Fan Cheng-kang) had formally relinquished their positions, however, and both assumed that they would be responsible for the postwar rehabilitation. Delicate negotiations over several months led to agreement on Lin as head of the university.[13] Scars remained, however, and it was understood that one weakness of Van's position was that he had remained in Shanghai after Japan assumed control. The wartime president of St. John's, William Z. L. Sung, was accused in 1946 of collaboration with the Japanese, and the faculty and students were deeply divided during Sung's two years of imprisonment and trial. Though Sung was finally acquitted, his usefulness to St. John's had ended, and finding a replacement did not prove easy. The vacuum created by President Hawks Pott's retirement in 1939 after fifty years of service was never really filled. From 1939 on St. John's was administered by acting presidents, temporary presidents, and executive committees.

Other Christian colleges also experienced discontinuity in leadership. Yenching lost the services of President Stuart when he became United States Ambassador to China in 1946. After illness forced C. J. Lin to leave the presidency of Fukien Christian University in 1946, the school had a succession of leaders, none of whom stayed long enough to bring stability. At several schools student protests made an issue of the college leadership. The students of Fukien in May and June, 1947, threatened to strike over the departure of the popular acting president, Theodore H. E. Chen; and then in November 1948 the student government demanded the resignation of the university president as being "too religious" and the dean of discipline as "too severe." Dissatisfaction with the college administration was not, of course, the fundamental source of student discontent. Student demands also included a call for more adequate rice subsidies and an end to the civil war; moreover, the demonstrations coincided with nationwide student campaigns. Nevertheless, the frequent changes in administration, the vacancies in the presidency, and in some cases the dependence on Westerners to fill the vacancies left many of the Christian colleges ill prepared for revolutionary change. Communications between the administration and activist students broke down in many of the colleges, and at the time of the communist victory school officials frequently did not have the sympathy and guidance of student leaders and left-wing faculty members.

[13] John B. Hipps was a key figure in the negotiations; see his account in *University of Shanghai*, pp. 141–151.

The years from 1945 to 1949, nevertheless, were not entirely negative ones. Concentrating on the tasks at hand, faculty and administration moved to the home campus and restored buildings to academic use. Almost as soon as the school doors were opened, social service programs were revived and plans for village reconstruction projects reactivated. Though the growth in enrollment created problems, it also enabled some of the schools to round out their programs and expand their offerings. Hangchow, which had added to its engineering courses during the war, secured recognition of its engineering department as a separate college and thereby qualified for registration as a university in 1948. St. John's fell in step with the other Christian colleges and registered with the Chinese government in 1947. Yenching developed a five-year course in industrial training which emphasized applied science and included one year in factories and three summers of field work. Most of the funds for the program came from local industrialists, and Yenching hoped eventually to have a school of engineering with a strong practical emphasis. In addition to restoration, schools undertook new building programs. Huachung, as part of a ten-year development plan, purchased several plots which eliminated private enclaves and consolidated campus property. Colleges were pleased that much of their support was coming from within China and from a variety of sources, and they interpreted this as evidence of their acceptance as permanent features on the Chinese scene. The Christian colleges, however, were to have only a few brief and turbulent years in which to attempt restoration.

Political Protest and Kuomintang-Student Relations, 1945–1946

College administrators were forced to recognize that political revolution was occurring in China, and with China's tradition of student participation in politics, revolution meant a positive role for youth in the transfer of power. Between 1945 and 1949 students became increasingly independent of academic discipline. Political activities began to supercede academic responsibilities, and the normal requirements of membership in a college community became unenforceable. The Christian colleges had historically been able to maintain tighter discipline over their students than the national universities, but by 1948–1949 many could no longer claim this distinction. The demands of students were forcing the resignation of college presidents and deans in Christian colleges as well as public institutions. Examinations had to be delayed or suspended and academic work for the semester abruptly ended. Decisions concerning the expulsion of student agitators had to be reversed. The Christian colleges had not experienced such turmoil since the Northern Expedition of 1926–1927. Not even the Sino-Japanese War of 1937 had seemed so ominous for the future of the Christian colleges as the revolution of the 1940's.

What were the students demanding and what were they seeking to accomplish? Examination of several student campaigns between 1945 and 1949 will illustrate a general shift to revolutionism among the students, as well as the specific role of Christian college students and the response of Christian college leadership to the move left. The loss of faith in Kuomintang legitimacy and the willingness of youth to accept communist leadership was based primarily on national rather than ideological loyalties. During the course of the student movement, New Youth came to believe that the communists, not the Kuomintang, could bring the peace and unity necessary to national growth and sovereignty.

Political activities by students during the first months after Japanese surrender underscore the desire for peace that pervaded the land. Though there was no coordinated national campaign during the fall or winter of 1945–1946, students had not abandoned their tradition of public expression on political issues. They sent petitions to the Kuomintang, addressed open letters to United States and Chinese leaders, and held parades and protest meetings. They expressed their longing for a new era of democracy and freedom or they attempted to influence specific policies of the government, but above all they protested against renewal of civil conflict. Two major characteristics of later student campaigns were already present in protests against civil war: criticism of the United States and the coincidence of demands by the communists, the third parties, and the students.

One of the early protests came from the Christian colleges center at Chengtu in mid-October, and it clearly revealed a consciousness of the unique relationship of the Christian colleges to a foreign power. In an open letter to Americans, eighteen Chengtu organizations criticized the use of American marines in communist occupied areas of north China.[14] Such action, they said, might encourage further hostilities rather than successful conclusion of a coalition agreement between the Chinese Communist Party and the Kuomintang. The letter called for clarification of United States policy and for United States respect of the right of the Chinese to establish their own national government. Signers included representatives of West China Union University, Yenching, and other Christian universities in Chengtu along with several Christian and literary organizations. The theme was picked up by the Chungking communist organ, *Hsin-hua jih-pao*, which published almost daily articles and editorials urging the withdrawal of United States forces from China. The Preparatory Committee of the China Liberated Areas Youth Association, a communist organization, sent a message in November 1945 to a world youth conference in London urging them to protest the presence of United States troops in China, and left-wing students in Chungking sent an open letter to American students with a similar message.[15] All these documents argued that the troops were a threat to peace, though occasionally they also condemned the troops as an infringement of Chinese sovereignty. The issue of peace also occupied the attention of the Democratic League, which founded an All China Anti-Civil War Association in November.[16] Kuomintang organs generally indicated their support of demands for an end to civil conflict and the formation of a coalition government, but they argued that the major deterrents to peace were the actions of the Chinese Communist Party.

The protests took a dramatic turn in Kunming, wartime home of several institutions, including National Southwest Associated Uni-

[14] Selections from the letter are quoted in *Hsin-hua jih-pao*, Oct. 22, 1945, trans. in *Chinese Press Review*, Chungking, Oct. 28, 1945. See the publicity in the *Hsin-hua jih-pao* issues of Nov. 6, 7, 8, 15, 16 in 1945, trans. in *CPR*, Chungking.

[15] *Hsin-hua jih-pao*, Nov. 7 and Nov. 27, 1945 in *CPR*, Chungking. The message of the Youth Association was actually sent by Feng Wen-pin, a party member long associated with youth organizations.

[16] *Kuo-min kung-pao*, Nov. 15, and *Hsin-hua jih-pao*, Nov. 20, 1945, in *CPR*, Chungking, Nov. 15, 21, 1945.

versity.[17] On November 25, 1945, the Kunming students staged a mass meeting to protest the renewal of civil war. At this time negotiations between the Kuomintang and the Chinese Communist Party were stalemated, Chou En-lai was leaving Chungking, General Patrick Hurley was quitting his post as United States ambassador in disgust, and there had already been military conflict between communist and Kuomintang troops near the Great Wall. As the assembled students listened to speeches decrying civil war and calling for a coalition government and withdrawal of all foreign troops from China, shots rang out over their heads. No one was hit, but the electricity for lights and microphone was cut and the university campus was surrounded by troops. The students called for investigation and apology and declared a protest strike. This in turn precipitated a raid of Kunming schools on December 1 in which four students were killed. Demands for apology and redress, continuation of the strike, a long period of mourning, and finally a public funeral in which the four were eulogized as martyrs to freedom climaxed the series of incidents.[18] Protests came from newspapers, professors, and many student groups; but academic work at other centers was not seriously disrupted by sympathetic strikes and demonstrations.

No national student campaign grew out of these incidents in part because many students were preoccupied with the homeward trek and others remained isolated in inland schools and out of touch with national politics. An effective national student union would have been needed to coordinate the actions of students in various cities, and nationwide student organizations and communication links had not yet been revived. Moreover, students and Kuomintang leaders showed a certain tolerance toward each other during the first months after the war. Though relations between students and the Chungking government had deteriorated during the war, the

[17] National Southwest Associated University had been formed from Peita, Tsing Hua, and Nankai; it continued operations in Kunming during the academic year, 1945–1946, with most of the students and teachers leaving for east China in May 1946.

[18] Robert Payne was lecturing at Southwest University at this time and participated in negotiations seeking a settlement; he is quite successful in conveying the emotional reaction of the Kunming students and teachers in *China Awake* (New York, 1947), pp. 199–236, 258–261. See also trans. of newspaper reports in *CPR*, Chungking, esp. Nov. 30, 1945 and Hu Lin, *I-erh-i ti hui-i* (Reminiscences of December 1), (Hong Kong, 1949).

Kuomintang was now identified with victory, and there was still hope for an era of peaceful reconstruction. Students generally addressed their petitions to the Kuomintang as the legitimate political authority in China. The Kuomintang leadership, for its part, tried to avoid direct confrontation with the students. Though there was pressure on students to concentrate on their academic responsibilities and there were attempts at censorship, student demonstrations did not ordinarily meet with force during the fall and winter of 1945–1946. Kuomintang officials as well as members of the Democratic League addressed the demonstrating students on November 25, 1945. The gunfire in Kunming on November 25 and December 1 was officially condemned, local commanders were blamed for the incidents, and the individuals alleged to have opened fire were punished.

The relationship between the students and the Kuomintang remained uneasy but tolerant until the student campaign of June 1946. Two aspects of the campaign seemed ominous for future Kuomintang-student relations, however: the students were rebuilding their national organizations, and the third parties and the left were making an open bid for student support in order to use student protests against the Kuomintang.[19] Incidents of violence, furthermore, bred ill will between students and Nanking. The campaign itself was relatively brief and was concentrated in the colleges of the Yangtze Valley, where economic hardship was particularly severe. After a period of relative stability during the fall of 1945, prices in the Yangtze Valley began a rapid rise in January. By the end of June the price index in east China stood at almost 2.5 times what it had been six months earlier. As in most campaigns between 1946 and 1949, the students quickly moved into the political realm. The civil war seemed so clearly the source of many problems that its end almost inevitably became their major demand. In their parades and

[19] Choi, "Students Unite to Put over $2 Billion Drive," *China Weekly Review*, June 1, 1946, pp. 7–8. Incidents during the campaign furnish evidence of student attempts to revive national organizations. See, for example, the story of the contest between the Tientsin Student Union and the head of a small medical college, a contest which the union won, thereby establishing its right to represent the students: S. E. Shifrin, "Da Jen Medical College Students Get Youth Reinstated, School Reopened," *ibid.*, June 8, 1946, p. 31; Nance, *Soochow*, pp. 125–126; Lamberton, *St. John's*, p. 218.

demonstrations, the students shouted a wide variety of slogans: demands for peace, national reconstruction, famine relief, increases in the salaries of government employees, democracy, and greater government attention to the problems of education and the people's livelihood.[20] The students, however, appealed specifically to all parties to extend the fifteen-day truce currently in effect in Manchuria and to bring the civil war to an end.

As the movement evolved, it became increasingly critical of the Kuomintang. The Nationalist government was still generally accepted as the legitimate government of China; the students quite naturally turned to it in appealing for peace and famine relief and in placing the blame for failure to achieve these. The Kuomintang government, furthermore, was responsible for maintaining law and order, and any attempt it made to restrict student activities was certain to arouse the antagonism of students. Both the Democratic League and the Communist Party were apparently aware of the difficult position of the Kuomintang vis-à-vis the student movement, and they encouraged students to concentrate on the civil war issue and helped them select tactics to make their demands heard.[21] Since negotiations concerning the extension of the truce in Manchuria were then in progress and the Kuomintang had made sweeping demands on the Communist Party as the condition of peace, the Communist Party and the Democratic League were eager to put as much pressure as possible on the Kuomintang.

Three schools which were to be important centers of left-wing leadership in the student movement from 1946 to 1949 were Chiaotung University and St. John's in Shanghai and Chekiang University in Hangchow. Students in the government institutions, Chekiang and Chiaotung, played a prominent role in organizing the initial

[20] Ta-kung pao, June 14, 1946, in CPR, Shanghai, June 13, 14, 1946.

[21] The Communist Party was especially eager for an extension of the Manchurian truce at this time and was using its influence in numerous quarters to obtain extension. The assumption was that a delay in renewal of hostilities would be primarily to their benefit. In a parade by Hangchow students on June 13, the economist Ma Yin-ch'u assumed the lead. Professor Ma, though apparently not a member of the Communist Party at this time, was associated with left-wing groups as well as the Kuomintang government, and he frequently participated in student campaigns. He had been a member of the Marxism Research Society and had been imprisoned, 1941–43, as a leftist critical of the Kuomintang (Wen hui pao, June 17, 1946, CPR, Shanghai, June 17, 1946).

moves of June 12 and 13. Students from St. John's were important in the next major action, an attempt to found a national organization to propagandize against the civil war. On June 19 the Federation of Student Organizations of Shanghai Municipality held a meeting to inaugurate a "Win the Peace Student Federation." Representatives from over seventy-two educational institutions, including most Christian colleges and many Christian middle schools in the Yangtze delta, were reported to have attended the assembly; students from St. John's and Soochow University were said to have presided over the meeting.[22] The goal of the peace federation was to unify the anti-civil-war campaign and to enlist support from labor unions, women's organizations, business groups, and cultural associations. As spokesmen for China, the students would draw up a peace manifesto to be signed by people of all occupations; they would call a one-day strike and hold a parade to publicize the peace movement; and they would send a delegation to Nanking to urge all parties to work for peace.

In translating their program into action, the students immediately ran into difficulty, and the incident arousing the greatest resentment occurred in connection with the peace delegation to Nanking on June 23. The composition of the delegation was indicative of its support as well as of the orientation of many student leaders. It included a representative of St. John's, Chen Chen-chung, and of Soochow University, Lei Chieh-chiung, and a number of civic and industrial leaders.[23] Most of the individuals belonged to neither the Communist Party nor to the Kuomintang, but to third parties such as the China Association for Promoting Democracy (Chung-kuo min-chu ts'u-chin hui), the China Democratic National Construction Association (Chung-kuo min-chu chien-kuo hui), and the National Salvation Association. Most of the delegates had grown increasingly critical of the Kuomintang, were in touch with the Communist Party, and were sympathetic with the communist proposals for ending the civil war and organizing a coalition government. A number

[22] Ibid., June 20, 1946.
[23] Members of the delegation included Ma Hsu-lun, Yen Pao-hang, Kwei Yen-fang, Sheng P'ei-hua, Pao Ta-san, Chang Chiung-po, and Hu Chueh-wen. Information on Ma, Yen, Sheng, and Hu may be found in Who's Who in Communist China, which calls the delegation communist instigated.

of them were beginning to assume the role they would play in the first People's Political Consultative Conference of 1949 and subsequently in the People's Republic of China: that of willing cooperation as representative of a third party in a communist-controlled coalition regime.

Shortly after their train pulled into the station in Nanking, the delegates were assaulted and several members injured before the police established order. The cries of outrage were immediate, and they implied that the attack was the responsibility of the Kuomintang government, if not actually its work. Chou En-lai expressed sympathy for the victims and demanded punishment of both the attackers and the negligent police; he announced that he would go to the hospital to visit the injured. The Democratic League issued a letter of protest. The Shanghai students were especially indignant because the most severely injured victim was their own representative, Chen Chen-chung of St. John's; their "Win the Peace Student Federation" decided to send a protest delegation to Nanking. The Kuomintang government was much more ambivalent in its reaction than the communist or third party leaders. After some hesitation, President Chiang expressed concern over the violence and government officials granted interviews to the peace delegates. The Kuomintang organ, *Chung-yang jih-pao*, however, had already blamed the incident on the "excessive propaganda" of such groups as the peace associations.[24]

The assassination a few weeks later of two leaders of the Democratic League in Kunming, Li Kung-p'o and Wen I-to (Wen Yi-tuo), did not improve the government's relations with the students or the third parties. Though the assassinations seem to have been the work of a local faction, the perpetrators were identified with the Kuomintang government, and Nanking could not escape the antagonism aroused by such terrorist tactics.[25] The peace protests, nevertheless,

[24] The parade and the conflict arising out of the peace delegation received publicity in most of the Shanghai newspapers of June 24 and 25, 1946. See *Wen hui pao, Shih shih hsin pao, Hsin wen pao, Chung-yang jih-pao*, trans. in *CPR*, Shanghai.

[25] Li Kung-p'o had gained fame earlier when he had been arrested as a leader in the National Salvation Association; Wen I-to was a poet and popular teacher at Tsing Hua. Protests thus came from many quarters: National Salvation Associations, Democratic League, Tsing Hua alumni, etc. Though Chiang

gradually subsided. Their decline may be attributed partly to the ending of the formal truce in Manchuria on June 30 and the realization that the readiness of both sides to renew hostilities made pleas for peace seem futile. Also, the academic year was drawing to a close and the students were dispersing for summer vacation.[26] The major consequence of the campaign had not been peace, but an alteration in relations between the students and China's competitors for political power.

Why should St. John's and to a lesser extent Soochow University become centers of political activism before most of the other Christian colleges? For one thing, St. John's, along with Chekiang and Chiaotung universities, was a locus of leftist influence, and there can be little question of the crucial role of left-wing leadership in initiating and orienting campaigns. Subsequent student campaigns in which a number of St. John's teachers and students were revealed as members of the Communist Party or other radical parties and in which St. John's was the source of radical literature will make the role of the left clearer.

The ability of radicals to exercise such influence first in St. John's and then in many of the east China Christian colleges was, in turn, related to the accentuation of postwar difficulties in these particular institutions. They had been deeply altered by the war experience and were continuing to pay the toll exacted by the chaotic Chinese environment and the uncertainty of their future. No longer were they small, tightly knit academic communities in which college tradition and a few dynamic administrators could exert a decisive influ-

---

Kai-shek condemned the assassinations and launched an investigation, many continued to believe that certain Kuomintang leaders had sanctioned the assassinations. Chou En-lai publicly implicated Ch'en Li-fu in the affair, filed a protest with Nanking, and requested an interview with U.S. Ambassador Stuart to discuss the matter ("Political Assassination," editorial, *China Weekly Review*, July 27, 1946, p. 191; Peter S. W. Wang, "Terrorism, Economic Chaos Make Kunming's Unhappy Lot," *ibid.*, Sept. 7, 1946, pp. 16–17). See articles in *Ta-kung pao, Wen hui pao*, and *Shun pao* from July 14 through July 31, 1946, CPR Shanghai.

[26] Southwest Associated University had disbanded in May 1946, but Peita, Tsing Hua, and Nankai had not yet resumed normal work on their campuses; this was one reason for the minimal response of the Peiping-Tientsin institutions to the famine relief and anti-civil-war campaign. It doubtless helps explain why the protests over the Kunming assassinations were largely verbal.

ence. Control over students was less effective and opportunities for communication between students and faculty less frequent than before 1937. With the inflation and government subsidies, the colleges attracted a number of students for whom economic support or political action was more important than academic achievement; the rapid expansion of the colleges meant that a high percentage of the student body belonged to the freshman and sophomore classes. During the war the Shanghai colleges had offered classroom instruction, but otherwise the students had been on their own in the rootless urban life of China's largest city. Normal campus routine had not been re-established before inflation and civil war occupied attention. Thus, the congregating of the students in the heart of the city, the lack of normal outlets for youthful energies, and the minimal sense of identity with their college facilitated the task of activists who would organize the students for purposeful activities. Youth, alienated from the older generation, found meaningful goals and a sense of community in student organizations and protest campaigns.

On the question of national loyalty, both the administration and student bodies of the Shanghai colleges were on the defensive. Since migration westward had been treated as a patriotic duty, those institutions which had remained in coastal China during the war felt a need to offer proof of their patriotism to those returning from Free China. St. John's was particularly vulnerable because its president in the spring of 1946 was under arrest for alleged collaboration. It hardly seemed appropriate for Western advisers temporarily holding administrative positions to insist on strict fulfillment of academic responsibilities in a time of national revolution. W. B. Nance of Soochow and James Pott of St. John's did not find it easy to set their students apart by forbidding activities in which students from the public universities were participating. Newly appointed Chinese administrators often lacked the authority to hold out against the demands of the students. China's political struggle was beginning to be fought out in the Christian colleges as well as the public institutions.

The Anti-American Issue, December 1946

The next major student campaign of the postwar era illustrates dissatisfaction with the Kuomintang regime and also a tendency to identify the United States with that regime. Since a protest strongly tinged with anti-Americanism demanded a clear response from students of the China Christian colleges, their role was a prominent one. The campaign began in December 1946, when hopes for a real coalition government were fading. General George C. Marshall was preparing to admit defeat and end his role as mediator. Major civil conflict seemed imminent. Instead of dictating peace as one of the five global powers, China was disintegrating into impotence and chaos, and the role of the United States seemed symbolic of a century of Western interference in China's internal affairs. The student campaign of the winter of 1946–1947 established a new image for the United States, at least in the minds of many Chinese: that of leader and symbol of Western imperialism. It also enabled the Chinese Communist Party and the third parties to establish an identity readily distinguishable from that of the Kuomintang and to increase their influence among the students.

The movement was touched off by an attack on a Peita girl student, Christmas Eve, 1946, by two American marines. Public reaction was relatively mild at first. Editorials of December 27 and 29 deplored the frequency of incidents in which American servicemen injured Chinese; they asked for investigation of the episode and punishment of the culprits. The Peiping municipal government lodged a formal protest with American authorities, who expressed regret and arrested the soldier accused of rape.[27] It looked as if the hope of Nanking and United States officials that the case would not be given "undue prominence" might be realized. The affair was not to be so quietly settled, however. Peiping students and the Democratic League took up the issue and initiated a campaign which was to spread to most of the educational centers in China and to last into February. Few of the Christian colleges enjoyed a peaceful January.

As newspaper editorials had stated, incidents involving injury to Chinese by Americans were of distressing frequency: jeeps running down pedestrians or rickshaw men, the sinking of junks by American ships, and brawls involving drunken servicemen. Though there was

[27] See the reports and commentaries between Dec. 26 and 30 in the Peiping-Tientsin newspapers, *Ching-shih jih-pao, Min-kuo hsin pao, Hsin chung-kuo pao,* and *Hsin pao, CPR,* Peiping-Tientsin.

resentment, most of the cases were settled or were dropped without much fanfare. Why, one might ask, was this particular incident made a cause célèbre? One reason was certainly the elitism of the students; assaulting a student had a different emotional impact on New Youth from assaulting a farm girl or a laboring woman. Not only was the crime considered more heinous, but the students could make their protests heard. During the year and a half since the end of the war, students had begun to re-establish their avenues of communication and organization and had gained experience in the techniques of organizing mass demonstrations. By calling on loyalty to New Youth as in the December 9th Movement, Peita students could once again win support for coordinated protests in the academic centers of China.

An examination of student demands, however, suggests that there were additional reasons for the vehement reaction of the students. That Yenching would join with other Peiping students in declaring a strike and organizing a massive parade on December 30 was hardly cause for surprise. Nor was it unexpected that the students would demand a formal American apology, punishment for the culprit, and compensation for the victim. Other demands were more far-reaching, though; a guarantee by American authorities against future incidents of this kind, an open trial with both Americans and Chinese participating, and the withdrawal of all American troops from China. Yenching professors supported this latter request in a petition asking troop withdrawal, and they also joined other Peiping teachers in a letter to Ambassador Stuart asking a guarantee against further incidents. Yenching students tried to give additional proof that they were not guilty of pro-American bias by taking the initiative in calling for a nation-wide protest by schools and universities.[28] Taking up the issue, Shanghai students demonstrated on December 30 and carried placards identical with those of the Peiping students at their parade on the same day. The following day, Ginling students joined other Nanking youth in a protest demonstration, and soon protests and parades were organized in Hangchow, Tientsin, Hankow, and even Chungking. Associations to coordinate the protests

[28] Reports on the activities of Yenching are in *Yi shih pao*, Dec. 30, 1946, *Shih-chieh jih-pao*, Dec. 30, *Ching-shih jih-pao*, Dec. 31, and *Ta-kung pao*, Jan. 10, 1947; *CPR*, Peiping-Tientsin.

sprang up like mushrooms after a rain, the "Student's Protest Association against Stationing American Troops in China" and the "Association for Protesting Against American Atrocities," for example.

The intensity and popularity of the anti-American sentiment shocked some Westerners, who had traditionally thought of the United States as having a unique relationship with China. For the students, the affair had become a question of national sovereignty and prestige. Phrases such as the American sense of racial superiority, insult to Chinese sovereignty, and affront to the whole Chinese people came into use. Many Chinese had hailed the ending of extraterritorial rights during the war as proof of China's acceptance as an equal and sovereign state, but almost simultaneously, treaties giving special privileges to the American military contingent in China had been negotiated, and by the end of the war the American military had its own communication lines, postal facilities, and court system in China. What had seemed barely tolerable during the wartime emergency became intolerable as American troops remained in China after Japanese surrender. The privileged position of American servicemen seemed to belie the renunciation of extraterritorial rights. Every incident in which a soldier injuring a Chinese was immune to prosecution by the Chinese judiciary revived memories of China's inferior status in foreign affairs.[29] The rape incident of December 24 simply touched fire to smoldering resentment. It was a cruel reminder of crumpling hopes for a sovereign and respected China. Because every incident grated on sensitive nerves, students demanded the impossible: an absolute guarantee by American military authorities that there would be no more such incidents. The United States was becoming heir to a century of anti-imperialist sentiment.

As the campaign progressed, another reason for the demand for troop withdrawal began to appear. The anti-civil-war cry was heard, and demonstrators began to correlate the presence of American troops with the continuance of civil war. Protesters asked whether the presence of American marines in China was in harmony with

[29] There had actually been a brief protest over this issue earlier when a group of students from National Chungking University had filed a protest with U.S. officials over injury to a Fu Jen student by an American soldier.

the United States role as mediator and whether the use of American soldiers in supporting the Kuomintang contributed to Marshall's efforts to arrange an agreement between the Communist Party and the Kuomintang. By early February the American marine had been tried and found guilty of rape [30] and Peiping students were saying relatively little about the original incident; their demands had shifted to an immediate end to civil conflict, an independent and sovereign foreign policy for China, and the withdrawal of American troops. The call for withdrawal of American troops was closely related to despair over the failure of General Marshall's mediation efforts and the imminence of war.

As open civil war approached, the communists had special reason to desire the departure of United States troops supporting the Kuomintang, and they worked hard to transform the movement into one which blamed the hostilities on American and Kuomintang policies. In this effort, they had the support of the Democratic League which also had special reason to foster policies in contradistinction to the Kuomintang. The League had broken with the Kuomintang in November 1946, when it had joined the Communist Party in refusing to participate in the National Assembly or a coalition government.[31] If it were to continue to have influence, the Democratic League would have to advocate policies different from those of the Kuomintang; it would have to strengthen its ties among the academic and literary communities normally supporting it; and it would need to cooperate with other anti-Kuomintang parties. Both the Democratic League and the Chinese Communist Party, therefore, took up the popular anti-American and anti-civil-war issues with alacrity. The North China Branch of the Democratic League, which included a number of prominent Yenching professors, proposed to issue a bulletin recounting atrocities of United States troops. The Liberated Areas Youth Association and Liberated

[30] There was a retrial in the United States in June 1947; the decision in this instance was that there was insufficient evidence for conviction.

[31] The Democratic League, an indeterminate grouping of associations and individuals, had split over the issue of participation in the National Assembly, with the National Socialist Party choosing to break with the League and participate. Earlier, the Youth Party had dissociated itself from the League in return for a Kuomintang offer of a large representation at the Political Consultative Conference.

Areas Women's Association in Yenan protested against the presence of United States troops in China and condemned Chiang Kai-shek for not protecting the national dignity of China.[32] On February 3 the Executive Committee of the Peiping Association for Protesting against American Atrocities supported a student petition to the forthcoming Foreign Ministers' Conference in Moscow for withdrawal of United States forces from China and voiding of recent Sino-American commercial and navigational treaties.[33]

Government authorities had initially tried to act as a restraining influence; and they had met with Peita students to argue that the case was a legal matter to be handled by American and Chinese officials. When such arguments availed little, however, the government resorted to sterner measures. On January 5 the Ministry of Education announced that university authorities would be held responsible for student misconduct and that they should take appropriate measures to prevent students from using the incident as a "pretext to mar and insult the dignity of our friendly ally." [34] With civil war being renewed, the government wanted to take out of circulation or intimidate individuals who were considered opponents of Kuomintang policy. On February 17, 1947, some two thousand were arrested, about one hundred of them students. The Democratic League, Peiping professors and students protested strenuously.

The change in Kuomintang policy was doubtless related to the change in the emphasis of the campaign; nevertheless, the Kuomintang paid a high price for its use of force. A protest which had originated with the assault of a Chinese student by an American soldier had ended in condemnation of the Kuomintang for totalitarian repression. In the course of the campaign the Democratic League and the Chinese Communist Party had represented themselves as defenders of peace and Chinese sovereignty whereas the Kuomintang had been labeled a client of the United States unable

[32] NCNA releases, Jan. 9 and 14, 1947.

[33] *Hsin-min pao*, Feb. 4, 1947, CPR. Mao Tse-tung, Chou En-lai, and Soviet leaders had on previous occasions made an issue of the presence of U.S. troops in China and had demanded their withdrawal as essential to peace. See the statement of Mao on June 22, 1946, of Andrei Gromyko to the UN Security Council on Sept. 23, 1946, of Joseph Stalin on Sept. 24, 1946, and of the Chinese communists to the UN in October 1946.

[34] *Ching-shih jih-pao*, Jan. 7, 1947, CPR, Peiping-Tientsin.

to guarantee either peace or independence for China. Those not wishing to identify themselves with either the Kuomintang or the Chinese Communist Party found less and less room for maneuver, and both the United States and Chinese liberals were forced to make choices. Although many of the latter began to move left, the United States retained its commitment to the Nanking regime, thus isolating itself from other political groupings and, like it or not, becoming associated with the continuance of the civil war and of China's weakness. The campaign had revealed that Christian college students, in the alleged dichotomy between China's welfare and United States friendship, would not be the last to attack United States policy; they would in some cases be the first.

Toward Revolutionism

For the educational world the academic year 1946–1947 had been one of sore disappointments, and the next student campaign, the protests of May–June, 1947, seemed to reflect the mood of all. Christian college administrators had looked forward to the year, for it was to be the first full one on the home campus for many. Instead, turmoil, hardship, and discontent had been typical. Even though the anti-American issue was not important enough in the May–June demonstrations to require special proofs of loyalty by Christian college students, their participation was more widespread than ever before. The knowledge that the source of most difficulties could be found in national events, not their own policies, furnished cold comfort to college officials. Some Christian leaders began to wonder whether it was advisable for Christian groups to stand apart from national affairs which affected the very existence of Christian institutions. Did Christian organizations not lose support because of their neutralism? The widespread alienation of youth revealed in the student demonstrations of May–June, 1947, pointed to the urgency of these questions.

Though protests had become almost endemic, they picked up momentum with commemorations of the May 4 anniversary. Under the leadership of the Association for Protesting against American Atrocities, Shanghai youth plastered up protest posters. Prominent slogans were: "Oppose Civil War," "Protect Human Rights and Freedom," "Down with Bureaucratic Capital," and "Unfreeze the

High Cost of Living Index." Conflict between students and police led to the injury and arrest of several students and strikes were called. With the meeting of representatives of the Shanghai college and middle school students on May 6 and the formation of the "May 4th Incident Protest Committee," the campaign was under way. There were also conflicts between students and authorities in Peiping over commemorations of May 4, 1919.[35]

To recount the dozens of protests led by students during the month of May would be tedious. Though the students had grown more efficient in organization and propaganda techniques, the campaign itself lacked form and focus. The protest was ostensibly against hunger and the civil war, but inflation and warfare had become two areas in which the students could hardly hope to have influence. In many of the schools the students also went on strike over side issues. The campaign illustrates the extent of demoralization by late spring, 1947. The techniques of the students showed the sense of hopelessness. Physical violence, clashes between opposing groups of students, scurrilous attacks on individuals in wall bulletins, and ultimatums were more common than before. The students, in their frustration, made demands which they could not legitimately expect to be met, and the campaign could not come to a clean end. There was little room for negotiation on some of the issues, no way of answering student ultimatums without a drastic reversal of Kuomintang policy. Rather, the demonstrations were kept alive by government arrests and raids; after the protests of May 4, 1947, many of the parades and mass meetings were held to protest injury or arrest of students. Thus, the movement fed on itself; it lacked a clear pattern of development. Throughout the movement, there were indications that some student leaders were primarily interested in expressing their dissatisfaction with Kuomintang rule and under-

[35] *Ta-kung pao*, May 5–7, 9, 12, 1947, *CPR*, Shanghai. The Peiping controversy, which began over Peita's presentation of two plays banned by the dean of discipline, led to demands for abolition of the position of dean of discipline. During the communist take-over of north China in 1948–49, the Peita drama group was revealed to be a communist front organization, and it seems likely that left-wing leaders already dominated the association in 1947. Certainly the two plays were sharply critical of existing conditions; one entitled "Return in Triumph" was an anti-civil-war tract and the other "A Woman and A Dog," was full of biting sarcasm about living conditions.

mining its legitimacy; since it had become dangerous to attack the government directly, they used hunger and the civil war as their public targets.

The student campaign of May–June, 1947, marked a turning point in relations between Nanking and the students.[36] Previously, those Kuomintang leaders who advocated keeping open the avenues of communication with the students had generally prevailed. At least until the arrests of February 1947, Nanking had officially deplored the use of violence. During May and June, 1947, Nanking began to use campus raids, arrests, and suppression of demonstrations frequently and readily. It was as if the Kuomintang had acknowledged loss of support by educated youth and was accepting its isolation. Student leaders, for their part, indicated that they no longer felt bound by the normal obligations of citizens under a legitimate government. A revolutionary environment existed in the sense that leaders of both sides ignored the regular channels for communication and negotiation. Both seemed to be losing faith in the possibility of meaningful exchange. Revolutionism, however, did not yet dominate the rank and file of students, and some members of the Nanking government were not reconciled to the growing isolation of the Kuomintang and the abandonment of legality. Thus, sharp internal divisions characterized both groups.

Partly because of divisions within their ranks but primarily because of government repression, student leaders saw the need to tighten their organization. First, regional administrations for the student unions were created, and then in late May students began to plan the revival of the National Student Union. When the organizational meeting was banned by the government, the executive group continued its work underground. Organization under such circumstances, of course, encouraged domination by a few disciplined and dedicated leaders. The union came under the control of individuals whose major goal was the overthrow of the Kuomintang, not concessions from the government or alterations in its policy. The outlook of the union was set forth in a letter to an American Student Conference on Christian Frontiers in the fall of 1947.

[36] This point is made in Dorothy Borg, "Students in Kuomintang China," *Far Eastern Survey*, Jan. 14, 1948, pp. 4–7. She is, however, referring primarily to the change in Kuomintang policy.

The struggle is basically one of the whole people against the fascist oppression of the Nationalist reactionaries. . . .

We therefore urge you to call for the immediate cessation of all military aid to the Kuomintang dictatorship and for an abandonment of America's imperialistic policy. . . .

Dear friends! The tide of democracy is already running high in China. It will not be turned back. The people of China are fully awakened and are determined to take their fate in their hands. The days of the reactionary regime, however much outside help it receives, are numbered. Its downfall is inevitable. A democratic coalition government of the people, for the people, and by the people, cannot and must not be prevented.[37]

The statement obviously coincides in language and argumentation with communist appeals and it was more radical than many students might wish in 1947, but the federation leaders were not likely to be repudiated in the face of government oppression.

What was the role of the Christian college students in the protests? The disparate nature of the campaign, the lumping of protests under the broad slogans, "anti-hunger and anti-civil war," and the role of government repression in the continuation of the campaign make assessment difficult. There were more strikes in the Christian colleges, and a greater number of institutions were represented in the protest demonstrations than ever before. Christian college students were no longer immune to government arrests, and the majority of their student government associations participated at one time or another in protests against arrests and the use of violence. The Ginling girls and the middle school students of West China Union University went on strike. Students at St. John's, the University of Shanghai, and Yenching consistently supported their colleagues and sometimes took the initiative in organizing action. On the other hand, there were also strikes which seemed principally concerned with campus issues. Though Hangchow Christian University students participated in the national protests, they also organized a strike in May to lower the passing grade in the school and to alter

[37] Excerpts from the letter are printed under the title, "Chinese Students Speak," in *The Nation*, CLXVI, 155. The letter is signed by Chang Liao for the National Student Union of China. Resolutions passed by the union on July 10, 1947, are in Ch'en Lei, *Hsiang p'ao-k'ou yao fan-ch'ih* (Demanding Food before the Cannon's Mouth), (Shanghai, 1947), pp. 131–134.

428 | CHINA AND THE CHRISTIAN COLLEGES, 1850–1950

the grade-point system. Fukien Christian University students joined in demonstrations over rice subsidies, government allocations to education, and inflation, but they also organized a strike because of the departure of the acting college president.

Perhaps the contemporary statements of university professors in Peiping are the most helpful assessments of the movement. A manifesto issued by thirty-two Yenching teachers on May 25 declared: "The recent student movement voicing opposition to the civil war and to starvation and demanding educational reform is the natural consequence of the students' dissatisfaction with the existing political chaos and of their anxiety over the present distressful situation they are in." [38] A May 30 statement signed by 585 Peiping-Tientsin teachers (including 141 Yenching professors) and comparing the situation in China with conditions on the eve of the French and Russian revolutions contained an element of truth. There was no established authority which commanded the respect of intellectuals. Ethical standards and a decent existence were becoming incompatible, and normal avenues for securing redress were ineffective. That most of the Christian colleges were also plagued by dissension and disruption indicates the pervasiveness of the revolt against authority. Just as American influence and aid could no longer protect the Kuomintang from military and moral defeat so the American connections could no longer cushion the Christian colleges against the effects of national disintegration.

Most demonstrators could hardly have had high hopes for the end of civil war and economic distress. More than anything else, the protests were an expression of frustration and of loss of faith in the older generation. Some student leaders were idealistic; some were working for the communist cause; many joined because they wanted to castigate those whom they held responsible for their troubles. Since the disintegration of normative sanctions affected all in authority, not just government officials, protests against all sorts of regulations might be expected. The corrosive negativism of revolution was abroad, and the students moved quickly and with little compunction into rebellion. The Christian college students were not different from other students in their alternation between protests over national issues and campus issues. It was a recognition that

[38] *Ta-kung pao,* May 26, 1947, *CPR,* Shanghai.

revolutionism had reached the Christian college students when in May–June, 1947, they ceased to be immune to government raids and arrests.

The students were rejecting the Kuomintang, and only a drastic alteration in Kuomintang policy and personnel could win back their confidence. Though most students in the spring of 1947 had not found a substitute on which to pin their hopes, the Kuomintang was commonly being identified as the war party while the left-wing groups were becoming associated with peace. Such a reputation may not have been justified in terms of the readiness of the Communist Party to accept a compromise solution, but the students saw that the Kuomintang tried to suppress anti-civil-war protests while left-wing leaders gave them support and guidance. The Kuomintang itself came to label all such campaigns as communist inspired. To a certain extent the Kuomintang was correct, for until 1948 the Communist Party was not in a position to bargain for more than a coalition government. The party could and did encourage the student movement in order to increase the pressure on the Kuomintang in any negotiations, and the timing and goals of the student protests from November 1945 to May 1947 correlated closely with the purposes and actions of the Communist Party. As the movement became more an expression of general disaffection than a demand for specific goals, it began to serve the communist cause in a different way; it created the impression that the Kuomintang had lost the right to rule China.

If the Christian college students were typical, and their actions indicate that they were, some student leaders in May 1947 had already decided that the Communist Party represented the only alternative to the Kuomintang; most students, however, had not transferred their loyalty to the Communist Party.[39] One effect of the Kuomintang's identification of all student campaigns as communist was to force a choice on students and to hasten the transfer of loyalties to the left.[40] In this sense the turning point in relations be-

[39] J. L. Stuart estimated that in Sept. 1947, 90 to 95 percent of the students in Tsing Hua and Yenching "did not want China to become communized" but that the percentage had dropped significantly a year later (*Fifty Years in China*, p. 189).

[40] This effect was frequently pointed out in newspaper editorials and educators' statements: see *Ta-kung pao*, May 31 and June 2, 1947, *CPR*, Shanghai.

tween the Kuomintang and the students occurred during the spring of 1947, approximately a year before the rapid disintegration of the Kuomintang's military position began. It is undoubtedly correct to give attention to military defeats in explaining the Kuomintang loss of the mainland, but it has never been easy to rule China without the loyalty of the educated class, and the Kuomintang had begun to lose this loyalty well before 1948.

The experience of the Democratic League and the Democratic Socialist Party demonstrate the inability of the third parties to offer a rallying point for the intellectual community. The Democratic League, which had gone into opposition to the Kuomintang, was by the fall of 1947 issuing public statements of short range goals which were hardly distinguishable from those of the communists. The Democratic Socialist Party, whose members had broken with the Democratic League over the issue of cooperation with the Kuomintang, also found its range of maneuver severely restricted. To students it did not seem any more an effective alternative to the Kuomintang than the Democratic League did to the Communist Party. The paucity of leadership offered during the student campaign of May–June, 1947, is exemplified in a muddy essay by Carsun Chang (Chang Chün-mai), head of the Democratic Socialist Party. In an article entitled "My Views on the Student Unrest," he stated that youth should concentrate on gaining knowledge and should refrain from using appeals to emotion, but that there were times when youth could not avoid appealing to the emotions.[41] The authorities, he wrote, should try to understand youth and not drive them to desperation; they should accept those demands which could be accepted and explain as fully as possible those demands which could not be accepted. About all that could be said for such an essay was that it was not likely to get its author in trouble with Nanking.

For the Christian college administrators the student campaign of May–June, 1947, dramatized the depth and extent of student discontent, and a number of them were disturbed by the politicization of the students and by their rejection of authority. They were cognizant that the Christian church had taught a doctrine of social responsibility and that now they needed to offer guidance to stu-

[41] *Tsai sheng* (The National Renaissance), May 31, 1947, *CPR*, Shanghai, June 9, 1947.

dents seeking to influence the future of Chinese society. Concentration on the immediate task of reconstruction was insufficient in a time of national revolution. Belatedly and generally a step behind the students, groups of Christian leaders turned their attention to politics. Many Christians, it seems, knew relatively little about communist theory, but what they knew appeared to contradict basic Christian values; what they heard about communist policy toward Christians and toward church property seemed in 1947 to offer little possibility of coexistence.[42] Christians, though, were no more successful than others in discovering alternatives to the disintegrating Kuomintang and the self-confident communists, and so in the fall of 1947 many Christian institutions and organizations remained reluctant to take a formal stand on political issues. After recognizing the legitimacy and patriotism of the student protests and condemning the conservative Intervarsity Christian Fellowship for ignoring political realities, a national conference of YMCA secretaries decided that members of the Student Christian Movement should only participate in student movements as individuals; the Student Christian Movement as an organization could not become involved in politics. Acknowledging that students were demanding a change, the YMCA secretaries decided to launch a movement under the slogan, "Reform thyself and change the status quo." [43]

Other Christians felt that calling for national revival through individual reform was a vain hope. Only a reformist government with nationwide power could serve the needs of China; thus, they sought to exercise direct political influence. Their approach was that warfare could settle nothing, the civil war should be ended and an effective coalition government organized. At the same time, they criticized American military aid as contributing to the continuance of the civil war and called on the United States to confine its assistance to relief and reconstruction. They still looked to the Kuomin-

[42] In 1947 John H. Reisner, formerly of the University of Nanking and currently executive secretary of Agricultural Missions, Inc., wrote from Peiping that communists were everywhere in the area and that wherever they were it was almost impossible to carry on church work. Letter of Reisner to Rowland M. Cross, secretary of China Committee, Foreign Missions Conference of North America, April 11, 1947 (mimeo., UB).

[43] Kiang Wen-han, "Chinese Student Christian Movement," CB, Dec. 22, 1947.

tang as the leading political force but asked drastic reform of the party. Various techniques were used to secure consideration of their proposals.

There were attempts to influence the United States to use its economic power to force Kuomintang acceptance of their program. When Lt. Gen. A. C. Wedemeyer came to China in August 1947 to gather information on future aid to the Kuomintang government, a group of fourteen Christian leaders offered him their recommendations. Most of the signers of the document were prominent in the Christian colleges, the YMCA or YWCA councils, or the National Christian Council.[44] They stated that Chiang Kai-shek was still recognized as China's national leader but that the present Chinese government could not expect to continue unless it regained the confidence of the populace. To do this, it must broaden the government coalition, guarantee civil liberties, insure the people's livelihood, and enforce rule by law. As to United States policy, its purpose should be to help China join the world community as a free, united, strong, and democratic nation. Such a goal could be best achieved not by military aid but by economic aid accompanied by measures to insure its efficient and honest use.

Christian leaders also tried to exert pressure on the Kuomintang. During the height of the student campaign in May 1947, they offered their services as mediators between the government and student representatives. Then, they conceived of a public appeal to both the Kuomintang and the Chinese Communist Party to accept an immediate armistice and open negotiations for a permanent settlement. On discovering, however, that there was the possibility of an interview with President and Mme. Chiang, they decided not to issue the appeal. The interview took place on July 12, 1947, and included first a conversation with Mme. Chiang and then a formal audience with President Chiang.[45] Spokesmen were Y. C. Tu, president of St. John's, and T. H. Sun, dean of studies at Cheeloo. After explaining that they came as eighteen Christian individuals, not as representatives of any Christian organization, they conveyed to Mme. Chiang their belief that the government had lost the confidence of the people and that it could win back the populace only

[44] CB, Sept. 17, 1947.
[45] "Report on a Visit to Nanking, July 11–12, 1947," CB, Aug. 7, 1947.

by assuring them of a minimum livelihood, personal security, and greater freedom. They hoped President Chiang would sacrifice party leadership for leadership of the whole Chinese people. Mme. Chiang's reply was that the party was aware of the hardships of the people, and it too desired peace, but not at the cost of appeasement. Christians could best serve the masses and the cause of real peace by giving unconditional support to the government. Chiang Kai-shek answered the plea of the Chinese Christians even less directly; he called on Christians not to stand aloof from the government and he chided the Protestants for not taking a clear stand for the Kuomintang as the Roman Catholics had done. After such an unsatisfactory attempt to influence government policy, some Christian leaders as well as Christian college students questioned the usefulness of appeals to the Kuomintang.

Revolutionary Politics in Command

Events in China between May 1947 and May 1948 increased the revolutionism of the students, and the tide in favor of the Communist Party began to run strong. There was less talk about a negotiated peace and more about military victory and political domination by one party. With a Mobilization Law, stringent press regulations, and the outlawing of the Democratic League in October 1947, the Nationalist government signified that China was once more under a war regime. Pleas for the civil liberties of peace time were out of order; disobedience and criticism were identified with treason. If Nanking was going to rely on the military to determine future control of China, then it behooved the Kuomintang to gain victories on the battlefield. Such victories did not occur; instead, communist armies began to seize the initiative. By the end of 1947 the communists had disrupted Manchurian railway service so that the Kuomintang had difficulty supplying troops in the major cities; in April 1948 communist troops captured Loyang, Weihsien, and their old capital of Yenan. With their military victories, the communists altered their political strategy, and they too began to find coalition proposals inacceptable. The decline in student demands for a representative coalition coincided closely with this change in the military balance of power and communist policy. Student activists were beginning to picture a China in which the Kuomintang played no role.

The third party members who in 1947 had called for a truce and coalition government doubted a year later that this was still a possibility. Of the six members of the university staff interviewed by the *Yenching News,* not one held out hope of a mediated peace.[46] Chang Tung-sun of the Democratic League had called for United States mediation in June 1947, but in March 1948 he was saying that a basis for peace negotiations no longer existed. Both he and Chancellor Lu stated that the communists could not be expected to make concessions in order to revive peace parleys while they were winning victories. Several of those interviewed went on to conclude that American aid was no longer of benefit ot China; it was instead a positive evil since it contributed to the continuation of the war. The statements on American aid had a special significance at that time, for the United States Congress was then considering a China Aid Act to bolster the Nanking regime, and left-wing groups were strenuously opposed to the continuation of aid. What was also noteworthy was the assumption of Yenching teachers that neither the Kuomintang nor the third parties could dictate the terms of peace and a coalition government. The initiative, they believed, had passed to the communists. Lei Chieh-chiung, who had been injured as a member of the delegation to Nanking in June 1946, and later had become a member of the Yenching department of sociology, stated: "It is certainly . . . fanciful to think that peace and a democratic China can be realized following the organization of a third party composed of a few Chinese intelligentsia who are good-intentioned. . . . This is because what they lack is substantial strength." [47] These Yenching professors were doubtless more pessimistic about the future of the Kuomintang than many Chinese who were farther from the area of communist victories, but the interviews do document the movement to the left of liberal intellectuals. Dissatisfaction with the Kuomintang-dominated coalition and the limited influence of other parties left individuals like Chang Tung-sun with the alternatives of political impotence or acceptance of left-wing guidance. To some, the latter seemed preferable.

Without making a conscious choice for communism, a growing

[46] Excerpts quoted in *CPR,* Shanghai, March 13, 1948.
[47] *Ibid.*

number of students had been maneuvering themselves into the same position. In truth, the position of students in China was full of contradictions. They considered themselves a privileged elite and in many ways they were; while receiving government subsidies, they were sharply critical of government policies. Some of their demands, ultimatums, and pressure tactics would not have been tolerated by much more liberal governments. At the same time many students were living just above the subsistence level, and they were subject to spying, blacklisting, and frequent raids and arrests by government authorities. The need to protect their position as national spokesmen and the importance of giving proof of loyalty to New Youth were persuasive arguments in gaining support for demonstrations at a time when they felt threatened.

The students had tightened and extended their organizations during 1947–1948. By the fall of 1947 actions were being taken in the name of the National Student Union of China, and there were even more effective working units available in the two regional federations: the North China Student Union and the union embracing the Shanghai, Nanking, Hangchow, and Soochow area. Despite their illegality, these federations were powerful enough so that government and university authorities were forced to negotiate with them regarding student demands. The numerous associations founded during specific campaigns as well as the student government associations of individual institutions were expected to work through the regional unions. Each association elected three representatives to the union and these in turn elected a standing committee to meet regularly. Through such an organization, a protest involving the majority of colleges in the area could be launched and directed. On more than one occasion the Yenching student government refused to negotiate with the Yenching administration without prior consultation with the standing committee of the North China Student Union. Below the regional organizations were city-wide units which during 1948 were almost continuously active. The student government associations of Peita, Yenching, Tsing Hua, and St. John's controlled practically all extracurricular activities in these schools; according to one report on Peita, the drama clubs, glee clubs, wall newspaper societies, and other organizations were expected to coordinate their actions with those of the student government associations and contribute their talents and energies to protest demonstrations.[48]

The Nanking government had become deeply concerned over the improving coordination of student associations as well as their political orientation and anti-Kuomintang outlook. It directed that student associations confine their interest to the internal affairs of the schools and tried to force the school administrators to restrict student activities. In consequence much of the planning and coordination had to be done in secret, in front organizations, or by executive committees; and as fewer individuals dominated policy decisions, radicals could more easily exercise control. These changes in the student associations, as well as shifts in the political climate and military balance of power after May 1947, influenced the nature of the last major student campaign before the communist victory, the protests of May–June, 1948. Confrontation politics was to be used to undermine the legitimacy of Kuomintang rule.

The campaign in the spring of 1948 gives evidence of deliberate planning. No one incident touched off protests as in the rape case, and it is difficult to select an opening date. Yet on several occasions similar demonstrations were simultaneously initiated in numerous cities. Students in Shanghai, Nanking, and other cities revealed the power and discipline of the student union when they passed almost identical manifestoes on May 4. Even the planning stages were typical of the campaign in that the radicalism of student leadership brought protests and violence. In one melee following a strategy session on May 3, school authorities had to call the police to restore order among Tahsia (Great China) and St. John's students. The selection of a central issue for the protests also seems to have been deliberate. Though all the negative themes of previous campaigns were present and economic hardship and government oppression loomed large, the unifying theme was anti-Americanism. The issue was United States aid to Japan, not a policy over which Chinese students could expect to exercise influence.

Unquestionably, protests over aid to Japan were to some extent a blind for attacking the Kuomintang government. Because of the

[48] A. Doak Barnett, *China on the Eve of Communist Takeover* (New York, 1961), p. 45.

close identity of Kuomintang and United States policy in China, an attack on the United States would readily be understood as an attack on Nanking. The criticism of the Kuomintang was made obvious by the constant reference to American aid to Japan as rebuilding the fascist regime; fascism and fascist regime were terms commonly used in pejorative references to the Kuomintang government. The attack on United States aid to Japan was also a criticism of American aid to China, for many Chinese were unhappy over the recent passage of the China Aid Act by the United States Congress.[49] Chou En-lai had long ago labeled American aid to the Kuomintang as unwarranted interference in China's internal affairs and a factor in the continuance of the civil war. As the tide of battle had turned against the Nationalists, many educated Chinese were coming to view peace as dependent upon communist victory; bolstering the Kuomintang government only prolonged the war. The rapid disintegration of Kuomintang authority in 1948, furthermore, meant that even economic aid and relief were not serving the purposes for which they were intended, so that they too no longer seemed desirable to many Chinese. The issue of American aid and interference was one on which the Christian college students were particularly sensitive, and as far as they were concerned, this was the area where they should concentrate their criticisms.

To ignore completely Chinese and communist interest in the future of Japan would be a mistake, however. A recent United States mission to Japan and Korea led by Major-General William H. Draper had brought the matter to the attention of many Chinese. Wishing to decrease Japanese economic dependence on the United States and to make Japan an outpost against the spread of communism and Soviet influence in Asia, the Draper Commission had recommended restoration of Japanese industrial capacity to a higher level than formerly advocated. This policy, of course, was not one which would find favor with the U.S.S.R. or the Chinese communists, and the Chinese Communist Party had reason to encourage protests against American aid to Japan. Condemnation of United States policy elicited a ready response from the academic community. One example of public support for the student protests was a

[49] Though the China Aid Act had been passed in April 1948, an appropriations bill still awaited action and was not passed until June.

telegram sent by Shanghai professors and academic leaders to President Truman and Secretary of State Marshall. Japan, they said, had not given up her militaristic ambitions, and aid would only help Japan achieve her war goals in Asia.[50] One of the signers was Ling Hsien-yang (Henry H. Lin), a businessman and the president of the University of Shanghai, who was later condemned by the communist regime as the "faithful running dog of the American imperialists." The issue of American aid in rebuilding Japan was a popular one with a many-faceted appeal.

As coordinated protests continued after May 4, the leadership role of the left wing became clearly discernible, and the communists seemed to be living up to their reputation among students as activists and organizers.[51] St. John's and Shanghai College of Law provided some of the most obvious evidences of left-wing influence. The St. John's Student Government Association prepared a poll on the subject of United States aid to Japan with wording so blatantly biased that unless a student wished to be accused of being a "running dog" of the Americans, he would choose the answer desired by the composers; the vocabulary was that of communist propaganda. The poll, based on the answers of 940 students and faculty members, was publicized in the Soviet-supported publication *Shih-tai jih-pao*.

(1) Japanese fascism has revived. Do you think this will result in another invasion of China?

    860   yes
     56   no
     14   other

(2) What will Japan's recovery represent?

     60   emancipation of the Japanese people and revival of the forces of peace

[50] *Ta-kung pao,* June 1, 1948, *CPR,* Shanghai.

[51] Maria Yen of Peita wrote concerning 1948: "The older liberals whom we admired we also knew were as leaderless as they were courageous. . . . Except our Communist friends. They were organized. They had discipline. They offered us leadership and the certainty of action. We could only sense vaguely the proportions of the Party underground in Peking, but we saw enough of the results it could produce to know it was there. While others debated, Communist comrades acted. They circulated illegal literature; they pasted up wall newspapers under cover of night telling Peking about the success of their armies. They organized strikes and protest parades" (*The Umbrella Garden* [New York, 1954], p. 6).

856 revival of Japan's imperialist aggressive forces and of her militarists and plutocrats

(5) What is the U.S.'s purpose in building up Japan?

726 American self-interest and desire to monopolize control of the Far East and Asia

21 true interest in the welfare of the Japanese people

271 counteract the U.S.S.R. and Communism and establish bases for this purpose

12 other

(7) As intellectual youth with college education and elite sons and daughters of the Chinese republic, what attitude should you take vis à vis the question of revival of Japanese aggression?

30 remain reticent

806 use every ounce of energy to enlarge propaganda to protest and oppose the American imperialists' building up of Japan

110 other [52]

Tsing Hua issued a pamphlet opposing United States aid to Japan, and the Shanghai Student Union helped found branches of the Shanghai Students' Federation for Opposition to America's Building up Japan and for Relief of the National Crisis. Public opinion polls closely modeled on St. John's were conducted among Shanghai students and their results publicized as proof of student support for the movement. As the activists grew bolder, posters at St. John's demanded a change in the Chinese government as well as in United States policy toward Japan. At Shanghai College of Law cartoons posted in late May illustrated the procommunist orientation of a few students. One poster was a portrait of Mao Tse-tung glorified as leader of the People's Liberation Army; another showed President Chiang and Vice-President Li Tsung-jen marching to Yüan Shih-k'ai's grave and was entitled, "Time Will Soon Arrive." A third portrayed Chiang kneeling before America with a new group of Twenty-one Demands.[53] Some students, for whom this exhibit was too radical, tried to tear the cartoons down; a free-for-all ensued. There was also dissension at St. John's, where leaders of student factions were assaulted by opposing groups. Violence became a more frequent accompaniment of student protests as the revolutionary mood spread. The Kuomintang was increasingly

[52] *Shih-tai jih-pao,* May 26, 1948, *CPR,* Shanghai.
[53] *Ta-kung pao,* June 1, 1948, *CPR,* Shanghai.

presented as the main deterrent to China's peace and prosperity, and the protests were a technique for undermining Kuomintang legitimacy, not for seeking concessions.

By early June strikes, arrests, protests over arrests, and riots over rice subsidies were making a farce of educational work in numerous Shanghai and Peiping institutions. Both educational and political administrators began to concentrate on restoring order. Kuomintang organs called for summary arrest of professional agitators, and special criminal courts began to handle those accused of conspiring against the government. Even the older generation of intellectuals, many of whom sympathized with the protesters' goals, were offended by the tactics and extremism of the activist leaders. College administrators tried to enforce bans on extracurricular activities and unauthorized associations; at the University of Shanghai the Students' Federation for Opposition to America's Building up of Japan was declared illegal because the students had not followed proper procedure in its founding, and at St. John's students were forbidden to have any outside speakers at their meetings. Even Ambassador Stuart, ordinarily sympathetic with the students, reprimanded them in a public speech on June 4. Stuart warned the students against allowing themselves to be used by anti-Kuomintang organizations; he indicated that student agitation against United States policy threatened the traditional friendship of China and the United States and might have serious consequences for the whole United States aid program in China. He implied a lack of gratitude among students for the assistance given China by the American people. The reaction was instantaneous and hostile.

The campaign of 1948 received a new stimulus from Stuart's speech, and the Christian colleges led the protestations. Among many Chinese, gratitude for American aid coexisted with resentment over American influence resulting from this assistance. It was not easy to be grateful in a relationship which implied inequality. Dissatisfaction with United States policy or belief that American actions were injurious to China could easily convert resentment into intense hatred. This conversion was taking place among those Chinese who had come to view United States aid as a deterrent to peace and to the rapid departure of a disintegrating regime. The bitterness of disappointed hopes for the postwar era was being focused on the Kuomintang and its ally, the United States of America.

It was understandable that those students who had benefited most from American aid were the ones whose resentment was most easily aroused. They were the ones most sensitive to any implication of inferiority, any implication that they were beholden to their benefactor. Yenching students called on all schools in Peiping to protest Stuart's statements, and even Yenching professors met to formulate a letter of reproach. The Peiping Federation for Opposition to America's Building Up of Japan called a strike and a mass demonstration against United States imperialism. A number of University of Shanghai students protested through a one-day hunger strike, and others held a comfort rally for the fasters. In Canton, Lingnan students and members of the Association of Returned Students from America publicly expressed their dissatisfaction; and in Nanking students at Ginling, the University of Nanking, and Central University instructed Ambassador Stuart to reexamine his thinking if he did not wish to destroy his record of service to China.[54]

Students particularly resented the implied threat of an end to American aid because of fostering an anti-American policy, and to demonstrate their independence some students at Yenching and Peita refused American food supplies and defiantly pasted crossed-out egg and soybean milk coupons on the wall boards. Some one hundred Tsing Hua faculty members returned their coupons with the statement: "In order to show the dignity and integrity of the Chinese people, we refuse to accept all aid supplies which the U.S. is extending us with the purpose of purchasing our souls." [55] Letters protested that Stuart lectured to the Chinese as if they were not the equals of Americans. Others asked why the Chinese should be grateful when the main purpose of American aid was to alleviate the economic crisis in America and earn profits for monopolistic capitalists. YMCA and Student Christian Movement leaders accused Stuart of slandering student patriotism and stated that the threat to end aid amounted to an attempt to use coercion in Chinese internal politics.

[54] *Hsin-wen pao,* June 8, 1948, *CPR,* Shanghai. Stuart's statement is contained in the Annexes of U.S. Dept. of State, *The China White Paper, August, 1949* (Stanford, 1967), pp. 869–871.

[55] *Hsin-wen pao,* June 21, 1948, *CPR,* Shanghai.

The sense of outraged nationalism which permeated all statements permitted no opposition and no explanations. Recognizing this, the communists gave all possible publicity to the issue.[56]

Revolutionary negativism had become so prevalent in Shanghai and Peiping that almost any incident or even rumor of an incident seemed sufficient to launch a protest. The goal of most college administrators was simply to close the academic year as quickly and decently as possible. St. John's held final examinations early and shut down; under criticism from the university administration for his irresolute policy toward students, President Tu resigned. Yenching lost its acting dean to a less difficult position. Other institutions dismissed large numbers of students, though this was likely to incur the ire of student organizations. When, for example, Soochow University dismissed more than one hundred for "poor academic records," the student government association launched an investigation and demanded explanations of each case.[57] Fukien Christian University managed to complete the academic year despite a four-day strike just prior to examinations. College administrators could only look forward with trepidation to the next academic year.

Surprisingly enough, academic work in many of the schools during 1948–1949 was less frequently disrupted by student strikes and demonstrations than in the previous years. This was true particularly in the schools in north China nearest the locus of communist power.[58] The year proved to be more one of transition to communist rule than one of struggle against the Kuomintang regime. Both students and administrators seemed preoccupied with their response to the impending communist victory in their area. For some of the schools, of course, the communist takeover was literal as well as psychological; the territory where Yenching and Tsing Hua were located came under communist control in December

[56] See the letter by a number of editors to *Ta-kung pao*, June 10, 1948. The Shanghai Playwriters and Artists Association was one of the groups issuing a protest; *ibid.*, June 17, 1948.

[57] *Yi-shih pao*, August 6, 1948, *CPR*, Shanghai.

[58] Some of the schools farther south, Fukien Christian University, for instance, were seriously disrupted by strikes during the fall of 1948; and, of course, the actual takeover of territory where schools were located involved some dislocation, but less so initially than many administrators had feared.

1948; the communists took Tsinan, the home of Cheeloo, in September 1948.

Why did protest demonstrations decline in Peiping and the Yangtze delta after the almost continuous disruption of the late spring and summer? One explanation is that many students did not return to their schools in September 1948; they remained at home to await the outcome of the military conflict; others departed precipitately as warfare threatened the locale of the school. At Ginling enrollment dropped from 480 in 1947–1948 to less than 100 students in October and November, 1948. Some of the institutions made a concerted effort to prevent the registration of known agitators when school reopened in the autumn, and the Ministry of Education ruled in September that students should be expelled from school simply on the basis of interrogation for suspected communist affiliation by the special criminal tribunals.

The radical leaders were less interested in protests; some left school for areas already under Communist Party rule; they feared last minute purges by the Kuomintang, and they wanted to aid the communists in assuming administrative control as they moved south. Protests were no longer needed to demonstrate that the Kuomintang had lost the Mandate of Heaven. Even those least enthusiastic about communism were no longer prepared to defend the Kuomintang; they had even abandoned hope for a Kuomintang-Communist coalition. The student activists had effectively used student discontent to encourage protests which poisoned relations between the Kuomintang and the educated class and which destroyed faith in the Kuomintang's ability to provide order and justice. The decline in agitation as communist rule approached supports the hypothesis that demonstrations were deliberately initiated and fostered by the leftists. In 1948–1949, leftist leaders had before them the task of smoothing the transition to control by the Communist Party, of convincing academicians that it would be possible to continue their work under the People's Republic. Protests and strikes would not serve this purpose and were no longer desirable. Christian college leaders, like others, were grateful for the indications that the transition would be orderly and began to make the necessary adjustments in their thinking and in the administration of their institutions.

XII | Amalgamation

The immediate postwar years had been characterized by the growing impingement of national affairs on the life of academic institutions and individual students. Though some students had remained aloof from politics, inflation and civil war had forced most of the academic world to give attention to national concerns. By 1948 the atmosphere on many campuses was revolutionary and intensely political. This impingement of politics on academic life was to be a continuing theme after the communist victory, but the political demands and the doctrinal guidelines henceforth would come directly from the ruling party rather than from student organizations or competing political organizations. Few Chinese in 1948–1949 understood the thoroughness with which education would be subordinated to national and party politics during the coming decade. Few anticipated apparently that even the life of their institutions would be threatened in the national revolution to be undertaken by the Communist Party. It seems probable, in fact, that party leaders themselves had no clear picture of the educational system to be instituted for new China.

The officials who in 1948–1949 became responsible for governing the world's most populous state had had long experience in revolution and in warfare. They had also exercised political authority in certain sectors of China, though under highly abnormal circumstances. They were now to function as the legitimate rulers of China, and adjustments in technique and orientation were essential. Revolutionary goals and lack of experience at first contributed to a certain naiveté in the conduct of foreign affairs and ambiguity in educational policy. While the dual tasks of completing the military

444

conquest and restoring political and economic order occupied the attention of party officials, moderation characterized educational policy. To have pushed through a new educational program immediately, to have ousted numerous teachers and administrators would have created a vacuum that the Communist Party was not yet ready to fill; furthermore, the party had not yet formulated a detailed educational program for the new circumstances in which it found itself. The years 1948–1951 formed a transitional era often labeled the period of New Democracy, though pragmatism as much as New Democratic theory guided the actions of Peking. By 1951 anti-Americanism had become one of the earmarks of China's foreign policy, and the guidelines of an educational policy to foster national revolution were being drawn. Neither offered favorable prospects for the future of the China Christian colleges.

Transition to Communist Control

Amid the initial uncertainty about the regime's policy toward religion, education, and Westerners, certain party actions seemed to indicate that Christians would be permitted to continue their social service work and religious activities. According to Mao Tse-tung, the culture of New Democracy should be national, scientific, and popular; and glosses in 1949 disclosed that the main task of education would be to help create a New Democratic culture by replacing "feudal, comprador, Fascist ideology" with an ideology of serving the people.[1] Christians generally believed that the Christian colleges could work within this framework, at least as far as they understood the terms. The People's Political Consultative Conference, called in September 1949 to legitimatize the new regime, included five Christians and two Buddhist representatives; and it passed the Common Program, in which religious freedom was promised and strengthening of middle and higher education was advocated. The communists, furthermore, appeared to have abandoned their policy of open antagonism toward religious institutions as they had extended their territorial control during 1948–1949.

[1] Mao Tse-tung, "On New Democracy," in *Selected Works of Mao Tse-tung*, III (New York, 1954), 153–155; "The Common Program," *China Digest*, VII, no. 1 (Oct. 1949), pp. 3–9. Articles from the Common Program on education are reprinted in Stewart Fraser, comp. and ed., *Chinese Communist Education: Records of the First Decade* (Nashville, 1965), pp. 83–84.

Earlier, Christian institutions and families had often suffered property loss when territory came under communist sway, and their buildings had been favorite targets in the billeting of troops, but during 1949 the orderliness of the conquering Red Army and its respect for property had become cause for comment. Christian churches and schools were sometimes able to continue operations even during the period of occupation.

Uneasiness was, of course, mixed with the rising hopes. Marx's views on religion were well known, and in light of previous policies by the Chinese Communist Party, Christian educators had no assurance that the current policy of tolerance would be permanent. Throughout its history the party had shown ambivalence toward intellectuals, who had been attracted to Marxism quite early and had furnished much of the party leadership; the party had often used students and other educated groups when interests coincided; yet the party could not fully accept the intellectuals as trustworthy, for they were classified as bourgeoisie and much of their training had been within the West European tradition. Anti-Americanism, closely associated with opposition to the Kuomintang, was not a battle cry to be lightly abandoned, and Christian institutions could not be certain that they would not be a focus for anti-Americanism in the future.

While the military conquest was in progress, the party provided general guidelines but left local military administrators considerable autonomy in applying them. The treatment of Christians and their institutions therefore differed. After Cheeloo College of Arts and Sciences and College of Medicine fled communist rule in the summer of 1948, the party opened an institute for training cadres in the unused buildings; when Cheeloo returned a year later, it had great difficulty repossessing all of the buildings. The communists also made it known that President Wu K'e-ming was no longer acceptable and must be replaced by someone who had remained in Tsinan through the transfer of authority. The arts college suffered gradual attrition, as no new students were allowed to matriculate in this division. Yenching, on the other hand, continued in operation while the communists took control of the Peiping suburbs in December 1948, and Westerners reported that, except for restrictions on travel, they encountered little interference with their activities. Individual communists were said to have established contact with sympathetic students and to have organized lectures, but official representations to the university administration were avoided until more specific guidelines on religious and educational policy had been provided. In certain cities the communists looked to the students to organize welcoming demonstrations as evidence of popular enthusiasm for the new regime.[2]

The reactions of the academic communities varied as they realized that communist rule was about to become a reality. Some Chinese Christian leaders, some teachers in the Christian colleges, and quite a number of students in the Christian institutions were in contact with party members before the arrival of the Red Army and looked forward eagerly to a new era under communist control. One member of Ginling expressed her reaction in a poem written soon after the communists took Nanking.

The dictator sat in his palace, clad in gorgeous garments,
    fed with rare foods
Produced by the labor of ordinary men.
He was waited on by numerous attendants,
Flattered by boisterous or deferential advisers
Who bribed or endowed their followers,
And who sucked the blood and lives of the frustrated and honest people.
They did not know about duty and responsibility.

Then came the storm and wind one night
From the howling of the offended people.
Palaces collapsed and the remnants of the favored ones fled.
Where could they hide with their sin?
The Liberation Army will pursue them to defeat,
And in hell will be their eternal palaces of fire and torment.
The people will be united to lash their souls and bodies;
Like water flowing into the earth the traitors vanish.
Such is the end of these treacherous imperialists.

Behold, a new-born kingdom of the people has come at last.
It came as a blessing from Heaven,
And as a free and righteous gift to us from God.

[2] See reports in *CB* for Dec. 28, 1948; Jan. 10 and 13, 1949. See also, Barnett, *China on the Eve*, pp. 316, 329, 339–347; Yen, *Umbrella Garden*, p. 139; Corbett, *Shantung*, pp. 255–262; *Yenching News*, XXVII (June 1949).

All the victims of the old kingdom will stand up and fight;
For duty is not neglected and souls are not blind.
The voice of our people will reach to the four corners of the world.
The people—the keepers of the light—will brighten the earth
Under the guidance of providence the patriots march to victory.[3]

Perhaps a larger number of Chinese had lost faith in the Kuomintang without really accepting the implications of communist rule. Some hoped for a coalition government in which they would have a voice as members of the third parties. Many, though unenthusiastic about communism, had concluded that rule by the Chinese communists was preferable to the chaos of China in 1948. Their hope was that communist rule would restore peace and order so that individuals and institutions could aid in the reconstruction of China and at the same time have the opportunity for concentration on their own growth and interests.

A number of Chinese Christians acted as mediators between the opposing armies in order to minimize disruption by eliminating useless resistance and assisting in the transfer of authority. In January 1949, Chang Tung-san of the Yenching department of philosophy helped negotiate the peaceful surrender of Peiping by General Fu Tso-yi, and in the spring of 1949 W. W. Yen and President Henry Lin of the University of Shanghai made a trip north to try to ease the transfer of control in the Yangtze Valley area.[4] The task of all those seeking to evolve policies for the changing circumstances was complicated by difficulty in obtaining accurate information on the course of the civil war or the intentions of the communists regarding religious and foreign-supported institutions. Many were uncertain whether the communist military victories signaled the birth of a new and long-lived regime or simply another episode in the continuing Chinese revolution.

Often the attitude of leaders of Christian institutions seemed to go through several phases as the Red Armies approached and they pieced together information about the Chinese communists. The initial reactions were fear of rule by those who were known to be atheists and concern about the future of institutions supported

[3] Feng Ming-yu, Ginling College, "Letter to the Editor," *China Monthly Review*, May 1951, p. 272.
[4] Barnett, *China on the Eve*, pp. 324–333.

by the United States, an ally of the Kuomintang. In April 1948, Wu Yao-tsung of the National Committee of the Y.M.C.A. published an article in the Christian magazine *Tien Feng* criticizing the church for its negative attitude toward a developing world revolution; the church and its institutions, he believed, needed drastic reform if they were to cease being reactionary forces molded by anachronistic capitalistic society.[5] Cries of outrage from Christian groups forced the resignation of Wu as one of the editors of the magazine. Acquiescence to communist rule might become a necessity, but it was hardly to be considered an opportunity, and relatively few Christian leaders could in early 1948 muster Wu's enthusiasm for revolution under communist guidance. The National Christian Council of China in March 1948 sent a "special word of comfort and exhortation" to its members as they faced a time of trial and suffering.[6] In July 1948 Victor Hayward of the National Christian Council still doubted that Christian institutions would be permitted to exist under a Chinese Communist regime.[7]

Some Westerners left their posts in north China, and mission boards delayed assigning replacements for retiring missionaries. Cheeloo's flight in the summer of 1948 did not, however, set a pattern for Christian college response. This was partly because of the rapidity with which Kuomintang power was disintegrating by late 1948. Migration to a section of mainland China beyond communist control with the intention of returning with the Kuomintang began to appear less feasible than the wartime flight before the Japanese armies. If the communists became the rulers of all mainland China, and this appeared more and more likely, a migrating college would have difficulty returning to its home campus. The best hope of retaining control over college property was to keep it in use.

Fear and contemplation of flight were followed by an attitude of acquiescence in the face of communist victory. In late 1948 encouraging reports about communist treatment of Westerners and of Christian institutions in areas already under communist control

---

[5] For a translation of Wu's article, see National Council of Churches of Christ in U.S.A., *Documents of the Three-Self Movement* (New York, 1963), pp. 1–5 (cited as NC, *Documents*).

[6] *Ibid.*, pp. 6–7.

[7] Hayward, "Overseas Newsletter," *CB*, no. 30 (July 22, 1948), p. 2.

inspired hopes of coexistence. A second message by the National Christian Council of China in November 1948 said little about a time of troubles, but attempted to answer the demand of Chinese Christians for political guidance and a statement of policy by the Chinese Protestant churches. Communists could no longer be portrayed as simply instruments sent to test the faith of Christians. Communist victory seemed too close to reality and the New Democracy program contained too much that was worthy. Still incapable of taking a formal stand in favor of communist rule, however, the council argued that the church was a spiritual fellowship and that its stand could only be "a religious one, and not a political one"; the church could never identify itself with any political party; it reminded members that the basic problems of man were spiritual, not political.[8]

Such a statement, though it showed movement on the part of the Protestant leadership in China, indicated much less change than many Chinese thought desirable; and some, especially those in educational work and social service, were ready for a more positive approach to communist rule. In December 1948 the United Board promised continued support to colleges under communist rule as long as they were able to remain loyal to their Christian principles and practices, and by January some of the Westerners who had taken refuge in Shanghai were returning to their posts in north China.[9] Various Christian organizations sponsored lectures and discussions on the meaning of communism and the doctrines of the Chinese communists. Some Christians were shocked to discover that the communists often couched their pronouncements in idealistic and even ethical terms. The techniques of the Communist Party might differ from those of Christians, but in their concern with social welfare and rural reform, the communists seemed to be pursuing goals that closely paralled those of the Christian reformers.

During 1949 a note of optimism began to creep into some of the reports on the present and future of Christian institutions in China.

[8] NC, Documents, pp. 7–8. See also, Frank T. Cartwright, "Protestant Missions in China," Far Eastern Survey, XVIII (Dec. 28, 1949), 301–305; "The Churches and U.S. Policy," ibid., pp. 305–306.

[9] The China Colleges, XVI (Dec. 1948), 4; XVI (Feb. 1949), 3; Victor Hayward, "Overseas Newsletter II," CB, no. 48 (Jan. 10, 1949), pp. 1–8.

Perhaps the enthusiasm of student leaders at the prospect of national reconstruction under communist guidance influenced some.
Perhaps those who had been unhappy over the refusal of Christian
organizations to take a stand grew bolder or were heard more
readily as communist victory came closer. Certainly the favorable
reports about the discipline of communist troops and the minimal
disruption experienced by most Christian colleges engendered hope.
Goals might have to be narrowed and Christianity would have to be
taught in the Christian colleges primarily by example rather than
direct exhortation. Complete Chinese control of administration
would be necessary immediately. But colleges pointed out that
China would need all available educational facilities and teachers
for a long time to come. If Christian institutions cooperated with
the new government and supported its reform program, would there
not be a place for the unique contribution of the Christian colleges? [10]

By the fall of 1949 and the actual inauguration of the People's
Republic of China many Christian college leaders were convinced
of the possibility of coexistence and were even proceeding on the
assumption that if they met the minimal demands of the new regime
in administration and curriculum, there would be room for individual variations. Cooperation, while necessary, would also enable the
institutions to have a voice in their destiny. The third message of
the National Christian Council of China, issued after the inauguration of the People's Republic, contrasted sharply with its previous
messages in 1948 and illustrated the change of attitude that had
occurred. It opened:

Brothers and Sisters in Christ:
Our country has already entered upon a new era in its history, and as
Christians we should with the greatest enthusiasm give praise and glory
to God for that awakening of the social conscience which we see spreading day by day under the New Democracy. . . .
Although the Christian Church in China has had a history of little more
than a hundred years, within this short period it has made a very real
contribution to the early beginnings and humble struggles of this movement which has now awakened China to a new destiny.[11]

[10] *The China Colleges,* XVII (Oct. 1949), 2; "Quarterly Notes," *International
Review of Missions,* XXXVIII (July 1949), iii.
[11] NC, *Documents,* pp. 9–11.

The council then pointed out the pioneering work of the church in such areas as the emancipation and education of women, rural reconstruction, introduction of science, welfare aid to workers, and promotion of vernacular literature. Christians should be happy that these tasks were now to be pursued on a much larger scale and should give their support to the regime; at the same time they had reason to believe that the church could continue to supplement the work of the government in education, medicine, and social service.

Toward Integration, 1949–1950

By late 1949 the Christian colleges were learning some immediate consequences of communist rule. Most Chinese accepted with equanimity complete Chinese control of college administration; this seemed to them a normal evolution which had been too long delayed. Since much progress had already been made, the replacement of Western administrators with Chinese was accomplished smoothly. Boards of directors were generally reorganized so that all members were Chinese, or Westerners participated without voting rights. When it came to the transfer of property titles from the Western board of governors to the Chinese board of directors, however, Chinese were likely to emphasize the legitimacy of the request, whereas the Western body would ask more time to arrange an orderly transfer with adequate safeguards for interested parties. Chinese Christians urged missionaries who had special talents and who could accept Chinese control of Christian institutions and communist control of China to remain and continue their work; these Westerners had a contribution to make and would be welcome. Those Westerners who had been closely associated with the Kuomintang and those who would find their new status as subordinates intolerable should depart.[12]

Christian college leaders soon discovered that the Chinese who would participate in policy decisions included not just faculty and administrators but also students and even the workmen and clerks employed by the school. One of the first changes demanded by members of the academic community in touch with the Communist

[12] "Message from Chinese Christians to Mission Boards Abroad," *CB*, no. 73 (Dec. 1949). The message was issued by an informal group of Christian leaders, a number of whom were prominent in education and youth work.

Party was the establishment of a university executive council with representation by all these groups. At Hwa Nan, for example, two-thirds of the members of the council came from the faculty and one-third from students and employees; in another instance the professors, lecturers, instructors, and students each had three representatives while the office staff and workmen had one representative each.[13] The wisdom of including on the council individuals who were in good standing with the Communist Party hardly needed to be emphasized, and the words of those in direct communication with the new authorities carried weight. The office of Dean of Discipline, anathema to the students because of its use by the Kuomintang as an informational source, was abolished, and its functions were assumed by the executive council or more frequently by a student guidance committee. By the end of 1949 approximately half of the Western faculty in the Christian colleges had departed for reasons ranging from retirement to opposition to the communist regime. Those who remained continued teaching but found it prudent to restrict other activities. They were able to travel only with government permission, a permission that was not always readily obtainable. Thus, the administrative changes in 1949–1950 were not generally disruptive, but they resulted in significant alterations in the personnel holding the top positions and in the general tone of the administration. Avenues for close supervision by the party were established.

Though the colleges were permitted to receive funds from Western supporters, financial problems grew ever more worrisome. The communist authorities levied taxes on all property that was not used for strictly educational purposes; this included income property and also land and buildings used for faculty residences, social service activities, and in some instances dormitories; schools with experimental farms paid taxes on the produce. Since the taxes were relatively heavy and the collection was sure, this extra expense was not an insignificant item. In 1950 Hangchow reported that its taxes on buildings, land, and agricultural produce amounted to almost US$4,000; several of the schools had to request emergency grants from the United Board to meet their tax obligations. At the same

[13] Hwa Nan, *Report of the President, 1949*, p. 3; *The China Colleges*, XVII (Oct. 1949), 2; *Yenching News*, XXVIII (June 1950).

time the colleges were discouraged from cutting staff, and they were expected to provide additional scholarships in order to attract a larger percentage of students from the proletariat. Chinese should have full control over the disposition of funds and students might well participate in budgetary decisions, but Western supporters should no longer be permitted to allocate monies for specific purposes. College budgets should be public, and an auditing committee with members from the student body, the faculty, and the workmen should be organized.[14]

Changes in college curricula during 1949–1950 were not drastic but were significant. Some changes seem to have resulted from the desire of students to anticipate the emphasis of the new regime as much as from direct demands of the party. It was, of course, understood that all religious instruction and activities should be voluntary and that Christians should receive no preferential treatment in matters such as scholarships. Since many students were responsive to the communist attitude toward religion, enrollment in religion courses and participation in chapel services and Christian fellowship organizations declined. Quite a few students even took the precaution of transferring to a government instituition or a private one not connected with the church. Enrollment was heavy in the technical and scientific courses, and liberal arts majors, especially those in philosophy and the social sciences, showed a sharp decline. At Hangchow in 1949–1950 over half the students elected engineering as a major, whereas less than one-eighth went into the liberal arts program.[15] Responding to a demand for short term and practical courses, Ginling introduced a two-year course in nursing and Soochow initiated programs in pharmacy and nursing. Such an emphasis had, of course, been encouraged by the Kuomintang throughout the 1930's and 1940's, but had been resisted by students who looked forward to careers in education or in the government. Now the students were assuming that the government would actually follow through with its program of social and economic reconstruction and that it would have an important role in the allocation of jobs to graduates.

[14] Hwa Nan, *Report of the President, 1949*, p. 3; *Ta-kung pao*, Aug. 12, 1949, in *CPR*, Shanghai, no. 950; "Inside Communist China," *China Century*, Aug. 23, 1950, p. 996; Day, *Hangchow*, pp. 136–137.

[15] Day, *Hangchow*, pp. 136–137; *The China Colleges*, XVII (Dec. 1949), 3.

The most important curricular change specifically dictated by the party was the elimination of courses in San Min Chu I and all other courses in history and politics not in accord with Marxist theory. Variously titled courses were substituted: Problems of the Chinese Revolution, Current Events, History of Social Development, Dialectics, History of Economic Thought, Imperialism, or Mao Tse-tung's View of Life. All had a Marxian orientation, and generally they fell in one of three categories: the political theory of Marxism-Leninism; courses in history, international relations, and current events as interpreted by Chinese communism; and "education in communist morality," that is, the cultivation of patriotism and a mass viewpoint. The classes were taught by instructors acceptable to the Communist Party, preferably a party member or a cadre who had received special training for the assignment. Yenching, for example, was requested to appoint three professors with knowledge of communist doctrine, one each in political science, social science, and economics.[16] Since political indoctrination and ethical instruction had long been considered a legitimate function of Chinese education, the introduction of required courses in the current orthodoxy met with little resistance on philosophical grounds.

The new regime intended to go much further than previous ones in placing education at the service of the state, however, and it would have greater power to enforce its demands than any previous Chinese government. The Communist Party, for example, organized institutes called revolutionary universities in which short term training programs for cadres were offered; students were encouraged to transfer to these institutes so that they could aid the party in organizing the new administration and initiating the land reform. Some two-hundred Yenching students volunteered to accompany the Red Army south and help ease the transition to the new regime. As the land reform movement gathered momentum, students and faculty responded to calls to serve for two or three months or even a year. Among Christian students national service was interpreted as a chance to give concrete expression to Christian ideals and to their support for the new regime. College administrators found it impossible to demand the normal academic routine, since students were used to perform numerous minor political tasks and were frequently called out of class to aid in celebrations. They paraded,

[16] Edwards, Yenching, pp. 431–432.

cheered, booed and provided audiences for special demonstrations. Much time in and out of the classroom was spent in discussions of dialectical materialism and its application to specific national problems. At Ginling during the spring of 1950 students and teachers spent a month between semesters in intensive study of the "History of Social Development" and students received four credits for their work. Before the opening of the fall semester in 1950 teachers in many areas of China were required to attend special courses on Marxist theory and to illustrate in discussion sections their understanding and acceptance of the Chinese communist interpretation of Marxism-Leninism. The party also specified the revision of textbooks to make them accord with Marxist dogma and the viewpoint of the people.[17]

One early indication of the all-pervasive role to be given politics was the fate of the University of Shanghai, whose president symbolized to the communists the evils of the previous regime. Before becoming university president, Ling Hsien-yang (Henry H. Lin) had had a successful business career in paper manufacturing; as an official in the Central Trust of China and the China Printing and Engraving Works, he had also been closely associated with the Kuomintang currency policy. During the summer of 1948 fifteen University of Shanghai students had been suspended as radicals and trouble makers, and the school administration had been subsequently accused of cooperating with the Kuomintang in restricting student political activities and in compiling a list of left-wing sympathizers. Communist supporters quickly made it clear that President Ling would not be acceptable to the new regime. At the first faculty meeting after the fall of Shanghai in May 1949, an assistant professor denounced the president, declared an end to his authority, and walked out of the assembly. Following a prearranged program, the professor called a rival meeting of teachers, staff members, students, and workmen and announced that they were taking control of the institution. They launched a campaign to reorganize the administration, and ideologically unacceptable teachers and administrators became the object of denunciation in public meetings and wall newspapers; even a show of military force was

[17] S. B. Thomas, "Recent Educational Policy in China," *Pacific Affairs*, XXIII (March 1950), 30; Edwards, *Yenching*, p. 429; Thurston, *Ginling*, pp. 143–144.

used. By the end of 1949 most Westerners and quite a few Chinese had concluded that they could no longer serve the university effectively and had left. President Ling had been replaced by an executive committee of three and an administrative council, both dominated by communist supporters. The administrative council had assumed most of the functions of the board of directors, including control of the budget; and for all practical purposes, ties between the university administration and the board of founders in the United States had been severed. The university had also been required to house a summer institute for training 1,500 cadres to accompany the army south despite severe overcrowding.[18] To some Chinese it seemed that the communists were making an example of the University of Shanghai because of antagonism toward President Ling and his administration. The extent to which academic considerations would generally be subordinated to the demands of party politics and the national revolution was to become apparent only after the outbreak of the Korean War.

Even as optimism about the continued existence of the individual institutions persisted, astute observers began to realize that the Christian colleges were being required to relinquish much that had made them distinctive. Variations in the administrative structure and the academic programs of the separate schools were rapidly disappearing. Though Christian colleges had met many of the demands for Sinification made by nationalistic Chinese during the 1920's and 1930's, integration had never been complete. The Christian colleges, with their stress on the liberal arts, carried in 1949–1950 the marks of their earlier models, the church-related institutions of the United States. The China colleges had added a social service emphasis to the extracurricular program, but this particular emphasis had been defined within the context of the Christian purposes of the institutions, and social service projects had often been initiated in collaboration with or under the auspices of religious organizations. Christian college leaders had at the same time fostered the development of a campus community among students and faculty. Though a majority

[18] Chao Wei-ming, "Ling Hsien-yang," *Chieh-fang jih-pao,* Shanghai, May 29, 1951, trans. in *Survey of China Mainland Press (SCMP)* under title, "Ling Hsien-yang—Faithful Running Dog of American Imperialists." See also, Hipps, *University of Shanghai,* pp. 166–198.

of the faculty was Chinese, the staff was international in membership, and Westerners had often been more influential than their numbers would indicate because of seniority and of Western financial support.

With each new government directive, the incompatibility of these distinctive characteristics with the evolving educational program of the Chinese communists became more obvious. In July 1950 the Government Administrative Council issued guidelines in a document entitled "Resolutions Concerning the Leadership of Institutions of Higher Learning." [19] This statement, drawn up by the First National Conference on Higher Education, left no doubt that the one legitimate purpose of higher education was preparation for national reconstruction as defined by the party. The institutions should require that their graduates have scientific and technical skills, appreciate the importance of serving the people, and attain a high cultural level within the Marxian ideology. Most curricula in the higher institutions, it was stated, would have to be reformed because they did not accord with these New Democratic ideals. In addition to dictating educational policy, the Ministry of Education would have control over the establishment, revision, or closing of an institution, the appointment and dismissal of the president, teacher's salaries, and minimal standards of expenditure.

Short term courses, highly specialized and narrowly defined majors, scientific and technical programs were favored. At Hsiangya, for example, the medical curriculum was shortened to five years, and a special two-year program to train high school graduates as public health workers was instituted; texts, scientific theories, and pedagogical techniques from the U.S.S.R. began to displace Western models.[20] While courses in English language and literature continued to be offered, Russian quickly became a popular field. The new regime regarded the liberal arts program as a luxury that China could not afford during the initial period of national reconstruction, or at least it believed that such a program should be followed by the

[19] For a translation of this document, see Fraser, *Chinese Communist Education*, pp. 92–97.

[20] Ling Ming-yu, "Medicine for the People," *China Monthly Review*, Oct. 1951, p. 171; "The New Hsiangya Medical College," *ibid.*, April 1951, pp. 204–206; A. M. Dunlap, *Behind the Bamboo Curtain: The Experiences of an American Doctor in China* (Washington, 1956), pp. 75–76.

very few. Within a year after the establishment of the People's Republic, professional training had so far eclipsed the liberal arts that some of the Christian colleges could no longer be called liberal arts institutions.

As ties with the party became a more important source of influence than contact with Western supporters, the Chinese leadership of the Christian colleges changed. National politics often determined the appointment or dismissal of Christian college administrators just as had long been the case in the national universities. Westerners and those Chinese closely identified with the United States had difficulty defining a useful role for themselves, and so the exodus of staff members from the mainland continued. In 1950 five of the Christian colleges were without presidents, and though a few representatives of the West were still on the faculties, the academic communities could no longer be considered international in atmosphere or personnel. The diversity of Chinese higher education was rapidly giving way to one national system centrally controlled in all important facets.

In the field of religion the People's Republic had also begun to delineate its basic policies by mid-1950. During May 1950 a small group of Christian leaders met with Premier Chou En-lai to discuss the role of the Protestant church in the new regime and the ways in which the church could contribute to national reconstruction. The Christian leaders had no official mandate from church organizations, but in general they were persons of influence in the Y.M.C.A. and Y.W.C.A., the Christian colleges, and the Church of Christ in China; most of them also already had a reputation as enthusiastic supporters of the new regime. Out of the series of meetings emerged a Christian Manifesto, drafted by Y. T. Wu, approved by Chou En-lai and issued after minor revisions in July 1950.[21] Fifty Christian leaders sponsored the manifesto as a guide for all Protestant churches under the People's Republic; included were Wu Yi-fang, president of Ginling; Chen Yu-kuang, president of the University of Nanking; Chao Tzu-ch'en, dean of the Yenching School of Religion; and Y. C. Tu, formerly of St. John's and the University of Shanghai.

[21] See NC, *Documents*, pp. 19–20, for a translation of the Christian Manifesto; see Jones, *Church in Communist China*, pp. 51–61, for a history of the document.

Though certain church officials expressed concern over the irregular manner in which these individuals became spokesmen for Protestantism in China and unhappiness over use of Marxian dogma and phraseology in the description of relations with the Western church, the outbreak of the Korean War undercut open criticism and opposition. The document, officially entitled "Direction of Endeavor for Chinese Christianity in the Construction of New China" eventually secured the signatures of some 400,000 Chinese, almost half the total Protestant membership.

The purpose of the Christian Manifesto was said to be threefold: to point out the use of missions by imperialists in the past and to place Chinese Christians on guard against future imperialist attempts to use missions to destroy the Chinese revolution; to indicate Christian support of New China; and to hasten the building of an independent Chinese church. These goals foreshadowed some of the changes which could be expected in Chinese Protestantism. Since the United States was considered the principal source of imperialist plots, the maintenance of personal and fiscal ties with Americans would be difficult. A major facet of Christian endeavor would no longer be under church control as the government assumed responsibility for agrarian reform and social service projects. Finally, the Protestant Church in China should be self-governing, self-supporting, and self-propagating. Unification of Protestant denominations into one Chinese church under the leadership of individuals acceptable to the new regime became the focus for a campaign known as the Three-Self Movement. The officials of the united church would act as channels of communication between the party government and Christian laymen.

Though many leaders in the new Protestant movement were associated with education, youth organizations, and social service, the place of religion on the college campuses was steadily eroded. The range of religious activities was being restricted in the very areas emphasized in the academic communities; doctrinal instruction and church ceremonies, the major functions left to the church, had never seemed sufficient to most Christian college students and had not generally been as attractive to them as the social gospel. It was not enough that all work in religion be voluntary; in case of schedule conflicts academic and political obligations took precedence. Many of those who had taught religion courses and acted as advisers to Christian organizations were the first to lose favor with the new regime. Western missionaries, who had been particularly prominent in these areas, had two strikes against them as representatives of "the opiate of the people" and of the imperialist West, and they had little choice but exodus. Another emphasis of the Christian colleges was rapidly losing ground.

The Korean War and the Christian Colleges

Until Chinese "volunteers" entered the Korean War in October 1950, however, Chinese Christians generally remained hopeful about the survival of the colleges as separate and identifiable institutions. Except for Cheeloo and the University of Shanghai, institutional integrity seemed to have been retained. The colleges were still permitted to receive fiscal aid from the West, and the United Board, though disturbed by the growing importance of politics and party doctrine, was willing to continue contributions for operating expenses. There were still a few Westerners on the faculties, and religious activities could continue if they were not overly obtrusive. Annual reports and letters home during 1949–1950 spoke of the continuance of academic routine, of classes taught, holidays celebrated with traditional festivities, and examinations held. The frequent interruptions of academic work for political purposes were probably no more disruptive than during 1947–1948. The outbreak of the Korean War in June 1950 inspired a rash of anti-American demonstrations, but these were not new to the Christian colleges.

What made the position of Americans untenable and led eventually to the disappearance of the Christian colleges on the mainland was the actual participation of China in the Korean War through its "volunteers." By 1951 attempts to distinguish between United States policy and the actions of individual Americans ceased to be acceptable. America and imperialism became synonymous. To be an American, to be pro-American, even to be closely associated with Americans was to be an enemy of the people. Politics pervaded all. In the emergency all should serve the state, and service to the state should come before all. Even after the departure of practically all the remaining Westerners in 1951, the China Christian colleges seemed too closely associated with America to be allowed to continue. They were considered sanctuaries for bourgeois ideology, and their very presence was interpreted as an insult to the Chinese revolution. The techniques by which the Christian colleges and other educational institutions were persuaded to reorganize themselves out of existence are worth noting because they are typical of the techniques used in many of the reform campaigns.

The first units of Chinese troops apparently began moving into North Korea in mid-October 1950; and when United Nations forces under General Douglas MacArthur pushed steadily northward, the Chinese initiated limited action against the United Nations' troops on October 26. This meeting of Chinese and American soldiers in battle was accompanied in China by an outburst of highly emotional nationalism and anti-Americanism, and the sound waves of protest reverberated from city to city and from campus to campus. In many schools class work was suspended for two weeks or more as students organized rallies and engaged in intensive discussions of the Korean conflict. Great numbers of students volunteered for military service, and the small percentage actually accepted into the armed forces departed from their campuses with much fanfare. Then on November 4 it was reported that all parties belonging to the government coalition had issued a joint declaration supporting a Resist America, Aid Korea Movement. To those experienced in Chinese Communist techniques, this signaled that the Korean conflict was to be the focus for a major national campaign. Factories, schools, professional groups, and other organizations began to found branches of the Resist America, Aid Korea Association to act as communication links between the party and the people. Both Chinese and Westerners appreciated the importance of conspicuous manifestations of loyalty to China by schools, churches, hospitals, and other institutions supported by Christian missions. The goal was to prevent the institutions from becoming favored targets of the campaign. Urgent pleas for immediate completion of the devolution process were telegraphed to New York: transfer of all property titles and all authority to a Chinese body, registration with the government and acceptance of its regulations for higher education if this had not already been done. Many who had hesitated to ratify the Christian Manifesto now affixed their signatures, and those who had counseled moderation in the drive for self-support, self-government, and self-propagation, retreated into silence. Yenching students held a mass meeting to inveigh against those who listened to Voice of America broadcasts.[22]

In mid-December the Resist America, Aid Korea campaign reached its first peak in the China Christian colleges. Though both sides in the Korean conflict engaged in complex diplomatic and military maneuvers during November and early December, the result was not a peace settlement. Rather, the position of both sides hardened as the issues of Taiwan's status and United Nations representation for the People's Republic became intertwined with proposals for a cease-fire in Korea. Chinese rejection of a December 14 cease-fire proposal by twelve Arab and Asian nations facilitated United States attempts to have the United Nations condemn China as an aggressor. By mid-December the war had become part of the contest between China and the United States for influence in East Asia. With the administrative apparatus already in existence, the Resist America, Aid Korea campaign could be pursued with vigor. Among the Christian colleges attempts to maintain ties with the Western world had to be abandoned. Even the measures proposed in October and November to complete Chinese control would no longer be sufficient proof of loyalty. Most Western teachers ceased meeting their classes, since even social contacts between individual Chinese and Westerners might place Chinese under suspicion. Some individuals were attacked as instruments of American imperialism, and Chinese Christian leaders finally reached a conclusion which they had hitherto resisted: summary departure by American missionaries would best serve the Christian institutions in China. They offered to help the foreigners obtain exit permits, and despite fiscal difficulties and administrative delays, most Americans managed to leave China early in 1951. By May 1951 eight Christian colleges did not have a single American on their staffs.[23]

To those acquainted with the student movements of 1935 and of the late 1940's, the campaign tactics must have seemed familiar. Branch leaders of the Resist America, Aid Korea Association were

[22] Theodore H. E. Chen, *Thought Reform of the Chinese Intellectuals* (Hong Kong, 1960), p. 26.

[23] *The China Colleges*, XVIII (Feb. 1951), 1–2; *ibid.* (May 1951), 3; Leonard M. Outerbridge, *The Lost Churches of China* (Philadelphia, 1952), pp. 215–217.

guided by a handbook, *Know America,* which provided both factual detail and the overall party line to be used in mass rallies and discussion groups. The party, having chosen the specific incident to be the focus of protests, indicated its choice in the *Jen-min jih-pao* (People's Daily) of December 14, 1950; the government replied to a speech made on November 28 to the United Nations Security Council by Warren Austin, United States representative. Austin's comments, delivered during the period of diplomatic and military maneuver, had consisted principally of protestations of long-standing Sino-American friendship and had spelled out the kinds of aid and support given China by the United States. Austin had emphasized the large numbers of Chinese educated in the Christian colleges and in the United States with American assistance, and he had asked if these were imperialist acts. He had concluded that "thousands upon thousands of Chinese and Americans share a community of experience and a compatibility that cannot be erased by evil propaganda." [24]

Such an argument did not make the position of the China Christian colleges any easier. Among the reasons for selecting Austin's speech as a focus for the Resist America, Aid Korea campaign were undoubtedly Austin's very emphasis on the traditional friendship of China and the United States and his assumption that many Chinese retained a sense of gratitude and of special kinship with the United States. Whether Austin were right or wrong, his comments seemed to confirm Communist Party suspicions that Chinese individuals or institutions formerly associated with the West were not trustworthy and should be required to give public proof that they had cut old ties and accepted new loyalties. At the same time many nationalistic Chinese reacted negatively to Austin's implication of graitude due the United States. The Chinese reply, interestingly enough, was heavily interlarded with quotations from anti-Christian tracts of the 1920's.

Both personal indignation and political insecurity encouraged

[24] *U.N. Security Council Official Records,* no. 68, Speech of Warren Austin to U.N. Security Council, 526th meeting, November 28, 1950, pp. 12–26; the Chinese reply was also issued by the New China News Agency; for English translation, see Pi Ying, "Exposure of American Churches' Aggression against China," *SCMP,* no. 46, pp. 14–16.

immediate response by Christian leaders, but the timing of some of the protests indicated coordination as well as spontaneity. The day after the Chinese reply, joint statements condemning Austin's speech were issued in Wuhan by a group of American returned students and by various Christian institutions; prominent supporters were Wei Cho-min (Francis C. M. Wei), president of Huachung, and Huang Fu, vice-president of the university. In Changsha on the same day, an Anti-U.S. and Accusation Rally was held by various divisions of the Hsiang-Ya Medical School and Hospital. Lingnan students and teachers in Canton demanded replacement of the university charter written in English and of the school song which expressed a "slave ideology." Fu Jen and Yenching students joined in a demonstration against Austin's hypocrisy and American cultural aggression. Within two weeks protest meetings had also been held at five other Christian college centers. Though schools remained nominally in session during late December and early January, students devoted themselves to the patriotic campaign, and politically astute teachers did not give tests, check attendance, or require homework during the period.[25] Some of the colleges ended the semester without holding examinations.

According to Tseng Chao-lun, vice-minister of education, the Resist America, Aid Korea campaign in the Christian colleges should serve "to expose the crimes of American imperialist cultural aggression, to raise the students' understanding of the aggressive nature of American imperialism, and to increase their hatred against the American imperialists."[26] The public demonstrations, however, were used to rally support and volunteers for the Korean War as well as to denounce American aggression. One tactic was to have individuals who were influential with the students set an example. At a Shanghai rally on December 20, Y. T. Wu of the Y.M.C.A. and Y. C. Tu, formerly of St. John's, encouraged students in the Christian

[25] Other Christian college centers holding protest meetings were Chengtu, Nanking, Tsinan, Shanghai, and Hangchow. Reports of protests by the Christian colleges were publicized by the *New China News Agency* between Dec. 21 and 31, 1950 (see *SCMP*, nos. 36–39); Wang Yu-chuang, "Letter to the Editor," Jan. 30, 1951 (erroneously dated Jan. 30, 1950), *China Monthly Review*, March, 1951, p. 109; Yen, *Umbrella Garden*, pp. 153–154.

[26] *Hsin kuan-ch'a* (New Observer), Feb. 10, 1951, reproduced in Fraser, *Chinese Communist Education*, pp. 98–103.

colleges to transfer to military schools; Wu revealed that he had already urged his son to withdraw from St. John's and enter a military institute.[27] Other speakers immediately arose to advocate this course of action. Though Christians were in a minority in most Christian colleges, Christian organizations and students were expected to help initiate and organize rallies, and the need to prove their trustworthiness became a motivation to fulfill expectations. Individual students sought to expiate guilt by public confession of sin. A Boone middle school student stated at a rally: "Formerly I considered it an honor for Americans to teach me English; I imitated the foreigner's type of walking; I dreamed of going to America. I even indulged in obnoxious American movies."[28] Another student confessed to having once regretted not being born an American. Such public displays of penitence served a dual purpose: they were a warning to those who might be guilty of similar attitudes or actions; the penitents were committing themselves publicly and irrevocably to the new regime. Within the latter group activists and leaders could be found or created.

Indignation was, in certain instances, focused on specific individuals who became symbols of American cultural imperialism. Americans were initially chosen, and a few months later Chinese Christians became suspect. Among those signaled out for attack at Huachung were John Coe, treasurer, and Margaret Sheets, professor of English; and the accusations were typical of those used against other missionaries. Coe, it was said, had discriminated against Chinese in salaries, housing, and other forms of remuneration as if Chinese were lesser creatures than Americans; he was charged with opposing the construction of a dormitory for workers on the grounds that servants could sleep on tables or under staircases.[29] Students of the department of foreign languages charged Miss Sheets with spreading imperialist propaganda and slandering China by accepting the American version of the Korean War and Chinese action in Tibet. The students took their indictment to the Student Union, which first held an accusation meeting of students in all mission schools in Wuhan and then called a meeting of all academic groups

[27] NCNA, Dec. 23, 1950, *SCMP*, no. 36.
[28] *Ibid.*, Jan. 12, 1951, *SCMP*, no. 47.
[29] *Ibid.*

in Wuhan. The Wuhan Student Union issued a formal statement condemning the views of Miss Sheets and Warren Austin and supporting the Resist America, Aid Korea campaign. On the recommendation of the Teachers' and Workers' Union, the Huachung Administrative Council terminated Miss Sheets' classroom work immediately and began action for her dismissal.[30]

Through such accusation campaigns, missionaries were relieved of their positions without a direct attack on their Christian faith or activities, an attack which it would have been difficult for Chinese Christians to support. These accusations, and others against former Christian college leaders such as Stuart of Yenching and John Ferguson of the University of Nanking, provided a focus for the Resist America, Aid Korea campaign in the Christian colleges.

On December 17, 1950, as the campaign was gathering momentum, the United States government froze all Chinese communist assets in the United States and made it unlawful to remit funds to mainland China without special license; within two weeks the People's Republic had replied in kind.[31] The Christian colleges immediately found themselves in a dilemma with serious implications for their continued existence. Under government regulations, raising tuition to make up for the lost income was not permissible; nor was it likely that sufficient support would be forthcoming from private Chinese sources. Christian college leaders had to seek government aid or accept drastic retrenchment. Though the former might threaten institutional independence, the latter was unacceptable, and so the colleges publicly welcomed the ending of ties with imperialism and turned to the government for guidance. They supported the party's official interpretation of United States action in their public statements; the United States had cut financial ties, it was said, because the attacks on Warren Austin and American imperialist policy had demonstrated that the United States would no longer be able to use the educational and religious institutions for

[30] *Ta-kung pao,* Hong Kong, Dec. 23, 1950, Dec. 25, 1950, *SCMP,* nos. 36, 37.

[31] The United Board requested a special license to enable it to continue to send funds but was unable to secure such permission until May 1951; by this time relations between China and the United States had so deteriorated that the colleges were no longer willing or able to accept the proffered aid.

cultural aggression.[32] Yenching issued a statement on January 3, 1951, condemning United States attempts to threaten the livelihood of Chinese personnel in American-subsidized institutions and thereby to undermine their loyalty to the Chinese people and government.[33] On January 16, 1951, the Minister of Education convened a meeting of representatives of the foreign-subsidized institutions to discuss their future. They agreed that the Christian colleges would move toward nationalization and in the meantime greater emphasis would be given to exterminating American influence in the colleges.

A number of administrative changes were made in 1951. The University of Nanking and Ginling were merged as National Chinling University, and Fukien University and Hwa Nan were united. Both amalgamations had long been advocated, and an important obstacle to attainment had been removed with the termination of support by denominational mission boards. Yenching became National Yenching University and West China Union University became National Hua Hsi University, with substantial aid coming from the government. Lingnan also found that it could not subsist on income from private sources and turned to the government. A more far-reaching change was the union of Huachung with the normal college of Chung Yuan University to form National Huachung University, an institution to prepare middle school teachers; nevertheless, this move accorded with the long-standing interest of Huachung president Francis Wei in teacher education. In most of the above cases the Christian college administrators remained in office through the reorganization; Li Fang-hsün of the University of Nanking, for example, became president of National Chinling University and Wu Yi-fang vice-president. Approximately a year was to pass before most Christian colleges disappeared as part of a drastic reorganization of the institutional structure of higher education.

Accusation Campaigns, 1951

Much of the energy of students and teachers during 1951 went into campaigns to rid higher education of American influence. This

[32] "U.S. Pressure on China Backfires," *China Monthly Review*, Feb. 1951, pp. 86–87.
[33] NCNA, Jan. 4, 1951, *SCMP*, no. 41.

action was deemed necessary not only because the United States was considered the number-one enemy of China, but also because Western influences were considered the major deterrent to attaining the educational goals of the People's Republic. The important targets were Chinese who gave evidence of being deeply influenced by Western Christianity, Western education, or loyalty to Western friends. Many Chinese in Christian institutions, it was said, were willing to condemn American imperialism but tried to make exceptions of the missionary effort, or their particular institution, or specific Western acquaintances. Some adopted an above-politics attitude, and some thought it was sufficient to praise the present without condemning the past. Realization of the ways in which American imperialism had used Christian institutions and of the ways in which seeming American friends had been exponents of bourgeois ideology had to be brought to the conscious level. Those who thought it possible to give general support to the new regime while fostering Western educational goals, curricula, and techniques must be helped to realize their error. During 1951, therefore, Christian institutions were encouraged to hold accusation meetings in order to expose imperialist influences and wipe them out.

Instructions on the staging of a mass rally are given in "How To Hold a Successful Accusation Meeting" by Y.M.C.A. secretary Liu Liang-mo.[34] An accusation committee should first be organized to study what to accuse and who should do the accusing. Potential participants should be instructed in the purposes and techniques of the accusation meeting, and then a practice meeting should be held to select those individuals who were most effective and to aid them in perfecting their speeches. During the meeting itself care should be taken to maintain decorum and at the same time build an atmosphere of high tension; thus, the initial speaker, who should create high tension, should be followed by one in a somewhat lower key before the meeting moved toward a climax. At all stages of the campaign the accusation committee should maintain contact with local party representatives and with the local branch of the Resist America, Aid Korea Association. Especially effective speeches should be recorded and published; especially useful materials collected for public exhibit, and evidences of disloyalty reported to the

[34] NCNA, May 15, 1951, reprinted in NC, *Documents,* pp. 49–51.

police. Though not all accusation meetings attained the standards set forth by Liu Liang-mo, the emotionally charged atmosphere was clearly designed to overcome the doubts of the reluctant and the qualifications of those wishing to avoid absolutes. Individuals who had tried to remain apart from politics or had thought it un-Christian to engage in public denunciation were urged to participate in order to make their commitment public and irrevocable. If possible, accusations should be made by those closely associated with the accused. A twofold purpose would then be served; the audience would be convinced of the truth of the accusation since it was made by a friend; in order to make the accusation and still maintain his self-respect, the accuser would need to cultivate within himself a highly emotionalized hatred of the crimes of the accused.

In some instances the accused no longer held influential positions in the Christian colleges. Ling Hsien-yang had been ousted from the presidency of the University of Shanghai in 1949 and had been living in seclusion since then, but he could still be considered representative of those who had committed crimes against the people. In April 1951 he was arrested and his service to American imperialism and Kuomintang "feudalism" widely publicized.[35] Frank Price, who had been closely identified with rural reform, was condemned by former colleagues as a retainer of Chiang Kai-shek; and John Cox of Hsiangya was accused of stealing national treasures when he tried to export his Chinese coin collection and other curios.[36] More typically, however, the object of struggle in a Christian college was a Chinese currently holding an administrative position, one who seemed to symbolize and embody the distinctiveness of the Christian colleges. To be most effective, the confession by the accused should take an autobiographical form; through his self-examination he should destroy his old self and also force other participants to hold up a mirror to their own lives.

One confession during the accusation campaign of 1951 was made

[35] *Chieh-fang jih-pao*, May 29, 1951; trans. in *SCMP*.

[36] "The New Hsiangya Medical College," *China Monthly Review* (April 1951), pp. 204–206; Sophia Chang, "Reply to an American Friend," *ibid.* (Feb. 1951), pp. 91–95; Jones, *Church in Communist China*, pp. 64–65. For a discussion of some of the techniques of persuasion, see Chen, *Thought Reform*, pp. 59–71 and Robert J. Lifton, *Thought Reform and the Psychology of Totalism* (New York, 1961).

by Lu Chih-wei, president of Yenching University. Lu had cooperated with the new government in instituting curricular and administrative changes, but he had been reluctant to repudiate as evil all of the Yenching heritage from the West or the whole of his past relations with Americans. At a time when Yenching was having to turn to the government for support and guidance, he still hoped that the institution could maintain its individuality. Lu was called upon, therefore, to examine Yenching's past and present for evidences of cultural aggression by United States imperialism; and in February 1951 he made public confession of his own role in making Yenching an outpost of American influence.[37] Lu's confession, though it provides insights into the agony of an individual asked to destroy his past, could hardly have been judged satisfactory by the party. Lu admitted that he had not previously viewed all within the Marxist-Leninist framework and had therefore made mistakes, but he denied that he had ever been the willing tool of American imperialism, and he offered examples of his opposition to Western interference in university administration. Though he condemned specific actions by individual Americans, he still refrained from denouncing all previous ties with the West. Though he admitted that J. L. Stuart had eventually become the tool of the United States and Kuomintang governments, he offered excuses and explanations for the earlier work of Stuart at Yenching. He obviously could not bring himself to a wholesale condemnation of his former colleagues and his own self, and he pled old age as an excuse for any inadequacy in his confession; young cadres, he indicated, had more thorough understanding and so he would leave the task to them.

Undoubtedly more satisfactory to the authorities was a confession by Chang Hsiang-lan (Helen Djang), dean at Ginling College, made in the fall of 1951 after three months of reformative study at a political institute.[38] Miss Chang revealed that she too had found it difficult to denounce former associates, and during the Resist America, Aid Korea campaign in November 1950 had been reluctant

[37] *Hsin kuan-ch'a,* Feb. 10, 1951; for translation, see Fraser, *Chinese Communist Education,* "U.S. Imperialist Cultural Aggression as Seen in Yenching University," pp. 104–110.

[38] *Chieh-fang jih-pao,* Shanghai, March 31, 1952; for trans. see NC, *Documents,* pp. 66–69.

to join in the condemnation of the American Helen Ferris. Though she had believed herself a patriot and had participated in the May 4 and May 30 movements, she had been proud of her training in Ginling and the United States of America. Even after the establishment of the People's Republic, she had hoped as dean to continue the Ginling tradition; and only as a result of her experiences at the political institute had she realized that it was not possible to be above politics and above class. To attempt to do so, as she had at Ginling, was to harm the people. With the new revelation of truth, she would stop offering excuses for herself and Ginling and would spell out in detail the way American imperialism had used Ginling to serve its ends. She would rid herself through criticism and self-criticism of "pro-America, revere-America, fear-America" attitudes, and both she and Ginling would henceforth serve the people.

Accusation campaigns in various Christian colleges emphasized the means by which the institutions had Americanized the students. Echoing the themes of the anti-Christian campaigns of the 1920's, the accusers condemned the use of English as a medium of instruction, the reliance on American textbooks and equipment, and the modeling of the curriculum on that of the American liberal arts college. Such practices instilled American bourgeois ideology in the students. Even the offering of scholarships for study in the United States was interpreted as a way to make the students amenable to the dictates of missionary educators during their college careers and cultural slaves of imperialism through their American training. The purpose of American aid was providing a market for American capitalism and keeping the colleges under the control of Westerners, the threat to cut off aid being deliberately used as blackmail to obtain obedience from the Chinese. The importation of American educational programs and standards, it was said, had actually harmed the people by delaying work toward truly democratic education. Thus, the seeming good of Hsiangya's preparation of some three hundred doctors in thirty-four years had been more than offset by the harm of its insistence on standards unsuitable for China that had deterred the rapid expansion of medical education.[39]

[39] For information on the campaigns in the Christian colleges, see "New Direction for St. John's," *China Monthly Review* (March 1951), pp. 146–147; "The New Hsiangya Medical College," *ibid.* (April 1951), pp. 204–206; "Three Former American Colleges," *ibid.* (Nov. 1951), pp. 242–243.

As far as the party was concerned, the accusation campaigns served a variety of functions. Students were encouraged to volunteer for services needed by the government. At St. John's and Hsiangya medical students offered to treat the wounded of the People's Liberation Army, to undertake medical surveys for the government, and to send teams to Korea, whereas they had formerly sought to concentrate on their studies and avoid politics, it was stated. Students at West China Union University volunteered to transfer to the National Military Cadres' Academy and to serve with the army in Tibet. Students who had previously ignored their obligations to the people were now contributing aid for Korea, working on land reform projects during vacations, and accepting government recommendations in the assignment of jobs after graduation. Perhaps the primary goal of the campaign in the Christian colleges, however, was to instil the idea that neither individual nor institution could remain above politics. Members of the Christian college communities must not only realize the error of their American bourgeois attitudes but also come to hate their former ideological framework and desire a sharp break with the Christian college tradition. They must realize that the national good should take precedence over individual or institutional ambition.

Demise of the Christian Colleges on the Mainland

Despite the preparatory campaigns, the government encountered opposition and delaying tactics when it moved toward institutional reorganization. Institutional loyalties, it seemed, did not die easily. In April 1952 a blueprint for restructuring most institutions of higher education in north China was revealed.[40] The government appeared ready to implement fully its emphasis on scientific and technical education; in order to train experts as rapidly as possible, previous trends toward highly specialized and narrowly defined

[40] Chang Ts'ung-lin, "Reform of Higher Technical Education Begins," *Jenmin chiao-yü*, Jan. 1952, *SCMP*, no. 349; "Reorganization of Technological Colleges in China to Meet Needs of National Construction," NCNA, April 16, 1952, *SCMP*, no. 317. There were to be several reorganizations of higher education in the People's Republic, and so the number of higher educational institutions varied from year to year; but in 1953, 182 higher educational institutions were listed and fourteen were classified as comprehensive universities. See I Wo-sheng, "Education in Communist China," in Union Research Institute, *Communist China, 1949–1959*, III (Hong Kong, 1961), 110.

curricula would be accentuated, and professional institutes concentrating in one or two fields were deemed the most efficient units for accomplishing these goals. A few universities would have a variety of curricula, including the humanities and social sciences, and most existing colleges and universities would be reorganized so that faculties in similar disciplines could be brought together to form professional institutes. Professional institutes could be either polytechnic schools offering work in several related fields, or institutes which concentrated in one specific area and were highly specialized (for example, East China Water Conservancy College, Peking Steel College, and Peking Aeronautical Engineering College). The Ministry of Education thus expected to shorten many of the professional programs and to incorporate practical experience.

In the Peking area Peking National University would become the comprehensive university and would absorb Tsing Hua's colleges of arts, science, and law, in addition to Yenching's liberal arts program. Tsing Hua would become an advanced polytechnic school and would incorporate the engineering college of Peita and the science and engineering departments of Yenching. Yenching would disappear both as an institution and as a name, though its campus was to become a main campus of Peita. Tsing Hua, on the other hand, would continue to exist as the name of a separate institution, and it could claim some continuity with its past despite the basic changes in its nature. Numerous other divisions and amalgamations were also outlined for the Peking schools. Fu Jen was to go out of existence with the transfer of most of its faculty to Peking Normal University or to the Central College of Finance and Economics, an institution to be formed from the economics and business administration departments of Fu Jen, Yenching, Tsing Hua, Peita, and Central Finance College.

As reorganization was instituted in other sections of China, Christian colleges there nearly always vanished from the scene. A break in continuity between the Christian institutions and the new schools was apparently deliberate. The experience of Hangchow Christian University was fairly typical in that its faculty and students were dispersed and it was almost impossible for alumni and members of the college community to retain any sense of continuing identity through the successor institutions. The Hangchow Colleges of Arts and Sciences merged with divisions from three other institutions to form a new school, Chekiang Normal College located on the Hangchow campus; the Hangchow engineering departments were incorporated into Chekiang University, and the Hangchow department of finance and economics was made into an independent institution, the Chekiang College of Finance and Economics.[41] Many faculty and alumni were unenthusiastic about the disappearance or revamping of their institutions and compared the amalgamations to promiscuous marriages which could not endure. Tsing Hua professors, for example, immediately protested against their school's becoming a professional institute and tried to obtain a modification of the plan so that Tsing Hua could be one of the multipurpose universities.

The Ministry of Education intended not only to overcome opposition to the changes, but to persuade the college educators to carry out the reorganization themselves. In the institutions of higher learning, therefore, the Three-Anti Campaign against corruption, waste, and bureaucratism was deliberately oriented to lay the groundwork for reorganization. On January 12, 1952, the Study Committee of Teachers of Institutions of Higher Education of Peking and Tientsin decided to stop examinations and other regular academic routine in order to devote all energies to the Three-Anti and ideological remolding movements. Numerous examples of waste, corruption, and bureaucratism were uncovered and several "tigers" were said to have been overthrown during the next few weeks. Nevertheless, the Study Committee and an Austerity Check-up Committee of the Peking Higher Educational Institutions remained dissatisfied with the progress made toward the elimination of bourgeois ideology and called for continuation of the campaign; regular school work was not resumed until March 1.[42]

In order to create readiness for institutional reorganization, examples of waste were spelled out in terms of departmentalism and institutional duplication and competition. There had been no rational geographical distribution; numerous schools were concen-

[41] "Hangchow Colleges Reconstituted on More Rational Basis," *Shanghai News*, Feb. 3, 1952, *SCMP*, no. 271; *The China Colleges*, XIX (April 1952), 2.

[42] *Jen-min jih-pao*, Feb. 8, 1952, *SCMP*, no. 277; *ibid.*, Feb. 26, 1952, March 4, 1952; and *Ta-kung pao*, Hong Kong, March 13, 1952, *SCMP*, no. 294.

trated in a few cities where they offered duplicate work in many small classes. Lack of correlation between colleges of science and technology had meant overlapping courses, and scientists had often refused to offer courses tailored to the needs of the technology programs. Institutional and departmental pride, it was said, had led to the hoarding of specialists and to the expansion of offerings or purchase of equipment simply to keep up with a competitor. Many specific examples of waste were undoubtedly accurate, and the demands for greater efficiency and for a greater sense of national responsibility were well founded. Nevertheless, some accusations were carried to such absurd lengths as to ignore academic considerations; one example of waste cited at Cheeloo Medical College was the purchase of milk and cod liver oil for one hundred experimental rats when two rats would do just as well.[43]

During the ideological remolding campaign the obligation of educational institutions to serve the people and the nation was emphasized. Curricular and institutional organization, teaching methods, and the definition of academic responsibilities should be altered to attract a larger percentage of students from the proletariat and to enable these students to overcome inadequacies in their preparation. At the same time every effort should be made to eradicate bourgeois imperialist ideology from text books and from the thinking of academic personnel; use of the English language and of translated American texts had led to the Americanization of students; one way of combating the "pro-America, revere-America, fear-America" attitude was to use Soviet texts and to emphasize the study of Russian. Loyalty to one's discipline and pride in personal contributions to knowledge were examples of sectarianism and individualism, bourgeois attitudes which must be replaced by dedication to the welfare of the people. Teachers were organized into committees to carry out the study necessary for ideological reorientation and application of the Three-Anti goals to the university. These committees in their organization generally coincided with departmental or sub-departmental lines, and since they were usually responsible for the methodology and content of the departmental offerings, they could be rigorous in demanding that individual courses meet the prerequisites set by the party. Some of the committees required that every in-

[43] *Ta-kung pao*, March 7, 1952, *SCMP*, no. 293.

structor submit detailed plans for each course before the beginning of a semester and alter the plans to accord with comments and criticisms of the committee; the committees were to meet regularly to review the work of its members and to discuss student criticisms.[44]

An editorial in *Jen-min jih-pao* on April 16, 1952 indicated that the time had come for specific action. According to subsequent articles, Peking teachers had acquired a new attitude toward their work; they had realized the importance of putting national interests before individual or institutional interests and had given their support to the reorganization. An Office of Readjustment of Colleges and Departments of Instruction of Higher Learning was organized by the Ministry of Education, and school committees began discussions regarding the reform of departments and curricula. Work teams of cadres tried to stir up enthusiasm and provide guidance. Since technical education was slated for rapid expansion, professors had to be persuaded to assume heavier work loads, help direct laboratory work, and teach the courses dictated by institutional needs rather than personal preference. For the increased percentage of students from proletarian background, teachers should organize short-term remedial courses. Perhaps most important of all, teachers should form the habit of turning immediately to a party representative when they needed guidance.[45]

Renewed campaigns at the Christian colleges demonstrated how completely the institutions had been tools of American imperialism and how thoroughly permeated with feudal and bourgeois attitudes they still were. Even though ties with Western supporters had been cut and schools like Yenching and West China Union University had already been nationalized, the government had concluded that the colleges would be havens of reactionism until they disappeared as institutions. Special drives were undertaken in the Christian schools, therefore, to convince their members that dismemberment was necessary and persuade them to take the leadership in the

[44] E. M. Kiesow, *China, The Challenge* (London 1954), pp. 7–10. Mrs. Kiesow, appointed to Cheeloo as a pharmaceutical chemist in 1948, continued to teach for a year (1952–1953) after the reorganization of medical education in Shantung.

[45] The campaign received wide publicity; see *Jen-min jih-pao*, May 20, 1952; *Chin-pu jih-pao*, Tientsin, May 21, 1952; NCNA, May 27 and 30, 1952; trans. in *SCMP*, nos. 345, 346.

process. Students and teachers at Yenching and Peking Union Medical College were given access to the presidential files of the institutions and to correspondence with the United Board so that they could prepare exhibits on United States cultural aggression and could gather materials for accusation meetings.

Historical perspective was abandoned. The United States of America was characterized as having always been the capitalist, imperialist enemy and therefore, the past contacts of Chinese teachers with Americans were retroactively considered examples of collaboration. Sociologists who had collected data on Chinese population and land tenure and had published their findings in the West were accused of having contributed information to the opposition. Exchanges of plant and insect specimens in previous years were condemned as thefts contributing to American imperialism and even to United States germ warfare. Hopes expressed by Westerners that the colleges would train Christian leadership for China or would offset Bolshevik influence seemed proof of the nefarious goals of the institutions. To have followed the pattern of the Missouri School of Journalism in planning Yenching's journalism program was to have succumbed to the American point of view, i.e., to have accepted the guidance of the enemy.[46]

Yenching faculty members who had been educated in the West were not the only ones who had to purge themselves of American influence; every single Yenching teacher had, simply by his association with Yenching, served the enemy and would need to undergo self-criticism. All too many thought it sufficient to condemn bourgeois ideology while continuing to believe that "the Americans established Yenching for the sake of education and did a good thing." By April 22 it was said that 111 Yenching teachers had undertaken self-criticism and 78 had completed their ideological reformation to the satisfaction of an austerity check-up committee.

Other individuals endured more severe trials, among them Presi-

[46] Wu Jui-p'ing, "An Examination of My Worship-American Thought and My Decadent Bourgeois Concepts," *Chin-pu jih-pao*, Tientsin, May 27, 1952, *SCMP*, no. 354; Shen Yun, "PUMC as Viewed in Exhibition for Accusation of U.S. Cultural Aggression," NCNA, June 9, 1952, *SCMP*, no. 352; James Endicott, "A Report on How American Imperialism Used Religion in China," *China Monthly Review*, June, 1952; Hsiao Feng, "What Did the U.S. Open Yenching University For?" *Ta-kung pao*, Hong Kong, April 22, 1952, *SCMP*, no. 322.

dent Lu Chih-wei, who once again became the focus for struggle against American influence. The autobiographical confession emphasizing extenuating circumstances that President Lu had made a year earlier was no longer sufficient. This time Lu was publicly denounced by his own daughter, a graduate student in the Yenching department of biology. Lu Yao-hua stressed her father's hypocrisy. He had condemned American imperialism, but he had not really rid himself of pro-American attitudes; he had not in every case condemned those with whom he had worked; he was a Christian with no political sympathy for the Communist Party. Several sentences in the denunciation by Miss Lu Yao-hua, however, seemed to indicate that Lu Chih-wei's real crime in 1952 was opposition to the disappearance of Yenching: "But here in Yenching it is just because of you, Lu Chih-wei, that imperialist influence is still making such a ferocious attack on the thought of every school mate. . . . You have kept this bastion for cultural aggression and continued to do harm to China. . . . I definitely will not permit the remnant influence of U.S. imperialism to exist in the land of China, in the vicinity of the capital, or even by the side of Chairman Mao Tsetung." [47]

In May 1952 Peking repeated its claim of the previous month that all opposition to reorganization in north China had been overcome, and professors who were willing to give public support were widely quoted; said one member of the Yenching department of Chinese literature: "In the past I was 'proud' of Yenching and did not want to see it merged with other schools but today I do not feel sad but very happy about it, as such a bulwark for cultural aggression by U.S. imperialism really should not be kept on." [48] Relapses, however, must have made it as difficult for the People's Republic as for later research scholars to judge the commitment of educators to the reorganization plan. Members of Peking Union Medical College (PUMC) were reported to have welcomed the transformation into China Medical College in the spring of 1952, but by July the campaign had to be renewed because, it was said, some individuals had just surrendered unconditionally in order to

[47] *Hsin yen-ching*, April 14, 1952; English trans. in NC, *Documents*, pp. 71–72.

[48] *Ta-kung pao*, Hong Kong, May 29, 1952; *SCMP*, no. 353.

avoid undergoing ideological reform.[49] These individuals were in mid-1952 still talking about maintaining PUMC standards and still admired the PUMC system which had stressed high quality training for a small number of students; many still hoped to concentrate exclusively on their academic work and avoid political involvement.

Whatever the real attitude of the students and faculty in the Peking institutions, the government had persuaded or coerced them into voting for the reorganization plan even when it necessitated the disappearance of their own institution. In the fall of 1952, the institutional structure of the colleges and universities in the north China area would look quite different from the way it had looked the previous autumn. Among those missing in Peking would be Yenching and Fu Jen. Cheeloo also disappeared; its science and theology divisions were transferred to Nanking, and Shantung Medical College, composed from the Cheeloo College of Medicine and the Shantung Provincial Medical College, was organized on the Cheeloo campus.

The focus of the campaign for educational reorganization could move south. With a political astuteness characteristic of numerous movements during the regime's early years, the party had worked out its techniques and propaganda line and had developed experienced personnel in one sector of the country before it attempted nationwide application. In February 1952 educators in the Shanghai area had begun to plan a period of intensive ideological reform such as Peking had initiated in January; and following the Peking model, they had organized a Study Committee with branches in various East China institutions to coordinate the campaign. A conference called by the Study Committee heard a report by the president of Peita on the ideological reform campaign at his school and its relation to the reorganization of the institutions of higher education.[50] The report was, with good reason, made by the president of the Peking institution which would lose least under the new structure. Austerity check-up committees were founded as in north China to ferret out examples of waste and corruption due to institutional duplication and individual ambition. Perhaps because of

[49] Ta-kung pao, Shanghai, July 26, 1952; Ta-kung pao, Hong Kong, July 31, 1952; SCMP, no. 398.
[50] Ta-kung pao, Shanghai, Feb. 2, 1952, SCMP, no. 272.

the opposition met in north China, creation of a Committee for the Reorganization of East China Institutions of Higher Education was delayed until midsummer. Events moved rapidly thereafter, though.

A meeting held August 2 to 5, 1952, planned the specific measures to achieve the new institutional structure. Since the Christian institutions were slated to disappear, public support by their leaders was desirable. Pan Shih-tzu of St. John's, Yu Jih-hsüan of the University of Shanghai, Hu Wen-yao of Aurora, Wu Yi-fang of Ginling, and others voiced their enthusiasm, it was reported.[51] In many instances, the institutional reorganization was actually put into effect in east China with the fall semester. The nationalization of the institutions in Hangchow, Shanghai, Nanking, and Foochow generally divided the faculty and students of the Christian colleges in each area among several specialized colleges or institutes. Though most of the administrators and teachers found academic positions in the new divisions, the identity of the individual Christian college was destroyed. For example, eight units were organized in Nanking, where Ginling and the University of Nanking had earlier been amalgamated, and former president Wu Yi-fang became an administrator in Nanking Normal College. Foochow National University became the comprehensive university for Fukien and located its College of Agriculture on the campus of Fukien Christian University and its College of Science on the Hwa Nan campus. Wang Shih-ching (Lucy Wang) of Hwa Nan was a vice-chairman of the administrative committee of Foochow National University.

South China was next in line. Again, reports by government and party officials and by individuals who had carried out this stage in other areas helped initiate the program; in July, for example, Professor Huo Jen-chih of Yenching narrated the experiences of his institution before a mass meeting at Lingnan and offered guidance as Lingnan teachers and students mobilized for a campaign against bourgeois ideological influence. Within a few weeks the Canton area had its own study committees, austerity check-up committees, and other paraphernalia of the campaign and was moving toward

---

[51] *Chieh-fang jih-pao*, Shanghai, Aug. 3, 1952, *SCMP*, no. 393; *Shanghai News*, Aug. 9, 1952, *SCMP*, no. 402; Wu Yi-fang, "I Happily Exert My Efforts at the Work of the People's Education," *Ta-kung pao*, Hong Kong, Oct. 13, 1952, *SCMP*, no. 438.

institutional reorganization.[52] Lingnan became a part of Chung Shan University (Sun Yat-sen University) as its engineering and agricultural work was transferred to special institutes and its campus became the locale for Chung Shan's College of Arts; President Ch'en Su-ching was made a vice-president of Chung Shan.

In Chinese tradition education had generally served a professional goal, entrance to the bureaucracy, but the emphasis of the curriculum had been humanistic. Through the examination system, the central administration had placed a premium on orthodoxy and had seen that education instilled loyalty to the Great Tradition; Confucian ideology had sanctioned the establishment. The People's Republic was, in some sense, continuing the professional emphasis of education, though widespread acceptance of the goal of modernization meant that professional education in the 1950's was technical and scientific training. There was historical continuity also in that the government attempted to define and control orthodoxy.

The discontinuities were, nevertheless, more fundamental than the continuities, and one major difference was the degree of government control and responsibility. Practical limitations on the power of the central administration and a narrow interpretation of its responsibilities had formerly meant considerable autonomy and even variety in education. The educational process had been largely a private responsibility, and many scholar-bureaucrats had studied both the heterodox philosophies of Taoism and Buddhism and non-orthodox interpreters of the Confucian teachings. In the modernization process most governments have assumed responsibility for educating their citizens, and the prestige of science has led to emphasis on science and technology in the curriculum. The Chinese Communists' search for efficient techniques of modernization and their commitment to Marxist revolutionary ideology have accentuated these trends in China. Professional education has been defined as the acquisition of specific skills and an orthodox ideology rather than the training of a complex individual and social being. Variety and private experimentation in education have been denied a place on the grounds of inefficiency and disloyalty. Thus, the People's Republic had no room for the Christian colleges with their liberal

[52] *Ta-kung pao*, Hong Kong, May 27, 1952, *SCMP*, no. 343; "American Imperialist Crimes at Lingnan," *SCMP*, no. 409 (Sept. 5–6, 1952).

arts orientation, their origins in bourgeois tradition, their attention to the campus community, and their private status. This held true whether or not the colleges maintained formal ties with the West. Cultural and ideological homogeneity was demanded, and so the Christian colleges along with numerous other educational institutions went out of existence.

Reorganization had been resisted, but through various techniques of persuasion, the regime had managed to have the reorganization carried out by the educators themselves. Though in most cases administrators and educational leaders from the Christian colleges were able to continue academic work, they were generally relegated to secondary administrative positions or they retreated to research. Few were imprisoned or suffered physical oppression. Subsequent self-criticisms and reorganizations reveal, however, that relations between the party and the educators continued to be marked by tension. Trust between the two groups was less than complete, and resentment over the subservience of education to politics was common. Though many educators had appreciated the importance of efficiency in training for national reconstruction and had accepted the need for specialization at the expense of a broad, general education, resentment of party educational policy continued to be fed by institutional loyalties ignored during the 1952 reorganization. As late as the Hundred Flowers Campaign of 1956, there were protests over the disappearance or transmutation of certain schools. Chao Chi-yuan, head of the department of law, University of Nanking, stated: "I have been in an unhappy mood for the past five years, since the college of law was abolished. My time was wasted and my specialty was rendered useless. I just don't understand what was the reasoning behind this measure." [53]

Chinese who had been prominent in the Christian colleges had little sense of security as they sought a place within the educational program of the People's Republic. They had tried to make their peace with the new regime and in some cases had openly welcomed it, but individual educators continued to find themselves the objects of distrust and criticism. Sometimes it was because they themselves had become disillusioned and thus reluctant to support new poli-

[53] *Jen-min jih-pao*, May 19, 1957; quoted in I Wo-sheng, "Education in Communist China," p. 128.

cies; dreams of cooperation in a common cause had been shattered by the all-pervasive and paramount power of the party. At other times it was because of the party's ingrained distrust of bourgeois learning and influence or the need of the party for concrete objects of criticism during a mass campaign. T. C. Chao of the Yenching College of Religion had undergone self-criticism during 1952, but was called upon on numerous later occasions to protest his loyalty to the regime and to confess his past mistakes. Since he had international renown as a Christian leader and had been an executive of the World Council of Churches, his assurances concerning religious freedom in China were demanded frequently and were given wide publicity by the People's Republic.[54] Francis C. M. Wei, former president of Huachung and then professor at the normal college replacing Huachung, had joined T. C. Chao and others in leading the Three Self Movement; nevertheless, he and several others from Huachung were denounced in 1957 for anticommunist and rightist activities. The Communist Party seemed unconvinced that Western influence as exercised through the Christian colleges had expired even with the expiration of the Christian institutions.

Successors

It would be inaccurate, however, to say that the China Christian colleges had no institutional successors. Small scale efforts continued the Christian College tradition outside the mainland. Along with the Western educators who left the China mainland between 1948 and 1952 were Chinese scholars committed to Christian education. These individuals joined Western supporters in seeking ways to aid refugee students and teachers and to carry on the work of the Christian colleges. A few examples may illustrate the extent to which continuity was maintained.

In 1951 a group of refugee teachers secured from the United Board a $20,000 grant enabling them to organize classes in downtown Hong Kong. The name Chung Chi College was adopted, and Chinese students, both refugees and permanent Hong Kong residents, were welcomed. Under the guidance of former Christian

---

[54] See the report of criticism of T. C. Chao in 1952, Chao's address on religious freedom in China in 1956, his poem criticising America in 1957, all quoted in NC, *Documents*, pp. 70–71, 138–139, 150–151.

college staff members such as Lei Ying-lam (Y. L. Lee), president of Lingnan from 1937 to 1948, and with the support of missions previously associated with the China Christian colleges, Chung Chi College acquired a site in the New Territories. Meanwhile, other institutions of higher education for Chinese in Hong Kong were being founded, schools with small enrollments, minimal income, and low academic standards. Among these were the United College of Hong Kong and New Asia College, the latter a Christian institution under its own independent board. When in the early 1960's the government of Hong Kong considered establishing a Chinese university to complement the English language University of Hong Kong, Chung Chi, United College, and New Asia College proposed that they unite to form the Chinese University of Hong Kong. They would thereby gain government support and would be able to expand and improve their educational programs so that their students would qualify for a university degree. The merger was formally declared in 1963, and Chinese University of Hong Kong (Chung-wen ta-hsüeh) with approximately 1100 students came into existence. Actual union of the three colleges on one campus awaited construction of buildings adjacent to the Chung Chi campus and came only in 1966–1967. Chung Chi and New Asia both hoped to retain their identity as Christian institutions despite federation and government support and regulation, and Chung Chi continued to receive aid and faculty members through the United Board.[55]

While maintaining its interest in Chung Chi, the United Board had undertaken to assist a number of Christian colleges in other parts of Asia: Silliman University and the Philippine Christian Colleges, Satya Watjana in Indonesia, and Yonsei University in Korea. To indicate its broadening interests, the United Board for Christian Colleges in China changed its name to the United Board for Christian Higher Education in Asia in 1955. Other organizations traditionally associated with the China Christian colleges joined the United Board in this expansion, the China Medical Board helping Yonsei University build its medical college, and Princeton-in-Asia, Yale-in-China, the Oberlin Shansi Memorial Association, and others

[55] This brief summary is based on publicity brochures about Chung Chi and various issues of the newsletter of the United Board, *New Horizons*, 1963–1969, plus occasional notes in the *China Bulletin*.

contributing personnel and building funds to the institutions associated with the United Board.

Several institutions on Taiwan were founded by faculty members and alumni of the China Christian colleges. Fu Ren University was revived. In 1951 refugees from the Shanghai Law College of Soochow University opened Soochow Law College in Taipei with Methodist support. The Law College, which offered a five-year program leading to an LL.B. degree, was later supplemented by an Arts College and a College of Commerce; under President C. Y. Stone (Shih Ch'ao-yung), formerly of Soochow on the mainland, the name Soochow University was revived, and in 1966 the institution entered into association with the United Board.

Tunghai University at Taichung, Taiwan, was the school which was most consciously founded to carry on the work of the China Christian colleges, and both Chung Chi and Tunghai had many of the distinctive features of the mainland Christian institutions. As early as 1952 Christian leaders in Taiwan had urged church leaders in the West to join in establishing a new Christian college; in 1953 a board of directors was organized, and the following year, Theodore Chen, former president of Fukien Christian University, came to Taiwan to guide detailed planning for the school. Tunghai University opened with 200 students in September 1955 and looked forward to a maximum of 800 to 1000.[56]

In reaction to the experiences on the mainland, the founders of both Chung Chi and Tunghai hoped to give special emphasis to the Christian purpose and Christian atmosphere of the institutions. Religious activities and courses in religion would be voluntary, but the religious goals would be achieved by maintaining a high proportion of Christians among the faculty and student body and by fostering an active campus community. This Christian emphasis could be preserved, it was argued, if Tunghai accepted the fact that the institution could play only a limited role in higher education on Taiwan, if in other words the school restricted its ambitions as to size of enrollment and diversity of curriculum. During their first

---

[56] Theodore Hsi-en Chen, "A Progress Report on Tunghai University," Aug. 9, 1954 (mimeo. statement to Tunghai board of directors, in files of the president, Tunghai University); 1958 statement in pres. files, no title; *Report of the President, 1958–1959*.

years of existence both Chung Chi and Tunghai did in fact draw a higher percentage of Christians to the faculty and student body than had many of the Christian colleges during the 1930's and 1940's.[57] Many of the faculty members were alumni of the Christian colleges.

Within a decade of founding, nevertheless, conflicts between the educational goals and the Christian purposes of the institutions had appeared, and the old question of the compatibility of Christianity and Chinese nationalism had been raised. Some supporters of Chung Chi, for example, were uncertain that the Christian atmosphere and purpose could be retained after the college became part of the government-supported Chinese University of Hong Kong and were not enthusiastic about the change in status despite the assistance in raising educational standards. On Taiwan Christianity has in certain quarters been associated with anticommunism and a conservative approach to economic and social problems, and this has not enhanced the appeal of Christianity for many college students. The conservative interpretation of Christian ideology, furthermore, has come into conflict with officially supported attempts to revive elements of the Chinese tradition. The extent to which the unique aspects of Christianity should be preserved and the extent to which the similarity and universality of Christian and Confucian approaches to ethics and truth should be emphasized have been controversial issues. Those who have espoused liberal Christianity have often found themselves on the defensive.

Among the distinctive features of the China Christian colleges had been their emphasis on a general liberal arts program, the attention given to the creation of a campus community, and composition of the campus personnel. Tunghai has made a deliberate attempt to retain these features and has had considerable success despite contradictory trends in higher education on Taiwan. The government colleges and universities have encouraged early specialization, whereas Tunghai has stressed work in the liberal arts as a

[57] United Board, *Annual Report, 1965–1966,* pp. 10–11; personal interview with Wu Teh-yao, president of Tunghai, Taiwan, July 8, 1962. The Tunghai board of directors recommended that at least four-fifths of the teaching staff be Christians. In 1965–1966, 32 percent of the Tunghai students and 42 percent of the Chung Chi students were Christians.

necessary foundation for the major field and as a prerequisite to the awarding of a B.A. degree. Protests have not been lacking. Students have complained that they are at a disadvantage in competing with students who have had more specialized training. Since the students on Taiwan enter college and obtain civil service positions and scholarships by government examination, they are intensely competitive and there is pressure for uniformity of educational programs. Instructors in certain fields, especially the sciences, have complained that the liberal arts courses reduce the amount of work possible in the major field.[58] Despite the pressures, Tunghai has retained its liberal arts program and continued to experiment with the basic courses, encouraged by the fact that its graduates have generally fared quite well in the examinations.

The site chosen by Tunghai, on a hill five miles from the city of Taichung, was considered desirable for a variety of reasons: the setting with its view of the eastern mountains was magnificent, and the city of Taichung donated the land, but perhaps decisive was the fact that the semi-isolation of the site would be conducive to an active, closely knit campus community. Arrangements which would contribute to a residential campus community received special attention. All faculty as well as all students were required to live on campus, and teachers were prohibited from accepting supplementary employment. Numerous campus organizations and frequent informal social gatherings of students and teachers were fostered. Time and energy went into planning and administering a student labor program whereby each student had to contribute four hours of work a week during his first two academic years. The goal of the program was to overcome a traditional aversion to manual labor and "to develop a sense of responsibility, cooperation and loyalty to the institution or group."[59] Though many have considered Tunghai's emphasis on the campus community one of its major strengths,

[58] For criticisms of the general education program, see Chu Yu-kuang, "General Education and Cultural Change in the Far East," *Comparative Educational Review*, IV, 35–42; Tunghai, *Report of the President, 1960–1961*, p. 3; "Minutes of the Committee on Reviewing the General Education Program," March 26, April 9, 30, 1959 (president's file on general education).

[59] Tunghai University, *Student Labor Program*, 1959 (pamphlet); see also numerous reports on the student labor program and minutes of the Student Labor Committee, 1958–1961 (president's file on the labor program).

there have been criticisms, some of them familiar. The life of Tunghai, it has been said, is isolated from the life of Taiwan, and students become alienated from their heritage and their environment. Much of the university income has been devoted to building a beautiful campus and more particularly to constructing numerous faculty residences and student dormitories; Chinese and Westerners have asked whether this is the most judicious use of limited funds.

Both Tunghai and Chung Chi have continued the tradition of the China Christian colleges in that they have an international faculty composed primarily of Chinese, Americans, Canadians, and a few Englishmen. There was, in fact, considerable continuity of person-nel during the first decade, with individuals from the China colleges playing a prominent role in the founding, administration, and instruction in the new institutions.[60] The trend toward Chinese control has been continued, though through its financial aid, the United Board has exercised some influence. The China colleges made important contributions in the areas of medical and women's education, and these emphases continue, though Yonsei University in Korea rather than Tunghai or Chung Chi has become the major medical center under Christian auspices. At both Tunghai and Chung Chi, women compose over one-third of the student body. As before 1949, the colleges have generally drawn their students from families of some affluence and from families with a business or civil service background.

The efforts in Taiwan and Hong Kong have been severely limited in comparison with the former thirteen Christian colleges on the mainland, and the new institutions can make no attempt to serve the great bulk of the Chinese nation. But those who had known the mainland institutions would not be likely to deny the new institutions the title of successors to the China colleges. Academic creativity and new directions based on the mainland experience have been much more difficult to achieve than the founders had anticipated during the 1950's. In both their strengths and their weaknesses Tunghai and Chung Chi continue many of the traditions of the former thirteen.

[60] Ku Tun-jou, dean of the College of Arts of Hangchow Christian University for many years, was, for example, also dean of the College of Arts of Tunghai.

XIII | Assessments

The period 1850–1950 was not a happy one in Chinese history. Disintegration of Chinese tradition and especially of gentry society proceeded at an accelerating rate, undermined by both internal factors such as population growth and bureaucratic corruption and external pressure from Japan and the West. By 1930 the social structure and cultural life of urban China bore scant resemblance to that of the cities of traditional China, and even in the rural villages stability existed no more. The growth of a modern society to replace the old had been uneven; in certain limited sectors there had been movement toward modernization while in other areas the characteristics of modern society were hardly perceptible.[1] Though efforts at modernizing and reintegrating Chinese society were undertaken by the Kuomintang, China endured war, civil conflict, and a communist revolution before hopes for a new and integral China were revived.

The life of the Christian colleges and of China became closely intertwined during these years, and interesting parallels in their histories can be cited. As the disintegration of Chinese tradition gathered momentum during the nineteenth century, Christian missions became in many ways the West's most direct challenge to the

---

[1] In an assessment of Chinese modernization before 1919, Knight Biggerstaff has used the eight characteristics of modernization proposed by a Conference on Modern Japan at Hakone, Japan, in 1960; see Marius B. Jansen, ed., *Changing Japanese Attitudes toward Modernization* (Princeton, 1965), ch. i. Biggerstaff concludes that the development of modern society in China was both limited and uneven prior to 1919. See "Modernization and Early Modern China," *JAS*, XXV (1966), 607–619. Much the same could still be said of the modernization of China by 1930.

Chinese heritage. Missionaries came to China to propagate an alien faith, which they rarely distinguished from Western civilization; they had few qualms of conscience about undermining the Confucian ethic, and they invaded interior China in order to do so. This was in contrast to Western traders who were interested in profits, not ideology, and whose associations were ordinarily limited to treaty-port Chinese and other Western traders. For many Chinese, contact with Christian missionaries represented their first experience with the alien culture of the West—a fact that was significant for Chinese understanding and adoption of aspects of modern society.

The Christian colleges gradually became a major focus of Protestant missions despite protests by evangelists. Like most other examples of Western influence in nineteenth-century China, the colleges originated out of the need of Westerners, not as a result of Chinese demand. They, however, by their very existence in China became more important as contributors to the disintegration of the Chinese heritage than as agents of Christian evangelism. They were Western-type institutions transplanted to China, and their Western administration, support, and curricula, their general atmosphere made them mediators of Western civilization. Since the values and structure of Western civilization differed in fundamental ways from the Chinese tradition based on an agrarian economy and a Confucian ethic, the colleges could not but become disruptive forces in China. The colleges might be relatively isolated from the intellectual life of nineteenth-century China and they might be scorned by Chinese literati, but they remained a visible alternative to the classical system of education.

A major turning point in Chinese history and in the history of the Christian colleges came with official recognition that adoption of a few Western military and industrial techniques would not bring China power and prosperity; many of the fundamentals of the Chinese heritage would have to be abandoned. The abolition of the traditional civil service examinations in 1905 denoted a break in Chinese history; negatively, this move by the Ch'ing dynasty hastened the decline of the scholar-gentry as a cohesive and socially dominant group, but positively it laid the basis for modernization in the realm of education and ideology. Not the classical tradition alone, but a combination of Western and Chinese studies, as exemplified by the mission schools since 1850, would be considered the norm. Henceforth, the Christian colleges became more active participants in the revolutionary process of modernization. They would have a constructive role as well as a destructive one.

Though hopes that the colleges would produce the leaders to remold China into a liberal, democratic society were disappointed, the institutions were prominent in several areas where change was greatest during the twentieth century. The institutions helped inspire the growth of nationalism among educated, urban Chinese. There was first the alienation of the educated from their heritage, a painful process which seems a necessary phase in the growth of nationalism outside the Western tradition. The Christian colleges initially participated in this process through their preparation of youth for study abroad; these new members of the educated elite could return to China, but Chinese tradition could never again be their home. During the 1920's when educated, urban Chinese began to define the Chinese nation in anti-imperialist and anti-Western terms, Christian education and Christian institutions became a major focus for nationalist movements. Some of the Christian colleges became associated with Chinese nationalism in a more affirmative way during the 1930's and 1940's as their students gained acceptance among the generation of New Youth and participated actively in nationalist movements. Urban-centeredness in economic and cultural life, politicization of the educated elite, and the assumption of increasing responsibility by the central government were other aspects of modernization in which the history of China and the history of the Christian colleges became intertwined.

In the area of rural revolution and the reintegration of Chinese society under a new ideology, many found the contributions of the Christian colleges disappointing. These tasks required both political power and unlimited self-assurance, and in the 1940's Christian missions could claim neither. A Sino-Western synthesis for a modern China would not come from the Sino-Western Christian institutions. Chinese would modernize without Christianity, and they alone would guide the process. The new modernizers, the Chinese Communist Party, made this clear as they merged the Christian colleges into other institutions in the hope of eradicating bourgeois influence. The Christian colleges performed their last function as identifiable entities when they became the object of anti-American campaigns. Their disappearance marked the closing of a century of intercourse between China and the United States.

For magnitude, the Christian missionary effort in China, 1850 to 1950, has few parallels, and not all of the influences flowed eastward. Missionaries served as interpreters of China to hundreds of thousands of church members in the West. The period of active dialogue between China and the West coincided precisely with the climax of the Protestant missionary movement, and the image of China held by the average American before World War II was largely the creation of the missionary.[2] At the same time the missionary represented Western civilization for many Chinese. With the interruption of contact and the termination of missions, images held on both sides of the Pacific Ocean have altered. Disappointment of high hopes, hopes of Westerners for a liberal Christian China and hopes of Chinese for real acceptance as one of the major powers, contributed to what has often seemed a virulent over-reaction during the 1950's and 1960's.

Although or perhaps because the modernizing of China and the history of the China Christian colleges were closely associated, it is not easy to isolate the specific contributions of the colleges. Influence is difficult to determine under the best of circumstances, and China was in a state of flux throughout the century of Protestant effort. The building up of numerous internal and external pressures during the nineteenth century led to the destructive explosion of the twentieth and the need for reconstruction of almost all aspects of society. The Western missionary might seem a more direct challenge to Chinese tradition than the trader, and yet the unique evolution of international settlements in the treaty ports became a grave infringement on Chinese sovereignty. Japanese imperialism and population pressure doubtless contributed more directly to communist victory than any failure by individual Chinese committed to village reconstruction or liberal democracy. Conclusions, therefore, must be tentative and must emphasize the contributory rather than the causal role of the Christian colleges in the continuing Chinese revolution from 1850 to 1950. The history of the colleges is revealing precisely

[2] For a detailed discussion, see Harold R. Isaacs, *Scratches on Our Minds: American Images of China and India* (New York, 1958).

because it became so closely interwoven with the creation of a nation out of a culture.

Graduates as an Index of Influence

One concrete way of appraising the influence of the Christian colleges is through their graduates. The social and intellectual background of the students, their purpose in entering mission schools, the courses taken, and their occupations, all tell something about the contribution of the institutions to China. Also to be taken into account is the number of students enrolled. The colleges were until 1925 small institutions affecting only a limited number of individuals. Before 1900 all Protestant schools combined enrolled an annual total of less than 200 college students; not until 1926 did their enrollment regularly exceed 3,500. After 1930 several eastern colleges expanded quite rapidly and by 1936 the number of college students in the Protestant institutions was almost double that of a decade earlier and approximately 12 percent of the total number of college students in China.[3] Partly because the government exempted students from military service and encouraged youth to continue their education, enrollment in institutions of higher education generally increased during the Sino-Japanese War and the subsequent civil war, and the Christian colleges shared in this trend; the Christian institutions had 12,000 college students in 1947, and in some years the Christian schools were training between 15 and 20 percent of the college students in China.[4] For a brief period, then, the Christian colleges made a significant contribution to the total number of college-educated Chinese, but during most of their history their contribution was in terms of the work of a comparatively small group.

During the early years the missionaries were successful in guiding into religious work the great majority of those who stayed to gradu-

[3] As of 1926 the colleges had a combined total of 4,463 graduates since their founding, according to Cressy, *Christian Higher Education*, p. 193. Graduates of the Christian colleges generally totaled 1,000 a year in the mid-1930's. See T. L. Tan, "Status of Christian Higher Education in China," *ER*, XXX (1938), 4; Lin Ching-jun, "Christian Education in China," *CCYB*, 1936–37, pp. 215–216.

[4] Oliver J. Caldwell, "Chinese Universities and the War," *School and Society*, Feb. 1942, pp. 232–233; "Events," *ibid.*, Oct. 1948, p. 245.

jority of the first students on Boxer indemnity scholarships had studied in mission schools.[7] In the 1910 Shanghai examinations for indemnity scholarships, twenty-six out of thirty-one men chosen were St. John's students. In the 1910 Canton examinations, there were 260 applicants; five of the six scholarships went to Canton Christian College students; three of the five alternates were also from Canton Christian College.[8] Even after the establishment of Tsing Hua to prepare students for study in the West, some students found training in a Christian school good preparation for the Tsing Hua examinations. A Who's Who of American Returned Students, issued by Tsing Hua in 1917, listed 401 students; 132 of these received all or part of their higher education in the Christian colleges.[9] Twenty-four more attended Christian secondary schools.

A list of the courses of study followed by the Christian college students after they came to the United States gives some insight into the purpose of the students and into what they considered the needs of China. Over one-fourth of the students majored in engineering, approximately one-fifth in the social sciences, and one-tenth in education. Though personal ambition obviously was a factor in the choice of studies, the Chinese students were intensely conscious of their role as future leaders of China. Since the Chinese government also exercised some influence over the courses taken by scholarship students, the concentration in these three fields presumably represented a strongly felt need for engineers, government administrators, and educators. The neglect of pure science and mathematics (five students) is somewhat surprising, and so, too, is the fact that only two students selected theology.

Upon their return to China, the students frequently did not follow the occupations for which they had studied in the United States. It is interesting to compare the occupations of the former Christian college students with those of other American "returned students" before 1917 (Table 6). Students who had not attended the mission schools frequently went into government work, whereas the Chris-

[7] James L. Barton, "An Adequate System of Christian Education in Non-Christian Lands," Proceedings of the Men's National Missionary Conference of the U.S.A. (New York, 1910), p. 263.

[8] Pott, "History," St. John's, p. 23; "Editorial Notes," ER, III (1910), 116.

[9] Who's Who of American Returned Students (Peking, 1917). The list obviously contained few students who left China after 1913.

Table 6. Occupations in China of students returned from America, 1916–1917

Occupations	Christian college students		Other students	
	Compo-nents	Totals	Compo-nents	Totals
Educators		35		100
Administrators	8		30	
Teachers	27		70	
Government workers		28		82
Technical and professional workers		45		52
Architects	0		2	
Editors and correspondents	4		2	
Engineers	29		33	
Legal practitioners	3		1	
Librarians	1		0	
Medical doctors	8		14	
Businessmen		10		19
Bank administrators and employees	1		7	
Managers and employees in industry and commerce	9		12	
Social and religious workers		10		1
Total		128		254
Listed more than once		5		32
Adjusted total		123		222

Source: Who's Who of American Returned Students (Peking, 1917).

tian college students were more likely to enter technical and professional vocations (especially engineering). Many from both groups turned to education and approximately the same proportion of each group entered business. Since all of the students received their advanced training in the United States, these statistics alone are insufficient basis for arguing that education in the Christian colleges influenced the choice of occupation. Several other factors, however, indicate that this trend toward professional and technical work rather than government employment was related to training in the mission institutions. Christian college graduates were at a disadvantage in securing government positions; they were considered by some Chinese to have compromised their nationality by attending mission schools. Their knowledge of classical Chinese was inferior, and they therefore had difficulty in winning the respect of traditional Chinese scholars, many of whom still had influential positions in the government. Using statistics compiled from the 1931 edition of *Who's Who in China,* one finds, furthermore, a similar and more pronounced trend (*Table 7*).

As was true among the returned students before 1917, so in the 1931 *Who's Who in China,* approximately the same proportions were engaged in business. Again, a larger percentage of the Chris-

Table 7. Occupations of Chinese in 1931 *Who's Who in China*

Occupations	Educated in Christian Colleges		Other Chinese listed	
	Compo-nents	Totals	Compo-nents	Totals
Educators		37		84
Administrators	18		43	
Teachers	19		41	
Government and party workers		48		408
Military men		0		101
Technical and professional workers		52		107
Agriculturists	1		1	
Architects	1		3	
Artists	0		6	
Editors and journalists	7		14	
Engineers	6		28	
Legal practitioners	16		37	
Librarians	2		1	
Medical doctors	10		8	
Scientists	2		1	
Writers	7		3	
Other	0		5	
Businessmen		22		90
Bank administrators and employees	7		22	
Merchants	7		31	
Men engaged in manufacturing and other businesses	8		37	
Social and religious workers		12		11
Other		1		2
Total		172		803
Listed twice		15		1
Adjusted total		157		802

tian college students went into technical and professional work, while a higher percentage of the other students had government positions. Contrary to the 1917 statistics, the Christian college students in the 1931 *Who's Who* led in the proportion engaged in educational work. The tradition that educated Chinese should seek government employment was still strong in China; the newer professions essential to a modern society—lawyers, engineers, agriculturists, doctors—still lacked the prestige of state service. If the Christian colleges interested their students in entering the newer professions, this in itself was a contribution.

Who's Who in China is certainly an incomplete listing of the leaders of China or of those Chinese who have made a significant contribution to China. The emphasis on government officials is strong, and the number of military leaders is high. As the preface of the 1925 *Who's Who* stated, obtaining information about outstanding Chinese in the coastal provinces was easier than learning about important Chinese of the interior. The work was compiled by *The China Weekly Review,* and Chinese capable of speaking English were undoubtedly favored. In spite of these shortcomings, the editions of *Who's Who in China* form a convenient listing of outstanding Chinese. In studying the 1925 and the 1931 editions of the work, one finds that approximately 12 percent of those listed in 1925 and 16 percent of those listed in 1931 attended Christian colleges.[10] More striking is the fact that from three-fourths to four-fifths of those from the Christian institutions had also studied abroad. Of the few whose entire education had been in China most were successful businessmen. The Christian colleges, it would seem, furnished only preparatory education for most of their students who became Chi-

----

[10] *Who's Who in China* (Shanghai; 3d ed., 1925; 4th ed., 1931).
The 1925 list includes the 1927 supplement. These percentages are only approximate; the education is not always given. In the 1925 volume, for instance, if I had compiled statistics on the basis of the number for whom some education is listed, the Christian college students would form 13 percent. Sometimes only graduate study is given. In some cases it is likely that anti-foreign and anti-Christian sentiment persuaded the individual not to mention training in a mission institution. These should, therefore, be considered as minimum rather than maximum percentages. Finally, I should point out that I have included all Chinese who attended a Christian college, not just graduates; I have not included those who attended mission institutions which were really high schools and which never attained college standing.

nese leaders. Among the Christian institutions, the college which provided the most thorough Western education, St. John's, trained the greatest number of Chinese listed. In the 1925 *Who's Who*, almost one-half of those who attended Christian institutions were St. John's men; in 1931, 38 percent. St. John's during this period drew a large number of students from well-to-do families, so, that they had both the financial resources for study abroad and the important personal connections helpful in securing government positions. If few Chinese rose to prominence solely on the basis of their Christian college education, the same was to some extent true of the graduates of government institutions; 57 percent of the Chinese in the 1925 *Who's Who* had studied abroad.[11] During this period education abroad was one of the quickest avenues to a position of responsibility and influence, and many considered preparation in the Christian colleges a convenient stepping stone toward the coveted status of "returned student."

The Christian college students listed in *Who's Who in China* and *Who's Who of American Returned Students* comprise, of course, only a small fraction of the individuals educated in the Christian institutions before 1925. Though quite an impressive list of Christian college students who became outstanding Chinese leaders could be compiled,[12] most Christian college alumni before 1925 achieved no

[11] H. D. Lamson, "Who's Who in China," *China Critic*, III (1930), 1113.

[12] The following men are among the individuals who might be included in such a list. (1) Chou Yi-ch'un (Y. T. Tsur)—president of Tsing Hua College, director of the International Famine Relief Commission and of the China Foundation for the Promotion of Education and Culture, 1924–1928; president of Yenching University, 1933–1934; minister of agriculture and forestry, 1945–1947; minister of health, 1947–1948. (2) Wu Chien (Zung Tse Kien Woo)—superintendent of Hanyang Iron and Steel Works and of Tayeh Iron and Steel Works; technical chief of Han-Yeh-P'ing Iron and Coal Company. (3) Yen Fu-ch'ing—dean of Hunan-Yale Medical College, 1914; dean, College of Medicine, National Central Medical College, 1927–1928; superintendent, Chinese Red Cross Hospital, 1928–1933. (4) Yen Hui-ch'ing (W. W. Yen)—minister to Germany; minister of foreign affairs, 1920–1922; prime minister, 1922, 1925–1926; ambassador to the U.S.S.R., 1933–1936. (5) Ts'ao Yün-hsiang (Y. S. Tsao)—president of Tsing Hua, 1922. (6) Shih Chao-chi (Alfred Sao-ke Sze)—delegate to Paris Peace Conference, 1918–1919; minister to Great Britain, 1914–1921, 1929–1932; minister to the U.S.A., 1921–1929, 1933–1935. (7) Hung Jung-liang (Hwang Yung-liang)—minister to Austria, Chinese representative to the League of Nations. (8) Niu Hui-sheng (Way Sung New)—prominent physician, one of the founders of the National Medical Association

such national distinction (*Table 8*). One explanation is that the Christian colleges persuaded a large proportion of their graduates to enter Christian work. To some extent the missions ploughed the graduates back into their own work rather than contributing them to the general welfare of China. This is not wholly true, since a large portion of the graduates taught in mission schools which educated thousands of China's school children. Slightly less than 10 percent of the Christian college graduates were teaching in non-Christian schools in 1925, whereas 26 percent of the alumni were teaching in mission schools. Only St. John's and Nanking had a large number of alumni teaching in government schools as well as mission schools.

A significant number of Christian college graduates who were interested in social service attended the mission medical schools and then worked in the mission hospitals. Since the figures for 1925 include only the graduates of the liberal arts colleges, the percentage engaged in all types of medical work is only 7.6 percent. If, as in 1924, the graduates of the separate professional schools were also included, the total number in medicine would be well over 10 percent of all graduates.

Fewer graduates became Christian ministers; the average was 5 percent, and the proportion was declining.[13] Hangchow and Hua-chung were proud of having approximately one-fifth of their alumni enter the ministry. For a number of reasons only a small percentage of Christian college students became clergymen. College-trained

---

of China. (9) Tiao Tso-ch'ien (Philip K. C. Tyau)—minister to Cuba and Panama; chief secretary to the Chinese delegation to the Washington Conference, 1921. (10) Tung Hsien-kuang (Hollington K. Tong)—newspaper editor and director, China Press, 1931–1935; managing director of *China Times, Ta wan pao,* and China Publishing Co.; vice-minister of information, 1937–1945. (11) Ku Wei-chun (V. K. Wellington Koo)—Chinese Plenipotentiary to Paris Peace Conference, 1919–1920; chief Chinese delegate to League of Nations, 1920; Premier and Minister of Foreign Affairs on several occasions during the 1920's; Ambassador to France, 1935, and to Great Britain, 1941–1947. (12) Sung Tze-wen (T. V. Soong)—Minister of Finance and Vice-President, Executive Yuan, 1928–1931; head of Bank of China, 1935–1943; Minister of Foreign Affairs, 1942–1945; President, Executive Yuan, 1945–1947. Though these individuals attended mission schools, most completed their education elsewhere; many were in positions where a knowledge of English was an important asset.

[13] *Statistical Report of Christian Colleges, 1924,* Table XIII, p. 18.

Table 8. Occupations of Christian college graduates in 1925 (in numbers)

College	From the year	Minis-try	Social and Religious Work	Teaching Chris-tian	Teach-ing Other	Medi-cine	Law	Engi-neering	Agri-cul-ture	Public Life	Business	Study in China	Study abroad	Other	No record	Total
Canton	1918	0	1	30	3	0	0	0	1	8	9	3	14	6	2	77
Central (Huachung)	1906	25	0	41	9	6	0	1	0	3	18	0	4	14	5	126
Fukien	1919	2	1	24	16	0	0	0	0	2	6	5	9	1	3	69
Ginling	1919	0	3	33	8	1	0	0	0	0	0	2	13	8	0	68
Hangchow	1849	49	13	53	24	5	0	7	0	8	34	2	8	3	12	218
Nanking	1896	11	5	77	76	40	0	1	27	11	26	2	22	31	64	393
St. John's	1890	23	9	90	106	73	4	21	1	42	159	9	48	15	61	661
Shanghai	1911	16	10	77	14	3	1	0	1	2	33	1	7	10	9	184
Shantung	1864	43	312	340	17	117	0	0	0	47	62	3	4	1	328	1274
Soochow	1907	2	16	60	47	3	0	2	0	10	47	10	11	15	0	223
West China	1910	6	1	18	1	16	0	0	0	0	2	1	1	0	0	46
Yale-in-China	1917	0	3	15	18	1	0	0	0	3	1	2	6	4	6	59
Yenching (male)	No records.															
Yenching (female)	1901	0	10	24	2	1	0	0	0	0	1	6	9	7	3	63
Huping	1913	4	0	13	0	0	0	0	0	0	6	1	2	0	2	28
Hwa Nan	1921	0	0	17	1	2	0	0	0	0	0	0	2	1	0	23
Lutheran	No graduates before 1925.															
Total		181	384	912	342	268	5	32	30	136	404	47	160	116	495	3512

Source: Handbook of Christian Colleges and Universities, 1926, Table XI, p. 38. These figures include only the graduates of the liberal arts colleges, not of the separate professional schools.

Chinese had to be accorded much higher social status and financial reward than those with a middle school education or less; without mission aid, few Chinese congregations could offer the salaries asked by college graduates. Also influential were the low esteem accorded most priests, whether Buddhist, Taoist, or Christian; the stigma of foreignness attached to Christianity and Christian workers, and a disinterest in the doctrinal and institutional aspects of Christianity among college students. Some Chinese were offended by the denominational divisions of Protestant Christianity and by the failure of some missionaries to keep abreast of recent scholarship in science and religion. The Christian missions produced many sincere and hard-working Chinese Christians; before 1928 they produced few outstanding religious leaders and no great Chinese theologians who could adapt Christianity to China and make it a Chinese rather than a foreign religion.[14]

Eleven percent of the graduates entered social and religious work exclusive of the ministry, and the proportion in this field had also declined between 1900 and 1925.[15] Cheeloo (Shantung Christian University) was the principal center for training social and religious workers—one-fourth of its graduates chose this occupation. Its preponderant place was related to its stress on the Christian purpose of the school and to its emphasis on the Chinese language rather than English as a medium of instruction. For most of the period before 1925 mission school graduates who had concentrated on Chinese rather than English were at a disadvantage in securing employment outside the mission or scholarships for study abroad; only seven of Shantung's graduates were studying abroad in 1925. These graduates, on the other hand, were well equipped for social work where a modest level of achievement in Chinese in addition to a knowledge of Western learning and of Christianity were necessary. Many were employed by the YMCA. Those schools that stressed English and admitted a large portion of non-Christians were less successful in persuading their graduates to enter evangelical and social work. If they did enter Christian service, the graduates in-

[14] "Report of the Christian Literature Council on the Present State and Future Task of Christian Literature in China," and "The Development of Leadership for the Work of the Church," NCC, 1922, pp. 432, 582.

[15] Statistical Report of Christian Colleges, 1924, Table XIII, p. 18.

creasingly preferred educational or medical work, occupations with higher standing and greater income.

Of the Christian college alumni, 4 percent were engaged in government work in 1925. Most Christian colleges had relatively few of their alumni in business, though several colleges in Shanghai and Soochow had about one-fifth of their graduates enter commerce. Approximately 6 percent of the total number of graduates were engaged in further study in 1925. For most alumni, the Christian colleges served one of two purposes: preparation for mission employment, particularly in the Christian schools; or training in English language and Western learning as preparation for teaching in government schools, for a business career in the treaty ports, or for graduate study.

This picture is incomplete, since the colleges lost a large portion of their students before graduation; for these students, statistics are unavailable. Some taught in elementary or middle schools and others became English tutors. Many apparently entered business. Certainly the missionaries' complaints about students' leaving to take lucrative positions in the port cities were loud and frequent. Quite a few apparently worked for foreign companies, where they acted as interpreters, clerks, or compradors. The British-American Tobacco Company, for example, required that a large proportion of its Chinese workers be able to use English; its interpreters and most of its bookkeepers were Chinese. Many of these reportedly were former mission school students.[16] *Men of Shanghai and North China,*[17] a collection of biographies published in 1933, contains accounts of both Chinese and Western leaders, and it is biased in favor of those Chinese with whom Westerners had greatest contact, generally those Chinese who spoke English. It emphasizes those who were successful in economic fields, whereas the *Who's Who in China* volumes are weighted on the political side. Of the ninety-three Chinese leaders listed, approximately one-third were educated in Christian colleges.

[16] Based on a questionnaire answered by Arthur W. Gregory and Quentin Gregory, both of whom were employed by the British-American Tobacco Co. in China from 1911 to 1918.

[17] George F. Nelliest, ed., *Men of Shanghai and North China* (Shanghai, 1933).

Training in English may have been only one of several considerations leading Christian college students to enter business. Marion J. Levy, in stating his belief that a large portion of the modern Chinese industrialists were educated abroad or in Western-type schools in China, offers another explanation.[18] Traditional Chinese society and education, which stressed family loyalty, land holding, and state service, did not provide an institutional structure or value system conducive to sustained and rapid industrial expansion. Levy concludes that a Chinese who had received a Western education, with its emphasis on competition, earned status, and other values incompatible with the Chinese heritage, would be better equipped to become a successful modern industrialist than a Chinese still immersed in the traditions of China. Chinese who attended the Christian colleges before 1925 had by this very act made a break with Chinese tradition; in fact, their choice of a Christian college often was an acknowledgment that they did not hope to rise within the traditional social structure; they looked to the college as a means of social mobility within that small sector of China that was undergoing change. Perhaps this is one reason why a few years in a mission school seemed to guide many toward membership in the business community of the treaty ports.

Conditions in China after 1925 make detailed analysis of the occupations and contributions of Christian college graduates during the 1930's and 1940's impossible. The CCEA, which under Earl Cressy had made surveys of many aspects of Christian education during the 1920's, did little in this realm during subsequent decades. To compile statistics that have validity from the biographical reference works published after 1931 is difficult. Training abroad continued to bring prestige, but as modern education became less of a rarity there was a tendency to omit mention of one's preparatory education in China. Chinese nationalism seems to have deterred some Christian college graduates from listing their undergraduate work.[19] Only general statements can be made, therefore, about the

[18] Levy and Kuo-heng Shih, *The Rise of the Modern Chinese Business Class* (New York, 1949), p. 13.

[19] An attempt to collect statistics on the educational background of individuals listed in the 1950 edition of *Who's Who in China*, for example, yielded no information on the undergraduate training of a large portion of the individuals,

contribution of Christian college graduates to Chinese national life during the 1930's and 1940's.

After 1925 there were apparently few major shifts in the types of occupations followed by Christian college graduates or in the general proportions entering various fields. The graduates, like the colleges, were beginning to play a more integral role in Chinese nation life; they were less likely than before to depend on mission employment. For example, approximately two-fifths of the Christian college alumni continued to enter educational work.[20] Since registration requirements and the war led to a significant decline in Christian elementary and secondary education, many of the Christian college graduates secured positions in the national educational system; in certain subjects such as agriculture, physical education, music, and English, the Christian colleges were a major source of supply. Chinese gradually displaced Westerners in the Christian colleges and the remaining secondary mission schools so that by 1937 the percentage of Chinese faculty members was much higher than that of Westerners in all the institutions and in all ranks. Education thus remained the occupation followed by the greatest number of Christian college alumni, but teaching no longer necessarily meant working in an institution dominated by Westerners and isolated from Chinese intellectual life.

The percentage of Christian college graduates entering the religious and social service fields declined somewhat during the

---

so that there was no assurance that those actually listing undergraduate degrees would provide a representative sample. Compounding the difficulty, the chaotic Chinese scene and the role of the Kuomintang led to a heavy emphasis on military and party leaders; leaders in other fields of endeavor were underrepresented. The *Biographical Dictionary of Republican China*, ed. by Howard L. Boorman and Richard C. Howard (New York, 1967–1970) is a valuable reference, but at the present writing only 3 vols. have been issued, and the biographies are fewer and more detailed than in the *Who's Who*.

[20] M. Searle Bates, *Missions in Far Eastern Cultural Relations* (New York, 1942), p. 11, gives the following statistics on the occupations of Christian college alumni in 1937: education, 41 percent; religion, 11 percent; medicine, 13 percent; commerce and industry, 11 percent; public service, 6 percent; unknown, 5 percent. Yenching reported on its alumni in 1938: education, 39 percent; public life, 18 percent; research and advanced training, 15 percent; social and religious work, 14 percent; business, 8 percent; other, 8 percent. *Yenching News*, XVII (Dec. 1938).

1930's, primarily because fewer were entering the ministry. Social service work, if anything, received greater emphasis because of the programs in rural reconstruction, industrial cooperatives, and urban welfare work. Although the percentage of Christian college graduates who entered medicine continued high, after 1925 they were less dependent on employment by mission hospitals; more entered private practice or became affiliated with government and private institutions.

The role of the Christian colleges in preparing Chinese for study abroad after 1925 continued to be an important one even if its nature changed somewhat.[21] During the 1930's and 1940's Tsing Hua became the leading single source of students going abroad on Boxer Indemnity scholarships. There were, nevertheless, fields which were encouraged because of their importance to national growth and power—agriculture and medicine, for example. Because Tsing Hua did not emphasize these studies while certain Christian colleges did, graduates of the latter often received government scholarships for advanced work in these categories. The Christian colleges also emphasized women's education, and a high proportion of the graduates of Ginling, Hwa Nan, and Yenching College for Women undertook advanced study. As a result of the policy of awarding some Boxer scholarships to women and the small percentage of women in government institutions, Christian college alumnae had considerable success in winning government grants. Many Chinese continued to go abroad without government scholarships, and for these the Christian colleges often provided English language training and Western contacts.

A small increase in the percentage of Christian college graduates entering public life was undoubtedly related to the fact that during

[21] It was reported in 1946 that more than 40 percent of the Chinese taking advanced work in the United States were Christian college graduates (*The China Colleges*, XIV [Oct. 1946], 2). A survey of Chinese students in the United States from 1854 to 1953 provided statistics for about half the students on the last schools attended in China; of these students, 38.3 percent were from the Christian colleges; 12.5 percent from Tsing Hua; 2.8 percent from Catholic schools and other colleges with Western support; and 46.3 percent from other Chinese institutions. See China Institute in America, *A Survey of Chinese Students in American Universities and Colleges in the Past One Hundred Years* (New York, 1954), pp. 36–37.

the 1930's an increasing proportion of the students in the Christian colleges came from affluent families. Personal contact was still crucial in securing government position, and this now worked to the benefit of Christian college alumni. At the same time few alumni attained positions of national prominence, since the party and the army provided the principal avenues to the top. Most of the alumni seem to have held routine jobs in the government hierarchy rather than the party hierarchy.

Those who did gain distinction often did so in fields where the Christian colleges had unique strength—in medicine, agriculture, or journalism. In 1947 over half of the staff of Peking University's College of Agriculture were graduates of the University of Nanking College of Agriculture and Forestry, and Nanking alumni dominated many other agricultural agencies and institutes, including the Ministry of Agriculture and Forestry and the provincial offices.[22] To a lesser extent Christian college graduates were prominent in medical education, the Chinese Medical Association, and the National Health Administration. Graduates of the Yenching department of journalism had an advantage in positions requiring a knowledge of both English and journalism so that they often became heads of China offices of international press services and Western newspapers. Journalists trained at Yenching were said to have introduced and popularized some of the methods of Western newspaper writing: feature stories, news photographs, and the use of the "lead" to introduce articles.[23] Since the Christian colleges had pioneered in higher education for women, the government and other institutions often turned to the officers and alumnae of the women's Christian colleges when they desired female representation; thus, Wu Yi-fang, president of Ginling, was delegate to the International Congress of Women, Chicago, 1933; member of the Presidium of the People's Political Council, 1940–47; and delegate to the United Nations' San Francisco Conference, 1945. Christian college graduates continued to hold diplomatic positions where facility in Western languages was important; they were, for example, heavily represented in the

[22] Letter of John H. Reisner to Rowland M. Cross, March 20–21, 1947, *CB*, no. 4 (April 11, 1947), 1; Bates, *Missions in Far Eastern Cultural Relations*, p. 27.
[23] *Yenching News*, XXVI (Nov. 1947).

Chinese staff at the United Nations immediately after World War II.

Even the People's Republic of China turned to Christian college alumni for certain types of positions. The editorial board of the English language periodical *China Reconstructs* and some of its more frequent contributors included Christian college graduates. Wu Yi-fang, Teng Yu-chih (Cora Deng), and others associated with the Christian colleges and the YWCA were prominent female representatives to numerous organizations and committees such as the People's Political Consultative Conference, the National People's Congress, and the Chinese People's Committee for World Peace. Kung P'eng, an alumna of Yenching, was for many years an interpreter and aide to Chou En-lai, and she served on such important occasions as the Marshall mission to China in 1945–1946 and the Geneva conference of 1954; she was director of the information department of the Ministry of Foreign Affairs from 1955 to 1964 and represented Peking at the 1961 Geneva conferences on Laos.

The Colleges and Chinese Nationalism

Both Chinese and Westerners have maintained that the contribution of Christian college students to China was diminished by the denationalization of the pupils. Statistics on the number of Christian college students who achieved fame or on the percentage of graduates who entered the newer professions tell only part of the story, it is said, because none of these individuals made the contribution toward the modernization of China that might have been expected. This criticism had been made both of those Chinese who began work immediately after graduation and of those who studied abroad. It has also been made of "returned students" in general, whether or not their preparatory training was in Christian institutions.[24] This

---

[24] Yang Hsiao-ch'un, "Chi-tu-chiao yü chiao-yü ch'üan," *CHCYC*, XIV, no. 8; Ch'iang Shu-ko, *Chung-kuo chin-tai chiao-yü chih-tu*, esp. pp. 154–170; Ch'en I-lin, *Chung-kuo chiao-yü shih*, pp. 346–372; Latourette, Personal communication, Dec. 12, 1953; Bates, *Missions in Far Eastern Cultural Relations*, p. 8; John Dewey, "American and Chinese Education," *The New Republic*, XXX (1922), 15–17; T. T. Lew, *China Today through Chinese Eyes*, pp. 98–99; Theodore Hsiao, *History of Modern Education*, pp. 130–131. For a detailed critique of "returned students" in general, see Y. C. Wang, *Chinese Intellectuals and the West, 1872–1949* (Chapel Hill, 1966).

criticism has an element of truth, but the term denationalization has been used to cover a multitude of sins. If by denationalization, it is meant that the individuals were alienated from rural China and from the Great Tradition of China, then few would deny the accuracy of the description. If, however, the critic also uses the term to imply a lack of patriotism, as it was used by nationalistic students of the 1920's, then the criticism is much less broadly applicable.

Many of the Christian college students were not masters of Chinese literary idiom and had difficulty adapting their learning to the Chinese environment. At the majority of the Christian institutions during the first quarter of the twentieth century, the students spent most of their time studying in the English language or learning the language itself. Courses in the social sciences were based on Western sources, and many of the science and mathematics textbooks were in English. Though government schools faced similar problems, alienation was undoubtedly more severe in the Christian institutions. Furthermore, when nationalism began to demand greater emphasis on Chinese culture and greater use of Chinese, the Christian college response was slow. Attempts to build strong departments of Chinese language and civilization met with many obstacles and few successes.[25]

Chinese lawyers and doctors have also been criticized for the use they made of their training. Many of the Chinese who studied medicine were said to have become so dependent on the well-

[25] Certain exceptions may be noted. With the aid of the Harvard-Yenching Institute, Yenching made important contributions to Chinese scholarship; the indexes to standard Chinese works published by the institute have been a boon to scholars. A partial list of the works in the Harvard-Yenching Institute Sinological Index Series compiled by William Hung, Nieh Ch'ung-ch'i, and others is given in Ssu-yü Teng and Knight Biggerstaff, *An Annotated Bibliography of Chinese Reference Works,* rev. ed. (Cambridge, Mass.; 1950), itself a monograph of *Yen-ching hsüeh-pao* (Yenching Journal of Chinese Studies). The Christian colleges had begun to emphasize the use of simplified Chinese style quite early; and several important writers in pai-hua or modernized Chinese style were educated in the Christian colleges. Hsieh Wan-ying (pen name Ping Hsin), the short story writer and poet; Hsu Chih-mo (pen names, Nan Hu and Shih Che), one of the pioneers in modern Chinese poetry; Hsu Ti-shan, novelist and short story writer; the playwright Hsiung Fu-hsi; and Yang Kang, novelist and newspaper reporter. Hsieh Wan-ying was one of the early supporters of the pai-hua movement; and during the May 4th Movement, he published propaganda articles written in the vernacular.

equipped hospitals of the treaty ports and the conveniences of city life that they were unwilling to work in rural China. Thus, the majority of the practitioners of modern medicine congregated in a few coastal cities, and the greater portion of the Chinese benefited little from the work of the Christian medical schools. Chinese who took legal training under Christian auspices learned Roman and English law, but knew relatively little about Chinese legal traditions; they were, therefore, handicapped in the attempt to work out a new Chinese legal system incorporating both Western and Chinese traditions.

At the same time, the very fact that educated Chinese in the twentieth century were the product of two cultures was important to the growth of Chinese nationalism. National consciousness is ordinarily based on a recognition of the existence of other nations and on a sense of competition with the people and culture of other nations. This attitude was foreign to the Middle Kingdom tradition of China. The Western presence in China, accompanied by a growing appreciation of the sources of Western power, was the catalyst of Chinese nationalism. And alienation from one's heritage seems a common phase in the development of Asian nationalist leaders. Few in the twentieth century have been men of tradition; they have, rather, been men of two worlds, men who could never go home again, men who could never return to the social structure and value system of their villages.

Some of the early products of the Christian colleges and government institutions and many of the returned students made only disappointing contributions to a new culture for a new China. They often lived compartmented lives in the "never, never world" of the treaty ports. A large percentage of the Christian college graduates who had not been abroad lived in the semi-isolated communities of the Christian institutions. Some gave up the struggle for change and, for the sake of personal security, made their peace with those in power. To modernize China was a mammoth task, and to accomplish much or even to remain committed when the leaven was so small was difficult. For most of these Chinese, however, education had contributed to national awareness and loyalty to the nation had become a primary value. Even those who were accused of being denationalized were in their contact with Westerners constantly reminded that they were Chinese. With their knowledge of the West, they often took the leadership in defending and explaining China to the West, a task which men of tradition could not perform.

By 1919 the forces for change had gathered momentum, and those living in the "two worlds atmosphere" of urban China could dominate the public image of China. Nationalistic movements and the forging of modern political instruments such as the Kuomintang and the Chinese Communist Party became possible. The younger generation in the government schools launched their first major nationalist movement with their demonstration on May 4, 1919. The fathers, those educators, professionals, and businessmen so often accused of being denationalized, gave support to their sons. With this illustration of the power and appeal of nationalism, May 4 quickly became a tradition, and the history of the 1920's was punctuated with nationalistic movements. Political leaders began to give expression to and to profit from the nationalism of educated Chinese. Nationalism had come to be a force to be reckoned with because it commanded the loyalty of both the New Youth and the older generation.

Though the returned students supporting the earliest nationalist movements included Christian college alumni, the Christian college communities themselves had been divided in their support and had been sharply criticized for their timidity and inaction. The nationalist movements demonstrated, however, that the separatism and autonomy of the Christian colleges were no longer acceptable; and the 1920's became a crucial era of transition for the Christian colleges. By the time of the Educational Rights Movement of the middle and late 1920's, the waves of nationalism were striking the Christian colleges and seemed about to inundate some of them. Even those accused of being denationalized, the Chinese students and teachers in the Christian colleges, supported demands that their institutions be made responsible to the Chinese government. Both sons and fathers among urban educated Chinese, both Christian college communities and public educators contributed to the pressure that made government registration and supervision a necessity. The first move toward the incorporation of the Christian schools into the national educational system was taken with the support of many in the Christian colleges. By the end of the 1920's integration of the Christian colleges with the Chinese environment had become a major theme among Westerners as well as Chinese. The criticism of Christian college students as denationalized with the implication that they were unresponsive to Chinese nationalism could therefore be considered generally applicable only for a brief period in the early 1920's.

During the 1920's when Christianity, Christian institutions, and the West were the focus of nationalistic movements, the distinctive traits of Chinese nationalism were being evolved. The movements contributed to an effort to distinguish Christianity from Western civilization, and they indicated that most Chinese found the secular and scientific strains of Western civilization more meaningful for the modernization process. Whatever their political loyalties, most educated Chinese accepted the Hobson-Lenin thesis on imperialism and documented it with examples of the symbiotic relationship between Christian missions and Western economic and political expansion. Anti-Christianism, anti-imperialism, anti-capitalism, and anti-Westernism became part of the very core of Chinese nationalism and at the same time molded its vocabulary.[26] Decisive also was the widespread acceptance of statism; few questioned the overriding importance of national unity or the leadership of the state in education, industrialization, and a host of other activities. In competition with integral nationalism and statism, neither individualism nor liberal democracy had great appeal. Educated Chinese, in giving content to Chinese nationalism during the 1920's, were providing a framework for the evolution of Chinese politics.

Moreover, the anti-Christian movement and the educational rights campaign illustrated the potency of the nationalist issue in power politics. The campaigns helped link youth movements with the new political parties, their power, and their political decisions. Student organizations and political parties began to assume an uneasy relationship in which each tried to use or influence the other in attaining what each considered the national interest of China. The competition of the students and the political organizations for

[26] In this connection it may be noted that the accusation campaigns against the Christian colleges in the 1950's echoed both the general themes and the specific criticisms of the 1920's movements. See articles on the colleges in the *China Monthly Review* for March, April, and Nov. 1951.

control of the nationalist issue encouraged reliance on the emotional appeal of anti-imperialism, anti-Westernism, and anti-Christianism, and these strains were enunciated again and again in the nationalist movements from the 1920's on.

Until the Sino-Japanese War of 1937, nationalism remained the monopoly of the urban educated elite. Conscious identification with the Chinese nation continued to be the consequence of experiences in urban China and the urban West, and it was almost invariably accompanied by alienation from rural Chinese life. Despite such programs as the New Life Movement, the nationalism of most Chinese remained largely negative in content for yet another decade and the ideological vacuum created by the destruction of Confucianism remained unfilled for many. During the 1930's Christian college youth participated more fully than before in national life and political movements; and in some of the demonstrations launched against the non-Western enemy, Japan, Christian college students even took the initiative. Christians, however, made no special contribution toward a new ideology for a new China. Though San Min Chu I, democracy, and liberal Christianity were espoused in the Christian college communities, Marxism-Leninism furnished the intellectual framework for many. The Christian college students were typical of the New Youth in that they frequently alternated between emotionalized nationalism directed at specific enemies and a privatism concerned only with personal interests and advancement.

When the Chinese Communist Party assumed control of China in 1949, the nationalist ideology which they used revealed many continuities with the nationalism of the 1920's and 1930's. Anti-capitalism and anti-imperialism as interpreted by Lenin were still important components. Anti-Westernism but at the same time alienation from the Confucian heritage and iconoclasm toward the Great Tradition were still significant themes. Both the desire for national unity and the readiness to accord power to the state had been accentuated by the civil war so that statism was an even more important aspect of nationalism in 1949 than it had been earlier. These continuities in addition to the Marxist-Leninist *Weltanschauung* popular among many educated Chinese facilitated the acceptance of communist rule by noncommunists. The New Youth in the Christian and government schools and many of the fathers welcomed the Chinese communists as spokesmen for Chinese nationalism.

Chinese nationalism also acquired new emphases after 1949. The tie between nationalism and revolution was revived after having been minimized for a quarter of a century, and revolution in this instance included social revolution. Though the communist leadership of the 1920's had belonged to the alienated, urban elite, the party had, since experiencing numerous disasters in the cities, built support by fostering social revolution in the countryside. Antibourgeois attitudes had been fed by practical experience as well as ideology. Urbanized intellectuals received an ambivalent welcome from the Chinese Communist Party since they were considered necessary to the regime, but not trustworthy. As the United States became the symbol of Western imperialism, of bourgeois democracy, and of continued Kuomintang resistance, nationalism became specifically identified with anti-Americanism. The consequences for the Christion colleges and for any assessment of the role of their graduates were multiple.

However nationalistic members of the Christian college communities might be, the institutions themselves were too closely associated with bourgeois ideals and with the United States to be permitted to continue for long. Whatever contributions the nationalistic fathers and sons had made, both in destroying the old and laying the foundations for the new, were lost from sight in the violence of the revolution begun in 1949. Modernization might require urbanization and industrialization, but it also includes agricultural and social revolution, and during their decade in the wilderness from 1927 to 1937 the communists had learned to use the revolutionary potential of rural China for their own political benefit. It was not that the Kuomintang elite had been denationalized but that their nationalism had ignored the need for revolutionary change in the countryside. Kuomintang nationalism, lacking roots in the peasantry, cut off from urban China during the war, and unable to exploit anti-Westernism, lost its base and focus. It lost also the support of many in the intellectual community. The Communist Party, by its emphasis on anti-Americanism could draw on the deep strain of anti-Westernism in Chinese nationalism. By its call for rural revolution, it could appeal to the revolutionary populism still attractive to many nationalists.[27] Many of the New Youth and many of the fathers transferred their loyalties in the hope of continuing their efforts to build a new China.

The Colleges and the Creation of a New China

In China between 1850 and 1950 the forces for change, both internally and externally, were so overwhelming that the destruction of Confucian China and the search for a new China would have occurred with or without the Christian educational effort. A people in contact with a foreign civilization, however, are highly selective; they adopt values, institutions, and techniques which seem meaningful and useful. The Christian colleges undoubtedly influenced Chinese selections from the West by influencing Chinese understanding and appreciation of Western civilization. Just as the attitude of many Chinese toward Christianity was partially determined by its association with imperialism, so the Chinese attitude toward the organization of higher education was influenced by the Christian college example. During the nineteenth century the Christion missionary was for many Chinese the personification of Western civilization, and the missionary's insistence on the dichotomy between Christianity and Confucianism contributed to a negative attitude toward many aspects of Western civilization.[28] On the other hand, the demonstrations of the benefits of Western medicine by mission doctors, hospitals, and medical schools facilitated the acceptance of medicine as an honorable profession. The same can be said of other aspects of Western civilization which Christian missionaries helped introduce. The history of the Christian colleges, therefore, provides insight into the changing attitudes of Chinese toward Western civilization and some indication of the reasons for the selections made by Chinese in the transformation of China.

[27] For further discussion, see Olga Lang, *Pa Chin and His Writings. Chinese Youth between the Two Revolutions* (Cambridge, Mass.; 1967), pp. 245, 265–267.

[28] Among the many arguments by Grand Secretary Wo-jen against the introduction of Western learning at the Peking T'ung-wen Kuan in 1867, one was the fact that Christianity was already gaining a foothold in China. To neglect Confucian learning for Western learning and to study under the Western barbarians would only encourage the growth of the foreign religion. See English translation of Wo-jen's memorial in Teng and Fairbank, *China's Response*, pp. 76–77.

The most conspicuous area of influence by the Christian colleges was naturally education. During the nineteenth century the Christian colleges were unique in China in that they presented a combination of Western and Chinese learning as the norm for educated Chinese. Most Chinese were not greatly impressed by the Christian college example, for to them the classical curriculum determined by the civil service examinations was the norm. Because the Christian colleges were a means of mobility for a limited number of Chinese, however, they could not be totally ignored. Because missionary educators were competing in an area generally reserved for the gentry, they represented a challenge to the traditional social structure. The mission schools were considered unworthy rivals fit only to be disdained, but nevertheless rivals. At the turn of the century when Chinese began to alter the educational system, the Christian educators and institutions began to have a more positive function. Ready at hand were Western-type institutions, and they could help in the formulating and answering of fundamental questions: What should be the relative emphasis given to mass elementary education and to higher education? Should professional education, a general liberal education at the college level, or highly specialized training at the middle level receive greater attention? Somewhat later the problem of the relation between the private and public sectors in education was made concrete in the educational rights campaign. And this, in turn, was closely allied with nationwide debate about the purposes of education and the relation between church and state.

As Chinese shaped their initial plans for a national educational system, they often turned to the missionaries and Christian college alumni for teachers, advisors, and administrators. At the request of Governor Yuan Shih-k'ai of Shantung, W. M. Hayes resigned as president of Tengchow College and accepted the presidency of a new provincial college in Shantung.[29] Hayes drew up a plan for a system of provincial grammar and high schools to act as feeders for the college. Governor Yuan not only approved the plan, but also sent it to the Empress Dowager who ordered copies sent to the governors and governors-general of all the provinces. When Yuan Shih-k'ai was made governor-general of Chihli, he had C. D. Tenney

[29] Headland, *China's New Day*, pp. 108–109.

draw up a similar educational plan for that province. In 1908 three graduates of Shantung Christian College were sent by the government to establish an institution of higher education in Yunnan. Two St. John's alumni, Hu I-ku as dean of Nanyang University and Ts'ao Yün-hsiang as president of Tsing Hua University, helped make their institutions leaders in higher education in China.[30] In addition to requesting help in organizing schools, Chinese administrators and teachers visited the Christian schools, observed their organization, and discussed with the missionaries Western curricula and pedagogical methods. The 10 percent of the Christian college graduates who taught in government or private schools carried with them much of the methodology and curriculum of the mission institutions.

The Christian educators had led in the introduction of the graded textbook to China, and many of the early textbooks used by the government schools had been written by missionaries. Though most of the works were eventually displaced by Japanese or Chinese texts, the Christian educators continued to make important contributions to both monographic and textbook literature in certain special fields such as medicine, agriculture, and English. In composing and translating this literature, the missionary educators had found it necessary to devise standard lists of scientific and medical terms in Chinese. They later cooperated with government-appointed committees in standardizing the translation of practically all medical and scientific terms in common use.

In the sciences and physical education the Christian colleges had particular influence. The colleges generally continued during the first quarter of the century to offer the best of the scientific programs given by the liberal arts institutions of China,[31] and, therefore, they remained important as models. The research activities of the Cheeloo College of Medicine, of the Lingnan and Nanking agricultural colleges, and later of Yenching University in sociology and Chinese studies helped demonstrate the valuable contributions which could be made by the application of the scientific method to

[30] For biographies of Hu I-ku and Ts'ao Yün-hsiang, see *Who's Who in China*, 1925, pp. 670–671, 741. Earlier, Peiyang College (later Peiyang University) and Shanghai School of Technology (Kung-i hsüeh-t'ang) had been founded with the guidance of educational missionaries.

[31] Morgan, *Teaching of Science to the Chinese*, pp. 63–64.

Chinese problems. Christian missionaries had met considerable opposition when they introduced physical education and recreation for students. As the mission school students had come to enjoy sports such as track, tennis, and soccer, however, the Christian colleges had organized intercollegiate athletic contests which included representatives from non-Christian institutions. The government eventually adopted the view that physical training could strengthen China by strengthening its citizens, and in 1909 the first program of modern physical education for China was organized under the leadership of M. J. Exner of the International Committee of the YMCA.[32]

The educational system initiated by the Chinese government during the early twentieth century thus employed many of the educational techniques devised in the West and exemplified in the Christian schools. The establishment of schools was not to be left up to individuals, families, or clans, but was to become a government responsibility. All Chinese were to be made literate, productive individuals and loyal citizens. As Chinese leaders had come to realize that a nationally conscious citizenry with a sense of civic responsibility could be a source of strength to a government, they looked to a national educational system to achieve this objective. The concept was in many ways compatible with the purposes served by classical education and the examination system, and Chinese needed little instruction from missionary educators to understand the political goals of education. The example of the mission schools did not go unnoticed, nevertheless; the Christian institutions had also been founded for purposes of indoctrination, as Chinese were well aware. The schools were for many Chinese a conspicuous illustration of the way in which Westerners used formal education for instilling a set of beliefs and a system of values. At the same time the clientele of the mission schools demonstrated the possibility of education on a mass basis; most of their pupils during the early decades had come from poor, illiterate families, and a number of these had completed a college education and became prosperous and valuable citizens. Missionary educators were among the early

[32] Gunsun Hoh, *Physical Education in China* (Shanghai, 1926), pp. 90–93, 163; S. Lavington Hart, *Education in China* (London, 1923), p. 9.

advocates of teaching in the vernacular, an essential innovation if the masses were to be educated.

As China began to seek more direct contact with the outside world, her dependence on the Christian educators and the mission schools for educational guidance declined. The 1912 revision of the Chinese educational system was strongly influenced by the Japanese model. The Boxer Indemnity Scholarships enabled hundreds of Chinese to go directly to the West for their knowledge of Western education, and furthermore, educational committees were sent to Japan, Europe, and the United States to observe educational methods and types of organization. Chinese complained that in the Christian schools the educational goals had been subordinated to the religious aims, and before 1911 this characterization was well founded. Though the narrowly evangelistic emphasis was generally abandoned during the twentieth century, the Christian colleges were most influential as educational models before this modification; this religious emphasis helps to explain why the Chinese turned so soon to other guides. The Chinese concept of the mission institutions which was formed during these early years lingered on and contributed to the strong nationalist reaction against the colleges during the 1920's, a reaction which in the case of certain colleges seemed more violent than current conditions warranted.

During the disrupted decade of the 1920's the Christian colleges became antimodels rather than models for Chinese educators and nationalists. Their major educational role during the 1920's was to stimulate national debate about the relation between public and private educational institutions. Partly because the Christian institutions preached doctrines deemed incompatible with the dominant ideologies of the 1920's, but primarily because of the Chinese definition of the purpose of education, there seemed no room for completely independent, private educational institutions. All schools would be subject to government regulation and all would be required to give instruction in the national ideology; courses in any other ideology could not be compulsory. Though the weakness of the government permitted some variation in practice, few political or intellectual leaders seem to have been philosophically committed to pluralism. In this realm there has been continuity from imperial China to communist China.

Christian education emerged from the 1920's with a mandate for Sinification and secularization, and during the next two decades it underwent significant changes along both these lines. Christian educators, however, have been criticized for not experimenting with new types of educational institutions and programs in carrying out this mandate. China was experiencing the problems typical of a heavily populated state moving from agrarian tradition toward modernization: overproduction of highly trained and urbanized professionals and a shortage of skilled technicians trained at the intermediate level. Why, it has been asked, did the Christian educators not evolve educational programs uniquely suited to China rather than import the expensive educational structure of the West? Why not, for example, concentrate limited funds and personnel on training large numbers of public health workers to serve the masses rather than a few M.D.'s for urban China? But the Western and Chinese educators in the Christian institutions were, after all, products of their own educational experience, and they quite naturally accepted the systems they had known as the norm. Institutional loyalties in China and among Western supporters were already established; in a time of depression and financial hardship, it was not easy to starve existing programs for experimental ones.

The few attempts by Christian educators to organize such intermediate programs, furthermore, had been resisted by the Chinese. Since tradition held those who worked with their heads superior to those who worked with their hands, any Chinese who got as far as middle school wanted to attain literati status, and he had no interest in becoming a technician or foreman. It seems probable that only a massive effort at the national level, a program involving government support and coercion and a complete restructuring of the school system could have made such a program acceptable. Even though the People's Republic has undertaken such an effort, the response has been mixed and its success uncertain. This does not mean that experimentation by the Christian institutions was impossible; it does mean that there was no widespread demand for it among the Chinese clientele and relatively little official support.

During its last two decades in China Christian education was represented primarily by the liberal arts colleges and a few professional programs. Many of the Christian institutions continued to be outstanding for their instruction in the English language and literature, and several had strong undergraduate programs in science. Their most distinctive characteristics during the 1930's, however, had little appeal for nationalistic educators or social reformers: administrative stability and relatively tight control over student activities, insistence on general liberal arts requirements before specialization, and the fostering of an active and cohesive campus community. Most of the institutions furnished their students with the means to a liberal arts education of good quality; and within the limits set by national crises, they tried to create an environment which would persuade the students to concentrate on their academic responsibilities. Though not the equal of the best government universities, the Christian colleges were generally well above average in the standard of education actually offered. This was in comparison with the many government institutions that failed to fulfill their potential because of political pressures and the inadequacy and irregularity of their support.

The Christian colleges thus supplemented the limited educational facilities of Kuomintang China; and to certain Chinese, especially those of some means, the distinctive features of the Christian colleges made them attractive, even preferable to the government schools. In the mid-1930's one of the institutions sent questionnaires to its graduates asking them to indicate what had meant most to them in their education at the school. The answers were in many ways true to the character of the Christian colleges; they emphasized the personal relationships among faculty and students, the spirit of the college, the friendships formed, and the emphasis on the spirit of service.[33] However valuable these might be, they did not represent the major interests of Chinese educators in planning higher education during the 1930's; the liberal arts college did not exert great influence on the evolution of Chinese education during this decade.

Only in certain special areas did the Christian institutions maintain a position of leadership. Agricultural education and research was one of these fields. The University of Nanking had pioneered in demonstrating the significance of modern agricultural research

[33] Fukien Christian University, *What My Education in Fukien Christian University Means to Me.*

and training for Chinese economic growth; and even after Lingnan, West China Union University, and a number of government institutions had entered the field, Nanking's College of Agriculture and Forestry remained in the forefront. The Chinese government was well aware of the fundamental work being done at Nanking, and relations between the university and the Chinese government and national schools were cordial. Nanking sponsored basic research in a great variety of areas, and some of the findings were significant for scholarship far beyond the realm of agricultural economics. In addition to evolving new agricultural techniques, developing some forty new varieties of seed, and training agriculturists; Nanking created the model for agricultural extension work, research programs, and curricula at the college and secondary levels.

The Nanking and Lingnan agricultural divisions worked with representatives from the Christian colleges and other associations in organizing rural reconstruction projects during the 1930's. In this work as in agriculture, the major achievement was a contribution to knowledge rather than significant improvement in the livelihood of the peasantry. Though some might consider such a contribution appropriate for academic institutions, others were disappointed that little progress was made toward revolutionizing the countryside. These rural reconstruction projects in China during the 1930's were among the first to give concrete demonstration of the internal cohesion of village life and the complexity of rural change. In addition, some of the essential techniques for initiating rural reconstruction programs were evolved. The initiation of a national program, however, was far beyond the capacity of the Christian colleges, and the Kuomintang government was not prepared to make such a massive effort with its risks of social revolution during the 1930's. For some of the Chinese committed to rural reconstruction the communists seemed after the war to promise fulfillment. Other individuals who had been associated with the University of Nanking or the rural reconstruction projects of the 1930's accompanied the Kuomintang to Taiwan and were able as members of the Joint Commission on Rural Reconstruction to put many of their findings into practice.

The missionary educators and doctors helped create among Chinese an understanding and appreciation of medicine as a profession. The missionaries not only established hospitals, but they founded some of the first medical schools in China, and these Christian institutions trained a large portion of the doctors educated in China. Taking their own experience as the norm, the medical educators steadily raised academic standards, thus, the model for medical training in China became the professional school producing a limited number of highly educated experts. The missionaries were the first in China to emphasize the scientific basis of medicine by requiring the use of cadavers in their anatomy classes; they prescribed the study of chemistry, biology, and physics as a foundation for the medical course; and in so far as possible they made compulsory the performance of laboratory experiments by the students themselves. They tried to introduce the professional ethics and the ideal of social service advocated by Western medical associations; and in order to regulate professional and educational standards, they organized the Chinese Medical Missionary Association in 1886. This organization performed a variety of other functions, such as publication of scholarly research, translation of medical works, and standardization of medical nomenclature in Chinese. By their research on diseases especially prevalent in China, the Christian institutions contributed to medical knowledge in general and to the improvement of health standards in China; the control of epidemics and the elimination of parasitic diseases resulting from the use of night soil were subjects receiving special attention. Almost inevitably the establishment of hospitals and the practice of modern medicine led to the importation of the nursing profession, and so Christian missions also introduced a new occupation for women.[34]

Two other areas where the Christian colleges were pioneers may be mentioned briefly. The Boone Library School, associated with Huachung University, made a small, but significant contribution to education and scholarship in China by introducing the study of library science. A modified Dewey system of cataloguing Chinese volumes was devised for small libraries, and its use made numerous Chinese collections more accessible to both readers and librarians.

[34] Actually, the emphasis on separation of the sexes meant that there was a strong preference for male doctors and nurses in the care of men and female doctors and nurses in the care of women. Though the division was not strictly maintained, neither of the professions became quite the monopoly of one sex that they tended to be in the United States.

The school trained a number of Chinese in the new profession of library science and sent them out to bring some system to the libraries in the schools of China. The work of the school, traditionally supported by Boxer funds, has been continued by Tunghai University, which offers courses in library science and which publishes *T'u-shu-kuan hsüeh-pao* (Journal of Library Science) and occasional books and pamphlets in the field (The Library Science Series). Yenching University's department of journalism introduced a new academic field and was for a brief period during the 1930's a center for training newspapermen for China. Its leaders also helped found the Chinese Journalists Association in 1936 in an attempt to defend freedom of the press.

Perhaps one of the more revolutionary moves by the Christian missionaries in the nineteenth century was to initiate formal education for women. Missionaries were not only saying that women were individuals worthy of education but also saying that women could earn a living in an honorable profession. Without necessarily being feminists, missionary educators were laying the foundation for a greater degree of independence than women had formerly known in China. The pressure of the missionary example and other influences from the West led the Chinese government early in the twentieth century to acknowledge some responsibility for women's education. The Christian institutions throughout their history gave greater emphasis to women's education than did the government schools, however. Chinese governments and organizations desiring female representation often looked to the Christian colleges, and this in itself was a recognition of their continuing leadership in women's education.

The main purpose of the missionaries in coming to China was the conversion of China to Christianity. In this they failed. The number of Christians in China never reached more than 1 percent of the total population, and though a Christian church survived in the People's Republic of China after the departure of the missionaries, it was a small and weak institution. Its future seemed uncertain. As part of the Three-Self Movement, some deeply committed Christians sought to organize a Chinese church within a generally hostile environment, but to most Chinese Christians the church had not become an institution which they could call their own; they did not maintain their ties with it. Chinese Christianity, furthermore, cannot be said to have had any great impact on the religious life of most Chinese. This is true despite the role of Christian missions in disrupting Chinese tradition and thereby undermining religious and social values; it was not primarily the Chinese Christian church nor Christian doctrines as such which challenged the Great Tradition; the challenge came from those missionary activities, institutions, and ideas which accompanied the preaching of the gospel. Since the communist victory of 1949, numerous students of Christian missions have tried to assess the reasons for failure. Why, they have asked, were so few Chinese attracted to Christianity? Why after a mission effort of unequaled magnitude was China left with an institution considered neither particularly vital nor especially interesting by most Chinese? Why was a nationalism with an anti-Western and anti-Christian base the most conspicuous residue?

Before 1925 the China colleges could say that the majority of their graduates were Christians and that at least half of their alumni entered some form of Christian service. On the other hand, a large portion of those Chinese who found employment outside mission institutions let their church activities lapse as soon as they left college. Only a few graduates entered the ministry, and very few of these became leaders who could translate Christian doctrines and institutions into Chinese terms. Christianity remained a foreign religion and the church a foreign institution. If anything, the tendency of Christian college alumni to dissociate themselves from the church became even more pronounced after 1925. Inability to staff the church with well educated Chinese ministers meant that many college graduates did not feel intellectually or emotionally at home in the institution. After 1925, furthermore, the proportion of Christians among the Christian college students declined and the number of conversions fell off. Many of the colleges were neither able to maintain a student body that was largely Christian nor able to find employment in Christian institutions for the majority of their alumni. This change in emphasis may be attributed partly to the campaign to raise educational standards, a change which meant that educational rather than religious objectives had to be given priority.

Moreover, Christianity had not been accepted as essential to

Chinese nationalism and the building of a new China. The Christianity brought to China had been heavily encrusted with elements of Western civilization and with church tradition. Perhaps in the nineteenth century it was not possible to separate Christianity from Western tradition. The Christian churches trying to appeal to people belonging to the mature and sophisticated Chinese heritage were themselves mature institutions, and Christian misions were the expressions of a culture confident of its superiority. This is in sharp contrast with the period of Christian expansion in the late Roman and early medieval times when the church was a flexible and evolving institution. In China in the nineteenth century the church showed little readiness to shake off any aspect of tradition as nonessential. Church organization, music, ritual, and the like remained Western. Even the various denominational doctrines and structures were considered essential and were brought to China as part of Christianity. Christianity was so deeply enmeshed in Western civilization that conversion often required adoption of many Western customs and values. Since Christianity was an exclusive faith, conversion demanded abandonment of much of the Chinese heritage.

At a time when most Chinese were reluctant to borrow from the West and to alter Chinese tradition, the close association of Christianity and Western civilization may have fortified the opposition to change. Chinese were offended by the foreignness of Christianity as well as by the arrogance of many representatives of Western Christendom, traders, diplomats, and missionaries. The implication that modernization required complete Westernization went against a natural desire of Chinese reformers to select those elements of Western civilization which seemed useful and meaningful. Intellectual and emotional resistance notwithstanding, China was changing. The Great Tradition was disintegrating rapidly by the turn of the century, and few educated Chinese could deny the necessity of seeking new bases of wealth and power. The activities of the missionaries had undoubtedly contributed to the process of change even while they had stiffened intellectual resistance. Their educational and medical work, their presence in China forced upon Chinese the recognition of the existence of another civilization. They became a part of the image which Chinese formed of that civilization.

By the 1920's, when the need for drastic change had been generally acknowledged by educated, urban Chinese, Westerners and Chinese alike were questioning the relevance of traditional Christianity for modern society. Programs with a statist, secular orientation seemed more meaningful, and none of the nationalist political movements included Christianity in its program for modernization. This was true despite attempts by liberal Christians to give meaning to their doctrine by fostering an ideal of social service and civic responsibility. The rural reconstruction projects were a contribution to China but not to Chinese Christianity. The same might be said of the Christian colleges. Their contribution to China was of lasting importance; their contribution to Christianizing China or Sinifying Christianity was marginal. The colleges aided the Chinese in defining themselves and in defining the West. The colleges helped make changes necessary and possible, and they stimulated the growth of Chinese nationalism. That nationalism had and continues to have a strong anti-Western bias.

| List of China Christian Colleges |

(with Dates of Founding, Amalgamations,

and Changes in Names—simplified)

Protestant Institutions

Canton Christian College, see Lingnan University

Cheeloo University (Ch'i-lu ta-hsüeh), Tsinan

Tengchow Boys' School, Tengchow, 1864 ⟶ Tengchow College, 1882 } Shantung Union College, Weihsien, 1902 ⟶
Tsingchow Boys' Boarding School, Tsingchow, 1894

Shantung Union College
Tsingchow Theological Institute, 1885 ⟶ Gotch-Robinson Theological School, 1903 } Shantung Protestant University, 1904 ⟶
Medical College, Tsinan, 1890's

Shantung Protestant University ⟶ Shantung Christian University, 1909 } Shantung Christian University, Tsinan, 1917 ⟶
Tsinan Institute, 1905

Shantung Christian University
North China Union Medical College for Women, 1908 } Shantung Christian University, 1924 ⟶ Cheeloo University, 1931

Fukien Christian University (Fu-chin hsieh-ho ta-hsüeh), Foochow

Foochow Anglo-Chinese College (upper classes)
St. Mark's Anglo-Chinese College   "   " } Fukien Union College, 1916 ⟶ Fukien Christian University, 1918
Foochow College   "   "

Ginling College (Chin-ling nü-tzu ta-hsüeh), Nanking, founding date, 1913; opening of Ginling College, 1915

Hangchow University (Chih-chiang ta-hsüeh), Hangchow
Ningpo Boys' School, 1845 → Hangchow Presbyterian Boys' School, 1867 → Hangchow Presbyterian College, 1897 →
Hangchow Christian College, 1914 → Hangchow University, 1948

Huachung University (Hua-chung ta-hsüeh), Wuchang
Boone School, Wuchang, 1871 → Boone University, 1909
Wesley College, Wuchang, 1885
Griffith John College, Hankow, 1899 } Central China University (Huachung), 1924 →
Huachung University, Wuchang
Huping College, Yochow, 1900's } Huachung College, 1929 → Huachung University, 1946
Yale-in-China, Changsha, 1906

Hwa Nan College (Hua-nan nü wen-li hsüeh-yüan), Foochow
The Foochow College Preparatory of Foochow Woman's College, 1908 →
Woman's College of South China, 1914 (two-year course) → Hwa Nan College, 1917 (four-year course)

Lingnan University (Ling-nan ta-hsüeh), Canton
Christian College in China, Canton, 1888 → Canton Christian College, 1903 → Lingnan University, 1926

University of Nanking (Chin-ling ta-hsüeh), Nanking
Nanking University, 1888
Nanking Christian College, 1880's } Union Christian College, 1906 → University of Nanking, 1910
Presbyterian Academy, 1880's

Peking University, see Yenching University

St. John's University (Sheng-yüeh-han ta-hsüeh), Shanghai
St. John's College, 1879 → St. John's University, 1905

University of Shanghai (Hu-chiang ta-hsüeh), Shanghai
Shanghai Baptist College and Theological Seminary, 1906 → Shanghai College, 1918 → University of Shanghai, 1931

Shantung Christian University, see Cheeloo University

Soochow University (Tung-wu ta-hsüeh), Soochow

Buffington Institute of Soochow, 1871 \
Anglo-Chinese College of Shanghai, 1882 } Soochow University, 1901, and \
Kung Hong School of Soochow, 1896 } Shanghai Anglo-Chinese College } Soochow University, 1911 →

Soochow University

The Comparative Law School of China, Shanghai, 1915 } Soochow University, 1915

West China Union University (Hua-hsi hsieh-ho ta-hsieh), Chengtu

West China Union University, 1910

Yale-in-China, see Huachung University

Yenching University (Yen-ching ta-hsüeh), Peking

T'ungchow Boy's School, T'ungchow, 1867 → North China College, 1889 → North China Union College, 1904 } Peking \
Gordon Memorial Theological College, 1893 → North China Union Theological College, 1904 } University, \
Methodist Boy's School in Peking, 1870 → Wiley Institute, 1885 → Peking University, 1890 } 1916 →

Bridgman Girl's School, Peking, 1864 → Bridgman Academy, 1895 → \
North China Union College for Women, 1904 } Peking University, 1920 → Yenching University, 1928

Peking University

Roman Catholic Institutions

Aurora University (Chen-tan ta-hsüeh), Shanghai

Aurora University, 1903 } Aurora University, 1938 \
Aurora College for Women, 1938

Catholic University (Fu-jen ta-hsüeh), Peking

Catholic University, 1925 } Catholic University, 1938 \
Women's College of Catholic University, 1938

Tsinku University (Tsin-ku ta-hsieh), Tientsin

Hautes Études Industrielles et Commerciales (Tientsin College of Industry and Commerce), 1923 → Tsinku University, 1947

Abbreviations

The following abbreviations are used in the notes and bibliography:

ABCFM	American Board of Commissioners for Foreign Missions
Chang, *TCSC*	Chang ch'in-shih, *Kuo-nei chin-shih-nien-lai chih tsung-chiao ssu-ch'ao*
CB	*China Bulletin*
CCEA	China Christian Educational Association
CCMC, *Records*	China Centenary Missionary Conference, *Records: Report of the Great Conference held at Shanghai, April 5 to May 8, 1907.*
CCYB	*China Christian Year Book*
CHCYC	*Chung-hua chiao-yü chieh*
CMYB	*China Mission Year Book*
CPR	*Chinese Press Review*
CR	*The Chinese Recorder*
ER	*The Educational Review*
FEQ	*Far Eastern Quarterly*
HI	Hoover Institution on War, Revolution, and Peace, Stanford University
IWSM	*Ch'ing-tai ch'ou-pan i-wu shih-mo*
MRL	Missionary Research Library, New York
NBT	New Brunswick Theological Seminary Library, New Brunswick, N.J.
NCC, 1922	*The Chinese Church as Revealed in the National Christian Conference, 1922*
NC, *Documents*	National Council of the Churches of Christ in the U.S.A., *Documents of the Three-Self Movement. Source Materials for the Study of the Protestant Church in Communist China.*
NCNA	New China News Agency

535

NWC	Nym Wales Collection at Hoover Institution, Stanford University
Pr	Princeton University Library, Princeton, N.J.
Records, 1877	*Records of the General Conference of the Protestant Missionaries of China, Shanghai, 1877*
Records, 1890	*Records of the General Conference of the Protestant Missionaries of China, Shanghai, 1890*
Records, EAC	Educational Association of China, *Records of Triennial Meetings*
SCMP	*Survey of the China Mainland Press*
SECCN	*Shih-erh-chiu chou-nien chi-nien t'e-k'an*
UB	United Board for Christian Higher Education in Asia, New York
Wason	Wason Collection, Cornell University Library, Ithaca, N.Y.
Yale Div.	Day Missions Library, Divinity School, Yale University, New Haven, Conn.

Bibliography

This selective bibliography excludes (1) general background works not specifically related to the China Christian colleges; (2) many items on Christian missions which were consulted but which contain little information on the educational work in China; (3) individual articles from serials, if consecutive issues of the serials were consulted; (4) individual items in the Correspondence and Reports Files on the colleges at the United Board for Christian Higher Education in Asia, in the Nym Wales Collection, in the Department of State Archives, and in the World Service Folders of the Y.M.C.A. Historical Library; (5) college catalogues and bulletins; (6) promotional brochures and brief reports issued by the colleges and the United Board, and (7) minutes of college boards and correspondence of college officers.

When items are not readily accessible, the library where they were used is indicated by abbreviations in parenthesis. (See Abbreviations.)

American Board of Commissioners for Foreign Missions. *Annual Reports, 1853–1902.* Boston.
——. *General Report of the Deputation Sent by the American Board to China in 1907.* Boston, 1907.
American Presbyterian Mission. *Report of the American Presbyterian Mission in Canton, China, 1890.* Hong Kong, 1891.
Anderson, Elam J. *English Teaching Efficiency in China.* Shanghai, 1925.
Anderson, Mary R. *Protestant Mission Schools for Girls in South China (1827 to the Japanese Invasion): A Cycle in the Celestial Kingdom.* Mobile, Alabama; 1943.

The Anti-Christian Movement: A Collection of Papers Originally Issued by the Anti-Christian Movement and Translated for the Student Y.M. and Y.W.C.A. of China. 2d ed. Shanghai, 1925. See also, Fan-tui chi-tu-chiao yün-tung.

"Appeal to the Whole People to Resist Japan and Save the Country (August 1, 1935)," *International Press Correspondence* (Inprecor), vol. XV, no. 64 (Nov. 30, 1935), 1595–97.

Asia. New York, 1932, 1939.

Associated Boards for Christian Colleges in China. *Annual Reports, 1939, 1941, 1942, 1943, 1945.* New York.

Associated Christian Students of Wuchang and Hankow. "Letter Addressed to Fellow Christian Students of the World," Nov. 15, 1937. (3 printed pages, HI.)

Association Progress. See *Ch'ing-nien chin-pu.*

Ballou, Earle H. *Dangerous Opportunity: The Christian Mission in China Today.* New York, 1940.

Balme, Harold. *China and Modern Medicine: A Study in Medical Missionary Development.* London, 1921.

Band, Claire and William. *Two Years with the Chinese Communists.* New Haven, 1948.

Band, William. *Science in the Christian Universities at Chengtu, China.* New York, ?1945. (MRL)

Barnett, A. Doak. *China on the Eve of Communist Takeover.* New York, 1961.

Bartlett, S. C. *Historical Sketch of the Mission of the American Board in China.* Boston, 1878.

Bates, M. Searle. *Missions in Far Eastern Cultural Relations.* New York, 1942.

Bennett, Adrian A. *John Fryer. The Introduction of Western Science and Technology into Nineteenth-Century China.* Cambridge, Mass.; 1967.

Bertram, James M. *First Act in China: The Story of the Sian Mutiny.* New York, 1938. The British edition is entitled *Crisis in China.*

Biggerstaff, Camilla Mills. "Home Economics at Yenching College, Peking University," *Journal of Home Economics,* XVII (1925), 160–162.

——. "Home Economics in China," *ibid.,* XVI (1924), 394–395.

——. "Yenching Progresses," *ibid.,* XIX (1927), 456–457.

Biggerstaff, Knight. *The Earliest Modern Government Schools in China.* Ithaca, N.Y.; 1961.

Bodde, Derk. *Peking Diary: A Year of Revolution.* New York, 1950.

Boone University. *Fiftieth Anniversary Report, 1871–1921.* (MRL.) After 1924, see Huachung University.

Boynton, Grace M. *At Yenching University, August, 1937.* (Pamphlet, 24 pp., HI.)

Britton, Roswell S. *The Chinese Periodical Press, 1800–1912.* Shanghai, 1933.

Brockman, Fletcher S. *I Discover the Orient.* New York, 1935.

Brown, Arthur J. *Report on a Second Visit to China, Japan, Korea, 1909, with a Discussion of Some Problems of Mission Work.* New York, n.d.

Bryson, Mary F. *John Kenneth Mackenzie: Medical Missionary to China.* London, 1891.

Buck, J. Lossing. *An Economic and Social Survey of 150 Farms, Yenshan County, Chihli Province, China.* Publications of the University of Nanking College of Agriculture and Forestry, Nanking, China, Bull. no. 13, 1926.

Buck, Pearl S. *My Several Worlds: A Personal Record.* New York, 1954.

Burton, Margaret E. *The Education of Women in China.* New York, 1911.

Candler, Warren A. *Young J. Allen.* Nashville, 1931.

Canton Christian College. *Annual Reports, 1894–95, 1900–1901, 1904, 1911–12.* (Occasionally entitled President's Report.) After 1926 see Lingnan University.

——. *Canton Christian College, 1919–1924.* (UB.)

Carlson, Ellsworth C. "The Wu-shih-san Incident of 1878," *A Festschrift for Frederick B. Artz.* Durham, N.C.; 1964.

Catholic University of Peking. *Bulletin, 1926–1934.*

Central China Presbyterian Mission. *Jubilee Papers of the Central China Presbyterian Mission, 1844–94.* Shanghai, 1895.

Chang Chih-tung. *China's Only Hope.* Trans. by Samuel I. Woodbridge. New York, 1900.

Chang Ch'in-shih (Neander C. S. Chang). *Kuo-nei chin-shih-nien-lai chih tsung-chiao ssu-ch'ao* (The Tide of Religious Thought in China during the Last Decade). Peking, 1927.

Chang Tao-chih. "Tui-yü chiao-hui ta-hsüeh wen-t'i chih kuan-chien" (Opinion Concerning the Problem of the Christian Colleges), *Chung-hua chiao-yü chieh* (Chung Hua Educational Review), XIV, no. 8 (Feb. 1925).

Cheeloo Monthly Bulletin. Tsinan, Shantung, 1935–1937.

Chen, Carol. "Progressive Education in the Days of Old, Hwa Nan College, 1915–18," *World Outlook*, Nov. 1947, pp. 483–484.

Ch'en Ch'i-t'ien. "Wo-men chu-chang shou-hui chiao-yü-ch'üan ti li-yu yü pan-fa" (The Causes and Methods of Our Demand for Restoration of Educational Rights), *Chung-hua chiao-yü chieh*, XIV, no. 8 (Feb. 1925).

Ch'en I-lin. *Tsui-chin san-shih-nien chung-kuo chiao-yü shih* (History of Chinese Education during the Last Thirty Years). Shanghai, 1930.

Chen Theodore Hsi-en. *Thought Reform of the Chinese Intellectuals.* Hong Kong, 1960.

Ch'en Tu-hsiu. "Chi-tu-chiao yü chung-kuo-jen" (Christianity and the Chinese People), *Hsin ch'ing-nien* (La Jeunesse), VII, no. 3 (Feb. 1, 1920).

"Chi-lin chang-ch'un wai-kuo hsüeh-chiao tiao-ch'a" (An Investigation of Foreign Schools in Changch'un, Kirin), *Chung-hua chiao-yü chieh,* XV, no. 2 (Aug. 1925).

Chiang Nan-hsiang and others. *The Roar of a Nation. Reminiscences of the December 9th Student Movement.* Peking, 1963.

Chiang Wen-han (Kiang Wen-han). *The Ideological Background of the Chinese Student Movement.* New York, 1948.

Ch'iang Shu-ko. *Chung-kuo chin-tai chiao-yü chih-tu* (The Modern Educational System of China). Shanghai, 1934.

"Chiao-yü-chia yü hsüeh-sheng ti ai-kuo yün-tung" (The Nationalist Movement of the Educationalists and the Students), *Chung-hua chiao-yü chieh,* XV, no. 6 (Dec. 1925).

"Chiao-yü wen-t'i" (The Educational Question), *Hsin ch'ing-nien,* VII, no. 3 (Feb. 1920), 145–146.

Chih, André. *L'Occident "Chrétien" vu par les Chinois vers la fin du XIXe siècle, 1870–1900.* Paris, 1962.

China. Ministry of Education. *Revised Regulations for Private Schools Promulgated by the Ministry of Education, October 21, 1933.* Trans. by Chester S. Miao. (Pamphlet, 46 pp., MRL.)

China Bulletin. See National Council of Churches of Christ.

China Centenary Missionary Conference. *Records: Report of the Great Conference held at Shanghai, April 5 to May 8, 1907.* Shanghai, 1907.

China Christian Educational Association. *The Christian College in New China: The Report of the Second Biennial Conference of Christian Colleges and Universities in China, Shanghai College, February 12 to 16, 1926.* Bull. no. 16. Shanghai, 1926.

——. *The Correlated Program for Christian Higher Education in China, 1933, as Revised by the Council of Higher Education.* (Pamphlet, 8 pp., NBT.)

——. *Handbook of Christian Colleges and Universities, 1926, Including Statistical Report for the Year 1925.* Bull. no. 14. Shanghai, 1926.

——. *Report on the Religious Life in the Christian Colleges in China.* Bull. no. 37. Shanghai, 1936.

——. *Statistical Report: Christian Colleges and Professional Schools of China, 1929–1930.* Bull. no. 27. Shanghai, 1930.

——. *Statistical Report: Christian Colleges and Professional Schools of China, 1930–1931.* Bull. no. 28. Shanghai, 1931.

——. *Statistical Report of Christian Colleges and Universities in China, 1924.* Bull. no. 8. Shanghai, 1925.

The China Christian Year Book, 1931–1938/39. Shanghai. (A continuation of *The China Mission Year Book.*)

The China Colleges, 1934–1952. Published by the Associated Boards for Christian Colleges in China. (Succeeded by *New Horizons for the China Colleges,* 1953–55; succeeded by *New Horizons,* 1956–.)

The China Critic, 1928–1940. Shanghai.

China Foundation for the Promotion of Chinese Education and Culture. *Annual Reports, 1924–1940, 1947, 1948.*

China Institute in America. *A Survey of Chinese Students in American Universities and Colleges in the Past One Hundred Years.* New York, 1954.

China Medical Board. *Annual Reports, 1915, 1916.*

The China Medical Journal, XL (Aug. 1926). (Special number on medical education.)

The China Mission Handbook. First Issue. Shanghai, 1896.

The China Mission Year Book, 1910–1919, 1923, 1925. Shanghai. (In 1926 became *The China Christian Year Book.*)

China Monthly Review. See *China Weekly Review.*

China Weekly Review, 1922–1936, 1946, 1951. Shanghai. (Entitled *Millard's Review of the Far East,* 1917–1921.)

The China Year Book, 1912–1914, 1916, 1919–1925. London, 1912–1919; Peking and Tientsin, 1921–1925.

Chinese Christian Education: A Report of a Conference Held in New York City, April 6, 1925, under the Joint Auspices of the International Missionary Council and the Foreign Missions Conference of North America. New York, 1925.

The Chinese Church as Revealed in the National Christian Conference held in Shanghai, May, 1922. Shanghai, n.d.

The Chinese Medical Journal, 1934, 1935. Shanghai.

Chinese Press Review. Issued by American Consulate. Chungking: Oct.–Nov., 1945; Jan. 1946. Peiping-Tientsin: Dec. 1946–March 1947; June–July, 1947. Shanghai: June–Aug., 1946; May–June, 1947; Nov.–Dec., 1947; May–Oct., 1948; July–Aug., 1949.

The Chinese Recorder, 1867–1941. Shanghai. (Title varies: *Missionary*

Recorder, 1867; Chinese Recorder and Missionary Journal, 1868–1912.)

The Chinese Social and Political Science Review, 1919, 1920, 1922–1939. Peking.

The Chinese Students' Christian Association Year Book, 1928. Ed. Alfred S. T. Pu. (Pamphlet, 40 pp., NBT.)

The Chinese Students' Monthly, 1915–1916, 1918–1919. New Haven.

"Chinese Students Under Fire," The Student Advocate, March 1936, pp. 12–13.

The Chinese Year Book, 1936–1940/41. Shanghai.

Ching Ch'ang-chi. "Lun hsüeh-sheng yung-hu tsung-chiao chih pi-yao" (Discussion of the Need for Student Support of Religion), Hsüeh heng (The Critical Review). 1922, no. 6.

Ch'ing-nien chin-pu (Association Progress), 1922. Shanghai Organ of the Y.M.C.A. of China (Yale div.).

Ch'ing-tai ch'ou-pan i-wu shih-mo (The Management of Barbarian Affairs of the Ch'ing Dynasty from Beginning to End). Tao-kuan series 72. Peiping, 1930.

Chou T'ai-hsüan. "Fei tsung-chiao chiao-yü yü chiao-hui chiao-yü" (Against Religious Education and Parochial Education), Chung-hua chiao-yü chieh, XIV, no. 8 (Feb. 1925).

Chow Tse-tsung. The May Fourth Movement: Intellectual Revolution in Modern China. Cambridge, Mass.; 1960.

——. Research Guide to the May Fourth Movement. Cambridge, Mass.; 1963.

Christian Education in China: A Study Made by an Educational Commission Representing the Mission Boards and Societies Conducting Work in China. New York, c.1922.

Chu Chia-hua. "British Boxer Indemnity Fund Activities," The China Quarterly, VI, no. 6 (1941), 437–441.

Chu, Clayton H. American Missionaries in China: Books, Articles, and Pamphlets Extracted from the Subject Catalogue of the Missionary Research Library. 3 vols. Cambridge, Mass.; 1960.

Chuang Wen-ya (W. Y. Chyne), comp. and ed. Handbook of Cultural Institutions in China. Shanghai, 1936.

Chung Shih. Higher Education in Communist China. Hong Kong, 1953.

Cochrane, Thomas. Survey of the Missionary Occupation of China. Shanghai, 1913.

Coe, John L. Huachung University. New York, 1962.

Cohen, Paul A. China and Christianity: The Missionary Movement and *the Growth of Chinese Antiforeignism, 1860–1870*. Cambridge, Mass.; 1963.

Commission on Christian Education of China. *Report on Christian Education in China: Its Present Status and Problems*. New York, ?1910.

Conference on Missions Held in 1860 at Liverpool: Including the Papers Read, the Deliberations, and the Conclusions Reached. London, 1860.

The Continuation Committee Conferences in Asia, 1912–1913. New York, 1913.

Corbett, Charles H. *Lingnan University*. New York, 1963.

——. *Shantung Christian University (Cheeloo)*. New York, 1955.

Cressy, Earl H. *The Advisory Council of the East China Christian Colleges and Universities, 1922–1928*. East China Studies in Education no. 4. Shanghai, 1929.

——. *Christian Higher Education in China: A Study for the Year 1925–1926*. CCEA Bull. no. 20. Shanghai, 1928.

——. *Costs of Christian Higher Education in China*. CCEA Bull. no. 15. Shanghai, 1926.

——. *Information for Admissions Officers Concerning Christian Colleges in China*. CCEA Bull. no. 31. Shanghai, 1933.

——. *Minimum Standards for Christian Colleges in China*. CCEA Bull. no. 21. Shanghai, 1927.

——. *The University of London and Christian Higher Education in East China*. East China Studies in Education no. 1. Shanghai, 1925.

Current Background, no. 20, Oct. 26, 1950–no. 100, July 18, 1951. Issued by U.S. Consulate, Hong Kong.

Day, Clarence B. *Hangchow University: A Brief History*. New York, 1955.

Death Blow to Corrupt Doctrines. A Plain Statement of Facts. Published by the Gentry and the People. Trans. from the Chinese. (Shanghai, 1870).

Decker, William M. "The Foundations and Growth of Shantung Christian University, 1864–1917." M.A. thesis, Columbia University, 1948.

Dewey, Evelyn, ed. *Letters from China and Japan*. London, 1920.

Dewey, John. "America and Chinese Education," *The New Republic*, XXX (March 1, 1922), 15–17.

Dunlap, A. M. *Behind the Bamboo Curtain. The Experiences of an American Doctor in China*. Washington, 1956.

Edmunds, C. K. *Modern Education in China*. United States Bureau of Education, Bull. no. 44. Washington, D.C.; 1919.

The Educational Association of China. *Triennial Reports, 1893, 1896, 1899, 1902, 1905, 1909.* Shanghai.

The Educational Directory of China, 1914–1918. Shanghai. (In 1920 became *The Educational Directory and Year Book of China.*)

The Educational Review, 1907–1938 (Entitled *The Monthly Bulletin of the Educational Association of China,* 1907–1909; merged with *The Chinese Recorder* in 1938.)

Edwards, Dwight W. *Yenching University.* New York, 1959.

Faber, Knud. *Report on Medical Schools in China.* League of Nations Publications Series, III, Health. Geneva, 1931.

Fairbank, J. K. "Patterns Behind the Tientsin Massacre," *Harvard Journal of Asiatic Studies,* XX (1957), 480–511.

Fan-tui chi-tu-chiao yün-tung (The Anti-Christian Movement). Shanghai, 1924. Jointly compiled by the Chung-kuo ch'ing-nien she (China Youth Society) and Fei chi-tu-chiao t'ung-meng (Anti-Christian Federation).

Fan Yüan-lien. "Hu-an yü chiao-yü" (Shanghai Case and Education), *Chung-hua chiao-yü chieh,* XV, no. 2 (Aug. 1925).

Far Eastern Survey, 1946–1949. New York.

Fisher, Daniel W. *Calvin Wilson Mateer: Forty-Five Years a Missionary in Shantung, China.* Philadelphia, 1911.

Foreign Missions Conference of North America. *Addresses on China at the 34th Annual Session.* New York, 1927.

———. *Reports of Annual Meetings, 1938, 1942, 1944, 1948, 1950.* New York.

Fraser, Stewart, comp. and ed. *Chinese Communist Education: Records of the First Decade.* Nashville, 1965.

Freyn, Hubert. *Chinese Education in the War.* Shanghai, 1940.

———. *Prelude to War. The Chinese Student Rebellion of 1935–1936.* Shanghai, 1939.

Fukien Christian University. *Report of the President, 1919–1922, 1925–1927, 1930–1935, 1939, 1942, 1945* (often entitled, *Bulletin of Fukien Christian University*). (MRL.)

———. *Twelve Years of Progress, Fukien Christian University, 1916–1928.* Foochow. (UB.)

———. *What My Education in Fukien Christian University Means to Me.* Foochow, 1938 (Pamphlet, HI.)

Galt, Howard S. "Yenching University, Its Sources and Its History." New York, preface dated 1939. (MS on microfilm, UB.)

Garside, B. A. *One Increasing Purpose: The Life of Henry Winters Luce.* New York, 1948.

Gascoyne-Cecil, Lord William (Rupert E.). *Changing China*. New York, 1912.

Gee, N. Gist. *Criteria of a Standard College*. CCEA Bull. no. 2. Shanghai, 1924.

Ginling College. *Report of the President, 1915–1918*. (MRL.)

———. *A Six-Year Review, 1915–1921*. Nanking, 1921.

Ginling College Magazine, II (Dec. 1925). (Tenth birthday issue, UB.)

Graves, R. H. *Forty Years in China or China in Transition*. Baltimore, 1895.

Gregg, Alice H. *China and Educational Autonomy: The Changing Role of the Protestant Educational Missionary in China, 1807–1937*. Syracuse, N.Y.; 1946.

Hangchow Christian College. *President's Report, 1904–05, 1907–08, 1911–12, 1912–13, 1918–19, 1919–20, 1925–26, 1927–28*. (Presbyterian Board of Foreign Missions, NYC.) (Known as Hangchow Presbyterian College until 1914.)

Hart, S. Lavington. *Education in China*. London, 1923.

Headland, Isaac T. *China's New Day: A Study of Events that Have Led to Its Coming*. West Medford, Mass.; 1912.

Henry, B. C. *The Cross and the Dragon or Light in the Broad East*. 2d ed. New York, 1885.

Hipps, John B. *A History of the University of Shanghai*. Richmond, 1964.

"Ho Ying-ch'in pei shang jen-wu" (Ho Ying-ch'in's Mission in Peiping), *Yen-ta chou-k'an* (Yenching University Weekly), Dec. 6, 1935, pp. 1–2.

Hoh, Gunsun. *Physical Education in China*. Shanghai, 1926.

Holden, Reuben. *Yale in China: The Mainland, 1901–1951*. New Haven, 1964.

Hsiao Kung-ch'üan. "K'ang Yu-wei and Confucianism," *Monumenta Serica*, XVIII (1959), 96–212.

———. "Weng T'ung-ho and the Reform Movement of 1898," *Tsing Hua Journal of Chinese Studies*, I (1957), 111–243.

Hsiao, Theodore E. *The History of Modern Education in China*. Peiping, 1932.

"Hsüeh-lien t'ung-kuo ti fei-ch'ang shih-ch'i chiao-yü fang-an yüan-tse" (The Principles of the Emergency Education Platform Passed by the Student Union), *Yen-ta chou-k'an*, Feb. 9, 1936, pp. 1–2.

"Hsüeh-sheng tsung-hui chieh-shu wu-sa ts'an-an pa-k'o yün-tung chih t'ung-kao" (Notice of Student Union's Ending the Strike Movement of the May 30th Incident), *Chiao-yü tsa-chih* (Educational Review) XVII, no. 10 (Oct. 1925).

Hu Shih. *The Chinese Renaissance*. Chicago, 1934.

——. "What I Believe," *Forum*, Jan. and Feb., 1931. Reprinted in *Living Philosophies, A Series of Intimate Credos* (New York, 1931), pp. 235–263.

Hughes, E. R. *The Invasion of China by the Western World*. New York, 1938.

Hume, Edward H. *Doctors East, Doctors West: An American Physician's Life in China*. New York, 1946.

Hung, William (Hung Yeh), ed. *As It Looks to Young China: Chapters by a Group of Christian Chinese*. New York, 1932.

Hwa Nan College. *Brief Book of the Woman's College of South China*. 1920. (Pamphlet, Methodist Church: Division of World Missions, NYC.)

——. *President's Report, 1929–30, 1933–34, 1942–43, 1949*. (MRL.)

I Ch'ien. "Kao ch'üan kuo t'ung hsüeh" (To All Fellow Students of the Whole Country), *Shih-erh-chiu t'e-k'an* (The December 9th Special), Dec. 17, 1935.

I Wei. "Tsai lun tsung-chiao wen-t'i" (Another Discussion of the Problem of Religion), *Hsüeh heng*, 1922, no. 6.

I Wo-sheng. "Education in Communist China," pp. 99–152 in Union Research Institute. *Communist China, 1949–1959*. Vol. III. Hong Kong, 1961.

Ilyushchechkin, V. P. "Studentcheskoe dvizhenie 9 dekabria 1935 g. v. Kitae" (The Student Movement of December 9, 1935 in China), Institut Vostokovedenia, *Kratkie soobshcheniia* VII (1952), 3–19.

International Missionary Council. The Madras Series. 7 vols. New York, 1939.

The International Review of Missions, 1928–1951. Edinburgh.

Israel, John W. *Student Nationalism in China, 1927–1937*. Stanford, 1966.

Jones, Francis P. *The Church in Communist China: A Protestant Appraisal*. New York, 1962.

Kiang Wen-han. See Chiang Wen-han.

Kiesow, E. Margaret. *China: The Challenge*. London, 1954.

Kilborn, Omar L. *Heal the Sick: An Appeal for Medical Missions in China*. Toronto, 1910.

Kirby, James E., Jr. "The Foochow Anti-Missionary Riot—August 30, 1878," *Journal of Asian Studies*, XXV (Aug. 1966), 665–680.

Ku Chieh-kang. *Autobiography of a Chinese Historian*. Leyden, 1931.

Kuno, Yoshi S. *Educational Institutions in the Orient with Special Reference to Colleges and Universities in the U.S.*, Part II, *Chinese Educational Institutions: A Preliminary Statement*. Berkeley, Calif.; 1928.

"Kuo-nei chiao-yü hsin-wen" (National Education News), *Chung-hua chiao-yü chieh*, XV, no. 1 (July 1925).

Kuo Ping-wen. *The Chinese System of Public Education.* New York, 1915.

Lamberton, Mary. *St. John's University, Shanghai, 1879–1951.* New York, 1955.

Lang, Olga. *Chinese Family and Society.* New Haven, 1946.

Latourette, Kenneth S. *Christianity in a Revolutionary Age.* 5 vols. New York, 1958–1962.

——. *A History of Christian Missions in China.* New York, 1929.

——. *A History of the Expansion of Christianity.* 7 vols. New York, 1937–1945.

Laymen's Foreign Missions Inquiry. *Fact Finders' Reports.* China, vol. V, Supplementary Series. New York, 1933.

——. *Regional Reports of the Commission of Appraisal.* China, vol. II, Supplementary Series. New York, 1933.

League of Nations' Institute of Intellectual Cooperation. *The Reorganization of Education in China.* Paris, 1932.

Leger, Samuel H. *Education of Christian Ministers in China.* Shanghai, 1925.

Levenson, Joseph. *Confucian China and Its Modern Fate.* Vol. I, *The Problem of Intellectual Continuity.* Berkeley, 1958. Vol. II, *The Problem of Monarchical Decay.* Berkeley, 1964.

——. *Liang Ch'i-ch'ao and the Mind of Modern China.* Cambridge, Mass.; 1953.

Lew, Timothy T'ingfang (Liu T'ing-fang) and others. *China Today through Chinese Eyes.* New York, 1922.

——. *The Contribution of Christian Colleges and Universities to the Church in China.* CCEA Bull. no. 4. Shanghai, 1924.

Lewis, Ida Belle. *The Education of Girls in China.* New York, 1919.

Lewis, Robert E. *The Educational Conquest of the Far East.* New York, 1903.

Li, Anthony C. "The History of Privately Controlled Higher Education in the Republic of China" Ph.D. dissertation, Catholic University of America, 1955.

Li Ch'ang and others. *"I-erh-chiu" hui-i-lu* (Memoirs of "December Ninth"). Peking, 1961.

——. "Recollections of the National Liberation Vanguard of China." In *Selections from China Mainland Magazines*, no. 296 (Jan. 15, 1962), pp. 27–36, and no. 297 (Jan. 22, 1962), pp. 28–43. Translated from *Chung-kuo ch'ing-nien* (China Youth), no. 22 (Nov. 16, 1961), pp. 6–16.

Li Huang. "Lun li-chiao-yü yü tsung-chiao chiao-yü," Discussion of Ethical Education and Religious Education), *Chung-hua chiao-yü chieh,* XIV, no. 8 (Feb. 1925).

Li Ju-mien. "Chiao-hui ta-hsüeh wen-t'i" (The Problem of the Christian Colleges), *Chung-hua chiao-yü chieh,* XIV, no. 8 (Feb. 1925).

Lifton, Robert J. *Thought Reform and the Psychology of Totalism.* New York, 1963.

Linden, Allen B. "Politics and Education in Nationalist China, The Case of the University Council, 1927–1928," *The Journal of Asian Studies,* XXVII (Aug. 1968), 763–776.

The Lingnaam Agricultural Review, 1922–1927. Canton.

Lingnan, 1937–1938, 1943, 1946–1949. New York.

Lingnan University. "The Spirit and Purpose of Lingnan." New York, ?1928. (Pamphlet, MRL.) Before 1926, see Canton Christian College.

Ling-nan hsüeh-pao (The Lingnan Journal), 1929, 1947. Canton.

Liu Kwang-ching, ed. *American Missionaries in China: Papers from Harvard Seminars.* Cambridge, Mass.; 1966.

Liu Po-ming. "Fei tsung-chiao yün-tung p'ing-i" (Comments on the Anti-Religious Movement), *Hsüeh-heng,* no. 6 (June 1922).

Lü Shih-ch'iang. *Chung-kuo kuan shen fan-chiao ti yüan-yin, 1860–1874* (The Origin and Cause of Anti-Christianism among Chinese Officials and Gentry, 1860–1874). Taipei, 1966.

Lutz, Jessie G., ed. *Christian Missions in China: Evangelists of What?* Boston, 1965.

——. "December 9, 1935: Student Nationalism and the China Christian Colleges," *Journal of Asian Studies,* XXVI (Aug. 1967), 627–648.

MacGillivray, D., ed. *A Century of Protestant Missions in China (1807–1907), Being the Centenary Conference Historical Volume.* Shanghai, 1907.

Martin, W. A. P. *A Cycle of Cathay, or China, South and North with Personal Reminiscences.* Edinburgh, 1896.

——. *The Awakening of China.* New York, c. 1907.

Mateer, Robert M. *Character Building in China: The Life Story of Julia Brown Mateer.* New York, 1912.

Miao Chu-seng (Chester S. Miao), ed. *Christian Voices in China.* New York, 1948.

Mo Ning. " 'Shih-erh-chiu' ti chiao hsün" (Lesson of "December 9th"), *Shih-erh-chiu t'e-k'an,* Dec. 17, 1935, pp. 1–2.

Mok Poon-kan. "The History and Development of the Teaching of English in China." Ph.D. dissertation, Columbia University, 1951.

Monroe, Paul. *China, A Nation in Evolution.* New York, 1928.
——. *Essays in Comparative Education.* New York, 1927.
——. "Student Politics in China," *Forum,* LXXVI (Aug. 1926), 186–193.
Morgan, Leonard G. *The Teaching of Science to the Chinese.* Hong Kong, 1933.
Morse, William R. *The Three Crosses in the Purple Mists: An Adventure in Medical Education under the Eaves of the Roof of the World.* Shanghai, 1928.
Mu Han. "Fei-ch'ang shih-ch'i chiao-yü yü hsüeh-sheng yün-tung" (Emergency Education and the Student Movement), *Yen-ta chou-k'an,* Feb. 9, 1936, pp. 3–4.
Myers, C. H. *Final Report of the Plant Improvement Project Conducted by the University of Nanking, Cornell University, and the International Education Board.* Nanking, 1934. (Wason.)
Nance, W. B. *Soochow University.* New York, 1956.
Nanking, University of. *11th Annual Report of the College of Agriculture and Forestry and Experiment Station, 1924–1925.* (Wason.)
——. *Chin-ling hsüeh-pao* (Nanking Journal), 1931, 1932, 1935.
——. *Report of the President, 1910–1912, 1915–16, 1918–19, 1924–25, 1936.* (UB)
The Nation, 1946, 1948.
National Christian Council of China. *Annual and Biennial Reports, 1933–1935.* Shanghai, 1935.
——. *Education for Service in the Christian Church in China: The Report of a Survey Commission, 1935.* Shanghai, 1935.
——. *A Five Years' Review, 1922–1927.* Shanghai, n.d.
National Council of the Churches of Christ in the U.S.A., Division of Foreign Missions, Far Eastern Joint Office. *China Bulletin,* 1947–1959. New York. (Until 1952 listed under Foreign Missions Conference of North America, Far Eastern Joint Office, China Committee, and numbered consecutively, 1–124; Vol. II begins with the Feb. 25, 1952 issue and is entitled *China Bulletin.*)
——. *China Consultation,* 1958, 1960. New York.
——. *Documents of the Three-Self Movement. Source Materials for the Study of the Protestant Church in Communist China.* Francis P. Jones, consultant and ed. New York, 1963.
National Review, XIV. Shanghai.
Nellist, George F., ed. *Men of Shanghai and North China.* Shanghai, 1933.
North China Union College. *Annual Report, 1914–1915.* (After 1917 see Peking University.)

North China Union Women's College. *Report, 1916–1918.* (UB.) (After 1918, see Yen-ching Women's College.)

Nym Wales Collection. China: Student Movement, 1936. (HI.)

Outerbridge, Leonard M. *The Lost Churches of China.* Philadelphia, 1952.

Paterno, Roberto. "Davello Z. Sheffield and the Founding of the North China College," *Papers on China,* Harvard University, XIV, 110–160.

Payne, P. S. Robert. *China Awake.* New York, 1947.

Peking Language School. *Some Aspects of Chinese Life and Thought: Being Lectures Delivered under the Auspices of Peking Language School, 1917–1918.* Shanghai, 1918.

Peking Leader Press. *Documents on the Shanghai Case.* Peking Leader Reprints no. 12. Peking, 1925. (Wason)

Peking Union Medical College. *Addresses and Papers, Dedication Ceremonies and Medical Conference, September 15–22, 1921.* Peking, 1922.

Peking University. *President's Report, 1909–10, 1912, 1917–1923.* (UB.) After 1923, see Yenching University.

——. *Report of the Board of Managers, 1917.* (UB.)

"A Petition from the Native Pastors, Licentiates, and Elders of All Denominations in the Province of Canton, China, to the Trustees of the Canton Christian College, U.S.A." (Typewritten copy, c. 1890, UB.)

"A Petition to the Trustees of Canton Christian College by the Gentry of Kwangtung, Requesting the Establishment of a Scientific College in Canton." (Typewritten copy, c. 1886–1887, UB.)

Pien (pseudonym?). "Wo-men ying-tang chin tai-piao chin ching ma!?" (Should We Send Representatives to the Capital!?), *Shih-erh-chiu t'e-k'an,* Jan. 9, 1936, pp. 1–2.

Pott, F. L. Hawks. "How St. John's College is Helping to Solve the Problems of China's Future," *The Spirit of Missions,* XLVII (1902), 405–412.

Potter, H. "Letter of March 14, 1877 by Bishop H. Potter to Bishop William B. Stevens." (Wason pamphlets.)

Price, Frank W. "History of Nanking Theological Seminary, 1911 to 1961, A Tentative Draft." New York, 1961. (Mimeo., NBT.)

——. *The Rural Church in China, A Survey.* New York, 1948.

Princeton-Peking Gazette, 1925–1938. (Pr.)

Proceedings of the General Conference on Foreign Missions held at London, October, 1878. London, 1879.

"The Projection of the Christian College in China Located at Canton,

Including A Review, Its Present Status and Prospects." (Pamphlet, c. 1897, UB.)

"Prospectus of a Christian College in China." (Wason pamphlet, c. 1886–1887.)

Records of the General Conference of the Protestant Missionaries of China held at Shanghai, May 10–23, 1877. Shanghai, 1878.

Records of the General Conference of the Protestant Missionaries of China held at Shanghai, May 7–20, 1890. Shanghai, 1890.

Reeves, William. "Sino-American Cooperation in Medicine: The Origins of Hsiang-Ya (1902–1914)," *Papers on China,* Harvard University, XIV. 161–214.

Report of a Conference on the Preparation of Educational Missionaries, 1916. New York, n.d.

Report of the Centenary Conference on the Protestant Missions of the World held in London, 1888. Ed. James Johnston. 2 vols. London, 1888.

Report of the Conference on the Church in China Today, 1926. Shanghai, 1926.

Report of the Ecumenical Missionary Conference. 2 vols. New York, 1900.

Richard, Timothy. *Conversion by the Million in China: Being Biographies and Articles.* 2 vols. Shanghai, 1907.

———. *Forty-five Years in China: Reminiscences by Timothy Richard.* London, 1916.

Russell, Bertrand. *The Problem of China.* New York, 1922.

St. John's University. *The 1925 Johannean,* XI (1925). Shanghai.

———. *President's Reports, 1900–01, 1905–06, 1911–12, 1914–16, 1920–21.*

———. *St. John's University, 1879–1929.* Shanghai, 1929.

St. John's University Alumni Association. *Diamond Jubilee, 1879–1954, In Commemoration of the 75th Anniversary of the Founding of St. John's University.* Taipei, 1955.

Schereschewsky, Samuel I. J. *An Appeal for Establishing a Missionary College in China, March 17, 1877.* Philadelphia, 1877. (Wason pamphlet.)

School and Society, 1921, 1925–1950. New York.

Schwartz, Benjamin. *In Search of Wealth and Power: Yen Fu and the West.* Cambridge, Mass., 1964.

———. "The Intelligentsia in Communist China," *Daedalus,* Summer 1960, pp. 604–621.

Scott, Roderick. *Fukien Christian University: A Historical Sketch.* New York, 1954.

Seabury, J. B. *The Vision of a Short Life: A Memorial of Warren Bartlett Seabury, One of the Founders of the Yale Mission College in China.* Cambridge, Mass.; 1909.

Shanghai, University of. *Annual Reports, 1914–1922, 1925–1928, 1930–1939.* Known as Shanghai Baptist College until 1931. (MRL.)

——. *Dr. Herman C. E. Liu, In Memorium, April 7, 1939.* (Pamphlet, UB.)

——. "Letters from the President," 1929–1937. Often entitled "U. of Shanghai Newsletter." (Mimeo., MRL.)

——. *Thirtieth Anniversary Report, 1906–1936.* (MRL.)

Shantung Christian University. *Annual Report, 1907, 1910, 1912, 1915, 1917–1918, 1923–1926.* (Various titles: *President's Report, Annual Register and Report*). Known as Shantung Protestant University, 1907–1909; after 1926, see Cheeloo University.

Shen Ting-i (*tzu* Hsüan-lu). "Tui-yü 'Chi-tu-chiao yü Chung-kuo-jen' ti huai-i" (My Doubts Concerning Christianity and the Chinese People), *Hsing-ch'i p'ing-lu* (Weekly Review, Shanghai), no. 36 (Feb. 8, 1920).

Shu Hsin-ch'eng, ed. *Chin-tai chung-kuo chiao-yü shih-liao* (Historical Materials on Modern Chinese Education.) 4 vols. Shanghai, 1923.

Smith, Edward L. *Fifty-two Days in China, Representing the Board of Trustees, Peking University.* 1918. (UB.)

Snow, Edgar. *Journey to the Beginning.* New York, 1958.

Snow, Helen F. *Notes on the Chinese Student Movement, 1935–36.* Stanford, 1958.

——. *Red Dust, Autobiographies of Chinese Communists.* Stanford, 1952.

Society for the Diffusion of Christian and General Knowledge among the Chinese. *Eleventh Annual Report, 1898.*

Soochow University. *The Tung Wu Magazine of Soochow University*, III, no. 4 (Nov. 1935).

Soothill, William E. *A Mission in China.* Edinburgh, 1907.

——. *Timothy Richard of China. Seer, Statesman, Missionary and the Most Disinterested Adviser the Chinese Ever Had.* London, 1924.

Speer, Robert E. *Report on the China Missions of the Presbyterian Board of Foreign Missions.* 2d. ed. New York, 1897.

Spence, Jonathan. *To Change China: Western Advisers in China, 1620–1960.* Boston, 1969.

"Statements Concerning Christian Higher Education Institutions in China, July, 1928." (Mimeo., 136 pp., MRL.)

Stauffer, Milton T., ed. *The Christian Occupation of China.* Shanghai, 1922.

——, ed. *Youth and Renaissance Movements.* New York, 1923.

Stevens, William B. "Letter by Bishop William Bacon Stevens to Bishop H. Potter, March 5, 1877." Philadelphia, 1877. (Wason pamphlets.)

Stuart, John Leighton. *Fifty Years in China: The Memoirs of John Leighton Stuart, Missionary and Ambassador.* New York, 1954.

A *Survey of Chinese Students in American Universities and Colleges in the Past One Hundred Years.* Under the joint sponsorship of National Tsing Hua University Research Fellowship Fund and China Institute in America. New York, 1954.

Survey of the China Mainland Press, no. 1 (Nov. 1, 1950)–no. 50 (Jan. 17, 1951); no. 266 (Feb. 1, 1952)–no. 449 (Nov. 8, 1952). Hong Kong, U.S. Consulate.

Tai, T. C. *The Library Movement in China.* Chinese National Association for the Advancement of Education, Bull. on Chinese Education, II, no. 3, Shanghai, 1923.

T'ang Liang-li. *China in Revolt: How a Civilization Became a Nation.* London, 1927.

Taylor, Joseph. *History of West China Union University, 1910–1935.* Chengtu, China, 1936.

Thomas, S. B. "Recent Educational Policy in China," *Pacific Affairs,* XXIII (March 1950), 21–33.

Thomson, James C., Jr. *While China Faced West: American Reformers in Nationalist China, 1928–1937.* Cambridge, Mass.; 1969.

Thurston, Matilda and Ruth M. Chester. *Ginling College.* New York, 1955.

Ting Chih-p'ing. *Chung-kuo chin ch'i-shih-nien lai chiao-yü chi-shih* (Events in Chinese Education During the Last Seventy Years). Shanghai, 1935.

"Ts'ai Chieh-min hsien-sheng tsai, hsin-chiao pai-yu hui chih yen-shuo" (Address of Mr. Ts'ai Chieh-min (Ts'ai Yüan-p'ei) to the Society for Religious Freedom), *Hsin ch'ing-nien,* II, no. 5 (Jan. 1, 1917).

Ts'ai Yüan-p'ei. "Chiao-yü tu-li-i" (Educational Independence), *Hsin chiao-yü* (The New Education), IV, no. 3 (March, 1922), 317–319.

———. *The Development of Chinese Education: A Paper Read before the China Society on April 10, 1924.* London, 1924.

Tsang Chiu-sam. *Nationalism in School Education in China since the Opening of the Twentieth Century.* Hong Kong, 1933.

Tsien Tsuen-hsuin. "Western Impact on China through Translation," *Far Eastern Quarterly,* XIII (May 1954), 305–327.

Tso I-li. "Wo ti ta-hsüeh sheng-huo" (My University Life), *Wen-hua* (Culture), I, no. 5 (June 1934).

Tsui-chin san-shih-wu-nien chih chung-kuo chiao-yü (Chinese Education in the Last 35 Years). Ed. Chuang Yü and Ho Sheng-nai. Shanghai, 1931.

Tung-fang tsa-chih (The Eastern Miscellany). 1904–1909, 1916, 1922–1925.

Tunghai University. Files entitled "Aims and Purposes," 1952–1962.

——. Files entitled "General Education," 1957–1962.

——. President's file on the "Labor Program," 1958–1961.

——. *Report of the President, 1958–59, 1959–60, 1960–61, 1964.*

Twiss, George R. *Science and Education in China: A Survey of the Present Status and a Program for Progressive Improvement.* Shanghai, 1925.

Tyau, M. T. Z. *China Awakened.* New York, 1922.

United Board for Christian Higher Education in Asia. *Annual Reports, 1945–1948, 1961–1967.* Original organization was Associated Boards for Christian Colleges in China, q.v.; from 1945 to 1955 the organization was known as United Board for Christian Colleges in China.

U.S. Department of State. Archives. Files on China, 1922, 1925.

U.S. Department of the Interior. Bureau of Education. "Progress of Western Education in China and Siam." Washington, D.C.; 1880. (Wason pamphlets.)

Van Putten, J. Dyke. "Christian Higher Education in China: Survey of the Historical Developments and Its Contributions to Chinese Life." Ph.D. dissertation, University of Chicago, 1934.

Van Slyke, Lyman P. "Liang Sou-ming and the Rural Reconstruction Movement," *Journal of Asian Studies,* XVIII (1959), 457–474.

Varg, Paul A. *Missionaries, Chinese, and Diplomats: The American Protestant Missionary Movement in China, 1890–1952.* Princeton, 1958.

"Wai-kuo chiao-yü ti ya-p'o" (Oppression of Foreign Education), *Chung-hua chiao-yü chieh,* XV, no. 2 (Aug. 1925).

Wallace, Edward W. *The Place of Private Schools in a National System of Education.* CCEA Bull. no. 5. Shanghai, 1925.

Wallace, L. Ethel. *Hwa Nan College.* New York, 1956.

Wan Min. "The New Policy of the Communist Party of China," *International Press Correspondence* (Inprecor), XV, no. 70 (Dec. 21, 1935), 1959–1967.

Wang Feng-gang. *Japanese Influence on Educational Reform in China, from 1895 to 1911.* Peiping, 1933.

Wang Hsiao-feng. "Chung-kuo fa-hsi-szu yü jih-pen" (Chinese Fascism and Japan), *Yen-ta chou-k'an,* Dec. 6, 1935, pp. 23–25.

Wang Ju-mei (Huang Hua). "Chung-kuo fa-hsi-szu yün-tung hsien-chuang" (The Present Status of the Chinese Fascist Movement), *Yen-ta chou-k'an,* Dec. 6, 1935, pp. 12–14.

Wang, Tsi C. *The Youth Movement in China.* New York, 1927.

Wang, Y. C. *Chinese Intellectuals and the West, 1872–1949.* Chapel Hill, N.C.; 1966.

Webster, James B. *Christian Education and the National Consciousness in China.* New York, 1923.

Wee, Kok Ann. *Physical Education in Protestant Christian Colleges and Universities of China.* New York, 1937.

Wehrle, Edmund S. *Britain, China, and the Anti-Missionary Riots, 1891–1900.* Minneapolis, 1966.

Wei Cho-min (Francis C. M. Wei). *The Spirit of Chinese Culture.* New York, 1947.

Wellons, Ralph D. *The Organizations Set up for the Control of Mission Union Higher Educational Institutions.* New York, 1925.

Wen Tsung-yao. "On Education," *Hsin ch'ing-nien,* II, no. 1 (Sept. 1916).

West China Missionary Conference. Chengtu, 1908.

West China Union University. *Annual Reports, 1910–11, 1913–14, 1924–25.*

——. *Reports of the West China Union University Senate to the Board of Governors, 1916, 1919, 1924–25, 1926–27.*

Wheeler, W. Reginald. *Flight to Cathay: An Aerial Journey to Yale-in-China.* New Haven, 1949.

——. *John E. Williams of Nanking.* New York, 1937.

Who's Who in China. 3d ed., 1925; 4th ed., 1931; 6th ed., 1950. Shanghai.

Who's Who of American Returned Students. Peking, 1917.

Wieger, Léon, ed. and trans. *Chine Moderne.* 10 vols. Hsien-hsien, China, 1920–1932.

Williams, Bascom W. *The Joke of Christianizing China.* New York, 1927.

Wong, K. Chimin and Wu Lien-te. *History of Chinese Medicine.* 2d ed. Shanghai, 1936.

World Missionary Conference, 1910. Vol. III, *Report of Commission III, Education in Relation to the Christianisation of National Life.* Edinburgh, n.d.

Wright, Henry B. *A Life with a Purpose: A Memorial of John Lawrence Thurston, First Missionary of the Yale Mission.* New York, 1908.

Wu Chao-kwang. *The International Aspect of the Missionary Movement in China.* Baltimore, 1930.

"Wu-sa ts'an-an ch'ien chih liu ying hsüeh-sheng keng-k'uan t'ui-hui yün-tung" (The Movement for Return of Boxer Indemnity by English Overseas Students before the May 30th Incident), *Chiao-yü tsa-chih,* XVII, no. 8 (Aug. 1925).

The Yale Mission, Changsha, China. *Annual Reports, 1908, 1910, 1911.*

The Yali Quarterly, 1922, 1924–1927, 1935–1936. New Haven.

Yamamoto, Tatsuro and Sumiko. "The Anti-Christian Movement in China, 1922–1927," *Far Eastern Quarterly*, XII (1953), 133–147.

Yang Hsiao-ch'un. "Chi-tu-chiao chih hsüan-ch'uan yü shou-hui chiao-yü ch'üan yün-tung" (Protestant Propaganda and the Restore the Educational Rights Movement), *Chung-hua chiao-yü chieh*, XIV, no. 8 (Feb. 1925).

Yen, Maria. *The Umbrella Garden: A Picture of Student Life In Red China*. New York, 1954.

Yen, Y. C. James. *The Ting Hsien Experiment*. Peiping, 1934.

Yenching Journal of Social Studies, 1938–1941, 1949. Peiping, (Pr.)

Yenching News (China ed.), 1935, 1937. Peiping. (MRL.)

Yenching News (New York ed.), 1933–1950. New York. (MRL.)

Yenching University. *Concerning Yenching University's Department of Journalism in 1936*. (Pamphlet, MRL.)

——. *President's Reports, 1931–1937*. (UB.)

——. *Report of the Registrar of the University, July, 1928–July, 1931*. (MRL.)

——. *Report of Yenching College for Women, 1935–1936*. (MRL.)

Yen-ching hsüeh-pao (Yenching Journal of Chinese Studies), 1927–1936, 1950. Peiping. (Wason.)

Yen-ching ta-hsüeh hsüeh-sheng tzu-chih hui (Yenching University Student Self-Government Association), ed. *Shih-erh-chiu chou-nien chi-nien t'e-k'an* (Special Issue on the Anniversary of December Ninth). Peiping, 1936. (Wason.)

Young China, 1920, 1921. Urbana, Ill.

Young Men's Christian Association Historical Library. World Service Folders, Correspondence, Sept. 1935–Oct. 1936.

Young Women's Christian Association of China, Student Dept. "Chinese Students and Religion. A Symposium." Prepared for the Pacific Area Conference of the WSCF, Aug. 23–Sept. 2, 1936. (Pamphlet, MRL.)

Yü Chia-chü. "Chi-tu-chiao yü kan-ch'ing sheng-huo" (Christianity and Emotional Life), *Shao-nien chung-kuo*, II, no. 11 (May 1921).

——. "Chiao-hui chiao-yü wen-t'i" (The Problem of Church Education), *Chung-hua chiao-yü chieh*, Oct. 1923.

——. "Shou-hui chiao-yü ch'üan wen-t'i ta-pien" (Answers to Questions Concerning the Restoration of Educational Rights) *Chung-hua chiao-yü chieh*, Feb. 1925.

Yün Chen. "Lü-mei kung-hsüeh tsa-t'an" (Comments by an Engineering Student Abroad in America), *Shao-nien chung-kuo*, II, no. 11 (May 1921).

Index

Administration of the Christian colleges, 36, 50–54, 108, 113–114, 120, 128–129, 155, 164, 183, 197, 235, 252–253, 261, 264, 274, 320, 331, 361, 369, 378, 384, 391, 407–408, 418, 430–431, 451–453, 456–457, 459, 468, 489, 523

Advisory Council of the East China Christian Colleges and Universities, 121

Agriculture, Christian colleges: education, 2, 80, 110, 117, 119, 180–183, 285, 288–289, 292, 303, 309–310, 400, 508–509, 523–524; extension work, 286–295, 376, 400, 524; research, 284–289, 293, 375–376, 519, 523–524; see also Nanking, University of, College of Agriculture and Forestry; and Lingnan University

Agriculture, Ministry of, 285, 509

All China Anti-Civil War Association, 411

Allen, Young J., 34, 45–47, 69, 83–85, 111–112

Alumni, Christian colleges: attitude toward their alma mater, 73, 120, 134, 180, 199, 240, 245, 306, 368–369, 401, 513, 523; employment by missions, 75–77, 100, 134, 138, 157, 163, 494–495, 502–505, 527; graduate study by, 2, 133, 135, 137–138, 153, 175, 196, 317–318, 496–505, 508; occupations, 27, 47–48, 76–77, 134, 152, 175, 182, 186, 302, 389, 494–509, 526; role in China, 48, 91, 100, 134, 152, 152n, 156, 157, 175, 285, 289–290, 311–312, 317–318, 345, 391–392, 495–502,

505–512, 519, 524, 526; role in the Christian colleges, 51, 54, 62, 110, 112, 138, 291, 486; see also Graduates

American Baptist Foreign Missionary Society, see Baptists, U.S.A.

American Board of Commissioners for Foreign Missions, 6, 13–14, 18, 30–31, 133, 146

American Church Mission, see Episcopal Church, U.S.A.

Anderson, D. L., 111–112, 164

Anglical Church, 6, 119

Anglo-Chinese College of Shanghai, see Shanghai Anglo-Chinese College

Anglo-French War in China, 7–8

Anti-Americanism, 118, 398, 419–424, 436–441, 445–446, 461–478, 493, 516; see also United States, criticisms of

Anti-Christian Movement, 1922, 174, 204, 215–232, 233, 236, 240–241, 267, 276, 514

Anti-Christian Student Federation, see Fei chi-tu-chiao hsüeh-sheng t'ung-meng

Anti-Christianism: Chinese tradition of, 6–7, 9, 40, 92, 219, 230; during nineteenth century, 6–9, 38–42, 48–49, 88–89, 92–94; during twentieth century, 92–96, 128, 174, 208, 233, 236, 240–243, 247, 250–251, 254–262, 268–269, 277, 464, 472, 514–515; see also Anti-Christian Movement, 1922

Antiforeignism, 1, 10, 39–42, 88, 92–95, 104, 118, 128, 174, 230, 245–246, 260, 267, 398, 514–515, 529

557

National Association for the Advancement of Education (Chung-hua chiao-yü kai-chin she), 233, 241, 251
National Association of Vocational Schools (Ch'üan-kuo chih-yeh hsüeh-hsiao lien-ho-hui), 180
National Bureau of Agricultural Research, 285, 287
National Central University, Nanking, 136, 287, 441
National Christian Council of China, 246n, 294, 298, 432, 449–452
National Economic Council, 294, 298
National Emergency Committee for Christian Colleges, 370
National Federation of Provincial Educational Associations, 251
National Health Administration, 160, 509
National Institute for Compilation and Translation, 335
National Liberation Vanguard of China, 353, 355, 356
National Medical Association of China, 144, 149
National Salvation Association, see Resist Japan National Salvation Association
National Southwest Associated University, 411, 412n, 417n
Nationalism, 88–90, 173–174, 207–212, 216, 267–269, 329–330, 374, 492, 512–517, 527; and Chinese Christians, 214–215, 231, 245, 247–249, 251, 513, 526–528; and Chinese education, 88–89, 208, 232–233, 236–237, 239, 241, 268, 326, 337, 348, 512, 514, 520; and the Christian colleges, 2–4, 172–173, 208, 214–215, 225, 232, 236–241, 245–252; 261–262, 268–269, 282, 323, 325, 329, 337–341, 347–348, 358, 366–367, 418, 441–442, 462–468, 492, 506, 510–517, 529; and Christianity, 90, 208, 219, 229, 237, 241, 247–248, 260, 267–269, 276–277, 487, 527–528; and communism, 204, 211, 244–245, 269, 323, 356, 410, 515–517; emphases of, 207–211, 244–245, 269, 492, 514–517, 529; and student movements, 173–174, 207–212, 225, 238–239, 244–245, 267–270, 320–323, 329, 341, 347–348, 512–515

Nationalist government, 263, 282, 284, 298, 322–324, 327–328, 341, 346, 348, 352, 367, 401, 413–416, 422–423, 426, 432–437, 524; and occupied China, 364, 366–367, 372–373, 389, 407–408
Nationalists, see Kuomintang
New Asia College, 485
New Culture Movement, 176, 188–190, 207, 216, 310, 374
New Democracy, 444–445, 450–451, 458
New Life Movement, 298–299, 335–336, 515
New Youth, 170, 173–174, 210, 241, 244–246, 265, 270, 296–301, 327–333, 337, 340, 347–348, 351, 355–358, 363, 410, 418, 420, 435, 492, 515–517
Nineteenth Century—A History (Mackenzie), 84
Ningpo Boys' Academy, see Hangchow Christian College
Ningpo Methodist College, 17n, 278
Niu Hui-sheng (Way Sung New), 501n
North China Christian Rural Service Union, 399
North China College (after 1916, see Peking University), 29–31, 55, 60–61, 69–72, 94, 106–108, 116, 168–169, 187, 189, 533
North China Council for Rural Reconstruction, 295, 298
North China Educational Union, 108, 121–122, 133, 146, 151
North China Industrial Service Union, 295
North China Theological Seminary, 123
North China Union College, see North China College
North China Union College for Women (also Yenching College for Women; before 1904, see Bridgman Academy), 121, 122, 132–133, 136, 151, 162n, 164–165, 195, 508, 533
North China Union Language School, 192, 312
North China Union Medical College, see Lockhart Memorial Medical College
North China Union Medical College for Women, 121, 136, 151, 156, 164, 531

China and the
Christian Colleges, 1850–1950

Designed by R. E. Rosenbaum.
Composed by Vail-Ballou Press, Inc.
in 10 point linotype Caledonia, 3 points leaded,
with display lines in monotype Perpetua.
Printed letterpress from type by Vail-Ballou Press
on Warren's 1854 text, 50 pound basis,
with the Cornell University Press watermark.
Bound by Vail-Ballou Press
in Interlaken ALP book cloth
and stamped in All Purpose black foil.